HUMAN MEMORY

HUMAN MEMORY

GABRIEL A. RADVANSKY

University of Notre Dame

Boston ▪ New York ▪ San Francisco
Mexico City ▪ Montreal ▪ Toronto ▪ London ▪ Madrid ▪ Munich ▪ Paris
Hong Kong ▪ Singapore ▪ Tokyo ▪ Cape Town ▪ Sydney

Executive Editor: *Susan Hartman*
Editorial Assistant: *Therese Felser*
Marketing Manager: *Pam Lasky*
Production Editor: *Patrick Cash-Peterson*
Manufacturing Buyer: *JoAnne Sweeney*
Composition and Prepress Buyer: *Linda Cox*
Cover Administrator: *Kristina Mose-Libon*
Electronic Composition: *Omegatype Typography Inc.*

For related titles and support materials, visit our online catalog at www.ablongman.com

Between the time Website information is gathered and then published, it is not unusual
for some sites to have closed. Also, the transcription of URLs can result in unintended typographical
errors. The publisher would appreciate notification where these errors occur so that they may be
corrected in subsequent editions.

Many of the designations used by manufacturers and sellers to distinguish their
products are claimed as trademarks. Where those designations appear in this book,
and Allyn and Bacon was aware of a trademark claim, the designations have been
printed in initial or all caps.

Library of Congress Cataloging-in-Publication Data
CIP data on file.

Printed in the United States of America

10   9   8   7   6   5   4   3   2   08   07   06

Dedicated to:
Mark Ashcraft and Rose Zacks,
who taught me about memory from A to Z

CONTENTS

CHAPTER FIVE

Working Memory   91

CHAPTER SIX

Nondeclarative Memory   113

CHAPTER SEVEN

Episodic Long-Term Memory   133

CHAPTER EIGHT

Memory for Space and Time   161

CHAPTER NINE

Semantic Memory   187

CHAPTER TWELVE

Memory and Reality   259

CHAPTER THIRTEEN

Memory and the Law   279

CHAPTER FOURTEEN

Metamemory   299

CHAPTER FIFTEEN

Memory and Development   319

CHAPTER SIXTEEN

Amnesia   339

PREFACE

This book is a guide to human memory, its properties, theories about how memory works, and how an understanding of memory can give us a better idea of who we are and why we do what we do. Although I have tried to provide a reasonably comprehensive survey of many issues of the modern study of human memory, my main concern is audience. Most college classes on human memory consist mostly of psychology majors who are planning to go on to some field of psychology other than memory research, such as clinical or social psychology. Many others plan to go on to nonpsychology fields, such as medical or law school. Other students are not psychology majors, but they are taking the class because they think human memory would be something interesting to learn about (and they are right). Only a small minority of students will plan to do research on memory. As such, I have tried to write this book with the goals, interests, and backgrounds of the majority of the students in mind, while still providing enough information and detail to satisfy the "memory" student. I have taken a number of steps along these lines.

First, in addition to fundamental topics that are necessary for a basic understanding of how memory works, I have tried to focus on topics that will be helpful and useful whatever the student's ultimate goal. I have tried to avoid going into detail about the minutiae of various topics and have instead focused on the big picture. However, there may be cases where I do present a number of different experimental outcomes or theoretical positions. I have done this to provide the student with a sense of the difficulty and complexity of studying human memory, and the degree of careful and rigorous thinking and action that are needed to get at the truth of the human condition.

I mention several times that a particular study was conducted using students from this college or that university so readers can associate with the information presented in this book. The participants in these studies are the same sort of people sitting in your classroom. I have tried to avoid language that would alienate a student—for example, "subject," which can put up a barrier between the student and the material.

I have also tried to present the materials about memory from a number of different perspectives. Some of these come from experimental research on memory itself, such as perspectives from behavioral data, neurological data, and computational modeling. In addition, I present details about how various topics relate to work outside the realm of memory research, such as work in social, clinical, or developmental psychology, or even as fields as far-flung as law enforcement.

ACKNOWLEDGMENTS

I would also like to thank the following reviewers whose invaluable comments helped in the writing of this book: Harriet Amster, University of Texas at Arlington; Bryan C. Auday, Gordon College; Ira Fischter, University of Florida; Dawn McBride, Illinois State University;

Joanna Salapska-Gelleri, University of Nevada, Reno; J. Scott Saults, University of Missouri; Dominic Simon, New Mexico State University; and Annette Taylor, University of San Diego.

I would like to thank all those students at Notre Dame who helped me refine the text as I was writing it, including Janie Alderette, Katie Allberry, Valerie Baur, Sarah Benton, Lisa Brintnall, Chris Broughton, Gretchen Bryant, Jimmy Carrera, Carrie Coffield, Ashly Cumberworth, Kyla Davis, Kate DeCarlo, Catherine Eichers, Elizabeth Goodhue, Richard Herbst, Katie Hesmond, Lauren Hogel, Sally Hosey, Jeneka Joyce, Laura Kent, Beth Kessler, Jessica Kinder, Michael Kwiatt, Margaret Laracy, Chris Letkewicz, Celine McConville, Gerald Meskill, Tiffany Milligan, Mary (Clare) O'Brien, Colleen O'Connor, Kevin O'Rourke, Leslie Pechkurow, Laurie Perez, Jon Pribaz, Maggie Priest, Meghan Rigney, Kristy Robinson, Austin Santesteban, Emily Schulte, Lindsay Slevinski, Brian Stouffer, Jon Streit, Scott Sutton, Justin Szalanski, J. R. Teddy, John Wahoske, Lauren Walsh, and Lauren White.

Thanks to all the help from Allyn and Bacon: Karon Bowers, Patrick Cash-Peterson, Susan Hartman, Therese Felser, Carolyn Mulloy, and Lara Torsky.

CHAPTER ONE

OVERVIEW AND HISTORY OF MEMORY RESEARCH

Memory is perhaps the most central aspect of human thought. Any question about human behavior, cognition, development, and nature requires an understanding of memory. Our memory makes us who we are, and it is one of the most intimate parts of ourselves. This may be why when we get close to someone, when we want them to know who we are and we want to know who they are, there is a sharing of memories. Many feel that the study of human memory is the closest one can get to a systematic study of the human soul. The aim of this book is to provide you, the student, with a survey and guide to what is known about human memory. As with most courses, there are a number of facts and ideas to learn. However, as any good professor will tell you, the slow accumulation of facts is not the main point of course work. The primary aim is to provide you with a deeper understanding and appreciation of some aspect of the world—and, hopefully, yourself. I hope that the ideas presented in this book are useful in your life after this course is completed.

A SMATTERING OF DEFINITIONS

Before we get too involved in the subject matter, there are some points we need to establish so you can readily understand the material. Specifically, we need to define how the terms *memory* and *learning* are used. The primary subject of this book is, of course, memory. So what is memory? Well, the problem, and the beauty, of this term is that is has many meanings.

Memory

The word **memory** has three definitions (Spear & Riccio, 1994). First, memory is the location where information is kept, as in a storehouse, or memory store. Second, memory can refer to the thing that holds the contents of experience, as in a memory trace or **engram.** In this sense, each memory is a different mental representation. Finally, memory is the mental process used to acquire (learn), store, or retrieve (remember) information of all sorts. Memory processes are acts of using information in specific ways to make it available later or to bring back that information into the current stream of processing, the flow of one's thoughts.

Learning

The other term that needs to be defined is **learning,** which is any change in the potential of people to alter their behavior as a consequence of experience. Obviously, learning and memory are closely related: For something to be remembered, it must first be learned. Because of historical circumstances, however, these terms have become somewhat disconnected in the language of psychology. "Learning" has come to refer more to the acquisition of associations, often in the context of studies of conditioning. Moreover, these studies are often performed on animals, such as a rat learning a maze. This is not the learning people often refer to when they are in school. In this book I use the term the way it is conventionally used, although I may occasionally use the more restricted sense.

Synopsis

The terms *memory* and *learning* are used in specific ways in experimental psychology. In general, memory is used to refer to the storage of information and the processes used to retrieve it. When referring to research, there is a greater likelihood that this will be work with humans. Learning is a term that has a greater association with studies of conditioning that are more likely to involve animals. However, both are clearly relevant to the topic of this book.

METAPHORS FOR MEMORY

There are several things that are striking about the human mind. One is that it is the part of ourselves of which we have the most intimate awareness. Our experiences are our thoughts. Another is that many, if not most, of the operations of the human mind are not open to direct inspection. In addition, there is the problem that every experience that the mind has changes it in some way. These issues lead to a number of problems in trying to understand memory. One has to be clever and develop ways to assess how memory works. Many issues of studying memory are covered in Chapter 3. More relevant here is the idea that there is no simple and direct way to talk about what memory is and how it works. Because of this, people often talk in indirect ways, using **metaphors.**

Roediger (1980) has compiled a list of metaphors that have been used over the centuries to capture various aspects of the nature of memory (see Table 1.1). Some of these metaphors express that memory is a recorder of experience, such as a wax tablet, a record player, a writing pad, a tape recorder, or a video camera. Other metaphors imply that different types of memories, different types of knowledge, and different times in our lives are stored in different places. These include such metaphors as memory being like a house, a library, or a dictionary. In contrast to the idea that some memories are somehow distinguished from one another, another concept is that they can also become intertwined and interconnected, like a switchboard or network.

Memory is not a passive thing. Some metaphors capture some of its more dynamic characteristics. For example, the process of retrieving a specific memory from the chaotic jumble we have accumulated during our lives has led to the idea of searching for memories

TABLE 1.1   Metaphors Used to Describe Memory

METAPHOR	EXAMPLES
Recorder of Experience	Wax tablet, record player, writing pad, tape recorder, video camera
Storage Locations	House, library, dictionary
Interconnections	Switchboard, network
Jumbled Storage	Bird in an aviary, pocketbook, junk drawer, garbage can
Temporal Availability	Conveyor belt
Content Addressability	Lock and key, tuning fork
Forgetting of Details	Leaky bucket, cow's stomach, acid bath
Reconstruction	Building an entire dinosaur skeleton from fossils
Active Processing	Workbench, computer program

as being something like trying to catch birds in an aviary or searching for something in a junk drawer. This also goes along with the idea that memories become harder to get at over time, as if they were being led away on a conveyor belt. Often a search is required to find the appropriate memories that match or meet the current need, like a lock and key. Memory retrieval is further complicated by the fact that much of what gets stored is forgotten, leaving only a portion of the original, like water in a leaky bucket. This loss of knowledge requires people to recreate the missing pieces of a memory, using a constructive process, perhaps like reconstructing a whole dinosaur from the fragments of bones left behind. Finally, metaphors capture the active nature of memory in manipulating information, as if it were a workbench or a computer program.

The large number of metaphors should give you the idea that memory is a complex thing that we have only begun to understand. Because of its ephemeral nature, we must rely on our knowledge of other more concrete and better understood concepts to help us make sense of it.

Before moving on, let's look at one more metaphor for memory that is very inaccurate: the idea that memory is a muscle. The idea here is that the more you use your memory, the better it will be. In other words, simply memorizing any information will make memory better in the future. There is no evidence to support this. Instead, it is not how much you use your memory but how much information you have in it that is important. So memory is not like a muscle but more like a key collection. The more keys you have, the more locks you can open.

Synopsis

Memory is not open to direct inspection. As such, we must use a variety of metaphors to capture various aspects of memory, such as its recording of experience and its organization and chaos. While each of these metaphors carries a degree of imprecision, each one effectively captures some characteristics of memory that makes it easier for us to understand.

HISTORY OF MEMORY RESEARCH

Questions about the nature of memory extend back millennia to the ancient philosophers. However, a true systematic, quantified, and rigorous assessment of the nature and limits of human memory did not begin until the end of the nineteenth century. In this section, we review some of the major players in the history of memory research starting from the ancients and leading up to about 50 years ago.

The Ancients

A great deal of Western scientific thought has developed from or has been influenced by the concepts of the great philosophers of ancient Greece. One of the first philosophers to influence our understanding of memory was Plato (428?–347? B.C.). Plato was the seminal rationalist philosopher. That is, he emphasized rational thought as a means of deriving an understanding of the world, and he deemphasized empirical observation, which he argued could be distorted by difficulties with perception. He was also a dualist in that he believed the mind was a different and separate entity from the body. Understanding how the mind and memory worked in the Platonic view depended on understanding the nature of innate, inborn knowledge that served as the foundation of all human thought. Memory serves as the bridge between the perceptual world and a rational world of idealized abstractions (Viney & King, 1998).

Plato also provided the metaphor of memory as a wax tablet, holding the impressions of experience. This metaphor also contributes the elements that memory varies depending on quality of the wax (the state of the person) and the pattern that is impressed (how well the information is encoded). The better the impression, the easier it will be to retrieve it later or to compare it with other impressions. Furthermore, the wax can be altered or erased so the impression is lost, thus leading to the concept of forgetting.

Plato's most prominent pupil was Aristotle (384–322 B.C.). Like any good student, Aristotle's ideas were at odds with his mentor. Specifically, whereas Plato was a rationalist, Aristotle was an empiricist, who believed reality itself was the basis of inquiry, not an abstract, perfect realm. One of Aristotle's most powerful contributions is the theory that memories are primarily composed of associations among various stimuli or experiences. This simple idea continues to have a far-reaching influence on how we think about human memory. As you will see, there are many theories of memory that are associationistic, such as accounts of priming, interference, or even the creation of some false memories. There is a pervasive idea that understanding how various elements are mentally linked to one another can capture the structure and processes of memory. These linking relationships often follow Aristotle's three laws of association: similarity, contrast, and contiguity. That is, memory associations provide links to ideas that are similar in nature, are the opposite on some critical dimension (and thus a form of similarity in that the dimension is present and is important), or occurred near one another in time.

Important Modern Precursors

The desire to understand memory did not stop with these great philosophers. This line of questioning has been continuously pursued. For example, St. Augustine (354–430) spends a great deal of time in Book X of his *Confessions* on the topic of memory, covering the subject in a way that would be familiar to the modern psychologist. Although premodern thinkers developed ideas about how memory worked, their studies were not pursued. For example, Robert Hooke (1635–1703), a famous scientist/philosopher in the later seventeenth century, developed a theory of memory with a surprising number of modern insights. Hooke did not continue to research this area, however, and his work was overshadowed by Sir Isaac Newton, which further hurried his ideas into obscurity (Hintzman, 2003). However, rather than present a description of the insights and opinions from the ancients to the present, only those more recent, modern influences are considered.

Darwin and Evolution.   One person who had a tremendous impact on scientific thinking in general, including human memory, was Charles Darwin (1809–1882). Darwin, of course, is best known for his theory of natural selection. The central concept of his theory is that within a species, various changes occur as a result of variation that can be either passed down to or removed from subsequent generations through the process of "natural selection." Through this process a species can develop features or abilities that allow it to become more adaptive to its environment. The same could be said about human memory. Many memory theorists are either implicitly or explicitly guided by the idea that it has developed through the process of evolution to capture many of the major characteristics of the environment and to perform specific tasks (Glenberg, 1997; Klein, Cosmides, Tooby, & Chance, 2002; Shepard, 1984). That is, different types of memories capture meaningfully different types of information that we need to remember from our experience. Also, because many species have been developing from or along a similar evolutionary trajectory, nonhuman animals can sometimes be used to study issues about memory that would require more control than is either practically or ethically possible.

This evolutionary aspect of human memory has an influence on how people think about the mind, behavior, and genetic influences. First, it is important to note that in some sense all human behavior has a genetic component (Turkheimer, 1998). The very existence of our brains in the interiors of our skulls requires that we have brain-building DNA. Second, all of our thoughts and memories depend on our biologically constructed brain. Any psychological state corresponds to some neural state. Thus, our thoughts and memories have an important genetic component. However, our DNA does not directly cause our brains to have the exact configuration that we happen to have at the moment. This is due to our long history of experiences during the course of development. Similarly, although our thoughts depend on neural hardware and processes, it does not mean that the simplest, most direct way to understand memory is going to involve a detailed understanding of the underlying neurophysiology. That said, it should also be noted that the more a person understands the underlying neurological components and processes, the better he or she will understand the higher-order operations. For this reason, although it would be possible to write a textbook on human memory without discussing neural structures and processes at all, I have included several descriptions of this influence to broaden your understanding.

Philosophy of Mind.   Another important group of modern thinkers that has influenced contemporary ideas about memory are the British empiricists, including George Berkeley (1685–1753), John Locke (1632–1704), John Stuart Mill (1806–1873), and David Hume

(1711–1776). They had a number of ideas about the human mind that continue to be of importance. Perhaps the most significant of these is the idea of the association, a concept originally conceived by Aristotle but worked into grand form by the empiricists. Association maintains that memories are largely composed of interconnections between various simple concepts or ideas. The influence of this associative view will be seen most clearly in Chapter 10 when we discuss some formal models of human memory. This role of associations in memory can be easily illustrated. Things in the world are rarely treated by people as isolated entities or properties. Instead, we are often reminded of other, related experiences that also included them. For example, when I eat a certain brand of cookies, I am reminded of my childhood because those were the kind of cookies my mother bought.

The empiricists' idea that memory is composed of a broad set of associations has without question had a major influence on modern ideas of human memory. However, the philosophical antagonists of the empiricists, the rationalists, including Rene Descartes (1596–1650) and Immanuel Kant (1724–1804), have also had an influence. While the empiricists characterized memory as a passive collection of associations built up from the environment, the rationalists took the view that the mind is actively involved in the building of ideas. This can be seen in various contemporary theories of memory that involve the active construction and reconstruction of memories, such as those found in schema theories, as we will see in Chapter 9.

Early Memory Researchers in Psychology

Psychology as an independent discipline arose in the latter half of the nineteenth century. Since then many people have influenced memory research. While we cover a few prominent ones here, it should be kept in mind that the study of memory did not always move at a steady pace. Sometimes in science people develop ideas that move the field forward but, for whatever reason, are not noticed at the time. These theories fall by the wayside, never to be heard from again. However, a few may capture the attention of future generations, who discover in the earlier, neglected work parallels to modern ideas. For example, in memory research, Richard Semon (1859–1918) developed a theory of memory in the first decade of the twentieth century that incorporated many ideas about the process of retrieval. However, his contemporaries largely ignored these ideas, and his insights were not appreciated until 70 years later (Schacter, Eich, & Tulving, 1978). Now let's look at some people whose work had a more immediate impact.

Ebbinghaus.   One of the first true students of memory in a scientific form was Hermann Ebbinghaus (1850–1909). He is best known for his 1885 publication *Memory: A Contribution to Experimental Psychology*. This work conveyed his detailed studies of memory, using himself as both the experimenter and the subject, because formal methods of obtaining research participants were not available at that time. So Ebbinghaus turned to himself as a convenient source of study. Also, this was a time of psychological research when the study of one's self was more acceptable. Currently, it is viewed as more objective if the experimenter tests another person who knows little to nothing about the experimental hypothesis. There are still a few people who do test their own memories, but these efforts are quite rare.

Ebbinghaus tried to study memory in as pure a form as possible, in the absence of an influence of prior knowledge. To do this, he devised a form of test stimulus called the **nonsense syllable,** which is a consonant-vowel-consonant trigram that has no clear meaning in the language. Nonsense syllables for English would be PAB, SER, and NID. Ebbinghaus created and used about 2,300 of these. These nonsense syllables had a tremendous effect on the study of human memory for many decades. Researchers not only used nonsense syllables, but also spent a great deal of effort studying them, even to the point where nonsense syllables were rated for meaningfulness (Glaze, 1928). That is, people recognized that some nonsense syllables seemed more wordlike than others. For example, "BAL" is rated high in meaningfulness (because of "ball"), whereas "XAD" is rated very low. People used the ratings for their research.

Ebbinghaus spent a lot of time memorizing nonsense syllables of various lengths, under various learning conditions, and for various retention intervals before he tested himself. (In some of his later studies he did allow some real words to enter his lists on the premise that it would have little effect.) For memory retrieval he would give himself the first nonsense syllable, and he would then have to recall the rest in the series. Using this simple approach, he was able to discover a wide range of basic principles of human memory that have withstood the test of time. Some of the more important ones are the concepts of the learning curve, the forgetting curve, overlearning, and savings. It should be noted that although Ebbinghaus discovered these using nonsense syllables, these same patterns are observed with all types of information.

The **learning curve** reflects the idea that there is a period of time needed for information to be memorized, such as the number of times a person needs to practice information, and that can be affected by a number of things, such as the amount of information to be learned. The learning curve is a negatively accelerated function in which most of the action occurs early on, with smaller and smaller benefits gained later on. So the largest amount of information is learned in the first segment. In the second, although more is learned, it is not as much as during the first. A similar description applies to the third segment, and so on. Thus, through this process, the information is gradually committed to memory. Furthermore, Ebbinghaus showed that how a person went about learning, in terms of the distribution of practice, influenced how well information was learned. Specifically, memory is better when practice is spread out over time, rather than lumped together—a distinction that is currently known as **distributed practice** and **massed practice.**

The **forgetting curve** is the opposite of the learning curve, and yet it is strongly similar to it. It is the opposite of the learning curve in that it conveys the loss of old information rather than the acquisition of new information. However, the forgetting curve is like the learning curve in that it is also a negatively accelerating function. As we'll see in Chapter 3, most of what is forgotten is lost during the initial period. As time goes on, the process of forgetting continues but at a slower pace. The more time that passes, the slower the rate of forgetting.

Forgetting is clearly the most problematic aspect of memory, and the forgetting curve suggests that we are doomed, sooner or later, to lose just about every memory we acquire. However, it should be apparent that this is not strictly the case. There are some pieces of knowledge that you've had for years and are unlikely to ever forget. One way to do this is by a process called **overlearning,** in which a person continues to study information after perfect recall has been achieved. This continued learning insulates a person against forgetting. If there is substantial overlearning, forgetting may be delayed for quite some time, perhaps indefinitely.

When information has been forgotten to the point that no pieces can be recalled with accuracy or reliability, it might seem that a person must start at square one and repeat all of the previous effort. However, this is not the case. Ebbinghaus found that after seemingly complete forgetting, subsequent attempts to relearn the information required less effort than the first time. This difference between the amount of effort required on a subsequent and prior learning attempt is called **savings.** The existence of savings is very important. For one thing, it demonstrates that information that appears to be lost may be residing somewhere in the darkened corners of our mind. It is no longer consciously available, but it can still exert an unconscious influence on behavior—in this case, serving as a platform on which to build a new set of consciously available memories.

Bartlett.   Another major figure in the study of human memory is Sir Fredrick Bartlett (1886–1969). Bartlett was, in some ways, the opposite of Ebbinghaus. Whereas Ebbinghaus was interested in the operations of memory independent of prior knowledge, Bartlett was directly interested in how prior knowledge influenced memory. He found that prior knowledge has a profound influence on memory. Specifically, he suggested that what is stored in memory is often fragmentary and incomplete. When people are remembering, in some sense, they are reconstructing the information from the bits that are stored and from other prior knowledge that the person has about such circumstances. This reconstruction is guided by what Bartlett called "schemas." Schemas are general world knowledge structures about commonly experienced aspects of life. (There will be more about schemas in Chapter 9.) To illustrate the effects of schemas, Bartlett had people read a story and then later try to recall it anywhere from immediately after they read it to several months or years later. What he found was that as memories for the story became more fragmented, the story content was altered to make it more consistent with a stereotypical story.

Gestalt Psychology

Modern views of memory were influenced by a number of movements in psychology. Two important ones were the Gestalt and behaviorist movements. The **Gestalt** movement, mostly advanced by German researchers such as Wolfgang Kohler (1887–1967), Max Wertheimer (1880–1943), and Kurt Koffka (1886–1941), suggested that strictly reductionistic approaches to mental life were incomplete. Instead, one needed the idea that complex mental representations and processes have a quality that is different from the component parts that make them up. This is not to say that the Gestalt psychologists completely rejected reductionistism. They most certainly did not. Instead, they argued that an understanding of more complex phenomena was important in its own right because it could be qualitatively different. For example, a melody is something that is qualitatively different from the individual notes that make it up, although it is certainly very dependent on them.

One of the ideas of the Gestalt movement that has influenced thinking about memory was the idea that the whole is different from the sum of its parts. This idea can be seen in modern views that memories are built up of a configuration of simpler elements to take on a new quality. For example, the finding that people remember the causally important elements of a story better than others (Trabasso & van den Broek, 1985) is directly in line with this idea. Gestalt psychologists also stated that the observed behavior of a person depends on both the context in which people find themselves as well as a frame of reference. This is reflected in the context effects that are observed in memory and the perspective effects, such as the hindsight bias, that are sometimes observed.

A final concept to come out of the Gestalt movement is the idea that mental representations are isomorphic. That is, their mental structure and operation are analogous to the structure and function of information in the world. The influence of this idea is clearly seen when spatial memory is discussed (Chapter 8). The idea is that the structure of a memory trace reflects the structure of the event, as it would be experienced, although in not as complete a form. It should be noted that for the Gestalt psychologists this isomorphism was a functional one. The memory trace functioned "as if" it has the same structure as external events, not that it actually did. An analogy here is a clock that is functionally isomorphic to the daily rotation of the earth. Even though the physical mechanisms are very different, both capture the same basic principle of the amount of time it takes for Earth to rotate on its axis. Today, people talk about mental representations as being second-order isomorphs (Shepard & Chipman, 1970). A first-order isomorph would be a representation that has the same physical characteristics as the thing it represents. Photographs and statues are examples of first-order isomorphs. A clock is a second-order isomorph. An example of a second-order isomorph in memory might be a mental map having properties similar to an actual map.

Behaviorism

As we will see in Chapter 6, there are many aspects of memory that operate on a basic and unconscious level. Some of these involve the encoding, storage, and retrieval of relatively simple contingencies in the world that fall under the heading of "conditioning." This was the domain of the behaviorists. **Behaviorism** is a school of thought that originally sought to bring greater credibility to psychology as a science. It was a line of thinking that had a strong grip in psychology for much of the early to mid-twentieth century. Part of this effort was to avoid mentalistic constructs because they could not be objectively observed and to focus entirely on observables. Although the workings of the mind could not be observed, behavior could be. So much of the experimental work that was done during the behaviorist era did not directly address issues of memory. However, there were some important insights and discoveries that are relevant here.

Two of the more salient forms of conditioning are classical and operant conditioning. Classical conditioning is a form of memory that allows one to prepare for contingencies that are present in the environment, whereas operant conditioning allows one to remember the consequences of one's own actions. Both of these concepts came into the vocabulary of psychology early on in the twentieth century. Classical conditioning was first described by the Russian physiologist Ivan Pavlov (1849–1936), who had won the Nobel Prize for his work on digestion. Operant conditioning was first described by an until then little-known American named Edward Thorndike (1874–1949), who discovered these principles because, in part, he wasn't able to do what he really wanted to do as a graduate student: study hypnosis.

The discovery and study of these forms of conditioning are important because for decades they shaped much of the research in learning and memory. There was great interest in studying the principles that guided these forms of learning and the implications they had on behavior. One of the salient qualities of classical and operant conditioning studies is that one can take these principles pretty far without having to posit much about what is going on mentally. One can just observe the stimulus conditions and the responses produced by an organism.

Despite this generally antimentalistic view during the behaviorist era, there were some important behaviorists who had important insights into issues of memory. Perhaps the most prominent of these was Edward Tolman (1886–1959), who did a number of studies with rats running through mazes. According to strict behaviorist analyses of maze running, what the rat is learning is to make specific turns at specific junctures. Each turn that the rat makes in the maze would either be reinforced or not. If this is true, then any change in the maze should result in the rat needing to learn the route all over again. However, Tolman observed that rats often did not need to undergo a relearning but adapted to changes very quickly. This led Tolman to suggest that rats possessed a mental representation in memory for that spatial location. Tolman called this the "mental map." The rats presumably could consult this mental map in memory to adapt to the changes in the maze. Thus, working within the behaviorist context, people such as Tolman were able to bring a discussion of memory and mental activity back into mainstream psychology.

Tolman was a molar behaviorist, although the term he preferred was "purposive behaviorism." That is, he was interested in larger behaviors as opposed to the more microscopic behaviors that interested many of his behaviorist colleagues. An example of a molar behavior might be something like getting to the end box of a maze or going to a movie, whereas a microscopic behavior might be an instruction like "turn left." This interest in molar behavior can be seen in an approach to memory that takes into account the goals and context of a person in the memory situation.

Verbal Learning

The **verbal learning** tradition existed in the context of a behaviorist psychology and stemmed from Ebbinghaus's work with nonsense syllables. The term *verbal learning* itself reflects the behaviorism of many of its practitioners, although what was being studied was a form of memory. Because the verbal learners were interested in preserving the behaviorist attitudes, the studies they conducted often had clearly defined stimulus and response components. Memorization was referred to as "attachment of responses to stimuli," and forgetting was "loss of response availability." (For a nice summary of verbal learning and its relationship to memory, see Tulving & Madigan, 1970.) The verbal learning tradition gave psychologists a way to study memory during the antimentalistic era of behaviorism.

One of the dominant methods in the verbal learning tradition is the **paired associate** learning paradigm. In this approach, people memorize pairs of items, often words, letters, or nonsense syllables. An example of a pair would be something like "BIRD-GLOVE." During testing, people would be presented with the first item of the pair and would be asked to produce the second (e.g., "BIRD-?"). The first item served as the stimulus and the second as the response.

There were many variations on this theme. The simple A-B paradigm would present people with a list of paired associates and have them recall the B items in the presence of the A cues. This is clearly memory in a behaviorist guise. Other paradigms are more complicated, where people must learn a second list of items. If this second list was unrelated to the first, this was called an A-B C-D paradigm. If the second list retained the initial cues with the first list, it was called an A-B A-D paradigm (much harder). Alternatively, one could have the second list be combinations of the A items with synonyms of the B items, called an A-B A-B' paradigm or a recombination of the A and B items from the first list, an A-B A-Br paradigm (very, very hard). Often what researchers were doing was looking at the effects of interference of prior learning on new learning. Issues of interference continue to be of interest to memory researchers, and some still use paired associate learning paradigms. We'll see some of the ideas developed by the verbal learners explored in the sections on interference in Chapter 7.

Early Efforts in Neuroscience

Memories are stored in the brain, but the brain is a complex and busy place. So where exactly would each memory be stored? Is it possible to locate individual memories in the brain? This is the basic question asked by neuropsychologists such as Carl Lashley (1890–1958). Lashley (1950) conducted a series of studies in search of what he referred to as the "engram"—the neural representation of a memory trace. Lashley first trained rats to run a maze and then surgically removed part of the rats' brains. After the rats recovered from the surgery, they would be placed back into the maze. If memories for the maze were localized in one part of the brain, then destroying that part would destroy the memory, and the rats would then run the maze just as if it were entering it for the first time. The major outcome of these studies was that no matter what part of the brain was removed, the lesioned rats were still able to perform better than control rats that were placed in the maze for the first time. The critical factor was how much tissue had been removed, not where (see Figure 1.1). This led Lashley to conclude that engrams were not localized in one part of the brain but were distributed throughout the cortex. While more recent studies have shown that some forms of memory may be localized in different parts of the brain, the general conclusion that many different and distributed parts of the brain are used during memory processing is well supported.

In addition to understanding what different parts of the brain do, it is also important to understand how the brain works. That is, how do the interconnections among neurons influence the processing of information? One of the great pioneers along this line of research was Donald Hebb. Hebb's classic contribution to the field was his book *The Organization of Behavior* (1949). Hebb is considered one of the forerunners of computational neuroscience—mathematical modeling of brain activity. According to Hebb, memories were encoded in the nervous system in a two-stage process. In the first stage, neural excitation would reverberate around in cell assemblies. A collection of cells that corresponds to a new pattern or idea would be stimulated, and this stimulation would continue for some time. In the second stage, the interconnections among the neurons would physically change, with some connections actually growing stronger. This is similar to the idea of long-term potentiation, discussed in Chapter 2. According to Hebb, it takes some time for memories to

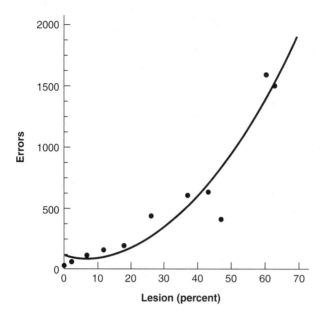

FIGURE 1.1   Results of Lashley's Experiment

Source: Lashley, 1950

move from stage 1 to stage 2. This is why if people suffer some sort of trauma to the brain, such as a blow to the head, they may lose recent memories. (We will discuss this in Chapter 16 when we examine amnesia.) In addition, these ideas of neural organization and change help lead to the development of computational models of the nervous system, such as the parallel distributed processing (PDP) models, discussed in Chapter 10.

The Cognitive Revolution

Over time, psychologists became frustrated with the constraints imposed by behaviorism. There was a desire to study mental activity as mental activity, not simply as a black box between the input of the stimulus and the output of the response behavior. The so-called **cognitive revolution** of the 1950s and 1960s marked a return of mental states to a state of legitimate study. This is important because it made the study of memory a palatable topic once again.

Many people contributed to the cognitive revolution. We focus here on one whose efforts serve as an example of the work and ideas that brought about this change. George Miller provided a number of important findings for memory research, such as his work on the capacity of short-term memory in his paper "The Magical Number Seven: Plus or Minus Two" (Miller, 1956). This work took the notion of mental processing seriously and demonstrated how it was a limited system, much a like a computer's processing is limited by the amount of memory it has. These studies were some of the first to come out of the behaviorist-dominated era to show that memory could be studied with the methodological rigor that the behaviorists were so fond of.

Miller also showed that how people mentally organized information has an influence on memory. Specifically, the more highly organized a set of information was, the better the memory. In other words, how information is actively thought about can affect later memory. In addition, the knowledge that a person has stored in long-term memory can influence current memory performance in profound ways. Thus, work by Miller, and people like him, showed that in order to understand how memory works in the current situation, one must understand how it is structured over the long term.

Synopsis

The study of memory has a long history stretching back to ancient times. There have been a long line of thinkers who have revealed important characteristics of memory that we continue to uphold, even to this day. While this history is long, it has not always been smooth. Even in recent times, there have been conflicting opinions about the importance and nature of various aspects of memory. By examining how we have progressed through time, we can better understand why we find ourselves in the state that we do.

THE MODAL MODEL OF MEMORY

The standard model of memory, or the **modal model** (Atkinson & Shiffrin, 1968), is a general theory of memory that is accepted by most memory researchers as a heuristic for understanding how memory works. However, it should be noted that no one uses this model as an accurate theory of memory. Nonetheless, it has been successful enough that it has limped along for years as one the primary guiding frameworks for discussing issues about how information is stored over time, so it is worth discussing. This model has four primary components: (1) the sensory registers, (2) short-term store, (3) long-term store, and (4) control processes. An outline of the model is shown in Figure 1.2.

The first component of the model, the **sensory registers,** is best thought of as a collection of memory stores. Each of these stores corresponds to a different sensory modality. For example, there is one sensory register for vision, one for audition, one for touch, and so

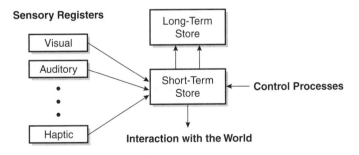

FIGURE 1.2   The Modal Model of Memory

Source: Atkinson & Shiffrin, 1968

forth. The world in which we live is full of information that is in a constant state of flux. Our sensory registers allow us to hold on to this information for brief periods of time to see if it is worthy of further attention. If we did not possess such memory stores, our minds would be constantly locked into only the very current state of affairs. In such a situation, we would not be able to detect patterns that involve very brief memories, such as determining that two frames of a film can be interpreted as continuous movement or that a sequence of sounds forms a word.

Once information has been attended to, it needs to be kept in the current stream of thought. Because what we are currently thinking about can change and drift relatively quickly, this information needs to be kept available for a short period of time. This part of the standard model is a **short-term memory** that generally retains information for less than a minute at a time if nothing is actively done with it. If consciousness is associated with any part of memory, it would be the information in short-term memory. This is knowledge that is either currently in conscious awareness or just beyond it. Another characteristic of short-term memory is its capacity—the amount of information that can be held in an active state. This amount is humblingly small—somewhere on the order of seven items. Issues dealing with the sensory registers and short-term memory are considered in more detail in Chapter 4.

The third component of the modal model is the idea that there are also control processes that actively manipulate information in short-term memory. This can include from rehearsing information to transferring knowledge to or from long-term memory, or perhaps even reasoning. This component of memory makes it an active participant in reality rather than just a passive absorption and retrieval mechanism. The idea that control processes in short-term memory work with knowledge in the service of some goal has led to the idea that short-term memory should be considered more of a working memory system. Issues of working memory are considered in detail in Chapter 5.

The fourth component of memory—the one that interests most people and that much of this text is devoted to—is long-term memory. **Long-term memory** encompasses a wide variety of different types of long-term knowledge and different ways of using that knowledge. Issues of long-term memory are covered extensively in Chapters 6 through 17.

Synopsis

The modal model of memory is the standard heuristic that is used to guide discussions of different aspects of memory. One component of this model is the sensory registers, which are brief memory systems that hold sensory information. Short-term memory holds small amounts of information for brief periods of time, usually under a minute. Long-term memory is responsible for storing information for very long periods of time. Finally, the control processes are used to actively manipulate information.

MULTIPLE MEMORY SYSTEMS

As is illustrated by the modal model, memory is not a unitary thing. Instead, it is composed of several different subcomponents. Each of these subcomponents has evolved, as a result

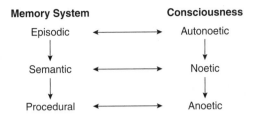

FIGURE 1.3   Tulving's Triarchic Theory of Memory

Source: Tulving, 1985

of environmental selection pressures, to handle a different job (Klein et al., 2002; Sherry & Schacter, 1987). Some of our long-term memories are implicit and act on us outside of consciousness. In contrast, others are explicit and can enter conscious awareness. Long-term memories can also differ in terms of whether they refer to specific events or to general knowledge.

A number of different classifications of long-term memory can be identified. One organizational guide is Tulving's (1985) *Triarchic Theory of Memory,* which is shown in Figure 1.3. This view divides long-term memory into three classes: procedural, semantic, and episodic. These divisions reflect the different tasks required of memory, as well as different levels of control and conscious awareness.

Procedural memory is an evolutionarily old memory system. Even relatively primitive organisms have some kind of procedural memory. More recently, people have referred to this as the nondeclarative memory and have grouped semantic and episodic memory in a declarative memory. This more elaborate view of the organization of long-term memory is illustrated in Figure 1.4, which first reflects the **declarative-nondeclarative distinction.** Declarative memory refers to memories that are easy for a person to articulate and talk about. In contrast, nondeclarative memory refers to information in long-term memory that is difficult to articulate but that still has profound influences on our lives. As can be

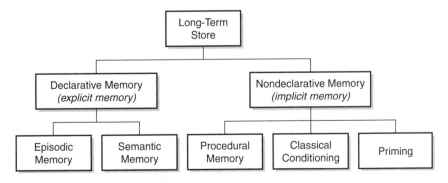

FIGURE 1.4   The Division of Long-Term Memory Systems

Source: Squire, 1986

seen in Figure 1.4, nondeclarative memories can be divided into various types, and in Chapter 6 we discuss many of these. One type of nondeclarative memory is the procedural memory of Tulving's classification. This is memory for how to do things, like ride a bicycle or speak your native language. However, other types of memories are included in this category, including condition responses and priming effects. This memory system is described as "anoetic" in Tulving's system because it does not require conscious awareness.

As shown in Figure 1.4, declarative memory can be divided into two categories as defined by the **episodic-semantic** distinction (Tulving, 1972). Semantic memories are generalized and encyclopedic and are not tied to a specific time or place. This is stable knowledge that you share with your community. For example, knowing what a bird is, what a stop sign means, and what you do in a restaurant are all semantic memories. Semantic memories are highly interrelated and are forgotten rather slowly once established. In **Tulving's Triarchic Theory,** semantic memory is noetic because it requires conscious awareness. You have to be consciously aware to know that an object is a bird or a tree and that it is similar to other members of that category.

In contrast, episodic memories refer to specific episodes or events in our lives. They are tied to the time and place in which the information was learned. For example, where did you go on your first date? Who told you that funny joke? Did you just see the word "apple" in a list of words. Also, unlike semantic memories, episodic memories for each event are compartmentalized and forgotten very rapidly. Episodic memory uses autonoetic knowledge in Tulving's Triarchic Theory because it requires knowledge of the self. For example, in order to know whether you've recently seen an action film, you need to have some memory of yourself as a separate identity to which past events can be referenced.

In addition to the different types of memory systems, we can also point out differences in how people use their memories. One of the more prominent of these is the **explicit-implicit distinction** (Schacter, 1987), which roughly corresponds to the distinction between declarative and nondeclarative memories. The important point here is how information is retrieved from memory, not the content of the information.

Explicit memory refers to when a person is actively and consciously trying to remember something. When you are trying to recall someone's name or when you recognize a suspect in a police lineup, this is explicit memory. Implicit memory refers to when a person is unaware that memory is being used. Even though most of this book is dedicated to issues of explicit memory, much of our lives, both thinking and action, are governed by implicit memory. The fact that familiar things are recognized more quickly, are preferred in choices, and guide our thinking are all examples of the influence of implicit memory operating. Other people have referred to this distinction based on the type of memory task used. This view might refer to direct and indirect tests of memory, without any claim on the nature of memory itself.

Synopsis

Human memory is not a unitary thing. Instead, there are multiple memory systems that perform different tasks and are responsible for different types of information. Often these capture various levels of involvement of conscious awareness, such as the Triarchic Theory of memory, the declarative-nondeclarative, and implicit-explicit distinctions. Other divisions capture the type of knowledge that the memory systems are processing, such as the episodic-semantic distinction.

RECURRING ISSUES

Before we move on to the specific topics, there are some issues that bear clarification. These issues reoccur throughout the chapters, so it would be helpful if you are alerted to them. In general, these issues have been lurking in the background of most memory research but are now coming to the forefront.

Neurological Bases

It is important to understand the neurological bases because memory exists as a property of the nervous system. The better one understands how the nervous system operates, the better one's insight into human memory. Early in the "cognitive age," much of the study of human thought, including memory, was dominated by the computer metaphor. Part of this metaphor was the distinction between the hardware and the software. The idea was that a person could have an understanding of how software operates with little knowledge of the underlying hardware. For example, some programming languages, such as C and JAVA, are designed to be hardware-independent. To an extent, human memory and thought, the software, can be studied without a detailed understanding of the neural hardware (sometimes called "wetware") on which it is instantiated.

However, some aspects of human memory can only be understood if one is familiar with the underlying neurophysiology, and there are many aspects of memory that are better understood or defined when the neurological underpinnings are made clear. Finally, if nothing else, knowing that a theoretical mental process can be associated with a real neural process lends confidence to one's findings and ideas. As we advance into the future, cognitive neuroscience becomes more and more important.

Emotion

A growing trend in cognitive psychology is to look at issues of emotion, which is a critical component of our everyday experiences. More and more memory researchers are incorporating emotion into their theories. The importance of emotions has been shown in both behavioral and neurological data. We will discuss the use of emotion to study human memory from time to time throughout the book to better capture its intertwined involvement with memory. Certain sections will present findings that are critically dependent on the emotional state of a person. In this way you will be able to see how these issues of memory, in general, that are often described apart from emotional experience are an important part of a larger psychological system.

Multiple Memory Sources

Another idea is that memory often uses multiple sources rather than a single source on nearly any memory task. Some of the clearest examples of this idea are what are known as **fuzzy trace theories** of memory (e.g., Brainerd, Reyna, & Mojardin, 1999). According to this view, there are at least two memory traces involved in any act of remembering. One is a memory trace that contains detailed information about a specific instance. The other is a more general, categorical trace that captures general information. What is remembered reflects a combination of these. Information in the detailed memory trace dominates when a person has a good memory of a specific event and is trying to remember what happened during that one event. In contrast, information in the general memory trace dominates when a person's memory for a specific event is poor or if knowledge is being used in a general way, such as trying to remember what a flywheel is.

Embodied Cognition

Recently, there has been increased interest in **embodied cognition.** While this phrase can mean many different things (Wilson, 2002), there are clear ways that this perspective can have particular influences on the study of human memory. The basic idea is that mental activity does not occur in a vacuum but is grounded in the type of worlds our bodies inhabit and the ways we can use our bodies in this world. Thought is affected by how we interact with the world. This can be seen when memory processes are affected by the situations people finds themselves in. That is, people use their context to help guide the encoding and retrieval of information. Second, memory often operates in real time as events are unfolding in the world. As anyone taking a college exam knows, memories often need to be adequately retrieved in a set time limit. Finally, memory is influenced by both the structure of the perceptual information it receives as well as the types of activities a person will likely need to perform in the future—for example, remembering how to navigate around town. All of these ideas are consistent with an embodied cognition perspective.

Scientific Rigor and Converging Evidence

Memory is a tricky thing to study. Each person's memories are different in important ways from everyone else's. There are also different aspects of memory that are qualitatively distinct. However, in order to have the clearest picture of what our memories are like, and who we are, we need to take as objective a view as possible. We need to avoid being led astray by our biases, momentary intentions, and other prejudices. Taking a rigorous, scientific approach can do this. Psychology, after all, is a science. To emphasize this, various approaches or methods of looking at the data from memory experiments are presented throughout the book to illustrate how the data from memory studies can be analyzed and interpreted to gain a more refined insight into the depths of our mental storehouses. Also, we will see that opinions and theories formed as a science are better supported when evidence comes from different methods of collecting and analyzing data. If these multiple sources of information are all consistent with the same explanation, this gives us greater confidence that the theory is closer to the truth. This is something known as converging operations.

Synopsis

While the focus of this book is on the various aspects of human memory, there are a number of recurring threads that will reappear across the various topics that represent emerging ways of thinking about memory. These include an increased desire to understand the neurological underpinnings of memory, the involvement of experienced emotions, the division of information across multiple memories, and a need to understand how memory operates in the real world. All of these, as well as every other topic in memory, are approached from a scientific perspective that seeks to drive answers about memory that help us have an accurate and durable understanding of ourselves.

SUMMARY

Understanding human memory is one of the most introspective tasks we can undertake as a species. By looking at how our own memories are created, structured, stored, and retrieved, we can gain a great deal of insight into who we are collectively and as individuals. The study of memory, however, is difficult. Memory is a very complex thing, incorporating issues of representation, storage, and process. People have been trying since ancient times to uncover the mysteries of human memory. Throughout history, particularly since the advent of psychology proper and especially since the advent of the cognitive revolution, we've gained a clearer and more consistent picture of what memory is all about, but much of the canvas is still obscured. Although there are many different theories about the nature of memory, many people at least implicitly follow the idea that short-term and long-term memory have different characteristics and that the operation of memory can be intimately influenced by the mental processes applied to the contents of memories. Moreover, different types of knowledge are handled by different memory systems. From this background, we will survey various aspects of memory, often touching on common themes of neuropsychological issues, multitrace influences, and issues of scientific rigor.

STUDY QUESTIONS

1. What do the terms *learning* and *memory* mean in the context of this chapter? How are they referring to similar things? How do they diverge?

2. Why do we need metaphors for memory? What are some metaphors? What do they tell us about the nature of memory?

3. What were some of the major figures and some of the major schools of thought that dominated thinking about human memory? What were the contributions of each?

4. What are some of the major divisions of human memory? What sort of processing is done by each of those divisions?

5. What are some of the emerging themes that will be recurring at various points in our discussion of memory?

KEY TERMS

behaviorism, cognitive revolution, declarative-nondeclarative distinction, distributed practice, embodied cognition, engram, episodic-semantic distinction, explicit-implicit distinction, forgetting curve, fuzzy trace theories, Gestalt psychology, learning, learning curve, long-term memory, massed practice, memory, metaphors for memory, modal model, nonsense syllable, overlearning, paired associates, savings, sensory registers, short-term memory, Triarchic Theory of memory, verbal learning

CHAPTER TWO

NEUROSCIENCE OF MEMORY

How are memories encoded? Where are they stored? How are they retrieved? Using the computer analogy, thoughts and memories are the software and data, and the nervous system is the hardware. A person can understand many aspects of the software without knowing much about the hardware. Think of how many computer users don't really understand how a computer works, but they can still operate the software. Still, to gain a truer insight into the computer software, how it represents information, how it processes that information, why some processes are fast and others are slow, one needs an understanding of the hardware. The same is true for memories and the nervous system.

Memory, like any mental process, is an **emergent property** of the nervous system. That is, it is not a property of the individual neurons, but it emerges when the neurons work together. To more clearly illustrate this, think of six square boards. None of those boards by itself has the property of containment. However, when the boards are arranged to make a box, then it is possible to place something in the middle of it. The property of containment emerges out of the arrangement of the elements that lacked that property individually (see Minsky, 1986).

Without a basic, working understanding of the nervous system, your knowledge of memory will be limited and incomplete. The aim of this chapter is to provide a general understanding of the major components of the nervous system and how they are involved in memory. We first consider the simplest component, the neuron; how neural communication occurs; and how this changes as a result of experience (the first step in encoding a memory). After that, we'll skip to higher levels of processing and discuss some of the major components of the brain, such as the cortex, and how they are involved in memory. Finally, we will examine ways to study how the underlying neurobiology is related to the observed psychology and how findings in memory research are related to such neurological structures and processes.

NEURONS

To adequately understand how neurophysiology relates to psychological experience, it is a good idea to have a working understanding of how the nervous system operates. Let's look at the basic components of individual neurons, followed by a presentation of neural communication.

Neural Structure

The most basic parts of the nervous system are the neurons themselves. A **neuron** is a specialized cell in the body that plays a role in the transmission and retention of information. The structure of a neuron is shown in Figure 2.1. Some of these components are shared with most other cells in the body. For example, the neuron has a cell body, or **soma,** that contains all of the general cell processing components, such as mitochondria, RNA, and so forth.

Other structures are important for the specialized jobs that neurons perform. Extending out of each neuron are dendrites. **Dendrites** are structures that are largely used for receiving signals either from sensory cells or from other neurons. Generally speaking, dendrites are responsible for collecting information for the neuron. Neurons also have another structure protruding from them called an axon. **Axons** are largely used for transmitting information out of the neuron either to other neurons or to other structures, such as muscles and glands. Thus, axons are generally responsible for sending information out of the neuron. At the end of each axon are nodules called terminal buttons. These **terminal buttons** contain the neurotransmitters. **Neurotransmitters** are the chemicals, such as dopamine, that are used to send signals to other neurons. Because axons can sometimes be quite lengthy, to avoid the loss or confusion of signals, some neurons have axons that are encased in a fatty substance known as a myelin sheath. This **myelin sheath** acts as an insulator for the neuron. The myelin sheath is not a solid continuous structure but has gaps along its length that are called the **nodes of Ranvier.** These nodes facilitate the transmission of information within a neuron by allowing the neural signal to jump from one point to the next without having to continuously traverse the entire length of the axon. Thus, the distance that the neural signal travels is functionally shortened.

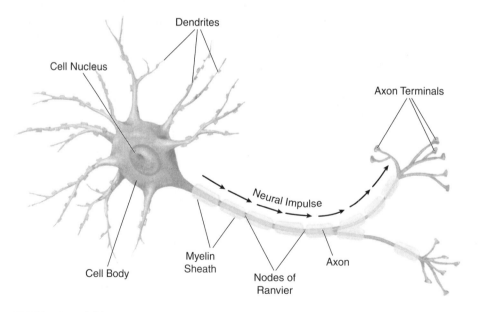

FIGURE 2.1   A Neuron

Neural Communication

As stated before, the job that neurons are designed for is the transmission and retention of information. Let's look at the transmission of information first. Neural communication can be roughly broken down into two components, one electrical and the other chemical.

Action Potential.   The electrical component occurs within the neuron itself and is called the **action potential.** When a neuron is sufficiently stimulated, an action potential occurs, and the neuron is said to "fire" (see Figure 2.2). When a neuron is not being stimulated, it has a resting electrical charge of –70 mV (millivolts). This is because there are a number of negatively charged ions in the interior of the neuron. When a neuron is stimulated, there is a depolarization of its electrical potential. If this depolarization shifts the neuron's electrical charge in a positive direction, the electrical charge may reach –50 mV. At this point there will be a dramatic change in the charge of the neuron, where it suddenly shifts to +40 mV. This is the action potential itself. After the neuron has fired, there is a brief recovery period where the neuron prepares itself to fire again and then resets itself at the resting potential of –70 mV. It should be noted that the action potential operates on the all-or-none principle. That is, there is either an action potential, which is always the same, or there is no action potential.

The action potential does not exist in the entire body of the neuron at one time. Rather, there is a wave of electrical energy flowing down the axon (see Figure 2.3). When a neuron fires, sodium ions in the surrounding extracellular fluid flood into the neuron. This occurs because the depolarization of the neuron has caused sodium "gates" on the cell membrane to open. The sodium ions themselves are positively charged, and this is what produces the positively charged component of the action potential. The electrical wave flowing down the axon is the wave of sodium gates opening and allowing these ions to enter the cell, much a like a row of dominos falling down. Each domino causes the next to falter. Immediately behind this wave of positive electrical charge, there is a second wave. This is

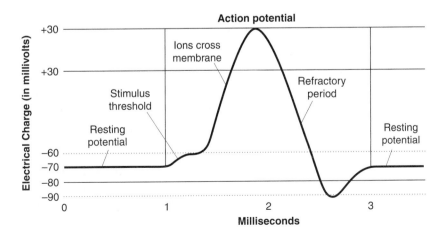

FIGURE 2.2   The Action Potential Over Time

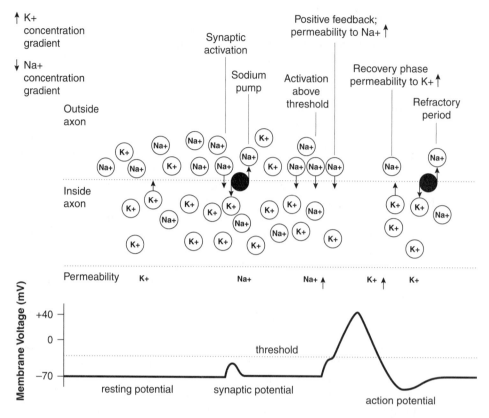

FIGURE 2.3   Movement of Ions In and Out of the Neuron's Cell Membrane During and After an Action Potential

Source: Eichebaum, *Neuropsychology of Memory*

a wave of potassium ions being forced out of the cell. This is part of the process of the cell recovering its resting potential level of electrical charge.

Neurotransmitters and the Synapse.   The other component of neural communication is chemical. This occurs at the **synapse** between two neurons. Although a single neuron may communicate with large numbers of other neurons, especially in the cortex, there is no direct physical connection between them. There is a small gap between the terminal button of one neuron and the cell membrane of another. This gap is called the synapse, which is about 100 to 200 angstroms wide (1 angstrom = $\frac{1}{10,000}$ of a millimeter). Neurons communicate across the synapse using special chemicals called **neurotransmitters.** While all neurotransmitters are involved in memory in some way, either directly or indirectly, some are more important than others. Perhaps the most important of these for memory is **acetylcholine.** When acetylcholine effects are enhanced, memory can improve, and it declines when acetylcholine effects are suppressed (Mishkin & Appenzellar, 1987). Other important neurotransmitters for memory are **dopamine,** norepinephrine, and gamma-amino butyric acid (GABA). Part of the problem with a condition like Parkinson's disease is the low level of dopamine available in the central nervous system. Neurotransmitters reside in the terminal buttons of one neuron, inside little synaptic vesicles, and are forced out into the synapse when there is an action potential. Ideally these neurotransmitters are absorbed by the subsequent neuron, altering its electrical potential.

There are two general classes of neurotransmitters. Excitatory neurotransmitters encourage the subsequent neuron to fire, causing the ion gates on the neuron's cell membrane to open and let in the sodium ions. In contrast, inhibitory neurotransmitters encourage the subsequent neuron to *not* fire, encouraging the ion gates to stay closed. At first, this may seem somewhat odd. If the goal of neural communication is to transmit information, why would one neuron inhibit the firing of a subsequent neuron? The reason is that one of the ways in which information is coded in the nervous system is the pattern of activation across a wide set of neurons. To create this pattern, some of these neurons need to be firing and others not. For example, computers code information by the patterns of 1s (on) and 0s (off), and this is roughly the same idea, although in a different form and with much greater complexity. Waves of neural firing that are dominated by excitation and little inhibition can occur in the brain and are called seizures (not a good thing).

Another important point about neurotransmitters is that they do not operate alone. Other chemicals in the nervous system can affect them. For example, neuromodulators can accentuate or diminish the influences of certain neurotransmitters. This adds a level of variability to the processing that occurs in the nervous system. Also, while some neurons interact with the body directly, such as through muscle systems, other neurons may eventually make contact with glands that can release various hormones into the body. In this way, the nervous system can influence parts of the body outside of itself.

Neural Change in Learning

Although communication between neurons occurs at the synapse, how do neural connections get altered as new things about the world are encoded into long-term memory? Obviously, these connections must be changed in some way. The precise mechanisms for how this occurs are not well understood at this time. One way is likely to be similar to a process known as **long-term potentiation**, or LTP (Bliss & Collingridge, 1993; Bliss & Lomo, 1973; Gustafsson & Wigstrom, 1988). LTP is a process that strengthens the connections between neurons by altering the ease with which postsynaptic neurons will fire. Often LTP can last for days or weeks, but it eventually dissipates. Thus, it seems to be a good model for the types of neural change that would occur in a memory. Overall, it is as if an LTP-like mechanism is serving as a temporary retention mechanism for information that is being stored in a more permanent form in other parts of the cortex. An important point to keep in mind is that LTP is not an actual process that occurs in the living brain but is a phenomenon that is observed by sending rapid pulse trains to sets of neurons in petri dishes (Eichenbaum, 2002). Still, some mechanism of this type is needed for memory at the cellular level.

Importantly, processes such as LTP illustrate that the connections among neurons are being altered, thereby storing information at a neural level. However, this process, known more generally as **consolidation**, takes a long time. Still, new knowledge and experiences actually physically alter the structure of the brain. This is true of every experience a person has in his life. Our brains, and thus our memories, are in a constant state of flux as we encounter new events, thoughts, and experiences.

A Blind Alley

One of the more interesting lines of study in neural encoding, which turned out to be a dead end, was done by James McConnell (1962), who studied learning in invertebrates, such as planaria (*Dugesia tigrina,* or flatworms). He conditioned worms to do a task, such as curling up in the presence of a light, which was predictive of an electrical shock. One of the interesting things about planaria is that if you cut them up, the missing parts regenerate into a whole worm. If you cut one in two, the head grows a new tail, and the tail grows a new head. McConnell found that if the worm is cut in two after learning, it regenerates, and the resulting planaria remembered what was learned just as well as those that had not been sliced and diced.

McConnell believed that memories were encoded not only in the structure of the neurons but also in the cell's RNA. To test this idea, he first trained a group of planaria. Then he ground them up and fed the pieces to other worms. He found there was a substantial savings in the rate at which the new worms were able to learn. It was as if they had in some sense acquired the memories of the worms they had eaten. This is the basic idea behind ritual cannibalism: By eating other people, you acquire their attributes. Of course, this is not true, but McConnell's work could be viewed as a scientific exploration of the theory that some information could be stored in RNA molecules and could be absorbed by another member of the species. As it turns out, McConnell's research was not consistently replicated and went nowhere. Still, it is interesting because it makes us think about other ways the body might store information. (For an interesting account of McConnell's career and his encounter with Ted Kazinsky, the Unabomber, see Rilling, 1996.)

Synopsis

The fundamental building blocks of the nervous system, and hence of memory, are neurons. Having a working understanding of how neurons work and communicate information provides a better understanding of how memory works. Neural communication occurs through electrical and chemical processes. The electrical component is captured in the action potential within a neuron, and the chemical component is captured by the neurotransmitters that cross the synapse. Neurons form memories by altering their connections to one another, such as by changes in the dendrites during long-term potentiation. How the nervous system acts in a memory system is not yet completely understood.

LARGER STRUCTURES

Up to this point, we have been talking about low-level processes. Now we are going to jump up to larger levels of neural organization. There are many structures that make up the brain. Most of these are involved in memory in some way, either directly or indirectly. Those that have a more direct involvement can be classified into two broad categories: (1) the subcortical structures, which are major parts of the brain that lie beneath the cerebral cortex and are evolutionarily more primitive, and (2) the various lobes of the cortex. In Chapters 16 and 17 we discuss various memory disorders that occur when one or more of these structures is damaged.

Subcortical Structures

Hippocampus. The subcortical structure that gets the most attention in memory is the **hippocampus** (see Figure 2.4). This is a seahorse-shaped structure (hence the name) that is part of the limbic system. The hippocampus, as well as the related surrounding complex of structures, is important for storing conscious memories of events (Mishkin & Appenzeller, 1987). It does not appear to be where long-term memories are actually stored, but it may help encode these memory traces in other parts of the brain, where they are held for long periods of time. More simply, the hippocampus may serve as a sort of waystation for the knowledge on the journey to permanent encoding (if it makes it that far). Some information is stored in the hippocampus but not for very long.

One type of information that the hippocampus is specialized in processing is memories for conjunctions of various stimuli that appear together in the environment. More specifically, the hippocampus seems well designed for the rapid encoding of episode-specific conjunctions—that is, whatever happens to be cooccurring at the moment. A slower, more generalized encoding of regular conjunctions is handled more by the cortex (O'Reilly & Rudy, 2001).

Damage to the hippocampus can lead to severe declarative memory deficits (e.g., Mahut, Zola-Morgan, & Moss, 1982). Often this takes the form of anterograde amnesia, described in detail in Chapter 16. Much of the research on long-term potentiation that was described earlier has been done by studying changes in neurons in the hippocampus.

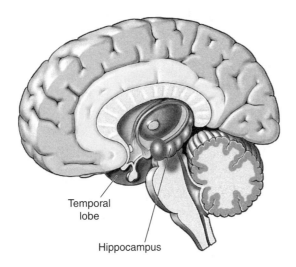

Temporal
lobe

Hippocampus

FIGURE 2.4   The Hippocampus and the Amygdala

Other Structures.   Another part of the limbic system important for memory is the amygdala (see Figure 2.4). The **amygdala** is an almond-shaped structure located at the lower part of the hippocampus, toward the front of the brain. The amygdala has been more difficult to understand because it appears to play different roles in humans and animals. However, there are good indications that the amygdala is responsible for processing emotional aspects of memories (Mishkin & Appenzeller, 1987). For example, if there were an emotional reaction to an event, that reaction would be encoded into the memory trace via the amygdala. This is not surprising given that limbic structures are important for emotion in general.

The **basal ganglia** are a collection of subcortical structures (including the caudate nucleus, the putamen, globus pallidus, and the subthalamic nucleus) located above and around the thalamus (see Figure 2.5). These structures are important for motor functioning—that is, the control of the voluntary muscle groups in the body. The basal ganglia have been implicated in memory for various unconscious types of memory processes, such as knowledge for habits and motor skills. A related set of findings is observed with the **cerebellum.** This is a relatively phylogenetically old structure located at the back of the brain (see Figure 2.6). Like the cerebral cortex above it, it has a convoluted surface structure, so it looks like a little brain underneath the larger one (and hence its name). The cerebellum is also associated with complex motor control and coordination. As such, it is used in memory for procedural skills that involve the complex coordination and control of the muscles, such as walking. This is a more primitive form of memory but very important nonetheless.

The **diencephalon,** including the **thalamus** and **hypothalamus,** primarily serves as a routing station for signals from different parts of the brain (see Figure 2.7). It is also involved in memory, although to not as great a degree as other structures. It seems to be

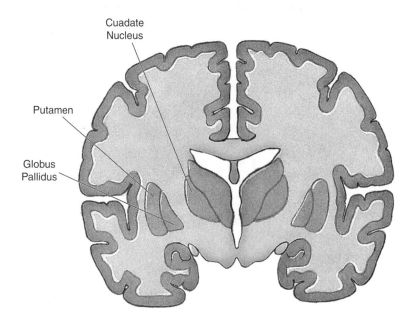

FIGURE 2.5   Basal Ganglia Structures

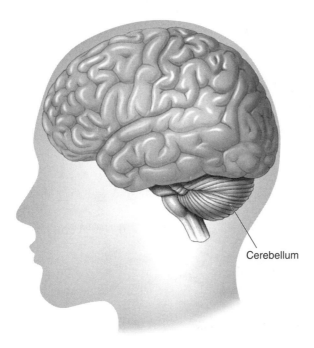

Cerebellum

FIGURE 2.6   The Location of the Cerebellum

involved in memory for conscious, factual knowledge. For example, it has been suggested that the diencephalon is important in storing information about the temporal sequence of events. More indirectly, the diencephalon is involved in controlling the sorts of neurotransmitters that are present in the nervous system at any given time, and so it has a roundabout influence on memory.

Cortical Lobes

The phylogenetically newest, and visually most prominent, part of the brain is the cerebral cortex. This is the wrinkly part that sits on top of what most people think of when they picture a brain. The wrinkled appearance of the cortex occurs because there is so much surface area being crammed into such a small volume. Many other parts of the brain have a smooth appearance. The brains of other animals, such as reptiles and amphibians, may be smooth in their entirety. In contrast, our brains are more powerful, so we need many more neurons, which, fortunately, we have. However, this increase in brain size brings with it an increase in head size. If the head becomes too large, then other problems arise, such as ease of birth and supporting and controlling such a large structure on the neck.

To keep the head small while increasing the number of neurons in the cortex, the cortex itself has become folded and wrinkled. If you could remove a person's cortex and lay it flat, you would see that it is very large. The average adult's cortex covers about 1,800 square cm (about 2 square feet) and is 2 to 3 mm thick. The wrinkling process preserves the

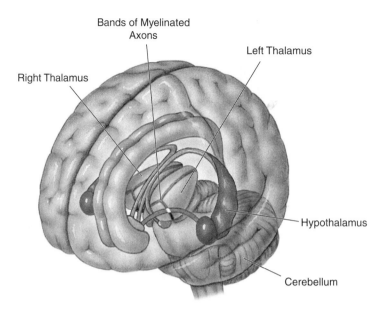

Right Thalamus

Bands of Myelinated Axons

Left Thalamus

Hypothalamus

Cerebellum

FIGURE 2.7   The Location of the Thalamus

amount of surface area while reducing the volume occupied. An analogy would be trying to get a sheet of paper into a coffee cup. The paper won't go in laying flat. However, if you wrinkle the paper up and stuff it in, you've taken a large surface area and enclosed it in a relatively smaller volume.

The cortex is divided into a number of major regions. First, it is divided into two hemispheres, a left hemisphere and a right hemisphere, and there are some memory functions that seem to be more dependent on one side of the brain than the other. This dominance of one hemisphere over the other is called **laterality.** There are a few cases where laterality might be important to memory function, and we will look at these. For now, it appears that the left hemisphere is generally regarded as being better at analytic processing, such as language and math, and the right hemisphere is better at holistic processing, such as spatial or music processing.

Each hemisphere is divided into four major subsections called lobes (see Figure 2.8). Each of these lobes is generally associated with different memory functions. At the back of the brain are the **occipital lobes,** which are generally involved in visual processing. In front of the occipital lobes, on the top of the brain and just behind the central fissure, are the **parietal lobes.** These are responsible for sensory processing from throughout the body, as well as spatial processing, such as knowing where something is. Also, in front of the occipital lobe but below the parietal lobe and under the lateral fissure are the **temporal lobes.** These are responsible for auditory processing and retaining knowledge about the identity of things in the world. Finally, at the front of the brain, in front of the central fissure and above the lateral fissure are the **frontal lobes.** These are the evolutionarily most recently developed part of the cortex and are involved in the control of action, emotion, and thought. If you are

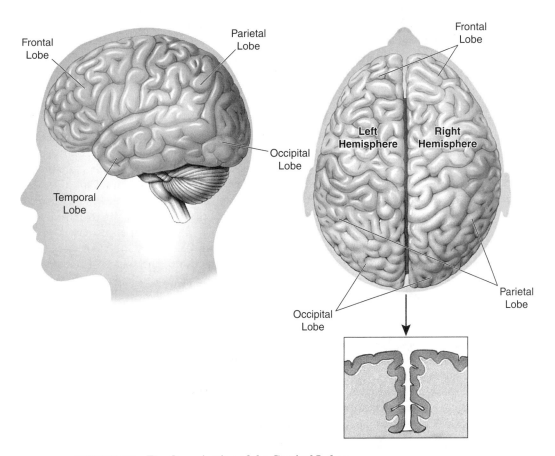

FIGURE 2.8   The Organization of the Cortical Lobes

trying to figure out how the names of the lobes correspond to a function or location in the brain, forget it! The lobes are named for the bones of the skull that overlay them.

Occipital Lobes.   The occipital lobes are involved more in perception than memory. However, there are some aspects of them that can be interpreted as memory. The occipital lobe detects features in the environment (Hubel & Wiesel, 1965), but the sensitivity to these features is based on experiences with the world. For example, if kittens are reared in an environment in which they only see horizontal lines, when they are adults, they will walk into a table leg because they cannot see vertical lines. They lack the feature detectors for vertical objects (Blakemore & Cooper, 1970). This suggests that our perceptual experiences are based on mental representations for the components that make up the world. These components are stored in the perceptual system over the long term. As such, they can be considered very long-term memory representations for the bits and pieces that make up the world.

Parietal Lobes.   The parietal lobes are less often thought of as being involved in memory than the temporal and frontal lobes, but they are used in a number of circumstances. For example, working memory processes that involve visual memory or the spatial manipulation of information (see Chapter 8) might involve the parietal lobes (Mishkin & Appenzeller, 1987). For example, animals that have had their parietal lobes surgically removed have trouble remembering spatial relations. This would include doing a task that involves mental imagery, such as scanning a mental image.

Temporal Lobes.   The lobes of the cortex most closely associated with memory are the temporal lobes. This is not surprising considering that the temporal lobes surround the hippocampus, which, as we have already seen, is one of the more important structures for memory. The part of the temporal lobe that is often studied with regard to memory is adjacent to or surrounding the hippocampus. This is the part of the brain where our long-term memories for several different types of information are believed to be stored. Damage to this part of the brain often results in some sort of memory loss. This part may be involved in remembering events from one's own life, something called autobiographical memory (see Chapter 11). It may also be the source of remembering ideas related to concepts you are pondering at the time. For example, when you think "wood" after hearing the word "lumber," this is a memory process called priming (see Chapter 6).

Frontal Lobes.   The frontal lobes are also important to memory. Again, these lobes are involved in the coordination of information, so the frontal lobes are important for working memory (see Chapter 5). This is important in a number of ways. The frontal lobes help a person select out those memories that are most relevant on a given occasion. They also coordinate various types of information into a coherent memory trace. For example, knowledge of the information itself, as well as knowing where information came from, must be put together into a single memory representation, called source monitoring (see Chapter 12). Sometimes we experience situations where information becomes separated, such as when we recall something but cannot remember where we remember it from. Alternatively, we may remember that someone told us *something,* but we cannot remember what that information was. The frontal lobes are also involved in the ability to remember what we need to do in the future, something called prospective memory (see Chapter 14). A failure to remember to tell your roommate that his mother called may be due to a problem with the memory processes controlled by the frontal lobes.

Synopsis

The brain is not a single structure but is made up of several, specialized substructures. A number of these structures play some role in memory processing. One of the more important structures for memory is a subcortical structure called the hippocampus. Other subcortical structures important for memory include the amygdala, cerebellum, basal ganglia, and structures of the diencephalon. The lobes of the cortex are also important to memory. The temporal lobe appears to play a prominent role, along with the frontal and parietal lobes, whereas the occipital lobe is the least involved in memory processing.

NEUROLOGICAL MEASURES

One of the most exciting areas of research in human memory is the development of methods and tools that allow us to look at how the brain itself is operating to encode, store, and retrieve memories. To provide a more complete coverage of the neuropsychology of memory, some of these methods are described here rather than in Chapter 3. In this section we look at measures of brain structure, as well as functions based on cortical electrical activity and blood flow.

Structural Measures

Although it is important to know the various functions that operate in the brain, it helps to be familiar with the brain's structure, especially of a specific person or group of people. Sometimes clues to patterns in the way a person thinks can be gained by understanding how their brains might be physically different from the norm. One thing to keep in mind about the brain is that its physical structure is not uniform; it differs from person to person, in much the same way that each person's face is unique. The best way to view the physical structure of a person's brain is to remove it from the skull (after death, of course). However, this approach still has its limits. Another way to view the structure is to surgically open up the skull of a living person and examine the brain, which can happen during surgery.

Computer-Assisted Tomography.   Short of death and brain surgery, there are ways to examine the brain with relatively little harm to a person. One way is to take a series of x-rays of the skull, each of them taking a different "slice" of the head, and then examine the brain structures revealed. This is a technique known as a **computer-assisted tomography** scan, or CT scan (formerly known as a CAT scan). An example of a CT scan is shown in Figure 2.9. CT scans show the structure of a living person's brain, such as the location of a tumor, damage from a stroke, or just general condition.

Magnetic Resonance Imaging.   A neuroimaging technique that has recently gained tremendous popularity is **magnetic resonance imaging,** or MRI. MRI works with the resonant frequencies of different molecules in the brain. When placed in a controlled magnetic field, the responses of those atoms can be detected and measured. An MRI brain scan is shown in Figure 2.10. Typically, the density of water molecules is used to determine structure, so it is not necessary to inject a chemical into the body, as with PET scans, or use harmful radiation, as with CT scans. Perhaps the biggest advantage of MRI scans is their clarity. The images that are produced are of much higher quality than those obtained with a traditional CT scan.

Electrical Measures

This section examines neurological measures of electrical activity generated by action potentials in the brain. Before covering more modern methods, we will look at some interesting reports made by Wilder Penfield in the 1950s (Penfield, 1955).

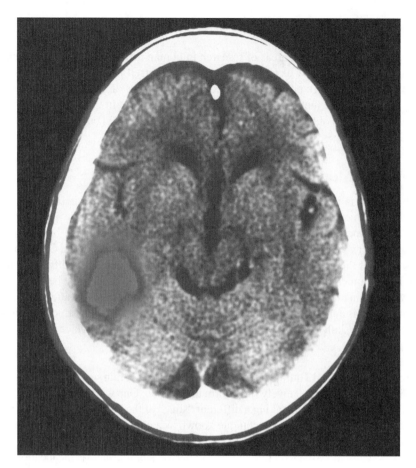

FIGURE 2.9   A CT Scan of the Brain

Electrical Stimulation.   Penfield was a Canadian neurosurgeon who was held in high regard for his work in mapping the sensory and motor homunculi in the cortex. He did this by probing people's brains with a mild electrical charge during surgery. Often these people had some intractable condition, so parts of the cortex were removed in an attempt at a cure (and often with a reasonable level of success). While the patient was awake, a section of the skull would be removed. Then the patient herself could report what effects the electrical stimulations had on her brain. This allowed Penfield to identify those portions of the brain that were critically important to survival. Although many functions are in the same area of different people's brains, there is some variability. While probing people's brains, Penfield often got interesting reports, usually when a portion of the temporal lobe was probed. Often it appeared that the patient was reexperiencing memories of long-lost episodes of their lives. Here is one example.

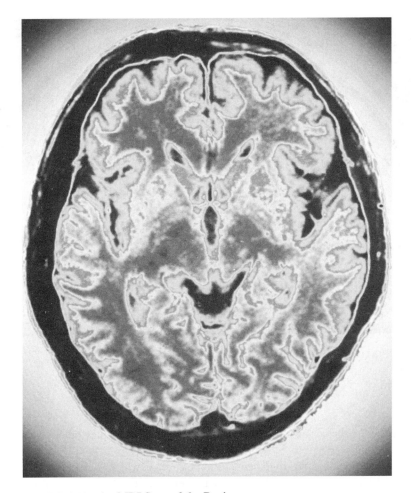

FIGURE 2.10   An MRI Scan of the Brain

The patient then said something about "street corner." The surgeon asked him, "Where?" and he replied "South Bend, Indiana, corner of Jacob and Washington." When asked to explain, he said he seemed to be looking at himself—at a younger age. (Penfield, 1955, p. 52)

Penfield reported that he had several responses of this quality from several different patients. He interpreted these reports as memories that the person had recovered or was re-experiencing. What was most striking to Penfield was that they were not the sorts of events that a person typically recalls from their lives, but rather boring and mundane memories. The vividness of these reports and their everyday quality led Penfield to suggest that the brain has the ability to record the stream of conscious throughout a lifetime. Long-term memory acted in some ways like a videorecorder. The electrical probe that he

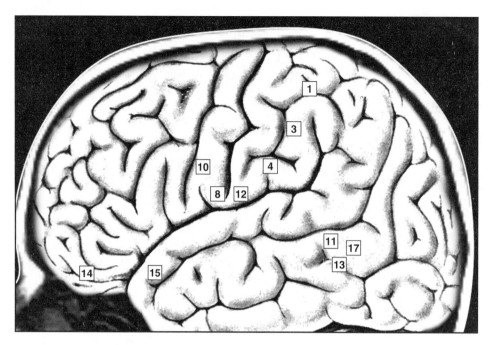

FIGURE 2.11   Penfield's Patient

Source: Penfield, 1955

had applied to the cortex allowed people to remember and replay otherwise forgotten aspects of their lives.

Although this is striking, there are some caveats, which were outlined by Loftus and Loftus (1980). First, it is unclear to what extent the reports were actually memories or were experiences generated at the time. These "memories" may be created in much the same way dreams are. According to the activation-synthesis theory (Hobson, 1988), during our sleep cycle, our cortex is stimulated with random electrical pulses from structures in the hindbrain. Because the brain does not like randomness, it attempts to impose structure on the information it is receiving. To do so, it uses readily available information that is reasonably close to the stimulation it is receiving. This is information in long-term memory. Penfield's reports could be of the same quality. His patients were receiving what amounted to random stimulation, and their brains were doing the best they could to make sense of this with whatever knowledge was available in long-term memory. Thus, these reports were mental constructs created at the time out of a combination of random information from the probe along with information that was actually stored in memory. (See Figure 2.11.)

Another problem with these reports is that there were very few of them. Of the 1,132 patients Penfield worked with, only 40 (3.5 percent) showed signs that he interpreted as memory reports. And most of these were not full-blown reports. Twenty-four claimed to have auditory experiences only (e.g., hearing voices or music), 19 claimed to have visual experiences only (seeing familiar people or objects), and only 12 gave what appeared to be complete memory reexperiences. Thus, there is very little evidence to work with.

Some of the reports Penfield received could not possibly have been actual reexperiences of past events. For example, in the report just given, the person states that he can see himself standing on the street corner. If memories of experiences were being faithfully recorded, this could not happen. You can't look at yourself from a distance without a mirror or a TV camera, for example.

Single-Cell Recording.   Although Penfield's electrical stimulation of the brain yielded intriguing, but perhaps misguided, results, there are other neuropsychological methods for examining cortical processing that rely on the electrical component of neural communication. The most direct use of this is called single-cell recording. In this method, an electrode is used to probe an individual living cell, somewhere in the nervous system, depending on the purpose and the tissue of interest. Using this electrode, the researcher is able to determine when it fires. Each time the electrical charge flows down the axon, it is recorded (although it should be noted that this technique may also pick up activity of other neurons in the proximity of the probe). The experimenter then has the subject engage in the task of interest, watching to see how the firing pattern of that individual cell changes. Obviously this is a very micro level of analysis. Information is only gathered about the operation of one cell in a brain made up of billions of cells. Also, this technique is invasive to the brain, so it is limited to animal research. Nevertheless, this technique can provide important detailed information about how different cells in the brain are processing different types of information.

Event-Related Potentials.   While single-cell recording provides information about what is going on in one cell, studies of event-related potentials provide information about larger groups of cells. Moreover, this approach has the advantage of being a noninvasive technique that can be used with ordinary people, such as university students, doing more complex tasks, such as remembering a poem. In this procedure electrodes are attached to a person's scalp so electrical activity in the underlying part of the brain can be recorded. These recordings are called *e*lectro*e*ncephalography, or EEG waves. Often there are several electrodes at regularly spaced and predetermined locations over the skull to help localize what the EEGs are actually recording.

EEG waves are used to measure **event-related potentials,** or ERPs. Basically, an ERP is a regular change in the pattern of electrical energy measured from the cortex at a given location as a function of the particular task or event that the person is thinking about (Coles, Gratton, & Fabiani, 1990). First, the memory researcher has an individual engage in various tasks at predetermined points in time. These are the "events" of event-related potentials. Then the researcher looks at the EEG waves that were recorded at that time relative to the time at which the events occurred. These electrical "potentials" in the EEG waves are what are "related" to the earlier "events"—hence the name event-related potentials, or ERPs.

If you've ever seen an EEG wave, it looks like a random bunch of vertical squiggles. And for each trial of an ERP study, this is largely what it is. Keep in mind that the brain is often being influenced by many things other than the particular task at hand, so there is a lot of electrical activity from these other processes. To get a clearer idea of what is going on in the brain, the researcher needs to average the electrical potentials across a large number of trials. This averaging process washes out much of the noise, leaving a clearer signal. An example of the effect of this averaging process is shown in Figure 2.12. As more and more trials are compiled, the ERP wave becomes more and more pronounced. This signal, or ERP signature, is often a relatively large wave of positive or negative electrical charge in a region of the brain occurring at a particular point in time after the original event. The ERP can then be related to theories of mental process. The existence of an ERP wave suggests that some sort of mental work is taking place. A difference between two waves corresponding to two different conditions in the study corresponds to different types of mental processes.

One of the biggest advantages to ERPs is temporal resolution—that is, knowing when things happen in the brain. Recordings can be made at 1 ms time slices. Thus, it is relatively clear when certain cognitive processes are kicking in or when different regions of the brain are becoming involved. People often talk about ERPs in terms of when certain interesting components arise in the waveform and the nature of these components. For example, people might talk about a P300 wave, which refers to an electrically positive wave occurring about 300 ms after the beginning of an event. An N400 wave refers to an electrically negative wave occurring about 400 ms after the beginning of an event (Bentin, 1989).

There are some disadvantages to ERPs. One is that the spatial resolution of ERP recordings—*where* things happen in the brain—is somewhat poor. Although one can get a general idea about what part of the brain is involved, determining a precise location is very difficult, although the technology is improving. Also, because there is so much activity going on in the brain at any given point in time, there is a lot of noise in addition to the signal one is interested in, which makes it more difficult to pick up on regularities that are in fact present. This is further complicated by the fact that there is a lot of "stuff" between the electrodes and the brain activity they are recording—skin, blood vessels, meninges, bone. One person described using EEG recordings to figure out what is going on in the brain as being a lot like trying to figure out what is going on in a factory by listening though the wall.

Blood Flow Measures

Not all neuropsychological methods rely on electrical impulses. Some approaches involve other measures of brain activity. One of these is a measure of cerebral blood flow. Collections of neurons that are working harder than other parts of the brain need more nutrients to be replenished and keep working. As a result, blood flow to those areas will increase to compensate for this change. The discovery of a relationship between blood flow and neural activity was somewhat serendipitous (as described in Posner & Raichle, 1994). In the early twentieth century, Walter K. had an abnormality in the blood vessels in his brain. Specifically, there was a large clump of blood vessels over his occipital lobe. Walter complained of a constant humming sound in his ears, which was the blood rushing through these vessels. He noticed the humming decreased when his eyes were closed and increased when his eyes were open and actively looking at something. The increased activity in the occipital lobes was associated with increased blood flow. In this section we look at two measures that rely on blood flow to assess what parts of the brain are being used for different tasks.

Positron Emission Tomography.   *Positron emission tomography,* or PET, is one method of measuring blood flow changes. Participants are injected with a radioactive

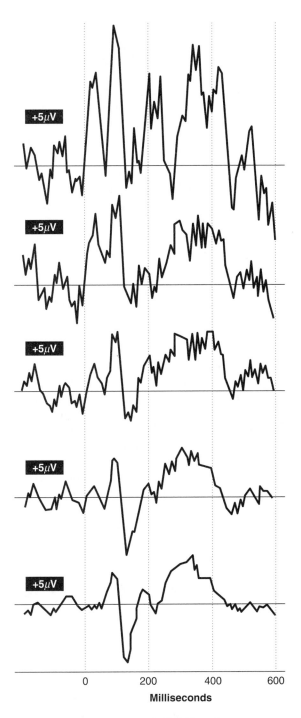

FIGURE 2.12   Averaging of ERP Waveforms

Source: Posner & Raichle, 1994

isotope of oxygen called oxygen-15 or ^{15}O. This isotope decays to ^{16}O, which is reasonably stable. The level of radioactivity is very low and relatively short-lived (it has a half-life of just over two minutes), so there is little harm to the body. Once the isotope is in the bloodstream, the person is placed into a recording device that measures the relative levels of the isotope in the brain. Recording levels in control conditions where the person is not doing much of anything are compared with experimental conditions where the person is engaging in the type of thought that is of interest for the study. Depending on the task, different parts of the brain are more or less active relative to the control state. These different levels of activity can be used to help determine which parts of the brain are being used.

Compared to ERP recording, the spatial resolution in PET scans is much better. Researchers have a clearer idea of what parts of the brain are being used for different cognitive activities. However, there are some problems with PET. One is that it takes a long time for a good image to be generated, typically no faster than 20 seconds. Think about how many different thoughts you could have if you were just lying on your back in a scanner for 20 seconds. Thus, while the spatial resolution is much better, the temporal resolution is relatively poor. So a person can determine *where* something is occurring in the brain but not *when*. It should also be noted that an averaging process is used with PET images similar to what is done with ERP recordings. What is revealed through these sorts of scans is averaged over many actual real-world events.

Functional Magnetic Resonance Imaging.   The MRI technology discussed earlier also has an advantage over CT scans in that it can be adapted to look at function as well as structure. This approach is called functional MRI or fMRI. fMRI uses the detection of oxygen atoms as a measure of mental activity. The density of oxygen molecules is associated with the operation of neural assemblies and the flow of blood to fortify those sets of cells. After all, the delivery of oxygen is one of the primary purposes of the bloodstream. The fMRI technique has the advantage over PET scans not only in the fact that there is no injection required, but that the images can be taken in a much shorter period of time, on the order of a few seconds, rather than the longer period of time that PET scans require. Still, fMRI scans still cannot match the temporal accuracy of ERP measurements.

At this point a number of neuroimaging methods have been mentioned. Each of these methods is used to take some sort of picture of either the structure of the brain itself or the neurological operations that occur during certain types of mental activity. There can be no question that such methods provide unique, intriguing, and valuable insights into the human experience. So why not use such methods exclusively? Well, it should be kept in mind that these methods provide only neurological information. They do not provide much information about content. To know what a person is remembering and to also gain some insight into how this occurs, we still need behavioral methods.

Altered Brains

Case Studies and Lesions.   Another source of insight into neurological underpinnings of memory comes from studies of people who have suffered some damage or lesion to the brain. This might be from an external event, such as a car accident or a gunshot; an internal event, such as a stroke or a virus; or, in very rare cases, from surgery. By examining the types of memory that are affected with damage to a specific part of the brain, it can be determined what role that structure plays. For example, if damage to the brain leads a person to be able to remember very little in the short term, it suggests that short-term memory uses this structure. Because of the very nature of these cases, it is not unusual for a single case to be studied in depth to help understand what has happened, what has gone wrong, and what sorts of techniques can be used to improve the situation.

Although brain lesions provide valuable insight, it is an imperfect method for studying neuropsychological processes. There are a number of reasons for this. One is that seldom is there is a pure lesion, with one structure being completely affected and no other structures being harmed. Lesions are often messy and affect a number of components. While this is especially true in humans, it is also true to some extent in animal studies in which lesions are intentionally introduced. Another problem with lesion studies is that rarely are there two cases in which people have identical lesions. Thus, it cannot be determined whether the consequences of the damage that occurred are unique to that person or are a generalizable consequence. Finally, lesions are very haphazard both in terms of where and when they occurred. There is not the sort of control one would hope to have in a systematic study. Thus, while there is important and valuable information to be gained from observing these cases, there are very clear limitations to the conclusions that can be drawn about how people think in general and how this thinking typically relates to the human brain. In spite of these limitations, as we'll see especially in Chapter 16 with amnesic patients, tremendous insight into memory can be gained.

Special Populations.   Studies of people who have some sort of altered neurological condition also provide pertinent data. For example, when we discuss amnesia (see Chapter 16), you'll see a number of studies using chronic alcoholics who have acquired a condition known as Korsakoff's Syndrome. Also, it is well known that as we age, there are systematic changes that occur in the brain as a result of the natural aging process. Thus, to some extent, age-related changes in memory can be viewed as neurological assessment of memory (see Chapter 15). Finally, some diseases, such as Alzheimer's, have systematic effects on the central nervous system (see Chapter 17). In these special populations, there is a high degree of regularity in the damage to the nervous system that is a result of the specific condition, so we can observe a systematic change in neurological functioning that results in altered thought and behavior. Of course, there may be some preexisting conditions that can complicate an assessment—for example, epilepsy can alter the brain's organization and structure.

Special populations are advantageous sources of information because they provide the researcher with a large number of people with a prespecified condition that has standard neurological changes associated with it. This allows for the removal of idiosyncratic changes that occur and are often observed in case studies. Because these groups are large, it also allows for a better understanding of the condition in a relatively short period of time and, hopefully, will lead to treatments faster.

Synopsis

A number of methods have been developed to look at how brain function relates to psychological experience, including that of memory. Some of these measures, like CT and MRI scans, look at structural characteristics, whereas others look at the actual functioning of the brain. For example, single-cell and EEG recordings examine electrical activity in the brain; PET and fMRI examine changes in blood flow as a function of mental work; and other methods examine how changes in brain structure affect memory. This includes damage to the brain from disease or injury, as well as groups of people who have well-known changes in brain structure, such as the elderly.

THE HERA MODEL

We've covered a lot of territory, so let's start putting some ideas together. As a reminder, in Chapter 1 we discussed that there are different types of long-term declarative memories called episodic and semantic memories. Is there anything about the organization of the brain that reveals any differences between how episodic and semantic memories are represented and processed neurologically? One theory of differential episodic and semantic processing is the **Hemispheric Encoding/Retrieval Asymmetry** (or HERA) model (Habib, Nyberg, & Tulving, 2003; Nyberg, Cabeza, & Tulving, 1996), which focuses on the prefrontal lobes in the left and right hemispheres of the brain during episodic and semantic encoding and retrieval. The prefrontal cortex is the most forward part of the frontal lobes.

Specifically, data from PET studies consistently show a greater involvement of the left frontal lobe in the retrieval of semantic information and the encoding of episodic information. Presumably, encoding new episodic memories involves using semantic knowledge to interpret the current situation. Conversely, there is consistently greater involvement of the right frontal lobe in the retrieval of episodic memories. This difference is even observed in behavioral data in which information is preferentially presented to either the left or right hemisphere (Blanchet et al., 2001). Thus, different parts of the brain appear to be more specialized for processing different types of information, and more precise studies of the prefrontal cortex show that smaller regions of the cortex are involved in more specific memory activities (Buckner, 1996; Shallice, Fletcher, & Dolan, 1998).

An important point to note about the HERA model is that it does not support the idea that episodic memories are stored in one hemisphere and semantic memories in the other. Nor is it the case that the frontal lobes are the primary brain regions where memory encoding and retrieval occur. For example, as mentioned earlier, the temporal lobes seem to be most critical for memory encoding, as evidence by people with severe brain damage and amnesia. Thus, we need to use the combination of information we get from both neuroimaging and brain lesion findings to better understand the facts (Mayes & Montaldi, 1999). What the HERA model does reveal is that different types of active controlled processing are involved in different memory processes. Even researchers who have a different interpretation of how neurological structures relate to memory processing seem to think that the brain handles semantic and episodic memories differently (e.g., Ranganath & Pallar, 1999; Wiggs, Weisberg, & Martin, 1999).

Synopsis

By understanding brain structure and function we can begin to build theories of memory that incorporate the realities uncovered by the results from the blossoming field of neuroscience. One example of this is the HERA model. This is a memory theory that attempts to take regularities emerging from neuroimaging studies—in this case hemispheric asymmetries—and map them onto what is known about different aspects of human memory.

SUMMARY

The operation of memory depends critically on the operation of the nervous system. At a basic level, we have covered the structure of the neuron and how the communication of information is accomplished at a neural level. This has involved both electrical and chemical components. We have also surveyed some of the larger brain structures that appear to play a major role in memory. This includes both subcortical structures, like the hippocampus, as well as parts of the cortex, such as the temporal lobes. Finally, because the study of neuropsychological processes involves an accurate assessment of the structure and function of the brain, we have described a number of neuroimaging techniques. It is also possible to gain insights into how brain structure and processes are related to memory performance by looking at people whose brains have been altered by lesions, disease, or the developmental process. After all, all thought, including and especially memory, occurs as an operation of the nervous system.

STUDY QUESTIONS

1. What are the basic components of a neuron?

2. How does the nervous system communicate information? What is the electrical component? What is the chemical component?

3. How do neurons change in order to encode information into memory?

4. What are some of the various neuroimaging methods available? Which are good for assessing structure? Which are good for recording electrical activity? Which are good for recording blood flow?

5. In what ways can changes in brain structure be used to assess memory?

6. What is an example of a theory of memory that takes into account findings from neuroscience?

KEY TERMS

acetylcholine, action potential, amygdala, axons, basal ganglia, cerebellum, computer-assisted tomography, consolidation, dendrites, diencephalon, dopamine, emergent property, event related potentials, frontal lobes, functional magnetic resonance imaging, HERA model, hippocampus, hypothalamus, laterality, long-term potentiation, magnetic resonance imaging, myelin sheath, neuron, neurotransmitters, nodes of Ranvier, occipital lobes, parietal lobes, positron emission tomography, single-cell recording, soma, synapse, temporal lobes, terminal buttons, thalamus

CHAPTER THREE

METHODS AND PRINCIPLES

Memory is an intimate part of who we are. However, despite the fact that it permeates all mental processes (or perhaps because of this), we have little conscious awareness of it. Intuitively, memory seems very ethereal. As described in Chapter 1, for most of history, memory was thought to be beyond objective study. It wasn't until the late nineteenth century that it became sensible to think about gaining a clear and accurate understanding of memory and the role it plays in our lives. Because it is so hard, if not impossible, to get a direct look at memory, we need good indirect methods. These often involve having an experimenter, manipulating what is to be remembered, recording an act of remembering, and then making inferences about memory based on what is observed. This may sound like an artificial process, but it's not unlike how other sciences proceed or how we conduct our day-to-day lives. For example, astronomers looking at computer readings can draw conclusions about planets circling distant stars without ever laying eyes on them. In this chapter we first address what an experiment is and how it compares to other types of data collection. Then we examine various methods of memory research. We first look at the learning situation itself, followed by some tasks that can be used to test memory contents and structure. Finally, we consider some issues about memory, such as conscious introspections. Along with each of these methods for understanding memory we also look at some basic, well-established principles whose discovery can be attributed, at least in part, to the methods being presented. For those interested students, methods of calculating some memory measures, perhaps for a laboratory section or a student research project, are provided in the Appendix.

COMPONENTS OF MEMORY RESEARCH

We approach memory from a scientific perspective to gain an objective understanding and minimize personal biases. As such, the ideas about memory discussed in this book reflect the work of scientists. To help you better understand how these people do their work, we first discuss what an experiment is and the different types of variables a researcher measures and control.

What Is an Experiment?

Most of our knowledge about memory comes from experiments. So what is an experiment? An *experiment* is a controlled situation in which a researcher manipulates variables of interest, measuring the effect of this manipulation. This is done while keeping many irrelevant variables as consistent as possible. Furthermore, participants are randomly assigned to the different conditions to make sure there is not any unwanted systematicity. The variables being manipulated are the independent variables, such as how much a person has to remember, how long she has to remember it, and so forth. The variables being measured are the dependent variables, such as how much is remembered, how accurate people are, how fast they remember, and so forth. In addition, irrelevant aspects of the situation are known as control variables. This can include such things as the room lighting, the instructions, the apparatus used, and so forth.

An experiment is done when a researcher has a hypothesis about the outcome. A hypothesis is an educated guess or prediction about how the variation of the independent variables will be related to the outcome of the dependent variables. Often this is the case in some theoretical language about how memory is operating in the context of the experiment.

Other Types of Studies

The experiment is not the only way to gather information about memory. Other methods are suitable when experimental control is difficult or impossible. One alternative is a *correlation,* where the performance of a dependent measure is assessed as a function of some preexisting change. For example, one can look at memory as a function of age. Age cannot be experimentally controlled, but it is information that can be used to make inferences about memory. Alternatively, a researcher may do a quasi-experiment in which preexisting conditions are combined with some controlled assignment of the independent variables—for example, if one class of students memorized a set of 100 words and another class memorized a set of 100 pictures. Here, the assignment of people to conditions is not random but is based on the classes they are already in.

Finally, in some situations, it is not possible to assess memory in large numbers of people. Instead, the researcher can do a case study. For example, when we look at the effects of brain damage on memory, we can assess memory in specific individuals because they are the only ones available with a specific type of deficit.

Synopsis

There are a variety of ways of studying memory. The most common are experiments in which a researcher has a great deal of control over the variables and can better assess what is affecting the observed outcome. The independent variables are manipulated, and the dependent variables are measured to see whether they conform to the hypothesis. In addition to experiments, it is also possible to use other methods, such as correlational, quasi-experimental, and case studies.

ASPECTS OF LEARNING

In order to test memory, some information first needs to be learned. How this happens is important. Was the information something that was consciously learned, or was it something that was just picked up along the way? What kind of information was it, pictures or words?

Intentional versus Incidental Learning

Methods.   An important factor in memory research is whether people explicitly *try* to learn. Explicit memorization is called **intentional learning.** The other possibility is that a person just happens to learn information during the course of other activities. This is called **incidental learning.** Intentional learning is when you study for this or any other class. Incidental learning is knowledge that you've picked up without having to try, such as knowing how often you've seen a movie in the past month.

An experimenter can explicitly alert a person that the information they are given is something that will be tested for later. These intentional learning instructions are direct, and they lead people to treat information more elaboratively. This elaborative processing can have profound effects on memory. Alternatively, if an experimenter gives incidental memory instructions, they are having the person pay attention to and think about the information but not expend any extra effort memorizing it. In such cases, a cover task is given to orient people to the information. These cover tasks vary from study to study, and they can include things such as pleasantness ratings, sensibility ratings, or sorting information into categories.

Principles.   In general, memory is better with intentional than with incidental learning. This section outlines four principles of memory that demonstrate the importance of the type of learning: levels of processing, mental imagery, the generation effect, and the automaticity of encoding.

Levels of Processing.   An example of the influence of the amount of effort exerted during memorization is the **levels of processing** effect (Craik & Lockhart, 1972). This refers to the degree to which people elaborate on information when they study it. When people try to learn, one thing they can do is simply repeat the information over and over. This is called **rote rehearsal.** In general, recall ability does not change with more rote rehearsal, and recognition is only slightly improved (Glenberg, Smith, & Green, 1977). You can see an example of the poor effectiveness of rote rehearsal in the results of a study done by Nickerson & Adams (1979). Students at Brown University were shown individual drawings of pennies like those in Figure 3.1. See if you can remember which is the correct one. In the penny study, students were shown pictures of pennies and asked to indicate whether they were accurate or not based on their memory of pennies they had seen in their lifetime and had to indicate whether it was correct. Students in this study were able to identify the correct drawing of the penny only 50 percent of the time. The penny that had the highest rate of acceptance was incorrect version I (with 67 percent of the students saying it was correct). Thus, repeated exposure to something does not improve memory.

In contrast, the more people think about the meaning of information, the more likely they are to use knowledge they already have, making inferences and thereby elaborating on the to-be-learned information. This connecting of knowledge is called **elaborative rehearsal.**

Information that receives little elaboration is processed less. For example, suppose a task is to think about a set of words and only determine whether the word is printed in upper- or lowercase letters. This is very shallow processing because it requires little attention to meaning and prior knowledge. However, if the task is to determine whether the word

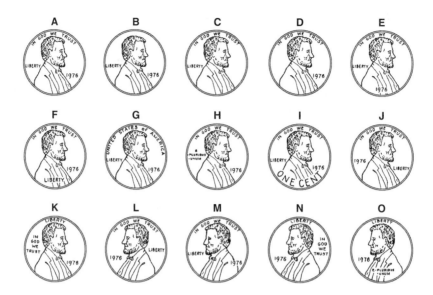

FIGURE 3.1   Which Penny Is Correct?

Source: Nickerson & Adams, 1979

makes sense in a sentence, this is deeper processing. In some sense, shallow processing evokes more incidental learning, whereas elaborative processing is more like intentional learning, although there may not be any overt effort to memorize. The levels of processing effect can occur for both incidental and intentional encoding (Hyde & Jenkins, 1973), although it is more likely to be observed during intentional learning.

Imagery.   One way people can elaborate on information is by creating a mental image of what is being learned. This greatly improves memory (e.g., Schnorr & Atkinson, 1969), as shown in Figure 3.2. People's memories were better when they formed mental images than when they were simply asked to rehearse the information. They had to make a concerted effort to form these mental pictures as well. The images did not appear spontaneously.

The discovery of the benefit to memory when a person creates mental images led to the development of what is known as the **Dual Code Theory** (Paivio, 1969). According to this view, people store information in memory in at least two forms: a verbal/linguistic code and a mental image code. These two codes can be associated to each other if they refer to the same thing. Memory improves in this view because with the use of mental imagery, there are multiple memory retrieval pathways to the same information and more memory traces containing the desired information. This makes successful remembering more likely.

Generation.   According to levels of processing, the more information is elaborated on, the better it is remembered. This can be done by the **generation effect:** Information that a person generates is remembered better than information that is simply read or heard (Slamecka & Graf, 1978). For example, suppose people are presented with a series of word segments,

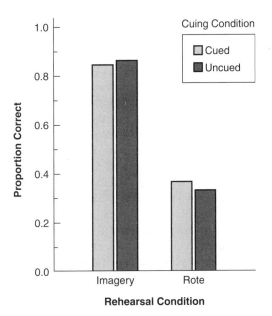

FIGURE 3.2   Impact of Mental Imagery on Memory

Source: Altered from graph reported in Schnorr & Atkinson, 1969

such as TAB_____, with the task of completing the word. This is a generation task because the person is generating the rest of the information. Alternatively, if people are simply asked to read a series of complete words, this is not a generation task because nothing is being created. The generation effect extends to a wide variety of different types of information, including memory for the context in which something was learned (Marsh, Edelman, & Bower, 2001).

A generation effect may also be observed when people solve a puzzle or problem when trying to understand something. This is called the **"aha" effect** (Auble, Franks, & Soraci, 1979). For example, a person may have trouble initially understanding a sentence such as "The man's back ached because the ends were too large." At some point, there is an awareness that this sentence is about the use of barbells and the person has an "aha" experience. Because the person generated her own explanation, memory about it is better. Similarly, if people complete a connect-the-dots puzzle, the picture is remembered better than if it was seen already assembled (Wills, Soraci, Chechile, & Taylor, 2000).

In addition to generating words and ideas, memory is also better when people actually perform a task in comparison to watching someone else do it or reading about it. This is called the **enactment effect**. Any type of performed action seems to produce this benefit. For example, it has also been shown that people remember words better if they are signed (as with American Sign Language) than if they are printed (Essen & Nilsson, 2003; Zimmer & Engelkamp, 2003). What appears to be happening is that people are mentally organizing and structuring information differently when they perform the action (Koriat & Pearlman-Avnion, 2003). This altered mental organization provides a better means of retrieving the information. However, it has also been suggested that this enactment effect may be a result, at least in part, of the objects used serving as memory cues (Steffens, Buchner, & Wender, 2003).

Automaticity.   It should be noted that under some conditions the type of learning might not matter much. Memory can be similar under incidental and intentional encoding conditions, depending on how people are thinking about the information at the time (Postman & Adams, 1956; Salzman, 1953, 1956) and may not be present with certain memory tests, such as recognition (Eagle & Leiter, 1964; Postman, Adams, & Philips, 1955). In other cases, there is an **automaticity of encoding** (Hasher & Zacks, 1979) in which information is stored in memory with very little effort. Because the information is automatically encoded, further efforts at learning do not provide additional benefit. Some types of information that are thought to be more automatically encoded are knowledge of event frequency, time, and location. For example, think of how many times in the past month you've eaten out. The answer comes to mind relatively easily, and it is unlikely that you deliberately learned this as it was occurring. If you think about the knowledge that you have, some of it was very easy to learn, whereas some of it was learned only with a great deal of effort.

Stimulus Characteristics

During learning, it is possible to manipulate not only what a person is doing, but the nature of the information itself. As already mentioned, some types of knowledge are easy to learn and remember. In contrast, others require more effort and are more likely to be forgotten.

Methods.   When studying memory, it is important to take into consideration what research participants think about the experiment. An adequate task analysis must be done. If not, there is the possibility that the researcher and the participant may interpret the materials in different ways. What an experimenter thinks the participant is memorizing is the **nominal stimulus.** The stimulus the subject identifies and thinks about is the **functional stimulus.** Usually, these are the same thing, but in some cases, they are very different. For example, a researcher might give people a list of nonsense syllables, one of them "DAX." In the experimenter's mind, this is just a meaningless series of letters. However, if the participant is a *Star Trek* fan, he would recognize this as the name of a character in the series.

Principles
Savings.   Stimuli affect memory in a number of ways. One of these, discovered by Ebbinghaus, is the principle of **savings.** After information has been learned and forgotten, a person requires less effort to learn it a second time. This is important for two reasons. First, this nicely illustrates the fact that although we may not be consciously aware of knowledge from our past, it may still affect our ability to learn and remember. Second, it shows that information we already know something about, even if we're not conscious of it, is easier to remember than information we are encountering for the first time. In general, the more information taps into our prior knowledge, the easier it is to remember. Thus, the meaning of a stimulus varies from person to person depending on the individual's experiences with and knowledge of a stimulus.

Pictures and Concreteness.   Pictures and words are treated differently by memory, even at a neurological level. For example, the right part of the hippocampus is more active for processing pictures, whereas the left is more active for processing words (Papanicolaou et al., 2002). Studies have found that pictures are remembered better than words (Shepard, 1967; Snodgrass, Volvovitz, & Walfish, 1972; Standing, 1973). This is the **picture superiority effect,** and it occurs because we are better attuned to processing perceptual than linguistic information. In addition, a picture is more likely to be unique and contain a higher degree of detail. However, even pictures can vary in how easily they are remembered depending on how meaningful they are. For example, people find it much easier to remember pictures of faces compared to pictures of snowflakes or inkblots (Goldstein & Chance, 1970).

It has also been found that concrete information—words like "car," "house," or "book"—is remembered better than abstract information—words like "truth," "betrayal," or "redemption." This is called the **concreteness effect.** Concreteness may aid memory because it involves more perceptual qualities. This is also consistent with the dual code theory mentioned earlier: Concrete information is more likely to be supported by an additional image code. This distinction between concrete and abstract information is supported neurologically. Concrete words are associated with greater basal extrastriate activation, suggesting greater perceptual processing (although there is some involved in abstract information processing as well) (Martin-Loeches, Hinojosa, Fernandez-Frias, & Rubia, 2001). Finally, there is greater activation of the right hemisphere by concrete words, whereas abstract words tend to involve more left hemisphere processing (Holcomb, Kounios, Anderson, & West, 1999; Kounios & Holcomb, 1994; Nittono, Suehiro, & Hori, 2002; Swaab, Baynes, & Knight, 2002).

Emotion.   Memory can also be influenced by emotions. Consider the difference between emotionally positive (e.g., courage) and negative (e.g., ordeal) information. According to the **Pollyanna principle,** there is a tendency to better remember positive than negative information. For example, positive words are learned more quickly than negative words (Anisfeld & Lambert, 1966; Stagner, 1933). Negative words are learned more quickly than emotionally neutral words (like *wood,* for example) (Carter, 1936; Carter, Jones, & Shock, 1934). However, there are circumstances where negative information is remembered better than positive information (Ortony, Turner, & Antos, 1983), such as with flashbacks about sudden, tragic events (see Chapter 13). Although there is no clear understanding of when memory is better with positive or negative information, it is clear that emotion can influence memory in important ways, with memories being more vivid for emotionally charged information (Kensinger & Corkin, 2003a).

Frequency.   This brings us to the final stimulus quality that can affect memory: **frequency.** Frequency is a bit odd in some respects. Memory is better for frequent information for recall tests (e.g., Taft, 1979), but it is better for rare information for recognition tests. Common things are easier to recall because there are more ways to get at them, which makes them more likely to be recalled. However, with recognition, less frequent items have fewer competitor memory traces, so they are recognized more easily (see the following sections on recall and recognition).

Synopsis

How information is learned and the nature of that information can affect memory. Memory is usually better when people intentionally learn something than when they learn it incidentally. This is reflected in the levels of processing framework, the influence of mental imagery, and the generation effect. However, some things seem to be learned more automatically. Memory is also influenced by what is remembered. For example, memory is better for things that a person already knows and for pictures, concrete information, and pleasant or intense experiences.

ASSESSING THE CONTENTS OF MEMORY

Questions about memory often center around issues of what information is in memory, what can be remembered later, and how easily it is remembered. There are a number of ways of getting at the contents of memory, and each has its advantages and disadvantages.

Recall

Methods.   The most straightforward way to test memory is the **recall** test. For recall, a person needs to report whatever he can retrieve from memory. There are many types of recall tests.

Free Recall.   The most basic recall test is **free recall,** in which people report as much information as they can. This is similar to answering an essay question on an exam. Because there is very little additional information provided, free recall is a good way to find out what a person knows very well. Presumably, this is what is reported. Information that a person knows, but not very well, is less likely to be reported because the person is less likely to successfully retrieve it.

Free recall data can also be used to study errors of omission (what people don't remember) and errors of commission (information that people report as memories that was not in fact part of the event). These are called **intrusions,** and they can be significant when studying false memories (see Chapter 12). Studying **recall order** can give insight into how memories are structured. This is discussed in more detail in the section on cluster analyses.

Forced Recall.   One problem with free recall is that there might be information that people remember, perhaps faintly, but that they are unwilling to report in case they might be wrong. The memories may seem unfamiliar or lacking in details. One way to encourage people to report these weaker memories is to give a **forced recall** test. Unlike a free recall, where a person can report as much or as little as desired, in a forced recall test a person is forced to report a certain amount of information. Typically, this is more information than what would have been reported under free recall. Using this approach, weaker knowledge in memory can be assessed as being present. Typically, this weaker knowledge is provided toward the end of forced recall. Forced recall can also be used to elicit intrusions. These errors can be informative about the processes people use to recover memories by illustrating how that process can break down. In other words, the mistakes that people make are not random, but they follow certain principles. Studying these errors can provide insight into how memory works normally when it is successful.

Cued Recall.   Memories are often associated with a context or setting. There are many things in the environment that can serve as context. To get a better idea about how context influences memory retrieval during recall, a **cued recall** test can be used. During memorization, people learn a set of information. The experimenter designates some of this information as target information the participant must recall. Associated with this target information are other sets of information that serve as retrieval cues. Thus, the experimenter is controlling the context that will be relevant later. The paired associate learning tasks that were discussed in Chapter 1 are a good example of this sort of cue and target knowledge learning.

During memory retrieval, the experimenter provides a set of cues, and the task is to report the information that goes with those cues. In this way the experimenter controls the context and can systematically observe how it influences memory. Memory retrieval is much more constrained than under free recall conditions. During cued recall, people respond to either as many cues as they can or to all of the cues, much like a forced recall test. Again, both accuracy and errors can be used to help understand the contents of memory.

Retrieval Plans.   During recall tests, people need to mentally organize the information to be able to adequately retrieve it later. This includes both recalling information that has not yet been reported as well as avoiding reporting something that has already been recalled. To monitor their memory retrieval during recall, people often develop a set of retrieval strategies known as a **retrieval plan.** This is a set of retrieval cues used to help guide a person through the information. As we will see in Chapter 7, if this retrieval plan is thwarted or disrupted by external influences, memory performance declines. This is true even when the cues are some of the elements that must be remembered, which, on the face of it, should help memory.

Principles
Forgetting Curve.   Perhaps the strongest finding to come out of research using recall tests is that the more time that has passed, the less likely a person will remember a given piece of information. Or, to put it simply, people forget more as time passes. The way forgetting proceeds was one of the first things discovered from recall tests. In Ebbinghaus's studies he was able to track his performance at various time intervals. What he observed is the **forgetting curve,** shown in Figure 3.3. The forgetting curve is a negatively accelerating function. That is, the rate of forgetting is most rapid initially after the information was learned. As time passes, although the cumulative amount of knowledge loss grows larger, the rate of this accumulation slows down accordingly. Forgetting curves are one of the most reliable observations in human memory and occur with all kinds of information, not just nonsense syllables.

Overlearning.   The consistency of the forgetting curve is reassuring in its stability. Yet, at the same time, it is deeply disturbing in its suggestion that everything we've ever learned or

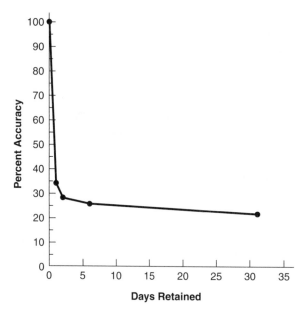

FIGURE 3.3 A Forgetting Curve

Source: After Ebbinghaus, 1885

known is fated to be forgotten at some point. While there is a truth in the forgetting curve, it is not always the case that forgetting inevitably occurs. In addition to the forgetting curve, another principle that Ebbinghaus discovered using recall was overlearning. **Overlearning** occurs when a person continues to study information after it is already possible to recall it without errors. This continued practice causes the forgetting curve to lessen and possibly disappear altogether. In such cases, the information becomes chronically available and is greatly resistant to forgetting. Thus, many of the fundamentals you remember from your schooling, such as the "A, B, C" song, have been greatly overlearned, and you are unlikely to forget that knowledge. This is one reason why education emphasizes repetition and practice.

Reminiscence and Hypermnesia.   Not only do we forget things all the time, but we can also remember things that were once forgotten. This principle of remembering previously forgotten information is known as **reminiscence** (Ballard, 1913). Generally, reminiscence is observed with a recall task, particularly free recall. Although reminiscence occurs, the processes of forgetting continue to operate. Thus, if the times that a person tries to remember are spread out, even though reminiscence is occurring, the person may be remembering less and less overall. However, if a person tries to recall information several times in a row, the rate of reminiscence may be greater than the rate of forgetting. Under such circumstances the person is cumulatively remembering more and more each time (Erdelyi & Becker, 1974; Wheeler & Roediger, 1992). This is called **hypermnesia** (the opposite of amnesia). Hypermnesia has been documented under a number of circumstances, but it is difficult to observe. It is more likely to be seen with pictures (Payne, 1987) and with shorter intervals between recall tests (Wheeler & Roediger, 1992). It is also more evident in free and cued recall situations than in recognition (Otani & Hodge, 1991). This occurs because the pieces of information in a set that are recalled earlier can serve as cues to assist the retrieval of the information that was previously forgotten.

It should also be noted that while shorter delays (e.g., a few minutes) are more likely to produce hypermnesia than longer ones (e.g., a few hours), at very short delays (e.g., a few seconds), whatever causes hypermnesia may not have time to operate. For example, using lists of words, hypermnesia does not occur if there is a delay of less than five seconds per word across memory tests, but it does occur if more than five seconds per word is given (Payne, 1987).

The existence and operation of reminiscence and hypermnesia have practical significance. When it seems that you have completely forgotten a piece of information, putting it out of your mind for a period of time may help you to remember it later. Of course, as with any type of memory, the more elaborately you think about the information during learning, such as forming mental images, the more successful later attempts to remember will be, even for reminiscence and hypermnesia.

Recognition

During recall, people need to generate the information, at least in part. However, in some cases, people need only to identify something already in their environment as being familiar or old, and thus recognized, or as being unfamiliar or new, and thus unrecognized. **Recognition** is a matching process in which the contents of the environment are compared with the contents of memory. If there is a match, then recognition occurs; otherwise it does not.

Methods

Old-New Recognition. The simplest form of recognition testing is **old-new recognition.** In this method a person is given an item and asked to indicate whether it is old or new. Often this is done by making yes-no decisions in which "yes" indicates old items. Memory is assessed based on the pattern of responses. This method simplifies the retrieval situation, making it easier to track and analyze. A great deal of information can be derived from such simple tasks. Sophisticated approaches can lead to penetrating insights into the contents and process of memory.

Correction for Guessing. When it comes to simple old-new responses, some accurately reflect a person's memory, but others involve a degree of uncertainty and are therefore guesses. Suppose a person identified 50 items correctly on a memory test. If that person had no incorrect answers, then it would seem that his memory was very accurate. However, if that person got 50 wrong and 50 correct, then it would appear he was guessing. What is needed is some way to correct for guessing, to provide a more accurate estimate of memory.

A simple way to correct for guessing is to subtract the number of incorrect responses from the number of correct responses. And in some cases this is what is done. However, this is a rather crude adjustment, and it can miss more subtle aspects of memory performance.

One must remember that guessing can be affected by two pieces of information. One is the degree to which old items can be distinguished from new ones in memory. This is called **discrimination.** Sometimes discrimination is relatively easy, such as identifying whether a person is a famous actor versus someone you've never heard of before.

The second piece of information is the degree to which a person is willing to accept what he remembers as new or old. This is called **bias.** In some cases, people may adopt a strict criterion and thus have a "conservative" bias. In this situation, people accept only cases in which they are very sure that the information is old so there are no false alarms. A **false alarm** is calling something old that is in fact new. A situation in which a person might be motivated to adopt a conservative bias would be in eyewitness identification. The eyewitness wants to be sure that the person she identifies is the criminal. Picking out the wrong person could lead to an innocent person being punished for a deed she did not commit and leaving the true guilty party at large, free to commit more crimes. In other cases, people may adopt a loose criterion and thus have a "liberal" bias. In this situation, people are more willing to accept a memory that has a more remote possibility of being old to avoid making any "miss" responses. A miss is calling an item new that is in fact old. A situation in which a person might be motivated to adopt a liberal bias would be in looking for a lost set of keys. The searcher wants to be sure that all plausible locations are searched.

A method of estimating discrimination and bias is called **signal detection theory** (Banks, 1970; Lockhart & Murdock, 1970). This approach has been adopted from psychophysicists, who borrowed it from communications theory. Using this approach, one can use a measure of discrimination, often called d', and of bias, often called β. (See Snodgrass & Corwin, 1988, for a discussion of various measures of discrimination and bias.)

The basic idea is to assess the ability to detect the signal (an accurate memory) from the noise (inaccurate memories). The thinking in signal detection theory is illustrated in Figure 3.4. This approach assumes that there are two distributions: one for the old items and one for the new items along some dimension, such as familiarity. The farther apart these two distributions are, the easier it is to distinguish between them and, thus, the larger the discrimination. Conversely, the more these two distributions overlap, the harder it is to separate them, the smaller the discrimination will be. Each of these conditions is also illustrated in Figure 3.4.

Keeping the distance between the two distributions constant, we can see how bias affects memory performance. The criterion a person uses to separate out what is identified as old and new is measured by β. If β is set very far to the right, the person has adopted a conservative criterion, and very few memories will be accepted as old. However, if β is set far to the left, the person has adopted a liberal criterion, and very few memories will be accepted as new.

Forced-Choice Recognition.   Another form of recognition is when people are given several items and are asked to indicate which one is old. This is **forced choice recognition.** Typically, there are two, three, or four alternatives. Forced choice recognition allows a researcher to manipulate the incorrect items in terms of the degree to which they resemble the correct one on some critical dimension. Such manipulations can provide insight into what sorts of knowledge people are using when remembering something. The wrong items that

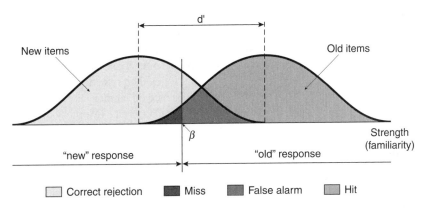

FIGURE 3.4   **Illustration of the Underlying Logic for Signal Detection Theory**

are more often selected as "old" would more closely match the information in memory, thus lending some insight into the contents of memory.

Social Influences

Many of the studies discussed here have a person largely alone in the environment. However, in the real world, people are in social situations, interacting with others in complex ways. These other people can influence memory. For example, people who work with high-performing individuals will recall more later than people who work with low-performing individuals (Reysen, 2003). Thus, how well we remember is influenced by how well the people with whom we interact remember. Now let us look at two other social influences on memory in detail.

Collaborative Inhibition.   Is memory affected by whether people are remembering things alone or in a group? Studies have found that when people in groups try to recall something, they typically recall less than if they were separated, asked to recall information, and had their individual efforts pooled (Basden, Basden, Bryner, & Thomas, 1997; Weldon & Bellinger, 1997). This decline in memory when working in a group is **collaborative inhibition.**

Collaborative inhibition may seem to reflect some sort of social loafing. However, what is actually going on is that a person is encountering different ways that other people have structured the information. Each person's recalls are based on his or her own retrieval plan. When confronted with an organization that is inconsistent with one's own retrieval plan, the ability to recall becomes disrupted, and performance declines (Finlay, Hitch, & Meudell, 2000; Weldon, Blair, & Huebsch, 2000). This is related to the part-set inhibition phenomenon (see Chapter 7). It should be noted that although people recall more as individuals than in groups, recalling in groups does increase the accuracy of the recalled information (Vollrath, Sheppard, Hinsz, & Davis, 1989).

Collaborative Facilitation.   Although memory is worse on recall tests in groups than alone, the opposite is true for recognition (Hinsz, 1990; Vollrath et al., 1989). This is

collaborative facilitation. In recall, the retrieval plan plays an important role in performance. In contrast, in recognition there is no retrieval plan. Memory only requires that something seem familiar, and anything more is a bonus. When people do recognition in groups, they can pool their resources to arrive at some consensus about what happened, although this is more effective at accepting old items than rejecting new items (Clark, Hori, Putnam, & Martin, 2000). Issues of social influence on memory are more prominently discussed in Chapter 12 (Memory and Reality) and Chapter 13 (Memory and the Law).

Synopsis

Two of the most common ways to test memory are recall and recognition. Recall involves producing information. Often people need a retrieval plan to help organize their recalls. Recall tests have helped illustrate such basic principles as the forgetting curve, overlearning, reminiscence, and hypermnesia. Recognition involves assessing whether something has been encountered before, such as with old-new recognition tests, although some correction for guessing may be needed. In more complex situations, people may be given forced-choice recognition tests in which they need to select one option from a set of alternatives. Finally, memory retrieval can be influenced by social circumstances. Sometimes other people can hinder memory, as with collaborative inhibition, whereas other times other people can augment memory, as with collaborative facilitation.

ASSESSING MEMORY STRUCTURE AND PROCESS

We have looked at methods that assess the contents of memory. In this section we cover ways of looking at memory structure and the processes that are used in retrieval. The structure of memories refers to both the organization of multiple pieces of information within a single memory trace or across multiple memory traces. The processes of memory refer to the mental activities that a person engages in when trying to retrieve a piece of knowledge. Basically, *how* do we remember?

Mental Chronometry

An important and frequently used source of information in memory research is the speed of responding. In many cases this **response time** is recorded on the order of milliseconds or seconds. The idea is that faster response times reflect simpler memory processes and/or more familiar memories, whereas slower response times reflect more complex memory processes and/or more unfamiliar memories.

Methods.   Response time is measured from the onset of some stimulus. For example, when asked to identify whether a series of faces has been seen before, the time will be recorded from the moment the picture was shown to the time the person responds. The time recorded for any given memory is not very informative by itself. That time must be placed in some context of other times to understand whether it is fast or slow. While there are many variations on this idea, the use of response times can be classified into two broad categories.

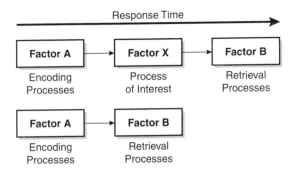

FIGURE 3.5 Donders's Subtractive Factors Logic for Response Times

The first description of mental chronometry, developed by Donders, was **subtractive factors logic.** This procedure is outlined in Figure 3.5. The idea is to have at least two conditions that are identical except for the inclusion of one step in processing. For example, both conditions include the same encoding (factor A) and response (factor B) processes. However, the condition of interest involves an extra step (factor X). After collecting the times, the time for the simpler process (A + B) is subtracted from the time for the more complex one (A + X + B). What is left over should be the time for the critical process. For example, in a simple condition one could have a person indicate whether a picture of a face is old or new. In a more complex condition the person would indicate whether a picture of a face is old or new and whether the person is living or dead. Based on subtractive factors logic, the difference between these two conditions would reflect the time it takes to remember a person's current heath status.

While subtractive factors logic is appealing, it has a number of problems. For one, it is unclear whether the process of interest is being added in a way that does not disrupt or change others and that occurs at a time when these other processes are not taking place. Another approach to mental chronometry is **additive factors logic,** developed by Sternberg (and discussed in more detail in Chapter 4). This approach is outlined in Figure 3.6. Rather than having two conditions that differ by the presence or absence of a mental stage, in

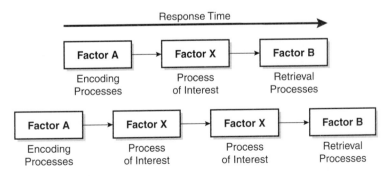

FIGURE 3.6 Sternberg's Additive Factors Logic for Response Times

additive factors logic the critical stage of interest (factor X) is always present. What varies is its degree of involvement—that is, how much of that process is added relative to a comparison condition. For example, it may be a stage that a person needs to go through many times or that involves various numbers of memory traces. By looking at the differences among conditions, one can provide an estimate of the influence of each increment of complexity. This approach is more likely to preserve a greater array of mental processes across conditions, making the comparison more reliable and meaningful.

Principles.   The analysis of response times has yielded a wealth of information about the structure and operation of memory. One of the most prominent of these is priming. **Priming** is a speeding up of response time to information that immediately follows related information. For example, when making lexical decision judgments (that is, deciding whether a string of letters is a word or not), people are faster to say the string "doctor" is a word if it immediately follows "nurse" than if it follows "bread" (e.g., Meyer & Schvanevelt, 1971). The idea is that "nurse" activates or primes a person's knowledge of nurses in long-term memory. The concept "doctor" is very related to "nurse," so, because it has been primed, information about doctors is retrieved more quickly than it would have been had the person been thinking about something unrelated (like bread) just previously.

Cluster Analysis

Some methods of assessing memory are aimed at directly indicating how information is organized. Knowing this can provide insight into how things such as remindings occur and why our thoughts drift in some ways but not in others. There are a number of ways to approach this question. Looking at the data from priming studies is one way. Regardless of the method, what is going on in such studies is an attempt to look at clusters of memories. In fact, there is a special domain of statistics known as cluster analysis where the goal is to detect groups or clusters of information in a set of data.

Methods.   There are number of methods that can be used to look at clusters of information in memory. Here we focus on two relatively simple measures to give you a feel for how this approach works.

Inter-Item Delays.   A time-based procedure for assessing memory organization with recall is if you keep track of the amount of time between each recalled item. What you'll find is that there is not a uniform pattern. Instead, people report a burst of a few items, then a pause, then a burst of a few more, and a pause, and so on (e.g., Patterson, Meltzer, & Mandler, 1971; Pollio, Richards, & Lucas, 1969). By using these **inter-item delays,** one can make inferences about memory structure. Memories that are structured together are likely to be recalled together during one of the bursts. However, information that is stored apart is more likely to be separated by a longer pause or delay.

ARC Scores.   There are also methods of obtaining memory clusters by looking at the content of recall, specifically the order in which information was reported. Pieces of information that are stored together in memory are likely to be recalled together. In many cases you can make some reasonable guess about how a set of information could optimally be organized. For example, a set of words can be organized into categories. It then becomes possible to test whether people have adopted that organization. This can be done by calculating Adjusted Ratio of Clustering (or ARC) scores (Roenker, Thompson, & Brown, 1971). ARC scores index the degree to which a recall sequence conforms to predetermined categories, taking into account how much organization would be expected by chance. The formula for calculating ARC scores is given in the Appendix.

There are many sorts of analyses that address the organization of information. For example, the ARC' score measures the degree to which a recall conforms to a predetermined sequential order (Pellegrino, 1971). The method for calculating ARC' scores is also provided in the Appendix.

Subjective Organization. There are also ways to get at subjective organization—that is, the organization imposed by the person himself or herself rather than the experimenter. This is useful when there is no clear a priori organization of the information. One of these is a measure that produces an ordered cluster tree (e.g., Reitman & Rueter, 1980). Basically, people are asked to recall a complete set of information a number of times. What this measure then does is look for consistencies in these repeated recalls, both in terms of the clusters that might be present as well as any stable sequential orders that might be produced.

Another way to assess how people subjectively organize information in long-term memory is to have them indicate where breaks should occur when they are viewing continuous events. For example, people might watch a film in which they are asked to press a button every time they think there has been an important shift in the situation. The locations that people select as break points are thought to correspond to separation of different types of information in memory (Newtson, 1976).

Principles. Clustering methods have shown that memories are highly structured. This structure may take the form of a hierarchy. The more structure a person can impose on a set of information, the better her recall will be (Mandler, 1967). When people are given a set of information, they often adopt that structure, which is seen in how they remember it. For example, in a study by Bousfield (1953), people were given a list 60 words to memorize. These words were from four categories (i.e., animals, people's names, vegetables, and professions), but they were presented in a random order. When people later recalled those words, there was a strong tendency to recall them in clusters based on the four categories. Moreover, as time passes and people have more experience with a set of information, their memories become more organized (e.g., Bousfield & Bousfield, 1966). In fact, experts in a domain have highly organized knowledge bases.

Finally, even when given what appears to be a random set of information, people impose some subjective organization upon it (Tulving, 1962). This subjective organization takes into account the various idiosyncratic interpretations people place on a set of items to create a structure that will help them remember. While space may abhor a vacuum, the human brain abhors randomness. It is always searching for regularities and structure.

Synopsis

There are a number of ways to look at the structure and function of memory. Mental chronometry allows us to look at how long it takes to remember something to help draw conclusions about memory structure, organization, and complexity. Priming is a classic example of the how mental chronometry can yield insights into memory. Cluster analyses more directly assess how knowledge is structured in memory.

CONSCIOUS EXPERIENCE OF MEMORY

Metamemory Measures

Another important characteristic of memory is the phenomenological experience of memory. The awareness of one's own memory and memory processes is known as **metamemory** and is highlighted in Chapter 14. A brief coverage of metamemory issues is presented here to illustrate how to study the experience and awareness of memory.

Methods.   Metamemory studies require people to report their own memory processes. This method of introspection has a long and checkered past dating back to the early days of experimental psychology, and many people are still cautious about using **verbal reports** (e.g., Nisbett & Wilson, 1977) because many of our thought processes lie outside of conscious awareness. However, despite this, there are still cases where verbal reports can provide insights about cognition (e.g., Ericsson & Simon, 1980), especially if one is concerned with conscious mental states and their consequences.

There are a number of metamemory methods. One of the most commonly used is remember vs. know judgment (Gardiner, 1988). With this approach, people are asked to recall or recognize a set of information. For those things that are recalled or identified as old, people then rate whether the information is something they consciously remember learning or something they know they encountered before but have no conscious memory of learning it. For example, if you can recollect where and when you learned of your acceptance into college, then you would say that you remember it. In contrast, if you have no conscious memory of this event, but you know it must have occurred, then you would say that you only know it.

Principles.   A number of insights have been gained by looking at what people attribute to their own memory processes. People can be led astray and become biased when assessing their own memories. This is clearly illustrated by the hindsight bias (a.k.a. the "knew-it-all-along" effect) (e.g., Fischhoff, 1975). The hindsight bias is a tendency to distort memories so they conform to one's current goals or circumstances. For example, people might be asked to make predictions about how likely an event is to occur. Then some time afterward one group (the experimental group) is presented with information about the actual outcome. Another group (the control group) is not given this information. If everyone then reports his or her original estimates, those in the experimental group are more likely to "misremember" their original estimates as being much closer to the actual outcome. We'll discuss this more in Chapter 14.

Implicit Memory

Again, implicit memory refers to memories and memory processes that are unconscious. It is rare to use memory so only implicit or explicit memory processes are involved. Performance almost always reflects a mixture of these two. However, there are some methods that allow for the effects and influences of each of these to be separated.

Methods. Measures that are aimed more at implicit memory use tasks in which people are not aware that memory is being tested or when there is little to no conscious control over the process. Implicit memory methods either tap preexisting knowledge or present people with a set of information and then test memory some time afterward. In the latter case, the memory tests are given under the guise of being unrelated to what had been done previously so people are not motivated to consciously remember. Implicit memory measures include such things as word fragment completion, perceptual identification, and priming.

One method for separating out implicit and explicit memory processes is the process dissociation procedure. Because there are no "process pure" tasks, with almost any task including both conscious and unconscious components, this procedure was designed to help estimate the relative influence of explicit and implicit processes (e.g., Jacoby, 1991). For example, suppose a person has read a list words and then takes a word fragment completion test. This procedure works by having people recall information under two conditions. In the inclusion condition, the person completes a series of word fragments with whatever words she can think of, even if they were words from the prior list. In the exclusion condition, a person uses any word he can think of as long as they are *not* words that were on the previous list. Using performance in these two conditions, it is possible to arrive at estimates of explicit and implicit memory. The procedures for calculating these components using the process dissociation procedure are given in the Appendix.

Synopsis

It is important to know what it feels like to remember something. Awareness of one's own memory is known as metamemory. Studies of metamemory reveal our insights into our own memories as well as how these insights can be wrong. It is also important to realize that many memory processes occur outside of awareness in what is known as implicit memory.

SUMMARY

This chapter reviewed a number of methods for looking at memory and some basic principles that are illustrated by them. Each method has its strengths and limitations. To gain the most accurate picture of memory, it is important to use multiple methods. The more methods that point to the same answer, the more reliable that answer will be. However, if different methods lead to different answers, then something is wrong. For example, suppose there are two conditions. In one, people are more accurate. However, if they also are much slower in that condition, then this is known as a speed-accuracy tradeoff. Because people are making fewer errors and slowing down, it may just mean that they are being more careful, not that these data reflect anything about memory per se. More generally, multiple sources of data can be used in combination to provide a more complete picture of how memory operates (Meyer, Irwin, Osman, & Kounios, 1988). Because of our lack of direct access to memory, we need a variety of methods. Converging operations allow us the greatest level of certainty about one of the more elusive topics in science.

STUDY QUESTIONS

1. What are the primary components of an experiment? Why is this a preferred way to study memory?

2. What are some ways to learn information so it will be better remembered later? Is this true of all kinds of information?

3. What kinds of information are easier to remember? What kinds are more difficult?

4. What are the various sorts of recall tests, and what can they reveal about memory?

5. What are the various sorts of recognition tests, and what can they reveal about memory?

6. What are some of the ways to correct for guessing on memory tests?

7. What are some of the ways that social situations can influence how well memory works?

8. How can mental chronometry be used to assess characteristics of memory? What is an example of some phenomenon of memory that is clearly shown using mental chronometry?

9. How are cluster analyses used to study memory?

10. What is metamemory, and what does it tell us about how people use their memories?

11. What is implicit memory, and why is it important to memory functioning more generally?

KEY TERMS

additive factors logic, "aha" effect, automaticity of encoding, bias, collaborative facilitation, collaborative inhibition, concreteness effect, cued recall, discrimination, Dual Code Theory, elaborative rehearsal, enactment effect, forced recall, forced choice recognition, forgetting curve, free recall, frequency, generation effect, hypermnesia, incidental learning, intentional learning, inter-item delays, intrusions, levels of processing, metamemory, old-new recognition, overlearning, picture superiority effect, Pollyanna principle, priming, recall, recall order, recognition, reminiscence, response time, retrieval plan, rote rehearsal, savings, signal detection theory, subtractive factors logic, verbal reports

CHAPTER FOUR

SENSORY AND SHORT-TERM MEMORY

When people think about memory, they typically think about retaining knowledge over long periods of time. When most people speak of short-term memory, they often refer to remembering over a few hours or days. However, for cognitive psychologists, memory in the short term means much briefer spans of time, often less than a minute. What is the point of studying such fleeting memories? Aren't changes in the world from one moment to the next just part of the noise in life? Well, no. Without these short-term memories, we would live in the permanent, absolute present—the eternal now. Language as we know it would not be possible. You would not be able to watch a film. Much of the world involves events that are spread out over time. Take the example of hearing a word. If you think about it, all words are made up of strings of sounds that are occurring at different points in time. To hear this string as a whole, you need to integrate the sounds. What allows you do this is the memory of what has occurred before, so the information you remember over a period of time helps you link together the sounds to form the whole word.

Two types of brief memories are considered in this chapter. The first are very short-term memories, known as the sensory registers. These modality specific systems allow us to do important sensory identification and integration, such as the preceeding word identification example. The second is what is more formally known as short-term memory. This is memory for ideas that are within or close to conscious awareness.

SENSORY MEMORY

The briefest memory systems are the **sensory registers.** These are modality specific systems. This means that each sensory register retains information specific to certain sensory information. For example, the visual sensory register retains visual information. It is easy to see that these are relatively primitive memory systems. Their primary purpose is for low-level processing that involves the sensory information itself.

Because different sensory systems process information with different physical properties, each sensory register has different qualities and characteristics. As such, some consideration is given to three sensory registers: (1) The visual sensory register or iconic memory, (2) the auditory sensory register or echoic memory, and (3) the haptic sensory register for touch information. There are other sensory registers, but these three have been selected to provide a relatively broad understanding of the sensory registers. The first two have been given a great deal of study. The third has received less attention, but we include it to illustrate how a sensory register operates even in a sensory modality for which humans are not particularly well suited.

ICONIC MEMORY

The first sensory register considered is the visual sensory register or **iconic memory.** Humans are primarily visual animals. As such, it is not surprising that iconic memory is the most extensively studied sensory register. Information is represented in iconic memory in a form that captures the visual stimulation we receive in our retinas, although there are some important differences. The mental representation in iconic memory is called an **icon** (hence the name *iconic* memory). To understand the role iconic memory plays, we need to understand how much information is held in iconic memory, how long an iconic representation is retained, and how iconic information is used to build up mental representation of the visual world, even though at any moment we are only seeing a small bit of it.

Span and Duration of Iconic Memory

The first two issues addressed are how much information iconic memory can hold and how long it holds it. In one study, Averbach (1963) presented two people (himself and one other) with sets of 1 to 13 dots for brief periods of time, anywhere from 40 to 600 milliseconds. The task was to say how many dots were in the display. The results are shown in Figure 4.1. For the briefest display (40 ms), people were fairly accurate when there was only a single dot, but they were pretty lousy at it when there were more than one. However, for the longer two durations (150 and 600 ms), they were fairly accurate when there were 4 or 5 dots, with performance declining gradually after that. Although there is a large time difference between the second and third conditions, the pattern of performance is roughly the same. The additional time did not provide much benefit.

Because this study looked at briefly presented displays, it is assessing iconic memory. From these data it is tempting to conclude that the amount of information that is being held in iconic memory is 4 or 5 items. Any more than that is beyond a person's capacity. Within that range, however, an accurate assessment can be made. However, this is an incorrect conclusion.

In a study by Sperling (1960), people were presented with brief displays, similar to the Averbach (1963) study. People saw displays of letters instead of dots, and there were 12 of them (in a 3 × 4 matrix). The task was to identify as many letters as possible. This display was presented for 50 milliseconds. The control condition (also called the whole report condition) simply asked people to name as many of the letters as possible. In this case, people were typically able to accurately name 4 or 5 letters. Again, by itself, this could be interpreted as showing that the number of items in iconic memory is 4 or 5.

However, there was an experimental condition in Sperling's (1960) study (also called the partial report condition). In this condition, one of three tones was sounded to indicate which row of the display people should start with. A high tone indicated the top row, a

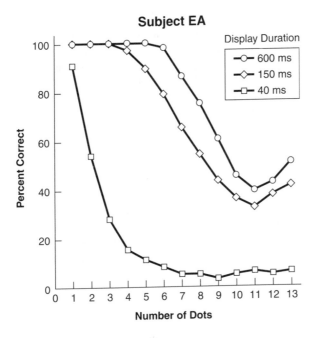

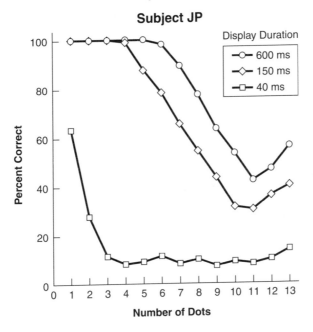

FIGURE 4.1   Span of Apprehension

Source: From Averbach, 1963

medium tone was for the middle row, and a low tone was for the bottom row. Moreover, this tone occurred anywhere from just prior to the display being removed to one second after the display had disappeared. Sperling used the sum of the performance at each of the rows to provide an estimate of what was available in iconic memory. If people could always report all 4 of the items in the cued row, this would indicate that all of the information was represented in iconic memory but that it decayed very quickly. Alternatively, if people could often report all 4 items from the first row but very few, if any, from the other rows, this would suggest that iconic memory can only hold very few items.

The results of this study are shown in Figure 4.2. Performance was near ceiling (very close to perfect) when the tone cue was presented at the time the display is removed. However, as the amount of time increased before the tone sounded, there was a decline in performance. Nearing the quarter-second mark (250 milliseconds), people are approaching their performance in the whole-report condition. These data indicate that a large amount of information is held in iconic memory—perhaps just about anything entering the visual system. However, iconic memory has a very brief duration. By about a one-quarter second, nearly everything has decayed. Anything that is left was presumably transferred into short-term memory before it was lost.

Anorthoscopic Perception

The effects of iconic memory can be observed in the distortions of reality produced by this sensory register. For example, a lightning strike appears to last longer than it actually does

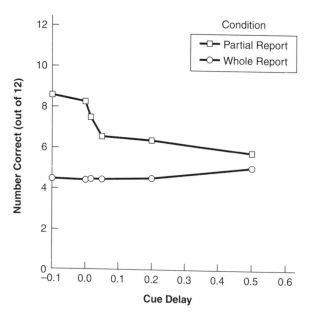

FIGURE 4.2   Availability of Information in Iconic Memory
Source: Sperling, 1960

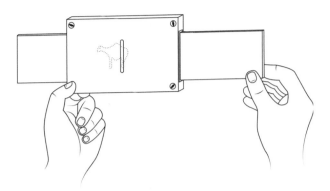

FIGURE 4.3   Example of a Device Used to Illustrate Anorthoscopic Perception

Source: Haber & Nathanson, 1968

because we are holding onto a memory of the strike. Another illustration is **anorthoscopic perception,** or the seeing-more-than-is-there phenomenon (Parks, 1965). This effect can be demonstrated by passing a picture behind a slit cut in a piece of paper or a board, as shown in Figure 4.3. If the figure is passed through the slit at a reasonably fast speed (e.g., 250–300 ms), people report seeing more of the figure than there actually is. This perception occurs because people are integrating information from different points in time in iconic memory to reconstruct the shape of the object.

What also happens is that the information in iconic memory becomes compressed to accommodate all that was seen in a small region of space (McCloskey & Watkins, 1978). Some examples of this compression are shown in Figure 4.4. Furthermore, the faster the objects behind the slit move, the more compressed the perception is (Haber & Nathanson, 1968). This cannot be the result of a simple retinal afterimage because if lots of different visual information were presented to the same place on the retina, and people were using a retinal afterimage to make their judgements, then all the information would be jumbled into the same space on the retina, and a perceptual blob would result. Instead, this suggests the active construction of a mental representation based on a memory of what was recently seen.

There is a clear evolutionary advantage to having such a sensory register. Suppose you were trying to identify an object as it moved behind a cluster of branches. If you can quickly integrate the bits and pieces you are able to see, you can identify the entity more quickly.

Trans-Saccadic Memory

We do not view the world in one glance. Instead, we must move our eyes, head, and body to scan our surroundings. In doing so, we view different parts of the world and then integrate them to build a complete mental picture of what the world is like. The typical eye movement is called a saccade. When our eyes land on some point in space, it is called a fixation. Fixations typically last around 300 milliseconds, whereas saccadic eye movements typically take 30 ms to execute. Moreover, we mostly perceptually process information during the fixations.

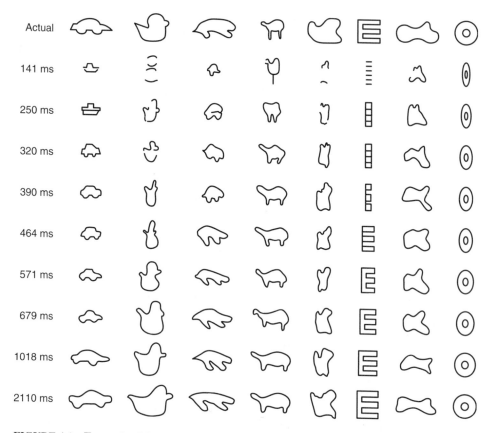

FIGURE 4.4   Example of Stimuli and Response Generated by People in the Study of Anorthoscopic Perception

Source: Haber & Nathanson, 1968

This characteristic of vision is important because it places demands on iconic memory. Specifically, we need to integrate information across saccades to build up a picture of the world. There needs to be a trans-saccadic memory (e.g., Irwin, 1996) that uses iconic memory. There are a number of ideas about how this is accomplished.

It has been suggested that trans-saccadic memory uses retinal coordinates, the position of an image on the retinas of your eyes. However, this is incorrect. For example, suppose people are presented with two displays composed of portions of a 3 × 3 grid of 8 dot locations. If the two grids were overlaid on top of one another, one could pick out the location of the missing ninth dot. This task is easy to do when the two grids are presented in the same position and people do not have to move their eyes. The process of using this idea to test trans-saccadic memory is illustrated in Figure 4.5a. The first dot display appears at the place where people are currently looking. Then a cross appears in the periphery, indicating where people should look next. When people move their eyes to the new location, the first display is erased, and a second is presented where the eyes have moved. This second dis-

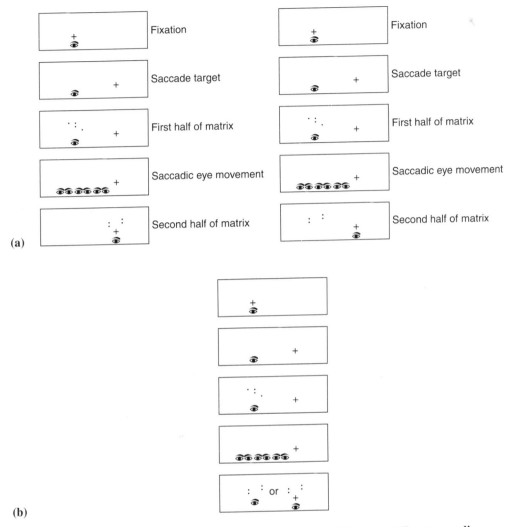

(a)

(b)

FIGURE 4.5 **Testing Retinally Based and Spatially Based Ideas about Trans-saccadic Memory**

Source: Irwin, Brown, & Sun, 1988

play overlaps the first in the same retinal coordinates (that is, the same place on a person's eye). Under these conditions, people are not able to integrate these two displays to identify the missing dot location.

Given that trans-saccadic memory does not use retinal position, it might use spatial information—that is, where entities are in space. A similar procedure can be used to test this idea. This is illustrated in Figure 4.5b, where the two dot patterns are in the same spatial location, even though the eyes are in motion. However, this does not appear to be the case either (Irwin, Yantis, & Jonides, 1983).

Instead, trans-saccadic memory appears to use representations of objects in the world, called object files (Kahneman, Triesman, and Gibbs, 1992), instead of retinal or spatial coordinates. Trans-saccadic memory is keeping track of basic characteristics of an object. Evidence for this comes from studies in which people are able to detect that something has been changed after an eye movement (Henderson & Anes, 1994), although this operation of trans-saccadic memory reflects some limited capacity (Irwin, 1991). Moreover, change detection is more likely to occur when the entity is at the focus of attention rather than in the background. This suggests that although we subjectively experience the world as stable and full of detail, this impression comes in part from our use of our memories to fill in the gaps with what we had seen before or with what our long-term memory assumes should be there (e.g., Henderson & Anes, 1994).

Although trans-saccadic memory seems fairly simple, working at low levels of thought, it can have important influences on higher levels of processing. For example, if people need to mentally rotate an image (see Chapter 5), this takes longer if they have to concurrently make an eye movement (Irwin & Brockmole, 2000). The execution of an eye movement and active operation of trans-saccadic memory put memory processes on hold while the eyes are doing their thing.

Change Blindness

The lack of accurate detail in visual memory has interesting consequences. For example, there are often errors in feature films that go unnoticed by most audience members, such as objects appearing and disappearing across cuts, clothes changing, and so forth. These are called continuity errors. In a set of studies, people saw films in which objects changed across cuts. For example, plates might change from red to white. However, people were very poor at detecting these changes and only did so less than 2 percent of the time (Levin & Simons, 1997).

In one study, people watched films in which one actor was changed across film cuts (the two people were of the same gender and ethnicity). Only 33 percent of the people noticed the change (Levin & Simons, 1997). In another example, an experimenter asked an individual (the subject) on the Cornell University campus for directions. While giving directions, two people passed between them carrying a door, thus blocking the subject's view of the experimenter. At this time, a second experimenter switched places with the first. After the door had passed, many subjects continued giving directions even though they were now talking to a different person. Only about 50 percent of the people noticed the switch (Simons & Levin, 1998).

Visual memory reflects our expectations. For example, for briefly presented scenes, people are more likely to detect a change in an object if it belongs in the scene (e.g., a blender in a kitchen) than if it does not (e.g., a live chicken in a kitchen) (Hollingworth & Henderson, 2003). This prior knowledge includes social constraints. In person-change experiments, college students were more likely to detect a switch when the experimenters were dressed like students than when they were dressed like construction workers. Students are in the same social group as the people being tested, but construction workers are not, so less attention is paid to them.

ECHOIC MEMORY

Echoic memory serves a similar purpose for audition as iconic memory does for vision. The mental representation in echoic memory is called the echo. However, because the demands on this system are different than they are in vision, echoic memory differs in important ways. Specifically, echoic memory must take into account the fleeting and temporary nature of sound.

Span and Duration of Echoic Memory

As a parallel to iconic memory, we would like to know the capacity and duration of echoic memory. In an analog to Sperling's (1960) iconic memory study, a study by Darwin, Turvey, and Crowder (1972) looked at these issues by reading to people wearing headphones three lists of three digits each. One list was presented only to the right ear, a second to only the left ear, and a third to both ears (so that it sounded like it was in the middle of the listener's head). After hearing the lists, the person was asked to report as many of the digits as possible (whole report control condition) or to report only one of the lists based on a visual cue that indicated left, right, or middle list. The data can be seen in Figure 4.6. Like Sperling's study, performance in the cued conditions indicated that more was available in echoic memory than that suggested by the whole report condition. Thus, it appears that echoic memory can retain a large amount of acoustic information.

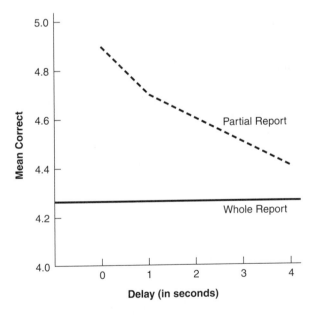

FIGURE 4.6   Assessment of Echoic Memory

Source: Darwin, Turvey, & Crowder, 1972

Now consider the duration of echoic memory. As can be seen in Figure 4.6, unlike iconic memory, echoic information is retained for a longer period of time, about 4 seconds. This makes sense given the natures of visual and auditory information. For vision, stuff in the environment is typically present all at once. Moreover, the eyes are constantly shifting to new locations, so old information must be removed to make way for the new. If a person needs to reprocess something, she need only to look at the thing again. In contrast, auditory information is stretched out over time and can typically be heard only once. Therefore, echoic memory needs to keep larger chunks of information and retain it long enough so it can be properly analyzed.

HAPTIC SENSORY MEMORY

While iconic and echoic memory have received the most attention, each sensory modality has its own memory store, with characteristics unique to that type of information. For example, take the sense of touch. Memory for touch, **haptic sensory memory,** must take into account the various qualities such as pressure and temperature. Moreover, it needs to account for both the spatial extent of what is in contact with the body, as well as how it changes over time. Thus, it is likely that this sensory register is going to be more like iconic memory than echoic memory. Furthermore, different parts of the body are differentially sensitive to tactile information than others (e.g., the hands and face are more sensitive than the knees or back). Thus, the sensory register may give differential preference to touch information from different parts of the body.

Span and Duration of Haptic Sensory Memory

Let's look at the capacity and duration of haptic sensory memory. A study by Bliss, Crane, Mansfield, and Townsend (1966) (Hill & Bliss, 1968) was also modeled after the Sperling (1960) iconic memory study. In this haptic study, people received jets of air at different locations on the fingers of each hand. People gave whole reports of all of the locations that were stimulated or gave partial reports after a light or a tone cue was given to indicate which parts of the fingers would be affected. The results showed that in the whole report condition people could report three or four skin locations, but in the partial report condition, performance was much better, with people having access to nearly all of the locations. There was also a rapid decay of information such that by about 1.3 seconds, much of the information was lost.

Synopsis

Memory is required even over very brief periods of time. Each sensory modality has a different sensory register dedicated to it. Iconic memory is the sensory register of vision. Echoic memory is the sensory register of hearing. Haptic sensory memory is for the sensation of touch. Each of these memory stores can hold a large amount of information for a very short duration. Although these memory stores interface with the world and ourselves in different ways, they all serve a common goal by using similar basic principles.

SHORT-TERM MEMORY

Short-term memory is the portion of memory responsible for processing and retaining information beyond the sensory registers, but not much longer than a minute or so at the most (without active processing). Short-term memory is unique in that its contents are included in consciousness or are at the very least quite near conscious awareness. Thus, when a person is thinking, he is actively using information in short-term memory. We'll examine the active manipulation of information in memory in Chapter 5 when we consider working memory.

Although it has been studied for years, the precise nature of short-term memory is unclear. Some people think short-term memory is a qualitatively different part of the human memory system. In contrast, others believe short-term memory is just a portion of long-term memory that is currently available. For those people, there is no clear distinction between short- and long-term memories. Instead, there is a continuum of availability within a single memory system. Regardless of which view is closer to the truth, there are aspects of memory that are very salient during short time periods. It is these aspects of memory that are of concern here.

Short-Term Memory Capacity

One of the most striking aspects of short-term memory is that it has a severely limited capacity. There are only a small number of things that can be actively processed at once. This limited capacity is easily demonstrated. For a quick, at-home study, have a friend of yours read you lists of random digits at the rate of about one per second. After you have heard the list, recall the digits in the order you heard them. Start out with a short list, such as only two or three digits, and have them get progressively longer. What you should find is that your short-term memory capacity is very small. Although this task starts out easy, it quickly becomes difficult. If you are like most people, you should be able to remember between five and nine digits in the correct order.

This small amount of information that can be held in short-term memory has been found for different types of information. It is generally accepted that a person's memory span is around seven items. The idea of short-term memory being an information processing bottleneck was first laid out in a classic paper in memory research entitled "The Magical Number Seven, Plus or Minus Two" (Miller, 1956). Thus, memory span is often described as being 7 ± 2 chunks of information. The term *chunk* is important because what can serve as a unit of information is flexible.

Although this 7 ± 2 figure is often cited as the capacity of short-term memory, some people have argued that its capacity is actually only about 4 ± 1 items (Cowan, 2000). People remember more information because they are using other cognitive resources to extend the functional size of short-term memory. For example, people may be chunking the information or using their long-term memories to augment short-term memory.

Chunking.   Regardless of whether the capacity of short-term memory is actually seven or four units, this is still not a lot. Yet, we seem capable of thinking about larger amounts of knowledge than this limit would imply. How do we do it? There are some mechanisms that can be used to expand short-term memory capacity. The most widely discussed is the concept of chunking. **Chunking** occurs when people take smaller units of information and group them into a larger unit. This functionally expands the capacity of short-term memory.

For example, if you were given a list of letters to remember, you are likely to be able to remember about seven of them. However, if those letters are grouped into words, then you can remember seven unrelated words, and the number of letters that you remember increases significantly. A word serves as a chunk to organize the letters. Any time there is an opportunity for chunking to occur, there is an opportunity to hold more information in short-term memory. So when you are trying to learn something new, if you can place that new information into some organization or structure, you are much more likely to be able to retain it.

So what guides the chunking process? Prior knowledge is a major influence. The more you know, the easier it is to form chunks. Chunking involves identifying patterns in information. The more knowledge you have, and the more efficient your application of that knowledge becomes, the greater your memory capacity will seem, even though it is really staying about the same. Thus, memory can be improved by gaining expertise.

Very Large Capacity.   This influence of expertise on short-term memory can be clearly seen in a study by Ericsson, Chase, and Faloon (1980). In this study, they brought a person, known as S. F., into their memory lab to test his short-term memory span for digits. At the beginning of the study his digit span was about seven items. They continued to test him for over a year and a half. They would have S. F. come to the lab and give him lists of digits. Over time, his digit span grew larger and larger. This can be seen in Figure 4.7. At the end of the study he could repeat back, in the correct order, nearly 80 digits that he had just heard read to him at the rate of about 1 per second. How did he achieve this superhuman feat of reaching such a large digit span?

Well, S. F. was a runner. He grouped the digits into chunks based on race lengths and running times, as well as using other devices, such as famous dates. For example, the sequence 3492 was recoded as "3 minutes, 49 point 2 seconds, near world-record mile time," and 1944 as "near the end of World War II." S. F.'s increase in his memory span was a result of his ability to acquire a skill of using long-term memory knowledge to organize the information in his short-term memory. This made his short-term memory capacity seem larger. Note that his chunks were often made up of 3 or 4 digits at a time. The fact that S. F.'s short-term memory span did not actually grow larger is illustrated by the fact that after his digit span had grow to gargantuan proportions, when he was given a set of letters, his memory span dropped back down to 6.

Another example of the influence of expertise is studies of memory for chessboards. People were first given a picture of a chessboard with chess pieces arranged on it. This board was then removed and the chess pieces were moved around. Chess experts are much better at remembering where the pieces were on the board compared to people who are novice chess players. The chess experts were drawing on their knowledge of the game to help them chunk the pieces on the board and thus remember their original locations. This is highlighted by conditions in which people were given chessboards that were not from the middle of a game but for which the pieces were randomly placed on the board. Under these circumstances, everyone's memory declined, and the chess masters performed no better than the novices (Chase & Simon, 1973).

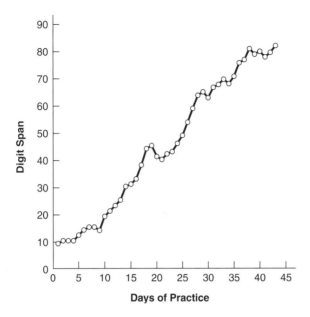

FIGURE 4.7 Example of Expertise Influences on Short-Term Memory Span. In this case, S. F.'s improved digit span with practice.

Source: Ericsson, Chase, & Faloon, 1980

Duration of Short-Term Memory

Short-term memory is not only a bottleneck because of its small capacity. It also only retains information, without active attention, for relatively short periods of time. Without active attention, information in short-term memory is largely forgotten in 30 seconds. The trick in showing this is that a person must first think about something so that it enters short-term memory and then not think about it until memory is tested.

There are a number of problems with this. First, it is next to impossible to tell people *not* to think about something and assume they have done so (Wegner, 1989). People cannot think about nothing. Their minds are always drifting around searching for something, anything, to think about. Second, whatever thoughts they are having cannot be related to what you are trying to test. Otherwise, they are attending to that information, and you cannot study how it is being forgotten over time.

Decay.   There have been a number of attempts to address short-term memory forgetting. The primary issue that has been studied is whether this forgetting is due to a decay or interference process. In a **decay** process, the primary cause of forgetting is the passage of time. The more time that has passed, the more the memory trace has decayed and some forgetting has occurred.

One of the first pieces of evidence to support a decay process interpretation was reported more or less simultaneously by Brown (1958) and by Peterson and Peterson (1959). As such, it is known as the Brown-Peterson paradigm. In the Petersons' study, students at

Indiana University were given consonant trigrams (e.g., TPZ) to remember. To keep people from actively rehearsing this, after seeing the trigram they gave the students a three-digit number (e.g., 274), with the task of saying the number aloud and then counting backward by threes (e.g., 274, 271, 268, 265,) until they were told to stop, at which point they were to recall the trigram. This study varied the amount of time between the presentation of the trigram and the cue to recall the information.

The data from this study is shown in Figure 4.8, which is a nice forgetting curve. The more time that has elapsed, the less likely it was that the trigram was remembered. By 18 seconds, nearly all of the information was lost. Because the to-be-remembered information did not appear to be involved in the current stream of thought, the only mechanism that seemed a likely candidate for forgetting was decay.

Interference.   While this decay theory has some intuitive appeal and is relatively simple (and science prefers simple explanations), there are serious challenges to it. Most of these challenges rest on the idea that this forgetting is caused by interference, not decay. With **interference,** information in short-term memory interferes with or in some way blocks or hinders the retrieval of other information. Because short-term memory has a very limited capacity, if new information is put into it, it is likely to displace the information that is already there. This is a form of interference.

One study that supported an interference interpretation of the Brown-Peterson data was done by Keppel and Underwood (1962). They suggested that some of the forgetting that was observed in this paradigm was due to interference from items learned on previous

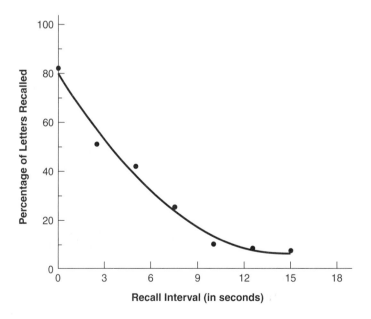

FIGURE 4.8   Results from Peterson and Peterson's Experiment

Source: Peterson & Peterson, 1959

trials. What they did was to have only three trials. They found that there was virtually no forgetting on the first trial. Forgetting only started to appear on the second and third trials. Thus, when there was no source of interference, there was no short-term memory forgetting.

Another study was done by Waugh and Norman (1965). They gave people lists of 16 digits. At the end of each list was a probe digit, which was also marked with a tone. The task was to state what digit followed the earlier occurrence of the probe digit in the series that was just presented. In this way the experimenters could control how much interference people had experienced. The further back in the list the probe digit was, the more interference there was. To get at issues of memory decay, they presented the digits at either a slow rate (1 per second) or a fast rate (4 per second). The results are shown in Figure 4.9. The more intervening items between the probe and its prior occurrence—that is, the more interference there was—the greater the forgetting. The rate of forgetting is similar in both the slow and fast presentation conditions. Thus, short-term memory forgetting is more a function of the amount of interference than the amount of time that has passed. Forgetting is observed in the Brown-Peterson studies because the task of counting backward produced interference and caused forgetting of the trigram.

In sum, interference is the primary cause of forgetting in short-term memory. This limitation on short-term memory has implications for everyday life. For example, if you are trying to keep information in your mind, such as telephone number or a person's name, and are disrupted by something else, it is likely you will forget it. When you are reading or listening to something, you often need to keep track of a number of ideas to understand what

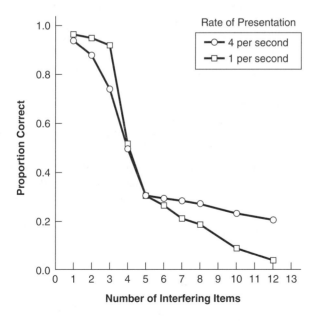

FIGURE 4.9   Results from Waugh and Norman Experiment

Source: Waugh & Norman, 1965—adapted by Ashcraft

is being communicated to you. If you are not able to do this effectively, then your comprehension, and your memory, of that information will suffer.

So if there is interfering information in the environment during comprehension, this displaces the information that you need in short-term memory. For example, if you are trying to study and the television is on, your ability to understand and remember what you are studying is compromised. If you are trying to reason through something, you often need to consider various possibilities and outcomes. This places a strain on short-term memory. If there is interference in the environment, your ability to reason is compromised. We all can remember situations in which there was a lot going on around us while we made a decision, and because we were not able to think clearly, we were left with a decision we regretted.

Synopsis

Short-term memory is a system that can hold only a small amount of information for a few seconds. However, we can increase our capacity by chunking information into larger units, thereby expanding how much we can be actively thinking. When forgetting occurs, this is due not so much to the passage of time as to interference caused by the intrusion of new information entering short-term memory and displacing older information.

Retrieval in Short-Term Memory

If a person encodes information into the limited capacity of short-term memory and avoids interference sufficiently to retain it, it may become necessary to then use it. At that point it needs to be retrieved from short-term memory. Somehow, the contents of short-term memory must be searched to select the one piece that is needed. How do you do this?

One of the most notable attempts to address this was a series of studies by Sternberg (1966; 1969; 1975). He used an experimental paradigm in which people were first given a list of one to six digits (e.g., 5, 2, 4, 3, 8, 0), well within the capacity of short-term memory. People were then given a memory probe (e.g., 4) with the task of saying whether the probe was in the list. Sternberg recorded how long it took to respond as a function of how many items were in the set and whether the probe was in the set.

Using this approach Sternberg tested three theories. The first is a **parallel search** theory. In a parallel search, all of the items in short-term memory are available more or less at once. It is accessed in parallel. This makes sense if one assumes that the contents of short-term memory are either in or close to consciousness. If people search short-term memory in a parallel fashion, then the amount of information in the search set should not matter. All of the information is available at once regardless of the size of the search set. As a result, response times should not vary with set size, and there should be little difference between the "yes" and "no" responses.

A second alternative was a **serial self-terminating** search. This involves going through items one at a time. Moreover, once people get to the target item, the search stops or terminates. In this type of search there is an increase in response time with an increase in set size. By going through the items one by one, the larger the set, the longer it should take. There is also a difference in the slope of the response times for "yes" and "no" responses. For "no" responses, the function is relatively steep because the person always needs to go through the entire set to verify that the probe item is not there. However, for "yes" responses, there is an increasing response time slope, but it should be half that of "no" responses. This is because people are going through the items one at a time, and on average they will get about halfway through the set before the target item is found.

The final alternative is a **serial exhaustive search.** This would again involve people going through things one at a time. However, rather than stopping when they found what they were looking for, people would continue until they had gone through the entire set. This search process would also result in an increasing response time function with increasing set size. However, if people searched in a serial exhaustive fashion, there is no difference in the response time slope for the "yes" and "no" responses. This is because in both cases people are going through the entire set of information.

The results of one of Sternberg's studies are shown in Figure 4.10. As you can see, the data support a serial exhaustive search. This outcome is instructive for you in two ways. For one, it shows you information about how short-term memory is searched. The other lesson here has to do with our ability to report on our own memory processes. When I list out the three possible outcomes in my classes and ask students to state which one they think is true, most people pick the serial self-terminating search. It may in some way be consistent with subjective experience. The fact that so many people get this wrong is important because we are talking about a simple process that occurs repeatedly throughout our lives in a portion of memory that is very close to conscious awareness. This is why memory researchers conduct so many studies in an attempt to understand what may sometimes seem like a simple question to answer. It is not unusual for the results of experiments to produce

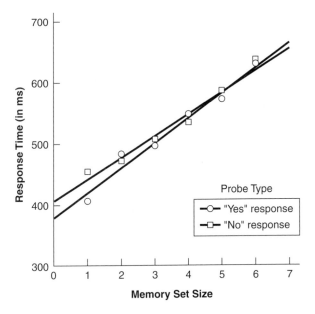

FIGURE 4.10   Results of Sternberg's Search of Short-Term Memory Task

Source: Sternberg, 1966

counterintuitive results. We do not have much conscious awareness of how our own memories operate. We need objective measures to test our theories.

Serial versus Parallel Issues

One important point about the search of short-term memory is that not everyone agrees that a serial process is necessarily involved here. Everyone agrees that this is a reasonable conclusion. The issue is that there are other possibilities that are just as reasonable that Sternberg did not consider. Specifically, some people have suggested that this pattern of data could result from a parallel process in which there are limited cognitive resources. When multiple elements are held in short-term memory, these resources become divided among them. This is like sending water down a pipe and then having the pipe divide into several smaller pipes, resulting in less water flowing down any one pipe. As a result, the more finely divided cognitive resources are, the less there is available to any one item, and thus the longer it takes for retrieval to occur.

This issue of serial versus parallel process has a long and tortuous history in memory research (e.g., Townsend, 1990). It is not unusual for someone to claim that a given memory process is either serial or parallel and then to have someone else come along and demonstrate that the opposite could be true. Currently, it is generally accepted that for any process, both a serial and a parallel process can be devised that produce a certain outcome. As such, it is very difficult to distinguish between the two. Often researchers select one based on what seems the most plausible and/or the simplest of the two.

For any complex memory process there are probably both parallel and serial components. The brain is composed of billions of neurons that are all regularly engaged in some sort of processing. Thus, because several neural assemblies are often simultaneously being used for memory, there is some element of parallel processing. For example, when a person is trying to remember where they heard something, they need to know both what the information is and the source of the information. Memory processes can also involve stages in which latter steps simply cannot be done without the results of other, earlier steps. For example, when deciding whether information was adequately learned, a person first needs to assess whether the knowledge is in memory and then produce a response based on that assessment.

Serial Position Curves

We will now consider temporal influences on short-term memory. One of the most durable short-term memory effects is the **serial position curve.** An example of one of these is shown in Figure 4.11. The serial position curve is a U-shaped function with memory being better for information at the beginning and end of a set, whereas information in between is less well remembered (Murdock, 1962). This serial position curve is found for various information types and set sizes.

Primacy Effect.   The superior memory for information at the beginning of a set is called the **primacy effect.** Traditionally, the primacy effect is not a short-term memory effect per se but is attributed to long-term memory. The idea is that when a person is given a set of in-

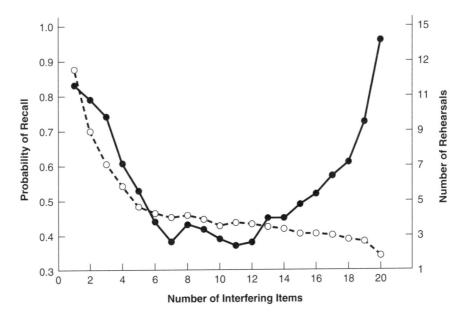

FIGURE 4.11   A Standard Serial Position Curve in Short-Term Memory. Solid dots show short-term memory, and open dots indicate the mean number of rehearsals per item.

Source: Rundus, 1971

formation, items at the beginning have more opportunity to be rehearsed. For example, for the first item, no other items have been given yet, so all of the rehearsal effort can be devoted to it. As such, it has the highest probability of being transferred into long-term memory. For the second item, attention is now split between the first and second items, so it is less likely that the second item will make it into long-term memory. This logic can then be extended to the rest of the list. After a number of items, the amount of additional rehearsal benefit will be negligible.

If people are given more time to encode information into long-term memory, then the primacy effect shows better memory. This was demonstrated in a study by Glanzer and Cunitz (1966), shown in Figure 4.12. In this study, people were given information at different speeds. When the information was presented at a slower rate, memory was better and the primacy effect was larger, but the recency effect was less affected.

Recency Effect.   The other half of the serial position curve is the superior memory for information at the end of the set, which is called the **recency effect.** Traditionally the recency effect is attributed to short-term memory. These items are those that have not been displaced by subsequent interfering information and so are less likely to be forgotten. As such, to maximize your own performance, it is best to try to recall the most recent things first, before you encounter potentially interfering information, and then proceed to whatever may be stored in long-term memory. The study by Glanzer and Cunitz (1966) also showed this aspect of the serial position curve. In a second experiment, people waited a period of time during which

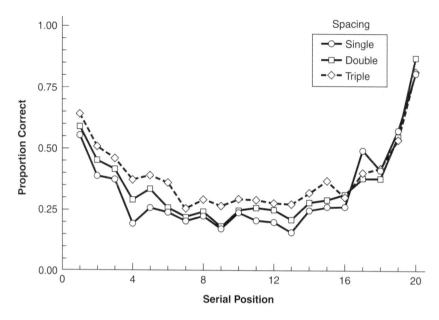

FIGURE 4.12   Effects of Additional Rehearsal Time on the Primacy Effect

Source: Glanzer & Cunitz, 1966

they did some distractor task before they recalled the information. The results are shown in Figure 4.13. The longer the delay, the less pronounced the recency effect. However, the primacy portion of the curve, which is attributed to long-term memory, is unaffected.

More evidence to support the idea that the recency effect is due to short-term memory and the primacy effect to long-term memory was found in a study by Rundus (1971). In this study people verbalized their thoughts during memorization. The bulk of this verbalization was made up of rehearsals. What was observed was that people rehearse the earlier presented items a great deal compared to the later items. The influence of rehearsal on memory is seen in Figure 4.11. One line is the standard serial position curve, and the other is the amount of rehearsal of any given item. As can be seen, early items were rehearsed substantially and remembered well. Presumably they are in long-term storage. However, later items are not rehearsed as much. The items at the end of the list are remembered not because of how much they were rehearsed, but because they are likely to still be in short-term memory.

Changing the Serial Position Curve

While the serial position curve is one of the more robust findings in memory research, it is not always observed. There are things that can reduce the primacy or recency effect or eliminate it altogether. We'll look at an example of each. With people's memory for actions they performed, the primacy effect is absent. In contrast, giving people something irrelevant at the end of a series can eliminate the recency effect.

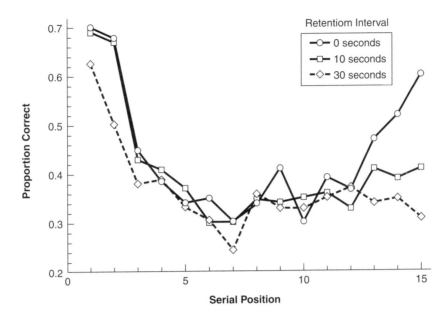

**FIGURE 4.13   Effects of Different Filled Retention Intervals (in Seconds)
on the Recency Effect**

Source: Glanzer & Cunitz, 1966

Memory for Actions.   Most of the research on serial position curves uses verbal materials, such as lists of words. However, we can also look at memories for activities recently
performed. As a reminder, memory for performed activities is generally better than memory for words (see Chapter 3), but there is still some forgetting. This forgetting is influenced
by serial position, but with performed actions there is no primacy effect (Seiler & Engelkamp, 2003). Performing activities leads a person to focus more of her attention on individual actions. As such, there is less opportunity to rehearse actions that were done
previously, and so this information is less likely to be transferred to long-term memory. As
a result, no primacy effect is seen.

Suffix Effect.   Another serial position phenomenon is the **suffix effect.** With the suffix effect the recency effect is diminished when extra information is presented at the end of a list
(Conrad, 1960; Crowder & Morton, 1969). For example, suppose you heard a list of words
in a short-term memory study. Then at the end of the list the experimenter either said nothing or said the word "go" to indicate that you should recall the list. In this case, the word "go"
is a suffix. Memory performance is worse in the "go" condition than in the silence condition.
The word "go" interferes with information in short-term memory, causing forgetting.

     The size of the suffix effect is related to the nature of the suffix itself. The more the
suffix is like the information on the list, the greater the amount of interference and the
greater the suffix effect (e.g., Ayers et al., 1979). For example, as illustrated in Figure 4.14,
when the suffix was human speech, the recency effect was greatly reduced, but this did not

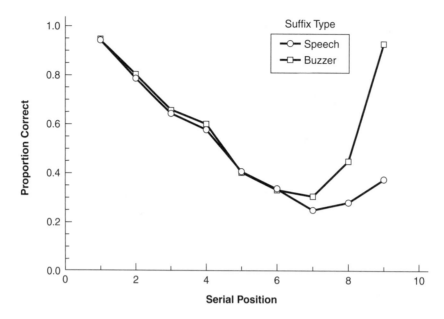

FIGURE 4.14 **Suffix Effects with Human Speech and Nonhuman Nonspeech Sound**
Source: Crowder, 1972

happen when it was a unrelated sound like a buzzer. It is also important what the person hearing the suffix thinks the suffix is. For example, if people hear a list of words and then hear a "baa" sound, if they are told that the sound was made by a person, there is a larger suffix effect than if they are told it was made by a sheep. This is true even though the exact same sound is used in both cases (Neath, Surprenant, & Crowder, 1993).

In general, the suffix effect is heavily influenced by physical characteristics of a suffix, leading many researchers to consider it as part of echoic memory. This was hammered out in a marathon series of 15 experiments reported by Morton, Crowder, and Prussin (1971). They found that the suffix effect was unaffected by the meaning of the suffix, its frequency, or its emotionality. However, the suffix effect was reduced if the suffix came from a different location in space, was of a different timbre (human voice versus noise), or was from a different person, particularly one of a gender different from the person reading the main set of items.

The suffix effect occurs not only for auditory short-term memory, but also for visual information, lip reading, tactile stimuli, and odors (Campbell & Dodd, 1982; Mahrer & Miles, 1999; Miles & Jenkins, 2000; Parmentier, Tremblay, & Jones, 2004). This presence of a suffix effect in all these sensory modalities suggests that it is a general property of short-term memory.

Memory for Serial Order

Short-term memory not only retains information content but the serial order as well. For example, if someone gave you a telephone number, remembering just the digits is not sufficient. You need to know the proper sequence as well. When people do forget the serial order, they do so in systematic ways. For example, there is a serial position effect. Also, if they remember things out of order, the things they mix up are likely to be close to one another. For example, if you mess up the telephone number 123-4567, you are more likely to misremember it as 123-5467 than as 163-4527. Using an organization adopted by Brown (1997), we look at a number of theories of memory for **serial order** information in short-term memory.

Slot-Based Models.   The simplest explanations for short-term serial order memory are **slot-based models** (Conrad, 1965). These theories assume that short-term memory is composed of a series of ordered slots (or boxes) and that information is dropped into each one as it is encountered. To convey order information, one simply reads off what is in the slots. The computer metaphor at work in cognitive psychology is particularly evident here. According to this view, item and order information are stored together because each piece of information is stored in a slot in a predetermined order. Thus, it should not be possible to forget content or order information without forgetting the other as well. Errors in order reports are thought to be due to loss of information about the content in each slot and are likely to be similar sounding items or items from adjacent slots. However, as appealing as this approach may be, there is little evidence to support it.

Chaining Models.   Another view of serial order memory is **chaining models** (Lewandowsky & Murdock, 1989). This view assumes that short-term memory information contains a series of associative links. Order information is recovered by moving along the associative chain. A problem with this view is that if people cannot remember an item, then the chain should be broken, and they should not be able to continue further. However, some sort of approximation of the lost item could be used to pick up further along the chain. Typically, forgetting results in only a partial loss of information. A similar line of reasoning can account for the prominence of local misorderings.

Perturbation Model.   Another theory of serial order is the **perturbation model** (Estes, 1972) in which information in short-term memory is organized into a hierarchy of chunks. Every item is regulated by a control unit that manages the chunk. These control units themselves may be grouped together by higher-order control units. At the highest level is a control unit for the entire set. An example of such a hierarchy is given in Figure 4.15. The item-to-control unit associations convey order information. This theory works well and can account for the fact that misorderings in serial memory are more likely to occur at a local level and within chunks than across levels. For example, a phone number, like 123–4567, is divided into two chunks: 123 and 4567. Based on the perturbation model, it is more likely that a person will misorder 4 and 5, because they are in the same chunk, than misorder 3 and 4, because they are in different chunks.

Inhibition Models.   Other theories of serial order information are **inhibition models** (e.g., Burgess & Hitch, 1992), which suggest that inhibition, a mechanism of attention, is used to recover serial order. As a person proceeds through a list, the retrieval process selects the most active or available one, which is usually the first one in the set. As each item is

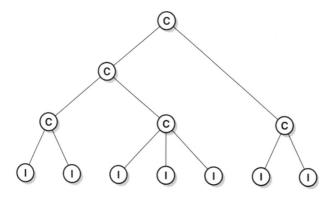

FIGURE 4.15   A Hierarchy of Control Units as Theorized by the Perturbation Model

retrieved and reported, the system then inhibits it and then sends activation to the next item in the order, which is now the most active. This inhibition keeps that previous item from being recalled again. This is similar to a phenomenon in visual search known as inhibition of return. For a search to be efficient, it is best if locations that have already been searched are not searched again too soon, allowing new locations to be checked. The same reasoning is applied here. To avoid recalling things that have already been recalled, inhibition is used. Serial order information falls out of this process.

This inhibition of recently processed short-term memory information can be seen in the phenomenon of **repetition blindness** (e.g., Kanwisher, 1987). Repetition blindness is observed in studies in which people read sentences presented in a rapid serial visual presentation (or RSVP) format. Essentially words are presented one at a time in the same location on a computer screen in a relatively quick fashion but still slow enough that people can read what they are seeing. It has been found is that if the same word is repeated within a relatively short time span, people claim to not have seen the word. For example, if given the sentence "When she spilled the ink, there was ink all over" people are likely to not report the second occurrence of the word "ink," even though this makes the sentence ungrammatical. This is because the word "ink" had been recently processed and inhibited in short-term memory. As a result, people have trouble processing it again, even though they are looking right at it.

Context-Based Models.   A final concept of serial order information in short-term memory is **context-based models** (Brown, 1997; Burgess & Hitch, 1992). These models exploit the fact that context is constantly in flux, even if at a very subtle level. This includes both what is going on in the environment as well as a person's internal context, including their physiological, emotional, and cognitive states. This shifting context is not random but varies in regular ways. It is also well known, as you will see in detail in Chapter 7, that contextual information is stored in memory. This context information can be used to help determine order information by reconstructing the order of the contextual change. In this view, misorderings occur because the contexts were similar. Items that are close together in time are likely to be associated with more similar contexts than items farther apart. This is why local misorderings are more common than distant ones.

Synopsis

Retrieval from short-term memory is affected by how much information is in memory, similar to what would be expected with a serial exhaustive search, although there are other possibilities. This retrieval is also affected by various aspects of time. People often show serial position curves, demonstrating a primacy effect (better memory for things early on) and a recency effect (better memory for the most recent items), although this latter finding can be disrupted with a suffix. Finally, people sometimes need to remember the proper sequence of information. This serial order memory is a complex process that is influenced by the associations formed between items, how the elements are chunked, a process of inhibiting recently reported items, and the context in which the information was encountered.

SUMMARY

This chapter examined issues of memory in the short term. Although the sensory registers can retain large amounts of information, when information moves closer to conscious awareness, short-term memory has a surprisingly small capacity. This is the bottleneck in our memory system. Short-term memory not only has a limited capacity, but it also loses information at an alarming rate due to interference. Despite this rapid forgetting, we are still able to retrieve information accurately. Our memory is better for things presented early on or near the end of a set. Also, we can reliably reconstruct the order in which it was originally presented, often by chunking the knowledge, suppressing recently encountered information, and exploiting changes in context.

STUDY QUESTIONS

1. What is the point of having sensory registers as memory systems?

2. What are the basic principles of iconic memory, and why does it have these characteristics? Echoic memory? Haptic sensory memory?

3. What does anorthoscopic perception tell us about memory?

4. What is the capacity and duration of short-term memory? How can this be extended?

5. How does forgetting typically occur in short-term memory?

6. How is information retrieved from short-term memory?

7. What is the serial position curve, and what does it have to do with short-term memory?

8. How is short-term memory able to keep track of the order in which things are to occur?

KEY TERMS

anorthoscopic perception, chaining model, chunking, context-based models, decay, echoic memory, haptic sensory register, icon, iconic memory, inhibition model, interference, parallel processing, parallel search, perturbation model, primacy effect, recency effect, repetition blindness, sensory registers, serial position curve, serial processing, serial self-terminating search, serial exhaustive search, serial order, short-term memory, slot-based models, suffix effect

CHAPTER FIVE

WORKING MEMORY

The previous chapter dealt with the retention of information in the short term. We saw that short-term memory includes conscious experience. However, conscious experience involves more than just retaining information over time. Things we are conscious of, or that are at least near conscious awareness, are being thought about. This "thinking" implies an active processing or manipulating of the information. For example, when you are thinking about how to get to a mall you have never been to before, you combine various bits of knowledge you already have: the layout of the city the mall is in, information from a map, knowledge of traffic patterns in that area, and conversations with your friends about the location of the mall. By actively using all of this information, you can determine the best route for you to take. This all involves the controlled use of information in short-term memory. Because of the special nature of this kind of processing, many people refer to this as a **working memory** system. The phrase *short-term memory* is reserved more for the brief retention of information. In fact, some researchers consider working memory and short-term memory to be two different psychological constructs (e.g., Cantor, Engle, & Hamilton, 1991).

This chapter provides an overview of some of the major issues involved with working memory. This overview uses the perspective of one of the more popular theories of working memory: the Baddeley and Hitch (1974) tripartite theory. We examine the role of each of the three parts of working memory and some of the memory phenomena associated with it. Finally, some applications of working memory issues at more complex levels of processing are considered.

BADDELEY AND HITCH MODEL

The most prominent theory of working memory is the **Baddeley and Hitch model** (1974). This is a tripartite theory that assumes that working memory is made up of three primary components: (1) the phonological loop, (2) the visuo-spatial sketchpad, and (3) the central executive. An overview of this theory is presented in Figure 5.1. The phonological loop and the visuo-spatial sketchpad are specialized slave systems under the control of a generalized executive controller. The **phonological loop** is the part of working memory primarily responsible for processing verbal and auditory information. The **visuo-spatial sketchpad** is responsible primarily for processing visual and spatial knowledge.

These two slave systems are relatively separate from each another. This is based on how different information types influence one another. For example, if you are trying to

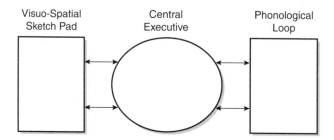

FIGURE 5.1   Baddeley Model of Working Memory

Source: Baddeley, 1986

think about verbal information, such as reading a chapter in a book, you are more likely to experience interference and distraction if you are exposed to other verbal or auditory information, such as listening to the radio. However, your reading would be relatively unaffected by some spatial task, such as tapping out a beat with your hand. Conversely, doing some visual-spatial task such as tracing a route on a map, would be disrupted by some other similar visual-spatial task but not by a verbal task (Baddeley & Andrade, 2000). There can be a great deal of interference if two tasks require resources from the same portion of working memory. For example, people have difficulty detecting visual and auditory signals if they are maintaining visual and auditory images, respectively, in working memory (Segal & Fusella, 1970; 1971) or, conversely, evaluating mental images when viewing distracting pictures (Lloyd-Jones & Vernon, 2003).

The *central executive* is the main control center of working memory. Although each slave system has some degree of processing capacity in and of itself, the central executive has additional capacity that it can devote to one of these slave systems if the demands on that system become excessively taxing. One of the more important jobs of the central executive is to regulate the flow of information in the current stream of thought, which can be done in a number of ways. Some believe the suppression of irrelevant information is an important determinate in how effective a given person's central executive is in controlling the operation of working memory.

While this tripartite model of working memory is a popular one, it should be kept in mind that this is not the only theory of how working memory operates. There are a number of aspects of thinking and memory that are not captured by this model. For example, as it is presented, the idea of working memory is relatively isolated from the rest of what a person is doing. However, it should be kept in mind that working memory is operating in the complex environment of a person in meaningful ways that can influence working memory performance. Take the example of people's body language while they are thinking problems through. It has been shown that people who gesture when solving problems, such as math problems, show better memory for that information than people who do not gesture (Wagner, Nusbaum, & Goldin-Meadow, 2004). Therefore, manipulating information in our working memory is a complex and intricate process. Let us return to the Baddeley and Hitch (1974) model.

PHONOLOGICAL LOOP

Of the three major partitions of working memory in the Baddeley and Hitch model, the **phonological loop** has received the most attention. This may be because much of the work on this part of working memory follows from research in the Ebbinghaus/verbal learning tradition, and the phonological loop is concerned with processing verbal information. In general, studies of the phonological loop have focused on linguistic materials, which are either read or heard, although other acoustic phenomena have also been studied.

Components

The phonological loop is composed of two primary structures: the **phonological store** and the **articulatory loop** (see Figure 5.2). The phonological store is a temporary storehouse of information, whereas the articulatory loop is the active rehearsal component. One helpful analogy is that the phonological store is like an inner ear that listens to what we say to ourselves, and the articulatory loop is like our inner voice that says what we are thinking. The way that the system works is that information is first entered into the phonological store. Over time, this information decays and eventually becomes lost. To prevent this, the articulatory loop can be engaged: By actively rehearsing the information in the phonological store, it is refreshed and preserved. Obviously, the more information that needs to be held in the phonological store, the harder the task of the articulatory loop becomes and the more likely information will degrade to the point that it cannot be adequately recovered and, thus, be forgotten.

Phenomena of the Phonological Loop

To better illustrate the role of the phonological loop in working memory let's look at some major effects that have been observed (Gathercole, 1997). These are consistent ways people perform when trying to use verbal information. These patterns of memory performance

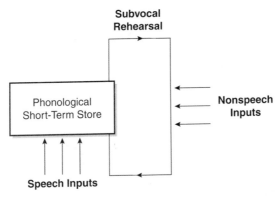

FIGURE 5.2   The Phonological Loop, with the Phonological Store and the Articulatory Loop

Source: Baddeley, 1986

provide us with insight into various characteristics of working memory. Along with the description of each of these is an explanation of why they could occur in this system.

Word Length Effect.   One of these patterns is the **word length effect,** which means a person's word span is smaller for longer words than it is for shorter words. This word length effect refers to articulation duration, not spelling or number of syllables (Baddeley, Thomson, & Buchanan, 1975). The longer it takes to say a group of words, the fewer words that can be readily recalled. This shows up in a number of ways. For example, keeping the number of syllables constant, more short-duration words, such as "wicket" and "bishop," can be remembered relative to long-duration words, such as "harpoon" and "Friday." Word length effects are even found in people who cannot speak (Baddeley & Wilson, 1985; Bishop and Robson, 1989), suggesting that the phonological loop captures the physical properties of spoken language as it is heard (however, see Hulme et al., 2004, for evidence that the word length effect disappears in mixed lists). The word length effect occurs because people spend more time rehearsing some items in a set. This causes these items not to be refreshed, making them more likely to be forgotten (Cowan, Baddeley, Elliott, & Norris, 2003).

A well-known finding related to the word length effect is that Chinese speakers have larger digit spans than English speakers, who in turn have larger digit spans than Welsh speakers (Hoosain & Salili, 1988). This is related to the length of the words for the various digits in the language. For Chinese, the digits are all monosyllables, whereas English has digit names that are multisyllabic, thereby lengthening articulation time and reducing how much the phonological loop can hold onto. An example would be "seven" in English, which is "qi" in Chinese. Welsh is even worse. It has also been shown that the digit span of Chinese-English bilinguals varies, depending on which language the person is speaking. Thus, it is not that Chinese speakers are necessarily smarter but that they are fortunate to have a language with simpler words for digits. The explanation for the word length effect is straightforward: The longer the words, the more information that needs to be refreshed by the articulatory loop. Because the articulatory loop is limited in how much it can refresh at one time, the longer the words, the harder the loop's, job and consequently, the more that is lost.

Articulatory Suppression.   Another characteristic of the phonological loop is **articulatory suppression.** This is a reduced verbal span when a person is engaged in a speaking task while simultaneously trying to remember a set of items (Murray, 1967; Peterson & Johnson, 1971). For example, suppose a person is given a set of words to hold in the phonological loop. While the person receives the words, she says some word over and over—for example, "the" (i.e., "the", "the", "the", etc.). This causes the person's memory span to be reduced. In other words, talking about one thing makes it very difficult to remember something else, especially if that is some verbal knowledge. For example, if someone tells you her name and college major at a party while you are engaged in conversation with someone else, this will impede your ability to rehearse and remember the name and major. In some sense, this is the suffix effect run amok. What happens here is that the articulatory suppression task, such as repeating the word "the," takes up resources from the articulatory loop. As a result, information in the phonological store cannot be adequately refreshed, and so it is lost.

Irrelevant Speech.   A third characteristic that is related to articulatory suppression is the **irrelevant speech effect.** This is the finding that the phonological loop is less efficient when people are listening to irrelevant speech in the background, even if it is in a language they don't understand (Colle and Welsh, 1976). You have probably had the experience of trying to read in a room where other people are having loud conversations. It is difficult to concentrate on what you are reading because this additional information (the background voices) enters working memory and takes up some of the resources of the phonological loop, causing other information (what you are reading) to be forgotten.

This has implications for students about the best way to study. In a study by Salame and Baddeley (1989) students were asked to keep a set of information in mind both while they had silence and while they listened to either instrumental music or music with vocals. The results of this study are shown in Figure 5.3. As you can see, memory was best when students were in quiet surroundings. When there was background noise that involved language, such as the vocals music, memory was worse. Listening to instrumental music had a moderate effect. The linguistic nature of the irrelevant speech of the vocals music interfered with the operation of the phonological loop. Therefore, when you study, it is best to do so under quiet conditions. If you must have background noise, choose instrumental music rather than music with vocals or, even worse, television.

Phonological Similarity.   A fourth finding is the **phonological similarity effect,** in which the more phonologically similar the items in a set are, the more errors that are made on recall (Baddeley, 1966; Conrad & Hull, 1964). In other words, when the words rhyme

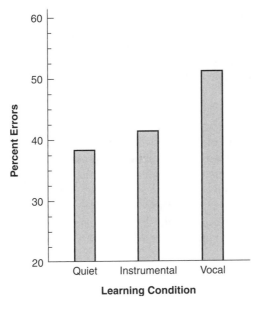

FIGURE 5.3   Working Memory Performance with Different Types of Background Music
Source: Salame & Baddeley, 1989

(e.g., "whole," "bowl," "stole," "pole," and "troll") people forget more and make more errors than when the words do not rhyme (e.g., "whole," "line," "milk," "fire," and "hunt"). Under these circumstances, people are more likely to misremember a similar sounding word. For example, if one of the words in a memory set was "whole," people might misremember this as "roll," which sounds similar but looks different, but not "while," which looks similar but sounds different. This is because information is degrading in the phonological store. When it comes time for an item to be rehearsed, some reconstruction may be needed. Because information in the phonological store is auditory in nature, this reconstruction process is based on the fragmentary phonological information that is available. When there are phonologically similar items, it is difficult to keep track of which ones have and have not been rehearsed. This makes it more likely that one of the unrehearsed items is not refreshed, and forgetting occurs (Li, Schweickert, & Gandour, 2000).

Lexicality.   It should be noted that all of these effects do not take into account knowledge in long-term memory. Working memory can be influenced by long-term memory. For example, memory spans are generally larger for lists of words than for lists of nonwords. This is known as a **lexicality effect** (Hulme, Maughan, & Brown, 1991). People use long-term knowledge to help support and reconstruct information in the phonological store. Information in long-term memory is powerful enough that it can even reverse some of the effects that are usually observed in studies of the phonological loop. For example, with the phonological similarity effect, performance is worse when the items in the set are phonologically similar. However, if these words are embedded in the context of meaningful sentences, this effect reverses: performance is better when the words are phonologically similar rather than different (Copeland & Radvansky, 2001). This commonly occurs with poetry and song lyrics. Presumably, people can draw on knowledge of the sentence along with memory of the basic rhyme scheme of the memory set to come up with the appropriate response. For example, you could remember "pole" if you know that all of the words in a set rhyme with "hole" and the sentence was something like "The vaulter was surprised when he discovered that he had somehow broken his _____." Thus, people can use their long-term knowledge to aid their short-term recall.

Synopsis

The Baddeley and Hitch model is one of the most well-known theories of working memory. The phonological loop portion of the model is geared toward processing verbal/acoustic information. This is done using the phonological store and the articulatory loop. Evidence for the operation of the phonological loop comes from a number of findings. The most prominent of these are the word length effect, articulatory suppression, the irrelevant speech effect, the phonological similarity effect, and the lexicality effect. All of these findings generally hang together quite nicely to provide a convincing story of how working memory handles verbal/linguistic information.

VISUO-SPATIAL SKETCHPAD

The other major slave system in the Baddeley and Hitch (1974) model is the **visuo-spatial sketchpad.** This component is primarily responsible for visual information, such as size or color, and spatial information, such as the relative orientation of entities, or spatially manipulating an object in one's own head. This section incorporates some aspects of spatial memory processing that some instructors may not typically consider part of working memory, such as dynamic memory. However, because they clearly involve the manipulation of spatial information, they are included here.

In general, it should be noted that the visuo-spatial sketchpad appears to typically involve more of a person's right hemisphere than the left. This is consistent with the idea that the right hemisphere is better adapted to spatial and holistic processing. More specifically, the premotor cortex (found at the back of the frontal lobes) seems to be important for the visuo-spatial sketchpad's active processing (Smith, 2000).

Mental Images

One of the main tasks of the visuo-spatial sketchpad is the construction, maintenance, and manipulation of mental images. This is done by creating images that bear some isomorphic relation to perceptual images. For example, mental images appear to be sensitive to object size and viewer distance. People are better able to identify the components of an image if the image is large or the viewing distance is close (Kosslyn, 1975).

These mental images must be actively maintained or rehearsed in the visuo-spatial sketchpad, or they will degrade. This is demonstrated in the CRT model of visual imagery (Kosslyn, 1975). When you watch television, the image you see on the screen (sometimes a cathode ray tube or CRT) is not projected all at once. Instead, the image is continuously being refreshed, with the cathode ray constantly scanning from the top of the image to the bottom and then starting over again. The speed at which this is done is called the refresh rate. Thus, even a static image is constantly decaying and being reconstructed. The CRT model of visual imagery assumes that a similar process is going on in the visuo-spatial sketchpad. The mental image is constantly constructing, decaying, and refreshing. This is similar to the operation of the articulatory loop described earlier.

In support of this, like the word length effect and the phonological loop, it has been found that people find it more difficult to maintain complex images than simple images (Kosslyn, 1975). The more components there are to the image, the more elements the visuo-spatial sketchpad needs to be constantly refreshing, and the greater the opportunity for forgetting to occur. Similarly, it has been found that larger images are harder to maintain than smaller images, presumably for similar reasons.

Visual Scanning

How does the visuo-spatial sketchpad manipulate information it has, and toward what aim? One of the roles of the visuo-spatial sketchpad is as a surrogate for physical reality. A person might make decisions about objects while at two different locations, which is done using working memory. When evaluating two spatial locations, a person may scan across his mental map of the area. This mental scanning increases proportionately with the distance that needs to be covered. Short distances are scanned in a short time, but longer distances require more mental effort and time. In a study of this mental scanning process, Kosslyn and his colleagues had people memorize a map of an island, much like the one in Figure 5.4. The task was to verify some aspect of one of the locations on the island. The

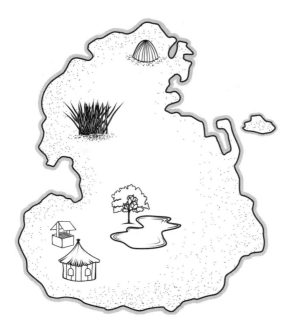

FIGURE 5.4   Map of an Island Used in Kosslyn's Mental Scanning Experiments

Source: Kosslyn, 1980

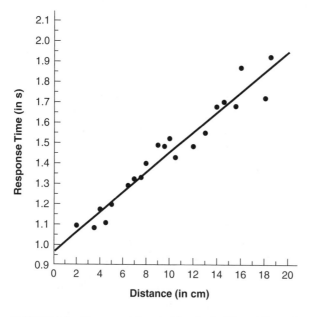

FIGURE 5.5   Response Time in Kosslyn's Mental Scanning Study as a Function of Distance on the Island Map

Source: Kosslyn 1980

results are shown in Figure 5.5. As can be seen, response time increased with increased distance from one location to the other. In general, mental imagery processes in working memory rely on similar visual and spatial processes as those operating during perception, except that a person needs to be constantly producing the images himself, rather than having them present in the environment. It is this constant image generation that can sometimes lead to errors in visuo-spatial working memory (Kosslyn & Pomerantz, 1977).

Thus, the processing of information in the visuo-spatial sketchpad takes on isomorphic perceptual qualities similar to what they would be if they existed in reality. A more striking example of this was demonstrated in a study done by Intons-Peterson and Roskos-Ewoldsen (1989) with students at Indiana University. In this study, students did a mental scanning task, much like in the Kosslyn study. However, rather than using a map of a fictitious island, the students used their knowledge of the Bloomington campus. More importantly, people were asked to imagine themselves going from one location to another, carrying either a balloon or a load of bricks. In both cases, response time increased with greater distances that needed to be mentally traveled. Moreover, the increase in response time was greater when the students imagined they were carrying the heavy load rather than the light one. Thus, the operation of working memory can capture aspects of the world in a direct fashion.

Mental Rotation

Another visuo-spatial working memory process is **mental rotation,** in which a person needs to mentally turn some object. This might be done so that a person can make a decision, such as identifying it. For example, a sign that is upside down is difficult to read. You must mentally turn the letters or numbers to decipher the message. Another possibility is that a person may need to compare two objects for some purpose. For example, a person working on a jigsaw puzzle may mentally rotate the pieces to see if they might fit together before actually picking up the pieces and trying them out.

Research has shown that, much like visual scanning, mental rotation has characteristics that mimic physical rotation. Specifically, the greater the degree of rotation required, the longer it takes a person to do the task. In a study by Shepard and Metzler (1971), students saw pairs of three-dimensional figures, like the ones in Figure 5.6. Participants had to say whether the figures were the same or different. These figures could either be rotated in the picture plane (as is the case with the figure pair on the top) or be rotated in depth (as in the case with the figure pair in the middle). The results, as seen in Figure 5.7, showed that response time increased linearly with the degree of rotation that was needed. It is almost as if people are actually mentally turning the object about in their visuo-spatial sketchpad.

Like other visuo-spatial sketchpad tasks, mental rotation shows some clear neurological underpinnings. Specifically, it appears that the parietal lobes are much more involved than other parts of the cortex, although there may be some coordinating support from the frontal lobes. Furthermore, if the mental rotation is particularly demanding, there may be greater involvement of the left hemisphere than the right, suggesting an increase in analytic processing in these cases (Just et al., 2001). This is different from what was stated earlier about visuo-spatial sketchpad processing in general. This illustrates that it is difficult to clearly identify one type of processing with any one brain structure. Although many

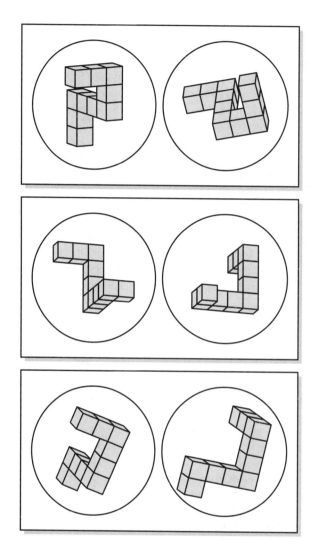

FIGURE 5.6 Object Pairs Used in Shepard and Metzler Mental Rotation Study

Source: Shepard & Metzler, 1971

visuo-spatial processes involve the right hemisphere, when more holistic processing is needed—in cases like mental rotation where more analytical processing is needed—there might be a greater dominance of the left hemisphere.

Boundary Extension

The operation of the visuo-spatial sketchpad can also be observed in a phenomenon known as **boundary extension.** As noted in the discussion of iconic and trans-saccadic memory in

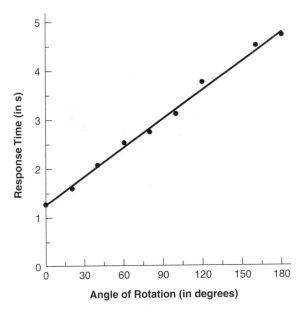

FIGURE 5.7 **Response Time Results from Shepard and Metzler's Mental Rotation Study**
Source: Shepard & Metzler, 1971

Chapter 4, when we view the world, we are only getting bits and pieces of it at a time. In part, what gives us the experience of being in a world filled with more visual information than is actually there is that we fill in around the edges with what we *think* should be there. This is especially striking in one's memory of pictures, television shows, or movies. For example, when you remember a movie, it is unlikely that your memory for the film contains your experience of the edge of the screen and the theater beyond that. It is as if you remember more of the scene than you actually saw. This memory for details beyond what is seen is called boundary extension (Intraub, Bender, & Mangels, 1992; Intraub & Berkowits, 1996; Intraub & Richardson, 1989).

In studies of boundary extension, a person was presented with a series of photographs, such as those in Figure 5.8. Then she would be shown photographs with the task of identifying whether the picture was one they saw before (old) or whether it was different (new). Some of these would be old pictures, Some shots would be close up, and others would be photos taken from a distance (and thereby extending the boundary of the original). It was discovered that people made more errors when presented with pictures that were photographed from a distance. And if people were asked to draw what they saw in the photograph, their drawings tended to include information that was beyond the boundaries of the photograph. It was as if the participants filled in the surrounding space when the information was being actively processed in the visuo-spatial sketchpad and then incorporated this into their memory of the scene. What is particularly striking is that this boundary extension occurs even when the photos were viewed very briefly (Intraub, Gottesman, Willey, & Zuk, 1996) or when people were warned ahead of time that boundary extension could occur (Intraub & Bodamer, 1993).

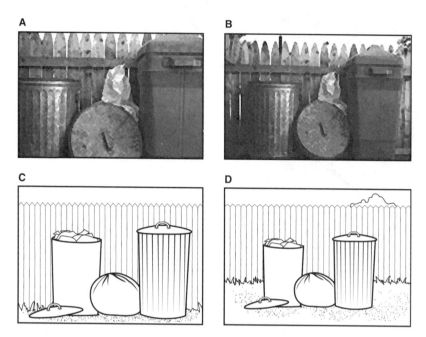

FIGURE 5.8   Example of Stimuli and Responses from a Study on Boundary Extension.
Subjects tend to remember having seen a greater expanse of a scene than was shown in a photograph. For example, when drawing the close-up view in Panel A from memory, the subject's drawing (Panel C) contained extended boundaries. Another subject, shown a more wide-angle view of the same scene (Panel B), also drew the scene with extended boundaries (Panel D). (Note: To evaluate the drawings in the figure, it is important to study the boundaries of each drawing and its associated stimulus.)
Source: Intraub & Richardson, 1989

Still, boundary extension is not an automatic, unconscious process of the visuo-spatial sketchpad that occurs whenever someone sees any kind of picture. For it to occur, a person must think that what is being viewed is a scene from the real world. There must be some sort of background, even if the background is only imagined (Intraub, Gottesman, & Bills, 1998). Pictures of objects without a background do not produce boundary extension (Gottesman & Intraub, 2002). This evidence of boundary extension only with the proper context is a case where the operation of the visuo-spatial sketchpad depends on knowledge stored in long-term memory. If the picture does not activate this knowledge, then no boundary extension occurs. More demonstrations that the visuo-spatial sketchpad uses long-term knowledge to make inferences about spatial aspects of the world are given in the next section.

Dynamic Memory

There are other unconscious processes that can occur in the visuo-spatial sketchpad that alter perceptual experiences based on physical characteristics of the world. Often, these involve the interpretation of either the real or perceived motion of objects. Because of this, it is called *dynamic memory* (see Hubbard, 1995b, for a review).

Representational Momentum.   When we watch objects in motion and blink or look away briefly, we still see them moving (unless they actually stop for some reason). This idea of continued motion is captured in the visuo-spatial sketchpad when memory for observed motion is tested. Specifically, there is a tendency for people to misremember the location or orientation of an object further along its path of motion than it actually was the last time it was seen (Freyd, 1987; Freyd & Finke, 1984; 1985). This is called **representational momentum.** It is as if people have difficulty stopping the object in their visuo-spatial sketchpad. An example of a representational momentum display is shown in Figure 5.9. In this display, a box appears to be rotating across a series of displays, much like a cartoon. After the last display there is a delay, and people are given a test display. The task is to say whether the object is in the same orientation as it was when it was last seen. These test objects can be the actual last display, a box rotated slightly backward, or a box rotated slightly forward. The results of one study are shown in Figure 5.10. There is a tendency for people to misremember the box as being further along in its rotation than it actually was.

Other studies have shown that representational momentum is observed in the path of the object's current trajectory when an object is moving along a path rather than rotating (Hubbard, 1990). Representational momentum is also influenced by the apparent speed with which the object is moving, with faster objects resulting in more representational momentum (Hubbard & Bharucha, 1988). This effect can take into account regular properties of the world. For example, one may claim to remember a pendulum beginning its backswing when that has not yet occurred (Verfaillie & Y'dewalle, 1991) or remembering a ball bouncing off a wall before it happens (Hubbard & Bharucha, 1988).

Representational momentum can also reflect properties such as a centripetal force (Hubbard, 1996). It is believed that this sort of dynamic memory involves active processing

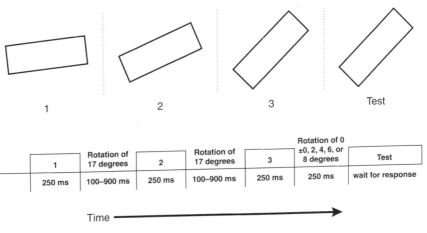

FIGURE 5.9   A Representational Momentum Display

Source: Freyd & Finke, 1984

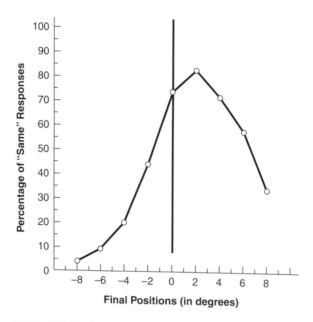

FIGURE 5.10 Results from a Study of Representational Momentum. Note that estimates of final position are distorted in the direction of the object's motion.
Source: Freyd & Finke, 1984

in the visuo-spatial sketchpad because the amount of distortion observed in a given person's reports is directly related to the speed with which he does mental rotation. The faster people mentally rotate, the greater their distortion (Munger, Solberg, & Horrocks, 1999). It should also be noted that the representational momentum that is observed in working memory tends to follow medieval impetus theories of motion rather than Newtonian or other more modern views of motion. This is true even in people who are experts in physics (Kozhevnikov & Hegarty, 2001), thus suggesting that this aspect of working memory is limited in terms of how it is influenced by knowledge in long-term memory (but see the influence of context effects following).

Representational Gravity.   Another influence of physical principles on visuo-spatial working memory is **representational gravity.** The basic finding is that memory for object positions tends to be distorted toward the earth, especially when the objects are not supported (Freyd, Pantzer, & Cheng, 1988; Hubbard, 1995a). An example of this is shown in Figure 5.11. Here, people view a plant that is initially on top of a table or suspended by a hook. Then in a subsequent display, the table or hook is removed. People are then tested for their memory of the location of the plant in the picture. When the table has been removed, people tend to remember it as being lower in the picture. This is consistent with the idea that some representational effect of gravity is influencing the visuo-spatial memory, moving the plant lower.

Similarly, if a circle is viewed on an incline, it is remembered as further down the incline, as if it had rolled down. Moreover, the greater the degree of the incline, the further the

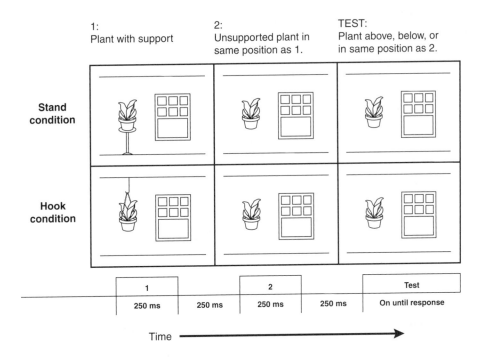

FIGURE 5.11   Representational Gravity Display

Source: Freyd, Pantzer, & Cheng, 1988

circle is misremembered as having rolled down the hill. Also, objects moving along a path in space may be remembered as being lower than they originally were, as if being pulled down by gravity (Hubbard, 1990). Moreover, larger, and presumably heavier, objects fall faster (show more effects of representational gravity) than do smaller objects (Hubbard, 1997).

Representational Friction.   Another quality of the visuo-spatial sketchpad that captures physical properties of the world is **representational friction.** This is the finding that objects moving in space slow down more quickly if they are moving along another object (such as the ground) that can produce friction (Hubbard, 1995). Furthermore, the greater the implied contact with a surface or surfaces, the greater the implied friction. In some sense, representational friction can put the brakes on representational momentum. Overall, it is as if people are trying to capture and predict the outcome of events in the world during the processing of information in the visuo-spatial sketchpad.

Context.   One final thing that should be noted about these dynamic memory effects is that they exhibit context effects. Specifically, the type of physical property that is exerted can vary depending on what that object is. For example, in one study people saw an object moving up a computer screen. This object was either a rocket or a church steeple. (These objects were used because of their similar shape, although they obviously have different

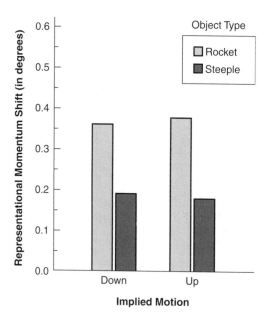

FIGURE 5.12   Influence of Object Context on Representational Momentum. Both a rocket and a church steeple were viewed moving upward across a computer screen. The representational momentum was greater in the rocket than in the steeple.

Source: Reed & Vinson, 1996

properties.) Rockets typically travel upward, whereas church steeples do not. As can be seen in Figure 5.12, there was greater upward displacement of the object in working memory when it was a rocket than when it was a steeple (Reed & Vinson, 1996).

Synopsis

The other slave system of the Baddeley and Hitch model is the visuo-spatial sketchpad. This part of working memory is thought to be dedicated to processing visual and spatial information. The visuo-spatial sketchpad appears to capture many qualities of the world in an analog and isomorphic format. This is illustrated by things such as mental scanning and rotation effects, as well as boundary extension. The dynamic operation of the visuo-spatial sketchpad on information in working memory can be seen in effects such as representational momentum, gravity, and friction. This characteristic of this part of working memory allows us to better function in a dynamic, fast-moving world.

CENTRAL EXECUTIVE

The final component of the working memory model is the **central executive.** This component is involved in the allocation of attentional resources (i.e., deciding what and what not to think about), as well as dealing with any active processing of information that is not directly handled by the two slave systems. As such, the central executive plays a critical role in working memory, and it is given the lion's share of what we normally consider as "thinking." Basically, the central executive does most of the work of working memory. However, despite this, little attention has been paid to it. In some cases, the central executive has become a sort of garbage can for researchers who need to account for working memory processes that are not readily understood in terms of either of the two slave systems. If it is unclear what is going on, researchers just ascribe it to the central executive and people move on.

That said, it should also be noted that there has been some serious investigation into what this component of working memory does. For example, if people are interested in studying working memory when this component is all tied up doing something else, researchers might give a person a task like generating a random set of numbers (which is much harder than it sounds). This causes people to do more poorly on tasks that require any sort of active thinking in which control over the flow of information is at a premium. This general control of attentional resources in working memory involves the operation of the frontal lobes, particularly the prefrontal cortex (Kane & Engle, 2002).

In some sense, the central executive serves as a distributor of memory resources. One thing that can improve memory performance is if there are more resources available. Activity that brings the body to a higher or optimal state of arousal is likely to have a positive effect on working memory performance. This is why you think more clearly when you've had enough sleep. An interesting demonstration of this effect of activity and arousal on working memory performance was a study by Wilkinson, Scholey, and Wesnes (2002). In this study, people who were or were not chewing gum were given a number of working memory tasks. What was found was that the people who were chewing gum (a physical activity) performed better on the memory tests than those who weren't. Of course, this does not mean that gum chewing is always a memory enhancer (and if you decide to try it out, *please* chew with your mouth closed), nor will it automatically boost you to the next grade level. However, it is clear that increasing your physical activity can increase your working memory performance.

Suppression

One mechanism of memory that the central executive controls is suppression. Suppression is used to keep irrelevant information out of working memory or to remove from working memory information that has become irrelevant or inappropriate (Conway & Engle, 1994). For example, in a reading span task in which people must remember the last word from each of a set of sentences, people with lower spans, and presumably less efficient suppression mechanisms, are more likely to get the word wrong (Chiappe, Hasher, & Siegel, 2000). The operation of such a suppression mechanism of the central executive is closely tied to that of the frontal lobes—in particular, the prefrontal cortex, which is at the very front of the frontal lobes (Kane & Engle, 2000).

Dysexecutive Syndrome

The disruption of the central executive can be seen when there has been damage to the brain, particularly the frontal lobes. This can result in a condition known as the **dysexecutive**

syndrome, where people lose some of the central executive functions that help them control their thought processes. As a result of this syndrome, people may exhibit two types of behaviors. Some behaviors may be perseverations. Perseverations occur when a person has been performing a task one way and is asked to perform it another way. For example, if a person is first asked to sort a deck of cards by suit, she could probably do so easily. But if she were then asked to sort the cards by value, she would probably sort them by suit again. This is because there is a perseveration of the old mode of thinking, and the person cannot disengage from the first to move on to the second. What is especially odd about this condition is that people can report what the correct sorting strategy should be and may admit they are not following the new strategy even as they continue to sort based on the old one. Relatedly, some of their behaviors may exhibit elements of distraction. For example, if they are not currently processing information at the moment, their attention might drift and become locked on some other stimulus in the environment.

Overall, this dysexecutive syndrome illustrates some of the attentional control processes that have been attributed to the central executive component of working memory. When this component has been damaged and is not operating properly, the flow of the stream of thought is disrupted, getting stuck on old information and drifting out to unrelated areas.

Synopsis

The central executive is probably the most active, and least understood, part of the working memory system. Still, we do have a good idea about what it is capable of. For example, the central executive helps coordinate what information is attended to in working memory and what is not. Part of this attentional control is achieved through some sort of inhibition mechanism. People can have problems with their central executive, producing what is known as the dysexecutive syndrome.

SPAN TESTS

In Chapter 4, we briefly examined measures of short-term memory span, including word span and digit span. These are **simple span** measures because they require a person to do one simple task—for example. remembering something for a brief period of time and then reciting it. However, this is a relatively poor measure of working memory because the participant isn't doing anything complicated. To address this, a number of working memory span tests have been developed. These are **complex span** measures. For a test to be a complex span measure there must be at least two components. One is a retention component, such as the simple span measure in which the person retains a set of information for a period of time. The other part is some active processing component, depending on the type of working memory process that is of interest. Overall, this approach allows us to more closely measure working memory rather than short-term memory.

Reading Span.   Perhaps the most widely used of the complex span tests is Daneman and Carpenter's (1980) **reading span** test. In this test, a person is asked to read aloud a set of two to six sentences, such as "The taxi turned up Michigan Avenue, where they had a clear view of the lake." At the end of each set, the person must recall the last word in each of the sentences of that set. The largest set of words that can all be accurately recalled corresponds to that person's reading span score. The retention component here is that the person must remember the final words. The processing component is that the person must think about the sentence in order to read it effectively. This sentence span measure has been found to be a good predictor of language processing (Daneman & Merikle, 1996), much better than simple span measures. This is because language processing requires an active manipulation of knowledge. This would correspond to the processing component of the reading span that is absent in the simple span tests.

Comprehension Span.   In addition to the reading span test, there are a number of similar span tests that tap into linguistic working memory processes. One of these is the **comprehension span** test developed by Waters and Caplan (1996). In this test, a person is asked to read sentences and then recall the last word of each sentence after sets of a certain number from 2 to 6. However, unlike the reading span, rather than read the sentence aloud, the person makes sensibility judgments. Some of the sentences make sense, such as "It was the gangsters that broke into the warehouse," whereas others do not, such as "It was the warehouse that broke into the gangsters." This sensibility judgment requires the person to think more deeply about the meaning of the sentences, providing a better measure of higher-level working memory processes, such as those operating at the mental model level (see Chapter 7).

Operation Span.   Another popular measure of working memory is the **operation span** test developed by Turner and Engle (1989). In this test, a person is asked to read aloud a two-step math problem, such as $(2 \times 4) + 1 = 8$, and then to indicate whether the solution is correct. After this is done, a word is presented. Again, these math operation–word combinations are presented in set sizes from 2 to 6. At the end of each set the person must recall as many words from that set as he can. The largest set size that can be accurately recalled reflects that person's operation span score. The retention component here is that the person must remember the words from each set, and the processing component is that the person must accurately solve the math problems. The results of this complex span test have been found to be a relatively more domain-independent measure of working memory span relative to the reading span test, which is more closely tied to language processing.

Spatial Span.   One final complex span test is Shah and Miyake's (1996) **spatial span** test. The intent of this test is to tap more into spatial working memory than the other complex span tasks. In this test, a person is presented with a series of letters that have been rotated from the normal upright position. The person's initial task is to indicate whether the letters are normal or mirror reversed. This is the active processing component of the test. Then, after a set of letters, the participant is asked to indicate where the tops of the letters were in the set by pointing to a predetermined set of locations. This is the retention component.

Synopsis

There are a number of ways of assessing working memory capacity. These are known as span tests. Some tests, such as word span and digit span, are simple span tests that only measure retention capacity. More complex span tests, such as reading span, comprehension, operation span, and spatial span, require people to hold a set of information in mind while they do some other task simultaneously. Thus, this shows an influence of the working part of working memory. These span tests are useful because they are often related to performance with more complex types of thinking.

WORKING MEMORY AND COMPLEX PROCESSING

The various components of working memory influence other, more complex mental processes. For example, working memory capacity is related to long-term memory retrieval. Long-term memory retrieval is not an automatic process, but it requires the mental resources of working memory and can be disrupted by a person's other thoughts (Carrier & Pashler, 1995; Rohrer & Pashler, 2003).

This effect of working memory on long-term memory retrieval is also seen when comparing people with different working memory capacities. Specifically, people with larger working memory capacities are better able to retrieve information than people with smaller capacities. Cantor and Engle (1993) reported that people with larger working memory span scores showed less associative interference, or fan effects (see Chapter 7), than people with smaller working memory span scores. Similarly, Kane and Engle (2000) found that people with larger working memory span scores showed less proactive interference. In general, people with larger working memory capacities seem to be less affected by irrelevant, interfering information. One possibility is that this additional information can be more easily managed and worked around if a person has more capacity.

It is also believed that working memory span scores reflect the ability to coordinate the contents of working memory and not necessarily the amount of capacity or "size" of working memory per se. One way to accomplish this is removing irrelevant information from working memory and preventing irrelevant information from entering working memory and mucking up the works (Hasher & Zacks, 1988). People with larger working memory spans are better able to coordinate information in working memory. Those with larger spans show smaller interference effects in long-term memory retrieval because they are better at keeping the irrelevant information out of working memory (Cantor & Engle, 1993).

One source of irrelevant information that can disrupt working memory is negative emotions—for example, if the person is shown pictures of fearful faces (Kensinger & Corkin, 2003). Negative content and irrelevant information can also clog up working memory. It has been reported that students who engage in expressive writing that discloses some personal emotions can increase their working memory span (Klein & Boals, 2001). First-year college students might write essays expressing their thoughts about coming to college. This benefit is observed even weeks after the disclosure. Apparently, expressing this information decreases the implicit need or desire for a person to think about it, so there are fewer intrusive thoughts about the issue. Similarly, it was found that people who wrote about negative experiences showed a larger increase in working memory span than people who wrote about neutral or positive experiences. So if you express thoughts that are troubling you, it might help you increase your working memory capacity later, and it could improve your memory overall.

Another case of working memory affecting other types of memory can be seen when a person who is trying to understand a description creates a mental representation called a mental model (Johnson-Laird, 1983; van Dijk & Kintsch, 1983; Zwaan & Radvansky, 1998). This mental model serves as a mental simulation of the world. For example, when you read a novel or watch a movie, you create a mental representation of that fictional world that has many of the properties of the real world. There are several aspects of a situation that people need to understand to get a clear picture about the events. Two of these are causal relations among events and the spatial locations where events occur. That is, a person must know why various things happen and where they happen. Because these are two different aspects of situations, it would seem reasonable to believe different parts of working memory influence them, and this has been substantiated.

In a study by Friedman and Miyake (2000), people were given a measure of their verbal working memory capacity (the sentence span) and a measure of their spatial working memory capacity (the spatial span). The students then read stories in which they had to keep track of causal and spatial information that occurred in the text. Friedman and Miyake found that a person's ability to keep track of the causal information in the story was related to performance on the reading span test. However, the ability to keep track of spatial information was related to performance on the spatial span task. Thus, it appears that different types of thinking used different aspects of working memory.

Synopsis

How a person uses working memory has implications for the ability to do a variety of mental tasks. For example, people who score higher on working memory span tests may be able to do better at long-term memory retrieval. What seems to be important for effective thinking is keeping the contents of working filled with relevant information and keeping irrelevant information out. For example, people who express what they are worried about often do not have these thoughts intruding on their working memories, and their general mental performance improves.

SUMMARY

This chapter covered some of the ways that information is actively manipulated in working memory. The most prevalent view of working memory is the tripartite model of Baddeley and Hitch. In this model there is a phonological loop for processing verbal/acoustic information, a visuo-spatial sketchpad for processing visual and spatial information, and an executive control that actively manipulates information, as well as guiding the focus of attention in the various components of working memory. The active processing of information is influenced by the skill with which a person is able to process information, as well as unconscious factors, such as how knowledge of physical reality can alter memory of perceived scenes. Finally, it should be noted that working memory is critically involved in any sort of complex processing. Thus, by gaining an understanding of how memory operates at a more basic level, we can learn something about how memory is involved at higher, more complex levels of thinking.

STUDY QUESTIONS

1. What are the primary components of the Baddeley and Hitch working memory model?

2. What are the primary components of the phonological loop?

3. What are some of the major findings that support the idea of a phonological loop?

4. What is the nature of the information in the visuo-spatial sketchpad?

5. What evidence is there that the visuo-spatial sketchpad of working memory captures real-world, physical processes?

6. What is the role of the central executive in working memory?

7. What are the different types of span tests that can be used to assess working memory? What are each of their properties?

8. What are some of the ways that working memory capacity influences other types of thought?

KEY TERMS

articulatory loop, articulatory suppression, Baddeley and Hitch model, boundary extension, central executive, complex span, comprehension span, dynamic memory, dysexecutive syndrome, executive controller, irrelevant speech effect, lexicality effect, mental rotation, operation span, phonological loop, phonological similarity effect, phonological store, reading span, representational friction, representational gravity, representational momentum, simple span, spatial span, visuo-spatial sketchpad word length effect, working memory

CHAPTER SIX

NONDECLARATIVE MEMORY

When we think about "remembering," we usually think of times when we are consciously aware of using our memories, such as trying to remember a person's name, the answer to an exam question, or where we left the car keys. This conscious, explicit use of memory is readily understood and apparent to people. People are also painfully aware of when this conscious memory has failed them and they forget something. It would not be difficult to talk about our experiences with using these memories, the content of these memories, and our awareness of them. This is part of what makes them declarative memories. However, as prominent as this type of memory may seem, much of the work of human memory operates not at the conscious level but at an unconscious level. Some of these unconscious memories are so far removed from our awareness that it is very difficult, if not impossible, to accurately talk about them. These are **nondeclarative memories.** One of the interesting things about nondeclarative memories, aside from the fact that they often operate outside of conscious awareness, is that they are relatively spared in cases of amnesia. This supports the idea that this is a distinctly different way memory processes information.

This chapter covers a number of elements related to nondeclarative memories. We start with a discussion of some of the more basic forms of learning and memory encoding. One of these is classical conditioning, in which an organism learns to respond to signals in the environment that are predictive of future outcomes. In a sense, the organism is showing memory for previous environmental contingencies. Following this, we briefly discuss operant conditioning. Although not strictly a form of nondeclarative memory, we include it because of its conceptual proximity to classical condition and because many unconscious memories do function based on operant conditioning principles. We also examine more "cognitive" sorts of nondeclarative learning, particularly procedural memories and implicit memories. These are memories we use for various tasks and that influence our behaviors without our conscious knowledge.

CLASSICAL CONDITIONING

Classical conditioning is one of the simplest forms of learning and memory. Its formal discovery is credited to Ivan Pavlov (1849–1936), the famous Russian physiologist (see Chapter 1). As such, it is sometimes referred to as **Pavlovian conditioning.** In classical conditioning, an organism learns that certain stimuli are reliable predictors of the imminent onset of other stimuli that are important to the organism. We examine classical conditioning in three forms: abstract; concrete, with the experimental situation used by Pavlov, and an example that is more in line with understanding human memory.

Abstract Structure

The basic classical conditioning paradigm is illustrated in Figure 6.1. Classical conditioning starts out with a stimulus that elicits a response in an organism. This stimulus is called the unconditioned stimulus, or US, and the response it elicits in the organism is called the unconditioned response, or UR. Both are considered unconditioned because no learning is needed. It is a stimulus-response relation that is prewired into the organism. Another stimulus is introduced in the situation that initially elicits no response in the organism. As such, it is referred to as a neutral stimulus, or NS. During learning, the NS is presented prior to the US in a reliable and consistent way. For quickest learning, it is best if the NS always precedes the US. Over time, the organism begins to associate the NS with the coming US. As a result, the organism makes a preparatory response, as if the US were about to occur, because the organism has learned this relationship. The stimulus is now called the conditioned stimulus, or CS, and the response that is made in the presence of the conditioned stimulus is called the conditioned response, or CR.

Pavlov

For an example of this, let's look at Pavlov's experiment. Pavlov received a Nobel Prize for his work in the study of digestion. While researching the initial stage of digestion, salivation, Pavlov collected saliva from dogs by surgically inserting tubes into their mouths and feeding them. To his annoyance, Pavlov found that the dogs would salivate even when they weren't fed. Pavlov noticed that the additional salivation occurred with some regularity: It often preceded the actual presentation of the food by a certain period of time. Pavlov suspected that the dogs had made a psychological connection between the presence of the person who gave them the food and food itself, so the dogs would salivate at the sight of the person. Pavlov decided to test his theory.

The structure of Pavlov's experiments is shown in Figure 6.2. In his actual study he used meat as the US and the dogs' salivation as the UR. The dogs did not need to learn to salivate to the meat. As an NS, he used a ringing bell. He rang the bell before he offered the meat to the dogs, so over time, the dogs learned that the ringing bell meant food. The dogs

Basic Paradigm

$$US \longrightarrow UR$$

$$NS \longrightarrow US \longrightarrow UR$$

$$CS \longrightarrow CR$$

FIGURE 6.1   The Basic Classical Conditioning Paradigm

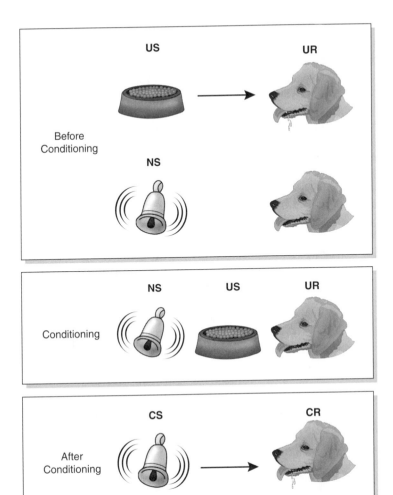

FIGURE 6.2   The Classical Conditioning Paradigm as It Occurred in Pavlov's Studies

began to salivate after the bell had sounded but before they were fed. The bell was now a CS, and the salivation was a CR.

Examples with Humans

Another example of classical conditioning that relates more to human activity is the development of phobias. These are irrational fears a person develops, such as a fear of elevators, open space, or public speaking. It is not unusual for these phobias to develop through a nondeclarative memory, a classical conditioning process of which the person is unaware. Specifically, a person has some initial experience with a situation that will come to elicit the phobia. For example, a person will have a negative public speaking experience, the anxiety experienced prior to public speaking is classically conditioned, and the person begins to avoid that situation, creating the phobia.

Happily, classical conditioning can also be used to get rid of phobias. This can be done through a process known as systematic desensitization. In this clinical method, people are first asked to think of situations that are very remote from the situation that elicits the phobia. Over time, the person is slowly brought closer and closer to the situation that produces the phobia. At each step along the way the person remains at that stage until she is not disturbed by that situation. When this feeling of calm has become associated with the situation at each stage, the person moves on to the next stage. This continues until a person finally reaches the phobia situation, which then is classically conditioned to a relaxed feeling. At this point the phobia has been conquered.

Associative Structure

What sort of association is being learned in classical conditioning? There are two general possibilities, which are shown in Figure 6.3. The first is that the CS is directly associated with the CR. That is, the CS directly causes the CR to occur. This is called a **stimulus-response association.** The other is that the CS is directly associated with a memory representation of the US, which then leads to the production of the CR. In other words, the CS is interpreted as predicting the onset of the US, so this elicits a CR in preparation for the CS. This is called a **stimulus-stimulus association.** This is one of those few cases where both possibilities are true. Classical conditioning can occur with either type of learning. However, in any given learning situation, only one type of association is stored. In the vast majority of the cases, stimulus-stimulus associations are learned. That is, the organism learns some predictive relationship. There are some cases, however, where stimulus-response associations are learned instead.

Because of the prominent influence of the stimulus-stimulus associations being used, what appears to be important in classical conditioning is not contiguity but contingency. **Contiguity learning** refers to the idea that learning may occur when an NS and a US occur near one another in time. However, while timing is important to a degree, it does not appear to be the critical factor. Instead, what is driving learning in this case is the establishment of some form of cause-effect relationship (however primitive) in order for contingency learning to occur. **Contingency learning** is when an organism appears to be sensitive to the causal structure rather than simply relying on occurrences in the same period of time.

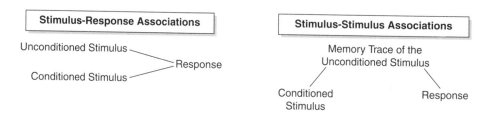

FIGURE 6.3   The Difference Between Stimulus-Response and Stimulus-Stimulus Associations in Classical Conditioning

Important Phenomenon

Initial Learning.   There are many important features of classical conditioning that clarify the role this type of memory plays and the nature of classical conditioning itself. First there is an acquisition period, or learning curve. The association is not effective immediately but takes a period of time to be learned. For example, it takes a while for a dog to learn that the sound of a bell is a signal for the presentation of food. This is because not all cooccurrences in the environment are going to be meaningful over the long term. Most will not. Because an organism has only a limited number of resources, such as a short-term memory capacity, those resources must be used wisely. By only encoding and using those relationships that are stable and meaningful, classical conditioning allows the organism to more effectively direct the ways that it prepares for events in the environment.

Forgetting.   Of course, the environment is not always stable, and an organism needs to adapt to change not only by learning new associations, but also by ceasing to respond to associations that are no longer relevant. When a CS is presented many times without a US, the organism will stop responding to that CS. This is called **extinction.** For example, if a bell rings but no food is offered, the dog will no longer salivate when it hears the bell.

What's interesting is that even when extinction has occurred, forgetting is not complete. This is revealed most clearly by two phenomena. The first is **spontaneous recovery.** This occurs when, after extinction, there is a long delay, and then the CS is presented again. The CR, which was extinct, reemerges, but it is not as strong as before. The organism remembers the original association with the CS and forgets that it no longer has meaning. This may be advantageous to an organism because environmental conditions might be present that make the CS meaningful again after an absence.

The other phenomenon related to extinction is **savings.** This is similar to the savings finding described in the discussion of Ebbinghaus in Chapter 3. Savings shows that after extinction has occurred, when an organism relearns a previous association, less time is required to do so than the first time it was learned. This suggests that some memory for that association remains, even though it appears to be forgotten.

Other Situations.   The learning and memory provided by classical conditioning is a helpful nondeclarative memory as long as it is applied in the correct situations. To monitor when this sort of information is retrieved and used, two mechanisms are available. The first is that the memory for the conditioned stimulus can be activated not only by the particular stimulus the organism was trained on, but also any stimuli that resemble that original stimulus. This is called **generalization.** The greater the similarity, the greater the generalization. In addition, the opposite process is needed as well. The association learned in classical conditioning may not always apply. The set of circumstances must be limited. This can be done by the process of **discrimination.** In this case, the organism learns that some stimuli that are similar to the original CS are not predictive.

Effects of Prior Conditioned Memories.   One of the primary mechanisms of forgetting is not the loss of information but the competition among memory traces in a process known as interference (which we discuss in Chapter 7). Something similar occurs in classical

$$CS_1 \;\longrightarrow\; US \;\longrightarrow\; UR \qquad\qquad CS_1 \;\longrightarrow\; US \;\longrightarrow\; UR$$

$$CS_1 \qquad\;\longrightarrow\; CR \qquad\qquad\qquad CS_1 \qquad\;\longrightarrow\; CR$$

$$CS_2 \;=\; CS_1 \;\longrightarrow\; CR \qquad\qquad CS_2 \;\longrightarrow\; CS_1 \;\longrightarrow\; CR$$

$$CS_2 \qquad\neq\qquad CR \qquad\qquad\qquad CS_2 \qquad\;\longrightarrow\; CR$$

FIGURE 6.4   The Blocking Paradigm in Classical Conditioning

FIGURE 6.5   The Higher-Order Conditioning Paradigm in Classical Conditioning

conditioning with the phenomenon of **blocking,** shown in Figure 6.4. To get blocking, an organism first develops some association with a CS. Once this is firmly established, a second NS is presented at the same time. Because an organism is already retrieving information about the prior association, the new association is not noticed and thus is not learned and encoded into memory. This is because it has no added predictive value.

A situation that can be similar to blocking is when there is a very different outcome, known as **higher-order conditioning.** The higher-order conditioning paradigm is illustrated in Figure 6.5. In higher-order conditioning, the organism first learns an association with a CS. After the association is learned to a high degree, a second conditioned stimulus is presented. However, in this case, the second conditioned stimulus occurs prior to the first, so old memories cannot interfere with the awareness of the new associations. The new stimulus is now predictive of the CS, and a CR is observed for the new CS as well.

It should be noted that while classical conditioning is a form of nondeclarative memory that is often operating outside of conscious awareness and does not seem to require consciousness, it does not blindly cause the learning of just any association in the environment. Instead, some associations are learned more readily than others that an organism may never learn.

One of the mechanisms guiding whether an organism can learn an association is **biological preparedness.** This is the concept that different organisms are biologically prepared to learn some associations more easily than others. For example, rats find it easier to learn associations having to do with smell than with vision because they are more olfactory animals. In contrast, the opposite is true for pigeons. They depend more on sight than on smell.

Mere Exposure Effect

The operation of classical conditioning at an unconscious level can even influence our preferences. This is illustrated by the **mere exposure effect** (Zajonc, 2001), which states that people prefer the things they already have been exposed to one or more times. The idea is that when we are exposed to something, we register that information, sometimes only at a subconscious level. As long as there are no negative connotations associated with that stimulus, a positive association is attributed to it. That is, the absence of negative associations in nondeclarative memory is interpreted as something we have experienced but not in any meaningful way and thus will not hurt us. In general, we prefer things we have been exposed to before, even if we don't remember them.

The effects of mere exposure can have dramatic influences on our lives and our culture. As an example of this, James Cutting (2003) showed that the development of the standard Western canon (the set of works that are identified by experts as the core or most important ones) are that the paintings that define French Impressionism are highly related to exposure. Specifically, adults' preference judgments were related to frequency of exposure in the culture rather than whether the adults consciously recognized the painting, the complexity of the painting, or their prototypicality. On the other hand, children who have not had this sort of exposure do not show such bias. So there does not seem to be anything special about the paintings at the core of the canon. What puts these paintings at the core is their frequency of exposure influencing people's ratings of preference.

This influence of memory on preferences is different from explicit memory of whether something is old or new. This is highlighted by the finding that different parts of the brain are activated in these situations, depending on the judgments people are making. Specifically, the preference judgments that drive the mere exposure effect seem to uniquely involve the right lateral frontal lobe, which is not observed with standard memory judgments (Elliot & Dolan, 1998).

The strength of the mere exposure effect is not constant, but it can vary under a number of different circumstances (Bornstein, 1989). The mere exposure effect grows larger with more exposures to the information, up to a point. With large numbers of exposures (e.g., over 100), the effect starts to decline. The effect is also more likely to occur when the information is presented in multiple contexts rather than the same context over and over. Similarly, the mere exposure effect is greater when there is a delay between the time the information was received and the preference ratings assigned compared to when ratings were given immediately after the information. These findings suggest that some change in context makes the information more distinct and, therefore, more preferable.

The mere exposure effect is better when the encounter with the information is brief. When it is longer, people are more likely to rely on declarative memory, although it can occur both when conscious recognition does and does not occur. This suggests that some degree of distinctiveness is helpful in creating the effect. Finally, although it is observed with most types of stimuli, the mere exposure effect does not appear to be particularly strong when people are exposed to abstract art drawings or paintings. This suggests that people have to understand what they see to be positively disposed to it later.

INSTRUMENTAL CONDITIONING

The other major tradition in conditioning research is **instrumental conditioning.** Unlike classical conditioning where an organism is learning to prepare for an upcoming event, in instrumental conditioning the organism is acting on the environment and then remembering and evaluating the consequences of those actions. Much of instrumental conditioning can be captured by Thorndike's Law of Effect. This states that the consequences of an action that have a positive outcome will be reinforced, whereas consequences that have a negative or neutral outcome will not be reinforced. *Reinforced* means that the behavior is more likely to occur in the future. Essentially, with the Law of Effect, the energy that an organism has available can be directed to activities that benefit that organism and directed away from activities that either provide no benefit or may actually harm the organism.

The domain of instrumental conditioning is far too extensive to be adequately covered here. However, it should be noted that we have many nondeclarative memories that have been brought about through this instrumental conditioning paradigm. Often a person is unaware that his behavior is being influence by prior memories of both pleasant and unpleasant events. Instrumental conditioning is, in some cases, the use of unconscious memories to shape our behaviors and thoughts.

Synopsis

One of the fundamental forms of nondeclarative memory that influences a great deal of our behavior is classical conditioning. In most cases, this involves the learning of a predictive association between two stimuli, one that is already important and one that is learned as a predictor of the occurrence of the first. Thus, what are learned are stimulus-to-stimulus associations, not stimulus-to-response associations. These associations take some time to be learned, but they can be forgotten, at least on the surface, through extinction. Phenomena like spontaneous recovery and savings illustrate that even after extinction/forgetting has occurred, there is still some representation of this association deep in memory. One example of an effect of classical conditioning in human memory is the mere exposure effect. Although also a conditioning paradigm, while some aspects of instrumental conditioning may have a nondeclarative component, this type of learning is different enough not to be consider a form of nondeclarative memory as classical conditioning can be.

PROCEDURAL MEMORY

Knowledge of how to do things, such as play the piano, throw a ball, or walk, is an important part of implicit memory. People may have skills and not know how they acquired them. We will now look at the acquisition of procedural skills and the influence of expertise.

Skill Acquisition

Many of the tasks we do improve with practice. These sorts of tasks are called **skills.** Skills can include activities where expertise is widely recognized, such as being able to play a sport, play a musical instrument, or write a best-selling novel. Most skills, however, are very mundane, and you may not consider them "skills." These include activities like walking, reading, riding a bicycle, driving a car, and having a conversation.

Stages of Skill Acquisition

Although there are a wide range of skills that can be stored in nondeclarative memory, the process of skill memory development is similar in all of them. There are three basic levels or stages of skill acquisition that are recognized by memory researchers: the cognitive stage, the associative stage, and the autonomous stage. In essence, this reflects a transition from very arduous and clumsy execution of a skill to more easy and fluid execution. The fact that there are three distinct stages does not mean a person must necessarily be in one particular stage. It is possible for an expert in a certain skill to spend most of her time operating at the autonomous stage but still have nondeclarative memory operating at the associative and cognitive stages for aspects of that skill she may be trying to refine or that, for whatever reason, she has yet to develop.

Cognitive Stage.   The beginning of a skill is the cognitive stage. This is the period of skill development where a person consciously and deliberately goes about performing the actions of the task. For example, when learning to play a game of chess, a person exerts a great deal of cognitive effort trying to consciously assess what is going on to keep the game progressing and either not get wiped out or, better yet, to defeat the opponent. This often takes the form of comparing the current state with the desired state and taking whatever action will bring him closer to the desired state.

Associative Stage.   After spending some time in the cognitive stage, a person will move on to the associative stage. At this stage a person can more quickly retrieve the knowledge needed to perform the task. That is, different memories become directly associated with different aspects of the skill. The need to mentally verbalize to think things through becomes less necessary. Information is quickly and easily recalled into consciousness, although substantial amounts of deliberate and conscious effort are needed. For example, a chess player would be able to directly retrieve information about what certain moves would entail. Different alignments on the board begin to be viewed as offensive or defensive.

Autonomous Stage.   After more practice with a skill, a person may move to the final stage: the autonomous stage. It is during this stage that the execution of the skill has become more proceduralized and progressed from involving consciousness to being largely unconscious. That is, the person's memories and knowledge have moved from being dominated by declarative knowledge to being dominated by nondeclarative knowledge. This is most clearly seen in cases where a person is learning some sort of motor skill, such as learning to play an instrument. When a person becomes an expert in this area, the execution of various components is done with very little conscious involvement other than the desire to execute a particular series of moves to accomplish some goal. There is very little in terms of overt, conscious involvement in the actual execution of the smaller steps of the skill.

In most cases the automation of skills in memory is helpful. However, there are cases where it can have the opposite effect. This occurs when people try to consciously think about what they are doing in cases where the skill is already highly developed. An example of this is when sports players choke under pressure. The athlete's conscious thoughts about what she is doing intrudes on and conflicts with information automatically retrieved from procedural memory (Beilock & Carr, 2001). In fact, when performing at a low level of skill (novices), people do better if they focus on accuracy, whereas at a high level of skill (experts), people do better if they focus on speed (Beilock, Bertenthal, McCoy, & Carr, 2004). This is illustrated in Figure 6.6.

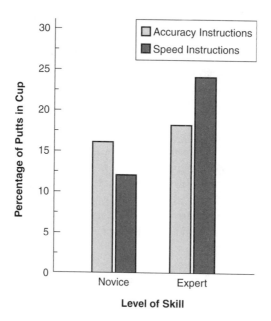

FIGURE 6.6   Mean Percentage of Putts Made for Novices and Experts as a Function of Whether They Were Instructed to Focus on Accuracy or Speed

Source: Beilock, Berthenal, McCoy, & Carr, 2004

Long-Term Working Memory

The automization of procedural memory is an important part of the development of expertise. However, this cannot account for all that is involved in memory in becoming an expert. Of course, there is also the amassing of more and more memories about the domain of expertise. Still, this also cannot fully explain how a person is able to deal with novel aspects of individual situations in an expert's domain of specialty. In addition, and of more interest for this chapter, there must be a development of ways to coordinate large amounts of information. **Long-term working memory** is one way experts do this (Ericsson & Kintsch, 1995). Long-term working memory is composed of a set of retrieval cues held in working memory that reference information in long-term memory. The effectiveness and organization of these long-term working memory cues increase proportionately to a person's skill in a domain. By using these cues, an expert can have ready access to the information that is needed to think through the current situation rapidly and accurately.

Synopsis

Procedural memory refers to nondeclarative memories for how to do things. The operation of procedural memory can be seen in the development of skills. Skills start out in memory as conscious, declarative memories, but with practice, people develop a more and more automatic procedural memory system that is not open to conscious awareness. In fact, conscious awareness can actually disrupt this system. More cognitively oriented skills, such as those of experts, reflect the more efficient operation of long-term working memory abilities for any given domain of knowledge.

IMPLICIT MEMORY

The last form of nondeclarative memory examined here is implicit memory. **Implicit memory,** in general, is any form of memory that does not require consciousness and can potentially operate without a person being aware that he is using his memory. In some sense, the other forms of nondeclarative memory and other types of memory we have examined can manifest themselves as some type of implicit memory. For example, procedural memories can be implicit, such as a person's knowledge of how to walk. The concept of savings, as originally described by Ebbinghaus, is a form of implicit memory in which a person is unaware of how previous, unconscious memories are influencing later learning (Nelson, 1978). This section considers how information gets into memory without our awareness, how implicit memory is assessed using indirect memory tasks, the differential effects of data-driven and conceptually driven processes on implicit memory, and the unconscious learning of sequential orders.

Incidental Learning

We have already discussed implicit memory in terms of the initial encoding of information. As we saw in Chapter 3, people can learn things either explicitly—intentionally trying to learn them—or implicitly—incidentally learning them. Incidental learning is a form of implicit memory because a person is not consciously aware at the time that the knowledge is being stored in memory. Although it is difficult to observe incidental learning as it is happening (because it is incidental), neurological measures can provide some insight into what will and will not be remembered later. For example, EEG recordings show that information that is remembered later shows up as different wavebands. Specifically, there is evidence of increased theta band synchronization and decreased alpha band synchronization (Klimesch, Doppelmayr, Russegger, & Pachinger, 1996). Moreover, people who remember more show a greater alpha band change in the lower half of the band, whereas people who remember less show more desynchronization in the upper alpha band (Klimesch et al., 1996).

Much of this tacitly acquired information from incidental learning makes up the contents of implicit memory. That is, the influences that are exerted on our thoughts and behaviors by implicit memory retrieval rely on knowledge that was unconsciously acquired. For example, a person moving to a new part of the country may start altering his speech patterns to conform to the local accent. This occurs without the person being explicitly aware that he is speaking with the new accent. You may have noticed this in your own experience. If you've gone away to college, you may find that the way you speak when you are at school differs from the way that you speak at home.

Indirect Tests of Memory

It is difficult to clearly understand what implicit memory is and does because its operations and effects are largely unconscious. To see its effects, a person must show an influence of prior experience (memory) without consciously being aware of doing so. That is, we need an indirect way of testing memory. There are a number of indirect memory tests that have been developed, some of which we examine in this section. Because most of these tests focus on verbal memory, many of the tasks use verbal information. However, to give you a feel for the broader range of indirect memory tests, some nonverbal tasks are described as well.

Priming.   One of the most extensively studied forms of indirect memory testing is **priming.** Priming occurs when a person is faster and/or more accurate at retrieving information when the target item has been facilitated by some earlier prime trial (Tulving & Schacter, 1990). There are many different types of priming, but here we focus on the most basic type: repetition priming. **Repetition priming** is when people are faster and/or more accurate to respond to an item when that same item has been encountered recently. This occurs even if people are unaware that they are using a memory of a prior experience to help them. For example, if you had seen the word *assassin* earlier in the day, you will recognize it faster and more accurately when you see it again later.

Repetition priming is often better when the information in the world is presented in the same way it was encountered. For example, it has been shown that people have a better memory for rotating objects if the objects are rotating in the same direction as the first time they saw them (Liu & Cooper, 2003). This suggests that even seemingly irrelevant details about things in the world can get into memory and influence the ability to remember them later.

The amount of benefit a person gets from repetition priming varies depending on how the information was learned in the first place. Let's look at memory for information read in a book (see Raney, 2003). If repetition priming is operating, a person will show the rereading benefit of reading the text faster the second time. However, the nature of priming can vary under different circumstances. Suppose the reader was relying primarily on memory of the text itself (such as surface form or textbase memory). This can occur in situations where people do not comprehend what they are reading and so cannot build adequate mental models of what is being described. Under these conditions, repetition priming is more likely to be affected by perceptual characteristics of the information, such as the handwriting it was presented in, the font used, or the word order. In contrast, if the reader fully understood what he was reading, and was able to build adequate mental models, repetition priming would extend to reading other texts that refer to the same state of affairs. Moreover, this repetition priming is less likely to be influenced by the perceptual properties of the text itself.

One of the interesting things about priming is that it appears to involve a decrease in neural activity in different parts of the brain, depending on what type of priming is occurring (Schacter & Badgaiyan, 2001). For example, repetition priming is more associated with decreases in activity in the visual cortex, whereas semantic priming is more associated with decreases in activity in the frontal lobes. This decreased activity in the brain likely reflects the lower amount of work that must be done because those memory engrams are already at a heightened level of availability based on the recent experience.

Indirect tests of memory, such as repetition priming, have influences at multiple levels of representation (see Chapter 7). For example, people respond faster to words they have seen in a word list than a paragraph. However, people read text faster if that same text had been read earlier but not if they see the same words out of context, such as in a word list (Levy & Kirsner, 1989). This suggests that whatever is being affected to create the repetition priming effect, the appropriate level of representation (in this case either the word level of the text level) needs to be retrieved. Retrieving the wrong sort of memory representation is less helpful.

In a more profound demonstration of indirect tests using reading, a study by Kolers (1976) had people first read a series of texts. These texts were presented in either a normal font or by inverting the letters. An example of an inverted text is shown in Figure 6.7. People were then asked to read the same texts again more than a year later. It was found that people read these texts faster the second time, both for normal and inverted texts, even after a substantial degree of forgetting had occurred. Thus, not only were the words and ideas of the text remembered, but even nominally superficial characteristics, such as the orientation of the letters, seemed to be stored in memory, producing a savings that made later reading easier.

Other Verbal Tasks.   Many indirect memory tasks involve having people reconstruct partial or degraded information in some way. The basic idea is that if people have this information in memory, even at an unconscious level, they should find it easier to do this reconstruction. One example of such a reconstructive process is a **word-stem completion** task (e.g., Graf, Mandler, & Haden, 1982). In this task people are presented with the initial

When we think about remembering, what most readily comes to mind are cases where we are consciously aware of using our memories, such as trying to remember a person's name, the answer on an exam, or where you put your car keys. This conscious, explicit use of memory is readily understood and apparent to people. People are also painfully aware when this conscious memory fails us when they forget. It would not be difficult to talk about our experience of using these memories, the content of these memories, and our awareness of them. This is part of what makes them declarative memories. However prominent as this part of human memory may seem, much of the work of human memory operates at the conscious level, but at an unconscious level. Some of these unconscious memories are so far removed from our awareness that it is very difficult, if not impossible, to accurately talk about what is going on with them. These are non-declarative memories. One of the interesting things about nondeclarative memories, aside from the fact that they often operate outside of conscious awareness, is that they are relatively spared in cases of amnesia. This supports the idea that this is a distinctly different way that memory is trying to process information.

This chapter covers a number of topics on nondeclarative memories. We start with a discussion of some of the more basic forms of learning and memory encoding. One of these is classical conditioning in which an organism learns to respond to signals in the environment that are predictive of future outcomes. In a sense, the organism is showing memory for previous environmental contingencies. Following this, a brief discussion of operant conditioning is given. Although this is not a strict form of nondeclarative memory as it is typically defined, it is also

FIGURE 6.7   Inverted Text

Source: Kolers, 1976

few letters of a word (the word "stem"), with the task of completing it with the first word that comes to mind. What is observed is that people are more likely to complete these stems with words they had seen previously. Often, the participants are unaware that they are using prior knowledge. This isolation of implicit memory processes in tasks such as stem completion can be shown by using methodologies such as the process-dissociation procedure (see Chapter 3) (Toth, Reingold, & Jacoby, 1994).

Another indirect memory task that uses reconstruction is **word fragment completion.** In this task people are shown words with letters missing at various locations, such as A _ _ A _ _ IN, and asked to complete the word. Again, it was found that people are better at completing the words if they had seen the words before (e.g., Tulving, Schacter, & Stark, 1982). Moreover, as shown in Figure 6.8, this ability to complete the fragments remains stable even after a long period of time, whereas more conscious and explicit recognition memory continues to decline over time. This shows the enduring influence of implicit memory processes on a person's behavior.

Another test of indirect memory that involves reconstruction is anagram solution (e.g., Srivinas & Roediger, 1990). On these tasks people are shown anagrams, such as "tderhun" for the word "thunder." People were better at solving the anagrams if they involved words they were familiar with. Again, people were not consciously using their memories.

Another verbal indirect memory task is the **lexical decision** task (e.g., Duchek & Neely, 1989). For this measure, a person is presented with a string of letters with the task of indicating whether a given string is a word or not (hence the term *lexical decision*). What is often of interest is how fast people respond to words depending on what has occurred earlier. Specifically, people are faster to respond to words when they have been exposed to them recently or to words that are related to ideas they have been thinking about recently. In addition

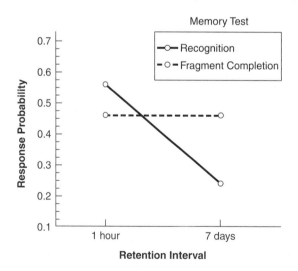

FIGURE 6.8   The Enduring Influence of Implicit Memory (Word Fragment Completion) Relative to Explicit Memory (Recognition)

Source: Tulving, Schacter, and Stark, 1982

to lexical decision, similar sorts of effects can be observed with a **naming** task. In these tasks, people must read out loud, as quickly as possible, words that are presented visually (e.g., Hashtroudi, Ferguson, Rappold, & Chrosniak, 1988). It is assumed that the word will be recognized faster if the participant has seen it before or if he can connect it to something in his experience. The advantage of a naming task, compared to lexical decision, is that, in some cases, this measure can be more sensitive to what is actually being activated in memory.

Some Nonverbal Tasks.   Indirect memory tasks are also used under conditions in which the actual perceptual availability of a word has been compromised. For example, imagine a word is presented for only a fraction of a second, such as for 35 ms. Under these conditions, it is very difficult to consciously identify the word. However, if the participant is already familiar with the word, this **perceptual identification** is sufficent (Jacoby & Dallas, 1981), although this is more likely when people actively observe these events before (Crabb & Dark, 2003). That is, it is easier for people to identify what they are seeing. The prior memory makes it easier to detect the presence of that item in the environment. This sort of process also can be seen in pop music. Often song lyrics are unclear, and you have to guess what the singer is saying. However, if you *read* the lyrics, you can easily follow the lyrics the next time you hear the song.

Although many of the indirect memory tasks described so far apply to verbal information, it should be made clear that implicit memory is important for all types of information. One example of a nonverbal indirect memory task is priming for pictures of possible and

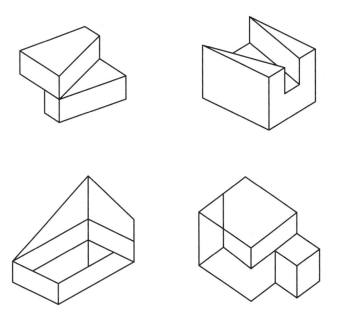

FIGURE 6.9   Examples of Possible and Impossible Objects
Source: Liu & Cooper, 2001

impossible objects (see Figure 6.9). Basically, what happens is that people first view a set of objects as part of some task, such as judging whether an object faces left or right. Then they are asked to make possible-impossible decisions. Some of the objects in the second test are the same as the first test. The degree to which people respond faster and more accurately to old objects relative to new objects is an indicator of priming. It has been found that nonverbal priming for these pictures occurs only for possible objects but not for impossible objects (Liu & Cooper, 2001; Schacter, Cooper, & Delaney, 1990). This suggests that memory takes into account an understanding of the object as a whole and not the parts that make up the image.

Implicit memory works on us in many ways. Even information that we are unaware of in the first place can influence our memories. For example, Kunst-Wilson and Zajonc (1980) had a set of randomly generated geometric shapes that were presented subconsciously by being displayed for only 1 ms. Some time later, people were given a forced-choice recognition test to select which objects they had seen earlier. Remember that a forced-choice recognition test is one in which people must select one element from a set of two or more, much like a multiple-choice test. It was found that people performed above chance. That is, they selected the previously seen shapes more often than would be expected if they were just guessing. This is interesting because they had no conscious awareness of seeing the shapes before, and their conscious identification later was random.

Data-Driven and Conceptually Driven Processes

Although the distinction between explicit and implicit memory is complex, a number of attempts have been made to describe the differences between them. One of the more successful of these is the belief that implicit memory tends to be driven more by the perceptual characteristics of the information. This is often referred to as data-driven processing because the mental activity is driven by information in the environment more so than the contents of a person's thoughts. In contrast, explicit memory is thought to be driven more by the conceptual characteristics of the information. This is often referred to as conceptually driven, because the mental activity is driven more by a person's prior knowledge, expectations, and goals. Seeing a cloud in the sky as a cloud is an example of data-driven processing, but seeing shapes in the clouds is an example of conceptually driven processing.

This distinction between data-driven and conceptually driven processing is significant when studying the effects of each on implicit and explicit memory. The general idea is that implicit memory is more affected by the way the information was originally presented—for example, written or oral. Thus, implicit memory is more influenced by data-driven processing. In contrast, explicit memory is more affected by the amount of processing that a person did during original encoding, such as whether it was generated or not. Thus, explicit memory is more influenced by conceptually driven processing (e.g., Blaxton, 1989).

Sequence Learning

Another type of nonverbal information that is encoded into nondeclarative, implicit memory is information about the order of events. There are repeating patterns of events in the world of which we may not be consciously but to which our implicit memory has become attuned. This was clearly shown in a study by Nissen and Bullemer (1987). In this study, students were shown a display of four lights in a row, with a button below each of the four lights. The task was to press the buttons below a light *after* the light lit up. There were two groups in this study. In the random, control group, the lights came on in a random order throughout the study. In the experimental group, the lights would come on in a consistent ten-light sequence. It was discovered that the speed with which people pushed the buttons dramatically increased (i.e., response time decreased), with even very little exposure in the experimental group (see Figure 6.10). Obviously, people were using their memories of the sequence before they were consciously aware of doing so. Moreover, when people were asked to explicitly report the sequence, there could not.

Another, more complex type of sequence learning involves implicit learning of **artificial grammars.** In these studies, people are presented with sequences of letters. These sequences are created using an algorithm such as the one shown in Figure 6.11. For example, in this case, the sequences VXVPS, TPPTS, and VXXXS are all valid or "grammatical" sequences, whereas the sequences XVSPV, PPTTS, and SXXXV are not. During the initial learning phase, people are shown a series of letter strings that were generated using the algorithm and asked to copy the letter sequence. It was found that even in the absence of explicit memorization, people appeared to be learning not just the sequences that were presented but the "grammar" or production algorithm used to generate the sequence. This implicit memory shows itself in people's ability to also accept (at above chance rates) valid sequences that were never seen before and to accept new sequences that used different letter sets but that followed the same rules (Reber, 1967; 1969). However, it should be noted

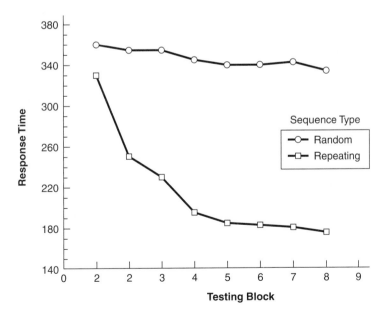

FIGURE 6.10   Improvement on a Serial Order Task with Random and Repeating Sequences

Source: Nissen & Bullemer, 1987

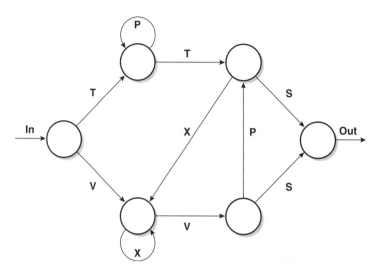

FIGURE 6.11   Algorithm Used to Generate Artificial Grammar

Source: Reber, 1967

that although this is a largely unconscious, implicit process, some conscious influences might also play a role if a person becomes aware of the repetition (Dulany, Carlson, & Dewey, 1984).

Memory Under Anesthesia

Most of the learning and memory that we have seen so far in this chapter has involved memory for information initially presented when people are conscious and aware of their surroundings. One way learning and memory can occur when a person is unconscious is during anesthesia. This is an issue of general interest. One purpose of anesthesia is so the person does not remember what happened during surgery (for example, feeling the incision being made). The brain is not completely dormant when a person is unconscious, but the question is whether it is active enough to learn.

In these cases, people are given information to learn while they are anesthetized during surgery. It might be a list of words or sentences, or a story. After surgery, people are tested to see if they have any memory for what they heard while they were unconscious. Based on an extensive review by Andrade (1995), there is definite evidence of learning while under anesthesia. This has been shown a number of ways, including a greater likelihood of repeating words heard during anesthesia on category generation, free association, stem completion, ratings of familiarity, recognition, and preference ratings tasks. Some tests have also looked at more complex forms of learning, such as providing people with answers to general knowledge questions, false fame effects, classical conditioning, behavioral suggestion (such as touching one's ear or chin), and therapeutic suggestions.

In one study, Schwender et al. (1993) had 15 patients listen to a tape of *Robinson Crusoe* while they were anesthetized and undergoing surgery. After surgery, when asked to free associate to the word *Friday,* 10 of these patients responded with "Robinson Crusoe," but 5 of them did not. In contrast, none of another group of 15 patients who did not hear the novel gave this response.

What a person remembers after surgery when they were anesthetized is important because it can impact recovery. For example, it has been suggested that derogatory comments made about the patient, such as commenting on an obese patient's weight, can cause the person to recover more slowly from the procedure. This is known as "fat lady syndrome." Some surgeons make a point of speaking about how well the surgery is going during the surgery, even if it's not true.

In general, most of the effects of information learned on memory appear to be at an unconscious, implicit level. People often have very little, and more often no, conscious awareness of having learned this information. While this is all very interesting, it should also be pointed out that it has been very difficult to replicate many of these findings. In almost every case where studies have found evidence of memory, there are similar studies that have not. There are many reasons for why this might be true. In some cases, it may be that the data just happened to fall in such a way that an effect was observed and reported. Researchers are less likely to report not finding an effect, unless one has already been shown. Alternatively, it could be that these are often very weak memory effects that are difficult to measure in the first place, so it would not be surprising if some people have trouble finding similar effects. Finally, it is difficult to control many factors that could influence the results in these cases. These include the type of anesthesia used, how deeply the patients go under, the extent of the surgery, and so forth. So as it stands, there is the intriguing possibility that there may be some nondeclarative learning going on when a person is under anesthesia, but at this point it is unclear when this happens and to what extent.

Synopsis

Implicit memory is memory that is largely outside of conscious awareness, although we may occasionally be made aware of its outcomes. Incidental learning is a form of implicit memory. To test implicit memory, a number of ways have been developed to look at the influence of memory without making the person aware that they are using their memories. These tasks include priming, word stem completion, lexical decision, word naming, and perceptual identification. The operation of implicit memory involves not only memory for specific content, but can also be seen in memory for how things fit together in the world, such as sequence learning. Finally, implicit memory can be seen in cases where conscious awareness is not present and general neurological functioning should be absent, as well as when a person in under anesthesia. This illustrates the durability and pervasiveness of unconscious, nondeclarative forms of memory.

SUMMARY

This chapter reviewed a number of forms of nondeclarative memory. These are memories that are difficult to articulate and that may fall outside the realm of conscious awareness. Nondeclarative memories include some of the most primitive forms of memory and learning, such as classical conditioning. It was also shown how nondeclarative memories could become involved in the development of skills, as with procedural memories. This type of knowledge allows us to perform many activities, such as walking and chewing gum at the same time without using much, if any, conscious mental effort. Finally, the operation of implicit memory was discussed. Although implicit memories operate and influence us below the radar screen of awareness, a number of methods have been developed for looking at how this vastly important component of our memories is involved in our lives.

STUDY QUESTIONS

1. What are the primary components of classical conditioning, and how does learning occur?

2. What are some of the important phenomena of classical conditioning?

3. How is the mere exposure effect a nondeclarative memory phenomenon? How is it a classical conditioning phenomenon?

4. What are the stages that knowledge goes through to develop skilled procedural memories?

5. What is implicit memory, and how is it measured?

6. What are some sorts of effects of implicit memory that can be observed?

7. What sort of knowledge can be learned and can influence later behavior with implicit memory?

KEY TERMS

artificial grammars, biological preparedness, blocking, classical conditioning, contiguity learning, contingency learning, discrimination, extinction, generalization, higher-order conditioning, implicit memory, indirect memory tasks, instrumental conditioning, lexical decision, long-term working memory, mere exposure effect, naming, nondeclarative memory, Pavlovian conditioning, perceptual identification, priming, repetition priming, savings, skills, spontaneous recovery, stimulus-response association, stimulus-stimulus association, word fragment completion, word-stem completion

CHAPTER SEVEN

EPISODIC LONG-TERM MEMORY

Memories help define who we are. Our opinions, attitudes, likes, and dislikes are a result of our previous experiences. Memory is the repository of those experiences and the shaper of our actions in the future. Thus, it is important to understand our memories of our individual experiences. These are the memories for the events and episodes of our lives. In the attempt to understand how memory works, it has been found that memories of personally experienced events are stored and remembered in ways that have unique characteristics. Memories for events that we experienced are **episodic memories,** whereas memories for general world knowledge are **semantic memories.** An example of this distinction is the difference between remembering the last movie you saw (episodic) versus remembering what a movie is (semantic). This chapter covers episodic memories. Semantic memories are covered in Chapter 9.

Several aspects of episodic memory are covered in this chapter. We first look at the information that can make up episodic memories and then examine how episodic memories can compete with one another or combine to form composite memories of different actual events. Although episodic memories are of specific experiences, we can sometimes have repeated exposure to the same and similar information. We look at how different types of practice of information can influence memory. Finally, some attention is given to how we either separate out information in memory or integrate several pieces of experience and the effects these actions have on later memory.

THE CONTENTS OF EPISODIC MEMORY

Like most long-term memories, episodic memories are amalgams of various types of information. These different components can be used either as whole units or as separate pieces. For example, when you remember a birthday party, you may recall the people, food, music, and gifts. Alternatively, you may remember a conversation you had with someone at the party but have no memory of songs that were sung, what other guests were wearing, or the party decorations. Our overview looks at different kinds of information that are in episodic memory and how it is used later during remembering.

Serial Position Effects

Chapter 4's discussion of short-term memory introduced the serial position curve, with superior memory for things at the beginning (primacy effect) and at the end of a sequence (recency effect). Serial position curves are also seen in long-term memory, such as memories of going to the theater (Sehulster, 1989), although the recency effects are larger (Hitch & Ferguson, 1991).

The explanations for serial position curves in episodic memory are different from those for short-term memory. For example, these primacy and recency effects can be attributed to the distinctiveness of those positions (Healy, Havas, & Parker, 2000). They are more constrained by the sequence—their position in the order—and so the first and last items are better remembered. In addition, the primacy effect reflects a novelty process. The first item is unusual relative to the context that preceded it, and so it is remembered better. Also, the recency effect reflects a standard forgetting curve, with more recent events being remembered better than older events. Finally, events at the beginning and end of a sequence are less susceptible to interference (see later in the chapter). The primacy effect reflects less proactive interference, and the recency effect reflects less retroactive interference.

Levels of Representation

When we experience an event, we do not think of it simply and directly. Instead, we process it at multiple levels. Each of these levels leaves a memory trace. One illustration of this is in memory for texts, where there are three levels of representation: the surface form, the textbase, and the mental model (van Dijk & Kintsch, 1983). The surface form represents the verbatim text. This knowledge is more important initially but is usually quickly forgotten (Sachs, 1967; 1974), although it may last for several minutes (Hayes-Roth & Hayes-Roth, 1977). The textbase is an abstract representation of the text. For example, the sentences "The girl hit the boy" and "The boy was hit by the girl" have different surface forms but the same underlying meaning, which is captured by the textbase. At the highest level is the mental model (Johnson-Laird, 1983; Zwaan & Radvansky, 1998), which represents the state of affairs described by the text rather than the text itself (Glenberg, Meyer, & Lindem, 1987). The mental model is a mental simulation of the described events.

In general, mental models are remembered over long periods of time. People may use knowledge at this level to mistakenly believe they had read one sentence when they had actually read a different, but similar, one (Bransford, Barclay, & Franks, 1972; Garnham, 1981; Rinck, Hähnel, & Becker, 2001). For example, people who read "The turtles sat on a log, and the fish swam beneath them" are more likely to say later that they read the sentence "The turtles sat on a log, and the fish swam beneath it."

In a study by Kintsch, Welsch, Schmalhofer, and Zimny (1990), people read a text and then took a recognition test either immediately, 40 minutes later, 2 days later, or 4 days later. The results are shown in Figure 7.1. It was found that the surface form memory decayed rapidly. The textbase memory, although better than the surface form, continued to decline over time. However, memory for the mental model was relatively durable and did not show much change. As a real-life example, think about when you read a newspaper article. You quickly forget the exact wording of the article, but you remember the basic ideas in the article for a while, at least. However, your memory for the situation described in the article (what the article was about) is much more enduring and is what you remember over the long term.

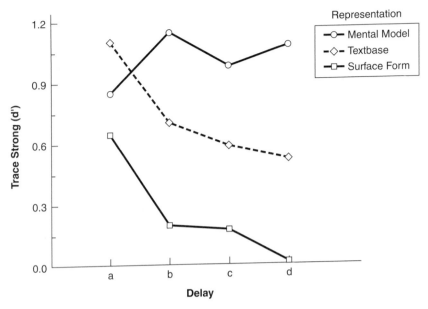

FIGURE 7.1 Episodic Memory Retention for Information at the Surface Form, Textbase, and Mental Model Levels

Source: Kintsch, Welsch, Schmalhofer, & Zimny, 1990

Cueing.   When we recall an event, we may do so easily, but sometimes we need a prompt to direct us, called **cuing.** In general, memory cues improve retrieval (e.g., Tulving & Pearlstone, 1966). Read the sentences in Table 7.1, but do not try to memorize them (Bransford & Stein, 1984). After you have read them, wait a minute, and then try to recall as many as you can. When you are done, draw a line under the last one you were able to remember. Then read the words in Table 7.2. Did the words in Table 7.2 help you to remember the sentences in Table 7.1?

What happened here is that the words in Table 7.2 are retrieval cues that help you remember what you forgot. When you read the sentences, you stored a number of pieces of information. Later you discovered that you could not remember some of the sentences. However, when you read the words in Table 7.2, they prompted the appropriate memories. This happened because the information in the cues is also in the memory traces. Long-term memory is a content addressable system in that we can access information using the components that make it up rather than only on some other principle (e.g., time of learning).

Types of Cues.   There are two types of episodic retrieval cues: feature cues and context cues. Feature cues involve components of the memory itself, like the words in Table 7.2. One of the best feature cues is yourself. If you can relate information to aspects of who you are, your memory will be better (e.g., Bellezza, 1992). In contrast, context cues involve some part of the environment. For example, one sentence from the list probably reminded you of other sentences, because each sentence was part of the context of the other sentences.

TABLE 7.1   Sentences from Bransford and Stein Study

A brick can be used as a doorstop.	A ladder can be used as a bookshelf.
A wine bottle can be used as a candle holder.	A pan can be used as a drum.
A record can be used to serve potato chips.	A guitar can be used as a canoe paddle.
A leaf can be used as a bookmark.	An orange can be used to play catch.
A newspaper can be used to swat flies.	A TV antenna can be used as a clothes rack.
A sheet can be used as a sail.	A boat can be used as a shelter.
A bathtub can be used as a punch bowl.	A flashlight can be used to hold water.
A rock can be used as a paperweight.	A knife can be used to stir paint.
A pen can be used as an arrow.	A barrel can be used as a chair.
A rug can be used as a bedspread.	A telephone can be used as an alarm clock.
A scissors can be used to cut grass.	A board can be used as a ruler.
A balloon can be used as a pillow.	A shoe can be used to pound nails.
A dime can be used as a screwdriver.	A lampshade can be used as a hat.

Source: Bransford & Stein, 1984

There are a variety of contexts that can influence memory. Three important types are linguistic, external, and internal context. Linguistic context refers to other bits of language (e.g., words, phrases, or sentences) that cooccurred with a particular piece of information. Paired-associate learning paradigms, such as those used by the verbal learners, depended heavily on linguistic context. In these cases, words were paired together, and then at retrieval, one of the words served as a linguistic context cue and the other was the to-be-remembered word. External context refers to the environment outside a person, such as the room one is in, the lighting level, or the objects and people present. Internal context refers to the environment inside a person, such as physiological state, emotions, and people's thoughts at the time. As you will see, these contexts can have profound influences on memory.

TABLE 7.2   Do These Words Help You Remember the Sentences in Table 7.1?

Brick	Rock	Pan	Barrel
Wine bottle	Pen	Guitar	Telephone
Record	Rug	Orange	Board
Leaf	Scissors	TV antenna	Shoe
Newspaper	Balloon	Boat	Lampshade
Sheet	Dime	Flashlight	
Bathtub	Ladder	Knife	

Source: Bransford & Stein, 1984

Context

Context can be a powerful cue to memory. In this section we focus on how the similarity between contexts at learning and remembering can influence retrieval.

Encoding Specificity. The most well-known form of this is the **encoding specificity** principle (Thompson & Tulving, 1970). This is the superior ability to remember when recall occurs in the same context as information that was learned as opposed to a different context. For example, if you learn something in one room, it is easier to recall it when you are in the same room. It is not unusual to fail to remember something until you return to the room where you got the information in the first place. Smith (1988) provides a clear account of the power of encoding specificity.

> Having lived most of his life in St. Louis, Missouri, except for two years at the University of Texas at Austin, and four years in the military service during the Second World War, my father returned to Texas after 42 long years of forgetting. Although previously certain that he could recall only a few disembodied fragments of memories of his college days, he became increasingly amazed, upon his return, at the freshness and detail of his newly remembered experiences. Strolling along the streets of Austin, my father suddenly stopped and animatedly described the house in which he lived in a location now occupied by a parking lot. He recalled in vivid detail, for example, how an armadillo had climbed up the drainpipe one night and became his pet, and how the woman who had cooked for the residents of his house had informed them of the attack on Pearl Harbor, abruptly ending his college career. Not until he returned to the setting in which those long-past events had occurred had my father thought or spoken of them. (p. 13)

The encoding specificity principle is illustrated nicely in a study in which scuba divers learned lists of words. Some lists were learned on land, and others were learned underwater. Later the divers were tested in either the same or a different context. As shown in Figure 7.2, memory was better when the words were recalled in the same context than in the different one (Godden & Baddeley, 1975).

The effects of encoding specificity are quite reliable. They occur when an environment is actually present or only thought about (Smith, 1979; 1984). Also, although it was initially suggested that encoding specificity was stronger with recall than with recognition (Smith, Gilenberg, & Bjork, 1978), more recent work suggests that it operates in both (Smith & Vela, 2001). Recognition, however, benefits from conscious recollection to see an influence of context (Macken, 2002), although it is not mandatory. If people distract themselves from the immediate environment during learning (Smith & Vela, 2001), then encoding specificity may not be apparent.

As a student, you may think it is better to study in the same room where you will take the exam. However, this is applying encoding specificity in a less than optimal way. Memories become strongly associated with a context when information is always presented in the same one. If something is learned in many different contexts—if you study in many different places—then there is no strong encoding specificity influence. The information becomes more context independent (Smith et al., 1978). That way, you can use your knowledge when you need it, not just when you happen to be in the right place.

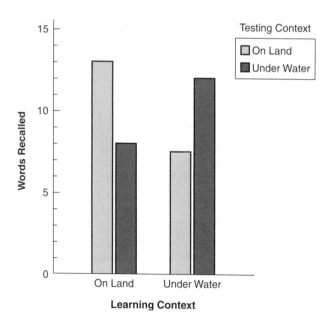

FIGURE 7.2   Results of Study Illustrating the Effect of Encoding Specificity on Memory for Word Lists

Source: Godden & Baddeley, 1975

State-Dependent Memory.   Encoding specificity often refers to external contexts, such as a room. However, there are other contexts that are internal to a person. One of these is a person's physiological state, such as being sleepy, drunk, or excited. This information is also stored in memory. As such, some things are better remembered when people are in a similar physiological state during recall as they were during learning. This is called **state-dependent memory.** An example of this can be seen in a study in which people learned while they were sober or drunk. They then took a memory test in either the same or a different state. As shown in Figure 7.3, memory was better when people were in the same physiological state (Goodwin et al., 1969). If people studied while they were drunk, they did better on the test if they took it while drunk. (It is important to keep in mind, however, that memory is worse overall if a person is drunk while learning or testing.) Similar state-dependent memory effects occur with nicotine (Peters & McGee, 1982), marijuana (Eich, Weingartner, Stillman, & Gillin, 1975), and Ritalin (Swanson & Kinsbourne, 1976).

Mood-Congruent Memory.   Another internal context is mood or emotion. We are always in some mood. These emotional states are stored in memory, allowing for **mood-congruent memory.** Our memory for information is better if we are in the same mood we were in when we got the information (Blaney, 1986; Bower, 1981). So when you are happy, you remember things you learned when you were happy. Say you have a fight with your boyfriend. While you are angry, you think of reasons why he is a big jerk. Later, you calm down and think about his good qualities. When you have another fight weeks later, all those

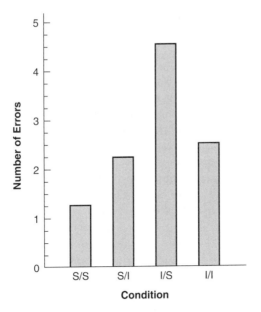

FIGURE 7.3   Results of a Study on State-Dependent Memory. The various condition labels represent "Study state" / "Test state" with S = sober and I = intoxicated.

Source: Goodwin et al., 1969

negative thoughts will come back to mind more easily because you initially thought of them while in a more angry emotional state.

Mood-congruent memory is supported by neurological work. Maratos et al. (2001) tested memory for words that were read in emotionally positive, emotionally negative, or neutral sentences. Later, a recognition memory test was given during an fMRI scan. Words that were read in emotionally positive or negative contexts were accompanied by brain regions associated with emotion processing, such as the amygdala and oribitofrontal cortex of the frontal lobe, being more active than the neutral context words

Mood-congruent memory also plays a role in depression. People who are depressed have a greater tendency to retrieve depressing memories than happy memories. It is not that they recall more negative memories than people who are not depressed, but they recall fewer positive memories (Blaney, 1986).

A case for the importance of mood-congruent memory was made by Eich (1995), who suggested that encoding specificity and state-dependent memory are forms of mood-congruent memory. Different external environments elicit different emotions. If two different places elicit similar emotions, they lead to better memory. A similar argument is made for state-dependent memory. Different physiological states tend to produce different affective states, which then influence memory.

Overall, context influences episodic memory in a wide-ranging fashion. As noted by Terry (2000), other types of context that influence memory include music (Smith, 1985), odors (Cann & Ross, 1989), temperature (Richardson, Guanowsky, Ahlers, & Riccio,

1984), time of day (Holloway, 1978), body position (lying down or standing up) (Rand & Wapner, 1967), phone calls (Canas & Nelson, 1986), and pain (Pearse et al., 1990).

Transfer Appropriate Processing.   Memory can also be influenced by the person's thought processes during learning. Memory is better when retrieval uses mental processes that are more in tune with those used at learning, a principle known as **transfer appropriate processing** (Kolers & Roediger, 1984; Roediger & Blaxton, 1987). As you will see, this principle is related to the depth of processing work discussed in Chapter 3. Information that is learned using processing that emphasize meaning has a greater positive impact on explicit memory tests such as recall or recognition. In contrast, information that is learned while emphasizing shallow surface characteristics has a greater impact on implicit memory tests. For example, in a study by Morris, Bransford, and Franks (1977), people responded to words using either a meaning-based (deep-level) task, such as whether the word "plane" made sense in the sentence "The _____ had a silver engine" or a rhyme-based (shallow-level) task, such as whether the word "eagle" made sense in the sentence "_____ rhymes with legal." Later, students took either a standard recognition test (an explicit memory test) or a rhyming recognition test (an implicit test) in which they indicated whether a new word rhymed with one that they had heard earlier (e.g., "regal"). The results are shown in Figure 7.4. Memory was better when the encoding and retrieval processes matched than when they did not. Thus, depth of processing (as discussed in Chapter 3) is not a clear guide to future memory. Instead, how successful memory is in the future depends on how people think about information.

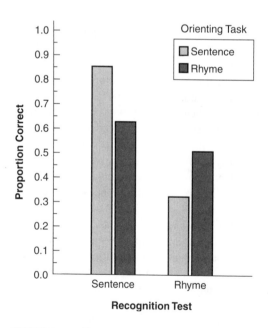

FIGURE 7.4   Results of a Study of Transfer Appropriate Processing
Source: Morris, Bransford, & Franks, 1977

Synopsis

Episodic memory is for individual events a person experiences. These memories are influenced by the order in which information was learned, showing a serial position curve. They also contain both content information about the event itself as well as the context in which the information was learned. These pieces of information can be used as cues to help people remember. Finally, episodic memories also contain information about how they were created in the first place. As illustrated by transfer appropriate processing, people find it easier to remember when they are in the same emotional state as they were when they learned the information.

IRRELEVANT MEMORIES

Each experience we have alters our memories, and we are constantly storing new memories. Even the act of remembering alters memory because the *experience* of remembering gets stored. One consequence of this multiplication of memory traces is that episodic memories compete with one another. This competition is known as **interference.** Interference, rather than decay or disuse, is one of the primary mechanisms of forgetting in long-term memory (McGeoch, 1932). Furthermore, there must be a way to control the confusion brought about by interfering memories. One such mechanism is the process of **inhibition.**

Interference

Interference occurs in memory retrieval when there is competition between memory traces. When there are two or more traces that have overlapping information, and you only want one of them, interference develops. For example, suppose you are trying to remember your friend Mary's phone number. You remember getting the number from Mary when you met her for lunch, but Susan was there, too, and you also got her number. These two memories are in competition because they both contain phone numbers and the element of having lunch, thereby producing interference. Here, several kinds of interference are presented, including negative transfer, proactive interference, retroactive interference, and associative interference.

Negative Transfer. **Negative transfer** is a form of interference in which the prior knowledge impedes the ability to learn new information (Anderson, 2000). For example, if a person has learned to drive a standard-shift car and then goes to drive one with an automatic transmission, there may be some negative transfer when the person tries to push down on the clutch (because there is no clutch). The memory traces for old information are well established when new information is encountered. Because these older memory traces are so strong, they are activated each time a person is trying to learn something new. This memory activation blocks the acquisition of the new information.

The amount of negative transfer experienced is a function of the degree of overlap between the old and new information. For example, in a study by Postman and Stark (1969), Berkeley students memorized lists of paired associates. After learning an A-B list, negative transfer was observed in the ability to learn a second list when the old responses were paired with new cues (C-B), new responses were paired with old cues (A-C), the pair items were recombined (A-Br), or synonyms were used (A-B') relative to a control condition using new lists (C-D). Whenever the new information overlapped the old information, learning was impeded.

The amount of negative transfer was greater when memory was tested using recall than recognition (Postman & Stark, 1969). This is because there are more memory traces that can get involved and compete for output during recall, whereas for recognition, the memory search is much more targeted on a few, or one, memory trace(s).

Proactive Interference. **Proactive interference** occurs when old knowledge results in the increased forgetting of new knowledge (Underwoood, 1957). For example, if a person studies psychology and then studies sociology, there will be greater forgetting and thus worse performance on a subsequent sociology test. Although proactive interference and negative transfer seem alike because they both involve older information impeding memory for newer information, negative transfer applies to the acquisition of new information, whereas proactive interference refers to the forgetting of memory traces for new information.

The degree of proactive interference experienced depends on the amount of overlap between different sets of information, not on how much information was learned earlier (Postman & Keppel, 1977). If it is difficult to differentiate between memory traces because of their content, then proactive interference is experienced. This is why sociology and psychology interfere with one another. Any effort that you can make to distinguish and differentiate sets of information reduces the amount of interference, and memory improves accordingly.

This influence of trace relatedness on proactive interference has been studied extensively. One basic principle is that the more related the information a person has memorized, the more proactive interference there is. Moreover, there is a buildup of proactive interference over time. This buildup continues until people are given information that differs from the old knowledge. At that point, memory improves, and there is release from proactive interference.

An example of release from proactive interference is a study by Wickens (1972) in which people were given successive lists of words to remember (see Table 7.3). The words in the first three lists were all names of fruits. If the fourth list were fruits again, then memory continued to decline, as shown in Figure 7.5. However, if the words in the fourth list belonged to a new category, release from proactive interference occurs. Moreover, the greater the difference, the greater the release. For example, vegetables are different from fruits, but they still have some traits in common, whereas professions are quite distinct from fruits.

Retroactive Interference. **Retroactive interference** occurs when new knowledge makes it difficult to remember old knowledge (Melton & Irwin, 1940). A classic demonstration of this is a study by Jenkins and Dallenbach (1924) in which students at Cornell University learned lists of ten nonsense syllables. They were then tested one, two, four, and eight hours later. What is important is what they did during this time. Half of the time, they were given the lists early in the day, so they were awake the whole time. The rest of the time they were given the lists at night, so they were asleep during the retention period. The

TABLE 7.3   Stimulus Lists from Proactive Interference Study

CONDITION	TRIAL 1	TRIAL 2	TRIAL 3	TRIAL 4
Fruits (control)	banana peach apple	plum apricot lime	melon lemon grape	orange cherry pineapple
Vegetables	banana peach apple	plum apricot lime	melon lemon grape	onion radish potato
Flowers	banana peach apple	plum apricot lime	melon lemon grape	daisy violet tulip
Meats	banana peach apple	plum apricot lime	melon lemon grape	salami bacon hamburger
Professions	banana peach apple	plum apricot lime	melon lemon grape	doctor teacher lawyer

Source: Wickens, 1972

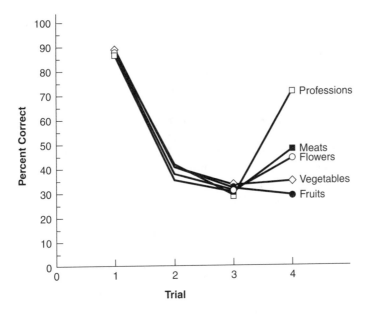

FIGURE 7.5   Results from a Study of Release from Proactive Interference

Source: Wickens, 1972

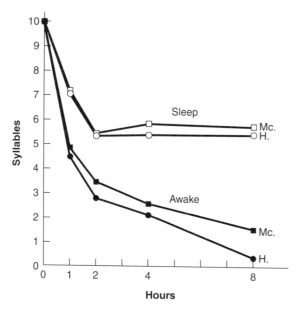

FIGURE 7.6   Results from a Study of Long-Term Memory Interference. Mc. and H. are the initials of the two subjects used in this study.

Source: Jenkins & Dallenbach, 1924

results in Figure 7.6 show less forgetting when the students slept than when they were awake. When people are awake, there is a continuous stream of new information (including thoughts). This new information produces retroactive interference, making the older information harder to remember. However, if people are asleep, there is not as much new information, so there is less retroactive interference and less forgetting.

With retroactive interference, new experiences make it harder to remember older, similar experiences. For example, if you study psychology and then study sociology, you forget some of the psychology you studied because the newer sociology memory traces interfere with your attempts to retrieve the older psychology information. Alternatively, imagine that you move to a new city. Your memory for the new telephone numbers, street names, and stories cause retroactive interference, making it harder for you to remember information about the city you used to live in. Again, keep in mind that the more dissimilar the information, the less interference.

The study by Postman and Stark (1969) also looked at retroactive interference. Retroactive interference was seen in a wide variety of cases when there was overlap between two sets of paired associate lists. Also, like negative transfer, retroactive interference is more pronounced with recall than it is with recognition. During recall people are trying to sort through a large number of competing memory traces, thereby allowing interference to be observed, whereas during recognition there are fewer memory traces involved.

In the verbal learning literature, retroactive interference was discussed as an "unlearning" of prior associations in memory (McGovern, 1964; Melton & Irwin, 1940). The idea was that new information causes older information to be lost or disrupted. However, this "unlearning" idea is not completely correct. There are cases where retroactive interference can subsequently be reduced or eliminated, suggesting that the original memories are still intact, even if they are difficult to use in a particular set of circumstances. For example, one idea is that retroactive interference involves a disruption of the set of retrieval cues that would otherwise be used to access information. If people are provided with the appropriate retrieval cues, then the effects of retroactive inhibition can be attenuated or eliminated (Tulving & Psotka, 1971).

Associative Interference.   **Associative interference** reflects the associative complexity of the information that was learned. The disruption of memory is not based on the temporal sequence (as is the case with the other forms of interference). Here, the more associations there are with a concept, the greater the interference and the worse the memory. For example, if you have just learned five things about Jenny, you will be slower to verify any one of these than if you had learned only one thing.

Often, associative interference is described in terms of the **fan effect.** The term *fan effect* assumes that information is stored in a propositional memory network with nodes representing individual concepts and links representing the associations among them (see Chapter 10). During retrieval, the more links "fanning" off of a concept, the greater the level of interference from the competing associations, and retrieval time increases accordingly.

In a study of associative interference, Anderson (1974) gave students lists of sentences to memorize, such as "The doctor is in the park" or "The lawyer is in the museum." The number of learned associations with the person and location concepts (e.g., doctor or park) was varied from one to three. Thus, there could be from one to three places that a person could be in and one to three people in a location. After memorizing a list of these sentences, a recognition test was given in which people indicated whether the sentence was studied or not. The nonstudied sentences were recombinations of people and locations, such as "The doctor is in the museum." The results showed that as the number of associations with a concept increased, response time also increased, as seen in Figure 7.7. Like other types of interference, associative interference is reduced by extensive practice (Pirolli & Anderson, 1985). Repeated exposure to each fact continues to make it distinct relative to the others, thereby reducing competition during retrieval.

A worrisome implication of associative interference is that the more you know, the harder it should be to remember. However, people who are experts in an area can actually learn more information than novices with little to no deficit in the ability to remember. This is known as "the paradox of the expert" (Smith, Adams, & Schorr, 1978). A way out of this paradox is through the use of chunking. Information that is organized into a common memory trace or chunk reduces the amount of interference because there are fewer traces that can compete with one another. Chunking can be done around a common theme, causal structure, ownership relations, spatial locations, time frames, or people (Myers, O'Brien, Balota, & Toyofuku, 1984; Radvansky, Spieler, & Zacks, 1993; Radvansky, Wyer, Curiel, & Lutz, 1997; Radvansky & Zacks, 1991; Radvansky, Zwaan, Federico, & Franklin, 1998; Smith et al., 1978).

Let's look at this chunking in detail. Suppose a person memorizes sentences about objects in locations. For some sentences, a single object is in several locations, such as "The

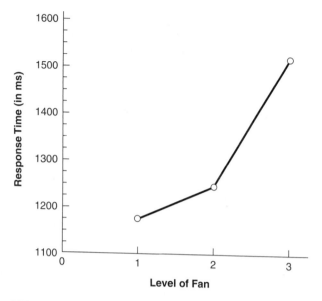

FIGURE 7.7   Results from a Study of Associative Interference Producing a Fan Effect
Source: Anderson, 1974

potted palm is in the hotel," "The potted palm is in the barbershop," and "The potted palm is in the airport." In these cases, multiple mental models are created, because each sentence refers to a different situation. So there are three memory traces that compete at retrieval. In contrast, for other sentences, multiple objects are in a single location, such as "The pay phone is in the laundromat," "The oak counter is in the laundromat," and "The ceiling fan is in the laundromat." In these cases, a single mental model is created that includes all of this information because it all refers to a single event. As such, there is only one memory trace, and thus no interference (Radvansky & Zacks, 1991). These differential interference effects are shown in Figure 7.8. This outcome is also observed when people retrieve information from maps that have been studied (Bower & Rinck, 2001) or make metamemory judgments of learning (McGuire & Maki, 2001).

Inhibition

Interference in memory is a problem if you want to remember accurately and quickly. There are ways that interference can be reduced or controlled. One of these is the mechanism of **inhibition** that actively reduces the activation of interfering information. There are a number of ways that inhibition influences memory (see Anderson, 2003, for a review, but see MacLeod et al., 2003, for an alternative view).

Part-Set Cuing.   As you learned, providing retrieval cues can aid memory. However, there are exceptions. If a person tries to remember a set of things, such as the names of sports teams, the probability of recalling any one of them is higher if a simple recall test is

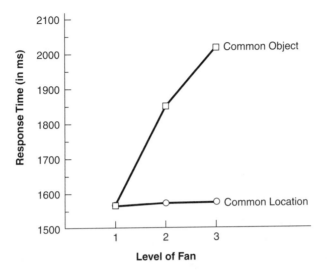

FIGURE 7.8 Differential Interference Effects when Information Can and Cannot Be Integrated Into Mental Models

Source: Radvansky, Spieler, & Zacks, 1993

used than if some of the names are given as cues to help a person get started. This poorer memory when provided with partial information is called **part-set cuing** (Nickerson, 1984; Slamecka, 1968), and sometimes part-set inhibition. Part of the explanation for this is that giving people part of the set disrupts their retrieval plan (Basden, Basden, & Galloway, 1977; Basden, Basden, & Stephens, 2002; Sloman, Bower, & Rohrer, 1991), similar to the collaborative inhibition discussed in Chapter 3.

Another part of the explanation involves inhibition. When people recall an item from a set, it is at a higher level of activation than the rest, and it blocks access to the other set members (Roediger, Stellon, & Tulving, 1977). This occurs in part because to reduce the interference from the other set members, they are inhibited (Anderson & Neely, 1996). As a person gets further and further into the set, the unrecalled memory traces get more and more inhibited, making it harder to recall them. So for part-set cuing, providing people with part of the set leads them to inhibit memory traces that might otherwise have been more available if they had been left alone.

Directed Forgetting. Inhibition can also regulate sources of proactive interference in which information learned in the past produces forgetting of more recently learned information. One way to get around this is to use **directed forgetting.** This involves telling people that some of the information they learned is irrelevant and can be forgotten (Bjork, 1970). For example, people might be presented with a list of words, instructed to forget those words, and then asked to remember a new set of words. Under such circumstances, memory for the to-be-remembered words is the same as if the participant had never been given the to-be-forgotten words. There is no proactive interference from the to-be-forgotten words. This is the directed forgetting effect. However, directed forgetting may not occur if people believe that the information they are told to forget will become relevant later (Golding, Fowler, Long, & Latta, 1990).

Part of the explanation for directed forgetting is that people inhibit the irrelevant to-be-forgotten memory traces (Bjork, 1989). This inhibition is due to an effort to keep the irrelevant memories out of the current stream of processing and not to the continued practice of the to-be-remembered information (Basden, Basden, & Morales, 2003). This inhibition of the to-be-forgotten information is pervasive. It occurs both for explicit memory tests, like recognition and recall, as well as implicit tests, like word fragment completion and repetition priming (MacCleod, 1989). Moreover, inhibiting irrelevant memories is an effortful process, even if we are not consciously aware of it. For example, when people are disrupted by an unrelated secondary task, the inhibition of to-be-forgotten information is greatly reduced or eliminated (Conway et al., 2000).

Negative Priming.   The operation of inhibition is also observed with associative interference. By focusing on those memories that compete and produce interference, we can assess whether inhibition is operating. If people need these interfering memories immediately after they have been used, they are less available (Radvansky, 1999). This decreased availability of memory traces that were recently inhibited is called **negative priming.** It is the opposite of what is seen in normal (positive) priming, in which related information becomes more available (see Anderson, Garavan, Rivardo, & Chadwick, 1997, for an example of negative priming in working memory). More generally, this is a case of **retrieval-induced inhibition,** in which remembering one thing makes remembering related things more difficult. In other words, remembering causes forgetting.

Repeated Practice.   Finally, inhibition is seen when people repeatedly retrieve part of a set of information. This repeated retrieval or practice causes competing memory traces to become inhibited, similar to what is seen in part-set cuing (Bäuml & Kuhbandner, 2003). As a result, the probability of recalling the nonpracticed memories decreases (Tulving & Hastie, 1972). It is as though people are forgetting that information faster. This retrieval-induced inhibition for related but unpracticed memories is called the **repeated practice effect** (Anderson & Spellman, 1995). It is important to keep in mind that this phenomenon occurs only when memory retrieval actually occurs. Merely exposing people to information is not sufficient (Ciranni & Shimamura, 1999). Furthermore, there must be some competition or interference during retrieval (Anderson, Bjork, & Bjork, 2000). However, this retrieval can be part of some other task that the person thinks is unrelated to the original presentation of the information (Bäuml, 2002).

Here's an example of how the repeated practice effect is produced, using the diagram in Figure 7.9 as a guide. Suppose a person is given categories to learn, such as "red things," like "blood" and "tomato," and "foods," like "strawberry" and "crackers." Now if a person practices some of the items, such as "red-blood" and does not practice others, the effects of inhibition will be observed. The repeated rehearsal of certain items makes them easier to remember (not surprising). What is interesting is that, compared to a control condition, such as practicing "tool-pliers," this repeated practice makes unpracticed items less available because they are inhibited each time the "red-blood" item is rehearsed (because they are interfering competitors). This is also true for other items learned in that category, such as

Related Condition

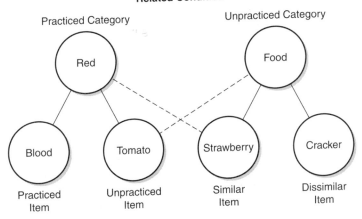

Unrelated Condition

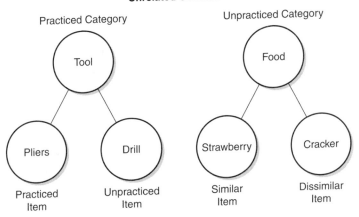

FIGURE 7.9 Operation of Retrieval-Induced Inhibition in a Repeated Practice Paradigm

Source: Anderson & Spellman, 1995

"tomato," but, more importantly, for other things that are part of that category in the real world, like "strawberry." This repeated practice effect can be observed with both recall and recognition (Hicks and & 2004; Veling & van Knippenberg, 2004), so it is a pervasive phenomenon.

The repeated practice effect shows that memory inhibits related but irrelevant memory traces that produce interference. It occurs when the competitors share similar categories, like "red things" or "foods" (Anderson & Spellman, 1995), or syntactic class, like "nouns" (Dopkins & Ngo, 2002), and even for sentences sharing similar concepts (Anderson & Bell, 2001). Although retrieval-induced inhibition is observed both in explicit and implicit memory tests, it is only seen in implicit memory tests that tap into conceptual knowledge (such as generating category members) but not perceptually based knowledge (such as completing word stems) (Perfect, Moulin, Conway, & Perry, 2002). As described in Chapter 6, the difference between conceptual and perceptual knowledge is related to the operation of explicit and implicit memory. Thus, these findings suggest that the repeated practice effect is more of an explicit memory phenomenon.

The repeated practice effect is a form of retrieval-induced inhibition that can be modified depending on how people think about the information. For example, if people integrate the information, then the repeated practice effect is reduced or eliminated (Anderson & McCulloch, 1999). By integrating information into a common memory trace, there are fewer competitors. If there is no competition, there is no need to suppress related but irrelevant memories. Alternatively, if memory traces are made more distinct and separated from one another, this can also reduce the repeated practice effect (Anderson, Green, & McCulloch, 2000; Smith & Hunt, 2000). When memory traces are more distinct, they compete with each other less and thus reduce the need for inhibition. However, if an unretrieved trace is highly related to the target, it may actually be facilitated rather than inhibited (Anderson, Green, & McCulloch, 2000; Bäuml & Hartinger, 2002). Also, for highly salient information, such as knowledge of one's self, this retrieval-induced forgetting is not observed (Macrae & Roseveare, 2002).

Inhibition, Working Memory, and Episodic Memory

The concept that long-term memory retrieval involves inhibition is basically claiming that attention is needed to remember (Anderson & Neely, 1996). In Chapter 5, we saw that one of the roles of working memory is in the regulation of inhibition. As such, it is reasonable to think that people who are better at this working memory inhibition should also be better at long-term memory retrieval. In fact, people who do well on working memory span tests tend to show less proactive interference than people who do not (Kane & Engle, 2000).

Synopsis

Part of effective retrieval in episodic memory is sorting out relevant and irrelevant memories. Where there are multiple, related episodic memories, this can produce interference, including proactive interference, retroactive interference, and associative interference. To regulate this interference, inhibition may be used to keep unwanted memories from entering the current memory process. This inhibition can make later retrieval of the inhibited memories more difficult. This includes phenomena such as part-set cuing, directed forgetting, negative priming, and the effects of selective, repeated practice. The operation of this inhibition in episodic memory may be similar to that found in working memory.

REPETITION AND PRACTICE

The more a person is exposed to information, the more likely it will be remembered. This is called a **repetition effect.** For example, information that is studied twice is more likely to be remembered than information studied only once. However, repeated exposures vary in their effectiveness on memory. How information is practiced can have a profound impact on memory.

Massed and Distributed Practice

Practice can affect memory depending on whether repeated attempts to memorize information are grouped together or spread out over many sessions. This is a distinction between massed and distributed practice. **Massed practice** is when there is a single, lengthy study session. For example, if a person decides to spend five hours studying, massed practice would be a single five-hour session. In contrast, **distributed practice** (also called spaced practice) occurs when the effort is spread out across multiple study sessions. For example, a person studies for five hours by studying for one hour per day for five days. In other words, massed practice is like cramming, and distributed practice is like consistently studying across a term. The difference between massed and distributed practice is important because, in general, memory is better following distributed practice than massed practice, and the longer the spacing between the distributed practices, the better the memory (Glenberg & Lehmann, 1980).

For example, in the results of the study shown in Figure 7.10, memory improved at a greater rate for distributed practice compared to massed practice. What is odd about the impact of different kinds of practice on memory is that people are generally unaware of it. In a study by Zechmeister and Shaughnessy (1980), students reported that they thought that

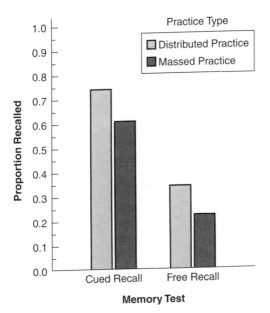

FIGURE 7.10   Effects of Massed Versus Spaced Practice on Subsequent Memory (with a Constant Context)

Source: Glenberg, 1979

memory was better after massed practice than after distributed practice. This is the opposite of reality.

There are three major explanations for why this difference in practice types occurs, and researchers are working to determine which of these provides the best account (Greene, 1989; Toppino & Bloom, 2002). These are deficient-processing, encoding-variability, and two-process accounts.

Deficient Processing.   The first class of explanations is deficient-processing accounts. These theories assume that massed practice reflects a deficiency in processing. There are a number of ways that this might come about. One is a neurological consolidation hypothesis that suggests that massed practice is inferior because two massed trials are stored as a single memory trace because consolidation has not run its course. With distributed practice, there is more consolidation, so memory is better (Landauer, 1969). A second is a habituation/attention hypothesis in which people habituate to information during massed practice and so do not as actively attend to it, leading to poorer memory (Rundus, 1971; Zechmeister & Shaughnessy, 1980). Finally, the accessibility/reconstruction hypothesis suggests that massed practice is worse because less effort is need to retrieve it because it is so fresh. As a result, people assume it is learned and do not devote the needed amount of time and effort to learning it. In all these explanations, there is something about massed practice learning that is less than optimal because of a deficiency in how the to-be-learned information is processed.

Encoding Variability.   The second class of explanations is encoding-variability accounts. These theories suggest that differences in the type of contextual information being stored in the memory trace account for the difference between memory after massed and distributed practice (Glenberg, 1976; 1979). When a person does distributed practice, the contexts (both internal and external) of each session are more distinct from one another, whereas in massed practice, the contexts are roughly the same. Thus, a wider variety of learning contexts provide more retrieval pathways. The more retrieval pathways, the more likely the information can be remembered when needed.

An illustration of the influence of context on memory for different types of practice is a study by Verkoeijen, Rikers, and Schmidt (2004). People were given either massed or distributed practice, with all the items shown on the same background or with a different background (context) each time. The results are shown in Figure 7.11. For massed practice, showing each item on a different background helped memory because even though the information was presented together, each one was in a different context, thereby facilitating retrieval. In contrast, for distributed practice, because the information is already distinct, presenting each item on a different background actually made things worse. When information was already distinct by distributed practice, changing the context made it hard to remember previous study experiences, so memory was poorer. However, when the background was the same in distributed practice, this reminded a person of the previous study experiences and facilitated memory.

Dual Processes.   The third class of explanations is two-process accounts. These theories assume that two processes operate during retrieval, both deficient-processing and encoding

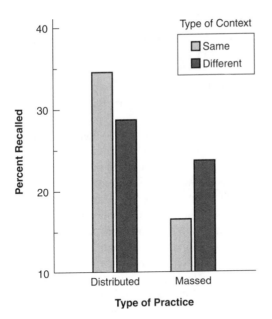

FIGURE 7.11   Effects of Massed Versus Spaced Practice on Subsequent Memory (with Varying Context)

Source: Verkoeijen, Rikers, & Schmidt, 2004

variability (Greene, 1989; Russo, Parkin, Taylor, & Wilks, 1998; but see Toppino & Bloom, 2002). The encoding-variability component is more automatic because it involves the use of contextual information, which has a largely unconscious effect on memory. In contrast, the deficient-processing component is more controlled and involves conscious, deliberate thinking.

Overlearning and Permastore

If a person continues to practice memorized information, then **overlearning** occurs. As reported by Ebbinghaus, overlearning strengthens memory traces, and there is increased resistance to forgetting. For example, musicians and actors continue to rehearse their parts even after they are flawless. This continued rehearsal strengthens their memory, making it much less likely that it will be forgotten when it comes time to perform.

What about things that you learn in school? You are in college right now. What is the fate of the information you are learning? Is it subject to the forgetting curve? What is the point of learning if you're only going to forget it all later? Why try to get an A when, after a few years, the natural process of forgetting will more or less even everyone out? Well, although there is an initial period of forgetting, a great deal of what is learned in school is retained throughout life.

Harry Bahrick, a memory researcher at Ohio Wesleyan University, has addressed these issues. His method is to take graduates who attend college reunions and test their memories for a college course, such as Spanish, from 3 months to 50 years after graduation. Bahrick has discovered that, although there is an initial period of forgetting, which lasts about three years, after that, little forgetting occurs (Bahrick, 1984; 2000; Bahrick, Bahrick, & Wittlinger, 1975; Conway, Cohen, & Stanhope, 1991). Whatever memory remains after three years is stable for the rest of your life and is said to be in **permastore.** Permastore can metaphorically be thought of as the deep freeze of memory. Entrance into permastore is an effect of distributed practice and overlearning.

An important thing to note is that forgetting occurs at about the same rate for everyone. That is, people who learned more in college forget at the same rate as people who learned less. Thus, even after the initial forgetting period, the same difference in knowledge levels persists. The people who got A's always know more than the people who got C's (Bahrick, 1984; Conway, Cohen, & Stanhope, 1991). So, study hard.

Still, for some types of information, there is no clear permastore benefit; it continues to be forgotten. These are generally things that have some isolated status and are difficult to relate to other things. This includes campus and town landmarks, things that a person is unlikely to have interacted with directly. Another example is knowledge learned in college mathematics classes (Bahrick & Hall, 1991). If people took advanced math classes in college, a great deal of information is entered into permastore. However, for students who get no further instruction, continuous forgetting of the information occurs.

Synopsis

A major factor that influences episodic memory is how it is practiced. Memory is better with distributed practice than massed practice. This occurs because under massed practice some items are not processed very well, and there are not as many contextual changes. Continued practice, even after the information is well learned, can cause overlearning and lead to it being placed in permastore. Once in permastore, the information is unlikely to be forgotten.

ORGANIZATION AND DISTINCTIVENESS

Organization

Episodic memory is improved if people use **organization.** This can be seen clearly in Figure 7.12, which shows data for people across a number of study sessions when a set of words was presented in either an organized (i.e., based on categories) or random fashion. This is an example of how the effects of chunking can work in long-term memory. An example of a preestablished structure that can aid memory is shown in Figure 7.13. Here, people used hierarchical organization to categorize 18 words into groups of 3 or 4 items. Each of these sets is chunked, and some of the chunks are chunked.

As described in Chapter 3, when people are not given an explicit organization, they engage in subjective organization (Bousfield, 1953) to impose a structure, even when there does not appear to be one. When people subjectively cluster, it often takes some time for the organization to develop, but it still aids memory.

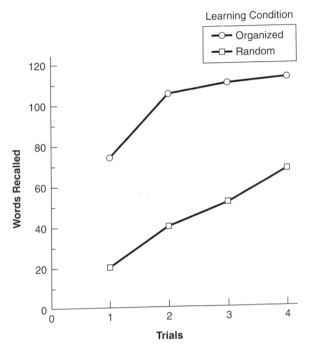

FIGURE 7.12   Influence of Organization on Later Memory Retrieval Across a Number of Learning Trials

Source: Bower, Clark, Lesgold, & Winzenz, 1969

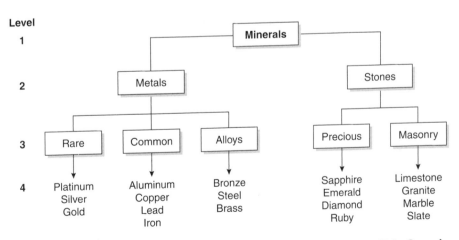

FIGURE 7.13   Example of a Hierarchical Structure that Can Be Used to Help Organize Memory

Source: Bower, Clark, Lesgold, & Winzenz, 1969

Distinctiveness

Episodic memory can be enhanced when a memory trace is separated out from competing ones that produce interference. Thus, memory is better for items that are distinct. For example, when people are given a set of items and one item is different from the others in some salient way, and there is some similarity among the other items. For example, one word might be printed in red in a list of black words. Or the word *tulip* might appear in a list of vehicle names. Memory for the unique item is better than memory for any one of the others. This is called the **Von Restorff effect,** after the woman who discovered it (Hunt, 1995).

Another example of distinctive processing is the effect of **bizarre imagery.** Here, people form mental images of something they are trying to remember. The very act of forming a mental image is a lot of work, so it improves memory (see Chapter 3). However, we can go a step further by creating bizarre images that are more distinctive. For example, to remember to buy ice cream, tomatoes, and carrots at the grocery store, you might imagine a bowl of ice cream with a face made with slices of tomatoes and carrots. Bizarre imagery can improve memory.

However, bizarre imagery only works when a small portion of the information gets the bizarreness treatment. If more than half or everything is bizarre, none of the information is distinct, so memory is not improved (McDaniel & Einstein, 1986). It should be noted that this effect is typically seen with free recall and not with cued recall or recognition. This is because bizarre imagery effects reflect an influence on the ability to access the information at retrieval rather than different amounts of attention paid to information during learning (Riefer & Rouder, 1992).

A related finding occurs with the enactment effect (see Chapter 3). As a reminder, the actions that a person performs or enacts are remembered better. Specifically, the enactment effect is observed when only some of the actions are performed. People who enact everything do not have superior memories (Engelkamp & Zimmer, 1997).

Relational and Item-Specific Processing

At this point there may seem to be a contradiction. On the one hand, organization helps memory, but on the other hand, distinctiveness helps memory. These processes seem to be working in opposition. The more organized information is, the less distinctive the elements are, because similarities are emphasized. Conversely, the more distinct information is, the less organized it is, because differences are emphasized. However, in the face of this apparent contradiction, it is also clear that both of these are at work (Hunt & Einstein, 1981; Hunt & McDaniel, 1993). On the one hand, relational processing is helpful in generating a retrieval plan for later recall. On the other hand, item-specific processing can help reduce sources of interference that may exist. Each of these has an impact on memory (Einstein & Hunt, 1980). The degree to which each of these aids memory is a function of the current set of information.

An illustration of the differential effects of relational and distinctiveness processing is a study done by Hunt and Seta (1984; see also McDaniel, Einstein, & Lollis, 1988). In this study, people learned items from categories of different sizes. People learned using either relational processing (sorting items into categories) or distinctive, item-specific processing (rating items for pleasantness). The results shown in Figure 7.14 illustrate that

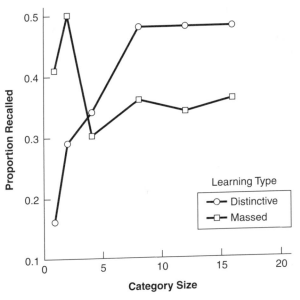

FIGURE 7.14   Effects of Learning Emphasizing Distinctiveness and Relational Processing as a Function of Category Size

Source: Hunt & Seta, 1984

memory was better for small categories when people engaged in relational processing (thereby helping them identify the interrelations among the few items as members of a category) but was better for larger categories when people engaged in distinctiveness processing (thereby helping them contend with the larger amounts of interference in those cases).

Material Appropriate Processing.   The distinction between item-specific and relational processing has implications for learning from a text. Memory for text information is better if the type of learning emphasizes the information for which memory is likely to be weak. For example, with a descriptive text, such as a college textbook, the emphasis is on a set of facts, or item-specific information. As a consequence, memory is better in this case if people engage in learning that emphasizes relational information. In contrast, with a narrative text, such as a fairy tale or novel, the emphasis is on the narrative flow and the interrelations among the events. That is, the emphasis is on the relational information. As a consequence, memory is better in this case if people engage in learning that emphasizes item-specific information. This distinction between types of learning and memory for different types of texts is called the **material appropriate processing** framework (Einstein, McDaniel, Own, & Cote, 1990; McDaniel, Einstein, Dunay, & Cobb, 1986).

This distinction between item-specific and relational processing has a broad range of applications. For instance, it can help explain generation effects, which involve an increase in relational processing for the generated item (Burns, 1992; McDaniel & Waddill, 1990; Mulligan, 2001). It also can help explain proactive interference. When a person learns a new association, because of the prior association, more item-specific processing will be done. As a result, people have poorer memory on a cued recall test (which depends on relational information). In contrast, if people are given only a free recall test, then the additional associations, which produce more forgetting in cued recall, lead to better memory. This is because free recall can take advantage of more item-specific processing (Burns, 1989).

Synopsis

How effective episodic memory is can be influenced by how information is related to other memory traces that share some affinity with it. Episodic memory can be improved by putting the information into some organizational structure. Episodic memory can also be improved by making new information distinct from other memories. While these two seem to be at odds, both are effective under the right circumstances. Relational processing improves memories for information for which a person does not have a large knowledge base, and it is unclear how it relates to what is already known. Conversely, item-specific processing improves memory when a person already has well-developed organization, thereby helping make this knowledge stand out and be less affected by interference.

SUMMARY

This chapter covered a number of issues about episodic memory. Episodic memories are defined by the individual events that they represent, including knowledge of both the content and context. The retrieval of episodic memories is aided by cuing with either content or context information. In episodic memory a great deal of forgetting is caused by interference, or competition with other memory traces that share similar content. People are able to reduce the effects of interference through organization and the use of inhibition. Finally, memory reflects the use of both organization and distinctiveness processes.

STUDY QUESTIONS

1. What is the influence of serial order of event types on episodic memory?

2. What are kinds of knowledge that are stored in episodic memories?

3. What kind of information can be used to cue episodic memory?

4. How does context influence episodic memory? What are the different types of contexts?

5. What does transfer appropriate processing tell us about what information is stored in episodic memory and how it is remembered later?

6. What are the different ways that interference disrupts memory retrieval?

7. What is the role of inhibition in episodic memory retrieval? What effects are produced by inhibition?

8. How does organization help episodic memory? How does distinctiveness help episodic memory? How are they opposites? How can this puzzle be resolved?

KEY TERMS

associative interference, bizarre imagery, cueing, directed forgetting, distributed practice, encoding specificity, episodic memory, fan effect, inhibition, interference, massed practice, material appropriate processing, mood-congruent memory, negative priming, negative transfer, organization, overlearning, part-set cuing, permastore, proactive interference, repeated practice effect, repetition effect, retrieval-induced inhibition, retroactive interference, semantic memory, state-dependent memory, transfer appropriate processing, Von Restorff effect

CHAPTER EIGHT

MEMORY FOR SPACE AND TIME

Space and time. According to physicists, this is the fabric that makes up our reality. Psychologically, these are the primary dimensions for orienting ourselves in our world. Space and time provide the framework for the events that we experience and remember.

Spatial information allows us to understand how different entities in the world are located and oriented with respect to one another. This is important when a person needs to do such things as navigate, locate objects, or estimate distances within that space. In this chapter we look at how people's memories for spatial configurations correspond to layouts in the world and the influences that cause distortions in memory for space. In general, space is a dimension of reality that is relatively static. We can move from one location to another and back again with ease and with little change in the actual spaces themselves.

In contrast, temporal information allows us to understand when events occurred, either with respect to the present, to other events in the past, or even to some more standard time scale, such as a calendar. Unlike spatial locations, our current place in time is always, inexorably, being pushed forward. We can't go back. This chapter also addresses how time information is stored and retrieved from memory, leading people to be either accurate or error prone in locating their memories in time.

MEMORY FOR SPACE

Although space may be the final frontier in science fiction, it is far from that in psychological research. There has been a large amount of research in memory that has focused on spatial information. In fact, study of memory and space was one of the areas of research with rats that helped bring an end to radical behaviorist views of psychology (Tolman, 1948).

From the viewpoint of an experimental psychologist, one of the appeals of spatial knowledge is that it is easy to understand exactly what was present in the world. We can get very precise measurements of spatial reality. We can measure distances, areas, curvatures, and so forth. We can then directly compare these measurements of reality to memory of these spatial properties. What is also interesting about memory space is that there seem to be parts of the brain that are specially dedicated to processing spatial knowledge. For example, single cell recordings of the hippocampus have shown that certain parts of this structure are important for knowing spatial location (Muller, Kuble, & Ranck, 1987; O'Keefe & Dostrovsky, 1971; Shapiro, Tanila, & Eichenbaum, 1997), and there is a region of the cortex, called the parahippocampal place area, that fMRI studies have shown to be critical to understanding the structure of the local space (Epstein & Kanwisher, 1998) and that can disrupt memory encoding if it is damaged in humans (Epstein et al., 2001). This part of the chapter discusses how actual spatial information relates to one's memory for a space by looking at memory psychophysics, memory for information learned from maps, and how our interaction with the world affects our spatial memory.

MEMORY PSYCHOPHYSICS

How well do our memories for space correspond to actual spaces? The part of psychology that deals with how experience of the world maps onto actual physical properties is called **psychophysics.** Basically, the question is how does our experience of reality correspond to actual reality? Many psychophysicists study issues of sensation and perception. Because of the high degree of sophistication of our perceptual systems, there are some well-established and consistent "laws" of psychophysical relations. One of the more prominent of these is **Steven's Law** of psychological magnitude (Stevens & Galantner, 1957). According to this law, the relation between actual and perceived magnitudes is a power function that is captured by the formula $\Psi = k\Phi^n$. Here, Ψ corresponds to psychological magnitude. This psychological experience is related to the actual physical magnitude, Φ, raised to some power, n, and modified by some constant, k.

The important point here is that the same principles can be used to study memory for the world. This is called memory psychophysics (e.g., Algom, 1992; Björkman, Lundberg, & Tärnblom, 1960; Moyer, Sklarew, & Whiting, 1982). Memory psychophysics is applied to a number of domains, including memory for size, area, loudness, and labor pains (Algom & Lubel, 1994; Algom, Wolf, & Bergman, 1985; Chew & Richardson, 1980; Kerst & Howard, 1978; Kerst & Howard, 1983; Moyer et al., 1977). However, we confine ourselves to memory psychophysics for spatial properties, such as distance and area.

In general, the relation between actual and perceived spatial distance is fairly good. The exponent in Steven's Law is very close to 1, although there is some distortion. This basically means that our perceptual experience of space is a near perfect one-to-one relationship. As for our memory for spatial properties, such as distance, the relation is still good, but there are more noticeable distortions (Wiest & Bell, 1985). Moreover, the amount of distortion is less when the space was originally viewed all at once compared to when the distance needs to be inferred from memory from separate experiences (e.g., estimating distances between buildings in a city that are separated by several other buildings, so the actual distance cannot be viewed directly). A number of theories have been provided to explain these relations.

Uncertainty Hypothesis.   One of the simplest theories is the **Uncertainty Hypothesis** (e.g., Radvansky, Carlson-Radvansky, & Irwin, 1995). According to this view, distortions in memory occur because there is forgetting over time. Some degree of uncertainty is introduced, with greater forgetting leading to greater uncertainty and more distortion. The more people have forgotten over time, the more uncertain people will become and the more likely they will be to make guesses about spatial distance based on the fragments that are in memory.

Reperceptual Hypothesis. Another explanation is the *Reperceptual Hypothesis* (Kerst & Howard, 1978). This view assumes that spatial information receives some (slight) distortion during perception. After all, our perception of the world is not perfect. Once information is perceived, it is stored more or less accurately. During retrieval, the information is passed through many of the same neural circuits that were originally used for perception. Thus, the space is reperceived. As a result, any distortion that was introduced during perception is doubled. This is consistent with research showing that during mental imagery, many of the same parts of the brain that are used in perception are also used in imagery (e.g., Kosslyn et al., 1993). This is also consistent with studies that have found that the memory exponent is close to the square of the perception exponent—exactly what would be expected.

Transformation Hypothesis. A third theory is the **Transformation Hypothesis** (Kemp, 1988). This states that the memory traces are gradually degraded and altered over time. As a result, there is almost certainly going to be some reconstruction. These reconstructions are likely to conform to more schema-consistent values (see Chapter 9). In this case, schematic values reflect the hierarchical structure of the space, such as major areas and regions, with the detailed information being lost.

Category Adjustment Theory. The final view, one that incorporates elements of the other three, is of the fuzzy trace variety. This is the **Category Adjustment Theory** (Huttenlocher, Hedges, & Duncan, 1991; Newcombe et al., 1999). According to this view, memory performance reflects a combination of both fine-grained memories and more coarse-grained memories. This theory assumes that objects in space are located within areas that serve as categories or schemas. Thus, a person remembers the object itself as well as the category to which it belongs. For example, if you are trying to remember where a certain city is located in the country, you may have a fine-grained memory of the actual location of the city on a map of the country, as well a coarse-grained categorical memory of the area it is in, such as which state it is in. Memory for space, then, is always a combination of these two influences. However, these two sources vary in their relative contribution at any given occasion. The stronger the fine-grained memories are, the weaker the influence of the coarse-grained memories. Conversely, the weaker the fine-grained memories are, the greater the influence of the coarse-grained memories.

Mental Maps

Of course, memory for space is more complex than remembering distances between locations. People have an ability to create complex mental representations of the environment to help guide their travels around the house, through town, and across the country. We carry around mental maps of the environments we encounter to help us navigate and do other sorts of spatial thinking. This section looks at theories of how mental maps are represented and used in memory.

Spatial Theories. The first class of theories can be defined as spatial because they assume that the memory of an environment is structured according to the same structure as is space. According to such views, mental maps are second-order isomorphs (Shepard & Chipman, 1970). That is, a mental map would functionally capture the structure of a real map, even though, neurologically, there is not a one-to-one relationship between the two (which would be a first-order isomorph). For example, a wristwatch is a second-order isomorph of the daily rotation of the Earth (because it captures that regular temporal quality of the Earth), but a model of the solar system in which the Earth spins each day would be a first-order isomorph.

This aspect of spatial theories of mental maps makes them the most straightforward to understand. The simplest version is that a mental map corresponds directly to the space it represents, called the **metric view.** Given the results in memory psychophysics studies discussed earlier, this seems reasonable. However, there have been few serious metric theories (e.g., Kosslyn, Ball, & Reisser, 1978; Levine, Jankovic, & Palij, 1982), because it is well known that mental maps are almost always distorted in some way.

One major influence on mental maps is areas or regions. Space is not uniform. The world is divided into continents, continents are (often) divided into countries, countries are divided into states or provinces, and so on. There are also many ways we chop up space. Locations are often assigned to superordinate locations, or regions. The **hierarchical view** (Stevens & Coupe, 1978) states that mental maps are organized the same way. Figure 8.1 gives an example of how a hierarchical representation might be structured for cities in Colorado and Ohio. Thus, a spatial hierarchy reflects the organization of smaller areas into larger areas. People often make errors that reflect a hierarchical memory organization. For example, people estimate the direction between two locations (e.g., Stevens & Coupe, 1978), but these estimates may be in error when the actual direction between the two places is different from the relation between the hierarchical regions. An example of this is shown in Figure 8.2. People often mistakenly report that San Diego, CA, is west of Reno, NV, because California is generally west of Nevada. However, Reno is actually farther west than San Diego. Thus, the direction of the superordinate regions influences spatial memory.

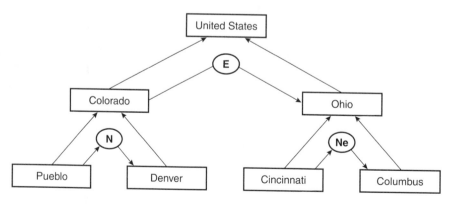

FIGURE 8.1 Hierarchical Representation of Space

Source: Stevens & Coupe, 1978

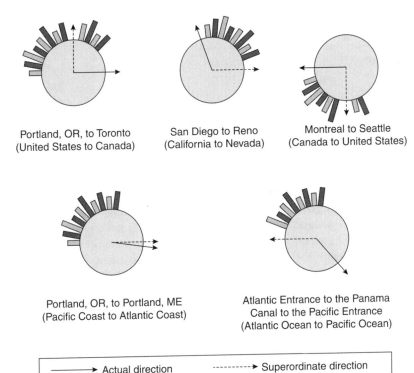

Portland, OR, to Toronto
(United States to Canada)

San Diego to Reno
(California to Nevada)

Montreal to Seattle
(Canada to United States)

Portland, OR, to Portland, ME
(Pacific Coast to Atlantic Coast)

Atlantic Entrance to the Panama
Canal to the Pacific Entrance
(Atlantic Ocean to Pacific Ocean)

───────► Actual direction   ‑‑‑‑‑‑‑‑► Superordinate direction

FIGURE 8.2   Distortion of Direction Judgments as Influenced by Superordinate Regions

Source: Stevens & Coupe, 1978

   A mental map that was based strictly on spatial regions would be categorical. That is, all of the locations within a region could be considered more or less the same, but this is not the case. More complex theories of mental maps use a combination of both metric and regional information. This is the **partially hierarchical view** (McNamara, 1986). Some of the best evidence for this view comes from spatial priming studies. In these studies people first memorized a map that was divided into regions. Within each region was a set of locations, such as cities or objects (see Figure 8.3). After memorization, people were given a primed recognition test (see Chapter 3). In this task, a series of location names are provided, and the participants were required to indicate whether those names were on the memorized map. What was observed was that mental map locations prime one another (McNamara, 1986). An example of such priming is presented in Table 8.1. In general, there is more priming (people are faster) for close locations (e.g., *key* and *spool* in Figure 8.3) than for far locations (e.g., *candle* and *needle*). Moreover, regions also mediate the amount of priming. For example, keeping Euclidean distance the same, there is less priming across different regions (e.g., *boat* and *stapler*) than within the same region (e.g., *key* and *spool*). This partially hierarchical influence is seen even when the division of an area into regions is subjective rather than objective (McNamara, Hardy, & Hirtle, 1989).

TABLE 8.1   Spatial Priming (in ms), Both Within and Across Spatial Regions

SAME REGION		DIFFERENT REGIONS	
Close	*Far*	*Close*	*Far*
705	768	763	790

Source: McNamara, 1986

Additional Mental Map Phenomena.   Also consistent with the partially hierarchical view are people's geographical knowledge of the locations of cities (e.g., Friedman & Brown, 2000a; Friedman, Brown, & McGaffey, 2002). People's reports of city locations are often clustered based on accepted political/climatic categories of regions. For example, as illustrated in Figure 8.4, when Canadian students were asked to estimate the latitude of cities in North America, four clear categories emerged. These were Canada, the northern United States, the southern United States, and Mexico (with Miami floating in between the

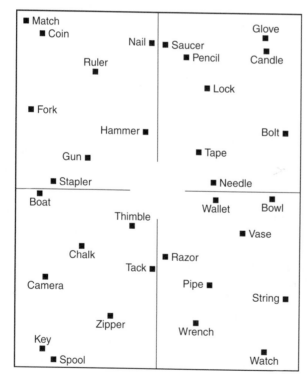

FIGURE 8.3   Map Used in Spatial Priming Studies

Source: McNamara, 1986

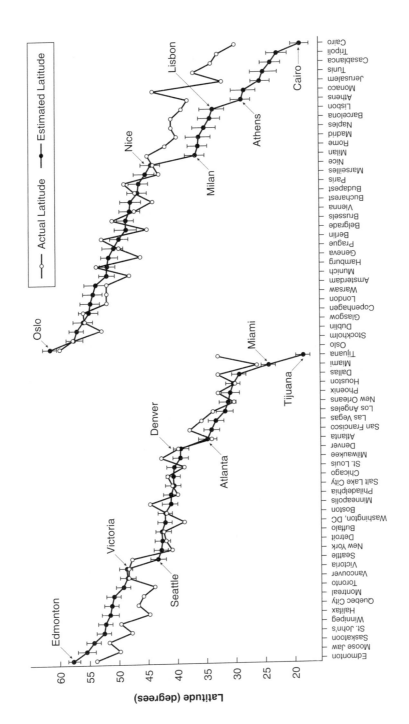

FIGURE 8.4 **Influence of Geographical Regions on Latitude Estimations in North America and Europe/Africa**

Source: Friedman & Brown, 2000a

United States and Mexico. A similar result is observed for students from Texas (Friedman, Kerkman, & Brown, 2002), so where people live is less important than how they divide the world into regions.

It is interesting to note that when accurate information about the correct latitudes or longitudes is provided as seed knowledge, people do make adjustments (Friedman & Brown, 2000a; 2000b), with the greatest adjustments occurring for those regions in which the seeds are provided. Interestingly, the amount of adjustment to other regions varies depending on their relation to the seeded region. If the regions are not directly adjoining, adjustment may be limited. For example, when European seed cities were provided, although there was an adjustment of the European cities northward, there was little change in the African cities. It is as if people just increased their idea of the size of the Mediterranean Sea.

Other spatial characteristics can influence mental maps and how they are remembered. One factor is the number of intervening locations on a route between two locations. In general, the more locations along a route, the longer people estimate distances on that route (Thorndyke, 1981). This increased crowding causes that part of the mental map to "expand" to accommodate all of the places. For example, in one study people memorized a map like the one in Figure 8.5. In this map there are a number of locations with varying numbers of intervening locations. When memory is tested by having people estimate the distances between pairs of cities, the more intervening cities there are, the greater the distance estimates (see Figure 8.6).

Route distance itself can also influence memory (McNamara, Ratcliff, & McKoon, 1984). Given the same Euclidean distance, priming is less if there is a long circuitous route between two locations compared to if there is a relatively short and direct route. In one study, students at Yale memorized maps like the one in Figure 8.7. The primed recognition memory test that followed had conditions in which map locations were either close in both Euclidean and route distance (e.g., Emmet & Davis), far in both Euclidean and route

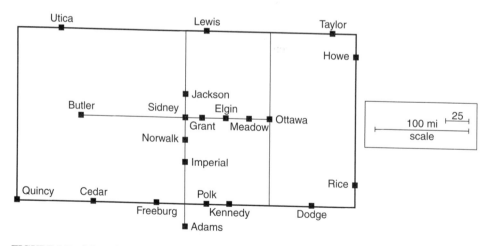

FIGURE 8.5   Map of Fictitious Area that Varies the Number of Intervening Locations Between Cities But Keeps the Distance Relatively Constant

Source: Thorndyke, 1981

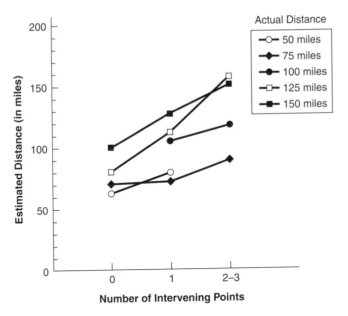

FIGURE 8.6 **Distance Estimate Results as a Function of the Number of Intervening Cities (see Figure 8.5)**

Source: Thorndyke, 1981

distance (e.g., Gallina & Sedona), or close in Euclidean distance but far in route distance (e.g., Mantee & Foster). As can be seen in Table 8.2, if the two map locations were far along the route, even if they were spatially close, the two places were perceived as being spatially far apart.

Finally, memories for space are distorted by prominent features, such as landmarks. Landmarks can be prominent buildings, natural features like lakes, or statues. Landmarks help define spatial regions or categories. As such, people tend to distort their memory for nonlandmark locations toward the landmarks (Sadalla, Burroughs, & Staplin, 1980). This is true even when the spatial memories are acquired verbally rather than through a map (Ferguson & Hegarty, 1994). This finding has been explained using the Category Adjustment theory (Newcombe et al., 1999), which we saw in the section on memory psychophysics. According to this theory, people store information about the landmarks as categorical information as well as fine-grained information about the locations themselves. Memory then reflects a combination of these, which often results in nonlandmark locations being mentally drawn to the landmarks.

Temporal and Hybrid Theories. Although it is clear that mental maps can be affected by spatial characteristics, they may also be organized by nonspatial information, such as temporal information. Here, temporal information refers to the sequential order in which map items are learned. Thus, places can be either close or far in temporal proximity in much the same way that they can be close or far in spatial proximity. Often spatial and temporal

TABLE 8.2   Spatial Priming as Affected by Both Euclidean and Route Distance. CE = close Euclidean, CR = close route, FE = far Euclidean, and FR = far route

CONDITION	RESPONSE TIME
Close Euclidean—close route	627
Close Euclidean—far route	682
Far Euclidean—far route	677

Source: McNamara, Ratcliff, & McKoon, 1984

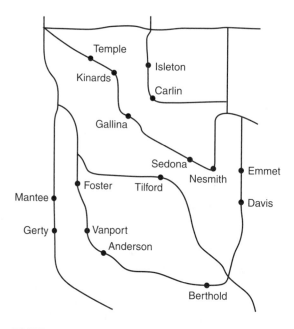

FIGURE 8.7   Map Used to Study the Effects of Spatial and Route Distance on Spatial Memory

Source: McNamara, Ratcliff, & McKoon, 1984

proximity are confounded during learning. Locations that are close in space are also studied close in time. However, these two dimensions can be disassociated. For example, imagine a person learns the map in Figure 8.8 in the order indicated by the arrows. Although people can derive spatial qualities (such as direction and distance) from their mental map, evidence from memory priming studies suggests that temporal, not spatial, structure is the primary basis of the mental map's underlying structure (Clayton & Habibi, 1991; Curiel & Radvansky, 1998; Sherman & Lim, 1991).

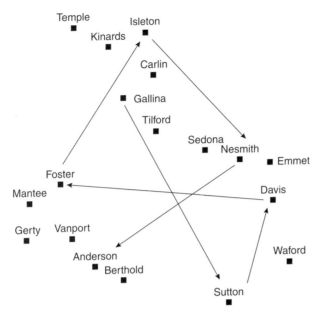

FIGURE 8.8 **Fictitious Map Illustrating the Deconfounding of Spatial and Temporal Proximity with a Partial Temporal Order Indicated by the Arrows**

Source: Clayton & Habibi, 1991

This dominance of a temporal structure for mental maps can vary. **Hybrid theories** assume that there is a contribution of both spatial and temporal information. For example, in a study by Curiel and Radvansky (1998), during memorization people either named indicated locations (focusing on identity information) or pointed to named locations (focusing on spatial information). As can be seen in Table 8.3, there was greater temporal priming when participants named the location but greater spatial priming when they pointed to the location. This suggests that the way people initially encode the information into memory can have a dramatic influence. It should also be noted that spatial and temporal information could work together to influence the structure of a mental map (McNamara, Halpin, & Hardy, 1992). That is, learning map locations that are close together in both time and space provides the greatest benefit to memory.

This hybrid theory of mental maps is supported by neurological evidence. Specifically, the parallel map theory (Jacobs & Schenk, 2003) suggests there are two types of information that are used in making mental maps, and these are observed by two different sets of neurological structures. One is the bearing map, which is a representation of the current heading in an environment. This corresponds to a rough representation of space based on the relative position to certain locations in the environment. The bearing map involves the neural structure of the dendate gyrus and a portion of the hippocampus called area CA3, as well as parts of the cortex that are linked to them. This map tends to be more developed in males, who are better at estimation types of navigation. More generally, this type of representation would be more sensitive to temporal order information.

TABLE 8.3 Differences in Spatial and Temporal Priming.
Whether people name map locations during learning in response to location cues or point to map locations in response to name cues.

CONDITION	NAMING	POINTING
Spatial		
Close	690	681
Far	714	730
Priming	24	49
Temporal		
Close	669	721
Far	709	718
Priming	40	-3

Source: Curiel & Radvansky, 1998.

The other neurological structure is a sketch map, which is a representation of a set of salient landmarks. This corresponds to a more accurate representation of space, based on the known positions of landmarks. The sketch map involves neural structures of a part of the hippocampus known as area CA1, as well as parts of the cortex that are linked to it. These sorts of maps tend to be more developed in females. More generally, this type of representation would be more sensitive to spatial structure information. The information from both the bearing and sketch maps can be used to form an integrated map that includes both types of information, depending on what is available.

Routes versus Surveys.   Many mental maps are created from a person's experience with an environment or from reading a map. However, there are other ways. Sometimes people create mental maps from language—for example, giving oral directions (e.g., "Go west on Cleveland until you get to Swanson. Turn north. Then turn right at the third stop sign"). People often can easily navigate through space with only this type of information.

While the manner in which this information is given sometimes does not seem to have major effects on the mental maps in memory, such as when map information is tested verbally (Taylor & Tversky, 1992), in cases where the maps are learned and tested visually, there is a preference for the orientation taken when the map was learned (Shelton & McNamara, 2004). In some cases people might be given **route perspectives,** in which spatial information is present as if a person were walking through an area. In other cases people might be given **survey perspectives,** in which the spatial layout is presented as if it were being viewed from high overhead, such as from a helicopter.

It has been found that when people are given the map information and asked to verify spatial inferences (spatial information derived from a mental map), they may be able to make them similarly in the two cases (Taylor & Tversky, 1992). If they are ask to verify pictures of the area (walking perspectives or overhead views), however, memory is better for the perspective in which the information was originally learned (Shelton & McNamara,

2004). This suggests that how information is represented in a mental map is influenced by how that information got into memory in the first place.

Semantic Effects.   Mental maps can also reflect the influence of semantic relationships. The degree to which different locations are meaningfully similar can accentuate priming, particularly if those places are already near one another (McNamara, Halpin, & Hardy, 1992; McNamara & LeSueur, 1989; Merrill & Baird, 1987). For example, people's memory of their college campus shows that their mental maps are somewhat semantically structured. In priming studies, buildings prime each other more if they serve the same function (i.e., dorms, administration buildings, sports facilities, etc.). Thus, how we interact with the world and the different functions of the elements (in this case different locations) influence how we remember that information.

Knowledge of the world can have more general effects. As with memory psychophysics, some spatial remembering is a mixture of fine-grained and coarse-grained information. This also applies to mental map memories. When given maps in the real world, there may be portions that are not quite straight but are at an angle with respect to a larger frame of reference. For example, on a city map, the streets may not be at 90-degree angles to one another, or the orientation of a town may not square with the standard compass points. Research by Tversky (1981) has shown that when these sorts of deviations are present, memories are distorted in such a way as to smooth out these irregularities. For example, streets are remembered as intersecting at something more closely approximating 90 degrees. One clear demonstration of this is the tendency of many North Americans to believe that South America is directly south of North America. It's actually more to the east. The western shore of South America is around the same longitude as the eastern shore of North America. This is because people's memories for maps reflect a combination of detailed information on the map and more general, schematic knowledge about orientations. These two types of memories cause people to make predictable errors in their mental maps.

Mental Maps and Thinking.   The structure of mental maps influences more than just memory for the map itself. It also influences other types of thinking. An example of this is when someone memorizes a map and then reads a story about events that occur in that area (e.g., Morrow, Greenspan, & Bower, 1987). In some studies people memorized a map of the research center shown in Figure 8.9 and then read a series of stories about situations that happened there. While reading, people use their mental maps in memory, and this influences comprehension. For example, if a story character is described as thinking about an object in the building, the time it takes a person to read that sentence varies as a function of the spatial distance between the character's current location and the object she is thinking about (Rinck & Bower, 1995). In general, the greater the distance, the longer it takes people to read. This is referred to as the **spatial gradient of availability.** The mental map in memory captures spatial characteristics of the building, and this spills over into comprehension.

This search of a mental map in memory during comprehension also shows the importance of map regions. People treat each room as a different chunk of information. As such, the spatial gradient of availability is influenced by the number of rooms between the character and the object, not by Euclidean distance (Rinck, Hähnel, Bower, & Glowalla,

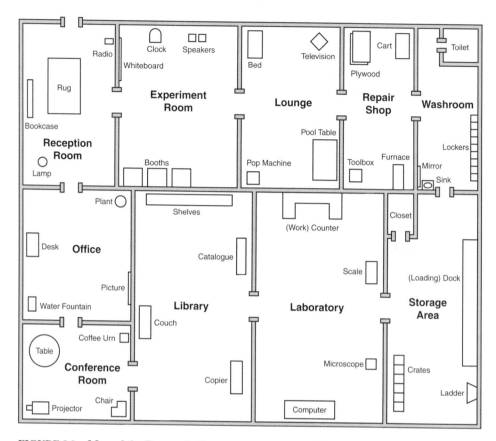

FIGURE 8.9   Map of the Research Center

Source: Morrow, Greenspan, & Bower, 1987

1997). Furthermore, the retrieval of information from the map is more affected by the number of rooms an object is in rather than the number of objects in that room (Bower & Rinck, 2001). These findings show that the same memory principles can be observed even with a task that does not primarily focus on remembering information from the mental map.

Spatial Frameworks

We spend our time in various spaces and regions that are defined in particular ways—a kitchen, a mall, a highway, and so forth. These spatial regions are called **spatial frameworks,** and how we interact with them affects our memories for them. In this section, we consider the influence of orientation and perspective on memories for space.

When we learn about a location, especially a large one that we cannot see all at once, such as a mall or a town, we may derive our understanding from a map. We study the map to create our own mental map. One consequence of this is that the orientation that the map was studied in becomes ingrained in our mental map. So when a person needs to estimate direc-

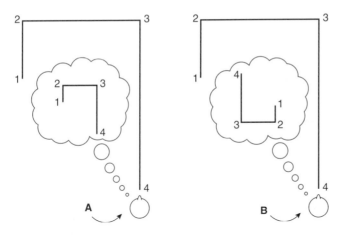

FIGURE 8.10   Direction Judgment When the Memorized Map Is Aligned or Misaligned with the Current Orientation

Source: Levine, Jankovic, & Palij, 1982

tions when facing a direction other than the original map orientation, he is slower to grasp the information and may make mistakes (Evans & Pezdek, 1980; Levine, Jankovic, & Palij, 1982; Waller, Montello, Richardson, & Hegarty, 2002). It is as if the mental map were being viewed as a mental image. The greater the deviation from the orientation the map was learned in, the more likely an error will be made in deciding which direction something is in. For example, in Figure 8.10 the person who has his mental map aligned with his current orientation is less likely to make errors than someone who has his mental map misaligned.

This **orientation effect** can be seen in the data presented in Table 8.4. This effect even extends to memory for observed spatial layouts (not just maps) that are either static or dynamic (like a soccer game) (Diwadkar & McNamara, 1997; Garsoffky, Schwan, & Hesse, 2002; Shelton & McNamara, 1997). It can also occur when a space is viewed from multiple perspectives. Each of the perspectives can be stored as an orientation-specific viewpoint (McNamara, Rump, & Werner, 2003; Valiquette, McNamara, & Smith, 2003). However, it

TABLE 8.4   Influence of Orientation on Mental Map Retrieval
This expresses error rates (in degrees) from the correct orientation, depending on whether the orientation during retrieval either matched or was counteraligned with the original orientation.

CONDITION	ALIGNED	COUNTERALIGNED
Small map	15.2	43.3
Large map	22.7	31.7
Path	20.2	28.3

Source: Levine, Jankovic, & Palij, 1982

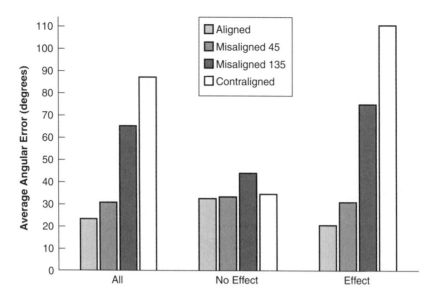

FIGURE 8.11 **Performance of Good and Poor Misaligned Map Populations**

Source: Rossano, Warren, & Kenan, 1995

may not be observed when people are active participants in the situation but only when they view it passively, such as watching a film (Sun, Chan, & Campos, 2004; Waller, Loomis, & Haun, 2004).

It appears that people can be broadly categorized into two groups (Rossano, Warren, & Kenan, 1995), as can be seen in Figure 8.11. One group of people seems relatively unaffected by how much their mental map must be rotated, whereas another group is highly susceptible to such errors. (Some people have such difficulty that they need to rotate a road map to their current driving orientation.) So there appear to be individual differences in the ability to rotate a mental map. This may be related to how well a person is able to use her spatial sketchpad in working memory.

However, if people learn a spatial area, such as a college campus, through experience rather than through a map, there may be no single orientation influence (Evans & Pezdek, 1980; Presson, DeLange, & Hazelrigg, 1989; see also McNamara et al., 1989). There may be general effects of a larger spatial framework, such as the walls of a room (Valiquette, McNamara, & Smith, 2003). Natural exploration exposes a person to a wide variety of perspectives. Hence, the mental map does not have a preferred viewing orientation. Figure 8.12 shows data from a study in which students were asked to make distance judgments for their own campus or for the map of an unfamiliar campus. An orientation effect was only observed for the unfamiliar campus.

A person's current perspective can have other influences. People often overestimate distances to locations near their current location but underestimate distances to places far away. This was embodied several years ago in some posters depicting the New Yorker's view of the world. These posters showed the locations of several places in New York as taking up a large

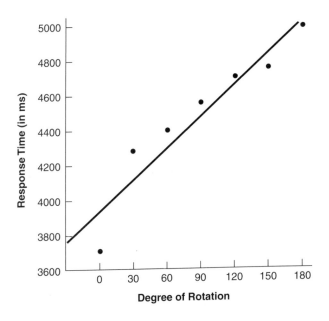

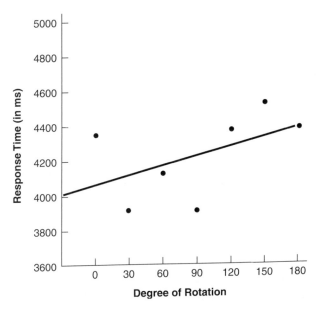

FIGURE 8.12   Mental Rotation Effects for Unknown and Known Campus Layouts. Mental rotation effects only observed for the unknown (map) campus condition.

Source: Evans & Pezdek, 1980

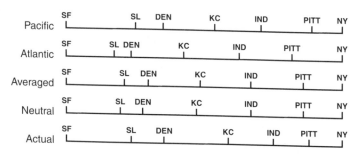

FIGURE 8.13 Effects of Relative City Locating Depending on the Point of View Taken at Retrieval. The cities tested here were San Francisco, Salt Lake, Denver, Kansas City, Indianapolis, Pittsburgh, and New York.

Source: Holyoak & Mah, 1982

area, but other, much bigger areas of the country were depicted as relatively small (and presumably insignificant). An interesting demonstration of the influence of perspective is a study by Holyoak and Mah (1982; see also Sholl, 1987). In this study students estimated the relative east-west locations of cities in the United States. Importantly, they were asked to make these judgments by imagining they were standing on the West Coast looking eastward, from the East Coast looking westward, or to simply make estimates (keep in mind the students were in Ann Arbor, Michigan). The results are presented in Figure 8.13. The estimated locations were biased based on the perspective. People who imagined themselves on the Pacific Coast reported the western cities being farther apart and the eastern cities being relatively close together, whereas the opposite was true for those who imagined they were standing on the Atlantic Coast. Finally, people who were simply asked to estimate the distances imposed a midwesterner's bias by spreading out the distance among cities in the middle of the United States.

Synopsis

Memory for space is generally pretty good. People's estimates of spatial qualities, such as distance, are very similar when made from memory as when they are looking right at something. People can create memories of spaces that they interact with, called mental maps. The organization and structure of these mental maps are influenced by various qualities of the spaces they represent. For example, they show influences of regions, routes, landmarks, semantic relations, and how the map information was originally learned. People's uses of spatial memories, such as mental maps, are influenced by the perspective people take when remembering. These perspective effects show that people often prefer a certain orientation of the mental map, especially for areas that are less familiar.

MEMORY FOR TIME

The other major physical property that we must deal with is time. In particular, we consider people's ability to remember *when* things happened. Like space, memory for time is not perfectly related to the actual flow of time. Instead, there are systematic distortions that vary with respect to the type of temporal information people are trying to remember.

There are three ways people can use memory for time (Friedman, 1993). The first is **temporal distance.** This is how in the past the event in memory occurred. The second is **temporal location.** This is knowing when an event took place, such as knowing a specific date. Finally, there is **relative time.** This is knowing the relative order of two or more events, such as knowing which came first. Friedman has used the analogy of an archeologist as a metaphor for understanding these three aspects of temporal memory. Temporal distance is like radiocarbon dating used to determine the age of an artifact. Temporal location is like looking at the characteristics of an artifact to determine to what time period it belongs, perhaps by comparing it to similar artifacts. Finally, relative time is used to place an artifact before or after other artifacts in time, perhaps based on the primitiveness or sophistication of one artifact relative to the others.

Phenomena

Using these three ways of thinking about time, we'll look at a number of phenomena that characterize memory for time and some of the theories that have been proposed to account for distortions in temporal memory.

Basic Memory Effects.   One of the most obvious things is that people have difficulty placing events in time. It is not unusual to misremember events as having occurred even several years before or after when they actually happened. This distortion of temporal memories, like most memories, is more likely to occur with older memories. That is, the further back in time the event was, the more likely it is that a mistake will be made in remembering when it happened. This is called the **memory age effect.**

This forgetting of older memories is really not that surprising. However, as with other memories, we can observe serial position curves in terms of the accuracy with which temporal information is retrieved (Toglia & Kimble, 1976; Zimmerman & Underwood, 1968). These serial position curves show a **primacy effect,** with people having better memory for the time of the first event of a certain type. For example, it is usually easy for people to remember when they got their first speeding ticket, but it is harder to remember subsequent tickets (I've only had one, so this is easy for me). There is also a **recency effect,** with people having superior memory for the time of recent events.

In addition, the ability to locate memories in time improves as the ability to identify the memory improves. That is, as memory for content information gets better, so does the accuracy with which a person locates the time from which it came. An illustration of this **accuracy effect** was provided in a study in which people were given either the melodies or titles to various songs that were popular anywhere from 2 to 56 years before. Although participants were able to locate songs in time better than chance when they did not consciously remember the song (25 percent accuracy), temporal memory was better if either the melody or the title was recognized (38 percent accuracy), and it was best if they could also remember the lyrics (60 percent accuracy) (Bartlett & Snelus, 1980). Essentially, the more information they could remembered from a song, the more accurately they remembered when it was popular.

Shifting in Time.   Another phenomenon is the **scale effect.** Scale effects reflect the fact that memory for when an event occurred may be accurate at one scale of time but be distorted at another. For example, a person may correctly remember that an event occurred on a Monday but misremember the week it occurred. An example of a scale effect is shown in Figure 8.14. This is data from a study done by Thompson, Skowronski, Larsen, and Betz (1996), in which they asked students at Kansas State University to record in diaries their experiences during the semester. At the end of the term they tested students' memories for events that transpired over the previous semester. Notice that along with the gradual shift in memory for the time of events, there are peaks that occur at regular intervals. Thus, as memory for the time of an event became distorted in terms of what week it occurred, there was some memory for the correct day.

Memories for when time events occurred can also be distorted by a process known as **forward telescoping.** This occurs when an event is placed more recently in time than when it actually occurred (Bradburn, Rips, & Shevell, 1985; Thompson, Skowronski, & Lee, 1988). For example, you might think something happened two years ago when it actually happened three years ago. Forward telescoping is likely to begin two months after the original event occurred, when sufficient forgetting has had an opportunity to set it. Furthermore, although it might seem that more vivid memories took place more recently because of their vividness, forward telescoping is unrelated to clarity of memory. Instead, the primary cause of telescoping is the amount of time that has elapsed since the event.

A related phenomenon is **backward telescoping.** This is when recent events are placed further back in time than they actually occurred. Backward telescoping is largely

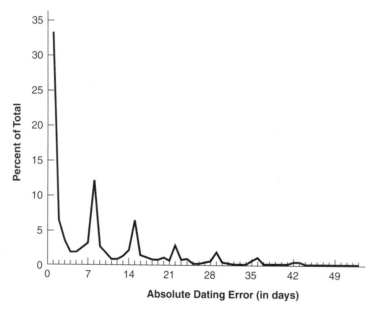

FIGURE 8.14   Results Showing a Scale Effect in Temporal Estimation

Source: Thompson, Skowronski, Larsen, & Betz, 1996

confined to recent memories (Rubin & Baddeley, 1989; Zacks et al., 1984). That is, very recent events can sometimes seem like they occurred a much longer time ago than they actually did. For example, in the evening, it may seem that the morning's events didn't even happen that day.

It has been suggested that these telescoping effects reflect uncertainty in time estimation and are a form of regression to the mean (Rubin & Baddeley, 1989). The presence of forward and backward telescoping can be assessed using memory psychophysics—that is, by looking at which component of the memory processes is being affected. Consistent with the presence of both these types of telescoping, psychophysical functions using Stevens's Law show slopes that are less than 1 and y-intercepts that are greater than 0 (Ferguson & Martin, 1983). This means that there is a general shift in memory for temporal events away from the extremes and more toward an average amount of time.

Ordering. Finally, memory for time can also refer to **order information.** People are fairly good at remembering the order in which events occurred. As a consequence of this, people can localize events in time by considering the order information. This can be either a forward order or a backward order. For example, Anderson and Conway (1993) found that people are better able to recall the sequence of events in their lives if they are recalled in a forward order, although a backward order of recall was fairly efficient as well. Recall attempts based on the relative importance of individual details of an event were the most difficult. In contrast, Whitten and Leonard (1981) found that students could recall their precollege teachers best when they tried to remember them in a backward order, worse in a forward order, and worst of all when they tried to remember them in a random order. Thus, in some way, temporal information is encoded as a part of the memory system.

Theories

A number of theories of temporal memory have been suggested. Following Friedman (1993), here are some of the more prominent ones. These theories can be broadly classified into distance-based, location-based, and relative time views. To help you keep track of the various theories and how well they explain the various phenomena just presented, all of this information is listed in Table 8.5.

Distance-Based Theories. Distance-based theories state that time estimates depend on how far in the past the original event is from the present. The simplest form are **trace strength models** (e.g., Brown, Rips, & Shevell, 1985). These theories believe that memory traces have strengths associated with them (see Chapter 7). The longer it has been since a trace was accessed, the weaker its strength will be. In contrast, stronger traces would refer to events that occurred recently. Thus, it would be straightforward to take the strength of a memory trace to determine its age. Such accounts can directly explain the memory age, recency, and relative ordering effects. This view can also explain why events that have been thought about frequently are remembered as being closer to the present. These memories gain strength each time they are retrieved (Brown et al., 1985).

There are a couple of related views. One is the **temporal sequence model** (e.g., Murdock, 1974), in which memory is compared to a conveyor belt. As memories are acquired,

TABLE 8.5 **Temporal Theories and the Effects They Predict**

	MEMORY AGE	PRIMACY	RECENCY	SCALE	TELESCOPING	RELATIVE ORDERING	ACCURACY EFFECT
Distance-Based Theories							
Trace strength	X		X		X	X	
Temporal sequence	X		X		X	X	
Contextual overlap	X		X	X		X	
Location-Based Theories							
Time-tag model	X			X		X	X
Perturbation	X	X	X	X		X	X
Reconstructive model	X	X	X	X	X	(X)	X
Relative Time Theories							
Associative chaining	X	X	X		X	X	X
Order code model	X	X	X		X	X	X
Category Adjustment Model	X	X	X	X	X	X	X

they are placed on the belt. The more time that has elapsed, the further away the memory is. Time information, from the present, could be directly determined. This is consistent with the idea that things that occur together in time may be associated in memory. This theory can account for some of the imprecision in time estimates (everything is relative).

Another view is the **contextual overlap model,** which is somewhat different in that it was not originally derived to deal with temporal memory (e.g., Glenberg et al., 1980). This view states that context is constantly in flux. Two events that are close in time are likely to be associated with contexts that have differed but only by a little. In contrast, events that are distant in time have very different contexts associated with them. Again, contexts can be either external or internal. According to this view, the greater the difference between the current context and the one associated with the memory trace, the older that trace is assumed to be. Your present situation is more similar to what it was last week, compared to a year ago, or even ten years ago.

It should be noted that, overall, distance-based theories have a number of problems. For example, they have difficulty with the primacy effect of the serial position curve, scale effects, and accuracy effects. In these theories there is no evaluation of the nature of the content of the memory, only its age. It should also be noted that this explanation of temporal memory does not have much to say about either forward or backward telescoping. There is no way to account for this regular plasticity in temporal memory.

Location-Based Theories.   Location-based theories state that the information needed to locate a memory in time is stored in the memory trace when it was originally encoded. The strength of the memory trace itself is not important. The simplest version of this view is the **time tag model,** in which people remember when something occurred because they store a tag with the memory for the event. That time tag would carry information about the hour, day, month, year, or whatever was relevant. All a person would need to do is read this information off of the memory trace. For example, I know that I officially started my current job on August 23, 1993. This is directly stored in my memory for that event. Some people have suggested that time tags may be associated with a biological clock (Tzeng, 1976), but although some memories have time information directly associated with them, most do not.

Another theory of temporal memory (which was also discussed in Chapter 4) is Estes's **perturbation model** (e.g., Estes, 1985). This theory assumes that memories are associated with contextual control elements that break up memories into chunks. Temporal information is derived from the control units, and errors in temporal memory are attributed to errors in the way perturbation changes have occurred. Thus, a person may remember that last week (a contextual control unit) she purchased a television and called her cousin in Virginia, but, because of perturbation errors, she might mislocate these memories to the wrong day. This theory does a good job of explaining scale effects.

A final location-based theory is the **reconstructive model.** According to this view, locating a memory in time is determined through a reconstructive inference process. This is based on the knowledge in the memory trace. People figure out the time of an event using information they know to be true, as well as similar events whose time is known. For example, I remember what happened to me on May 1, 1983. I remember seeing a number of people in old convertibles driving through Cleveland's near west side, shouting and waving signs. This was in the late afternoon on my way home from school. I remember it was May 1 because these people were members of the local Communist party, and there was also a brief segment about them on the news that night. They were shouting about how there should be a revolt of the workers and that communism should replace the current political system (it didn't happen). I know it was May 1 because this is an important date in communism, and I know it was 1983 because I was coming home from high school, which would have made it 1980, 1981, 1982, or 1983. I also remember discussing this with a girl I was dating at the time, and I did not date her until my senior year, so it must have been 1983. Thus, using my knowledge of the event combined with the circumstances of my life at the time, I can make inferences about the date. This is right in line with the reconstructive theory.

Location-based theories of temporal memory fare pretty well. The memory age effect can be attributed to a loss of either the time tag or context information needed to locate the memory in time, including the introduction of perturbations. Serial position curves can also be accounted for. Primacy effects are attributed to both the superior memory for the event itself, as well as for any temporal information associated with it. This is assisted by the fact that the early occurrence of events of a certain type makes those events more temporally distinct, which also makes them better remembered. Scale effects are accounted for by the loss of aspects of a time tag, an error at one level of contextual control but not another, or being able to use information in the memory to reconstruct temporal information more accurately. For example, remembering an event that occurred at church could be easily reconstructed to be an event that occurred on a Sunday, which is very likely to be accurate, but the memory is vague enough that the year cannot be accurately reconstructed. Telescoping effects are explained by the reconstructive model by assuming that memory traces may be distorted based on the amount of content recovered. Relative ordering effects can be directly accounted for by the timetag and perturbation models. They can also be explained to some degree by reconstruction theories, although not as well. Finally, accuracy effects are easily accounted for from this view. The more that is retained in a memory trace, the more accurate the time tag, the better the control units, or the more reliable the information used for reconstruction.

Relative Time Theories.   The relative time theory states that relative temporal order information is stored directly in memory. That is, information about other events and their relative temporal relation to one another is stored along with the memory of the event itself. According to a simple **associative chaining model** (e.g., Lewandowsky & Murdock, 1989), along with an event are stored associations of prior occurrences of events of the same type. To locate an event in time, one assesses how it is associated with other events to which it is related. Specifically, did it occur before or after these other events? Thus, by determining where the event is in a sequence, one can figure out its temporal location.

Another relative time theory is the **order code model** (e.g., Hintzman, Summers, & Block, 1975). According to this view, every time an event occurs, all of the related events become activated in memory. Thus, people are reminded of previous similar situations they have been in. These reminded events then get associated with the memory for the current event. So the more recent an event is, the more reminded events that are associated with it. Of course, the first event of that type has no additional memories associated. Thus, a person may be able to locate an event in time, at least relatively, by using information about other events that were associated with it during the reminding process.

Obviously, these theories can directly account for relative order effects. But they can explain other things as well, such as the memory age effect in that older memories are more likely to have lost the needed associations. They can also explain serial position effects. For the order code models, older memories would have the greatest number of associations, so they are the easiest to locate. They are also remembered better as well for this reason, accounting for the accuracy effect. Conversely, the recency effect occurs because these memories have had the least amount of forgetting and the largest number of associations. Forward telescoping is explained as a loss of associations, making the memory seem not so old. However, these theories do have difficulty explaining scale effects, because information about temporal scale is not preserved, only relative orderings and backward telescoping, because there is no reason to expect such a distortion.

Category Adjustment Model of Time.   Using an approach similar to understanding spatial memory, Huttenlocher and colleagues (Huttenlocher, Hedges, & Bradburn, 1990; Huttenlocher, Hedges, & Prohaska, 1988) have developed a theory of temporal memory. Again, it is assumed that memories are stored at two levels: a fine-grained level and a coarse-grained level. The information at the coarse-grained level would include large categories of time, such as 7, 10, 14, 21, 30, and 60 days. Estimates of when events occurred in time would reflect a combination of both the detailed and categorical information. The temporal categories serve the role of both placing limits on which events could have occurred (such as knowing that a lecture must have happened sometime between the beginning and the end of a semester), as a well as a basis for rounding estimates when there is uncertainty at the fine-grained level.

This fuzzy trace approach can account for memory age and accuracy effects because the forgetting of information at the fine-grained level is more likely to occur as memories get older. Serial position effects are also readily explained. Recency effects are due to a relatively small amount of forgetting, whereas primacy effects reflect memories that are more likely to occur at a temporal border and so are likely to be easily located within that category. The use of coarse-grained information explains scale effects because the scales often correspond to categorical values. Also, both forward and backward telescoping are explained as tendencies to rely more on categorical prototypes when fine-grained information has been forgotten. Finally, ordering effects are accounted for in a way similar to the perturbation model. In fact, this view of temporal memory is described as being very similar to the perturbation model.

Synopsis

Memory for time is worse than memory for space. Memories for when things happened are fraught with distortions and errors. In addition to general memory errors due to the age and serial position of the information in memory, there are a number of other factors that can distort memories of time. For example, temporal memories show effects, such as scale effects, involving categories of time, as well as consistent telescoping that shift memories in time in a regular fashion. Despite these errors, it should be kept in mind that people do seem to be able to remember the proper sequence or order in which event occurred, even if they cannot place them properly in time. Various theories of temporal memory have struggled to capture the qualities of temporal memory. These include distance theories that are based on the age of the memory, location-based theories that are based on knowing when the information occurred in time, relative time theories that derive estimates of time based on memory for the order of events, and mixture models, such as the category adjustment theory, that take into account a number of mental processes acting on memory for time.

SUMMARY

In this chapter we looked at memory for time and space. Memory for spatial information is fairly reliable. When distortions in spatial memory occur, they are very systematic to the point of obeying psychophysical principles. The mental maps that are stored in memory are rarely metric representations that directly capture the Euclidean information in a spatial layout. Instead, they are hierarchically distorted by the spatial regions that compose the map, as well as the temporal order in which the information was learned. The organization of mental maps is also influenced by semantic knowledge and important landmarks. When using a mental map from memory, accuracy is influenced by the initial orientation of the map, as well as the perspective a person takes on a space being thought about.

Memory for time is less reliable than memory for space. Memory for when events occurred is influenced by how old the memories are, when they occurred in a sequence, the particular time period in which they occurred, and how well the memory is remembered in general. A number of theories of temporal memory were presented that looked at how temporal memories were derived by using the age of the memory itself, information in memory that can use used to determine time, and the relative position of that memory with respect to other memories.

STUDY QUESTIONS

1. How can psychophysical principles be applied to memory?

2. To what degree and how are memories for space distorted with respect to actually perceiving a space? Why?

3. What are some of the major factors about a space that can influence the organization of a mental map?

4. What are the different ways of experiencing or learning the information that will go into a mental map, and how do they influence the final nature of that mental map?

5. How good is a person's memory for time?

6. What are some of the characteristics of memory that affect the ability to remember when something happened?

7. In what ways does memory for time get distorted?

8. What are the major classes of theories that try to account for people's ability to remember when things happened? What are the strengths and weaknesses of each of these theories?

KEY TERMS

accuracy effect, associative chaining models, backward telescoping, Category Adjustment Theory, contextual overlap model, distance-based theories, forward telescoping, hierarchical view, hybrid theories, memory age effect, metric view, order code model, order information, orientation effect, partially hierarchical view, perspective, perturbation model, primacy effect, psychophysics, recency effect, reconstructive model, relative time, reperceptual hypothesis, route perspective, scale effect, spatial frameworks, spatial gradient of availability, Steven's Law, survey perspective, temporal distance, temporal location, temporal organization, temporal sequence model, time tag model, trace strength model, transformation hypothesis, uncertainty hypothesis

CHAPTER NINE

SEMANTIC MEMORY

Sometimes our memories do not refer to specific events but are more encyclopedic. This general knowledge of the world is **semantic memory.** This type of memory allows us to take advantage of regularities in the world to make more accurate predictions about what will happen next. For example, if all you had to go on were episodic memories of specific instances, then every time you encountered a dog you would have to start all over again figuring out the safety of the situation or how you should react. Every time you saw a new chair, you would need to determine what its purpose was. Every time you went to a restaurant, you would have to learn the procedure for dining and how to get some food. Semantic memories are generalizations that can apply to a wide variety of similar but different circumstances.

In this chapter we look at a number of aspects of semantic memory. We first address the issue of semantic memory organization and how it provides us with not only the information we may need at the time, but also other related information that is likely to be relevant. This is semantic priming. We examine two types of semantic memories and how we use them to understand our world. One is how categories are structured and used. We will see how ordered relations are represented and how these relations influence memory more generally. The second types of semantic memories are scripts and schemas for commonly experienced aspects of life. Finally, we spend some time looking at cases where semantic memory falls short of our expectations and desires.

SEMANTIC PRIMING

A salient characteristic of semantic memory is its highly organized and regular structure. General knowledge is stored and/or remembered in such a way that remembering one concept brings related memories closer to awareness. This facilitation of related ideas is called *priming* (Meyer & Schvaneveldt, 1971), with people responding faster to a concept after it has been primed. In a typical priming study people are given a lexical decision task. That is, they are given strings of letters and asked to say whether they are words. For example, "doctor" is a word, but "dohter" is not. In these studies there are pairs of words. There is a critical trial, called a prime, that is followed immediately by a target. What is of interest is how fast people respond to the target (such as by pressing a button). If the prime is unrelated to the target, this is a baseline, control condition—for example, if the target "nurse" is preceded by the prime "potato." If the prime is semantically related to the target, this is the experimental condition—for example, if the target "nurse" is preceded by the prime "doctor." Generally, people are faster to respond to the target in the experimental condition relative to the control. Priming is even observed in ERP recordings as early as 250 ms after the target word is presented (Bentin, McCarthy, & Wood, 1985).

Semantic priming occurs because concepts are not understood in isolation but in terms of how they relate to other ideas. By activating related concepts, a person is bringing to bear a larger set of knowledge to help her understand what is happening. Priming also helps a person detect inconsistencies. When people encounter semantically anomalous information, such as hearing a sentence like "The doctor listened with his carrot," ERP recordings show an increased negativity in electrical potential around 400 ms after being given semantically anomalous information (Kutas & Hillyard, 1980). This semantic inconsistency detection is called the N400.

Semantic memory is structured based on shared aspects of meaning, not prior associations (Thompson-Schill, Kurtz, & Gabrieli, 1998). Thus, concepts that are similar are metaphorically stored closer in semantic memory. This can even include emotional states. For example, people respond faster to happy words such as "peace" when in a happy mood and faster to sad words such as "die" when in a sad mood (Olafson & Ferraro, 2001). When a concept is activated and retrieved from memory, this activation is not limited to that one concept but spreads to related concepts. Because these concepts have been activated somewhat, if there is then a need to use them, it is now closer to conscious awareness and can be used more quickly. This is priming.

The inclusion of information in semantic memory requires a great deal of exposure to move it from episodic to semantic memory. For example, in a study by Dagenbach, Horst, and Carr (1990), college students did not show significant priming of newly learned words until after five weeks of practice with the information. The learning of new relationships between existing concepts in semantic memory did not show priming even after such extended practice. Thus, the conversion of knowledge from episodic memory to semantic memory is a highly involved and drawn out process.

Controlled Priming

In general, priming is a more or less automatic process that is dominated by implicit memory. Still, it is possible for priming to be affected and redirected by conscious effort. This is shown most clearly in a study by Neely (1977) where people were given category names followed by a lexical decision task. These lexical decision trials came 250, 400, or 700 ms after the category name. This difference between the onset of the category name and the lexical decision trial is called the stimulus onset asynchrony, or SOA.

There were five conditions of interest. The pattern of results for each of these conditions is shown in Figure 9.1. The first condition was Nonshift-Expected-Related in which people expected that if a word followed the category name, it would be a member of that category, and it was—for example, seeing the category name "BIRD" followed by the word "robin." As can be seen in Figure 9.1, consistent positive priming was observed at all SOAs.

A second condition was Nonshift-Unexpected-Unrelated, in which people expected that if a word followed the category name, it would be a member of that category, but it was

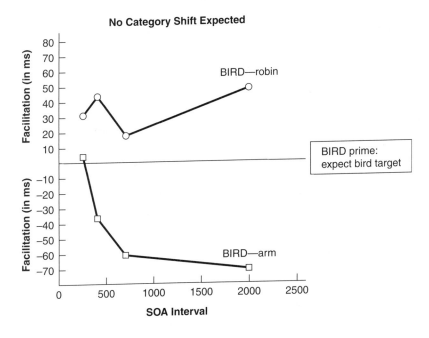

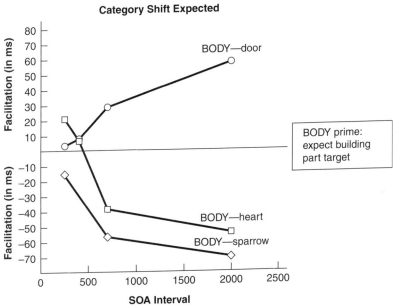

FIGURE 9.1   Automatic and Controlled Priming in Semantic Memory

Source: Neely, 1977

not—for example, seeing "BIRD" followed by "arm." As can be seen in Figure 9.1, there is initially no effect on response time, but later people are actually slower to respond to "arm" because the activation in semantic memory has all been directed to the "BIRD" portion. Thus, it takes longer to disengage from this part of semantic memory and move it to another one.

The third condition was Shift-Expected-Unrelated, in which people expected that when a word followed a category name, it would be a member of a certain unrelated category, and it was. An example of this would be seeing "BODY" followed by "door" when a building part was expected. As can be seen in Figure 9.1, positive priming develops over time. The idea is that if people expect a BUILDING part when they get "BODY," they can consciously activate that portion of semantic memory, but this conscious process takes time.

The fourth condition, Shift-Unexpected-Unrelated, was similar to the preceeding, except the word was a member of some other unrelated category—for example, seeing "BODY" followed by "sparrow." As can be seen in Figure 9.1, there is initially some negative priming, and this gets larger over time. The idea is that because people expect a BUILDING part when they get "BODY," they have consciously activated the BUILDING part of semantic memory, and it requires a great deal of effort to disengage this activation and move it to another portion.

The fifth condition was Shift-Unexpected-Related, which is similar to the previous two, except the word is a member of the same category as the prime—for example, seeing "BODY" followed by "heart." As can be seen in Figure 9.1, there is initially some positive priming. This suggests that there is an automatic process that activates the portion of semantic memory associated with the probe. However, over time, people have consciously shifted away activation to another part of semantic memory. As such, people need to engage in more effort to disengage from the part that is expected and move back to the original portion. This is supported by EEG recordings that show that the automatic activation of information in semantic memory emphasizes the parieto-temporal cortex, whereas the conscious evaluation of semantic information emphasizes the frontal lobes (e.g., Krause, Gibbons, & Schack, 1998).

Mediated Priming

The theory behind semantic priming is that when a concept in memory is activated, this activation spreads to related concepts, which are then at a higher level of availability than they were previously. From this perspective, the question becomes, how far does this spread go? Do only those concepts that are directly related to the first receive this spreading activation, or does it go beyond that? For example, when retrieving the concept "lion," it is likely that the concept "tiger" will be activated because these are both large, predatory cats. If "tiger" becomes primed, will concepts related to it, but not "lion," also be activated, such as the concept "stripes"? To test this, a memory researcher would have a person retrieve the concept "lion" and then look at how the ability to retrieve "stripes" is affected. This is called **mediated priming** because the connection between "lion" and "stripes" is mediated by "tiger."

In general, mediated priming does occur (McNamara & Altarriba, 1988), as shown by using both response times and ERP recordings (particularly the N400 component) of changes in cortical activity (Chwilla, Kolk, & Mulder, 2000; Hill, Strube, Roesch-Ely, & Weisbrod, 2002). However, as you might expect, mediated priming is smaller in magnitude than regular priming, and it is sometimes nonexistent (e.g., De Groot, 1983). The further away concepts are from the original, the less likely that meaningful priming will occur.

Semantic Interconnectivity

In episodic memory, it has been found that increased numbers of associations with a concept can slow down retrieval time. This is the fan effect. Semantic memory is composed of a very large number of associations among concepts. This interconnectivity can be thought of as a complex network of concepts and associations. These network models are described in more detail in Chapter 10. For now, it is important to note that there are a large number of connections among concepts in semantic memory. And so, based on the fan effect, one would expect that it should be very difficult to retrieve information from semantic memory. However, the opposite is true. Specifically, concepts in semantic memory that have a greater number of interconnections are retrieved faster (Kroll & Klimesch, 1992) and allow people to make responses based on partial information (Kounios, Montgomery, & Smith, 1994).

This is because in semantic memory these associations provide both direct and indirect connections between concepts. That is, two semantic memory concepts might be directly associated but also share a number of intermediate concepts, which functionally increases the number of retrieval pathways between them. As a result, there are many ways that concepts can prime one another. The more indirect connections there are, the more likely any one of those pathways would have been traversed by activation after a given period of time has passed. Think of this as a horse race. If there are a lot of horses running, the race being will be over faster than if only a few horses are racing because there is more likely to be a fast horse in the bunch.

Inhibition

Like episodic memory, **inhibition** can also be used to help narrow the appropriate part of semantic memory. During retrieval, related concepts may be inhibited, such as when a person generates information, but not when it is simply heard or read. For example, people retrieve the concept "salmon" for the category name "FISH" more slowly if they had recently retrieved several other examples of fish. Specifically, this inhibition occurs when people actively retrieve information than if they are passively reading (Blaxton & Neely, 1983; Johnson & Anderson, 2004; Roediger, Neely, & Blaxton, 1983). The need to select a specific semantic memory causes the inhibition of related competitors that could produce interference.

Nature of Semantic Information

The nature of semantic memories is complex because semantic memories are supposed to capture all of our general knowledge about the world. Although some of the theories we encounter give the impression that semantic memory has a clear structure, like a computer database, we must keep in mind that this is a memory system with a human face. Semantic memories, in addition to reflecting abstract relations among concepts and ideas, also capture how we interact with the world. For example, even simple things like how we represent nouns and verbs reflect different aspects of semantic memory. Using ERP recordings, it has been found that nouns, particularly concrete nouns of objects that you can see, tend to activate more of the sensory cortex in the parietal lobe, whereas verbs of action tend to activate more of the motor cortex in the frontal lobe (Pulvermüller, Lutzenberger, & Preissl, 1999).

This influence of embodied cognition is reflected in the fact that the availability of information about concepts shows evidence of perceptual effort during memory retrieval (Solomon & Barsalou, 2004). The amount of visual area taken up by the property can be used as an index of perceptual effort. For the concept "fish," the property "scales" is relatively easy to remember, whereas the property "eye" is more difficult. This embodied influence on semantic memories also applies to emotional responses to concepts (Olafson & Ferraro, 2001).

Synopsis

The activation of knowledge in semantic memory causes the priming of related concepts. After an initial, automatic priming process, a person may also engage a more consciously controlled search. This priming can extend beyond immediately related concepts, as in mediated priming. Semantic memory retrieval, more generally, is facilitated by more connections among concepts, which is the reverse of episodic memory. However, priming does have its limits, and people can actually be slowed if they have recently actively selected related concepts.

CONCEPTS AND CATEGORIES

An important job of semantic memory is the organization of concepts and categories. Rather than remember lots of bits and pieces about the world, we group together this knowledge. This similarity-based grouping is **categorization,** in which two or more entities are treated as though they are equivalent. Essentially, a **concept** is a mental construct that contains information associated with an idea, whereas a **category** is a class of concepts to which a set of assertions applies. The process of categorization allows us to draw on prior experience in a regular and reliable fashion in new situations. This way, a person does not need to spend as much time thinking about how to act in new situations. Some assumptions can be made that the elements of the new situation are like those that were observed previously. For example, having the category "dog" in semantic memory allows a person to treat members of that category as being more or less the same, such as knowing that all dogs eat dog food, may bite, and like to run.

In this section of the chapter we look at various ideas about how semantic memory categorizes information. We first look at some properties of human categories, followed by a number of theories of categorization (Medin, 1989; Medin & Smith, 1984). After this, we look at cases of human categorization in social situations, namely stereotypes and prejudice.

Properties of Categories

Human categories are complex, with the various category members relating to the category in different ways. One of the ways that people use categories can be seen in the **levels of**

categorization. Essentially, there are three levels of categorization: basic, subordinate, and superordinate (Rosch & Mervis, 1975). The basic level is the one we operate with most often. It is at this level that categories are defined by features that provide enough detail to allow us to treat different members of the category as similar but without providing more detail than is often necessary. Examples of basic level categories are things like saw, dogs, chair, or drum. The subordinate level provides detailed information about more specific portions of a basic category. Examples of subordinate level categories are things like camping saw, miniature poodle, leather recliner, and kettle drum. Finally, the superordinate level provides very general information that captures a wide range of basic level categories. Examples of superordinate categories are tool, pet, furniture, and musical instrument.

This distinction is psychologically important because this reflects differences in how people use categories. In general, basic level category information is retrieved better than the other two (Rosch et al., 1976). People are able to retrieve more attributes that are particular to basic level categories and are able to retrieve the names of basic level categories more quickly than the others (Tversky & Hemenway, 1984). This difference in retrieval speed is shown in Figure 9.2. This suggests that the basic level of categorization has some kind of primacy in semantic memory.

Categories have many members. Their combined influence gives rise to a category in memory and manifests itself in several ways. First, there is a **central tendency,** or averaged ideal for the category. Second, categories have **graded membership.** Some members of the category are thought of as being better members of the category than others. For example, "robin" is often thought of as being a better member of the category "bird" than "penguin."

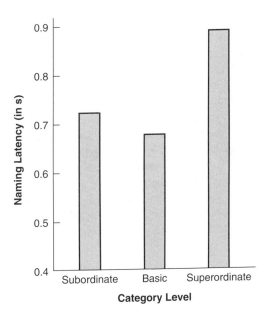

FIGURE 9.2   Naming Time for Concepts at Different Category Levels

Source: Tversky & Hemenway, 1984

Alternatively, some things are ambiguous category members that may be marked with linguistic hedges—for example, statements like "technically, a tomato is a fruit" or "loosely speaking, a bat is a bird."

Finally, members of a category might not be defined by a single set of features but may share characteristics. This is called **family resemblance** (Rosch & Mervis, 1975). An example of this would be the members of the category "furniture." Many types of furniture have legs, are made of wood, are intended to be used indoors, but this is not true of all types of furniture. These principles of categorization illustrate that people are sensitive to the correlations among features that define categories—for example, the idea that flying tends to go with birds and tire tends to go with bicycles. This is true both in terms of how categories are distinguished from one another, as well as the features that create a family resemblance within categories (Chin-Parker & Ross, 2002).

Classical Theory of Categorization

When you first think of categories, you might think of the rules that are used to define them—for example, knowing that a "bachelor" is an unmarried adult male, that an "even number" is divisible by two, and that "speeding" is going faster than the posted limit. The idea that categories are defined by necessary and sufficient features is the **classical view of categorization.** They are necessary in that these features must be present, and they are sufficient in that as long as they are present, something is a member of the category. Any additional information is irrelevant.

A study by Bruner, Goodnow, and Austin (1956) provided support for the classical view. In this study, people were shown figures in the set shown in Figure 9.3. In this set, each item can be identified along a number of dimensions, including the type of objects, their number, their color, and the number of borders. When people are given subsets of items, along with an indication of whether each one is a member of the category, people have little difficulty deriving the rules that define the categories. Three category derivation examples, from relatively simple to more complex, are provided in Figures 9.4, 9.5, and 9.6.

Although it may seem that human categories follow this rule-based approach, it quickly becomes clear that this theory has serious problems. For example, it cannot explain the ideas of central tendency, graded membership, and family resemblance. This is clearly seen when one looks at human memory for categories that should clearly and directly follow the rules of necessity and sufficiency. For example, the categories of "even numbers" and "odd numbers" are very well and simply defined. However, these categories show graded membership (Armstrong, Gleitman, & Gleitman, 1983). For example, in the data shown in Table 9.1, "4" is rated by people as being a better example of the category "even number" than "106" is, even though technically they are both equally acceptable members of this category.

Prototype Theory

It is clear that categories are organized around the unconscious mental statistics we keep about various categories. One approach to capturing these qualities is the **prototype model** of categorization. According to this view, categories are determined by a mental representation

FIGURE 9.3   Set of Stimuli Used to Illustrate the Classical View of Categorization

(*Source:* Bruner, Goodnow, & Austin, 1956

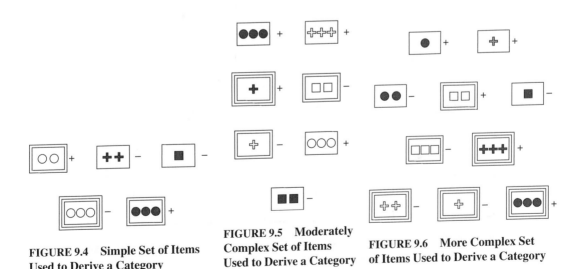

FIGURE 9.4   Simple Set of Items Used to Derive a Category

FIGURE 9.5   Moderately Complex Set of Items Used to Derive a Category

FIGURE 9.6   More Complex Set of Items Used to Derive a Category

TABLE 9.1   Ratings of Items (Out of 6) for a Well-Defined Category—in this Case, Odd and Even Numbers

EVEN NUMBER	RATING	ODD NUMBER	RATING
4	5.9	3	5.4
8	5.5	7	5.1
10	5.3	23	4.6
18	4.4	57	4.4
34	3.6	501	3.5
106	3.1	447	3.3

Source: Armstrong, Gleitman, & Gleitman, 1983.

that is an average of all of the category members. This averaged mental representation is called a prototype (Rosch, 1975). It may or may not correspond to an actual entity in the world. For example, the prototype for "dog" would be an average of all dogs ever encountered and may not correspond to any particular breed of dog. An example of prototype extraction using dot patterns is shown in Figure 9.7. The prototypes for the two categories are shown at the left. In this study, when people first learned the categories, they were shown deviations from the prototypes, such as those on the right. The prototypes were never shown. However, when people were later asked to sort both old and new patterns, the proto-

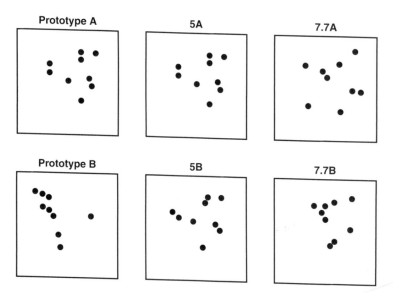

FIGURE 9.7   Dot Patterns of Deviations (Right) Derived from a Prototype (Left)
Source: Posner & Keele, 1970

types were identified and correctly sorted at a high rate of accuracy, suggesting that categorization was working to derive a prototype, which was then later easily and readily recognized (Posner & Keele, 1968; 1970).

This importance of prototypes can even be seen with more meaningful stimuli. For example, in some studies photographs of people's faces are used for making preference judgments along with morphed composites of these faces. What is found is that people prefer and rate as more attractive the composite faces, which are closer to the prototype face (Langlois & Roggman, 1990; Langlois, Roggman, & Musselman, 1994; Rhodes et al., 2003; but see Alley & Cunningham, 1991). That is, people show a greater preference for faces that are averages of the others. Because these faces are averages, they have fewer unusual and distinguishing characteristics. A pretty face is a boring face. This is part of the reason why attractive faces are more difficult to remember (Light, Hollander, & Kayra-Stuart, 1981). Similarly high attractiveness for more prototypical instances is also observed for dogs, cats, watches, birds, fish, and automobiles (Halberstadt & Rhodes, 2000; 2003).

The nice thing about prototypes is that they provide a clear explanation for central tendencies in a category (which would be the prototype itself) and graded category structure. The closer a given instance is to the prototype, the better it is a member of the category.

However, there are important aspects of categories that are not accounted for. For example, people are often aware of the size of a category—that is, about how many different members are in the category. With a prototype there is also no information about how much variability there is among members of the category. This kind of information cannot be derived from a single prototype representation. Also, our categories change as we continue to go through life. However, the prototype does not capture this kind of information. For example, a caricature (a category member with exaggerated features on one or more dimensions) is considered a better representative of a category than a prototype when the category is considered in the context of other, related categories (Goldstone, Steyvers, & Rogosky, 2003). That is, the caricature captures distinctive features of the category and emphasizes them in an extreme way rather than presenting them as an average of all the members. This helps distinguish a category from other, similar categories that might otherwise cause interference and confusion. However, although caricatures are better representatives of a category, at least for faces, they are rated as less attractive than the prototype (Rhodes and Tremewan, 1996).

Exemplar Theory

Another approach to understanding categorization is **exemplar theory** (Medin & Shaffer, 1978; Nosofsky, 1988). In this view, rather than deriving prototypes, people use all the category members to make memory decisions. Thus, this view captures central tendency, graded membership, and family resemblance, as well as information about category size, variability, correlated attributes, and any new information about it. Because categorization is always using all of the memory traces in that category, any new experiences will have an influence.

Another advantage of exemplar theories is their ability to explain the context sensitivity of categories. For example, the color gray is seen as being more similar to white in the context of hair color but as being more similar to black in the context of clouds (Medin & Shoben, 1988). The selection of exemplars constantly changes, depending on the particular memory traces that happen to be used. Also, more priming is experienced when the contexts are experienced similarly. For example, people are primed more for a pony *mane* after verifying a horse *mane* than a lion's *mane*. This is because the pony mane is more perceptually similar to a horse's than a lion's (Solomon & Barsalou, 2001). Finally, previously activated semantic meanings can bias how new information is interpreted (Gagne & Shoben, 2002). For example, a phrase like "adolescent doctor" is easier to interpret if it follows the phrase "animal doctor" than if it follows "country doctor." In this case, both "adolescent doctor" and "animal doctor" refer to the kind of patient the doctor treats, whereas "country doctor" refers to where the doctor lives.

A serious problem with both prototype and exemplar theories is an inherent circularity. Specifically, categories are defined by the experiences with members of that category. That is, the various members of the category all contribute to defining it. However, the memory traces that are selected are those that conform to the criteria of the category. In short, how can memory traces be selected to define a category if the category is needed to select them in the first place?

Explanation-Based Theory

Another view of categorization is that people are trying to provide some reason for why things should be grouped together. For example, wings often goes with having feathers, and people are sensitive to this probabilistic relationship. According to explanation-based views, when people form categories, they try to come up with some theory or explanation for why those things tend to go together. For example, feathers and wings tend to go together because feathers are well suited for helping a creature fly through the air. This idea that people are seeking out and using prior knowledge to understand how members of a category form a coherent group allows us to create categories (Rehder & Ross, 2001). Examples of this would be social groups, political events (e.g., revolutions), and social institutions (e.g., governments), which may not share physical features but that overlap in a thematic way.

Another aspect of how memory constructs categories is that people can create new categories on the fly. These are called **ad hoc categories** (Barsalou, 1983). For example, coffee, perfume, leather, and skunks can all be members of the category "things with a distinctive smell." These ad hoc categories are interesting because people can generate them off the cuff, but they have many of the same properties as standard categories, such as having a central tendency, graded structures, and family resemblance, and people know how large they are. This provides insight into how easily semantic memory structures can be generated, and it raises questions about the stability of semantic memory in general.

One theory of how we create categories in the pursuit of some explanation of the world is **psychological essentialism.** This is the idea that all the members of a category have some underlying essence that people may or may not be aware of. This usually applies to natural kind categories, which can be defined by chemical structure or DNA, such as "water" or "skunk," although some artifact categories, such as "scientific instruments," are treated by people as if they have essentialist category qualities, and some natural kind categories, like "humans," do not (Kalish, 2002). People create categories pragmatically, as is needed (Kalish, 2002), to serve a purpose. The degree to which members fit a category is a function of the degree to which they serve or fulfill that purpose. Overall, causal relations among category attributes is an important part in creating categories in semantic memory (Rehder & Hastie, 2001). Causally more important features are stronger determiners of a category. That is, they provide more of a psychological essence than peripheral features (Ahn, Kim, Lassaline, & Dennis, 2000).

The human impulse to explain how things are categorized can even be observed in cases where there is an attempt to provide categories without theories, such as with the American Psychological Association's *Diagnostic and Statistical Manual of Mental Disorders*. The original intent was to provide a means for clinicians to diagnose mental disorders without having to subscribe to a particular theory. This way, clinicians with a psychodynamic, humanistic, behavior modification, or any other perspective could all arrive at the same diagnosis of a person's condition, even if their theoretical view would provide different explanations of the causes and the treatments. However, despite this attempt to make the manual theory independent, individual clinicians still use the manual based on their theory-based understandings of the various diagnostic categories (Kim & Ahn, 2002). As a result, the same patient presenting the same symptoms might be diagnosed differently.

Stereotypes and Prejudice

There is no question that the process of categorization, on the whole, is a valuable aspect of semantic memory. However, this process can cause problems. One way that categorization can be problematic is when we engage in stereotyping and prejudice. Stereotypes are categories for various groups of people. When you stereotype someone, you are treating that person as if they are essentially the same as any other member of that group. When this stereotype causes one person to treat another person in an inappropriate manner, this is prejudice. So, overall, while categorization is useful, we must be careful to ensure that any categories we form about people are accurate and fair. More important, we need to be aware that categorization is a very human way to think about things, but we need to exert some effort to monitor our thoughts and behavior so that we do not inappropriately classify people.

Synopsis

A central aspect of semantic memory is the ability to create and use categories. People's categories seem to be oriented around a basic level and show evidence of central tendency and graded membership with family resemblance among the members. Human categorization does not appear to follow the rules of the classical categorization model. Instead, it operates using probabilistic information, as in prototype and exemplar theories. Moreover, it also exhibits characteristics to suggest that people are problem solving their way through category creation, with the use of explanation-based categories. This categorization process can go awry when inappropriately extended to people.

ORDERED RELATIONS

Another characteristic of semantic memory is the influence of the structures of knowledge ordered along some dimension, such as size, intelligence, age, and so forth. The influences of these orderings on remembering are called linear order effects (e.g., Banks, 1977).

One ordering effect is the **semantic distance effect,** in which people are quicker to make judgments about the relative order of two items as the distance between them increases (Potts, 1972; Rips, Shoben, & Smith, 1973). For example, it is easier to judge that an elephant is bigger than a rabbit than to judge that a dog is bigger than a rabbit. The idea is that the farther two concepts are along a given dimension, the easier it is to distinguish between them, and so people can retrieve and compute this information quickly. However, concepts that are relatively close in semantic memory are harder to discriminate, so judgments that require a person to distinguish between them are slower and more error prone.

With the **semantic congruity effect** people are faster to judge the relationship between two items if the valence of the comparison term matches the end of the ordered dimension at which the objects are located (Banks, Clark, & Lucy, 1975). For example, it is easier to judge that Jefferson was president before Monroe than to judge that Monroe was president after Jefferson because both are at the "early" end of the dimension. Information about that dimension is stored in semantic memory along with the concepts. For example, Jefferson and Monroe are both thought of as early U.S. presidents. As a result, the attribute of "early" would be stored directly with these concepts in semantic memory. When this information is needed, if the attributes match the judgment, people can respond more quickly than if there is a mismatch. If there is a mismatch, people need to engage in more thinking to get the information lined up properly.

Finally, with the **serial position effect** people are faster to judge relationships between items at the ends of an ordered dimension than those in the middle (Shoben, Cech, Schwanenflugel, & Sailor, 1989). For example, it is easier to judge that Rhode Island is smaller than Connecticut than it is to judge that Indiana is smaller than Ohio. Items that are at the ends of a dimension are more distinct and, therefore, easier to discriminate, so people can make semantic decisions more quickly. However, to some extent, people can make these sorts of semantic decisions on the fly. For example, if, during the course of a study, semantic memories, such as animal sizes, are broken down into two categories—large animals (e.g., horse, whale, rhino) and small animals (e.g., flea, rat, snail)—people show serial position effects for both subsets, not just for the extreme ends of the entire set (Cech, Shoben, & Love, 1990).

More generally, serial position effects, like those observed in short-term memory (see Chapter 4), are also observed in long-term semantic memory. When people recall information from semantic memory, there often are primacy and recency effects, with information being remembered better from the beginning and end of a series. For example, serial position curves have been observed for memories for U.S. presidents (Roediger & Crowder, 1976) and for church hymns (Maylor, 2002). In this case, the serial position curves are due to the frequency of exposure to information, with people encountering the names of the very early and the very recent presidents more so than the others (Healy, Havas, & Parker, 2000). This also accounts for the fact that Lincoln is remembered much better than he should be. His name is encountered quite a bit even though he is neither an early nor a recent president. Thus, there are a number of influences of ordered relations in semantic memory on the ability to retrieve knowledge.

SCHEMAS AND SCRIPTS

In life, there are many different types of situations that are fairly regular in how they unfold and operate and how we are expected to react to them. That is, commonly experienced aspects of life have some shared framework that unites them. We are able to capitalize on this to help us understand new situations, much as we use categories to understand new objects or creatures. A semantic memory that captures commonly encountered aspects of life is called a schema. This was an idea originally developed by Bartlett (1932) in his studies of how people's prior memories influence later performance. (If you have more than one schema, it is called either schemas or schemata. Both plurals are acceptable. I generally use the first when I'm being lazy and the second when I want to sound smart.)

The schema concept penetrates a number of domains in psychology, and you may have come across them before in another course. For those of you who haven't, a schema contains all of the basic information about the components of a certain aspect of life and how these parts interact with one another. A schema can be thought of as a blueprint for a situation that a person can draw upon to understand a specific case. In some sense, schemas are a type of theory-based category. As you will see, schemas can be used to help memory, but they can also hurt memory.

Primary Schema Processes

There are five primary processes that are involved in using schemas (Alba & Hasher, 1983). Four of them are for encoding information, and the fifth is important during retrieval.

Selection.   The first process is selection. When a person has a schema, she can tell which components are likely to be important and which are peripheral. For example, when watching a football game, it is important to understand how much time has elapsed. Thus, your schema for football would tell you to pay attention to the clock. In contrast, if you were watching a baseball game, the amount of time that has elapsed is of considerably less importance. Thus, your schema for baseball would select out information about the time. Information that is important in the schemas is more likely to be encoded and remembered.

Knowing which schema is relevant can greatly influence performance. For example, in a study by Bransford and Johnson (1972), people were presented with an ambiguous passage to read (see Table 9.2). If people are informed ahead of time that the passage is entitled "Washing Clothes," then they remember more of it later. The title allows people to activate the appropriate schema in memory. They can then appropriately select what is relevant in the passage and interpret it. The fact that this occurs during encoding is supported by the finding that this title benefit is only observed when it is given *before* reading, not afterward when a person is trying to recall the text (Summers, Horton, & Diehl, 1985).

Researchers have seen a similar outcome with pictures. A study by Bower, Karlin, and Dueck (1975) used droodles such as those shown in Figure 9.8. People were shown

TABLE 9.2   Ambiguous Passage that Is Clarified by Activating the Appropriate Schema

The procedure is actually quite simple. First arrange items into different groups. Of course one pile may be sufficient depending on how much there is to do. If you have to go somewhere else due to a lack of facilities, that is the next step; otherwise, you are pretty well set. It is important not to overdo things. That is, it is better to do too few things at once than too many. In the short run this may not seem important, but complications can easily arise. A mistake can be expensive as well. At first, the whole procedure will seem complicated. Soon, however, it will become just another facet of life. It is difficult to foresee any end to necessity for this task in the immediate future, but then, one never can tell. After the procedure is completed one arranges the material into different groups again. Then they can be put into their appropriate places. Eventually they will be used once more and the whole cycle will then have to be repeated. However, that is part of life.

Source: Bransford & Johnson, 1972.

these pictures either with or without labels indicating what they were. It was found that the labels helped people's memories.

Abstraction.   A second schema process is abstraction, which converts the surface form of information (e.g., verbatim wording) into a more abstract representation that captures the underlying meaning of what the person is hearing or seeing. For example, if a person hears a list of sentences and tries to comprehend them, within a few minutes he would not be able to distinguish the verbatim sentence from a paraphrase (Sachs, 1967; 1974). Similarly, if people see a picture, they are less likely to notice a change, such as adding or subtracting elements, rearranging entities in the scene, or changing the orientation of entities in the picture, if the re-

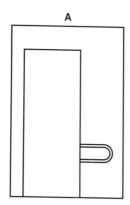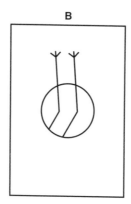

FIGURE 9.8   Droodles Used in a Study to Assess the Influence of Labeling and Schema on the Ability to Remember. Droodle A could be described as a very short person playing a trombone in a telephone booth. Droodle B could be described as an early bird who caught a very strong worm.

Source: Bower, Karlin, & Dueck, 1975

arranged picture fits their abstract, schematic memory of what they saw. For example, people are less likely to notice a change if the same basic situation is present, such as changing a specific instance of an entity (e.g., one type of car for another), moving the relative position of two entities, or even zooming in or out of the picture (Mandler & Ritchey, 1977).

This schema altering is not always in the direction of a more general concept, but it can sometimes be more specific if the person is going from a superordinate to a basic level category (Pansky & Koriat, 2004). For example, if one person hears "vehicle" (superordinate) and another hears "sports car" (subordinate), both will abstract this information to the basic level "car." However, people are more likely to notice changes that alter the meaning of what they saw.

An example of the process of abstraction for visual information is shown in Figure 9.9. In this study by Carmichael, Hogan, and Walter (1932), people were given the line

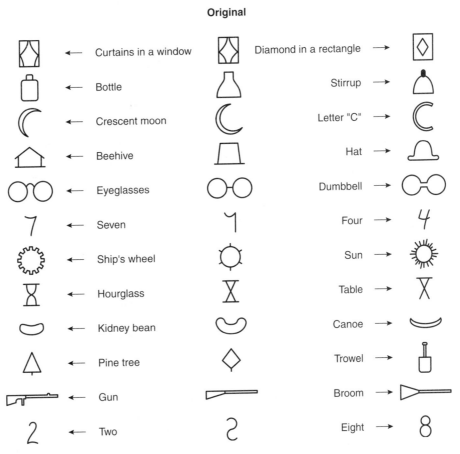

FIGURE 9.9   Ambiguous Line Drawings in the Middle Were Given One of Two Labels
Later reproductions by people, on the left and right, conform to the schema activated by the label.
Source: Carmichael, Hogan, & Walter, 1932

drawings in the middle column with one of two labels. Each of these labels is placed next to the drawing. After a period of time, people were asked to draw what they remember seeing. Examples of the types of drawings people would produce are given on the right and left sides of Figure 9.9. People tended to distort their drawings to have them conform to the label that was provided. People use their schemas to abstract away the relevant information and lose the ambiguous information. Thus, what is remembered is more schema consistent.

Interpretation.   A third schema process is interpretation. When we read a book, watch television, or even experience events in life, there is a lot of information we miss. For example, when you see a movie, there are a number of things that happen off-camera. Still, you have no troubling inferring what they are. Also, there are often large jumps in time and space. For example, you can watch a film in which a person is boarding an airplane one moment and then getting off the next. You don't think that the person got onto the plane and then immediately turned around and got off. Instead, you infer that there was a flight between the two actions, even though only a few seconds have elapsed in the theater. This interpretation can have a powerful effect on memory. People often remember having encountered information that they inferred from a schema of that event type. For example, people who view a sequence of events in which they see the effect of an outcome are likely to claim to remember seeing a schema-consistent cause, even if was never presented (Hannigan & Reinitz, 2001).

Integration.   The fourth aspect of schema processing is integration. In real life we are usually given information about an event all at once. However, sometimes we come across descriptions of events that are given to us piecemeal. For example, when reading a mystery novel, the author may present different aspects about the murder at different points during the story. If the reader has any hope of figuring out what happened and who the guilty party is before being spoon-fed this information at the end, these pieces of information must be integrated into a common mental representation of the event. This is done using schemas.

Reconstruction.   Up to now we have seen how schemas influence encoding. However, schemas can also affect retrieval. As mentioned already, memory traces are not complete records of the past. Instead, they are fragmentary. As such, only bits and pieces of the original experience are likely to be resurrected into consciousness. Sometimes there are a lot of fragments, enough to recover almost the entire memory, whereas in other cases the fragments are few and far between. In either case, some reconstruction is necessary—the fifth schema process. In reconstruction, people fill in the gaps in the memory traces. It would make little sense to fill in these gaps with random information. Instead, a person has a good chance of accurately reconstructing a memory if those gaps were filled with information that is likely to be true. This is much like a paleontologist reconstructing an entire creature from the fragments of fossilized bone.

There is a lot of evidence showing the operation of reconstruction in memory. Some of this comes from Bartlett's (1932) work on schemas. In one set of experiments, he gave British college students a Native American folktale to read called "The War of the Ghosts." This tale is shown in Table 9.3. Some time after reading—often several days, weeks, or months later—a participant was required to recite the tale. During recall, people not only

TABLE 9.3   "The War of the Ghosts," a Native American Folktale

One night two young men from Egulac went down to the river to hunt seals, and while they were there it became foggy and calm. Then they heard war-cries, and they thought: "Maybe this is a war party." They escaped to the shore, and hid behind a log. Now canoes came up, and they heard the noise of paddles, and saw one canoe coming up to them. There were five men in the canoe, and they said:

"What do you think? We wish to take you along. We are going up the river to make war on the people."

One of the young men said: "I have no arrows."

"Arrows are in the canoe," they said.

"I will not go along. I might be killed. My relatives do not know where I have gone. But you," he said turning to the other, "may go with them."

So one of the young men went, but the other returned home.

And the warriors went on up the river to a town on the other side of Kalama. The people came down to the water, and they began to fight, and many were killed. But presently the young man heard one of the warriors say: "Quick, let us go home: that Indian has been hit." Now he thought: "Oh, they are ghosts." He did not feel sick, but they said he had been shot.

So the canoes went back to Egulac, and the young man went ashore to his house, and made a fire. And he told everybody and said: "Behold I accompanied the ghosts, and we went to fight. Many of our fellows were killed, and many of those who attacked us were killed. They said I was hit, and I did not feel sick."

He told it all, and then he became quiet. When the sun rose he fell down. Something black came out of his mouth. His face became contorted. The people jumped up and cried.

He was dead.

Source: Bartlett, 1932.

forgot parts of the story, but they added new elements. Often this new information was less consistent with the original story but more consistent with typical English folktales. One recall is shown in Table 9.4. Schema-based reconstruction is reflected in the idea that if the warrior had been shot, he would have fallen unconscious and been carried off the battlefield. However, this did not occur in the original story.

People also show evidence of schemas with nonverbal information. In one study, students at the University of Illinois were asked to wait in a graduate student's office before the experiment began. However, what they did not realize was that the experiment had begun. After spending a few minutes in the "office," they were taken to another room, where their memory for the "office" was tested. What was found was that people tended to misremember items as being in the "office" when they were not. These were articles that were consistent with a schema of an office. For example, many people remembered seeing books, when there were none (Brewer & Treyens, 1981). In general, people use a combination of detailed memories and schemas to remember, just as in fuzzy trace theory. People are more likely to falsely remember schema-consistent information about a room at longer delays (e.g., 48 hours) than if tested immediately (Lampinen, Copeland, & Neuscatz, 2001). The verbatim memories are rapidly forgotten, leaving people more dependent on their schemas in semantic memory.

TABLE 9.4 Recall Attempt for "The War of the Ghosts" Four Months Later

There were two men in a boat, sailing toward an island. When they approached the island, some natives came running toward them, and informed them that there was fighting going on the island, and invited them to join. One said to the other, "You had better go. I cannot very well, because I have relatives expecting me, and they will not know what has happened to me. But you have no one expecting you." So one accompanied the natives, but the other returned.

Here there is a part I can't remember. What I don't know is how the man got to the fight. However, anyhow the man was in the midst of the fighting, and was wounded. The natives endeavored to persuade the man to return, but he assured them that he had not been wounded.

I have an idea that his fighting won the admiration of the natives.

The wounded man ultimately fell unconscious. He was taken from the fighting by the natives.

Then, I think it is, the natives described what happened, and they seem to have imagined seeing a ghost coming out of his mouth. Really it was a kind of materialization of his breath. I know this phrase was not in the story, but that is the idea I have. Ultimately the man dies at dawn the next day.

Source: Bartlett, 1932.

Forgetting can lead people to make judgments based on their schemas rather than a memory of a particular instance (Gilovich, 1981). Memory reports become more schematic. Information that is falsely recalled but that is central to a schema is often accompanied by a feeling of familiarity (see Chapter 14). This is in contrast to cases where schemas are used to infer information at the time of encoding. In this latter case, the information produces false memories where people claim to recollect seeing or reading about the cause of the event (Hannigan & Reinitz, 2001).

Scripts

When general knowledge refers to a sequence of events that occur in a stereotyped fashion, a special type of schema called a script is used. Scripts are temporally ordered schemas that are structured according to the major components of the event (Abbot, Black, & Smith, 1985; Barsalou & Sewell, 1985), with a preference for using script information in a forward order (Haberlandt & Bingham, 1984), although more central components may be more available (Galambos & Rips, 1982). People have good semantic memories for the order of events for common aspects of life. When people are asked to list the components of a script, such as what happens at a restaurant, many of the lists have the same entries (Bower, Black, & Turner, 1979), suggesting that there is a great deal of regularity captured by this type of semantic memory. A typical list for what to do in a restaurant is shown in Table 9.5.

The use of scripts has clear influences on how information is retrieved and used. For example, when people are reading a text of a scripted event, they take longer to read a sentence when the action is further along in the script from the prior sentence than if it is closer (Bower, Black, & Turner, 1979). For example, if people had just read a sentence about waiting to be seated, they would read the next sentence faster if it was about looking at the menu than if it was about finishing the meal. The idea is that people are scanning their scripts to help them make sense of what they are reading. When the information is close in the script,

TABLE 9.5   A Typical Script for What to Do in a Restaurant

Open door	Meal arrives	Pay bill
Wait to be seated	Eat food	Leave tip
Go to table	Finish meal	Get coat
Be seated	Order dessert	Leave
Look at menu	Ask for bill	
Order meal	Bill arrives	

Source: Bower, Black & Turner, 1979.

less effort is required. However, when the information is far in the script, more effort is required because more of the script needs to be scanned to bring the person up to date. A lot more knowledge must be inferred.

The influence of scripts is also seen when people are given pieces of information about a scripted event in a random order. When later recalling it, there is a tendency to report those bits and pieces in an order that more closely approximates the structure of the script (Bower, Black, & Turner, 1979). Moreover, if people provide summaries of normal and scrambled texts, their summaries are similar and fairly indistinguishable (Kintsch, Mandel, & Kozminsky, 1977). Thus, people use scripts to organize information to help them both understand it and remember it better.

Limits on Schema Usage

While schemas and scripts have a large influence on memory, they are not always used. There are important constraints on when memories do or do not conform to schemas. For example, people are likely to make causal inferences because understanding causal relations is important for understanding how the world is structured and operates. However, when given partial information about a cause-and-effect sequence, people do not always make these inferences. There is a strong bias to infer causes but not effects (Hannigan & Reinitz, 2001) because people can easily infer how they may have gotten to a current point in time (what caused this) if they access the appropriate schema. However, knowing what will happen next (what effects to predict) is more difficult because in many cases any number of possible outcomes could exist. This is not to say that people never use their schemas to make predictions about the future—only that they are much less likely to do so.

It is also possible to get people to disregard schema-generated information. This is more likely to occur when the schema has been discredited. This was done in a study by Hasher & Griffin (1978; see also Anderson & Pitchard, 1978). In this study people were given ambiguous texts, such as the one in Table 9.6. It is ambiguous because it could be either about an escaped convict or a deer hunter. Students were first asked to read this text from one of these perspectives. After a brief delay, the students were asked to recall the story. Some did this from the same perspective as they read it. In contrast, others were led to believe that the experimenter had given them the wrong title initially. They were then given the "correct" other title. The results are shown in Table 9.7. It was found that when there was a title switch, people recalled the same amount of information as when there was

TABLE 9.6   Ambiguous Story Consistent with Two Schemas—an Escaped Convict or a Deer Hunter

The man walked carefully through the forest. Several times he looked over his shoulder and scrutinized the woods behind him. He trod carefully, trying to avoid snapping twigs and small branches that lay in his path, for he did not want to create excess noise. The chirping of the birds in the trees almost annoyed him, their loud calls serving to distract him. He did not want to confuse those sounds with the type he was listening for.

Source: Hasher & Griffin, 1976.

no switch. However, there were important differences in the number and type of inferences made. When there was a title switch, people made fewer intrusions, whereas those who did not have the switch made a large number of schema-consistent intrusions. This suggests that people can disregard schemas and use more detailed, verbatim memories.

Synopsis

Semantic memories for commonly experienced aspects of life are called schemas. During encoding or learning, schemas can be used to select relevant ideas, abstract away the critical ideas, draw inferences through a process of interpretation, and integrate otherwise separate pieces of information. During retrieval schemas can help reconstruct details that were forgotten. For sequences of events, people can use specialized schemas called scripts. While schemas and scripts have a powerful influence on memory, they do not always dominate. Under the right circumstances people can disregard their schemas and scripts and remember more accurately.

PROBLEMS WITH SEMANTIC MEMORY

Semantic Illusions

How many animals of each kind did Moses take on the ark? Many people respond with the answer "two," but this is incorrect. Moses did not take any animals on the ark, Noah did. In

TABLE 9.7   Influence of a Schema Shift on Later Memory for Schema Consistent Inferences. The data are for the percentage of idea units recalled from an ambiguous story and the number of intrusions based on the initial theme, the alternate theme, or some other theme

CONDITION	IDEA UNITS	FIRST THEME	SECOND THEME	NEUTRAL
Same schema	35%	2.58	0.17	0.92
Schema shift	35%	0.54	0.08	1.33

Source: Hasher & Griffin, 1976.

their original study of this type of memory error, Erickson and Mattson (1981) found that 81 percent of the students at the University of California, San Diego, who were asked this question respond with the answer "two" even though they all knew the correct answer. So why do so many people make this mistake? Semantic memory, like other types of memory, is prone to error. In addition to general forgetting, semantic memory errors occur that involve the inappropriate retrieval of information.

One salient form of semantic memory error is the **Moses Illusion.** This illusion does not appear to be due to people mentally correcting the question or making rushed responses (Reder & Cleermans, 1990; Reder & Kusbit, 1991). It also occurs when there is overlapping lexical information, such as a similar name. An example of this is when people gives an inappropriate response to the question "What was the famous line uttered by Louis Armstrong when he first set foot on the moon?" (Shafto & MacKay, 2000).

There are three parts of the explanation for the Moses Illusion, as shown in Figure 9.10. First, semantic processing is very general unless people focus on the information of interest (Barton & Sanford, 1993; Erickson & Mattson, 1981). Second, people only engage in a partial assessment of semantic memory information (Reder & Cleermans, 1990; Reder & Kusbit, 1991). Third, similar language components, such as a similar name, can inappropriately activate information in semantic memory, giving the illusion that it is known (Shafto & MacKay, 2000). Thus, information in semantic memory is accessed in a less than precise way and can lead to errors that would not be made if people were being more deliberate and careful.

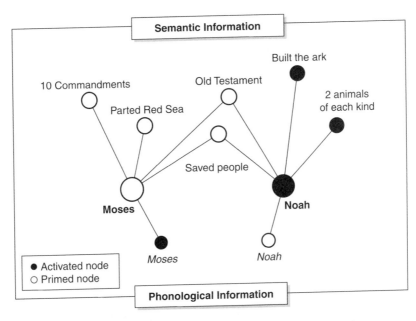

FIGURE 9.10   A Semantic Network Giving Rise to the Moses Illusion

Source: Shafto & MacKay, 2000

Naive Physics

Semantic memory illusions also apply to nonverbal knowledge. As was shown in Chapter 5, memory can incorporate physical principles and properties of the world, such as gravity and friction. How objects move in the world should be stored, to some degree, in semantic memory. And, to some extent, this is true. However, when we consciously try to apply this knowledge, errors in semantic memory can be revealed. This is clearly seen at the mental model level of thinking when people are asked to make predictions about the movement of objects. In studies of these sorts of errors, students at Johns Hopkins University were given diagrams, such as those shown in Figure 9.11. The task was to indicate (1) the trajectory of a ball shot out of the tube, (2) the trajectory of the ball when the string broke, and (3) the path of the bomb when the plane dropped it. The responses are shown in Figure 9.12.

Although people do give the correct responses in some cases, they also give incorrect responses based on having incorrect information stored in semantic memory (McCloskey, Caramazza, & Green, 1980). What is interesting about many errors is that people are responding as if they are holding medieval impetus theories of motion (but see Cooke & Breedin, 1994). Whereas these sorts of responses are more likely when people are viewing static diagrams, they are less likely to occur when they are viewing moving displays (Kaiser, Proffitt, & Anderson, 1985; McCloskey & Kohl, 1983), although not always (Rohrer, 2003). This suggests that the errors in semantic memory can influence working memory as well.

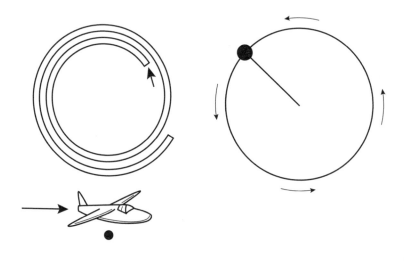

Ground

FIGURE 9.11 Stimuli Used to Illustrate Principles of Naive Physics. A person's task is to show the path of the ball once it leaves the tube or is released.

Source: McCloskey, 1983

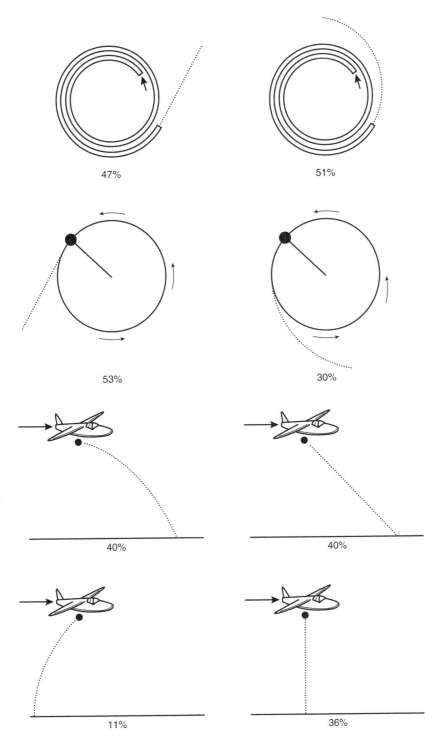

FIGURE 9.12 Responses Given in Naive Physics Studies

Source: McCloskey, 1983

This incorrect understanding can be extended to cases where people don't understand how a device works—for example, many people treat a thermostat not as a device for setting the ideal temperature but as a heat accelerator, setting the temperature much higher in the mistaken belief that the house will get warmer faster.

Another source of misinformation in semantic memory is people's understanding of how vision works. Vision works by light energy entering the eye and being absorbed by the photoreceptors (rods and cones) in the retina. However, there are a large number (33 to 86 percent, depending on the measure) of college-educated people who mistakenly believe that vision involves emissions from the eye (Winer et al., 2002). This is called the extramission view of vision and has been found in large numbers of adults tested using a variety of methods. It is reflected in people's responses when talking about vision, such as imagining rays coming out of the eyes or the belief that you can "feel" a person behind you is looking at you. This semantic misunderstanding of an intimate part of our human experience illustrates the degree to which our knowledge of the world may be completely erroneous.

Synopsis

Our semantic memory is only as accurate as the information in it or how it is used. While much of the knowledge in semantic memory is accurate, it can break down. Such breakdowns occur when knowledge is only superficially accessed, as in the Moses Illusion. Breakdowns can also occur when semantic memories, although based on experience, have somehow been stored incorrectly, such as errors people make on naive physics tasks.

SUMMARY

In this chapter we looked at how people store and retrieve general world knowledge in semantic memory. Semantic memory is highly structured. This organization brings related concepts to mind through the process of priming. Although priming is largely automatic, it can be controlled to some extent. In addition, inhibition may also occur if there is competition among concepts. The organization of knowledge is clearest when people form categories. The process of categorization appears to be less dependent on rules of necessary and sufficient features and more on information about overlapping properties or causal relationships among category members. We also looked at how ordered relationships can influence the use of semantic memory. We explored the operation of schemas and scripts during learning and retrieval. Although the use of schemas and scripts is quite pervasive, it does have its limits. Finally, we looked at cases where semantic memory can be in error, leading people to look at the world in ways that are incorrect.

STUDY QUESTIONS

1. What is semantic priming? What sorts of information get primed? How far does it extend?

2. How long does it take for information to be established in semantic memory?

3. To what degree can semantic priming be consciously controlled? When are semantic memories inhibited?

4. What are the basic properties of categories formed in semantic memory?

5. What are some of the major theories of how people form categories?

6. How is semantic memory retrieval affected by the order of information along a dimension?

7. What are the primary ways that schemas influence memory at encoding? At retrieval?

8. What are schemas for sequential event knowledge called? How do they operate?

9. How can a person avoid the influence of schemas and remember more accurately?

10. What sorts of problems can occur when semantic memory is used? How do these errors arise?

KEY TERMS

ad hoc categories, categorization, category, central tendency, classical view of categorization, concept, exemplar theory, explanation-based categories, family resemblance, graded membership, inhibition, levels of categorization, mediated priming, Moses Illusion, naive physics, priming, prototype model, psychological essentialism, semantic memory, semantic distance effect, semantic congruity effect, serial position effect.

CHAPTER TEN

FORMAL MODELS OF LONG-TERM MEMORY

Providing verbal descriptions of memory is nice. They give us a feel for how memory operates, but verbal descriptions can be vague. Worse, verbal descriptions alone do not distinguish among different ideas about how memory works. A more precise language is needed to capture the subtle flavors and nuances of human memory, and that language is mathematics. By casting our ideas in a language that can be described and tested mathematically, thereby creating a formal model, we can look at finer qualities of memory performance than would be possible using only verbal descriptions. Often this mathematical expression is done in the form of computer models of memory. Also, creating a formal model of memory in some mathematical guise forces us to be explicit about how everything works. This is a process where our assumptions are laid bare. With verbal descriptions it's easy to fudge things and make assumptions without realizing it. Also, formal models allow for more accurate predictions about how memory will work in the future, as well as provide more accurate descriptions of what happened in the past. If psychology is to continue to succeed as a science, there should be a reasonable level of predictability given a certain amount of starting knowledge. This does not mean that the goal of psychology is to predict every little behavior or thought (although that is a theoretical possibility, given infinite prior knowledge), but it at least must provide some general description of what will happen on average. For example, knowing that people will remember better over the long term if they spread out studying over several short sessions rather than a single long session.

Formal models provide a degree of precision and accuracy in describing mental life that is not possible with verbal descriptions. Formal models play the important role of explicitly pointing out errors in theory. Hintzman (1990) stated the following.

> The common strategy of trying to reason backward from behavior to underlying process (analysis) has drawbacks that become painfully apparent to those who work with simulation models (synthesis). To have one's hunches about how a simple combination of processes will behave repeatedly dashed by one's own computer program is a humbling experience that no experimental psychologist should miss. (p. 111)

In this chapter we look at a number of theories that have served as successful formal models of human memory. We first look at two simple formal models of memory that were proposed to account for recognition and recall. Then we look at how a formal comparison about these two simple measures of memory, recall and recognition, have led to some interesting and unexpected insights into human memory. Next, we cover four classes of theories: (1) network models, which assume memory is a highly integrated, associative structure; (2) global matching models, which assume that memory is accessed as a whole, and structure emerges from this process rather than being encoded in long-term memory itself; (3) parallel distributed models of memory, which use the nervous system as their inspiration; and (4) dual process models, which assume there are two fundamentally different types of memory processes that can operate, with performance always being a combination of the two.

Before turning to the models themselves, you should be aware that these are largely mathematical models that rely heavily on quantitative descriptions of memory. However, in this chapter I present relatively few formulas. The intent of this chapter is to provide you with a general overview of how these formal models characterize memory. The perspective taken here is not to assume a degree of mathematical sophistication and the ability to apply that knowledge.

SIMPLE MODELS OF MEMORY

We will first examine a couple of relatively simple models. Using these as a starting point, we then move on to more developed ideas. The first theory is the threshold model of recognition, followed by the generate-recognize model of recall.

Threshold Model

The first simple model of memory, the **threshold model** (see Anderson, 2000, and Murdock, 1974, for descriptions), addresses the concept that there is some threshold of activation that a memory trace must exceed before it is detected and identified as "old" (or recognized). This threshold is a subjective cutoff that a person uses (in some way, consciously or unconsciously) to evaluate information as either new or old. Now, not all memories that people think are old have in fact been seen before. Some of the thoughts are new, but for some reason, people recognize them as something that is remembered. According to the threshold model, these incorrect responses are essentially guesses. We must be able to account for how much guessing is going on to help us to better understand how well memory is operating. For example, if a person answers "yes" to all of the old items on a memory test, but never says "yes" to a new item, then we can assume that memory for this information is very good. However, if a person answers "yes" to all of the old items, but also always answers "yes" to all of the new items, this is a much less impressive feat. So to get at the true state of memory, one needs to correct for guessing.

The way to correct for guessing in the threshold model is to look at both the probability of correctly recognizing something, as well as the probability of incorrectly identifying something as recognized (a guess). Assume that p is the probability of correct recognition, and g is the probability of guessing correctly. The "|" sign stands for "given that." Therefore, the probability of giving a correct "yes" response on a recognition test can be written as follows.

$$P (\text{"yes"}| \text{ old item}) = p + (1 - p)g$$

Using this formula and logic, the terms can be rearranged to allow a person to gain an estimate of the likelihood that person is actually recognizing rather than guessing.

$$p = \frac{P(\text{"yes"} \mid \text{old item}) - P(\text{"yes"} \mid \text{new item})}{1 - P(\text{"yes"} \mid \text{new item})}$$

This model of memory is related to ideas in **signal detection theory** (see also Chapter 3), which is a more sophisticated development. When a memory trace of an old item exceeds threshold, a person correctly recognizes an old memory. This is called a hit. When a person fails to recognize previous items, it is because the level of activation of that memory is below the threshold, and so it is rejected. This is called a miss. When a new item is rejected because the representation in memory does not exceed threshold (because it is new), then this is called a correct rejection. Finally, if a new item does have a representation in memory that exceeds threshold, a person will inappropriately identify it as old. This is called a false alarm. Signal detection approaches to formal memory modeling play a larger and more obvious role in the global matching models discussed later in the chapter.

Generate-Recognize Model

The other simple formal model considered here is the **generate-recognize model** of recall (Kintsch, 1970). This model assumes that recall, particularly free recall, occurs in a two-stage process. It is possible to think of recall as being like recognition except requiring a higher threshold before a person can adequately report the information. However, the generate-recognize theory takes a more elaborate view. An important part of this model is the idea that recall involves a search of memory, whereas recognition simply involves a person indicating whether an item is familiar or not. Still, it would be nice if the memory processes involved in recall were not completely different from recognition. The generate-recognize model tries to accomplish both the identification of processes unique to recall as well as taking advantage of memory processes thought to operate during recognition.

The first stage of the model is the generate component, which is unique to recall. During this phase a person takes whatever retrieval cues are available and begins to build or generate a set of memory traces whose contents can be reported. This is done by the activation of information in memory that is associated with the cues, followed by the information that is associated with that, and so on. This information is cross-referenced to help the person generate a set of possible responses. In the second stage, the person then applies the standard recognition memory processes to the information that was generated in the first stage.

This model, although relatively simple, makes some clear predictions about how memory retrieval operates. One is that recall is more difficult than recognition, which is true. Another is that recall should be more clearly influenced by associations between concepts in memory, which is also true, although recognition can be influenced, as is seen in priming paradigms. Finally, this model also predicts that all of the influences that affect recognition should also affect recall. Recognition is a subcomponent of recall.

Modeling Recognition and Recall.   As described in Chapter 3, recall and recognition are popular ways of looking at memory. What we are going to look at here is a formal assessment of the relationship between these two retrieval methods. In some ways they might seem very similar—for example, they are both explicit memory measures—but there are important differences. For example, they differ in the degree to which they are influenced by the organization of information during learning. Suppose a person learns a list of words that are either grouped by categories (organized) or are presented randomly (unorganized). In such cases, the organized list is recalled better than the unorganized list. However, recognition memory is much less affected by this, if at all (Kintsch, 1968). This is consistent with the generate-recognize theory.

However, there is a problem. In many experiments of reasonable scope, there are a sizeable number of items that may be recalled but not recognized. This is called **recognition failure,** and it poses a serious problem for the generate-recognize theory. If all of the processes that operate during recognition also operate during recall, then anything that is recalled should be recognized. However, recognition failure is a regular occurrence. The consistency of this relation is shown in Figure 10.1. In this graph, if everything that could be recognized was also recalled, then the data points should all fall along the diagonal (with some accommodation for error), but we do not see this. There is a systematic deviation from this, with points regularly falling above the diagonal, indicating recognition failure (not recognizing items that were recalled). The first formal description of this phenomenon, called the **Tulving-Wiseman function** (Tulving & Wiseman, 1975), is as a mathematical relationship. In this function, Rn stands for recognition, and Rc stands for recall. (And as a refresher, p stands for "probability that," and I stands for "given that.")

$$p(\text{Rn} \mid \text{Rc}) = p(\text{Rn}) + .5[p(\text{Rn}) - p(\text{Rn})^2]$$

The explanation for this function is that recall and recognition use different types of retrieval cues (Flexser & Tulving, 1975; Tulving & Watkins, 1977; but see Hintzman, 1987; 1992, for a different interpretation). Recall uses the cues used to prompt retrieval, whereas recognition uses the item itself. For example, whenever I go to my favorite local used-CD store, they ask for the last four digits of my phone number (I am building up credits for free CDs). There are several times that I find this difficult to remember without recalling the first three digits (the exchange) first. This is a case where I have my phone number stored in such a way that the retrieval of the last four digits is highly associated with the context of the first three. If I were presented with only the last four digits without such a context, it would not surprise me if I did not recognize it as part of my phone number. This sort of differentially based retrieval system that uses different memory cues, with some relative independence between recall and recognition, is clearly at odds with the generate-recognize model and was only brought to light with a formal analysis of the data.

Synopsis

Simple models are able to capture basic characteristics of memory, as well as reveal where simple-minded thinking, which may seem intuitively plausible, is actually in error. The

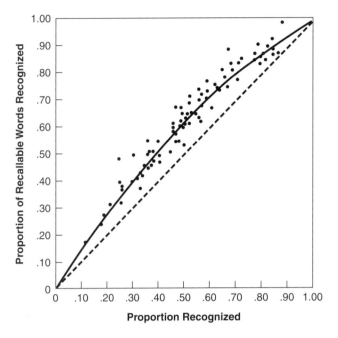

FIGURE 10.1   Data Plot Illustrating Recognition Failure and the Tulving-Wiseman Function

Source: Flexser & Tulving, 1975

threshold model is a theory of recognition memory that assumes that memories are retrieved when their activation level exceeds some threshold. This is similar to signal detection models discussed previously. The generate-recognize model is a simple theory of recall that incorporates all of the essential, basic characteristics of recognition in the retrieval process. As appealing as the generate-recognize model might be for its simplicity, consistent findings such as recognition failure indicate that it is in error.

NETWORK THEORIES

In Chapter 1 we saw that the work of Aristotle had a profound influence on current psychological thought through his ideas about associations. The influence of associations on the structure and function of memory has been seen in some degree in Chapters 6 through 9 with phenomena such as priming, encoding specificity, the organization of mental maps, and the structure of semantic memory. Many popular formal models of memory have taken this idea of associative structure and used it as the fundamental basis for their theories of memory. One of the clearest ways to see how memory researchers have used the concept of associations and the structure of memory is in terms of complexes of associations in network models. These are mental representations of knowledge in which there are large numbers of smaller units, often called nodes, joined together in tangled web of associations by an even larger number of links.

Semantic Networks

The first major **network theory** of memory was an attempt by Collins and Quillian (1969; 1972; elaborated on by Collins & Loftus, 1975) to capture semantic memory in the service of a computer program that would hopefully be able to use human language in a natural way (a goal that is still very far off). In **Collins and Quillian's network model** of semantic memory, the nodes were simple concepts, like "bird" or "canary," and the links were of several types. For example, in Figure 10.2, which shows a portion of a network, there are property associations and categorical associations. For property associations, some concepts are properties of other concepts they are associated with. For example, "feathers" is a property of "bird," "yellow" is a property of "canary," and so forth. Other types of associations were superordinate category relations—for example, "A canary is a bird." In semantic networks information is generally stored in one location in the network based on some cognitive economy. That is, rather than expending effort endlessly replicating concepts, individual concepts can be instantiated in the network only a few times, or even once.

Spreading Activation.   When a person accesses a concept in memory, like "canary," a search process begins by having activation move along all the links associated with that concept. This is a process known as **spreading activation.** A simple way to look at spreading activation is as electricity flowing through the wires of a circuit. Through this process of spreading activation, if the concept "feathers" were also accessed, the links associated with that would be searched, too. When two search paths meet to create an intersection, the person can verify that the concepts are associated and stored in memory. If the two searches

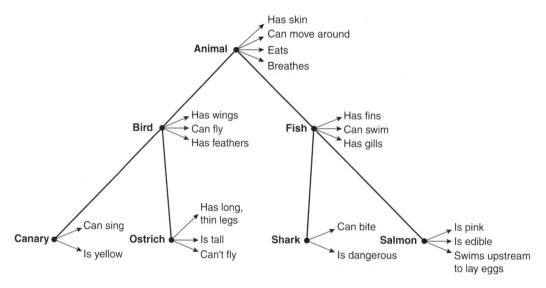

FIGURE 10.2   **Portion of a Network in Collins and Quillian's (1969; 1972) Model of Memory**

Source: Collins & Quillian, 1969

do not form an intersection because they are not connected in memory, then the information is not something that is recognized.

A prediction of this model is that the speed with which information is retrieved should be a function of the distance between two nodes in the network. For example, people should be faster to verify "A canary is yellow" than to verify "A canary has feathers." This can be defined in terms of hierarchical category representations, or degree of relatedness. Figure 10.3 illustrates a memory network in a way that captures this idea of relatedness. For example, red can be thought of being more closely associated with colors because

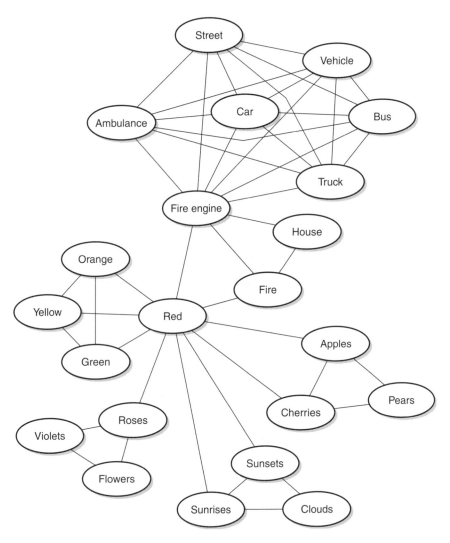

FIGURE 10.3 Portion of a Network in Collins and Loftus's (1975) Model of Memory

Source: Collins & Loftus, 1975

there are more links to other colors. However, red is less associated with vehicles because, in this network, there is only a single link from red to the vehicles cluster. Also, relative strength of individual associations is captured by the length of the links connecting the concepts, with shorter links standing for more strongly associated concepts. For example, while "sunsets" is associated with both "red" and "sunrises," it is more closely associated with "sunrises" than "red," because the association is stronger as illustrated by the shorter link length.

Although initial studies supported this idea (Collins & Quillian, 1969), subsequent work revealed some problems. This study suggested that structure of memory was more complex. For example, it was assumed that if nodes in a hierarchical structure were far from one another in the network, it should take a long time to verify one of those facts. However, it has been found that some facts can be verified much quicker than should be possible according to these network models (Rips, Shoben, & Smith, 1973). For example, people verify the statement "A pig is an animal" much faster than "A pig is a mammal," even though the opposite was predicted. Thus, the formal model made predictions that could easily and directly be put to the test.

Priming.   The attractive idea behind this sort of network theory of memory is that everything is defined in terms of everything else, much like a dictionary. However, this is also a major problem (Johnson-Laird, Hermann, & Chaffin, 1984). One of the appealing things about network models is that they provide clean, simple accounts of the basic finding of priming. As a reminder, in priming, when people encounter information, this not only activates those particular concepts in memory, but it makes related concepts more available as well. According to a network model, priming occurs because a concept becomes activated in memory. Activation then spreads along the associative links to related concepts. This is why it is easy to shift your thinking to related ideas (because they are already activated or primed to some degree) rather than to something completely different. However, information in the model is still internally defined within the model, not with reference to the world.

ACT

Another network model of memory is the **ACT** (Adaptive Control of Thought) family of models (Anderson, 1976; 1983). Of all the models discussed in this chapter, this one is probably the most advanced in the sense that it tries to be a model of many aspects of cognition rather than being just a model of memory (although some people would argue that just about everything in cognitive psychology is memory).

ACT Network.   According to this view, information is stored in a propositional network. A proposition is any simple idea unit. In the memory network a proposition is conceptualized as two nodes and a link. Information is retrieved from the network by nodes becoming activated and the activation spreading along the links. This is similar to the semantic networks just discussed. An example of a propositional network structure for the sentence "The sleepy student is in the old classroom" is given in Figure 10.4. As can be seen, this sentence is made up of large number of propositions that are organized by the network

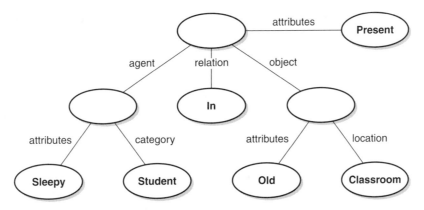

FIGURE 10.4   ACT Model Propositional Network for the Sentence "The sleepy student is in the old classroom."

structure. There are a number of other assumptions about the ACT model that make it different from semantic networks.

One important property of the ACT model is the distinction between type nodes and token nodes. **Type nodes** correspond to generalized concepts, such as those seen in the semantic network models. For example, a "bird" type node would stand for birds in general. In addition, **token nodes** correspond to specific instances. For example, a "bird" token node would stand for a specific bird, such as "that robin over there." An illustration of the type-token node distinction is provided in Figure 10.5. Here the specific instances of words in the phrase "Bill is tall, lazy, and hairy." correspond to token nodes (labeled in lowercase). Each of these token nodes is associated with type nodes (indicated by the labels in all capitals). In this example, it is also shown how there can be some decomposition of concepts. The word "tall" is partially decomposed into two token nodes for the first two sounds of the word (labeled as nodes 5 and 6) and their associated type nodes.

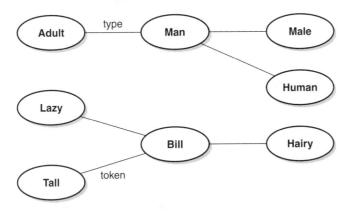

FIGURE 10.5   Type-Token Distinction in the ACT Model

The ACT model also contains the idea that there is only a limited amount of activation in the system. Not all associations with a concept in memory can be searched equally well, simultaneously, and to a high degree. Instead, activation is a limited resource in the system. The more associations with a concept, the more finely divided the activation becomes, and retrieval time is slowed accordingly. This is the ACT model's explanation for the fan effect (described in Chapter 7). In essence, the more facts a person learns about a concept, the more associations that are linked to it. When a person needs to verify any one of those facts, the number of associations with that concept divide up the activation, and retrieval along any one of those associative pathways is slowed (Anderson, 1974).

Memory Systems.   Finally, another characteristic of the ACT model is the distinction between production and declarative memory and how they interact in working memory. What has been discussed up to this point is the declarative memory aspect of the model, particularly the retrieval of information, but the other important part of the model is the production memory system. Production memories are basically the mental steps a person takes to proceed from one state of knowing to another. That is, the production actually manipulates information. Production memories are executed when the appropriate conditions in working memory match the relevance of the production. They are basically, "if . . . then" statements in long-term memory. If a condition is present, then the information is manipulated in a specified way. For example, when you learned addition in your elementary school math class, you were essentially developing production memories for how to manipulate the number information as it was encountered in problems you were given.

These production steps are initially very slow and cumbersome to execute and are stored very weakly in memory. However, they become more and more automatized and subconscious the more practice a person has with them. For example, when you solve a math problem—such as "What is 574 times 63?"—you invoke the appropriate mental procedures to arrive at the correct answer. The more practice you have with these types of problems, the stronger the production memories become, and the easier it is to solve the problems. At some point, your ability to solve such math problems will be nearly automatic.

Production memories essentially interact with the declarative memory network through working memory. Working memory is basically that portion of the declarative network that is currently active along with the productions that are operating on it. This inclusion of a production memory to the model makes it a very powerful tool. It allows for explanations of memory based not only on how information is structured but the way people are actively manipulating it in working memory and the consequences this has for later long-term memory.

Synopsis

Network theories of memory have been very influential in psychology in general. The Collins and Quillian, and Collins and Loftus semantic memory models were some of the first to provide clearly testable predictions that were, at least initially, verified by studies with people. Network models of memory have continued to develop over the years. The concept of spreading activation pervades a great deal of thinking about memory retrieval, especially in some accounts of priming. One of the most prominent theories of memory, the ACT family of models, has a propositional network as a primary part of the way that it stores information in long-term memory. This network structure is used as part of its explanation of working memory as well.

GLOBAL MATCHING MODELS

According to network models of memory, knowledge is stored in one very complex, highly organized, and highly integrated memory structure, in which portions of the network become selectively activated to meet the demands of the current situation. In comparison, for **global matching models** of memory, information is accessed through processes that consider the entire set of memory traces available. In such views, any relation between different memories occurs at retrieval, depending on the nature of the cues to the memory probe. That is, structure in memory emerges out of the process of retrieval rather than being a part of long-term memory storage, as is the case with network models of memory.

In these models information is either stored in separate memory records, in what are called **multiple trace models** of memory, or are patterns of information imposed on a common memory framework, in what are called **distributed storage models** of memory. In global matching theories, multiple memory traces are activated in parallel. What is retrieved at any given point in time is a function of (1) the familiarity of the memory probe, (2) the degree of overlap between the probe and the memory traces, and (3) the amount of activation of the memory traces related to the probe (Clark & Gronlund, 1996).

In general, global matching models have evolved out of signal detection theories of memory retrieval (see Chapter 3). The availability of memory traces are a function of their familiarity (discrimination), and successful retrieval in these frameworks involves activation reaching a certain threshold (bias). A couple of prominent multiple trace models of this type, SAM and MINERVA 2, are considered here. We also examine two distributed storage models, called TODAM and CHARM.

SAM

One of the most successful multiple trace models of memory is the Search of Associative Memory, or *SAM,* model (Gillund & Shiffrin, 1984; Raaijmakers & Shiffrin, 1980; 1981; 1992). According to SAM, memories are stored in traces that contain content, associative, and contextual information. In this theory, memory traces are formally called "images," but this is not related to perceptual images or mental imagery, such as we saw in Chapter 5. Because of this, we use the term memory *traces,* not images.

According to the SAM model, remembering occurs when some cue (something in the world or a thought) overlaps with information in a memory trace. This causes the trace to become active and potentially retrieved. Memory retrieval in this model is viewed as a probabilistic process—that is, the probability that a given memory trace is remembered is a function of its relation to the memory probe and its strength relative to other memory traces. The greater the strength, the higher the probability of retrieval.

Recall.   The retrieval process that SAM goes through during recall is illustrated in Figure 10.6. Initially, a person is presented with a recall cue, such as a question. To organize the information that needs to be recalled, especially if it is even a modestly complex set, a person

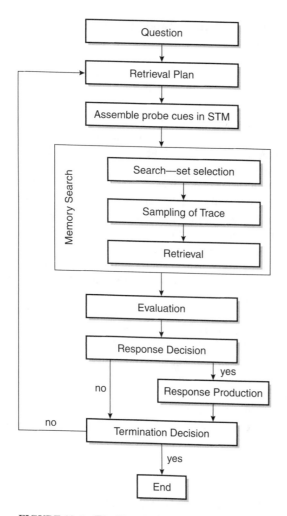

FIGURE 10.6   The Processes Involved in Recall in the SAM Model of Memory

Source: Raaijmakers & Shiffrin, 1981

must create a retrieval plan to keep track of the information. This retrieval plan then generates a series of probe cues that access long-term memory traces using a global matching process. During the memory search, the model first restricts itself to a subset of memory traces that are more likely to be relevant. It then searches through these memory traces, starting with the stronger ones and moving to the weaker ones. These are recovered into short-term memory, where they can be evaluated and either reported (output) by producing a response or not (similar to what happens in the generate-recognize model). After this a person either continues to search memory for more information or quits.

So essentially what is happening here is that information is retrieved through a sampling process that is influenced, but not completely determined, by the degree to which memory traces are related to a retrieval cue. Traces that more closely match the cue are more likely to be retrieved and evaluated. If they are relevant, they are reported; otherwise, they are not. After each recall, the person goes back to search for more information that could be recalled until some point is reached when the decision is made to stop.

Recognition.   In comparison, in recognition, whether or not a given item is recognized is a function of the sum of all of the memory traces related to the probe. This retrieval process is illustrated in Figure 10.7. First, information in both the recognition item and the context in which it is embedded are used to sample memory. This process essentially makes contact with all of those memory traces that share features with the recognition item and the context. The addition of the context helps narrow down the set of traces that contributes to recognition, thereby making it more accurate. If the familiarity value that is returned by this sampling process is above some threshold or criteria, then a person accepts the information as old (it is recognized). Otherwise, it is classified as something new (it is not recognized). Thus, something may be recognized even if a person has a large number of weak memories for that information, not just a single strong memory for a previous occurrence.

So this memory process during recognition essentially extracts thoughts one at a time, starting with those memory traces that resonate most strongly with the retrieval cue. This includes both information in the cue itself as well as the surrounding context. If this sampling process produces a memory trace that is strong enough, then the person recognizes the information as old. Otherwise, it is rejected as new. Once again, there is an element of probability associated with the retrieval process that is focused on the actual recovery of information from long-term memory.

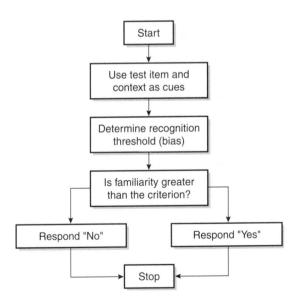

FIGURE 10.7   Processes Involved in Recognition in the SAM Model of Memory

Source: Gillund & Shiffrin, 1984

MINERVA 2

Another multiple trace model is called **MINERVA 2** (Hintzman, 1986; 1988) (MINERVA 1 did not last very long). This theory assumes that information is stored in memory traces, called vectors, that are strings of features that comprise the original memory. Each feature is represented by a number that indicates its presence or absence. These features can either be content or context information, allowing MINERVA 2 to explain effects like encoding specificity. One of the interesting things about MINERVA 2 is that during remembering, what is retrieved is not a single memory trace (as in the threshold model) or simply a level of familiarity (as in SAM). Instead, what is returned is a new memory trace called an echo, which is a weighted composite of all the memory traces that were activated. We will examine two characteristics of the echo in detail: echo intensity and echo content.

Echo Intensity.   The echo intensity refers to the activation strength of the echo that is returned by the retrieval process. This is a function of the intensity of the memory traces that were tapped by the retrieval process (see Figure 10.8). This is analogous to the familiarity value returned in SAM. Depending on the amount of overlap of the memory probe with a memory trace, the activation level varies accordingly. The greater the overlap, the greater the activation. So if a memory probe activates memory traces with a high degree of overlap with the probe, then the echo intensity is greater. For example, you have many memories of people speaking your name. Thus, if your name were a memory probe, the echo would have a high level of intensity because of the high degree of overlap of this information. In contrast, you are likely to have very few to no memory traces about St. Ignatius High School football during the early 1980s. Although this information can make contact with some memory traces—such as those about football, high school, and the 1980s—there is likely

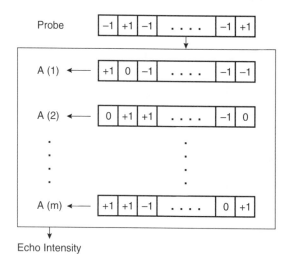

Echo Intensity

FIGURE 10.8   Echo Intensity in MINERVA 2

Source: Hintzman, 1986

little overlap with this memory probe as a whole, and the echo intensity will be weak, thereby indicating that this information is not known. Echo intensity can also be useful in determining frequency information. More intense echoes are likely to reflect frequent occurrences, whereas low-intensity echoes are likely to reflect rare events (Hintzman, 1988).

Echo Content.   The other aspect of the echo is echo content. Echo content in MINERVA 2 is a weighted average of the contents of all of the memory traces activated by the probe. Those memory traces with a greater overlap carry greater weight and so have a greater influence over the content of the echo. This is illustrated in Figure 10.9. Thus, what is returned during retrieval is a composite or blending of many traces. As a result, MINERVA 2 can produce generalized effects in memory, such as the influence of schemas (Hintzman, 1986). This is because specific features get averaged out, and what is left are the general abstract components. For example, if you are presented with the concept "grocery store," this activates all the memory traces about grocery stores that you have in long-term memory. What you experience remembering is a weighted average of all grocery store experiences you have ever had, with the individual contexts averaged out.

Specific and General Retrieval.   When a person is more interested in remembering a single event, the precision of the memory cue is more important. The more closely an original memory trace corresponds to the memory cue, the larger the role it plays in the structure of the echo. But there is always some contribution of other overlapping traces, even if that contribution is quite weak. In this way, memory retrieval is always a distorting process because what is remembered is always, in some way, a composite of several previous memories. To compound this distortion further, the echo that is returned is itself then stored as a memory trace. In this way, MINERVA 2 shows that our memories are constantly changing as a result of experience and even by the act of remembering.

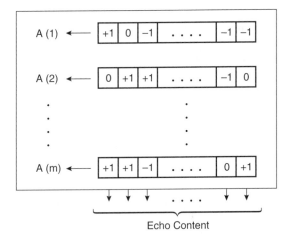

FIGURE 10.9   Echo Content in MINERVA 2

Source: Hintzman, 1986

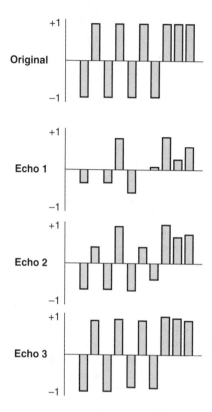

FIGURE 10.10   Echo Improvement in MINERVA 2

Source: Hintzman, 1986

Although the MINERVA 2 retrieval process has this constantly distorting property, this same process helps MINERVA 2 narrow in on a memory trace. By using the echo that was returned to help focus the memory search, thereby activating a smaller and smaller set of memory traces, a person can have much more accurate memory retrieval compared to getting only the first returned, most averaged, memory trace. This process is illustrated in Figure 10.10. Initially, the composition of the echo only remotely resembles the information that is being searched for. However, over time, by using the echos that were generated previously as part of the memory search process, the correspondence gets better and better.

Further Work

Work continues on the development of more sophisticated formal models of memory. One of the more recent developments is a model called REM, for Retrieving Effectively from Memory (Malmberg, Steyvers, Stephens, & Shiffrin, 2002; Shiffrin & Steyvers, 1997). REM combines properties of SAM and MINERVA 2, as well as other sources, to provided a wider-ranging, more effective account of human memory. Like SAM, REM assumes that information is stored in multiple memory traces or images. It also searches memory in a trace-by-trace, probabilistic fashion like SAM. Furthermore, information is represented as a vector of features, much like MINERVA 2. Furthermore, unlike the other models, REM assumes there is a probability that there will be some error in the information stored in a given memory trace. This more developed model of memory has been successfully applied to a wider range of memory phenomenon.

TODAM and CHARM

Formal models like SAM and MINERVA 2 are multiple trace models that store each experience separately in memory. Any blending of information occurs during retrieval. Now we consider a pair of global matching models that involve distributed storage. This is a sensible step to take if one thinks about how the brain most likely stores information. It is probably not a system where each experience is stored at a separate location in the cortex. Instead, many different memories are imposed on the same neural structure, and the information is distributed throughout this structure.

Two of these models are the Theory of Distributed Associative Memory, or **TODAM** (Murdock, 1982a; 1982b; 1983; 1993; 1995), and the Composite Holographic Associative Retrieval Model, or **CHARM** (Eich, 1982; 1985). Like MINERVA 2, these models assume that information is represented as vectors of features. These models were originally developed to account for memory for item and associative information, as well as processes such as serial order information. This largely reflects their development out of a verbal learning tradition of memory. In that research, emphasis was on memory for paired associates.

In these models, item information is represented by a different memory trace for each item. What is important here is that associative information is stored in the model as a memory trace that is a convolution of the two item memory trace vectors. So what is a convolution? The convolution process is graphically illustrated in Figure 10.11. Each item vector is combined with each and every element of the vector of another memory trace to create the composite vector trace. Thus, information from both items is distributed across a shared set of memory elements. This is actually an efficient way of encoding a set of information about items and associations, using a relatively small number of resources. Because of the regular structure of these convoluted vectors, the original information can be extracted using a correlation process. In this case, the properties of the convoluted vector are correlated with the values of some memory probe, thereby allowing for the extraction of the previous information.

One metaphor that has been used in describing this model is ripples on a pond (Murdock, 1982). Different objects, such as a textbook or a computer, make different types of waves when thrown in the water. If a number of objects are thrown in the pond, all of these waves are superimposed on the same surface. With enough sophistication, one could examine the wave patterns to determine what sorts of objects are likely to have been thrown in.

Synopsis

Unlike network models of memory, global matching models do not make strong assumptions about how information is organized in memory. Instead, the structures that are

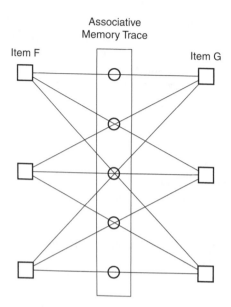

FIGURE 10.11   Process of Convolution in Models like TODAM and CHARM
Source: Eich, 1982

observed are thought to be more a result of the process of retrieval. The SAM model has been a very successful theory of recall and recognition that is based on probabilistic access of memory traces as a function of the match with the retrieval cue. Other global matching models, such as MINERVA 2, provide interesting accounts of how memory is changed by the act of remembering. Still other global matching models, such as CHARM and TODAM, demonstrate how multiple memory traces can be superimposed on a limited representational structure, as would be expected to be seen in the neurons of the brain.

PARALLEL DISTRIBUTED PROCESSING (PDP) MODELS

Another broad class of formal models of memory are **parallel distributed processing,** or PDP, models. These are models in which information is stored in a single structure with multiple memory traces that are superimposed on one another in a common representational framework. That is, there is a network of nodes and links like those in a semantic network. However, rather than the node being connected to those concepts that are associated with it, in a PDP model each node is massively interconnected with a very large number of other nodes. In many cases, memory representations are distributed across a number of shared components. That is, it is the pattern of activation, not the particular nodes that are activated, that produces the representation, learning, and memory in a PDP model.

Perhaps the most prevalent types are the models known as **connectionist models** (McClelland, 2000) or **neural networks.** These theories use the structure of the nervous system in the brain as a source of inspiration for trying to capture memory. The brain is in a real sense a distributed representation. Information is not stored in individual neurons, which can only fire, or not, at a given point in time. Instead, information is captured by the pattern of neural firing over a large set of neurons. As a result, any given neuron participates in the representation of a very large number of different memories, along with what other neurons are doing. Thus, information in the brain is distributed across a wide assembly of neurons.

Connectionist models can take a similar approach. An example of a connectionist network is provided in Figure 10.12. First, it is assumed that there is a network of nodes and links. A connectionist model is basically a collection of "units" that is interconnected to other units (and possibly to themselves as well). The units in these models would correspond to neurons, and the connections to axonal connections with other neurons. This is different from network models in that a given node does not stand for a particular concept. It is just a node. These nodes are massively interconnected with other nodes, forming layers of nodes, similar to the layers of cells in the brain for processing some types of information. Thus, there is a very high degree of interconnectivity. Information is represented in the pattern of activation in the nodes of the network. These patterns are established by shifting the weights of the connections among the various nodes. Thus, learning is a shift in connection strengths, which allows new patterns to emerge.

Further following the inspiration from the brain, these units are often divided into "layers" of units. This is consistent with neuropsychological work showing that brain cells are often grouped into layers or units along some path of information processing. A typical connectionist model might contain three such layers: an input layer, an output layer, and a "hidden" layer, whose presence allows for a great deal of flexibility in adjusting to experience. It is this hidden layer that gives a connectionist model its flexibility and power to learn and retain information.

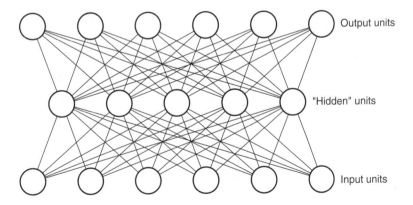

FIGURE 10.12   Sample Parallel Distributed Processing Network

Learning

The way in which information is represented in a connectionist model is in terms of the "strengths" among the connections between the units. These strengths are often referred to as connection weights. Some of these connections are excitatory and some are inhibitory. Information is basically represented as the pattern of units that are active. The model is thought to be operating well when the pattern of activity at the output stages bears a stable and consistent relationship to the pattern of information at the input stage.

The shifting of connection weights in a network is a gradual process. Furthermore, every experience that a person has alters the neural connections in some way. Those that correspond to the experience become stronger, whereas the others may become weaker or not be affected at all. However, over time, there is evidence clear differences in the representation of different types of knowledge. Figure 10.13 shows shifts in the activation levels of a number of output nodes in a network that has been trained on a number of concepts. The more training there has been, the more differentiated the representations. Moreover, notice that concepts that have similar meanings are represented by similar patterns of activation in the network. Thus, a connectionist model is able to capture such memory characteristics as semantic similarity.

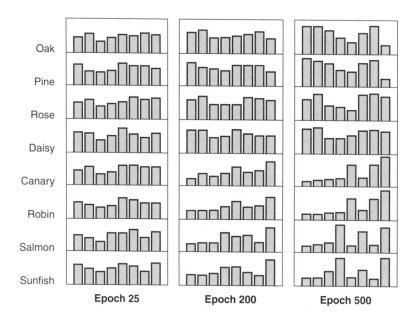

FIGURE 10.13   Representational Improvement across Various Epochs (Training Cycles) in a Parallel Distributed Processing Model. The height of the bars correspond to the activation level of a set of output nodes for each of the concepts.

Source: McClelland, 2000

Synopsis

PDP models are some of the most advanced and complex models of memory to date. The way they process information is inspired by the organization and processing of neurons in the brain. Information is encoded into these networks in a complex of massively interconnected units by changing the pattern of connection weights between them. This is in contrast to other memory models, such as network models, where individual concepts are represented by single nodes. In PDP networks, there is a great deal more flexibility and plausibility because any individual unit does not stand for anything. Instead, information is represented and processed in a distributed fashion across the entire network.

DUAL PROCESS THEORIES

One characteristics that many of the models we have seen so far share is that they assume that recognition memory is a single process function, probably involving some version of a signal detection theory. However, there are a number of other formal theories that take the view that recognition memory involves **dual processes.** One of these is a familiarity process that operates on a signal detectionlike principle in which information is identified as old (remembered) when it exceeds some threshold level of activation. The other is a recollection process that involves the conscious retrieval of many different components that are associated with the to-be-recognized information (see Yonelinas, 2002, for an excellent review). Both of these processes are operating normally, but we sometimes find ourselves in situations where one process is producing one result and the other is producing another (but see LeBoe & Whittlesea, 2002, for an alternative view). For example, suppose you meet someone who looks familiar, but you cannot remember her name or how you know her. This is an example of remembering using the familiarity process but not the recollection process.

Atkinson and Juola

One of the earliest dual process models was Atkinson and Juola's (1973; 1974) model. According to this view, people first try a quick familiarity process to see if the information is recognized. If this initial process fails, then a person engages in a more deliberate and effortful search of long-term memories. This more effortful search would presumably produce the richer set of knowledge that is associated with recollection. Thus, this is a model in which recollection is conditional on familiarity failure.

Recent Views

Subsequent dual process theories took the view that recollection and familiarity are operating concurrently and in parallel (e.g., Mandler, 1980). Because the familiarity process uses much less information, it is often finished before the recollection process. This is what is known as a "horse-race" model. The basic idea is that different mental processes (like different horses in a race) all start out more or less independently of one another and begin proceeding to some goal. The one that reaches the goal first is the winner. In this case, the process that produces a decision of recognition allows the person to give a response. In these views, the familiarity process is more unconscious and automatic, whereas the recollection process is more conscious and effortful (e.g., Jacoby, 1991). Also, familiarity can be thought of as providing more quantitative information about the strength of the memory trace(s). In comparison, recollection provides more qualitative information about things that are associated with the information (e.g., who? what? where? when? why? etc.) (e.g., Yonelinas, 2002).

One Process or Two?

One of the rules of thumb in science is, when all else is equal, accept the simplest possible solution. This is called Occam's Razor. The basic idea is that all of the irrelevant stuff is trimmed out. So why have a dual process theory of memory if a single process model, such as a global matching model, will do just fine? Well, one reason is that it has been observed that recollection is much more influenced than familiarity by (1) different levels of processing, (2) generation effects, and (3) full versus divided attention during learning or retrieval. In contrast, familiarity is more affected than recollection by (1) changes in modality (e.g., first hearing something (auditory) and then later reading it (visual)), (2) perceptual priming, (3) changing response bias (i.e., being more liberal or conservative), (4) familiarity information being forgotten more rapidly (Yonelinas, 2002), and (5) the influence of novelty (Kishiyama & Yonelinas, 2003). So there seem to be a number for factors that have a profoundly stronger influence on certain of these memory processes but not the others, suggesting that a model of recognition may need both of them.

The operations of familiarity and recollection also appear to involve different neurological structures. Specifically, familiarity appears to depend more on the temporal cortex surrounding the hippocampus and on the operations of the cortex as a whole. This is why brain damage typically has a much smaller effect on familiarity than it has on recollection. In contrast, recollection appears to depend more on the hippocampus itself and the frontal lobes. The influence of the hippocampus is seen in amnesiacs who have suffered damage to this part of the brain. The influence of the frontal lobes on recollection is also seen in older adults. Older adults have their most dramatic age-related changes in frontal lobe functioning. Similar results are observed in people who have sustained frontal lobe damage (Yonelinas, 2002). So, again, the pattern of observations suggests that there are two retrieval processes involved in recognition. We have also seen that these two different processes operate using different parts of the brain, thereby bolstering the plausibility of dual process models.

Synopsis

While most of the memory models we have discussed are single-process theories, it is possible that memory involves dual processes. In many dual-process models there is usually a simpler, automatic, familiarity-based process and a more complex, deliberative, conscious recollection–based process. Evidence for the operation of dual processes comes from work showing double dissociations. That is, something is changed that affects one process but not the other, and vice versa, or even that affects the two processes in opposite ways. This will be discussed more in Chapter 14.

SUMMARY

In this chapter we looked at a number of formal models of memory. The importance of formal models is that they allow for a level of precision in memory description and prediction that is simply not available with verbal descriptions. We began with a pair of simple models: the threshold theory and the generate-recognize model. We then discussed the recognition failure function and how this careful analysis of memory performance can reveal inadequacies in a formal theory. Four general-class models of memory were discussed. The first were network models of memory that describe the structure of memory. This structure was largely dependent on associative relations among concepts, which then had an influence on later memory. The second class of models was global matching models, which tried to address the processes and dynamics of memory retrieval under a variety of circumstances. The global matching process of these models assesses memory as a whole rather than acting only on a few select memory traces or components. Many of these global matching models have some form of signal detection theory as the basis for the explanation of memory performance. The third class of models was parallel distributed processing models. These are theories of memory that use the structure of the nervous system as an inspiration for how they account for memory. They are sometimes called neural network models. These formal models assume a high degree of interconnectivity among sets of primitive elements, with the pattern of connection strengths and activation levels corresponding to memories in the system. Finally, the fourth class of theories discussed was dual process models of recognition memory. These theories assume that there are at least two memory processes operating during recognition: a simple familiarity component and a more complex recollection component. Overall, there is great value to developing precise and well-articulated formal models because it allows us to more closely capture and understand the workings of our memories.

STUDY QUESTIONS

1. What are two simple models of recognition and recall? What evidence is there to suggest that such basic ideas may be in error?

2. What were some of the first network models of memory, and how did they structure information?

3. By what processes are memory retrieved from and activated in a network model of memory?

4. What are the primary characteristics of global matching models of memory?

5. What are some of the ways that information is thought to be stored and retrieved in global matching models?

6. What are some of the major features of PDP models of memory?

7. What are the two types of processes that are thought be operating in dual process models? What is the evidence to support this idea?

KEY TERMS

ACT, CHARM, Collins and Quillian's network model, connectionist models, distributed storage models, dual process theories, generate-recognize model, global matching models, MINERVA 2, network theory, neural networks, parallel distributed processing model, recognition failure, SAM, signal detection theory, spreading activation, threshold model, TODAM, token node, Tulving-Wiseman function, type node

CHAPTER ELEVEN

AUTOBIOGRAPHICAL MEMORY

Many of the issues presented in previous chapters may appear to be mundane aspects of human memory, such as knowing how to ride a bike, remembering whether a certain word has been seen before, or knowing what a bird is. While these are certainly important aspects of memory, there many other factors that involve what most of us would consider as being more central to distinguishing ourselves from other people. These are the memories that make us unique beings. They help form our identities and give structure to our lives. Knowledge of a person's memory is a very intimate thing. Often when we meet new people, an important part of getting to know one another is to exchange memories, often in the form of providing excerpts from our life story. The type of memory that forms our life story is **autobiographical memory,** and it is the focus of this chapter.

Autobiographical memory covers events, situations, and other knowledge about one's life that span a person's entire life. This chapter covers general characteristics of autobiographical memories and the various levels of detail in autobiographical memory. We consider how autobiographical memory has a narrative character. We'll look at changes in autobiographical memories over time and development, including infantile amnesia for our earliest memories and the reminiscence bump for central portions of our lives. Finally, we cover issues involved with flashbulb memories for surprising events that occur in our lives.

CHARACTERISTICS OF AUTOBIOGRAPHICAL MEMORIES

In this section we examine what sets autobiographical memories apart from other types of memories. This includes their relationship to episodic and semantic memories, the nature of autobiographical memories, and the ease with which they are retrieved.

Episodic or Semantic?

Because autobiographical memories are about a person's own life, are they a kind of episodic memory? In a way, they are. However, autobiographical memories are much more than that. They go beyond the information found in episodic memory alone. They are far more constructive and integrative, often spanning multiple events. In contrast, episodic memories are each generally confined to a single event.

Autobiographical memory also contains generic information about yourself, such as your address, phone number, where you work, and so forth. Much of our life story involves

relatively stable, semanticlike information. Still, autobiographical memories differ from semantic memories in that they are uniquely about our lives. There is an intimate relationship
between semantic and autobiographical memories. Not only does autobiographical memory have semantic aspects, but semantic memories are influenced by autobiographical
memory. For example, semantic knowledge of famous people is more available if they are
autobiographically significant, such as a personal hero, even accounting for frequency and
recency of exposure (Westmacott & Moscovitch, 2003).

Varieties of Information. Autobiographical memories are about individual events in our
lives and how they are interrelated. This may even involve integrating events separated by
long periods of time. Moreover, autobiographical memories contain many interpretive inferences about how an event relates to others and what it means to us.

We can gain some insight about the structure of autobiographical memories by looking at retrieval patterns. Typically, people report general information followed by specific
details (Anderson & Conway, 1997). For example, a person may report something like "I
remember when I was in high school back in Cleveland Ohio. I had this Latin teacher. He
used to constantly terrorize our class. It was horrible. I remember one day he gave a really
hard exam. To make sure we didn't cheat, he put a chair up on his desk at the front of the
class. He then sat on the chair, staring at us all, making us more nervous and tense than we
already were." It is more unusual for people to report information in the reverse order, starting with the details and working out to the general information. This suggests that autobiographical memories are organized around more general pieces of information. Within these
more generalized chunks are the details of our lives.

This organizational structure suggests that autobiographical memories are quite complex. They contain information at a variety of levels of detail and span broad periods of
time. This complexity also influences the retrieval time. It takes much longer to retrieve an
autobiographical memory than a typical episodic or semantic memory. Semantic and
episodic information can be retrieved in 1 or 2 seconds. However, it is not unusual for autobiographical memory retrievals to take 2 to 15 seconds (Anderson & Conway, 1997). This
slower processing time reflects a need to access more information and to sort through the
autobiographical structure to locate the specific memories needed.

Synopsis

Autobiographical memory is a complex form of memory with components that are borrowed from episodic and semantic memories by containing information about both individual events and stable characteristics of a person. Autobiographical memories are woven
out of basic knowledge about the events in our lives, along with the inferences and interpretations of these events.

LEVELS OF AUTOBIOGRAPHICAL MEMORY

Autobiographical memory cannot be simply and easily described because it is made up of
different types of information. One way of parsing this type of knowledge is by the length

of time that is covered (e.g., Conway, 1996). There are three levels that can be addressed: (1) the event level, which refers to specific, individual events; (2) general events, which refer to extended sequences or repeated series of events, often sharing a common component (as compared to a strict temporal sequence); and (3) lifetime periods, which are broad, theme-based portions of a person's life.

An example of how these different levels may be organized is presented in Figure 11.1 (Conway, 1996; Conway & Pleydell-Pearce, 2000). At the top of the figure are two lifetime periods, which in this case happen to overlap in time. These are the relationship and work themes. Within each of these are a number of subcomponents that make up that theme. Each

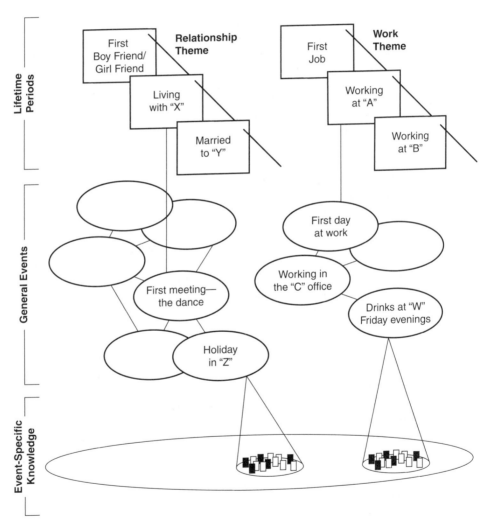

FIGURE 11.1   Hierarchy of Autobiographical Memories

Source: Conway, 1996

of these components is associated with a collection of general events. For example, in the work theme, "working at A" is associated with a number of general events, such as "first day at work," "working in the C office," and "drinks in the evening with W." Each general event is also associated with memories of specific episodes at the lowest level of the hierarchy.

Event-Specific Memories

At the most basic level are **event-specific** memories, which most closely correspond to episodic memories. These are memories for specific, continuous periods of time that involve a common activity occurring at a particular place. For example, the Latin teacher sitting on his chair while perched on his desk is an event memory. Event memories contain a lot of perceptual and contextual detail about what something looked or sounded like, as well as information about time and space. Finally, event memories contain internal contextual information, such as the person's emotional reaction to the event or his physiological state at the time.

While most event-specific memories are lost over time, others endure and become important as singular memories. This is the opposite of many memory processes that tend to move toward making information more semantic and schematic (Pillemer, 2001). In order for an event-specific memory to be retained as a single event, it needs to have some special quality. Pillemer has defined four ways this can be accomplished. First, they can be memories of originating events that have a large number of goal-relevant memories that follow them—for example, a memory of a childhood experience that sets a person on the path toward an eventual career. Second, they can be memories of turning points in which a person's life plan is suddenly redirected—for example, being injured in a car accident. Third, they can be memories of anchoring events that serve as the basis for a major belief system in life—for example, someone having what they believe is a religious experience. Finally, people have memories for analogous events that they use to guide their future behavior. For example, if a person remembers the embarrassing incident at work when she got caught goofing off, she would remember that event if the temptation to do that again ever arose. All of these types of event-specific memories can make them easy to remember and slow to forget.

General-Event Memories

At the intermediate level of the hierarchy are **general events.** One type of general event is a sequence of specific events that form a larger episode. For example, the first day on the job is a general event because it is made up of the various individual experiences of that day, such as given a tour of the building, assigned a desk, given literature on company policies and benefits, and so forth. The extension of an event across time and space occurs because people are able to unify smaller events by common themes based on the content of the memories (Burt, Kemp, & Conway, 2003). This may even involve linking events to multiple themes.

The other type of general event is the repeating event. For example, your memory for a class taken last year is a general event. The different class sessions are not considered a sequence of events because they were separated by large periods of in time. Still, the repeated event quality to the class can be used to organize experiences into a general event of being in that class. For both types of general events, there is often some personal goal that is being affected by the extended event.

The ability to create and store general-event memories requires integrative and interpretive thinking. Integration is required because different events must be brought together into a common memory trace. This is particularly clear for recurring situations, such as taking a class. Interpretation is also needed because a person must understand how the various events go together. For example, in a general-event memory of the class, a person's memory for receiving a grade on an exam must be related in some coherent fashion to her memory for taking the exam and its relation to the studying before that.

Lifetime Period Memories

At the highest level of the hierarchy are **lifetime periods.** These are long periods of life that are organized along some common theme, such as "early childhood," "education," or "career." Lifetime periods give a person a sense of structure about the progression and development of his life in the service of various goals or preferences. When people recall autobiographical memories, if they go beyond a single general event, they are likely to confine their retrieval to a given theme of their life (Barsalou, 1988). For example, when recalling information about previous work experience, they are unlikely to recall information about the various relationships they were involved in, unless those relationships in some way overlapped with their work experiences (such as dating a coworker).

Evidence for the Hierarchy

This autobiographical memory hierarchy is more of a heuristic than a hard and fast categorization. There are many cases where it is unclear at what level a given memory belongs. Also, information may be divided up into many subcomponents at the different levels. For example, a general event may be broken down into other general events. A memory for taking a class may be broken down into different parts of the semester. Thus, there is a recursive quality to autobiographical memories in which smaller and smaller parts can be nested into a larger description (Barsalou, 1988). An example of this recursive decomposition is shown in Figure 11.2.

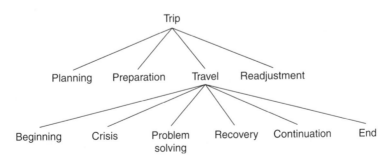

FIGURE 11.2   The Recursive Process of Breaking Down an Autobiographical Memory into Smaller and Smaller Parts—in this Case, a Memory of a Trip

Source: Barsalou, 1988

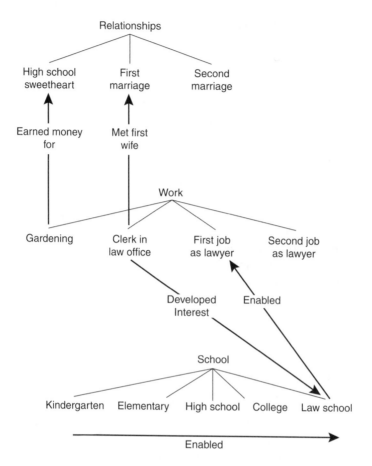

FIGURE 11.3   Temporal Overlapping of Various Lifetime Periods with Different Themes Based on Common, Shared Specific and General Events

Source: Barsalou, 1988

It should also be noted that people typically have different aspects of their lives going on concurrently. Thus, there is some overlap of various extended life events. As such, there are a number of ways that autobiographical memories relate to one another (Barsalou, 1988). An example of this overlapping quality is illustrated in Figure 11.3, in which there are events from different lifespan periods overlapping one another in time. After all, life does not start and stop depending on our goals and preferences.

Neurological Evidence.   Despite the fuzzy nature of this division of autobiographical memory, there is some neurological support that this takes place in memory. For example, some people with dense amnesia can recall lifetime period and general-event information but not memories for specific episodes from their lives. For example, a patient known as S. S. became amnesic after a case of herpes simplex encephalitis when he was about 40 years old (Cermak & O'Connor, 1983; McCarthy & Warrington, 1992). The virus damaged part of his left hemisphere. Although he was of high intelligence (I.Q. of 133), he had severe memory problems. S. S. cannot remember specific events from his life, but he can recount general aspects of his life experiences, such as his job. Thus, although he had trouble remembering at the event level, he could remember at the general and lifetime period levels.

A similar case is patient K. C., who suffered damage to the frontal-parietal region of his left hemisphere and the parietal-occipital region of his right hemisphere as the result of a motorcycle accident at the age of 30 (Tulving, Schacter, McLachlan, & Moscovitch, 1988). He is unable to remember any events from his life. For example, he cannot remember the circumstances of his brother's tragic drowning death ten years before. He does, however, have memory for general, semantic knowledge that extends to knowledge acquired about his job, which he had just recently begun, and even personally relevant information, such as being able to draw a floor plan of the house he grew up in as a child (although he can't say which room was his), recall the names of his school classmates, and describe places when he has vacationed. This distinction between what is and is not remembered reinforces the idea that autobiographical memory for events is a separate form of memory from more general knowledge.

In contrast, patient, K. S., who had a right anterior temporal lobectomy to control her epileptic seizures, was able to recall specific life events but not general knowledge about the people involved in them (Ellis, Young, & Critchley, 1989). She also had trouble with the identities of famous people and product brands. Thus, in some sense, she had the ability to store memories at the event-specific level but not more general information.

Synopsis

Autobiographical memory can be divided into three levels. At the event-specific level are memories of individual events, which is closest to episodic memory. At the general-event level are memories for extended and repeating events. Finally, at the lifetime period level are memories that span broad, thematically related parts of our lives. This hierarchy is supported by studies of the effectiveness with which people retrieve memories at different levels, as well as neurological evidence from patients who appear to be suffering memory problems at one level but not the others.

AUTOBIOGRAPHICAL MEMORY AS LIFE NARRATIVE

As mentioned earlier, autobiographical memories serve as our life stories. They are **life narrative** memories (McAdams, 2001). This follows a general human tendency to organize our experiences into some sort of narrative structure (Bruner, 1991), rather than simply a structure based on semantic information (Conway & Berkerian, 1987). Because this autobiographical memory is constructed to form a story, studies of this type of memory should reveal such characteristics. People are often able to access information in autobiographical memory using basic event components that are found in narratives, such as people, places, activities, and other thematic information (e.g., Barsalou, 1988; Burt, 1992; Burt et al.,

1995; Lancaster & Barsalou, 1997; Wagenaar, 1986). In general, autobiographical memories can be elicited by any source of information that is stored with the event. For example, odors are particularly effective at helping people remember events from their lives (Chu & Downes, 2002).

In addition, when people are probed for autobiographical memories, they tend to retrieve them in clusters of others that occurred at a similar time (Brown & Schopflocher, 1998b). Moreover, these reminded events are related to the original memory in systematic ways. People are most often reminded of events that are causally related to one another (either as a cause or an effect). They are also reminded of events that share the same person, place, or activity (Brown & Schopflocher, 1998a), similar to the ways that people organize their memories of actual stories (Zwaan & Radvansky, 1998).

To help make their autobiographical memories narrative in style, people often draw on their semantic memories. As you may recall from Chapter 9, people have organized event scripts and schemas. If these are used to structure autobiographical memories, then they should reflect the temporal order of the script. In fact, people are better at recalling life events when they do so in a forward order rather than a backward order, or by reporting event details based on their importance. Moreover, when people are asked to recognize details from a life event, they are fastest in responding to the first and more important details (Anderson & Conway, 1993). For example, if you remember a trip to a restaurant, when you think back on it, you are more likely to replay it back in your mind in a forward order, as it was experienced. However, if you were just thinking about one or two important details, such as a marriage proposal, you would to be able to retrieve it quickly and without the need to start at the beginning.

While narrative structure is important, it is not always observed. Information about things like temporal order may be missing. For example, in a study by Burt, Watt, Mitchell, and Conway (1998), people were asked to take photos during the course of their daily lives. When they returned to the lab, they were then shown the pictures for the first time with the task of putting them in the correct temporal order. Performance on this task was terrible. People were only correct about 9 percent of the time, although they did better if less than a week had passed, in which case they were 35 percent correct. This low performance most likely occurred because the snapshots were just random bits that did not create well-defined narratives and so were more difficult to correctly structure and order.

Perspectives in Autobiographical Memory

Narrative structure also shows itself in how we experience our autobiographical memories. When you think about events from your life, there is often an accompanying visual image. The thing is that these images can vary in their perspective. Sometimes we experience the memory from our original perspective in the situation, with the same perceptual field of view. These are called **field memories.** In contrast, at other times, we view the situation from outside of ourselves and may even see ourselves in that situation. These are called **observer memories.** The very fact that we can have observer memories emphasizes the constructed nature of autobiographical memory.

This distinction between memories (Nigro & Neisser, 1983) is influenced by three factors that involve how a memory is experienced (see Table 11.1). One factor is the age of

TABLE 11.1   Dimensions and Criteria for Field and Observer Memories

DIMENSION	FIELD MEMORY	OBSERVER MEMORY
Age of memory	Newer	Older
Emotionality	More emotional	Less emotional
Self-awareness	Less self-aware	More self-aware

the memory. In general, older memories are more likely to be observer memories. A second factor is the emotionality of the memory. Generally, the more emotional the memory, the more likely it is experienced as a field memory. Finally, the third factor is one's self-awareness in the situation. Generally, the more self-aware a person is, the more likely one is trying to understand one's role in the larger event, and so this tends to lead to more observer memories. For example, an observer memory is more likely to be generated when one remembers giving a speech.

This has been supported by work on posttraumatic stress disorder (PTSD). It has been found that when these people remember the traumatic events that produced their condition, they felt more stress and anxiety when they recalled them from a field memory perspective than from an observer memory perspective (McIsaac & Eich, 2004). Taking the view one had during the event is more likely to engage emotional reactions and reinstate the emotional and physiological states of the time. This makes the person more anxious. However, taking the perspective of an outsider in some sense helps detach the person from the event and reduces the anxiety from remembering it.

Schema-Copy-Plus-Tag Model

People use schemas and scripts to help reconstruct autobiographical memories that are incomplete. The older autobiographical memories become, the more schema-consistent people's reports are likely to be (Eldridge, Barnard, & Bekerian, 1994). Thus, in an important sense, schemas guide the formation of our memories and strongly influence how and what we remember. While this is true, it is also true that if you think about your life, it does not feel like you have a memory full of generic, stereotypical events. Instead, you tend to better remember the parts that are unusual. Memory is heavily schematic, but what is schema-inconsistent tends to be more memorable.

The Model.   So what is the solution to this apparent paradox? One idea is that our memories represent both schematic and unique aspects of an event. This is the schema-copy-plus-tag model (e.g., Graesser, Gordon, & Sawyer, 1979; Graesser & Nakamura, 1982; Graesser, Woll, Kolwalski, & Smith, 1980; Trafimow & Wyer, 1993). When you encounter a new event, you first activate the appropriate schema. That schema, or at least the more relevant parts of it, will be the basis for your memory of the event. The retrieval of this schema helps reduce the need to actively think about and process every little detail. One can simply assume that most of them are about the same as they usually are.

In addition, people associate "tags" with the memory trace to denote all of the important things that are inconsistent with the schema, thereby making the memory of that event unique. For example, if you go to a restaurant and the manager tells you that you do not have to pay the check, this is going to be represented by a tag in memory. People are less likely to remember schema-consistent information than unusual tag information when the event memory involves themselves or another familiar person as compared to when it involves an unknown person (Colcombe & Wyer, 2002).

Item-specific and Relational Processing.   This use of schemas and tags is part of the distinction between item-specific and relational processing (see Chapter 7). The schemas provide the relational processing, whereas the tags serve as item-specific processing. Memory for event information in terms of the schema and tags can further be influenced by how the information is learned. Learning that emphasizes the general structure of the event, such as sorting information based on themes, facilitates the schematic aspect, whereas learning that emphasizes item-specific information, such as filling in missing letters in sentences, facilitates the tag aspect (Hunt, Ausley, & Schultz, 1986). It should be noted that this distinction between the schemas and the tags also parallels fuzzy trace theories.

Representing autobiographical knowledge this way has two consequences. First, because most trivial details were not directly represented in the memory, it is difficult for people to distinguish between schema-consistent parts that were actually present and those that were not. Second, because the tag is part of the memory trace, it makes it easy for a person to remember what was odd about the event. This aspect of memory has some unfortunate consequences for education. In studies of students' memories for what happened during class, it has been shown that they better remember unusual things that happened during the lecture, such as spilling coffee or jokes that were told, as compared to the more central and typical aspects of the lectures (Kintsch & Bates, 1977; Nakamura, Graesser, Zimmerman, & Riha, 1985).

Synopsis

Autobiographical memory is structured as a life narrative, with the structure of memory paralleling that seen in memory for actual stories. This constructive aspect of autobiographical memory is seen in the distinction between field and observer perspectives in autobiographical remembering. Finally, although autobiographical memory construction and retrieval can be guided by schemas, people use memory tags to help remember odd and unusual but important aspects of an event.

AUTOBIOGRAPHICAL MEMORY OVER TIME

Like most memories, autobiographical memory has a forgetting curve. People better remember more recent events than older ones (Whitten & Leonard, 1981), and, consistent with the Pollyanna principle, there is a tendency to remember pleasant events better than unpleasant ones (e.g., Wagenaar, 1986), with the emotional intensity of negative events being tempered more so than positive events (Walker, Skowronski, & Thompson, 2003;

Walker, Vogl, & Thompson, 1997). Oddly enough, this forgetting curve extends to events that happened prior to birth (Rubin, 1998). This probably reflects interest in the historical events that led up to the current situation (Brown, 1990).

There are two major deviations to the standard forgetting curve discussed here, both of which concern events that a person actually experienced. The first is the very poor memory for very early life experiences, called infantile amnesia. The second is the very good memory for life experiences around the age of 20, called the reminiscence bump.

Infantile Amnesia

Now that we've reached the middle of this chapter, let's talk about the beginning of life—specifically, our memories from when we were infants. But wait. Where *are* they? Most adults, if they think about it, find that their earliest memory is not from when they were infants but more likely from when they were between the ages of 2 to 4. (It is even possible to have autobiographical memories from as early as ages 18 to 24 months, but not earlier (Howe, 2003).)

For example, my earliest memory is from when I was about 2½ years old. My parents had just moved to Wisconsin, and we were living in a trailer until they could find a house. It was late December, and I remember ice creeping in underneath the door—not a pleasant sight. Because my family was new in town, some of my father's new coworkers wanted to help out. So one of them came to the trailer one evening dressed as Santa Claus to give me a thrill. (He already had a Santa suit because he had discovered that when he wore it to a bar, someone always wanted to buy Santa a drink.) When he walked into the trailer, I was terrified. I remember crying and screaming and running into my bedroom to get away from this big, red, creepy-looking guy who had burst into my home and started ho hoing at me.

Occasionally, people report memories from earlier ages. However, many of these "memories" were generated in response to seeing pictures, hearing stories told by older relatives, or other sources. Thus, they are not memories of the event itself.

So what happens to memories of a person's life before the age of two or so? This is a period for which nearly no one has any reliable autobiographical memory. Clearly there is a lot of learning during this time, and information is being committed to memory, such as learning how to walk and talk. However, this learning does not have the quality that allows us to remember previous events from our lives. All of the events are forgotten. As such, this absence of early childhood memories is called **infantile amnesia.** Several explanations are now presented for why infantile amnesia occurs.

Psychodynamic View.   One of the first people to take note of infantile amnesia was Sigmund Freud (1899/1938). Freud's explanation was integrated into his psychodynamic theories. In Freud's scheme, many of people's psychological problems involved sexual thoughts and desires. Infantile amnesia was no exception. According to Freud, when we are infants we go through a period of sexual thinking and wishing. Part of that involves a desire to be sexually intimate with our opposite-sexed parent. As we mature, we take on the rules and norms of our culture as part of the development of the superego. During this time we learn that the incestual thoughts that we were having are taboo. To protect ourselves from this threatening and horrible knowledge about ourselves, our unconscious blocks from consciousness all memories from this time. This repressive activity is so successful that people often have no memory of when they were infants.

Freud's theory makes interesting reading, and it fits well into his broader theories. However, there are few people today who accept his view on infantile amnesia. Most contemporary explanations focus on other factors that influence how memory operates, especially memory traces that may have been formed during the first few years of life.

Neurological View.   A more modern explanation of infantile amnesia is a neurological account based on the state of various neural structures in the course of development. For example, the hippocampus is an important structure in laying down new memories (see Chapter 2). Damage to this structure in adults can lead to severe memory problems and amnesia (see Chapter 16). The hippocampus is relatively undeveloped at birth. It does not reach adult form until a child is a few years old. Thus, the ability to lay down new memories would be hindered, contributing to infantile amnesia (Nadel and Zola-Morgan, 1984).

Infantile amnesia may also be a result of a less developed frontal lobe, which is important for binding contextual factors in memory, allowing for such things as source monitoring (see Chapter 12). This inability to appropriately link different aspects of experience could lead to an inability to adequately form autobiographical memories (Newcombe et al., 2000). However, while neurological development is a contributing factor to infantile amnesia, it is not the whole story. For instance, it is well known that infants can acquire, but not retain, complex and neurologically sophisticated episodic memories (see Chapter 15).

Schema Organization View.   Another theory of infantile amnesia is that infants are trying to understand how the world works and are still developing how to use schemas, called the schema organization theory. For example, a child might remember what typically happens during a trip to McDonald's but not remember any of the details from a given trip. Relatedly, this theory suggests that young children also have underdeveloped schemas, and so they focus on inappropriate aspects of an event. When their schemas become more developed, they have difficulty retrieving the prior memories that were formed with the old schemas.

Language Development View.   An important thing to note about the time when infantile amnesia lifts is that this is also the time during which language acquisition is making significant strides (Nelson, 1993). Thus, we call this language development theory. From this view, infantile amnesia reflects an inability to organize information into a coherent life narrative, which can then be used to help retrieval. Early on, infant memory has two roles: either as a generic schema-driven memory or as a repository for temporary episodic memories. But with the advent of language, and the need to share experiences with others in our social context, autobiographical memory is developed. So the chaotic jumble of memories that is infantile amnesia is displaced with the organization of the new autobiographical memory. This is supported by work that has found that preverbal children do not translate that knowledge into verbal information after they learn how to talk about those events. The memories appear to stay nonverbal (Simcock & Hayne, 2002).

Emergent Self View.   A final view of infantile amnesia is the emergent self theory (Howe & Courage, 1993). According to this view, the removal of infantile amnesia is a function of a person developing a sense of self as a unique and identifiable entity. Newborn infants lack a clear sense of self as a separate entity from the environment. The development of the self is further divided into the acquisition of the "I" and the "me." The "I" is the subjective sense of self as a causal agent, whereas the "me" is the objective sense of self, such as your personal features. This latter sense of self emerges around 18 months of age and is fairly well established by 24 months. Once the concept of self is established, autobiographical memory can be constructed around it. Again, the offset of infantile amnesia corresponds to the onset of autobiographical memory.

Multicomponent Development.   After reading about all of these theories about infantile amnesia, many of which seem to have some plausibility, it seems as though there are many factors that bring on this infantile amnesia. There are a number of changes that move a person from a state of not remembering much about his own life to the awareness that is autobiographical memory. The multicomponent development theory (Nelson & Fivush, 2004) is that there are number of memory abilities or components that emerge to bring about this new type of memory. These components include not only the development of an adequate episodic memory system, but also the development of language and narrative skills, an understanding of how adults think and talk about the world and the passage of time, as well as how the person understands himself or herself. The interaction of these multiple influences is reflected in the fact that people in different cultures experience different offset ages for infantile amnesia. For example, people in Western cultures, such as the United States, come out of infantile amnesia six months earlier than people living in Asian cultures (Wang, 2004). This may be because in these cultures children interact differently with adults, with a greater focus on the self in Western cultures.

Reminiscence Bump

Another interesting characteristic of autobiographical memory that influences the standard forgetting curve is something that is easier to observe as a person ages. This is a finding that memories of a person's life tend to be dominated by events from around the age of 20 (between 15 and 25). In these studies, a free association paradigm is used in which people are presented with lists of words—such as "bird," "chair," "apple"—and are asked to recall the first memory from their life that comes to mind. Most of the memories are from the recent past, and the further back in time one goes, the fewer memories there are, just as in a standard forgetting curve. However, there is an oddity in that there is a bump in the curve around the age of 20, with people recalling more information from this period of their lives than would be expected in a normal forgetting curve (see Rubin, Rahhal, & Poon, 1998). This is the **reminiscence bump** (see Figure 11.4). There are a number of explanations for this finding that have been given by Rubin, Rahhal, and Poon, each of which seems to have some credibility.

Cognitive View.   One idea is oriented around basic cognitive processes, called the *cognitive account*. A general serial position effect exists in long-term memory. Part of this serial position effect is a primacy effect where initial memories are easier to retrieve than

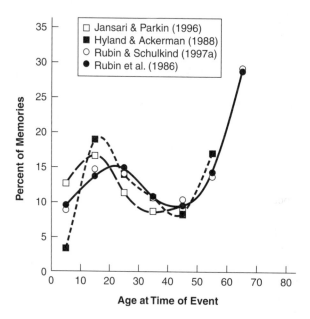

FIGURE 11.4   The Reminiscence Bump

Source: Rubin, Rahhal, & Poon, 1998

subsequent memories. In terms of autobiographical memory, events in a person's life are re-membered better if they were the first ones of that type. One of the things about the age around which the reminiscence bump is centered is that this is a time in life when there is a great deal of change and a number of experiences are occurring for the first time, such as one's first kiss, first car, first apartment, first job, and so forth.

Because there are so many firsts, it is not surprising that these memories are easier to recall than others. Thus, the reminiscence bump can be attributed to a large number of pri-macy effects. For example, it has been shown that people who immigrated to the United States from Spanish-speaking countries show reminiscence bumps at different times, de-pending on when they moved. The later they moved, the later their reminiscence bump. Moving to a new country with a new language provides a lot of initial and novel experiences (Schrauf & Rubin, 1998).

A related idea is that people may be using "life scripts" of what is expected to be major transition points in a person's life and that these scripts are used to guide memory retrieval (Berntsen & Rubin, 2004). This is supported by the idea that many culturally accepted posi-tive life events often occur at well-defined transitions (e.g., getting married), whereas this is not true for negative events (e.g., having a friend die). Consistent with this, the reminiscence bump is much more clearly observed for positive events than for negative events, and people indicate the position of life transitions points at around the time of the bump.

Neurological View.   Another explanation for the reminiscence bump is the neurological account. The period of the reminiscence bump is when a person is at her neurological and cognitive peak, when her nervous system is neither maturing nor declining. As such, people are at their best capacity to encode and store memories. Thus, memory should be more efficient at these times than at any other. Prior to this, people have difficulty encoding information into long-term memory. Furthermore, after this, beginning in the late 20s, one begins to see declines in memory ability, which becomes more prominent as aging progresses.

Identity Formation View. A final explanation for the reminiscence bump is the identity formation account. During the reminiscence bump a person is making a number of decisions about who he is with regard to preferences, ideologies, vocation, and so forth. Although people can make these sorts of decisions at any time during their life, more decisions than usual are made at this time. These are decisions that shape our choices and actions in the future and become associated with them. As a result of this increased interconnectivity, memories from this time are more available than normally.

Summary. So there are several explanations for the reminiscence bump. The cognitive theory focuses on the uniqueness of initial experiences. The neurological theory focuses on changes in neurological functioning. The identity formation account focuses on the important role that period of time plays in the development of one's own self-identity. None of these explanations has an advantage over the others. It seems likely that each of them plays some role in the emergence of the reminiscence bump.

There are still aspects of the reminiscence bump that need to be accounted for. For example, people are more likely to show a reminiscence bump for positive than negative events (Berntsen & Rubin, 2002). Moreover, the reminiscence bump is guided, in part, by cultural schemas. For example, in a study by Rubin and Berntsen (2003), college students were asked to estimate the likelihood that a typical 70-year-old would remember various events from the past. These students' estimates were very close to the actual pattern shown by adults in this age group. This suggests that cultural expectations can guide the maintenance of information in autobiographical memory.

Flashbulb Memories

So far, our discussion of autobiographical memory has focused on relatively mundane aspects of life. However, we also have memories for surprising and important events that are very vivid, have a great deal of detail, and are relatively resistant to forgetting. For example, many people remember where they were and how they heard about the assassination of John F. Kennedy. A generation later, people can tell you detailed information about how they hear about the explosion of the space shuttle *Challenger*. More recently, people are likely to have this quality of memory for the news of Princess Diana's death (Hornstein, Brown, & Mulligan, 2003) or the terrorist attacks on September 11, 2001 (Schmidt, 2004; Tekcan, Ece, Gülgöz, & Er, 2003).

Highly detailed memories for surprising events are called **flashbulb memories** (Brown & Kulik, 1977) because it is as if the mind had taken a picture of the events that were occurring when the surprising information was learned. What is striking about flashbulb memories is that they contain detailed information for not only the surprising event itself, but also for the context in which it was learned. It is not unusual to find people who remember who told them, what the weather conditions were, whom they were with, where they were, what they were wearing, and so forth. Obviously this contextual information is not directly relevant to what they learned. Still, it seems to be stored at a high level of detail.

Flashbulb Memories Are Special.   The original explanation for flashbulb memories was that there is a special memory process, called the "Now Print!" mechanism, somewhere in the neural coding of long-term memory (Brown & Kulik, 1977). This mechanism is triggered when something of great importance occurs, and it encodes so much detail because when something surprising happens, by storing everything in great detail, it allows a person to later sort out and identify the important components. This is especially important for rare events where memory is more critical because another experience of this type is unlikely. Thus, this sort of mechanism would have some survival value. However, future work on flashbulb memories failed to support this idea.

Flashbulb Memories Are Not So Special.   Some people have suggested that flashbulb memories are just normal memories for important events because flashbulb memories can contain errors, become distorted, and be forgotten over time (Christianson, 1989; Mc-Closkey, Wible, & Cohen, 1988; Schmolck, Buffalo, & Squire, 2000; Talarico & Rubin, 2003). They can also include misinformation from hearing other people's stories of the event (Niedźwieńska, 2003). In studies of flashbulb memories over time, it has been found that there is some forgetting, people's accounts change, and incorrect information can seep in. For example, a person might remember that she was having lunch with a particular individual when she heard the news, but in truth, the person she remembers having lunch with was somewhere else that day. Flashbulb memories may reflect a belief in the accuracy of the memories that emerges out of the emotional reaction to learning surprising news rather than the actual accuracy of the memory. The stronger the emotional reaction, the more the memory is believed (Talarico & Rubin, 2003). A clear example of how wrong a flashbulb memory can be seen in the following quote from memory researcher Ulric Neisser (1982).

> For many years I have remembered how I heard the news of the Japanese attack on Pearl Harbor, which occurred on the day before my thirteenth birthday. I recall sitting in the living room of our house—we only lived in that house for one year, but I remember it well—listening to a baseball game on the radio. The game was interrupted by an announcement of the attack, and I rushed upstairs to tell my mother. This memory has been so clear for so long that I never confronted its inherent absurdity until last year: no one broadcasts baseball games in December! (It can't have been a football game either: professional football barely existed in 1941, and the college season ended by Thanksgiving.) (p. 45)

Criteria for Flashbulb Memories.   It seems as though flashbulb memories are different from normal memories, even if they are created through normal memory mechanisms and subject to forgetting. It may be that flashbulb memories are better records of the autobiographical experience of a surprising event, but memory for the event itself may be more normal (Tekcan et al., 2003). What we remember better is our reaction, not so much the news itself. Although they are not perfect records, flashbulb memories do have some distinguishing qualities, at least phenomenologically. It is only under rare circumstances that all of the relevant factors are present, allowing the flashbulb memory to be created (Conway et al., 1994).

So under what circumstances are flashbulb memories more likely to be formed? An outline of the more important criteria was provided by Finkenhauer et al., (1998) and is shown in Figure 11.5. The first criterion is that the event be novel. That is, it should be a rare and, most likely, a new occurrence. For example, seeing the World Trade Center towers being attacked was a new event, but hearing about a murder on the evening news, sadly, is not. This novelty can lead to a feeling of surprise. This uniqueness and unexpectedness help it stand out in memory and thus be less likely to be influenced by interference. Also, because the event is surprising, people are more likely to dedicate a greater degree of effort in elaborative processing trying to make sense of the event and its consequences. This makes the flashbulb memory more complex and detailed as well as more enduring.

Also flashbulb memory creation requires that the event be important and have significant consequences for the person witnessing or hearing about it. It is critical to remember information that had an impact on our lives but not to remember more trivial information. For example, the events of September 11, 2001 were important and consequential, but a penny found in a parking lot is not.

The degree to which the events are surprising and important affects the person's emotional reaction. The more intense the emotional relation, the more likely a flashbulb memory will be formed. Emotionally intense events raise a person's arousal level, which can aid

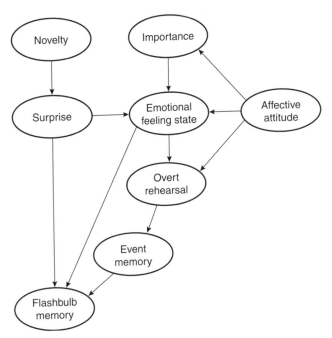

FIGURE 11.5   Outline of Major Factors in the Creation of Flashbulb Memories

Source: Finkenhauer et al., 1998

in memorization (Bradley, Greenwald, Petry, & Lang, 1992), perhaps influencing much of the effect of surprise (Hornstein, Brown, & Mulligan, 2003). It can therefore lead to more attention to the event, more elaborative processing, and more remindings as subsequent consequences are encountered. This all facilitates the retention of information in a flashbulb memory. The emotional reaction can even override the novelty and surprise components for events that are expected, even if they are repeated, but that are emotionally intense. For example, a survey of gay men in the New York City area found that although there were repeated experiences of loved ones dying of AIDS, and the death was expected with the progression of the disease, the emotional intensity of each experience of loss was sufficient to create lasting memories of hearing of the death (Mahmood, Manier, & Hirst, 2004). Thus, emotional reaction plays a pivotal role in forming flashbulb memories.

Another factor that influences flashbulb memory formation is a person's affective attitude. These are the person's opinions and beliefs prior to the event that can provide the basis for later elaborative processing in the creation of a flashbulb memory. If a person lacks the requisite knowledge to understand or think deeply about the event, a flashbulb memory is less likely to occur. For example, if a popular sports figure retires, people who are not fans of that sport will consider that news insignificant and will not form a flashbulb memory of it. In contrast, a person who is an avid fan would probably form a flashbulb memory.

Finally, people will engage in more overt rehearsal of the flashbulb memory event by discussing it with others. When these sorts of events occur, people spend a great deal of time thinking about it and how they heard about it, including discussing with others how they heard about it and their reactions to it. Finally, if it is a public event, the news media repeatedly devotes intense coverage to it. This dwelling on and sharing of the information affect memory. The memory traces are reinforced and strengthened, decreasing the likelihood that forgetting will occur, and it may actually be a form of overlearning.

Synopsis

Like other memories, autobiographical memories are affected by the passage of time and other influences that are more unique to this form of memory. For example, there is an abrupt drop in the ability to produce memories from the first few years of life with infantile amnesia. As we age, we also notice a change in the forgetting curve, so there is unusually better memory for events around the age of 20 with the reminiscence bump. Finally, memories of surprising and emotionally engaging events can lead to flashbulb memories that seem to be remarkably resistant to forgetting.

SUMMARY

Autobiographical memory refers to the ability to remember the events of one's life in a coherent life narrative. This life narrative can be examined at a number of different levels, from specific events through repeating or extended general events and expanding into thematically organized lifetime periods. This distinction is supported by evidence from people with brain damage, who can remember information at one level but not another. A great deal of autobiographical memory is reconstructed when a person is trying to remember, using scripts and schemas. The parts of an event that are most likely to be accurately remembered are the unexpected and important parts, not the mundane and trivial ones. Autobiographical memory changes over the life span. Adults have almost no autobiographical memories for the first few years of life. Moreover, although a person continues to lose memories due to the natural forgetting process, the period of time from around 15 to 25 years of age tends to be better remembered. Finally, there are some events that have such a profound impact on our lives in that relatively few of the details are forgotten, and the memories stay with us clearly throughout our lives.

STUDY QUESTIONS

1. In what ways are autobiographical memories like episodic memories? Like semantic memories?

2. What are the three levels of autobiographical memory? What are their characteristics?

3. During what period of a person's life does infantile amnesia occur?

4. What are some of the causes of infantile amnesia? How credible are each of these?

5. What is the reminiscence bump? Why does it occur?

6. What are flashbulb memories? What causes them? How much are they like or dislike regular memories?

KEY TERMS

autobiographical memory, event-specific memories, field memories, flashbulb memories, general events, infantile amnesia, life narrative, lifetime periods, observer memories, reminiscence bump

CHAPTER TWELVE

MEMORY AND REALITY

Our memory is our contact with the world beyond the present. We make assessments about the nature of the world, how it works, and what has happened in the past, based on what we remember. Most of the time our memories are fairly accurate and we get along fine. However, other times, what we remember and what actually happened may be two very different things. For example, if you misremember that you turned off the oven before you left for vacation when in reality you left it on, you risk burning down your house. It is important to understand when our memories can betray us and when they can be trusted. What are the circumstances that cause memory and reality to part ways?

In this chapter we discuss a number of factors related to how memory and reality square up and how our ideas of the past may be faulty. The first issue is how we keep track of where our memories come from. This is called source monitoring, and it includes situations of unconscious plagiarism, or cryptomnesia, and false fame effects. We also examine the sleeper effect and how this phenomenon affects our attitudes and opinions. We look at cases where memory and reality are at odds when people remember things that never happened, or false memories. This includes some discussion of both implanted memories and memories recovered under hypnosis. Finally, we look at how the apparently normal use of information in memory can change our memories. Specifically, we look at the processes of verbal overshadowing and the revelation effect.

SOURCE MONITORING

Many of the issues about memories that we have seen so far have been on what the memory is about. Although this is important, another critical factor is *how* a person knows where a memory came from. For example, did she hear a story on the news or from a friend? Was it all just a dream? The ability to keep track of where memories come from is called **source monitoring** (Johnson, Hashstroudi, & Lindsay, 1993), and it involves processes over and above those needed to assess whether something is old or new (Johnson, Kounios, & Reeder, 1994; Lindsay & Johnson, 1991). However, as complex as it is, accurate source monitoring does not necessarily require complete conscious awareness of the original source. Accurate source judgments are regularly made when people rely on vague and partial information more associated with less conscious feelings of familiarity (Meissner, Brigham, & Kelley, 2002).

Source monitoring requires people to first integrate information about source and content into a common memory trace. Later they actively and deliberately search memory for source information. Not surprisingly, each of these stages involves a different part of the brain. The integration of different types of information involves the hippocampus. The search for source information, being a controlled memory process, uses the prefrontal lobes, whereas the actual retrieval of this information emphasizes the temporal lobe areas (Senkfor & Van Petten, 1998).

Types of Source Information

A number of different types of information are used to evaluate the source of a memory. Although this information is used to make decisions about a memory's source, people don't need to have conscious awareness of the event itself but can make fairly accurate judgments based on partial or unconscious information (Hicks, Marsh, & Ritschel, 2002).

One criterion is perceptual detail. This is perceptual information that is encoded into the memory trace, such as what a person was looking at or hearing when the memory was created. Memories of events that were actually experienced often have a higher degree of perceptual detail than memories generated by hearing about an event from someone else or imagining it. For example, people find it easier to discriminate between words they actually said versus words they thought they said. The difference in perceptual experiences in these two cases is relatively pronounced. However, people find it more difficult to remember words that another person actually said versus "hearing" in their mind the words being said in that person's voice (Johnson, Foley, & Leach, 1988). This is because both have similar perceptual or pseudoperceptual qualities.

Another criterion is contextual information. This is information about the context in which the memory was acquired. For example, if people remember seeing a plane crash while they were in an airport terminal, it is more likely that the event was witnessed. However, if people remember seeing the plane crash while they were sitting in their living room, it is more likely they saw it on the local news. Thus, people can use expectancies based on the context to help make source monitoring decisions (Bayen, Nakamura, Dupuis, & Yang, 2000).

Overall, people better remember source information when the source is consistent with expectations than if the memory comes from an unexpected source, suggesting that some level of guessing is involved in source monitoring (Bayen et al., 2000). Also, these expectancies are more likely to be operating at retrieval than at encoding (Hicks & Cockman, 2003). For example, it is easier to recall that a reminder to call your mother came from your sister than from your professor because the first is more expected, even if the second were actually true. People can also be swayed by what others say. For example, if a person knows that other people claimed to have witnessed something, that person is more likely to make a source monitoring error by claiming to see something he only imagined (Hoffman, Granhag, See, & Loftus, 2001). Source monitoring is a complex and fragile memory process.

A third criterion is the amount of semantic detail and/or affective information that is available. This is how much the person was mentally and emotionally involved in the events in memory. This can include thoughts that a person had (e.g., "Man, Bob must really be stupid to ask if gravity's getting heavier") or emotional reactions (e.g., I remember feeling really queasy when I saw what the car accident had done to that girl's face). This information can be used to help a person figure out where the memory came from.

A final criterion is cognitive operations. These are any mental activities that were done when first thinking about the information. This includes retrieving information from long-term memory, manipulating information, trying to generate a mental image, and so forth. This is more likely to be found in memories of events that were only thought about. Ideas and images do not pop into our heads without effort. Instead, when we think things through, we not only remember what we were thinking about, but also the mental activity that we used to generate those thoughts. For example, if you were trying to remember something your significant other said in the middle of an argument, you might think, was this (1) a real argument or (2) something you imagined he said when you couldn't talk directly to him (most people seem to be brilliant at winning these arguments). An imaginary argument would have more cognitive operations associated with it.

Types of Source Monitoring

There are three basic types of source monitoring (Johnson, Hashstroudi & Lindsay, 1993): internal source monitoring, external source monitoring, and reality monitoring. Table 12.1 provides a summary of each to help you keep track.

Internal Source Monitoring. **Internal source monitoring** involves distinguishing between events a person thought about doing versus events she actually did. The person who is trying to remember if he locked the back door before going on vacation is engaged in internal source monitoring. Perceptual detail is important for making these decisions because actions actually taken have more perceptual detail in memory (e.g., remembering seeing the key turning in the lock), whereas events that were simply thought about may have little or no perceptual detail. A similar point can be made for contextual information. Semantic detail and emotional reactions are likely to be low because these actions were generated by the person and so are unlikely to be reacted to. Finally, cognitive operations are likely to be high in both because in both cases the person is actively planning to carry out the action. The question is whether or not it was done.

TABLE 12.1   Types of Source Monitoring and How They Relate to Different Types of Source Information

TYPE	PERCEPTUAL DETAIL	CONTEXTUAL INFORMATION	SEMANTIC DETAIL	EMOTIONAL REACTIONS	COGNITIVE OPERATIONS
Internal	—	X	—	—	X
External	X	X	X	X	—
Reality	X	X	X	X	X

External Source Monitoring.   A second type of source monitoring is **external source monitoring,** in which a person needs to distinguish between two external sources. Who told you this, Susie or Jane? Did you read about this in the newspaper or in a supermarket tabloid? Perceptual detail is important for making these decisions because different external sources have different types of perceptual detail associated with them (e.g., a man's voice or a woman's voice). The information about contextual information can be informative. For example, when you are trying to decide which of two people told you something, and you always see one person in your neighborhood and the other person on campus, then knowing where you heard this information can help you narrow it down. Semantic detail and emotional reactions can be used in a similar fashion. Finally, because the information is coming from outside the person, cognitive operations are likely to be low and not very informative about the source of the memory.

Reality Monitoring.   **Reality monitoring** (Johnson & Raye, 1981) involves distinguishing among memories of events that actually happened and those that were only imagined. For example, did a witness to a car accident actually see broken glass, or did she only hear just someone speak of broken glass later? It is not unusual for people to mistakenly think they saw things that were only read or heard about, but it is less common to think that something that was seen was only read or heard about (Belli, Lindsay, Gales, & McCarthy, 1994).

Obviously, perceptual detail is going to be important in reality monitoring. Events that actually happened have greater perceptual detail than those events that were only imagined. Moreover, events that were actually witnessed have a great deal more contextual information associated with them, whereas events that were imagined have little contextual detail. Also, semantic detail and emotional reactions are much more developed in memories for events that actually happened as compared to things that a person just thought about. Last, knowledge about cognitive operations is likely to be scarce for events that had occurred but plentiful for events that were imagined. However, reality monitoring errors do occur, even when it would seem a person could easily discriminate between what was thought and what actually happened. For example, a week after viewing photographs and reading descriptions of scenes, people made frequent mistakes when identifying pictures of scenes they had only read about but made fewer mistakes when identifying scenes they had seen photographs of (Intraub & Hoffman, 1992).

Source Monitoring Errors

Source monitoring is pertinent for this chapter's focus on memory and reality because information about source grounds memories in reality. Often, people are reasonably accurate about where their knowledge came from. However, this is not a perfect process, and errors can be made. For example, repeated attempts to remember, which can produce reminiscence and hypermnesia, can also increase the likelihood of confusing an imagined event with a real one (Henkel, 2004). This is because the repeated memory retrievals of imagined information may introduce more perceptionlike qualities to the memory (through the process of imagination) and make any given memory seem more like something that actually happened. As a result, people claim that imagined events actually happened.

When source monitoring errors occur, a person's understanding of the world and what actually happened are at odds. For example, if there is an error in internal source monitoring, a person might believe she had done something she had never done or had only thought about doing something she had actually done. An error in external source monitoring would result in a person thinking that they had gotten information from one source when in fact it was from another. For example, a person may believe that he read some fact about a president of the United States in a history book, when in reality, he had watched a historical movie. Finally, an error in reality monitoring could lead a person to think that events had actually happened when they had only imagined them or that an event that they thought they imagined, had in fact happened. For example, thinking that you came up with an idea that you actually heard from someone else is a reality monitoring error.

Source misattributions can occur because a person has forgotten the source and must his schematic knowledge to make decisions about it. In a study of choice making (Mather, Shafir, & Johnson, 2000), people chose between two alternatives—for example, which of two people they would go on a blind date with. A number of characteristics of each person were given. Some were positive, such as "always interesting to talk to," and others were negative, such as "awkward in social situations such as parties." Some time after picking which person they would go on the blind date with, people were asked to identify which characteristics belonged to which person. In general, people tended to misremember positive characteristics of other choice as belonging to the person they picked and to a lesser extent, misremember the negative attributes of the person they actually did pick as belonging to the person they rejected. This does not occur when options are assigned rather than chosen (Mather, Shafir, & Johnson, 2003). So the choices we make can distort our memories. We have a tendency to think of the things we choose as more positive than they are and the things we do not choose as more negative than they are.

Source Cueing

Finally, source information is not only important in verifying the nature of information in memory; it can also be used to retrieve information. When source information is used to help a person remember, it is called source cueing (Radvansky & Potter, 2000; see also Dodson & Shimamura, 2000). This is in contrast to most studies of source information that look at source discrimination, which involves determining the source of a retrieved memory. In source cueing, knowledge about source can be used to narrow down or access traces in long-term memory. For example, in music, the timbre on which a melody is played (e.g., piano, guitar, trumpet, etc.) can be source information. This is because different timbres are associated with different instruments and so would be different entities in the world. If you hear a melody on one instrument, you are more accurate at identifying it later if it is played on the same instrument than if it is played on a different one (Radvansky, Fleming, and Simmons, 1995). The source information is being used as a memory cue.

Cryptomnesia

Knowing where information comes from can have important consequences. For example, it is important to know whether an idea is one's own or someone else's. When we present someone else's idea as our own, it is plagiarism, but not all plagiarism is intentional. Some cases of plagiarism are unconscious and unintentional. This occurs when people come up with ideas they believe are their own but in fact were encountered in the past. This memory of the previous encounter has an unconscious, implicit effect on thinking, without the knowledge of the information's original source entering consciousness. This unconscious plagiarism is called **cryptomnesia** (but see Brown & Halliday, 1991, for a different account). I've had two clear cases of cryptomnesia in my own life. Once was when I was writing what I thought was the perfect introduction for a paper, only to discover an almost identical introduction in another paper when I was checking back over my references. The other time was when I had written a melody on my fretless bass and realized later that it was extremely similar to a bass line melody I had heard on a CD I had gotten about a month earlier.

There have been many explanations for how cryptomnesia occurs. One is that cryptomnesia is a source monitoring error—in particular, a reality monitoring error. A person retains the information in a memory trace. However, because of the amount of time that has passed and/or because little attention was paid during the original encoding, the memory trace is weak, and the source information associated with it will have little or no influence later. Whatever feeling of familiarity does happen to be associated will only serve to boost a person's confidence in the idea. In addition, it has been shown that memories of plagiarized ideas may have many of the same phenomenological characteristics as accurate memories (Brédart, Lampinen, & Defeldre, 2003). For example, people have a relatively high confidence in these memories, although not quite as high on average as in accurate memories.

False Fame

One of the more powerful ways to manipulate memory is to influence the frequency that something is encountered. For example, information that is repeatedly encountered is more likely to be remembered, may become overlearned, and subsequently be chronically available (see Chapter 7). However, different components of a memory trace are forgotten at different rates. For example, information content may be remembered for a long time, but source knowledge may be lost. Alternatively, source knowledge may never have been learned in the first place or learned very poorly. In either case, a person may be put in the situation of needing to reconstruct the missing information. One type of knowledge that people can use is how familiar the memory seems. Familiarity is, of course, related to how frequently something has been encountered.

One feature of human memory that shows this familiarity-based reconstruction is the **false fame effect** (Jacoby, Kelley, Brown, & Jasechko, 1989). This is the tendency to think that someone is famous or more famous than she really is because her name sounds familiar. For example, you may think that your favorite musicians or actors have lots of fans because they are well-known to you. The false fame effect is even more dramatic in that it may be possible to take a person who has utterly no fame whatsoever and make him "famous" overnight. This is done using the principle of mere exposure (see Chapter 6).

In a study, a memory researcher might give people a list of names. Some names may be people who are a little "famous" for a time, such as Roger Bannister, Minnie Pearl, and

Christopher Wren. These were names that most students probably heard of but couldn't quite remember who they were. The other names on the list would be people who were clearly not famous, such as Sebastian Wiesdorf, Larry Jacoby, and Gabriel Radvansky. The student's task would be to go through the list and pick out who is famous and who is not. Later, the students would be given a new list of names, which consisted of famous people, nonfamous people whose names they had seen before, and new nonfamous names. Half of the students were given this new list immediately after the first list, but the other half were not given this new list until the next day. The researchers found that the students who got the second list the next day were twice as likely to declare nonfamous people famous simply because they had seen those names on the list. Thus, those people became famous overnight!

This false fame effect can also occur if a person is distracted by some other task (such as listening to a person read a series of numbers, waiting for three odd numbers in a row) while they were either first learning the names or trying to remember if the name is famous (Jacoby, Woloshyn, & Kelley, 1989). In such cases, because the name was familiar, the person declared it that of somebody famous. Thus, the link between memory content and memory source was disconnected (Steffens, Buchner, Martensen, & Erdfelder, 2000). In a very real sense, there is an unconscious influence of previous memories (this name has been encountered before) on conscious efforts to make a decision (is this name famous?). This is one reason why some people say that there is no such thing as bad publicity. People may often remember that they've encountered a name before but not why. The more times a name has been seen or heard, the more familiar it will be, and the more famous that person will seem. (It's not a good idea to overdo it. Eventually the public will connect the unflattering information with the name.)

Another consequence of increased frequency is that people show a preference for things that are familiar. This probably has some survival value, so we are not tempted to try new things, which could be dangerous. If we stick with familiar things, we are more likely to survive because we've survived encounters with them before. This is also why publicists for actors, musicians, or politicians do everything they can to get their client's name heard as often as possible. The more the name is heard, the more familiar it is, the more famous the person will seem, and the more people will like them. This is also why advertisers try to get their commercials played as often as possible. The more familiar the product's name, the more people decide they like it, and the more they are going to buy it.

Sleeper Effect

A phenomenon in the area of social psychology that involves the use of source monitoring is the **sleeper effect.** This occurs when people are given some propaganda that comes from a source of either high or low credibility. If the source has low credibility, then people initially discount the information. However, after a delay of a few days, weeks, or months, people still remember the information but now consider it more credible than when it was heard the first time. What previously seemed unreasonable has, with the simple passage of time, become reasonable (Hovland & Weiss, 1951; Weiss, 1953). The sleeper effect is shown in Figure 12.1.

The sleeper effect occurs when people store both the content information of the message and the source information. As time passes, the content information is better

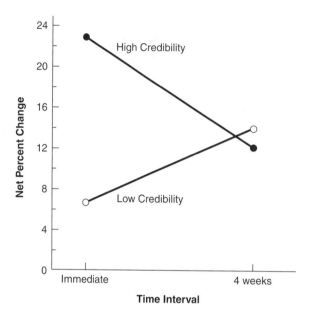

FIGURE 12.1   An Illustration of the Sleeper Effect
Source: Weiss, 1953

remembered than the source. Or at least, the source information in memory becomes disconnected from the content information. People then remember the content but forget the source. As a result, they are more willing to accept the information as credible because they no longer have available the source information that would make it suspect (Underwood & Pezdek, 1998).

Several components must be in place to even get a sleeper effect. The first is that people must pay attention to the information in the message. By doing so, they are setting up a memory trace of the content information. Second, the person receiving the message should not get the discounting source information until after the message has been given. Getting the source information later makes it less likely that people will discount the message from the outset and thus be less likely to learn it. Finally, the person should rate the trustworthiness of the source immediately afterward. This provides a longer amount of time for the source information to be forgotten (Pretkanis, Greenwald, Leippe, & Baumgarder, 1988).

Synopsis

In addition to remembering information content, it is also helpful to remember where information came from. This is source monitoring, and it can include discriminating between multiple external sources (external), whether one thought something or actually did it (internal), or some event actually happened or was just thought about (reality). Conversely information about source can also be used as a memory cue. Although people are reasonably accurate at source monitoring, errors can occur. Source monitoring errors manifest themselves in unconscious plagiarism (cryptomnesia), false fame, and sleeper effects. In all of these cases, people remember content information but forget where it came from. As a result, they handle it differently than if they accurately remembered the source.

FALSE MEMORIES

One of the more intensively studied aspects of memory in recent years is the question of when and how people "remember" things that never happened. These are called **false memories.** Our memories are important to how we function in the world. Sometimes errors in memory can cause serious problems. This is especially important when our memories are the only source of information. A good example is erroneous information from eyewitness testimony.

Deese–Roediger-McDermott Paradigm

A simple way to create false memories is by using a list-learning paradigm. First, people hear a list of words, such as those in Table 12.2. Soon after, they try to recall as many of those words as possible. Of course, people are able to recall only a portion of the list. The interesting thing here is that people often very systematically misremember words that were not on the list. For example, for the list in Table 12.2, people often mistakenly say that they heard the word "sleep" even though it was not there (Deese, 1959; Read, 1996; Roediger & McDermott, 1995). Try this with your friends. What makes this finding even more interesting is that over time people tend to forget the false memory information less than the true memories, even over periods as long as two months (Seamon et al., 2002).

As is clear in this example, false memories are more likely to occur when there is a plausible context. People are likely to misremember the word "sleep" because all the other words in the list refer to things having to do with sleep. In fact, these words were specifically selected because of their association with that word. This makes it more likely that people will have a false memory for that item.

In general, these sorts of false memories are guided by how many associations there are between the words that were actually seen (the more the better), as well as the general recallability of the actual list words (the fewer the better) (Roediger, Watson, McDermott, & Gallo, 2001). The larger number of associations makes it more likely that the false memory word will be primed or unconsciously activated. The less recallable the actual items are,

TABLE 12.2   Words that May Lead to a False Memory for the Word "Sleep"

bed	dream	doze	peace
rest	wake	slumber	yawn
awake	snooze	snore	drowsy
tired	blanket	nap	

Source: Roediger & McDermott, 1995.

the more likely a person will need to do some guessing or memory reconstruction, making it more likely that the false memory item will be "remembered." These false memory estimates are based on partial information (Heit, Brockdorff, & Lamberts, 2004). For example, a person may be misremembering the source of the information (it was thought about but not heard) or be using more gist memories than verbatim memories (Brainerd, Payne, Wright, & Reyna, 2003; Brainerd, Wright, Reyna, & Mojardin, 2001). Because people's memories for pictures are much more detailed and less gist oriented, they are less likely to show this effect for pictures (e.g., Hege & Dodson, 2004).

This is supported by ERP measures of the P300 component, which is a part of the ERP signal that reliably occurs *about* 300 ms after people are presented with a memory probe, and it is associated with recognition. With false memories, the P300 is observed earlier than with true recognition (Miller, Baratta, Wynveen, & Rosenfeld, 2001). This suggests that people are making these memory decisions faster perhaps because they are being less thorough and using less information.

This production of a false memory for an unpresented word can be influenced by a large number of factors. One such factor is the operation of inhibition, which was described in Chapter 7. Two memory processes that are thought to employ inhibition are directed forgetting and part-list cueing (Kimball & Bjork, 2002). When people are encouraged to forget a set of words that regularly elicits a false memory, the rate of producing false memories goes up. Apparently, the instruction to forget the list inhibits the memory for that list, thereby making access to the memories for the entire list harder. As a result, people have a more difficult time discriminating between what was actually heard and what was not, so more false memories are produced. In contrast, if people are provided with part of the original set of items, the part-set cueing effect is extended to the critical nonpresented word, as well as those that were actually heard. Because all the other information is being suppressed by the retrieval of the cued-for information, the rate of producing false memories actually declines. The rate of reporting a critical word can also be reduced if there is a more emotional connotation (e.g., words like "rape") than with emotionally neutral words (Pesta, Murphy, & Sanders, 2001). This again shows the influence of emotions on memory processing.

As with source monitoring, the occurrence of false memories can be influenced by social factors. As a reminder, people are more willing to say that they saw something that was only imagined if other people claim they saw it, a source monitoring error (see earlier). In fact, people are more likely to make a false memory error if they engage in a source monitoring task as compared to a simple memory task (Hicks & Marsh, 2001). Also, people are more likely to mistakenly "remember" events that never occurred or had been asked to imagine had occurred, if they are reported by other people (Roediger, Meade, & Bergman, 2001). Just hearing other people relate events may cause us to remember them as if we experienced them.

False Memories from Integration

Another way people can misremember is when information that was presented at different points in time becomes integrated into a single representation in memory. Thus, with integration, what were actually several events are misremembered as a single event. This is sim-

TABLE 12.3   Sentences Used in the Bransford and Franks (1971) Study

The ants ate the sweet jelly, which was on the table.	The ants ate what?
The ants in the kitchen ate the jelly, which was on the table.	The ants were where?
The ants in the kitchen ate the jelly.	What was in the kitchen?
The ants ate the sweet jelly.	The jelly was what?
The ants were in the kitchen	What was in the kitchen?
The jelly was on the table.	What was on the table?

ilar to the integration processes discussed with regard to schemas in Chapter 9. Thus, people are more likely to remember different pieces of information as being part of the same event if they "seem" like they should go together.

One example of integration is a study by Bransford and Franks (1971). In this study, people were presented with a list of sentences, shown in Table 12.3. During study, people had to answer simple questions about the sentences, also shown in the table. (Go ahead and read the sentences and answer the questions now.) Afterward, people were presented with a recognition test to identify which sentences they had seen before. In addition, people were asked to rate how confident they were in their answers. An example of this recognition test is shown in Table 12.4. Try to identify which sentences you remember seeing and which you do not. Also, rate how confident you are. After you are done, look at Table 12.3 to see which sentences were actually there.

The important result in Bransford and Franks's (1971) study was that memory did not simply reflect whether or not a sentence had been seen before. The study and test sentences contained various amounts of simple idea units (called propositions). Each of these sentences can be grouped into a theme and contains 1, 2, 3, or all 4 propositions from that theme. For example, in one theme the sentence "The ants were in the kitchen" is a one-proposition sentence, "The ants in the kitchen ate the jelly" is two propositions, "The ants in the kitchen ate the jelly, which was on the table" is three propositions, and "The ants ate the sweet jelly, which was on the table" contains all four propositions. On the memory test, the more propositions a sentence had, the more likely people "remembered" having read it before. A

TABLE 12.4   Recognition Test from the Bransford and Franks (1971) Study

The ants in the kitchen ate the sweet jelly, which was on the table.

The ants in the kitchen ate the sweet jelly.

The ants ate the sweet jelly.

The sweet jelly was on the table.

The ants ate the jelly, which was on the table.

The jelly was sweet.

The ants ate the jelly.

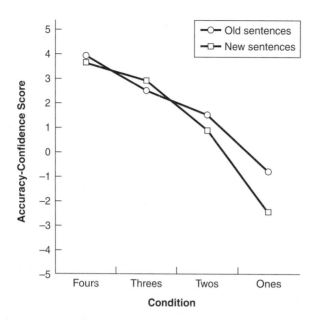

FIGURE 12.2   Recognition Test Data from the Bransford and Franks (1971) Study
The accuracy score reflects. . . .

sentence with four propositions that was not read was more likely to be "recognized" than a sentence with only one proposition that was read. Moreover, people's confidence ratings showed the same pattern. Confidence in their "memories" increased proportionately with the number of propositions in the sentence. This can be seen in Figure 12.2.

The explanation for this is that when people read the sentences, because there is overlap in content, they are likely to be interpreted as referring to a common situation (see also Chapter 7). This makes it easy to integrate the information. This integrated representation is then used to make the memory judgments. Because items that contain more propositions more closely match the memory trace, they are more likely to be recognized and given higher confidence ratings. Thus, people use memories of entire events that they created, not memories for what they actually experienced.

This sort of integration process is seen with normal reading as well. For example, when people read fictional stories about real people, they tend to misremember some of the fictional information as being real. More generally, the fictional knowledge gets integrated in with the real knowledge. Although people are aware that the story contained some fictional information, they also think that they knew some of the fictional information *before* reading the story (Marsh, Meade, & Roediger, 2003).

Implanted Memories

In the preceding examples, a person created false memories almost as a natural consequence of thinking about the information he was given. The false information was never explicitly given. However, it is possible to explicitly plant false memories in people (Loftus, 2004). One way this can occur is when people overtly question whether a person remembers something from her past. For example, somebody tells you that your mother claims that when you were eight year old, you got lost in a mall, and then she asks you if you remember that incident. Another way to implant memories is when a person overhears or reads another person's report. For example, if you hear me say that I remember seeing a story about whales on the news, you might be more likely to claim to have seen such a story as well, even if you had not (Meade & Roediger, 2002). These implanted memories are provided to people in such a way that they believe that they are real memories. This sounds strange, but it's true.

Implanted false memories have been observed for more autobiographical memories, not just for word lists. Again, the likelihood of creating a false memory is a function of how plausible the information is (Pezdek, Finger, & Hodge, 1997). In one study, people were asked about events from their lives to see if their memories corresponded with those of their parents. During this time, the researchers relayed a description of an event that was presumably described by the student's mother but that had never happened. This event was one that was either consistent with being raised Jewish or Catholic. Jewish students were more likely to have a false memory for the Jewish event than the Catholic event, and vice versa. This is illustrated in Table 12.5. Thus, the probability of having a false memory is a function of the plausibility of that event. However, it is possible for a person to have false memories of implausible events, such as witnessing a demonic possession, if the event is made to seem more plausible, such as reading articles about possession. This increased plausibility then makes it more likely that a person will indicate that the event occurred in his own past (Mazzoni, Loftus, & Kirsch, 2001).

In some unfortunate cases, people may inadvertently get implanted memories from overzealous and substandard therapists looking for repressed memories (Loftus, 1993). The suggestion that these "memories" have been repressed makes it more likely that a person will accept them as real, even if they are implanted false memories. The normal scrutinization of the memory content and source information does not seem to take place.

A technique that makes it more likely that implanted false memories will be formed is visualization or imagination. When people actively imagine false events, this makes it more likely that false memories will be created and that people will feel more confident about these false memories. This is called **imagination inflation** (Garry & Polaschek, 2000; Mazzoni & Memon, 2003). Imagination makes the memory traces richer in detail and gives them more pseudoperceptual qualities, making them seem more like real memories. Moreover, this imagination inflation is greater if people already have some experience of

TABLE 12.5   Number of People Reporting False Memories for Catholic and Jewish Events

PARTICIPANTS	NEITHER EVENT	CATHOLIC EVENT ONLY	JEWISH EVENT ONLY	BOTH EVENTS
Catholic	19	7	1	2
Jewish	19	0	3	0

Source: Pezdek, Finger, & Hodge, 1997.

the event. For example, if people only heard the sounds of a car accident but formed a mental picture of the cars involved, they are more likely to believe later that they saw the accident as well as heard it. (Henkel, Franklin, & Johnson, 2000). Moreover, the influence of imagination inflation is greater when people take a first-person perspective (Libby, 2003) or with repeated imaginings (Thomas & Loftus, 2002). Over time, people claim to consciously "remember" actually doing imagined events, even if they are bizarre activities, such as sitting on dice (Thomas, Bulevich, & Loftus, 2003; Thomas & Loftus, 2002).

Given the power of imagination inflation, it is not surprising that actually viewing pictures can make false memories even more likely. If people see photos of themselves at the age that some event was supposed to have occurred, they tend to create false memories at a much higher rate (Lindsay et al., 2004). Presumably, viewing old family photos of a certain time period gives memory some concrete perceptual information to put into the false memories, along with any additional memories that are triggered by seeing the pictures.

Although it seems very unlikely, it is possible for people to implant false memories into themselves. In a study by Zaragoza et al. (2001), students at Kent State University first watched a film. Afterward, they were asked a number of questions about the movie. Some of these people were told to answer all of the questions, even if the described event did not occur in the movie. For example, a question might be "The chair broke and Delaney fell on the floor. Where was Delaney bleeding?" when the character did not bleed. That is, the student was forced to manufacture an answer to a question they knew to be false. What is interesting is that during memory tests a week later, the students who knowingly confabulated answers during the first part of the study now accepted many (32 percent) of these answers as truth. Moreover, if the experimenter had provided supportive feedback during the made-up response (such as "Yes, that's right"), then the rate of accepting these self-implanted false memories was higher (38 percent) than if only neutral feedback (such as "Okay") had been given (26 percent). Thus, even minimal external support of these self-implanted false memories boosts their credibility tremendously (see also Thomas, Bulevich, & Loftus, 2003).

This social influence of implanted false memories is also affected by the people involved. That is, false memories are more likely to occur in people who are more prone to dissociative experiences (e.g., driving and not remembering what happened the past few miles). Presumably these people have a harder time distinguishing between what was real and what was only imagined or was only plausible. Furthermore, false memories are more likely to occur when the person who provides the implanted information is extroverted. This influence is particularly strong when the person doing the remembering is much more introverted (Porter, Birt, Yuille, & Lehman, 2000).

Although people can falsely remember implanted information, there are some tendencies that distinguish true from false memories. In particular, true memories are often richer in detail, are more emotional, are more likely to be "recollected," and are more likely to be field memories. In contrast, false memories are likely to be stereotypical events, more likely to be "known," and be observer memories (Frost, 2000; Heaps & Nash, 2001). However, these are not defining criteria because true and false memories overlap each other on all of these qualities. These are only trends that characterize the set of false memories as a whole from the set of true memories. This is like saying men are taller than women. While this is true in general, there is a great deal of overlap between these two distributions. Just as you cannot make any clear judgments about the sex of a person given information about height, you cannot use many of the qualities of a memory to determine if it is true or false.

Hypnosis and Memory

If you are not familiar with the concept of **hypnosis,** you should be aware that this is a real and acknowledged condition. The hypnotic state is an altered state of consciousness in which a person is more willing to accept and follow the suggestions of the hypnotist. People vary in the degree to which they can be hypnotized. Some people are not at all hypnotically susceptible and apparently can never experience the hypnotic state. Others are highly susceptible, to the point of being able to experience auditory, visual, or tactile illusions as suggested by the hypnotist.

While there are many interesting topics that can be explored regarding hypnosis, the issue at hand is how hypnosis can influence memory. Does hypnosis make memory better, make it worse, or does it have no appreciable effect? At first blush, it seems that hypnosis has a beneficial effect on memory. If you put people under hypnosis and ask them to recall things, they report more information than if they are not under hypnosis. There are also some very salient anecdotal reports about the effectiveness of hypnosis in memory retrieval.

One of the more well-known reports is of the Chowchilla kidnapping (as reported by Smith, 1983). In 1976, members of the Symbionese Liberation Army (a militant radical left-wing sect at the time) kidnapped at gunpoint a bus full of schoolchildren and their bus driver. They were herded into a couple of vans and driven to an old rock quarry. At the rock quarry students and bus driver were placed into a buried chamber. Eventually the bus driver and students were able to dig themselves out of their tomb and go to the police. When questioned by the police, the bus driver reported that he had tried to memorize the license plates of the vans as they were being loaded onto them. However, because he was so agitated at being held at gunpoint, he was unable to recall the plate numbers when questioned by the police. At this point a decision was made to hypnotize the bus driver in the hope that this would help him remember some critical piece of information. While under hypnosis, the bus driver called out two license plate numbers. One of these, except for one digit, turned out to be the plate number for one of the vans. This information eventually led to the arrest and conviction of the kidnappers. With reports such as this, it can clearly be seen why some people would view hypnosis as a memory technique with great practical potential.

Perhaps more familiar are cases where people are hypnotized under therapeutic situations. The movie *Communion* provides a striking example of this when a man is hypnotized and recalls his abduction by aliens. More down-to-earth and common are cases where people are hypnotized in therapeutic sessions to remember aspects of their past that they may have forgotten because they had been traumatized by the event. Often these approaches to using hypnosis take the view that memory is like a videotape that accurately records events that occur in the world and that can be played back with a high level of accuracy if the proper technique is used. This is clearly incorrect.

There is no doubt that people report more memories under hypnosis than otherwise, but there can be problems. For one thing, there is a much larger risk that the memories people report are inaccurate (Smith, 1983).

It has also been suggested that the new information that is reported when a person is under hypnosis is no different from the hypermnesia that one would normally see with repeated recall (see Chapter 3). As a reminder, when people are asked to remember something over and over again, they can often remember things in later attempts that they had forgotten previously. This was demonstrated in a study by Dinges et al., (1992). In the study people were given 40 line drawings to look at and memorize. The participants were then asked repeatedly to report what they had seen either when they were hypnotized, or not. A forced recall test (see Chapter 3) was used, in which the people were required to recall 40 things. In doing so, they were essentially equating hypnotized and unhypnotized people for the overall amount of information they were willing to report. What they found was that there was no difference in how much was recalled when people were either hypnotized or not. Furthermore, consistent hypermnesia was observed in all cases. The only possible benefit of hypnosis could be to calm a person who is highly anxious. However, this can also be accomplished by other methods and without the risk of the potential recall of false memories.

Synopsis

The separation between memory and reality is most salient when people have false memories of events that never occurred. These false memories can come from many different sources and take several different forms. For example, people can mistakenly think a word that is closely related to other words on a list was actually heard earlier. Other times, false memories come about through our natural impulse to integrate several pieces of information into a single, coherent memory, and we may misremember what individual pieces of information were learned apart from the others. More disturbing are situations where false memories are not created as a by-product of how our memories operate but by the failure of our memories at times to resist the implanting of false information from outside sources. These implanted false memories are even more likely to occur when the information comes from a trusted source, including, and very dramatically, when that trusted source is a hypnotist. However, it should be noted that while we can be easily misled in some circumstances, our grip on reality is fairly firm, and we tend not to create false memories wildly but create false memories of things that would likely have occurred anyway. Thus, with most false memories, little if any harm is done.

FALSE MEMORIES THROUGH NORMAL MEMORY USE

Every time we use our memories we change them in some way. Different things that we do with the information alter memories' content. In this section we look at two examples of apparently normal ways of using memory that can lead to false memories. These are verbal overshadowing and the revelation effect.

Verbal Overshadowing

When we talk about things we've seen, our memories can be changed by this verbalization. This is a process called **verbal overshadowing.** Essentially what happens is that when we describe an event, we create a verbal memory of our description. Because verbal information is different from other types of knowledge, such as visual information, our memory for what we said alters our memory for what we saw. This is consistent with fuzzy trace views of memory that assume that performance is a mixture of various memory traces. Overall, the effect is that our more recent verbal memories overshadow our older visual memories.

As an example of this, students at the University of Washington, in a study by Schooler and Engstler-Schooler (1990), watched a videotape of a bank robbery. Afterward, some people were asked to spend five minutes writing a verbal description of the robber's face. Everyone was then shown a set of eight pictures of similar faces and asked to pick out which one was the robber, if his picture was there at all. (In fact, the face of the robber from the film was present.) It was found that students who produced a verbal description of the robber's face correctly picked it out 38 percent of the time, whereas students who did not write the description were able to pick out the robber 64 percent of the time. Thus, memory performance was worsened by talking about what was experienced. It should be noted that verbal overshadowing does not occur if people only read a description—only when they actually generated it (Dodson, Johnson, & Schooler, 1997).

Moreover, it appears that verbal overshadowing of something like the face of a person involved in an event can occur even when it is not the face that is described. In a study by Dodson, Johnson, and Schooler (1997), verbal overshadowing was present even when people wrote descriptions of another face. Moreover, in a study by Westerman and Larsen (1997), people wrote descriptions of a car that was in a videotaped scene. Even under these conditions, memory for the face became more difficult. Thus, verbal overshadowing can also influence the types of information that are sought after during memory retrieval. In this case, there is a shift from visual to verbal information. Alternatively, it has been suggested that verbalizing may alter the recognition process and make people more conservative in their memory judgments, since the verbal overshadowing effect is less likely to occur when people are forced to make a choice between several alternatives (Clare & Lewandowsky, 2004). Either way, talking about things can sometimes make memory worse.

Revelation Effect

When we interact with the world, information is not immediately apparent but is revealed to us slowly over a period of time. During this time we may be trying to figure out what we are dealing with. As a consequence of this revelation process, people are more likely to both recognize old information as old and to misrecognize new information as old if the information is revealed gradually rather than all at once. This is called the **revelation effect** (Luo, 1993; Peynircioglu & Tekcan, 1993; Watkins & Peynircioglu 1990), and it can also occur when people make frequency judgments (how often something occurred) in addition to simple recognition judgments (Bornstein & Neely, 2001). There are several ways that the revelation effect is studied experimentally. For example, a word might be revealed one letter at a time until the person can make a recognition judgment (e.g., M _ _ _ _ _, M _ _ O _ _, M _ _ O _ Y, etc.). It should be noted that the revelation effect only occurs when people think they are remembering a prior episode. It does not occur if people either know that no such episode occurred or if they engage in semantic memory retrieval (Frigo, Reas, & LeCompte, 1999; Watkins & Peynircioglu, 1990).

The revelation effect appears to be a result of people using the familiarity of an item (Cameron & Hockley, 2000; LeCompte, 1995; Westerman & Greene, 1996; but see Hicks & Marsh, 1998, and Niewiadomski & Hockley, 2001, for explanations based on response criteria). Specifically, as people progress through the revelation process, the information feels more familiar, so people are more willing to claim they had seen it before. This even occurs when people have not heard something before but have been subjected to subliminal suggestions that they had (Frigo, Reas, & LeCompte, 1999). Consistent with this familiarity idea, the revelation effect is more likely to occur when people are less able to consciously recollect the circumstances in which information was encountered and have to rely more on feelings of familiarity. So when there has been a greater delay between the original presentation and the memory test or when the information is presented more quickly, it is harder for people to encode the information that would make conscious recollection possible (Landau, 2001). This familiarity may even come in the form of general activation by some presumably unrelated prior task, rather than revelation itself, such as performing a working memory span task just prior to making a recognition decision (Westerman & Greene, 1998). However, when retrieval does emphasize conscious recollection, the revelation effect may not be observed (Westerman, 2000). Again, people are making judgments based on familiarity rather than actual memory.

What is particularly striking about the revelation effect is that it not only applies to simple stimuli, such as words, but also to complex events (Bernstein, Godfrey, Davidson, & Loftus, 2004; Bernstein, Whittlesea, & Loftus, 2002). That is, if people are led through a process of trying to uncover their memories, this very uncovering process can increase the likelihood that a person will later falsely claim that the memories are real. Thus, efforts of trying to recover previously hidden memories about ourselves by engaging in imagination can lead a person to believe in false memories.

Synopsis

False memories can be created not only from special circumstances that encourage their creation, but also through what would seem the normal use of memory. For example, the seemly benign act of describing a witnessed event to someone can lead to distortions in later memory. This occurs even when the part of the event being described is not the one that is tested later. Also, the gradual recovery of information during the search of memory can also create false memories. In this case, the build up of partial memories of the revelation process lead to greater feelings of familiarity and the mistaken impression that the information was encountered before.

SUMMARY

In this chapter we looked at a number of ways that memory for the past can depart from the reality of the past. An important aspect of memory that is needed to help determine whether a memory corresponds to actual reality is knowing the source of the information. Source monitoring draws from a number of different types of information to make an assessment of where the information in memory came from. Source monitoring is usually accurate. However, from time to time there can be an error in which a person either loses the source information or misattributes information from one source to another. One example of an error in source monitoring is cryptomnesia, or unconscious plagiarism, the inappropriate attribution of others' ideas to one's self. Other problems in source monitoring include the false fame effect, where a recently heard name is inappropriately thought to be famous, and the sleeper effect, in which people forget the source of information and then accept information as more credible than they previously thought.

Another way memory can become disconnected from reality is through the creation of false memories, or memories for things that never happened. Sometimes these false memories are memories for things that are very likely to have occurred but in fact never did. A person more easily generates these sorts of false memories. False memories may also be implanted from outside sources when information has been suggested as actually having occurred, especially repeatedly. Implanted memories are more likely to occur if people repeatedly engage in visual imagery and are encouraged by other people. Finally, the creation of source monitoring errors and false memories is heightened by altered states of consciousness, like hypnosis. Basically, hypnosis leads a person to want to cooperate with the hypnotist more so than would otherwise be the case, leading to the acceptance of information as being actual memories that would have otherwise been rejected as imaginary.

Finally, we looked at some instances of where problems in memory can occur through its normal use. In one case, memory for visual information became worse after people talked about the events that were seen. This is verbal overshadowing. In the other case, information that is revealed slowly over time is more likely to be falsely remembered than information that is presented all at once. Overall, while people's memories correspond well to reality, there can be cases when there are major exceptions.

STUDY QUESTIONS

1. What is source monitoring? What are the different types of source monitoring?

2. Generally speaking, what happens when a source monitoring error occurs. More specifically, what are some of the ways that source monitoring errors produce problems?

3. How can false memories by created by hearing related sets of information?

4. How are false memories implanted?

5. What is the best way to describe the effect of hypnosis on attempts to remember?

6. What is the influence of providing a verbal description of a witnessed event on memory?

7. Does slowly revealing information to people make memory more or less accurate? Why?

KEY TERMS

cryptomnesia, external source monitoring, false fame effect, false memories, hypnosis, imagination inflation, internal source monitoring, reality monitoring, revelation effect, sleeper effect, source monitoring, verbal overshadowing

CHAPTER THIRTEEN

MEMORY AND THE LAW

Memory has practical and important applications in the world. Currently, for most of you, one of the more important applications involves memory of a large set of facts that can be written on an exam or used to write a term paper. Hopefully, some of what you have learned here can be applied to those efforts. However, there are other applications for using memory outside of the classroom. One of the more salient of these is how memory works, and how forgetting occurs, in the legal arena. There are many situations in which arriving at a just legal outcome involves people using their memories effectively. When memory is more accurate, police, judges, and juries can come to more appropriate conclusions. However, as we have repeatedly seen in this book, there are cases in which memory reports may be inaccurate, even though a person is doing the best he or she can. Such memory errors can lead to serious miscarriages of justice, with guilty individuals not being held accountable and still at large or innocent people being punished for things they did not do.

This chapter looks at five domains in which memory can influence legal matters. The first is the accuracy of eyewitness memory. The second is the confidence eyewitnesses have in their memories. The third area is the development of a cognitive interview that is used to gather information from witnesses in a way that gets the most out of memory. Fourth is the ability to identify a perpetrator from a lineup. And fifth, we consider some issues about how memory processes might influence the effective operation of juries in arriving at a verdict.

EYEWITNESS TESTIMONY

When an accident occurs or a crime is committed, one of the more important sources of evidence to help determine the best application of justice is the eyewitness report. Eyewitnesses often can provide the legal system with information about the event that could not be obtained any other way. Moreover, if it is a serious enough case to warrant a jury trial, eyewitnesses can provide some of the most convincing evidence to jurors. Thus, the accuracy, stability, and scope of eyewitness memories are of critical importance. It is vital to understand the degree to which eyewitnesses' accounts of an event are accurate portrayals, even in the absence of any desire to mislead on the part of a witness.

We approach the accuracy of eyewitness reports by looking at how various things can affect these memories. For instance, how can the wording of a question influence memory? What influence does misleading information have on memory, and why? How does the witness's emotional state at the time of the event affect later memory? Are there other aspects of the event itself that may have a profound effect on later memory?

Wording Effects

In order to get information from a witness, questions must be asked. It is critically important to understand that how questions are worded can influence what is remembered. People reconstruct their memories of an event based on the questions they are asked. Take the example of an automobile accident involving two cars. People will vary their estimates of the speed at which the cars were traveling, depending on the wording used in a question. In a study by Loftus and Palmer (1974), people watched a film of a car accident. After the film, they were asked, "How fast were the cars going when they smashed/collided/bumped/hit/contacted each other?," with each person receiving a different verb. What was found was that the estimation of speed varied, by nearly ten miles per hour, depending on which verb was used (see Table 13.1).

Furthermore, in the car accident film, there was no broken glass. However, in a second experiment, after asking the speed question, they asked the participants if they had seen any broken glass (there was none). In this case, only the verbs "smashed" and "hit" were used. Loftus and Palmer found that the more severe the verb, the more likely people claimed that they had seen broken glass. Participants reported seeing broken glass 16 percent of the time when they heard "smashed" but only 7 percent of the time when they heard "hit." People who were not asked the speed question said "yes" to the broken glass question only 6 percent of the time. So the wording of a question can influence a witness's memory.

This influence of wording even occurs in what might seem to be very subtle differences, such as whether a question contains the word "a" or "the." In one study (Loftus & Zanni, 1975), people saw a film of a car accident. They then wrote a summary of what they saw and answered some questions. One question was either "Did you see a broken headlight?" or "Did you see the broken headlight?" The difference between the words "a" and "the" is important because using the word "a" doesn't presuppose the existence of a broken headlight, whereas the word "the" does. Half the time the questioned item was present in

TABLE 13.1   Speed Estimates as a Function of the Severity of the Verb Used in the Question "How fast were the cars going when they _____ each other?"

VERB	SPEED ESTIMATE (MPH)
smashed	40.8
collided	39.3
bumped	38.1
hit	34.0
contacted	31.8

Source: Loftus & Palmer, 1974

the film, and half the time it was not. The most important finding here is when the item was not in the film (e.g., no broken headlight). Under these circumstances, people claimed they saw the (nonexistent) item 7 percent of the time when the word "a" was used but 18 percent of the time when the word "the" was used. This error is made more than twice as often as a result of a change in a seemingly small function word.

Misleading Postevent Information

As you may have guessed, because it is so easy to alter memory reports based on the wording of a question, it is also alarmingly easy to alter memory by giving misleading information afterward, whether intentionally or not. This is called **misleading postevent information.** This misinformation enters the memory, and people have difficulty distinguishing it from accurate memories. We first look at some ways of assessing the influence of misleading postevent information and then consider some theories that try to explain how this happens.

Methods.   A standard approach for looking at the influence of misleading postevent information on memory was first used by Loftus, Miller, and Burns (1978). First, people watch an accident or crime on video. For example, a person might see an accident in which a driver disobeys a yield sign. Then the participant is asked a question about the video. In some cases, the question refers to an object that was in the scene, such as "Did another car pass the red Datsun when it was stopped at the yield sign?" Because the sign mentioned in the question is consistent with the video, this is called the consistent condition. In other cases, this question refers to an object that was not in the scene, such as "Did another car pass the red Datsun when it was stopped at the stop sign?" Because no stop sign was in the video, this is called the misleading condition. Finally, a third control condition is used in which the question is neutral, such as "Did another car pass the red Datsun when it was stopped at the intersection?" Thus, this is called the neutral condition.

After viewing the event and answering the critical question (among others), people were asked to make a decision about what they saw—for example, choosing between pictures or verbal descriptions. For example, a person might make a choice about whether the car had stopped at a stop sign or a yield sign. Although memory is better in the consistent condition (relative to the neutral condition), performance is worse in the misleading condition. The results of one study are shown in Table 13.2. This misleading postevent information effect is fairly stable and occurs with a wide variety of situations. It is more pronounced the greater the delay between witnessing the event and the time the misleading information is encountered (Loftus, Miller, & Burns, 1978). It also occurs when the misleading information is presented prior to the witnessed event (Eakin, Schreiber, & Sergent-Marshall, 2003). People can even mislead themselves. Witnesses who provide false information (i.e., lie) after witnessing an event have a poorer memory when they later try to remember accurately. They retrieve less true information and are more likely to have their lies intrude on their attempts to remember exactly what happened (Pickel, 2004). In their minds, their lies have become truths.

Theories.   A number of explanations have been given for why eyewitness memory reports are altered by misleading postevent information. Four of them are the memory trace

TABLE 13.2 Proportion Correct for Selecting the Correct Item after Consistent, Misleading, or Neutral Information

QUESTION TYPE	PROPORTION CORRECT
Consistent	70
Misleading	43
Neutral	63

Source: Loftus, Miller, & Burns, 1978

replacement theory, the memory coexistence theory, the response bias theory, and the source monitoring theory.

According to the memory trace replacement theory (Loftus, 1979), when misleading information is encountered, the original memory trace is permanently lost or altered in favor of one containing the misleading information. The new information has overwritten the old, and it is impossible to recover the original information. An example of the power of the overwriting process can be seen in a study in which people were given three alternatives on the memory test. One was the original item (e.g., yield sign), one was the misleading item (e.g., stop sign) and a third was a new item (e.g., no parking sign). After giving an initial response, people selected their best second-guess. In cases where people initially selected the misleading item, the probability of selecting the correct item on the second-guess was at chance. If the original memory were still present, then performance should have been higher. The results were consistent with the idea that the original information was absent from memory.

A second view is that both the original and misleading information coexist in memory. This is called memory coexistence theory. Because misleading information is more recent, it obscures the original memory trace, making it difficult for a witness to be accurate. In a study by Berkerian and Bowers (1983), it was shown that if the appropriate context is given at the time the questions are asked, the misleading postevent information effect can be reduced or eliminated. This was done by having the questions match the order in which the event originally unfolded rather than in a different, more random order. In another study by Christiaansen and Ochalek (1983), people were warned prior to the memory test that some of the questions contained misleading information. With this warning, people were able to disregard some of the information and perform more like people who were not misled. Thus, they were able to remove the memory traces containing the misleading information and focus only on those traces from the original event. Finally, even when there appears to be no memory for the original information on an explicit memory test, like recognition, there is evidence that the information is still present when an implicit memory test is used, like lexical decision (Dodson & Reisberg, 1991).

The third view is that memory is not altered by misleading information, nor is it rendered inaccessible. Instead, the effects that are observed are due to a response bias that reflects how the memory tests are constructed (McCloskey & Zaragoza, 1985). Thus, this is the response bias view. The logic here is a bit complex, so we'll use Table 13.3 to sort it out.

TABLE 13.3   Rates of Responding Supporting Response Bias View of Misleading Postevent Information

MEMORY STATE FOR ORIGINAL INFORMATION	PERCENTAGE OF PEOPLE IN MEMORY STATE		EXPECTED TEST PERFORMANCE
PART A			
Remember	40%		100%
Forget	60%		50%
Total correct			70% (40% + 30%)
PART B			
Remember	40%	20%	100%
		20%	50%
Forget	60%	30%	0%
		30%	50%
Total correct			45% (30% + 15%)
PART C			
Remember	40%		100%
Forget	60%		50%
Total correct			70% (40% + 30%)

Source: McCloskey & Zaragoza, 1985

Imagine the standard situation where at the memory test people select between two alternatives: the original item and the misleading item. In the control condition, when the misleading information is not given (Part A), one of two things will happen. In some cases, people remember the item from the event. Suppose, for the sake of argument, that this occurs 40 percent of the time. All of these people (100 percent) will be correct. In other cases, people do not remember the item (60 percent). They need to guess, with a 50 percent probability of being correct. Thus, the rate of people being correct on the memory test is the sum of the performance of those people who remember (40 percent) and those who do not remember but guess (30% = 60% × 50%), which in this example is 70 percent (40% + (60% × 50%)).

In the misled condition (Part B) one of four things could happen. (1) People remember the original item from the event but not the misleading item. (For the sake of argument, assume that this is half the people who remember the original item: 20 percent.) (2) People remember both the original and misleading items, are uncertain which is correct, and guess between the two, so they are correct half the time (10 percent). (3) People forget the original item but remember the misleading one. These people will always be in error (0 percent). (4) People forget both items, so they choose between the two by chance (15 percent). Thus, the total for the misled condition in this example, assuming the same base rates as for the control condition, is 45 percent.

Presenting witnesses with a modified version of the memory test tested this response bias view. Instead of having people choose between the original and misleading items, the choices were the original item and a new one. The misleading item was not a choice. In this case the influence of memory for the misinformation is removed. In the control condition (Part C) two things can happen. (1) People remember the original item. Regardless of their memory for the misinformation, if they remember the original information, this is what is selected, and performance is at 100 percent. (2) People forget the original information. Also, regardless of whether they remembers the misinformation, they randomly select between the two alternatives. Thus, performance is 50 percent.

As can be seen in Table 13.3, if the response bias view is correct, performance will be similar for the modified version of the memory test for the control and misled conditions. This is what was observed. In a series of six experiments, McCloskey and Zaragoza (1985) found that performance with a modified memory test was not meaningfully different (72 percent accurate) from a nonmisled control condition (75 percent accurate). This illustrates that attempts to understand how remembering, forgetting, and misremembering occur may involve more complex thinking.

A fourth theory for the misleading postevent information effect is that a problem with source monitoring exists (see Chapter 12). Thus, this view is called source monitoring theory. In general, witnesses given misinformation often remember where it came from (Zaragoza & Koshmider, 1989). However, source monitoring errors do occur. People are more likely to make source monitoring errors if the memory retrieval tasks require them to engage in more reflective thinking, such as answering questions or properly arranging the order of a set of statements of a narrative describing the event. Witnesses are less likely to fall prey to misinformation if that information is presented in a simple narrative form (Zaragoza & Lane, 1994). Reflective thinking makes aspects of memory that distinguish source more obscure, leading to an increase in source monitoring errors. The more thematically similar misleading information is to the witnessed event, the more likely errors are made. Errors can also occur for more thematically distant information, but at a much lower rate (Lindsay, Allen, Chan, & Dahl, 2004).

Just because a person is given misleading information, it does not mean that the memory will be altered. It depends on the source of the postevent information. For example, misleading information about an accident is more likely to have an effect if people think it came from an innocent bystander than if it came from a driver who may have caused the accident. In the second case, people are much more likely to disregard the information (Dodd & Bradshaw, 1980). Furthermore, in an interesting twist, Assefi and Garry (2003) found that people were more susceptible to misinformation if they thought they had recently consumed alcohol (even though they hadn't), as seen in Figure 13.1. Thus, even implicit social demands can influence an eyewitness's memory. What was even more disconcerting was that not only did people who *thought* they had consumed alcohol make more errors, but they were also more confident in their answers.

Arousal Influences

Events involving eyewitnesses are often not standard, mundane events. Instead, they can involve emotion-arousing situations, as when someone witnesses a violent car accident or is

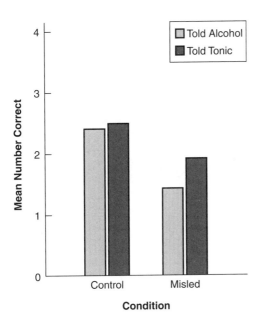

FIGURE 13.1   Influence of Perceived Alcohol Consumption on Memory Performance

Source: Assefi & Garry, 2003

a victim of a serious crime. Because intense emotions are involved, there is some question about what effect these emotions can have on an eyewitness's memory. Do emotions make it better? Do they make it worse? Well, the picture is somewhat complicated. There is no doubt that memory is affected by emotion, but the relationship between emotion and memory for an event is complex. This relationship is outlined well by Christianson (1992).

Yerkes-Dodson Law.   One of the views favored earlier in eyewitness memory research was the idea that emotion and memory followed the **Yerkes-Dodson law** (Yerkes & Dodson, 1908). According to this view, arousal is a continuum, with memory performance being an inverted-U-shaped function, as illustrated in Figure 13.2. At low levels of arousal, a person is relatively lethargic and does not encode information into memory very well. This is like trying to study when you are tired (not that you've ever done that). As arousal increases, memory performance increases as well, up to a point. There is a certain level where memory encoding is maximized. Beyond that point, a person becomes overaroused, and memory worsens. This is like trying to study when you are preparing to go out on an eagerly anticipated date. From this view, people who are bystanders to a violent crime are likely to remember more than a person who was the victim. Presumably, the bystander would be closer to the optimum level, whereas the victim would be highly aroused.

Easterbrook Hypothesis.   There is evidence that overall memory does follow this basic pattern. However, the situation is more complicated than this simple view implies. Specifically, the ability to remember details under different levels of emotional stress depends on

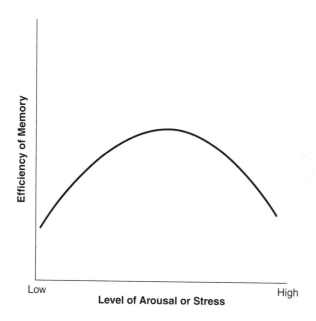

FIGURE 13.2   The Yerkes-Dodson Law

the type of details. At high levels of emotion, memory for peripheral details (e.g., the color of a car, someone's clothing, the actions of bystanders, etc.) becomes worse. However, memory for central details (e.g., what a robber said) becomes better. This contradicts the Yerkes-Dodson law, but it is consistent with another account called the Easterbrook hypothesis.

According to the **Easterbrook hypothesis** (Easterbrook, 1959), at higher levels of emotional intensity, people restrict their attention to a narrower range of details. Attention becomes more focused. This is a process called cue utilization. Basically, under normal emotional stress levels, people notice a wide variety of aspects of their environment, giving a more balanced amount of attention to various details. However, during an emotional event, people focus more of their attention on the principal parts of that event and less on other irrelevant details in the environment. Thus, peripheral details of an event become less well remembered, whereas the central details become better remembered. For example, if you encountered people as part of a nonstressful event, you might be able to remember their faces equally well. However, if you met those people as part of a stressful event, where one was a bank robber and another was a person in line, the cue utilization that occurs as a result of your narrowing your attention to the critical part of the event would lead you to pay more attention to, and thus better remember, the robber's face relative to the other customer's face.

It should be noted that although high levels of emotion can lead a person to accurately remember a narrower range of information, this does not mean that people do not report remembering a wide array of information. Although accurate memory is present for the details focused on, people can still fill in their memories with what they *expect* to be present in the rest of the situation based on their schemas and scripts. For example, people who are shown both emotional and neutral pictures show boundary extension effects (see Chapter 5) of similar magnitudes (Candel, Merckelbach, & Zandbergen, 2003). In effect, they are still interpreting their memories of the pictures they viewed using their expectations of what likely extended beyond the boundaries of the pictures.

Weapon Focus. A good example of emotional intensity and memory is the weapon focus effect. The **weapon focus effect** is an increase in memory for a weapon (such as a gun, knife, cleaver, etc.) that is present in an event along with a decline in memory for other details (Maass & Köhnken, 1989; Steblay, 1992). Recordings of eye movements while watching pictures that depict a crime show that people spend more time looking at what a person is holding if it is a weapon than if it is some more neutral object (Loftus, Loftus, & Messo, 1987). This even occurs when a weapon is present but does not necessarily involve some possibility of a violent action (Kramer, Buckout, & Eugenio, 1990). Basically, the barrel of a gun or the blade of a knife is a point of great interest to people, and they spend a lot of time looking at such things. At some level people want to know whether the weapon will be used against them. This increased attention to a weapon increases memory for that weapon, but it decreases memory for other aspects of the event, such as a perpetrator's face. While some of this weapon focus effect is due to the unusualness of a weapon (Pickel, 1998), there is also added memory disruption because it is a source of danger.

John Dean's Memory

One of the more famous cases of how memory was involved in legal proceedings is that of John Dean's memory for the coverup of the Watergate break-in during President Nixon's administration. This incident led to the president's resignation. John Dean, one of the White House advisors, was called upon to testify before Congress about the coverup in terms of what was going on in the White House. John Dean testified against President Nixon and the other coconspirators. What was most remarkable about Dean's testimony was the number of conversations he claimed to personally remember and the degree of accuracy with which he remembered them. (His initial statement to Congress was 245 pages.) His memory was so remarkable that reporters nicknamed him "the human tape recorder."

The interesting thing about this story is that soon after John Dean had given his testimony, real tape recordings emerged that Nixon had secretly made of White House conversations in the Oval Office. At that point, it became possible to compare Dean's own recollections of the conversations with the actual recordings. This opened up the possibility of a scientific study of memory for conversations that had legal implications. And this is just what was done (Neisser, 1981).

In comparing the initial testimony concerning things that were claimed to have been said and the actual conversation on the tapes, John Dean hardly ever got it right. Many of the things that he claimed were said were actually never said. For example, with regard to one of the White House meetings, Dean claimed that Nixon had asked him to sit down, had asked Halderman (another aid) to keep him posted, and praised Dean for doing a good job. Also, John Dean claimed that he himself had made statements about not really wanting to take credit for his efforts and that the coverup would eventually unravel. The tapes revealed that none of these statements were made during the meeting in question.

However, a comparison of Dean's statements and the tapes also indicated that there was no deliberate attempt to lie on Dean's part. The tapes do corroborate important points in Dean's testimony, such as the fact that the White House was aware of and was involved in the coverup of aspects of the Watergate break-in. Often the distortions in Dean's testimony reflected a schematization of his prior memory. That is, his memory reflected the events in a cleaned-up fashion that he believed should have occurred. Also, Dean misremembers himself as playing a more central role in the conversations than was the case. This self-centered bias is an expected aspect of anyone's memory of an event. This is because our memory of an event includes both the things that objectively occurred as well as our own subjective thoughts and emotions that would be stored as part of the memory trace. Any act of remembering is likely to involve these components.

Synopsis

While eyewitness testimony is generally accurate, this accuracy can be altered by factors that distort the memory reports. For example, the way a question is worded can lead people to misremember the event in the direction implied by the wording of the question. People also incorporate misleading information about events into their reports. This is likely due to problems in response biases and source memory. Finally, eyewitness memory is affect by the level of arousal that a person is experiencing. At very high levels of arousal, memory performance becomes worse. This seems to be because attention during memory encoding is focused on a few smaller, critical details, such as a weapon.

EYEWITNESS CONFIDENCE

When an eyewitness does give a report, is there any way to assess how accurate this testimony is, especially when there are few to no other sources of corroborating evidence? Intuitively it would seem that the more confident a witness is, the more accurate the information is likely to be. Conversely, a memory that a witness is unsure about is more likely to be inaccurate. However, metamemory, the monitoring of one's own memory performance, is far from perfect (see Chapter 14). The same basic principle applies to eyewitness accounts. For example, in the case of eyewitness identification, the average overall correlation between accuracy and reported confidence is quite low: $r = .29$. If only people who actually select someone are considered (leaving out people who say that they do not see the offender in the line-up), the correlation improves somewhat: $r = .41$ (Sporer, Penrod, Read, & Cutler, 1995). Still, the relation is far from perfect. It is quite possible to have people who are very confident that an innocent person committed a crime.

Eyewitness confidence can be influenced by a number of factors. One of these is postidentification feedback, which is information about the quality of an identification that an eyewitness might make. For example, if positive feedback is provided to a witness, such as "Good. You identified the suspect," the witness's confidence in his or her memory increases, compared to a condition where no feedback is given. This can also make the witness embellish claims about the quality of her view of the crime, the clarity of her memory of the event, and the speed with which she remembers identifying the person (Wells & Bradfield, 1998; 1999). Of course, there is no way for such a comment to actually improve any of these qualities of a person's memory.

It has also been found that telling a witness what other witnesses reported increases confidence. For example, after a lineup identification for an offender, if a witness is provided with feedback that another witness picked the same person, he feels more confident about his choice. However, if the person hears that another witness picked someone else, confidence decreases (Luus & Wells, 1994). Thus, the relation between a person's identification accuracy and his or her confidence can become distorted by subsequent information.

Witness confidence is also influenced by how many times questions are asked about information. The more times a person is asked about an aspect of a crime or an accident, the greater his confidence will be in the memory. This is true even for misleading postevent information (Shaw & McClure, 1996). Moreover, this level of confidence as a result of repeated questioning is unrelated to the accuracy of the memory for the event. What appears to be happening is that the repeated questioning makes that particular information easier to access and more salient in memory (remember it is impossible to probe memory without changing it). The increased fluency with which that information is retrieved may lead a person to be more confident in its accuracy (Shaw, 1996). This is important because judges and juries are often swayed by the confidence a witness appears to have in the memories that are reported. By the time a witness gets to trial, the same questions have been answered many times, thereby increasing confidence in memory without a corresponding increase in accuracy. To make matters worse, efforts to make a person aware of the relationship between her level of confidence and her memory accuracy may either have no real effect or actually worsen the relationship (Robinson & Johnson, 1998).

Finally, eyewitness confidence can be influenced by external motivation to remember accurately. In a study by Shaw and Kerr (2003), people were given either extra motivation to remember accurately (a possibility of winning money for being most accurate) or no motivation at all. Students at Lafayette College witnessed an event in their classroom and were then given a memory test five days later, either with or without the additional motivation. What was found was that, in this study, extra motivation did not significantly alter the accuracy of the memory reports and given confidence ratings on their answers. However, motivation did affect the relationship between accuracy and confidence. For the unmotivated students, the correlation between accuracy and confidence was relatively good: $r = .44$. However, for motivated people, the correlation was horrible: $r = .05$. Essentially, what happened was that by encouraging people to try harder, a great deal of effort is associated with each memory retrieval. As such, it becomes more difficult for people to identify what was easy and what was difficult to remember, and the usefulness of the confidence ratings drops tremendously. This is important because in many legal settings a witness is motivated to try hard to remember.

Synopsis

Although the confidence an eyewitness has in his or her memory reports is often used as an indicator of the accuracy of the memories, the real relationship between confidence and accuracy is quite low. Moreover, the relationship between accuracy and confidence can be worsened by a number of factors. For example, reinforcing feedback, even from someone who does not know what really happened, can artificially increase a witness's confidence. Eyewitness confidence can also be affected by repeated attempts to remember the event and external encouragement to try to remember more accurately.

COGNITIVE INTERVIEW

Given the problems with eyewitness memory that can make it so error prone, can anything be done to improve eyewitness reports? Research on eyewitness memory has led to methods of gathering information that should increase the amount of accurate information and decrease the likelihood of misinformation being introduced into an eyewitness's memory. One of the more prominent of these approaches is the cognitive interview. The cognitive interview is a technique developed using an understanding of basic memory principles to maximize the amount of correct information from a witness and minimize the amount of incorrect information (Geiselman et al., 1984; Geiselman, Fisher, MacKinnon, & Holland, 1985). The cognitive interview does this by focusing on five retrieval processes.

The first process is to use the principles of encoding specificity and mood congruent learning (see Chapter 7). Basically, there should be some attempt to reinstate the external and internal contexts of the event. This can include having the person imagine being back at the scene of the incident and feeling how he felt at the time. By reinstating the context, this serves as a retrieval cue, making it more likely that people will be able to access information in long-term memory. As a reminder, context is most likely to have an effect on memory retrieval during recall with weaker memory traces—just as in the case of many police interviews.

Second, because sometimes people can retrieve only part of the information, as with the tip-of-the-tongue state (see Chapter 9), witnesses are encouraged to report whatever information they can remember, however partial or insignificant it may seem to them at the time. For example, if a person cannot remember someone's name but can remember how many syllables it had or what letter it began with, then the person should report that. This sort of information, even in a fragmentary state, can potentially be useful to investigators.

Third, there are often many different retrieval pathways to a given piece of information. When we forget about information, we may be able to retrieve it later if we take a different approach to it (see Chapters 7 and 9). This can be accomplished by reporting the components of the event in a variety of orders. By starting at different points, this may emphasize different types of information, leading to different details being reported. This also serves to enhance eyewitness reports.

Fourth, a person may be asked to report the information from a different perspective (see Chapter 9). Altering one's perspective may make some information more salient and more likely to be reported. As a consequence, the witness's memory report becomes more complete. These alternative perspectives provide alternative retrieval pathways, allowing a person to remember information that might otherwise have been missed.

Finally, with the cognitive interview, police questioners are discouraged from interrupting a witness's report in the middle of a narrative, when possible. By disrupting a person, the flow of the natural retrieval process is disturbed, and some of the more weakly stored information might not be reported. This is similar to the part-set cueing effect (see Chapter 9), in which providing people with part of a learned set of information can actually result in the probability of recalling a given item decreasing rather than increasing. In short, interrupting people may disrupt their idiosyncratic retrieval plans, thereby worsening memory performance.

The cognitive interview is a very effective eyewitness memory tool. Using the cognitive interview can boost the reports of accurate information from actual crime victims by more than 50 percent without any noticeable change in the amount of false information that may inadvertently be reported (Fisher, Geiselman, & Amador, 1989). The cognitive interview takes a bit more time to administer than the standard police interview approach. However, given the amount of extra police work that might be required without that information, the cost is well worth it.

Synopsis

Although eyewitness memory can be altered in a number of ways, by using what we know about memory, we can develop ways of questioning people that are less likely to disrupt memories and increase the accuracy of the information that is recovered. The cognitive interview is one way of doing this. This question method takes into account what is known about the influences of learning context, partial retrieval, hypermnesia, and part-set cuing on memory to avoid situations that will deter accurate remembering.

EYEWITNESS IDENTIFICATION

One of the most important things an eyewitness to a crime or accident can do is identify the people involved, particularly criminal suspects. An eyewitness must reliably remember the prominent features of individuals in order to accurately identify them later. However, as we have seen in many other chapters in this book, people are prone to forgetting, which can cause them to make memory errors. In this case of eyewitness identification, this could lead to two highly undesirable outcomes: (1) failing to identify a perpetrator and (2) mistakenly identifying an innocent person as the perpetrator. The second of these is worse because it might lead to the prosecution of an innocent person, leaving the culprit free to engage in further crimes. There are a number of things that can influence a witness's memory of a person involved in a crime. Some of these are beyond the control of the legal system, such as whether a perpetrator was carrying a weapon (which will reduce eyewitness identification accuracy). However, there are steps that can be taken that will increase the ability of an eyewitness to accurately remember and identify a person (Wells et al., 2000).

Mugshots

Mugshots are a standard device used by investigators to help identify perpetrators of crimes. Essentially, an eyewitness is shown a series of photographs of people who have been involved in previous crimes. If the witness can identify the perpetrator from this set of faces, the police can work more quickly to solve the crime. However, mugshots can also have some negative effects on eyewitness identification memory. For example, if people are shown a series of mugshots, and the perpetrator is not among them, the eyewitness may sometimes pick out another person as the criminal. To make matters worse, when a person incorrectly identifies someone from mugshots, her ability to identify the perpetrator later (if she sees the person on the street, for example) is even lower than for those who do not incorrectly identify someone (Brigham & Cairns, 1988; Davis, Shepherd, & Ellis, 1979; Gorenstein & Ellsworth, 1980). Essentially, people's memory for the mugshot that was selected interferes with, and makes it harder to retrieve, the memory of the face of the person involved in the crime. However, this only occurs if people make a commitment to identifying one of the faces in the mugshots as the perpetrator (Dysart, Lindsay, Hammond, & Dupuis, 2001). There is no memory deficit that comes from just viewing the pictures.

Moreover, it has been found that in cases when the perpetrator was not among the mugshots, witnesses are more likely to pick out a person whose mugshots, even if they were not the one that was initially picked (Memon, Hope, Bartlett, & Bull, 2002). Most likely the witnesses picked these individuals because they seemed "familiar," not realizing it was because they were among the mugshots. More generally, people have better memory for having seen a face before than remembering *where* they had seen that face (Brown, Deffenbacher, & Sturgill, 1977). In other words, problems in source monitoring with mugshot viewings can lead to errors in eyewitness identification.

Lineups

One way to improve eyewitness identification is proper lineup procedure. Keep in mind that because of how memory naturally operates, there has been some forgetting of details on the part of the eyewitness, and memory will not be perfect. Witness identification of a suspect is essentially a recognition process. A person is comparing his memory with what is presented in the environment, such as faces in a police lineup. During identification, people are making judgments based not only on how well a given person matches their memory, but also how well the different people in the lineup compare to one another in terms of how much they resemble the offender. This is the **relative judgment principle** (Wells, 1984). According to this principle, people may select someone out of a lineup not because this was the person the witness saw, but because compared to others in the lineup, that person most closely resembled the criminal.

Therefore, **lineup similarity**—the physical resemblances of others in the lineup—is significant. For example, lineups created with fillers who do not resemble a suspect much are going to be biased in favor of having the witness chose the individual who most closely resembles the witness's memory of the offender more so than the others. However, when lineup fillers at least fit the basic description given to the police by the witness, people need to use their memories more carefully, and their selections become more diagnostic. It has been shown that with similar lineup fillers, the identification of guilty suspects is roughly the same, but the identification of innocent suspects decreases considerably (Lindsay & Wells, 1980).

Another factor that can influence eyewitness identification is the instructions given to a witness. Perhaps the most critical factor influencing a decision is whether the instructions include a statement telling the witness that the perpetrator might not be present. This "perpetrator possibly absent instruction" explicitly opens up the possibility of the witness not identifying anyone. Without this simple instruction, eyewitnesses appear to have a strong compulsion to select *someone*. As a result, an innocent person in the lineup may be identified just because they closely resemble the perpetrator. With this instruction, people are less likely to feel compelled to pick someone, and the false identification rate drops dramatically (Malpass & Devine, 1981). In general, it has been shown that the rate of false identification drops by about 42 percent when this instruction is included. The rate of not selecting a perpetrator only drops by about 2 percent when this instruction is included (Steblay, 1997).

Finally, eyewitness identification can also be strongly influenced by how the lineup is presented. The traditional lineup—the one you see in movies and cop shows—is a simultaneous lineup, where all of the alternatives are presented together and the witness is asked to select one. Another type is the sequential lineup, where the witness is shown one person at a time. Keeping in mind that people are making decisions in line with a relative judgment principle, errors in witness identification are much more likely to occur with a simultaneous lineup than with a sequential lineup (Lindsay & Wells, 1985). It is much easier for a witness to make relative comparisons between people when they are presented simultaneously. As such, relativistic judgments are more likely to be made. However, when a sequential lineup is used, people are put in a position of being forced to compare the person they are seeing at the moment with their memory of the perpetrator. This is because a witness does not know whom they will be seeing next or how many people they will see altogether. Using a sequential as opposed to a simultaneous lineup has the effect of greatly lowering false identifications, with little to no effect on positive identifications of actual offenders.

Unconscious Transference. In addition to aspects of eyewitness identification that investigators can control, such as the way a lineup is presented, there are other aspects that are not under control. One of these is **unconscious transference,** which occurs when a person mistakenly identifies an innocent bystander as the perpetrator of a crime (Ross, Ceci, Dunning, & Toglia, 1994). In such cases, a person remembers seeing the offender, but then becomes confused. So an innocent bystander is incorrectly remembered as having been the person who committed the crime. What happens in these cases is that people remember seeing the person as a bystander but also remember him as the perpetrator as well. This is a memory blending theory of unconscious transference (Ross et al., 1994). There is an assumption by memory retrieval processes that these two individuals are one and the same. However, if people are aware prior to witnessing the event that these are two different people, then people are less likely to make this error.

Another view that has been suggested is a source monitoring theory of unconscious transference (Read, 1994). According to this idea, people remember a person but fail to remember the situation in which they interacted with that person. As a result, people may be more likely to misattribute the source of that memory as a case of remembering the person as the perpetrator of a crime.

Synopsis

Understanding how eyewitness memories function is also important in situations where a person needs to make an identification of a possible criminal. As with regular memories, the very act of using memory can change how well memory works. For example, having seen a face previously, even in a set of mugshots, can mistakenly lead people to think that was the face of the perpetrator. Also, because people are prone to use relative judgments when assessing their memories, it is better to have sequential lineups rather than simultaneous. This forces people to rely more on a strategy of comparing each person with their memory of the perpetrator rather than with each other. In addition, lineup accuracy is increased if people are explicitly reminded that they can say "not present" to the lineup. While investigators can use some techniques to reduce memory errors of eyewitnesses, it is still possible for things to occur that is out of their control. For example, an eyewitness may make a blending error and misremember a bystander as the perpetrator because they remember that person's face as part of the event.

JURIES

The influence of memory on legal matters does not only affect gathering testimony and information from eyewitnesses but other areas as well. One other legal setting that the operation of memory may be important is in juries. Jury trials, while fairly efficient, are often not as crisp and clean as one would hope for in an ideal world. In this section we look at two ways that memory processes can influence jury decisions. These are the order in which information is encountered and the ability of juries to disregard inappropriate information.

Information Order

When jurors hear evidence, they try to mentally construct a memory for the evidence heard in the form of a coherent story, much like what occurs for autobiographical memory (see Chapter 11), only in this case the memory representation is for other people's experiences (Pennington & Hastie, 1986; 1988). The memories of jurors are further affected by the order in which they learn information, just like people in normal settings. What is important here is the fact that the order in which this information is stored in memory has an influence on the decisions that are rendered later. There are two ways to assess how order information affects jury decisions. The first is to use a step-by-step process in which people are asked to render preliminary decisions after each piece of information is given. Under these circumstances, people are more likely to show a recency effect (Furnham, 1986; Pennington & Hastie, 1992). That is, their decisions are more likely to be most influenced by the information they learned most recently. The most recent information is most available in memory, so people are going to rely on it more.

The other way to assess the influence of order information is to have people make decisions after all of the information is given. When this is done, one of two things can happen. If people are provided with background information, such as providing a motive for a killing, then decisions are more likely to show a recency effect. However, if people are not given such background information but are presented only with descriptions of the reports of various witnesses, then people are more likely to show a primacy effect (Kerstholt & Jackson, 1998). This happens because when background information is provided, it gives people a starting point, and they are more willing to adjust their opinions based on new information. However, without background information, people must try to make a coherent story with the information they have. As a result, they need to keep more information of their own creation active in working memory, and they are more reluctant to alter their prior understanding of the events.

Inadmissible Evidence

One problem that can arise before a jury trial (as with pretrial publicity) or during the trial itself (in cases presented by attorneys) is when jury members are exposed to evidence that a judge deems inadmissible. At that point, the judge has a couple of choices. One is to declare a mistrial, and the other is to instruct the jurors to disregard or ignore the inadmissible evidence. Clearly, the second alternative would be preferable if the jury can be trusted to do so because it would make the process quicker.

The instruction to a jury to disregard evidence is essentially a directed forgetting instruction (see Chapter 7). As a reminder, in directed forgetting, people are given a set of information. At some point, they are directed to remember some of the information but to forget the rest. In general, people are fairly efficient at doing this. Information that is designated as to-be-forgotten is recalled less well compared to information designated as to-be-remembered (Bjork, 1970). The question here is how well does this instruction to forget work in a real-world setting that may have serious implications for a defendant on trial?

When memory for inadmissible evidence is tested for using a directed forgetting paradigm, it is typically observed that jurors' memories for the inadmissible evidence is poorer than for admissible evidence. So there does appear to be some success in forgetting the information. However, when looking at assessments of a person's attributes (e.g., friendly, dishonest, etc.) and decisions to convict or acquit, there is a clear influence of the inadmissible evidence. Specifically, the presence of damaging inadmissible evidence biases jurors toward a guilty verdict, whereas supporting inadmissible evidence biases jurors toward a not guilty verdict (Golding & Hauselt, 1994; Thompson, Fong, & Rosenhan, 1981). More generally, people continue to use information they were supposed to disregard to make attributions about a person (Wyer & Unverzagt, 1985). Part of the reason for this is that because the memories for this inadmissible information may have been suppressed (this is essentially directed forgetting), people have difficulty accessing the source information in long-term memory (Bjork & Bjork, 2003). Thus, jurors may remember the information but not where it came from, and, thus, they also forget that they are supposed to disregard it. In essence, this is also a form of sleeper effect.

This influence of the supposedly to-be-forgotten information on decision making is also influenced by what jurors think about the source or nature of the information. Specifically, the directed forgetting is less efficient, and the opinions are more biased when the jurors believe that information is accurate and relevant to the defendant. This would occur when the information is described as confidential but inadvertently presented. However, the directed forgetting is very efficient and opinions much less biased when the jurors believe that the information is inaccurate and irrelevant to the defendant (Golding, Fowler, Long, & Latta, 1990). An example of this latter case would be if the jurors were told that the information they were given was to be disregarded because it actually referred to another person in a different case. Alternatively, if the jurors are suspicious of the source of the inadmissible evidence, it will also not have an effect on their decision making (Fein, McCloskey, & Tomlinson, 1997). For example, if people are exposed to pretrial publicity that is damaging to the defendant and then later learn that this information was leaked by a source trying to unfairly discredit the defendant, then jurors successfully forget that information.

There appear to be clear influences of inadmissible evidence on the decisions of individual jurors. Specifically, when the evidence is deemed relevant and coming from a reliable source, people have a hard time forcing themselves to forget it to the point that it does not influence their subsequent decisions. It still appears to be in long-term memory and have an implicit effect on thinking. While this information may sound depressing, the influences of this ineffective forgetting can be mediated or softened during the deliberation process where the jurors must discuss the case with the other members of the jury and come to a consensus about what verdict to render (London & Nunez, 2000). In this case, the collective memory efforts of the entire jury help serve to dampen the implicit influences of supposedly to-be-forgotten and inappropriate information. This information is so weak to begin with that it cannot compete with the stronger, explicit knowledge that is being openly discussed during deliberation.

As a final point, it should be noted that not all inadmissible evidence comes from external sources. Sometimes it comes from the jurors themselves. Specifically, when people are thinking about events, they sometimes think about the way things might have been if someone had behaved differently. This is called counterfactual thinking. When people engage in counterfactual thinking, they are more likely to focus on behaviors that are outside of a person's normal routine. Jurors are more likely to award a victim a larger compensation if the other party did something out of the ordinary because it is easier to imagine that person doing something different. However, if it was the victim who did something outside of her normal routine, then the juries tended to award a smaller compensation. It is as if they are in part unconsciously blaming the victim. Moreover, the smaller people's working memory spans, the less likely they are to suppress these irrelevant thoughts when making these decisions (Goldinger, Kleider, Azuma, & Beike, 2003).

Synopsis

Memory is important for juries. For example, juries' decisions, which are based on jury memories, are influenced by the order in which information was encountered. Thus, there is a serial position curve influence in this real-world setting. Also, juries vary in their effectiveness at being able to suppress, or forget, inadmissible evidence that was presented in a courtroom. Even when they try to conform to instructions to disregard irrelevant information, the decisions juries reach can be biased in the direction of the inappropriate information due to unconscious memory processes.

SUMMARY

In this chapter we looked at a number of ways that human memory can have an influence on legal issues. The clearest cases of where memory has an influence is in the reports of eyewitnesses to an accident or crime. The memory reports of such witnesses can be dramatically influenced by the way questions are worded or by being exposed to misinformation between their witnessing the actual event and subsequently having their memories tested. These inaccurate memory reports appear to reflect biases in how information is encoded in memory and is less likely to involve an actual change or loss of the original memory trace or problems in monitoring the source of the information. Eyewitness memory is further complicated by the influences of emotional arousal on the ability to accurately remember. In general, memory encoding becomes much more selective and focused on a relatively few critical details at the high levels of arousal that may often be present in these sorts of situations, such as a weapon. It was also pointed out that although distortions in memory reports from witnesses can occur, as was seen with John Dean's memory of the Watergate scandal, the general gist of eyewitness memory is fairly accurate. Unfortunately, it is difficult to detect discrepancy between an actual event and a person's memory for it based on the confidence a witness has in the memory, which further complicates matters. To get around such difficulties in witness memory, developments such as the cognitive interview are available to law enforcement personnel to help safeguard the investigative processes from such damaging influences on a person's memory. Also, further memory biases in eyewitness identification have been isolated, along with recommendations to better conduct identifications so such errors do not complicate and damage the legal process. Finally, some influence of memory on juror decision making was considered. This coverage focused on the ability of jurors to forget information that was deemed inadmissible in the context of a trial. The ability to accurately forget such information and have it not influence subsequent decisions is less likely to be successful when the information is thought to be relevant than when it is not. It was also noted that the jury deliberation process itself might serve to correct for some of these memory biases.

STUDY QUESTIONS

1. How can an eyewitness's memory be altered by what she hears after witnessing an event?

2. What are some likely effects of misleading postevent information?

3. How does an eyewitness's arousal level at the time of an event affect memory? What theory best captures this?

4. How does the presence of a weapon during a crime affect memory?

5. What is the relationship between eyewitness confidence and accuracy? How can this be altered, and with what outcome?

6. How does the cognitive interview work to produce more accurate memory reports?

7. How is eyewitness identification affected by the use of mugshots? By different types of lineups? By things that are said by an investigator? By the presence of bystanders?

8. How does the order in which they hear things affect jurors' memories?

9. What happens in the memories of jurors when they are instructed to disregard inadmissible evidence? How does this influence their decision making?

KEY TERMS

cognitive interview, Easterbrook hypothesis, confidence, eyewitness testimony, lineup similarity, misleading postevent information, relative judgment principle, weapon focus effect, wording effects, unconscious transference, Yerkes-Dodson law

CHAPTER FOURTEEN

METAMEMORY

Much of how our memories affect our thinking and behavior occurs out of conscious awareness. Still, we do have some conscious insight. There are cases in which we are very much aware of our efforts to remember and, more painfully, when we fail to do so. To remember more effectively, we must have some conscious awareness and control of our own memories. This is **metamemory**—the awareness of one's own memory. This refers to both the contents of memory as well as how we go about remembering. Our beliefs about ourselves can limit or expand what we can do. For example, in a study by Assefi and Garry (2003), students were given tonic water to drink. Students who were misled to believe that they had consumed alcohol had worse memory performance than people who were truthfully informed. So just the belief that memory is worse after alcohol consumption led people to use their memories less efficiently.

There are a number of ways we can look at the effectiveness of metamemory. First, we examine theories of metamemory, and then we look at a number of phenomena, including our ability to judge when we have learned something or whether we will later remember things that are currently forgotten. We also look at how we know that we *don't* know something. Other phenomena refer to how we experience an act of remembering and how what we currently know biases what we remember of the past. We discuss prospective memory, which is remembering to do things in the future, as well as things that can be done, such as mnemonics, to make memory more efficient. Finally, we look at some people who have exceptional memories.

GENERAL PROPERTIES AND THEORIES OF METAMEMORY

Before considering various aspects of metamemory, let's go over the difference between cues and targets. Then we'll look at some theories on how metamemory judgments are made—namely, cue familiarity, accessibility, and competition hypotheses.

Cues and Targets

As a point of terminology, the memory traces that people make judgments about are called targets, and the questions or prompts are called cues. For example, if someone were to ask you if you remember your thirteenth birthday, the memory for the birthday would be the target, and the question you were asked would be the cue.

In his review of metamemory, Schwartz (1994) outlined two types of information that are used to make judgments. One is target-based sources, which is information from the memory trace about which the judgment is made. This includes information that has been retrieved from memory, as well as the ease with which it is recovered. Target-based sources of metamemory are especially important in judgments of learning. The second type of information is cue-based sources, which includes information that is gleaned from a memory cue, such as a question, rather than target information. Metamemory judgments are likely to be better in proportion to the familiarity of the cue information. For example, if someone asks you a question about a topic you are relatively familiar with, you are more inclined to say that you know the answer based on how familiar the information in the question seems. Now, let's look at three general theories of metamemory.

Cue Familiarity Hypothesis

According to the **cue familiarity hypothesis** (Metcalf, 2000; Reder, 1987) metamemory judgments are made based on the familiarity of the information in a memory cue. The more familiar the cue information is, the more likely people will judge that the knowledge is in memory. Imagine if someone asked you if you know your grandmother's maiden name. If you know a lot about your family, you might recognize this as a familiar topic and say to yourself, "This is something I know." However, if you are not all wrapped up in your family's history, you might recognized this as a topic you know little about and say to yourself, "I have no clue."

Accessibility Hypothesis

According to the **accessibility hypothesis** (Koriat, 1993; 1995), metamemory judgments are inferential. People can make inferences about what is in memory based on what is at hand or even using partial retrievals of the relevant knowledge. There are two sources of information that are used to make these inferences. One is the amount of information that is activated when a judgment is made. The more information that is activated, the more likely that the knowledge is in memory. For example, if you can't think of someone's name, but you know what letter the name begins with, how many syllables it has, and so forth, then that is a lot of information, and you will judge that the person's name is in your memory. The other source of information is the intensity of the activated memory traces. This includes the ease of access, the vividness of any imagery, how specific the information seems, and so forth. The stronger the information retrieved, the more likely the knowledge is in memory. For example, if you are asked what your best friend's mother's maiden name was, a number of names might be activated in your memory, but only very weakly. As a result, you would decide that you do not know the information.

Competition Hypothesis

According to the **competition hypothesis** (Schreiber, 1998; Schreiber and Nelson, 1998), metamemory judgments are influenced by the number of memory trace competitors that are involved in retrieval. Metamemory judgments are greater when there is less competition. If there are only a few traces involved, people can be assured that the search process is fairly targeted and is likely to produce the desired information. In contrast, if a large number of traces are involved, then it is less likely that the knowledge is going to be retrieved. The more competition among the relevant traces, the more difficult memory retrieval will be.

Synopsis

There are a number of theories of metamemory. One idea is that decisions are based on the familiarity of the cues. Another is that judgments are based on a partial memory search. Finally, there is the idea that metamemory judgments are based on how much interference is experienced.

JUDGMENTS OF LEARNING

When people learn something, it is helpful to know how well it is stored in long-term memory. Information that is poorly learned should be studied more, and information that is well learned does not need much further study. Estimates people make for how well they have learning something are called **judgments of learning,** or JOLs (Arbuckle & Cuddy, 1969). Studies of JOLs have shown that these judgments are between poor and horrible assessments of how much has actually been learned. The question is, why?

Theories of JOLs

One theory is the inability hypothesis. According to this view, JOLs are so poor because people have little conscious awareness of their own mental processes (e.g., Nisbett & Wilson, 1977). They lack the ability to assess their own learning. An alternative is the monitoring-retrieval hypothesis, which states that JOLs are poor because people are assessing whether they can retrieve information and report it. When JOLs are made soon after the information was encountered, that knowledge is still in working memory. As such, people think that the information is better learned than it actually is.

These theories were tested by Nelson and Dunlosky (1991; Dunlosky & Nelson, 1994; Scheck, Meeter, & Nelson, 2004). They elicited JOLs either immediately or after a delay. If the inability hypothesis is correct, then the delay should not matter. However, if the monitoring-retrieval hypothesis is correct, then after a delay, working memory will have been cleared out, and people will depend more on long-term memory and more accurately judge their future performance. In one study (Dunlosky and Nelson, 1994), people learned a set of words either through rote rehearsal or by forming mental images. As discussed in Chapter 3, memory is better when people use imagery. As shown in Figure 14.1, when people made JOLs immediately after studying, there was little to no distinction made between how well people thought they learned in the different conditions. However, when there was a delay, there was a marked difference between the JOLs in these conditions in exactly the pattern that is revealed by actual memory performance (however, see Kimball & Metcalfe, 2003, for an explanation based on distributed practice).

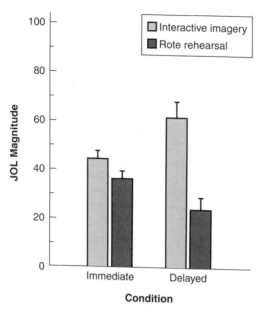

FIGURE 14.1 Judgments of Learning. Words were learned under imagery or rote memorization instructions, given either immediately or after a delay.
Source: Dunlosky & Nelson, 1994

These improvements in JOLs are also consistent with Koriat's (1993) accessibility hypothesis. While the clearing out of working memory may contribute to the enhancement of JOLs, the passage of time and the fluency with which information is processed have effects over and above the working memory component (Kelemen & Weaver, 1997). Specifically, JOLs are more accurate the closer the conditions at the time the judgments were made to those when memory retrieval occurred. When people can properly assess what is available in long-term memory and the strength of their information sources, JOL estimates are more accurate.

JOL Cues

Koriat (1997) outlines how JOLs are affected by three types of cues: extrinsic, intrinsic, and mnemonic. Extrinsic cues are information concerning aspects of the learning environment, such as massed or distributed practice, or presentation times. People are not attuned to how these external characteristics influence their ability to learn, and JOLs are not affected by extrinsic cues. Intrinsic cues are aspects of the information being learned, such as the perceived ease of learning each piece of information. In contrast to extrinsic cues, JOLs do appear to be sensitive to intrinsic cues. This is in line with the cue familiarity hypothesis. Finally, mnemonic cues are memory-based sources of information. These are assessments of how a person has done on previous judgments. Over time, with practice, if people continue to make JOLs, they tend to shift from using intrinsic cues to using mnemonic cues. This is in line with the accessibility hypothesis.

Additional information does not always improve JOLs. In some cases, JOLs can actually worsen. For example, multiple study-test cycles can worsen JOLs over time (Koriat,

2002). Declines in JOLs also occur when there is competition among memory traces. For example, in the fan effect (see Chapter 7) retrieval is more difficult with an increased number of associations with a concept. This also lowers JOLs (McGuire & Maki, 2001). When additional knowledge acts in competition with a desired memory trace, people judge that they do not know the information, so JOL estimates are decreased. This is in line with the competition hypothesis.

Allocation of Study Time

Although JOLs can be inaccurate, people do have some sense of their learning ability. One important adaptation people can make is how they allocate their study time. Ideally, study time should be planned to maximize the amount of new knowledge that is learned. For example, spending all your time on subjects you already know well is less effective. It may increase overlearning, but it does not help you learn new things.

People do regulate their study time based on how easy they think pieces of information are to learn. However, this allocation is not always effective. For example, people often choose distributed practice for easy items and massed practice for hard items, which makes learning less effective (Son, 2004). When people first encounter information, they tend to focus more effort on the difficult items, which manifests itself as massed practice (and also gives the illusion of harder studying). Moreover, because these items are so difficult, people have trouble learning anything new. They spend most of their effort on things that are far from being learned. As a result, there is little gain of new knowledge. This is the labor-in-vain effect (Nelson & Leonesio, 1988).

However, the picture is not completely dismal. As people gain experience with the material they are trying to learn, study time allocation becomes more effective. Rather than spending most of the time on the hardest items, people shift to spending more time on items that are just beyond their current ability level. This is called the region of proximal learning (Metcalfe, 2002; Metcalfe & Kornell, 2003). This method is more efficient because people spend less time on knowledge that is way beyond their ability. Instead, they focus on things that can help them ratchet up to the next level.

Synopsis

Judgments of learning are important for effective learning. Unfortunately, the relationship between JOLs and later accuracy is often disappointingly low. Part of this is because people make JOLs before clearing out what is left over in working memory. Understanding JOLs is complicated by the fact that their accuracy varies depending on the cues that are available. People use their JOLs to manage their study time in inefficient ways and may even spend much effort studying things that are too difficult. With more experience, however, the person learns to use what he already knows as a springboard for learning new things.

FEELING OF KNOWING

When you forget things, it does not always feel the same. Sometimes you don't know something and it seems like you never learned it. Other times, you don't know the answer, but you feel that it is somewhere in memory, and if you heard or saw it, you would be able to identify it. These forgetting differences are revealed by **feeling of knowing,** or FOK, judgments (Hart, 1965).

To get FOK judgments, people were asked a series of moderately difficult questions, such as "Who was Richard Nixon's vice president before Gerald Ford?" Some things were never learned, but others had been encountered but were no longer prominent. After failing to recall an answer, people made an FOK judgment by rating how likely it was that they would identify the information on a later recognition test. Then, at the end, people were given an actual recognition test to see how well their FOK judgments corresponded to their actual memory. In general, it was found that FOK judgments are reasonable predictors of future memory, although there are some deviations (Hart, 1965).

Problems with FOK Judgments

Although FOK judgments can be accurate, there is some inaccuracy. According to the cue-familiarity hypothesis (Reder, 1987), FOK judgments are based on the familiarity of information in the question or cue. One way to test this is by using the "game show" method (Reder, 1987), in which people are given a question and then either answer it (control condition) or indicate that they know the answer (game show condition). This is called the game show method because it is like a game show in which the contestants are asked a question and the one who hits the buzzer first gets to answer. This technique reveals that people know whether they have information in memory before they can actually retrieve it (Reder, 1987), as shown in Figure 14.2. Moreover, the rate that people indicate that they know an answer is related to the familiarity of the information in the question and not necessarily what is in memory (Reder & Ritter, 1992). Similarly, people give higher FOK ratings to things they think they *ought* to know, rather than what they actually know (Costermans, Lories, & Ansay, 1992).

Other Aspects of FOK Judgments

FOK judgments are related to how much partial information is remembered (Koriat, 1993; 1995). Most of the partial information are semantic attributes of the information people are trying to remember (Koriat, Levy-Sadot, Edry, & de Marcas, 2003), such as failing to recall a name, but knowing that the person was a nineteenth-century composer who lived in Germany. With a large amount of accurate partial information, there is a high correspondence between FOK ratings and future memory. However, if the partial information is incorrect, the correspondence is lower. This is why the overall relation between FOK ratings and actual memory is not ideal. Partial information also predicts whether what is eventually retrieved will be "remembered" or is just "known" (Hicks & Marsh, 2002; see the remember-know section later in this chapter). A cue-familiarity account applies more to the early stages of the processing, which is related to "known" information. However, an accessibility account applies more to later stages, when familiarity with the cue is high and people have gone past the initial evaluation stage (Koriat & Levy-Sadot, 2001), which is related to "remembered" information. Finally, FOK judgments are affected by the number of competitors involved. If people are trying to remember something, FOK ratings are higher if it has a small set of competitors rather than a large set (Schreiber, 1998; Schreiber & Nelson, 1998). This is in line with the competition hypothesis.

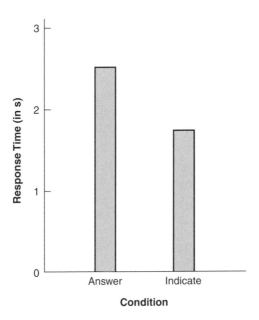

FIGURE 14.2 **Difference in Response Times.** People either had to answer a question (control) or indicate that they knew the answer (game show).

Source: Reder, 1987

Tip-of-the-Tongue State

A **tip-of-the-tongue (TOT) state** is when people fail to recall information but feel that they are about to retrieve it. It is on the tip of their tongues (Brown & McNeill, 1966). This seems like a FOK judgment. However, a FOK judgment assesses whether a person thinks the information will be remembered, whereas a TOT state indicates that remembering is about to occur (Brown, 1991; Schwartz, 2001).

Characteristics of TOT States. There are a number of characteristics of TOT states (Brown, 1991). First, people experience them about once a week on average. Second, there is often some information available. It is not unusual to be able to think of words that are similar to the one that is needed, either in terms of meaning, sound, or both. Third, people in a TOT state often are having trouble with a proper noun, such as the name of a person or place. Fourth, a person in a TOT state may be aware of the first letter or sound, and perhaps the last one as well, of the word, along with the number of syllables. Finally, the occurrence of TOT states does not appear to be related to feelings of stress or anxiety.

Theories of TOT States. One theory of the TOT state is the incomplete activation view (e.g., Brown & McNeill, 1966). A TOT state occurs when the search range has not been sufficiently narrowed. There are too many possibilities, so the person cannot retrieve the desired word. Another theory is a blocking view, in which TOT states occur when related but inappropriate competitors are activated to a greater degree and block access to the appropriate information. These blocking memories, rather than the appropriate one, are being retrieved, making it harder to access the target memory. People keep retrieving the wrong one. Moreover, because these wrong traces have been retrieved recently, they are more available and so are more likely to be retrieved again. This starts a vicious cycle, resulting in the TOT state.

KNOWING THAT YOU DON'T KNOW

Sometimes we feel like we know something, even if we can't remember it at the moment. Other times, we know that we just **don't know** something. No matter how long we search, we know that the target information will never be remembered. For example, if I asked you the question "When was the city of Lakewood, Ohio, founded?," "Is *scissel* a word?," or "Does President Bush use an electric toothbrush?," most of you know immediately that you do not know the answer. What is interesting about these "don't know" judgments is that people make them as rapidly, if not more rapidly, as they do about knowledge that is actually in memory (Kolers & Palef, 1976). Why does this occur?

One idea is that when people are asked about very unfamiliar topics, they can rapidly make a judgment based on the information in the question, consistent with the cue-familiarity hypothesis (Reder, 1987). When given a question with very unfamiliar information, because memory retrieval does not get very far in starting, people can quickly identify the information as being not known.

In support of this, in a study by Glucksburg and McCloskey (1981), people first explicitly learned that they did not know certain pieces of information, such as "It is unknown whether John has a pencil" (*explicit don't know*) along with facts that were known, such as "John has a shovel" (*true*) and "John does not have a chair" (*false*). After learning, people made "yes," "no," and "don't know" replies to these statements, as well as to new statements that the person would not know about. People were slower and less accurate in saying that they did not know something if they had previously learned that they did not know it than if they had never studied it (see Figure 14.3). Thus, by having something in memory for the "don't know" facts that were learned, there is now something for memory to access, so retrieval time slows down accordingly. However, when nothing was learned, there is nothing in memory, so rapid "don't know" responses are made. "Don't know" responses are faster when there is no relevant information in memory, but they are hindered when there is relevant information in memory, even when this is knowledge that the information is not known.

Another idea is that when asked questions about things people don't have in memory, if the information is distinctive, it will not make contact with many memory traces. As such, there is a failure to retrieve any information from memory in a very short period of time. Based on this lack of retrieval, a person can judge that the information is not known (Ghetti, 2003). This is consistent with the accessibility hypothesis.

Synopsis

When people forget something, they can estimate whether they know it, even if it is not currently available, as with feeling-of-knowing judgments. These judgments are fairly accu-

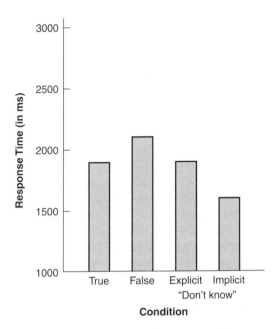

FIGURE 14.3   Difference in Response Times. Questions were true, false, or unknown. "Don't know" responses were for facts that were either learned earlier as "don't know" (explicit) or not (implicit).

Source: Glucksburg & McCloskey, 1981

rate, although not perfect. FOK judgments are based on either partial information or an assessment of the familiarity with a cue. When remembering seems imminent, it is known as a tip-of-the-tongue state. When FOK errors are made, it is often because the information is in a domain that the person has a lot of knowledge about, so they inappropriately judge that the knowledge is known, or in a domain that they have little knowledge of, so they judge that it is not known. Finally, when there is no information in memory, people are very quick to say that they do not know something.

REMEMBER VERSUS KNOW

Up to this point we have been talking about metamemory judgments for information that a person either does or does not remember. Now, let's consider cases where people rate the quality of something they remember by making a **remember-know judgment** (Gardiner, 1988; Tulving, 1985b). If the remembering experience is accompanied by a conscious recollection of the circumstances in which the information was learned, this is a "remember" experience (although Rubin, Schrauf, and Greenberg, 2003, suggest that "remember" responses reflect a belief that an event occurred). In contrast, if people do not consciously remember this but only have a feeling of familiarity, this is a "know" experience. This distinction between "remember" and "know" parallels some of the issues discussed in

Chapter 6, such as the difference autonoetic (remember) and noetic and anoetic (know) knowledge in Tulving's (1985b) Triarchic theory.

The Distinction Between "Remember" and "Know"

A great deal of the work has been done on the remember-know distinction and how it reflects memory processes and experience (summarized by Gardiner and Java, 1993, and Gardiner and Richardson-Klavehn, 2000). It appears that "remember" and "know" responses reflect relatively independent qualities of memory. Research has shown a double dissociation between these types of responses. This means that things that affect one type of response do not affect the other, and vice versa. This is important to demonstrate that remembering and knowing reflect different ways of using memory and are not just after-the-fact labels that people apply to their experiences.

Affecting "Remember" But Not "Know."   "Remember" but not "know" responses are affected by depth of processing, generation effects, the frequency of occurrence, divided attention at learning, the retention interval (if less than a day), reading silently or aloud, intentional versus incidental learning, and serial position. As an example of one of these, if you read something aloud, you are more likely to have a "remember" experience than if you had read it silently. However, the probability of giving a "know" judgment to anything you remembered would be the same, regardless of how you read the text.

Affecting "Know" But Not "Remember."   In contrast, "know" but not "remember" responses are affected by repetition priming, stimulus modality (e.g., visual or auditory), amount of maintenance rehearsal, and suppression of focal attention. For example, if you engage in maintenance rehearsal, such as repeating a word over and over, this would not alter the degree to which you are later able to recollect it. However, if you did happen to remember it, you would be more likely to say that you "know" that you learned it.

Affecting "Remember" and "Know" in Opposite Ways.   There are cases where "remember" and "know" responses are both affected but in opposite ways, such as "remember" responses being more common and "know" responses being rarer. Cases of this type are word versus nonword memory, massed versus distributed practice, gradual versus abrupt presentations, and learning in a way that emphasizes similarities or differences. For example, with massed practice, "remember" responses are less likely and "know" response are more likely. In other cases, "remember" and "know" responses are similarly affected, such as by the retention interval (if more than a day), the amount of unfamiliar information, and long versus short response deadlines (when people are forced to respond within a certain period of time).

Implications for the "Remember" and "Know" Distinction.   This distinction between "remember" and "know" metamemory responses corresponds to specific memory differences. For example, "remember" responses correspond to knowledge-based, conceptually driven processing, and "know" responses correspond to perceptually based, data-driven processing (Rajaram, 1993). The remember-know distinction is also supported by neurological evidence. For example, the parietal lobe may be more involved in cases where someone is more likely to "remember" (Wilding, 2000), and "remember" responses are associated with greater EEG activity than are "know" responses (Burgess & Ali, 2002).

Finally, this distinction resembles the difference between recollection and familiarity in dual process models of memory (see Chapter 10) or the difference between explicit and implicit memories (see Chapter 6). Whatever the actual correspondence is, people do have different metamemory experiences when they retrieve information from memory. Sometimes it is more vivid, whereas other times it is more a feeling of familiarity.

This distinction between "remember" and "know" responses is revealing about differences between expert's and novice's memories. The influence of prior knowledge, such as schemas, on memory retrieval are often observed with recall but less frequently with recognition. Experts almost always recall more accurately than novices, but these two groups do not differ less on recognition tests, and this seems to be related to the fact that experts are more likely to give "remember" reports, whereas novices are more likely to just say that they "know" it. For example, in a study of University of California, Davis students, Long and Prat (2002) had people read stories based on the television series *Star Trek*. Some of the students were experts (people who watch the show a lot), and some were novices (people who only watched the show occasionally). The two groups performed similarly on a recognition test of the stories. However, the experts were more likely to report that they remembered reading the information, whereas the novices were more likely to say that they knew it. The experts' prior knowledge allowed them to spend more time making inferences and elaborating on the memory traces they were creating, which then made it more likely that they would have an experience of remembering it.

Hindsight Bias

One characteristic of human thought is that people tend to think of events as being more deterministic after they occur than before. This is called the **hindsight bias,** and this increased deterministic thought after the fact is called "creeping determinism" (Fischhoff, 1975). For memory, the hindsight bias is observed when people remember their mental state as being different from what it really was. People misremember their mental state as being more similar to their current knowledge state.

As an illustration of this, in a study by Safer, Bonanno, and Field (2001), bereaved spouses rated their grief six months after the death and then four and a half years later. At the second rating, people also rated how much grief they felt at the six-month period. Although most people said they felt more grief at the six-month period, their memory of their experience was positively related to their current level of grief. Thus, they were misremembering their emotional states in hindsight based on their current state (see also Levine et al., 2001).

The hindsight bias pervades many aspects of life. Other examples of this effect are people's memories for their predictions of outcomes of the Rodney King civil rights trial (Gilbertson, Dietrich, Olson, & Guenther, 1994), the Clarence Thomas Supreme Court Justice confirmation vote (Dietrich & Olson, 1993), memory for the probability of a medical diagnoses being correct (Arkes, Wortman, Saville, & Harkess, 1981; Detmer, Fryback, & Gasser, 1978), the results of political elections (Blank, Fischer, & Erdfelder, 2003; Leary, 1982; Powell, 1988), the outcome of sporting events (Leary, 1981), and the inevitability of a layoff at work (Mark & Mellor, 1991). This reinforces the point made in Chapter 1 that our memories are constantly in a state of flux and that what we currently remember is in part due to our experiences and current state.

Let's look at how the hindsight bias applies to romantic relationships. People's memories of their relationships are biased in the direction of their current opinion of it. People who are pleased remember events more positively than people who are unhappy (McFarland & Ross, 1987). Moreover, even when relationship satisfaction has remained constant, people misremember it as improving over time (Sprecher, 1999). This leads to an unusual finding that people in satisfactory relationships, even for marriages over 20 years, are biased to remember the past as worse than it really was, although they remember the relationship positively overall. This negative bias is a trick of memory in that it makes it seem as though the relationship is getting much better than it actually is (Karney & Coombs, 2000). Thus, people have a more positive attitude toward their relationship than they would if memory were accurate; to make people think that things are getting better, people misremember things as being worse than they were.

The Knew-It-All-Along Effect.   A major variant of the hindsight bias is the **knew-it-all-along effect** (Fischhoff, 1977; Wood, 1978). In studies of this phenomenon people are asked to evaluate information in some way at Stage 1—for example, judging whether a series of statements are true or false. Then, at Stage 2, people are presented with feedback about the information encountered at Stage 1. This feedback is likely to be knowledge that the person did not have at Stage 1. Finally, in Stage 3, people indicate their memory for what they knew at Stage 1. This is compared to people who got no feedback at Stage 2. What was found was that metamemory reports of prior knowledge are biased toward the information learned during Stage 2. After learning something in Stage 2, people have a hard time remembering what it was like not knowing it, as if they knew it all along.

Thus, it is difficult for us to remember what it was like when we did not know something. College professors are no exception. If you have ever felt that one of your instructors acted in a condescending manner, it may be that because of the knew-it-all-along effect, she was just having trouble remembering what it was like to learn the course material for the first time.

Remembering Forgetting.   Another illustration of the hindsight bias is people's memories for their own memory. Specifically, how well do people remember whether they had remembered or forgotten something previously? In a study by Joslyn, Loftus, McNoughton, and Powers (2001), people were tested for information at one day and then six weeks after originally learning it. At the six-week session, people were also asked whether they had remembered or forgotten specific pieces of information at the day 1 session. People were more accurate at remembering their previous memory successes but were less accurate at remembering their previous instances of forgetting. About half the time a person had originally forgotten an item, it was later reported that it had been remembered. Thus, there is a bias in metamemory to think that we have better memories than we do.

Avoiding the Hindsight Bias.   While current knowledge can influence assessments of prior knowledge, it is not the case that people have completely lost the original information. If the current knowledge state is discredited in some way, people can disregard it in their metamemory judgments and gain more accurate access to the original knowledge state. In a study by Hasher, Attig, and Alba (1981), students were given a set of statements to rate as either true or false. In a second stage, they were told that some of the items were either true or false. Importantly, at the third stage, some of the students were told that the information they were given in the second stage was incorrect. When the information from the second stage was discredited, people accurately remembered their original opinion in the first stage. In contrast, people who received no discrediting feedback showed the standard knew-it-all-along effect. This reinforces the idea that our memories are using multiple sources of knowledge and that what we remember in a given instance is the degree to which these different memory traces and processes are emphasized.

A similar reduction of the knew-it-all-along effect can occur if people are asked only to retrieve information that was recently learned, rather than what they remember knowing before the new knowledge (Begg et al., 1996). People who are told to monitor source information are better able to assess whether their knowledge is recent. It is important to note that simply encouraging people to try harder has no influence (Fischhoff, 1977). Finally, while encouraging people to consider alternatives is helpful, encouraging them to try to remember even after it becomes difficult to think of other alternatives may actually increase the potency of a hindsight bias by making the known outcome seem a result of the difficulty of thinking of alternatives (Sanna & Schwartz, 2004; Sanna, Schwartz, & Small, 2002).

Remembering Beliefs.   Finally, memory can be affected more globally as well. In a study by Winkielman and Schwartz (2001), some of the people were told that sad events fade quicker from memory, whereas others were told that happy events fade quicker. People who were told that unhappy memories are forgotten quicker were more likely to rate their childhood as less happy, especially following a difficult autobiographical memory task. It is as if people are thinking that if they have forgotten many unhappy memories, then their childhood must have been less happy than they would have otherwise rated it. This is an influence of metamemory on another type of thinking.

Synopsis

Remembering is accompanied by different conscious experiences, such as the difference between "remember" responses, which are associated with conscious recollection, and "know" responses, which are associated with unconscious feelings of familiarity. This distinction is supported by reports of conscious experience, as well as by neurological and behavioral dissociations. Metamemory awareness sometimes leads people astray, as with the hindsight bias. Essentially, people assess the past in a way that is more consistent with the present.

PROSPECTIVE MEMORY

Prospective memory is used to remember to do things in the future (Loftus, 1971). Remembering to give your roommate a message and remembering to take the pizza out of the oven in 20 minutes are both examples of prospective memory. This is in contrast to **retrospective memory,** or memory for information learned in the past, which is the focus of much of this book. Prospective memory is mentioned in this chapter on metamemory because one must, in some sense, monitor one's own memory to know when some action is to be taken in the future.

Prospective memory has been tested in a number of ways. Some of these are naturalistic, such as having people remember to call at certain times (West, 1988). Others are laboratory-based, such as having people press a button when they see a certain word (Einstein & McDaniel, 1990) or after a certain amount of time has elapsed. This gives the researcher more control over what people can use to help them remember. For example, in naturalistic studies, people could write reminders on a calendar or a sticky note. This is less of a test of memory than a test of lifestyle organization.

Components of Prospective Memory

There are many difference between prospective and retrospective memory. For example, as we will see in Chapter 15, while aging has a profound effect on retrospective memory, the changes to prospective memory are more subtle (Burgess & Shallice, 1997; Einstein & McDaniel, 1990). In general, prospective memory performance has little to no relation to retrospective memory performance on tasks such as recall and recognition.

Prospective memory involves two components: (1) remember what to do in the future, and (2) remember to do it. Number 1 is similar to retrospective memory. Thus, prospective memory depends on retrospective memory ability, not vice-versa. However, the second part is unique to prospective memory. It involves deliberately monitoring of the environment for the cue to remember. This is an element that is absent in retrospective memory. Although there is some overlap, retrospective memory ability is relatively unrelated to prospective memory ability. For example, people with frontal lobe damage may be hindered in prospective memory, but their retrospective memory may be unaffected. Also, brain-damaged people with retrospective memory deficits may have some prospective memory problem as well, but it may not be as severe.

The importance of control over memory and thought in prospective memory, as evidence by the link with the frontal lobes, carries over to conscious awareness. Prospective memory requires control of thought that involves conscious experience to a greater degree. As a consequence, people are more aware of their prospective than their retrospective memory errors. People who complain about memory problems are more likely to have prospective memory problems (Mäntylä, 2003).

Types of Prospective Memory

There are two types of prospective memory: event-based and time-based (Einstein & McDaniel, 1990). Event-based prospective memory occurs when people need to remember to do something when some event occurs—for example, remembering to give a person a message when you see her. Event-based prospective memories differ from retrospective memories in that people are less likely to make prospective memory errors following a longer delay or a delay with multiple activities (Hicks, Marsh, & Russell, 2000), whereas longer delays and greater amounts of information make retrospective memory worse. This may occur because longer delays and more activities allow more opportunities for people to remind themselves to engage in the prospective memory task, thereby increasing the likelihood that it will be remembered.

Event prospective memory is complicated. For example, it can be influenced by the relation between the event that is supposed to signal people to remember and the action that is to be done (McDaniel, Guynn, Einstein, & Breneiser, 2004). When the event and the action are semantically associated (e.g., write down the word "needle" when you hear the word "thread"), prospective memory is more automatic and is less influenced by things like divided attention. However, if the event and action are not associated (e.g., write down the word "needle" when you hear the word "parasol"), prospective memory is more deliberative and can be more disrupted if attention is drawn elsewhere. Event-based prospective memory also is more difficult when there are multiple cues as opposed to one, and even more difficult if these cues are unrelated to one another (Marsh et al., 2003). In essence, attention is drawn further away from the prospective memory task when it is divided up among different things in the environment that one needs to watch out for.

Time-based prospective memory occurs when people need to remember to do something at a certain time or after a certain time interval. Remembering to call home on Mother's Day or to feed the dog at 4:00 are examples of time-based prospective memory. Time-based prospective memory is harder than event-based prospective memory (Einstein et al., 1995) because with event-based prospective memory, there is something in the environment that reminds the person what needs to be done. With time-based prospective memory, it is up to the person alone to remember. We can improve our time-based prospective memory by making it more event-based. For example, you could set a timer and just wait for the buzzer to go off (an event) to remind you to feed the dogs.

With time-based prospective memory, people make more errors if the tasks are repetitive—for example, taking medications after certain time intervals. The more a person has performed the task, the more likely an error will be made and the person will forget. Part of what is going on is that source monitoring errors occur, which then cause problems with prospective memory (Einstein, McDaniel, Smith, & Shaw, 1998; Marsh, Hicks, Hancock, & Munsayac, 2002). For example, it may be that a person is confused and thinks she has just taken the medication, when in fact she is remembering another time that she did so. This is a case where doing something more frequently actually makes memory worse, not better.

Synopsis

People need to know what to do in the future and when to do it. This is prospective memory. Although it shares some aspects with retrospective memory, it is also guided by some of its own processes. Prospective memory tasks can be either event-based or time-based. Event-based prospective memory is generally easier and may improve with the passage of time. In comparison, time-based prospective memory is harder and is more susceptible to source monitoring errors.

NEUROLOGICAL BASIS OF METAMEMORY

To date, the neurological investigation of metamemory has been rather meager compared to other memory processes. Some of the studies done involved participants who had people suffered some sort of brain damage. This work has pointed to the frontal lobes as being important for metamemory judgments. For example, people with frontal lobe damage are much more inaccurate on FOK tasks (Janowsky, Shimamura, & Squire, 1989) and prospective memory (Burgess & Shallice, 1997; Cockburn, 1995).

The importance of the frontal lobes in metamemory judgments is consistent with what is known about this part of the brain. If you remember from Chapter 3, one of the important jobs of the frontal lobes is the control of thought and action, as well as regulating and monitoring the stream of thought. In the case of metamemory judgments, people need to monitor and have some control over how they are using their memories. When the frontal lobes are damaged, this ability is compromised, and metamemory suffers.

MNEMONICS

When we are aware of the limitations of our own learning and memory, we can begin to take steps to correct this. One thing we can do is to use metamemory techniques, known as mnemonics. **Mnemonics** are mental or physical devices used to help people remember. There are a number of ready-made mnemonic devices that can be used as structured cue sets to help remember larger sets of information. One example is the peg-word mnemonic, in which people use a known sequence of items, or "pegs," on which to "hang" other pieces of information. For example, people might memorize the sequence "One is a bun, two is a shoe, three is a tree, (and so on)." This structure can then be used as a set of pegs for other information. For example, suppose you needed to go to the grocery store to buy onions, milk, and watermelon. You could use the peg word mnemonic by forming a mental image of sliced onions on a bun, a shoe full of milk, and watermelons hanging from a tree. When you get to the store, your sequence of pegs will help you remember the images you formed, which will help you remember what you need to buy.

Another common mnemonic is the method of loci. In this mnemonic a person first has a set of well-known locations. These can be rooms in one's house, locations along a familiar path, and so forth. A person then imagines things at each location. To use our grocery shopping example, a person might mentally place the onions in the living room, cartons of milk at the foot of the stairs, and watermelons in the dining room. Then, to remember, the person takes a little mental tour of her home.

Other mnemonics take advantage of the information itself. For example, a rhyming mnemonic takes all the information and forms a rhyme from it. For example, the rhyme "Thirty days hath September, April, June, and November" is a rhyming mnemonic for the number of days in the months. Acronyms are another mnemonic, in which the first letters of phrase are used to help people remember. For example, the word HOMES is an acronym for the names of the five great lakes: Huron, Ontario, Michigan, Erie, and Superior. Finally, acrostics can be used as a mnemonic, in which the first letters of the information are used as the basis of forming some new memorable phrase. For example, the phrase "On Old Olympus' Towering Top, A Finn And German Vault And Hop" can be use to help a person remember the names of the twelve cranial nerves in their correct order: Olfactory, Optic, Oculomotor, Trochlear, Trigemenal, Abducens, Facial, Auditory, Glossopharyngal, Vagus, Accessory, and Hypoglossal (premed students take note!). Remembering the phrase provides the cues to the appropriate names as well as preserving the correct sequence of the information.

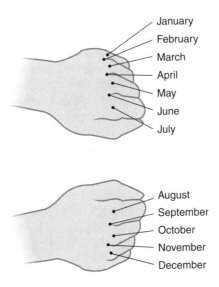

January
February
March
April
May
June
July

August
September
October
November
December

FIGURE 14.4   The Knuckle Mnemonic

There are many mnemonics people can use to aid memory. Sometimes a mnemonic is a simple cue, like tying a string around your finger. Other times, the structure of the mnemonic helps a person remember the information itself, such as the knuckle mnemonic, which is another way of remembering how many days there are in each month (see Figure 14.4) with the knuckles being the months with 31 days and the valleys standing for months with 30 days or fewer. Regardless of the specific mnemonic, in all cases, the ability to cue memory is at work, in much the same way as the other sorts of cues we've talked about (see Chapter 7).

Synopsis

People can use their metamemory knowledge to help them remember better, such as with mnemonics. Most mnemonics rely on some well-known or readily available, consistent structure that can then be used as a guide to help a person remember what they are interested in retrieving.

EXCEPTIONAL MEMORY

Having an awareness of one's own memory can help improve how it is used. Further improvements can occur as the range of knowledge is broadened. The more you know, the easier it is to remember because it is easier to organize and chunk information. Thus, expertise can cause a person to have what would otherwise seem an exceptional memory for certain types of information.

We saw some of this in Chapter 4 when discussing how to improve the capacity of short-term memory and still have 7 + 2 chunks of information. An example of this was the case of S. F., a runner who extended his digit span up to over 80 items (Ericsson, Chase, & Faloon, 1980). Another example of this is that taxi drivers' memories for street names are better than most people's. This superior memory is not due to their intelligence, but to both the large amount of knowledge they have about streets in their city and the highly organized way this information is represented. For taxi drivers, this information is chunked based on routes through the city (how they use this knowledge), rather than spatial proximity, semantic relatedness, or alphabetical order (Kalakoski & Saariluoma, 2001).

Other studies of exceptional memory found cases when the knowledge people are using is implicit. For example, speakers of tonal languages, such as Mandarin Chinese and Vietnamese, are better at memory for musical pitches and are more likely to have perfect pitch than speakers of nontonal languages, such as English (Deutsch, 2002). Because those languages place a greater demand on remembering pitch information for processing language, this knowledge can then be applied, at an unconscious level, to memory for the pitches of tones used in music.

Memorists

The development of exceptional memory with expertise is readily understood and is seen in our interactions with experts. However, there are also cases of people with exceptional memories. These people are called mnemonists or **memorists.** We use the term *memorist* because these people are not relying on mnemonics as described previously (Neisser, 1982).

Perhaps the best-known memorist was S., a man who lived in the former Soviet Union in the early to mid-twentieth century (Luria, 1968). S. worked as a newspaper reporter in Moscow and had the uncanny ability of accurately remembering large sets of details from an event without having to take any notes. S. was found to have a short-term memory span of over 70 items, with the additional amazing ability of recalling them in any order requested. He could also recall lists of items years after hearing them only once.

A major contributor to S.'s ability was the fact that he had synesthesia. This is a rare condition in which sensory qualities from different modalities intrude on one another. For example, different sounds may appear as colors. S. had a particularly strong case of this. This made his memory traces very rich and detailed, allowing them to endure, be highly structured in memory, and be recalled accurately later. While S.'s condition allowed him to remember exceptionally large sets of items, there were some drawbacks. For one, because he was so dependent on sensory and perceptual qualities, he found it difficult to comprehend and think about abstract ideas. Furthermore, over the years, S.'s condition became an overwhelming burden for him. He eventually was institutionalized in a mental hospital and died there.

Not all memorists have an unusual neurological condition. An example of this is the memorist Rajan Mahadevan (Biederman, Cooper, Fox, & Mahadevan, 1992; Thompson, Cowan, & Frieman, 1993; Thompson et al., 1991). Rajan made it into the *Guinness Book of World Records* when, on July 5, 1981, he accurately recited pi out to 31,811 digits (from memory) in 3 hours and 49 minutes. (This record was broken on March 9, 1987 by Hideaki

Tomoyori, who went out to 40,000 digits.) His unusual memory ability was first observed at the age of five when his parents hosted a dinner party of 50 people, and, to occupy himself, he memorized in just a few minutes the license plate numbers of all of the guests' cars and then reported them to the guests.

Rajan has a very large memory span, with a letter span of 13, a visual digit span of 28, and an auditory digit span of 43. One memory strategy that works well for Rajan is keeping track of the position of an item in a sequence. The sequence itself, with its various positions, serves as a mnemonic encoding and retrieval device. When he makes errors, they are often for digits at adjoining locations. This use of positioning as a memory aid makes Rajan treat information differently than other people do. For example, when presented with a list of words, Rajan is much less likely to use semantic relations to help him remember. His performance on more complex types of information, such as stories and spatial information, is well within the normal range, suggesting that his exceptional memory abilities are confined to digits and similar sorts of information.

Rajan earned a master's degree in clinical psychology from the University of Mysore in 1986 and a master's degree in cognitive psychology from Kansas State University in 1991. While he had good memory for digits, he had normal memory skills for other types of information. He would sometimes try to extend his memorization approach to other types of information but not always with the same level of success. He had a tendency to memorize information from a text or lectures. However, as many professors will tell you, while memorization is important, what is as important is the ability to apply and use that knowledge.

Eidetic Imagery

Some people think they have photographic memories, which is the ability to use mental images in a way that closely resembles perceptually viewing an image. This is called **eidetic imagery** (Gray & Gummerman. 1975). Someone with this ability would have extraordinary memory for information that was seen earlier, showing little to no distortion. In general, there is little support for the existence of eidetic imagery. People do not have photographic memories. Instead, people who appear to have this type of memory are instead using other memory skills to a higher degree. Moreover, this is often restricted to a limited domain or type of knowledge. If eidetic imagery does exist, it seems to be present in young children, but it gradually disappears as a person ages (Haber, 1979).

Synopsis

Some people exhibit exceptional memory. In some cases, this comes with expertise. More exceptional cases include memorists who have exceptional memory skills that seem to defy the imagination. Often these memorists have exceptional memory for certain types of information but normal memory for other types of information. Finally, despite claims to the contrary, there is little evidence to suggest that there is something akin to a photographic memory. People who make this claim often have special strategies for handling certain types of information, but they do not have memories that are highly detailed visual representations of what was seen earlier.

SUMMARY

In this chapter we looked at metamemory, the awareness and monitoring of one's own memory processes and content. There are a number of theories of metamemory. Some of these, like the cue-familiarity hypothesis, focus on the familiarity of external memory cues. Others, like the accessibility hypothesis, focus on information that is actually retrieved from memory. A number of metamemory processes were considered, including judgments of learning, feelings of knowing, and tip-of-the-tongue states. We have seen how one's current state of knowledge influences how we remember our own previous memories, as with the knew-it-all-along effect. We have also seen how memory can reach forward in time to allow us to plan and do things in the future (prospective memory). Many of these metamemory processes critically involve the frontal lobes, which control patterns of thinking in general. Finally, we discussed some mnemonic devices, as well as cases of people with exceptionally good memories, even if only for certain types of information. Being more accurately aware of your own memory abilities can serve you well.

STUDY QUESTIONS

1. What are the sources of information available to people when making metamemory judgments? How do these relate to the major theories of metamemory?

2. How accurate are judgments-of-learning and how are they made?

3. How effective are people at allocating their study time, and why?

4. What are feeling-of-knowing judgments? When are they given? How accurate are they?

5. What is the difference between feeling-of-knowing judgments and the tip-of-the-tongue state?

6. How do people assess that they do not know something?

7. What is the difference between "remember" and "know" responses?

8. What are the hindsight bias and the knew-it-all-along effect? How can they be avoided?

9. What are the types of prospective memory? What influences their effectiveness?

10. What neurological structures are strongly associated with metamemory performance?

11. How do mnemonics work? What are some examples of mnemonics?

12. What are some of the ways that people can exhibit exceptional memory performance?

KEY TERMS

accessibility hypothesis, competition hypothesis, cue-familiarity hypothesis, don't know judgments, eidetic imagery, feeling of knowing, hindsight bias, judgments of learning, knew-it-all-along effect, labor-in-vain, memorists, metamemory, mnemonics, prospective memory, remember-know judgment, retrospective memory, tip-of-the-tongue state

CHAPTER FIFTEEN

MEMORY AND DEVELOPMENT

As we have seen repeatedly in this book, memory is not a stable, static thing. Every experience we have alters our memories by making some things easier and some things harder to remember, distorting some information, and clarifying other information. To further complicate this picture, people are in a constant state of development. There is no such thing as a nondeveloping person. These developmental changes have profound implications for how memory functions. This chapter examines some of the major issues in memory and development, but rather than covering the entire life span, we look at three regions of development and the major changes in memory that occur within them. These are infancy and childhood at one end and old age at the other. By looking at infancy and childhood, we can see how our memory and memory skills became more and more sophisticated and efficient. By looking at the effect of aging on memory, we can get some idea of how our own memories are going to change as we enter into old age, which usually means some decline in our memory abilities. However, as you will see, there are some things that remain the same, or even improve.

INFANCY

The development of memory begins as soon as the nervous system is capable of retaining information. However, not all types of memories are available at the same time or for the same reasons. In this section we consider a number of ideas about very early memories and memory systems that are found in infants. We first consider some issues about how to test preverbal humans to give you an idea of the challenges facing memory researchers. After this we look at some of the findings indicating where people are in terms of different types of memories and memory processes when they are infants.

Testing the Very Young

Testing infants' memories is an exceedingly difficult task. The biggest challenge is the fact that infants can neither understand nor produce language, which is the medium for most studies of memory. Thus, researchers who want to study infants' memories are immediately faced with the problem of how to communicate with such nonverbal primates in a way that will provide meaningful information about their states of mind. A number of clever techniques have been created to address this problem. Some of the more prominent of these are discussed here. Each of these methods uses something that is already available to the infant—that is, some activity that the infant already engages in. What the memory researcher then does is look to see how this behavior changes as a function of whether something is remembered or not.

Looking Method. One method of studying infants is to use a gaze duration/direction or some sort of **looking method** (Friedman, 1972). Infants spend a lot of time looking around the world in a constant effort to understand it and gain some control over it. Infants do not look at everything for the same amount of time. Instead, they spend more time looking at things that are of interest to them and less time looking at boring things. This can be used to assess memory. New things in the environment are more likely to be interesting than old things (which seem uninteresting after a while unless there is some positive reinforcement). Thus, it is reasonable to infer that infants spend more time looking at new things compared to old things. In essence, things that are looked at less are things that are recognized, and thus are in memory, whereas things that are looked at more are not recognized and not in memory.

Nonnutritive Sucking. Another way to determine what infants are remembering is use the infants' natural sucking behavior. If you have ever interacted with infants, for any reasonable period of time, you are aware that babies love to suck on things. This sucking is important because it helps the infant to eat, but they also suck on lots of other things that do not provide any nutritional value, such as pacifiers. The memory researcher can take advantage of this **nonnutritive sucking** as a tool to study memory because the rate of sucking changes as a function of whether the infant is seeing or hearing something old (in memory) or new. This can be measured using what are effectively high-tech pacifiers that can record the sucking rate of an infant. When something is old, infants suck at a slower rate. They are bored, so they suck more slowly. However, when something is introduced, infants' sucking rates speeds up because the world around them is new and exciting (Cowan Suomi, & Morae, 1982).

Conjugate Reinforcement. A third task that has been used is a **conjugate reinforcement** paradigm (Rovee-Collier & Fagan, 1981). With this technique, infants are placed on their backs in a crib. One end of a ribbon is tied around one of the baby's ankles, and the other end is attached to a mobile. Whenever the baby kicks, the mobile moves, which is a very cool thing for infants. They soon pick up on the kicking–mobile movement relationship and spend a good deal of time kicking to get the mobile to move more. Memory for this event can be tested by varying any number of things, such as the amount of time that has passed or the context that can serve as a cue.

Elicited Imitation. It was believed for a long time that very young children did not possess the ability to recall information but only to recognize things. Recall was thought to be delayed until a person acquired the ability to use language. However, researchers have found that young children can recall information using techniques such as **elicited imitation** (Bauer, 1996; 2002). In these sorts of studies, an experimenter does some task, such as assembling a simple toy, while the child observes. Then after some delay, such as a month later, it is observed whether the child also engages in the task. This is evidence of recall in preverbal children because it requires the child to deliberately bring to mind a mental representation of the steps needed to do the task. This is recall. Using this technique, it has been found that some form of memory recall is starting in children as young as nine months and becomes stable by two years of age.

Memory and Infancy

Human memory is composed of several different components that develop at different rates. More primitive memories, such as nondeclarative memories, are present at birth. Almost immediately, people start developing new skills to help them get along in the world. Thus, implicit memory is well on its way at a very early age. There is even evidence that infants prefer familiar sounds that they heard while in the womb, such as the sound of their mother's voice.

The development of different types of memory is associated with the different rates of development of the parts of the brain responsible for them. For example, the thalamus and some medial temporal structures, which are more important for more primitive types of memory, appear to be nearly developed at birth, whereas the frontal lobes, which are important for controlling the flow of processing through memory are not completely functional until the age of one year or older (Chugani, Phelps, & Mazziotta, 1986). Thus, the patterns of memory abilities observed in infants are, to some degree, influenced by the readiness of their nervous systems to handle different types of information.

Semantic Memory. Memory in infancy is advanced enough to abstract away from the original information. This is a process we encountered in our discussion of schemas (see Chapter 9). Memories can be used to identify things that superficially resemble the original information. Even infants appear to create and use categories. As early as 3 or 4 months, they can make some basic level category distinctions for perceptually isolated categories, such as dogs and cats (Eimas & Quinn, 1994; Quinn, Eimas, & Rosenkrantz, 1993). However, it isn't until about 14 months old that infants can make distinctions based on superordinate category relations, such as knowing that properties like "drinking" and "sleeping" belong to the superordinate category of "animals" and that "needs keys" and "giving a ride" belong to the superordinate category of "vehicles" (Mandler, Fivush, & Reznick, 1987; Mandler & McDonough, 1996) and knowledge of finer basic level categories remains elusive until over 2 years old (Mandler, Bauer, & McDonough, 1991).

For another example of semantic memory processing, consider the identification of line drawings or other pictorial representations of real objects. To do this, one must match a more abstract picture with a memory of a real object, which is not as simple as it sounds. In an extreme test of this abstraction ability, Hochberg and Brooks (1961) raised a child from birth to age 19 months in an environment in which objects in pictures were never named and where pictures were relatively unavailable, even to the point of not letting the child see picture books and removing labels from baby food jars. Despite this lack of experience with visual abstraction, at 19 months, when the child was finally tested, he was able to identify pictures of objects, even line drawings, with no noticeable problems.

Episodic Memory. Complex forms of episodic memory appear to be present in infants even at very young ages. For instance, using the conjugate reinforcement paradigm, in which an infant's kicking causes a mobile to move, it has been found that even infants as young as three months old remember to kick when placed in that situation again five days later (Butler & Rovee-Collier, 1989). This is episodic memory, because the rate of kicking is context dependent. That is, when the crib liner is the same during the second session as it was during the first, the rate of kicking is higher. However, if a different liner is used, the rate of kicking is lower. The crib liner is an episodic memory retrieval cue, and this is a case of encoding specificity (see Chapter 7).

This is further supported by suggestions that infant memory can be distorted by misinformation, similar to what is observed in eyewitness testimony (Rovee-Collier, Borza, Adler, & Boller, 1993). Using a conjugate reinforcement paradigm, infants are first shown a mobile that moves when they kick. Then the infants spend some time with a different mobile. In this case, after some delay, when the babies see the original mobile, they are less likely to kick to try to make it move than if they had never seen the second mobile.

The ability to explicitly remember information over long periods increases in accuracy and duration as the infant matures. For example, using the elicited imitation paradigm, Carver and Bauer (2001) have found that nine-month-old infants are able to remember and reproduce a previously viewed action up to four weeks later. This remembering is even evidenced in ERP recordings (Bauer et al., 2003). In contrast, ten-month-old infants are able to reproduce the action up to six months later. Complex forms of memory, such as declarative memory, are developing at a rapid rate throughout infancy. As our methods of testing very young children become more sophisticated and reliable, we are able to discover more and more things that infant memories can do.

Synopsis

To test infant memories, researchers must develop skillful methods to determine what infants can remember. This includes things such as the looking method, nonnutritive sucking, conjugate reinforcement, and elicited imitation. Using these methods, it has been found that infants have well-developed nondeclarative memories. However, more advanced memories, such as semantic and episodic memory, are still in a process of developing and emerging and are not as efficient.

CHILDHOOD

As a person leaves infancy and moves into childhood, memory continues to develop and progress. The nervous system continues to show developmental changes well until a person reaches early adulthood. These changes, of course, influence memory processing. For example, the speed with which children can execute memory processing increases exponentially until the mid to late teens (Kail, 1991). The nervous system becomes much more efficient.

Semantic Memory

As children acquire more knowledge about the world, semantic memory becomes more complex. Even at young ages, a child can have a complex semantic network of concepts in a particular domain. For example, the portion of a 4½-year-old boy's semantic knowledge of dinosaurs is shown in Figure 15.1 (from Chi & Koeske, 1983). This boy's memory representation is fairly complex and well organized. For example, many of the armored dinosaurs are in a highly structured cluster and so are the large plant-eaters. When the boy was asked to recall the names of dinosaurs, the ones he could recall most often were those with the greatest number of links in his semantic network.

Children also begin to develop schemas and scripts for various common aspects of the world around the age of three (Nelson & Gruendel, 1981). Of course, these become more numerous and developed as a child ages. At first they are very simple descriptions of only the most basic parts of the action. However, as children mature, scripts become more complex, including many details and more minor steps in whatever the process might be. The prevalent use of scripts and schemas by young children can be clearly seen in their desire to cling to set routines where they can predict and clearly understand what is happening.

When it comes to categorization, even relatively young children show some proficiency in organizing their categories in memory. However, there are some changes that occur in categorization as a result of the process of development. For example, preschool children are likely to assume that members of the same basic level category have a similar internal structure (same kind of stuff inside) but do not do this for superordinate level categories. However, by second grade, children extend this to superordinate categories as well (Gelman & O'Reilly, 1988). Another thing that changes during childhood is how natural kind and artifact categories are developed (Gelman, 1988). Natural kind categories are categories for objects that exist in nature, such as animals and plants. These are often defined by adults based on characteristics such as mating practice and genetic structure. Members of a natural kind category are often superficially similar. Artifact categories are categories of items created by people for various uses. These sorts of categories are defined by how the artifact is used, not its appearance. For example, a screwdriver may be more similar in appearance to a butter knife, but the knife is more likely to be classified with a fork. This distinction between these different types of categories is made by young, preschool children but not by older children.

Episodic Memory

The ability to organize and structure information continues to change as a person matures (Paris & Lindaur, 1976). An example of this is inferring that a spoon is used when reading the sentence "The truck driver stirred the coffee in his cup." If this inference is made, then the word "spoon" is an effective memory cue for this sentence. Older children are more likely to infer implicit associations that can be used to help organize the information and improve memory. This also assists in the emergence and development of autobiographical memory.

This increase in the degree of structure and organization is also reflected in retrieval (Bjorklund & Zeman, 1982). For example, for memory of furniture at home, younger children (around age 10) tend to organize their memories based on furniture category (e.g., chairs, tables, etc.), whereas by age 16 children have switched over to organizing around spatial categories (e.g., living room, dining room, etc.) (Plumert, 1994). For retrieval,

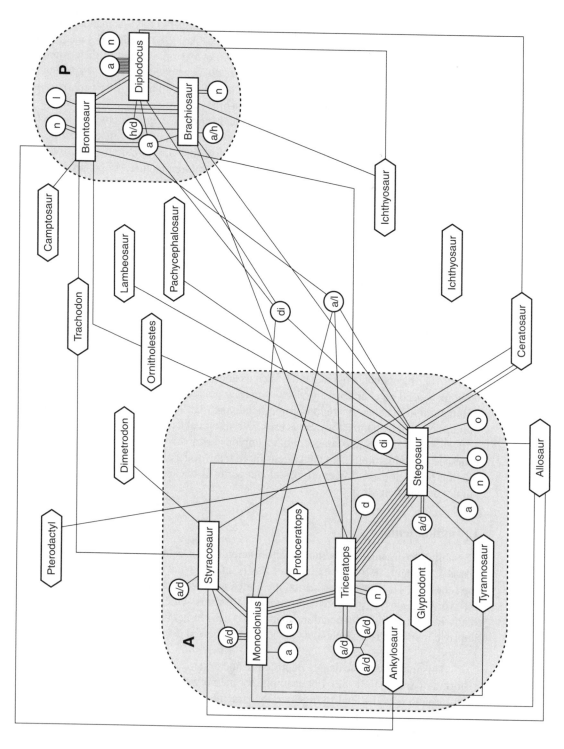

FIGURE 15.1 A Boy's Semantic Memory Network for Dinosaur Concepts

Source: Chi & Koeske, 1983

children show similar interference effects, such as a fan effect, as adults, and they can also organize information to eliminate that interference but only if the information is familiar (Gómez-Ariza & Bajo, 2003).

Some of the biggest changes in childhood memory involve a better use of strategies, as well as an increased awareness of the need for strategies to avoid forgetting. An awareness of the need to rehearse information to maintain it (i.e., short-term memory) emerges in two-year-old children (DeLoache, Cassidy, & Brown, 1985). For example, a toy might be hidden under some object, and children will continue to glance or point in that direction, suggesting that there is an active attempt to maintain this information in memory. However, this does not occur when the toy is placed on top of an object in full view and the need to remember the location is eliminated.

Working Memory

Although the sensory registers are well developed by childhood (Engle, Fidler, & Reynolds, 1981), the ability to use working memory consistently improves. For instance, there is an increase in the rate and effectiveness of rehearsing information to keep it in memory (Flavell, Beach, & Chinsky, 1966) during the childhood years. Partly, there is a consistent increase in the amount of information that is being rehearsed (Case, 1972; Ornstein, Naus, & Liberty, 1975)—that is, the child's memory span is getting larger. With the larger memory span, overall performance increases. An increased memory span makes it more likely that information is successfully transferred to and from long-term memory.

This developmental difference also reflects changes in how children use information in working memory. One factor is the speed with which children can articulate information. As a reminder, the word length effect in working memory is the finding that people remember fewer words as the articulation length of the words increases. This is because longer words are more likely to decay in the phonological loop (see Chapter 5). As children age, they can pronounce words more quickly. This increased speech rate along with the increase in age results in older children having larger memory spans (Hulme, Thomson, Muir, & Lawrence, 1984). This relation between rehearsal speed and span is shown in Figure 15.2.

Another factor that influences working memory is the child's interests. A study by Lindberg (1980) showed that when children were given words pertaining to subjects that interested them, such as the names of cartoon or television characters, memory spans improved to that of a college student, whereas college students' memories were better for categorized lists of words, as shown in Figure 15.3. In other words, the ability to retain a set of words in a memory span test is at least partially a function of the person's knowledge base. If a set of items is drawn from a child's knowledge base, her memory performance is much better.

Other factors also contribute to increasing working memory capacity in children. One of these is a general increase in the speed of cognitive processing (Kail, 1991). This speed change not only has an influence on verbal working memory, but on visual-spatial aspects as well (Kail, 1997). As children increase the speed with which they process information, they can more effectively maintain the information needed for whatever memory process is operating. At slower speeds, more information is forgotten and lost, and children's thinking is not as effective.

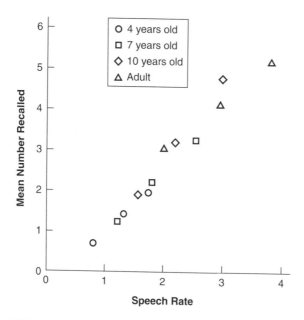

FIGURE 15.2   Relation between Person's Speech Rate and Working Memory Span Scores Broken Down by Different Age Groups

Source: Hulme, Thomson, Muir, & Lawrence, 1984

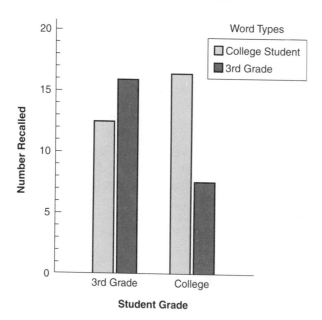

FIGURE 15.3   Influence of Domain of Interest Words on Memory Span in Children and Adults

Source: Lindberg, 1980

Finally, another factor that contributes to increases in working memory efficiency are changes in the ability to inhibit irrelevant information that seems to develop during childhood. As an illustration, Harnishfeger and Pope (1996) tested six-, eight-, and ten-year-olds, along with college students, on a directed forgetting task (see Chapter 7). As a reminder, in directed forgetting, a person needs to inhibit information that is to-be-forgotten. They found that the ability to inhibit information increased with age, with ten-year-olds doing as well as the adults.

Metamemory

Another important change is in metamemory awareness, which gets better as children grow older. For example, in a short-term memory serial position curve (see Chapter 4), memory is better for the first and last items of a list. These are the primacy and recency effects, respectively. However, to get the most out of the recency effect, people should recall the last items first before they are displaced out of short-term memory. People develop an implicit understanding of this, and adults often recall the last few items first, before moving on to items stored in long-term memory. However, young children are not this sophisticated and are less likely to start with the final items, thereby reducing overall retrieval. For example, a study by Samuel (1978) found that this strategy was used infrequently by first graders, but it became progressively and steadily more used as a person moved into the college years.

An important situation where episodic memory is important is in eyewitness testimony. As we saw (see Chapter 13), eyewitness memory is easily distorted for details, and it is worse when the witness has been exposed to misleading information after the event. How reliable are children's eyewitness accounts? The results here are a bit mixed and complicated. However, some simple points can be made (Ceci & Bruck, 1993). First, children are capable of providing accurate eyewitness testimony. In the absence of external influences, a child's memory of what happened is similar to an adult's, provided that a child has a good working understanding of the event. The other factor, unfortunately, is that children are more prone to suggestibility. In other words, they are less able to resist and discount inappropriate information that may come from other sources after the event has been witnessed.

In summary, there is a lot of change in memory that occurs during childhood. These changes reflect an increased sophistication in how memory is used by a person. They reflect the complexity of semantic memories, the structure and organization of episodic memories, the span of working memory, and the increased awareness and control of memory abilities in general.

Synopsis

Memory continues to develop in childhood. Semantic memory becomes more extensive and detailed. Episodic memory becomes more developed, with children organizing information more and developing better strategies for remembering. This increased effectiveness is also seen at the level of working memory, with greater working memory capacity, faster processing speed, and more efficient inhibition of irrelevant information. Finally, terrific strides are made in the awareness of the limits and abilities of their own memories and how well they can control them.

OLD AGE

Memory is one of the areas of our lives in which we expect to see some changes as we progress into old age. The basic stereotype is that old people are more forgetful than young people. There is some degree of truth to this, and we explore some of the reasons for this age-related change in memory. However, the natural aging process does not affect all types of memory in a negative way. There are some things that stay the same or even improve.

Neurological Changes

Age-related change in memory is a universal phenomenon seen across a wide variety of cultures (Park, Nisbett, & Heeden, 1999). This universality is a result of fundamental changes in the nervous system that occurs.

Neural Conduction Speed.   One of the most basic changes as a result of the natural aging process is a change in the rate or speed of neural firing. In general, neurons fire more slowly in older adults than in younger adults. As a consequence, older adults take longer to engage in any cognitive process than younger adults. The more complex the task, the more noticeable the slowdown.

Declines in Frontal and Temporal Lobes

Different parts of the brain change at different rates during aging. The frontal lobes of the brain appear to undergo the greatest change (Albert & Kaplan, 1980) and are used less effectively, or at least differently, in older adults (Rypma, Prabhakaran, Desmond, & Gabriei, 2001; Stebbins et al., 2002). The part of the frontal lobes that is most affected is the dorsolateral prefrontal lobe (the part on the top and sides in the front) rather than the ventromedial prefrontal lobe (the part on the bottom and middle) (MacPherson, Phillips, & Sala, 2002). The dorsolateral prefrontal lobe is more responsible for working memory, in particular the central executive, which controls the flow of thought. In contrast, the ventromedial part of the prefrontal lobes is more associated with emotional and social tasks, such as regulating one's feelings. Finally, this decline in the frontal lobes also involves a decline in the dopamine system of the brain (Braver et al., 2001).

There is some evidence that older adults perform similarly to people who have had damage to their frontal lobes (Dempster, 1992; Stuss et al., 1996). For example, the ability to recall unorganized lists of words, which requires some sort of controlled, strategic retrieval, is lower in older adults. Obviously, reduced functioning in the frontal lobes is going to reduce a person's ability to control the flow of information in memory, leading to a wide variety of problems.

In addition to declines in the frontal lobe, there are also more problems with processing in the temporal lobes. As described earlier (see Chapter 2), the temporal lobes are important for many different types of memory processes, including encoding, storage, and retrieval. As such, older adults show global problems with learning and retrieving information.

One way older adults' might compensate for a decline in functioning is to decrease lateralization. Lateralization is when one hemisphere of the brain (left or right) becomes more dominant or does more of the processing than the other. Lateralization may occur initially because a group of nearby cells can make the necessary computations faster than groups that are spread out and may need to pass information along the corpus callosum. However, in older adults, there is less evidence for lateralization (Cabeza, 2002). This may occur because older adults need to recruit a larger array of cells, across a wider range of the cortex, to do the same job that a more localized portion of cortex would be able to handle in younger adults.

Theories of Age-Related Memory Declines

The changes in memory that occur as we age are complex. Not surprisingly, there are a number of general theories of these changes. Some of the major theories are presented here. After this, we consider some more specific changes in memory that accompany aging.

Speed Theory. One of the more basic changes is a slowdown in the speed with which people execute various memory processes. Explanations that center on this change are known as **speed theories.** A change in processing speed can affect memory in many ways. One is that, during the course of processing, it is more likely that forgetting will occur of some of the information in the stream of thought. As a result, performance declines (Myerson et al., 1990; Salthouse, 1993). If older adults are forgetting more bits and pieces as they proceed through a line of thought, they are going to have more problems.

One way to capture the effects of general slowing is to create a Brinley plot (e.g., Myerson, Wagstaff, & Hale, 1994; but see Cerella, 1994; Perfect, 1994). In these plots, older adult processing time is plotted as a function of corresponding younger adult processing time. An example of a Brinley plot is shown in Figure 15.4. If there were a perfect correspondence between the two response speeds, then one would see data lining up on the

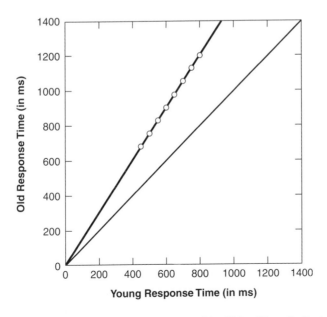

FIGURE 15.4   Example of a Brinley Plot Using Hypothetical (and Perfect) Data

45-degree vector. However, the older adult memory processing is slower than younger adults', as evidenced in the plot by the data points falling above the 45-degree line. What is important is that these data exhibit a linear function—that is, there is a consistent slope to the line, which reflects the rate of slowdown in older adults' processing speed. It is not unusual to have Brinley plots with a slope of 1.5, meaning that older adults are processing at 1.5 times the speed of younger adults.

Working Memory Declines.   Another theory is that older adults have reduced working memory capacity (Craik & Byrd, 1982). It is believed that older adults have reduced attentional resources that result in a functionally reduced working memory capacity. Because older adults are less efficient at keeping multiple pieces of information active in working memory, they are less able to effectively coordinate information to the degree necessary to allow for efficient thinking.

One example of a decline in working memory capacity can be seen in the ability to comprehend a brief story. In a study by Light and Capps (1986), younger and older adults heard brief three- to five-sentence stories in which the final sentence contained a pronoun that referred back to a story character. What was manipulated was the distance between the characters and the pronoun by varying the number of sentences between them. The greater the distance between the two, the more performance declined, especially in older adults. An example of one of these stories, along with some data, is shown in Table 15.1. Having more sentences between a pronoun and the name increases the amount of information that must be held in working memory. Because older adults have a smaller working memory capacity, they have a greater difficulty holding on to the name information and are more likely to forget it. As a result, when the pronoun is heard, they have a harder time determining to whom it referred.

Inhibitory Declines.   As mentioned earlier, one of the major changes in the brain that accompanies aging is a reduction in the frontal lobes. This has helped lead to the suggestion that there is a decline in the ability to inhibit irrelevant information with aging (Dempster, 1992; Hasher & Zacks, 1988). This is called **inhibition theory.** When older adults are

TABLE 15.1   Effects of Age-Positive and Age-Negative Words on Memory. Difference in pre- and postexposure conditions.

	YOUNG	OLD
Number of intervening sentences		
Zero	65.1	64.1
One	61.8	58.3
Number of intervening sentences		
Zero	64.9	63.4
Two	61.3	54.7

Source: Light & Capps, 1986

trying to remember information, they experience more difficulty because related but irrelevant information is activated, thereby clogging the stream of thought. In a sense, one of the reasons older adults have trouble with their memory is not that they are remembering too little but they are remembering too much.

As mentioned in Chapter 7, one way to observe the influence of inhibition in memory is with directed forgetting. We have seen that older adults have difficulty inhibiting information, but they show smaller effects in inhibition in directed forgetting (Andrés, Van der Linden, & Parmentier, 2004; Zacks, Radvansky, & Hasher, 1996). For example, if later asked to recall information that they were previously told to forget, older adults recall more than younger adults because this information was not sufficiently inhibited. This decreased ability to inhibit to-be-forgotten information can even lead a person to misattribute characteristics to people, as when a person is told that information about a suspected criminal was actually from a report on a different crime (Chen & Blanchard-Fields, 2000). In these cases, because they are using the to-be-forgotten information, older adults are likely to give different sentences to criminals. Thus, older adults' decreased ability to suppress irrelevant information can lead them to later use this information from memory to make judgments when that information is inappropriate.

Self-Initiated Processing.   The final, major theoretical view of changes in memory as a result of aging is that there are changes in the ability to self-initiate various types of memory processes when needed (Craik, 1986). Like the inhibition theory, this is related to the concept that there is a decline in frontal lobe functioning that accompanies aging. As a result of this decline, older adults are less able to monitor their own memory processes. As a consequence of this, they are more likely to not start some mental process when it is necessary.

This deficit is most likely to reveal itself in memory processes that require some form of self-initiated rather than environment-driven retrieval processes. For example, we have seen that memory is more compromised in aging when assessed with a recall test than with a recognition test. In general, the more a memory process relies on self-initiated processing to be successful, the more likely it is to be disrupted in natural aging. For example, because of this decline in self-initiated processing, an older adult would be less effective in meta-memory estimates.

Some Things Change

This part of the chapter focuses on changes that actually occur as a result of the natural aging process. The next section is concerned with a consideration of aspects of memory that do not change, even in the context of so many other changes.

Episodic Memory.   One of the most noticeable changes in memory that occurs as a result of getting older is a decline in the ability to accurately recall and recognize information. On the majority of memory tests for previously seen or heard information, older adults invariably score lower than younger adults. However, while there is a decline in the quantity of information that is remembered, there does not seem to be an overall change in the quality with which it is remembered. So although the overall rates of recall decline with aging, the degree to which people have organized the information that is recalled stays about the same (Kahana & Wingfield, 2000). Thus, declines in memory with aging do not appear to be a consequence of a decline in older adults' ability to structure and organize information. In fact, older adults may be more dependent on the organization of information in memory, leading them to be more susceptible to things such as the part-set cuing effect (Marsh, Dolan, Balota, & Roediger, 2004).

The degree of memory change that occurs as a result of the natural aging process can be impacted by a number of characteristics. One of these characteristics is the emotional tone of the information. One of the theories about aging is that there is a general tendency to emphasize positive information over negative information as one grows older. This reflects a greater interest in close interpersonal relationships and a desire to control emotions that occur as one ages. Perhaps as a consequence of this use of emotional information, it has been found that older adults show less of an influence of negative information in memory than do older adults (Charles, Mather, & Carstensen, 2003; Kennedy, Mather, & Carstensen, 2004). For example, when presented with pictures to remember, younger adults' memory for the pictures tends to be best for pictures of negative images. However, for older adults, the memories are not as dominated by such emotionally negative information. This does not mean that older adults are not sensitive to emotional information, but actually, the opposite. For example, it has been found that older adults show mood congruency effects in memory more often than do younger adults (Knight, Maines, & Robinson, 2002).

One of the consequences of a greater rate of forgetting is that it is much harder to observe hypermnesia in older adults as compared to younger adults. However, the rate of reminiscence is the same for both younger and older adults. The reason that there is so little hypermnesia is due to the much faster rate of forgetting for the older adults (Widner, Otani, & Smith, 2000). In other words, because the forgetting rate is so rapid, any recovered memories that may arise, because of reminiscence, do not outweigh the losses.

Finally, consistent with the idea that there are declines in the ability to inhibit or suppress irrelevant information, older adults are more susceptible to retroactive interference in working memory (Hedden & Park, 2001) and are less effective at directed forgetting (Zacks, Radvansky, & Hasher, 1996). That is, they have difficulty removing information that is currently being thought about. They also have trouble regulating what information enters into working memory from long-term memory. For example, older adults are more susceptible to associative interference and show larger fan effects than do younger adults (Gerard, Zacks, Hasher, & Radvansky, 1991).

Episodic versus Schematic Information.   A general characteristic of older adults' memory process that occurs as a result of declines in episodic memory is a greater reliance on schematic information that is already stored in semantic memory and less of an emphasis on details about specific instances, which is more likely to be lost due to a declining episodic memory. In general, it seems that older adults have well-preserved schemas and are able to use this schematic information to help them retrieve information as well as younger adults (Hess & Flannagan, 1992).

This differential use of semantic and episodic memory can also be seen in social judgments. Older adults are more likely to make predictions of other people's future behavior based on a general, schematic understanding, rather than in reference to specific episodic information about the person (Hess & Follett, 1994; Hess, Follett, & McGee, 1998). However, not all social judgments are more biased toward schematic information for older adults. For example, if people are asked to rate how likable a person is, younger and older adults use schematic and specific information similarly (Hess & Bolstad, 1998).

The type of information that is more readily forgotten, and so is most likely to suffer as a consequence of aging, is episodic memory for details. Keeping in mind fuzzy trace theories of memory, it is believed that memory can be composed of more detailed, specific memories and other more general, gist-related memories. In general, as the natural aging process proceeds, there are marked declines in episodic memory, whereas semantic memory is more stable and might even improve (Nyberg et al., 2003). As a result, older adults' memory performance is more likely to be influenced by general similarity of what had been encountered before, rather than a reflection of memory for details (Koutstaal & Schacter, 1997), which is not observed when older adults do not have prior knowledge (Koutstaal et al., 2003). This differential loss also has consequences for autobiographical memory. Specifically, older adults are more likely to report semantic details from their lives, such as their occupations, addresses, and so forth, rather than episodic details, such as how something looked (Levine et al., 2002).

Source Monitoring.   Older adults are less effective at source monitoring than are younger adults. For example, older adults are more likely to make reality monitoring errors, such as confusing perceived and imagined events, perhaps because of an increased use of memories for internal thoughts and feelings relative to memories for perceptual and contextual information (Hashtroudi, Johnson, & Chrosniak, 1990). This reality monitoring problems has been used to explain, in part, why older adults can be more susceptible to false memories because they mistake words they just thought of for words they have heard before (Dehon & Brédart, 2004).

Older adults are more likely to have source monitoring errors that involve confusing perceptually similar sources (e.g., two women) or conceptually similar operations (e.g., pleasantness ratings), or even confusing the words of another for something they themselves said. One example of a source monitoring error is older adults being more likely to pick a person from a police lineup even if the person was not the perpetrator seen in an earlier video but had only been seen before in a series of mugshots (Memon, Hope, Bartlett, & Bull, 2002). They are basing their decisions on inappropriate source information.

Unlike younger adults, older adults may be less able to integrate different types of source information (e.g., perceptual and conceptual) to help them in their source monitoring (Johnson, De Leonardis, Hashtroudi, & Ferguson, 1995). They are more likely to exhibit source monitoring errors if their attention is focused elsewhere, such as when emotions play a larger role in a situation (Hashtroudi, Johnson, Vnek, & Ferguson, 1994). This difference in attentional resources can be seen in ERPs recorded during source monitoring, with younger adults' ERP waves showing greater discrimination than those of older adults (Dywan, Segalowitz, & Webster, 1998). These sorts of source monitoring errors are more prominent in older adults who are also having greater difficulty with frontal lobe processing (Glisky, Rubin, & Davidson, 2001).

This decline in source monitoring can have broader effects as well. For example, older adults appear to be more willing to produce false memories (Gallo & Roediger, 2003).

In some cases, these false memories are schema or script-consistent information that was not actually encountered (LaVoie & Malmstrom, 1998). In other cases, when asked to report whether features belong to a option that was chosen or to some other option, older adults are more likely to make source errors of identifying positive attributes as corresponding to the choices they made (Mather & Johnson, 2000), including being more likely to rely on stereotypes when making source judgments (Mather, Johnson, & De Leonardis, 1999). However, it should also be noted that age-related changes in source monitoring do not always occur. For example, when two sources are defined based on some sort of value characteristics, such as being told that John always tells the truth and Mary always tells lies, older and younger adults do equally well at correctly identifying source information (Rahhal, May, & Hasher, 2002).

The changes in source monitoring that can occur as a result of the natural aging process parallel a general change in context dependency in memory retrieval (Duchek, 1984), such as encoding specificity (see Chapter 7). In general, older adults are less likely to use environmental cues to help them recall something. This is related to the more general theory that older adults are less able to self-initiate various memory processes.

Metamemory.   Another major area in which age-related changes in memory occur is prospective memory (see Chapter 14). As a reminder, prospective memory is when a person remembers to do something in the future, such as remembering to give your roommate a message the next time you see her. Like other types of memory, prospective memory declines in old age. However, there is some variation, depending on the type of prospective memory. Older adults tend to be noticeably worse than younger adults for both time-based and event-based prospective memory tasks, but this age difference may be larger for time-based prospective memory (Einstein et al., 1995; Henry, MacLeod, Philips, & Crawford, 2004). This is consistent with the finding that older adults have greater difficulty with self-initiated processing. Prospective memory, such as remembering to take the cookies out of the oven in ten minutes, requires self-initiated processing. This age difference in prospective memory does not appear to be due to the ability to form a plan of what to do in the future or in carrying that plan out once it is remembered, but in the ability to actually do the task when it needs to be done (Kliegel, McDaniel, & Einstein, 2000).

What is also interesting is that although older adults do more poorly on prospective memory tasks when tested in the laboratory, they actually tend to do better in naturalistic settings (such as remembering appointments) (Henry et al., 2004). This may reflect more time spent managing time and developing strategies to help remember to do things in the future. These strategies may be developed to such a high degree that they more than compensate for any natural declines in prospective memory that may be developing. For example, it has been found that time-based prospective memory in older adults is much better when they lay out a plan of implementation (e.g., taking medication) ahead of time rather than just rehearsing the information (Liu & Park, 2004), suggesting that the rehearsal process connected to the memory task can improve performance. This can help older adults overcome such a memory deficit.

The difficulty older adults have with prospective memory reflects more general problems with metamemory that occur as a person ages. For example, older adults' ratings of feeling of knowing are much poorer than those of younger adults (Souchey, Isingrini, &

Espagnet, 2000). Also, older adults may experience greater problems when in the tip-of-the-tongue state (White & Abrams, 2002). Again, these declines are attributed to problems associated with a decline in the frontal lobes.

Another metamemory process that is related to aging is JOLs. The picture is somewhat complicated in that older adults differ from younger adults in some ways but not others. Older adults differ from younger adults in the absolute accuracy of their judgments of learning, with the older adults being less accurate than the younger adults (Bieman-Copland & Charness, 1994). That is, older adults are less accurate in their assessments of whether they have learned something new or not. However, older adults are similar to younger adults in terms of relative accuracy (Dunlosky & Hertzog, 2000). That is, they adjust their judgments of learning based on the nature of the information being learned, such as whether the information is difficult or easy to learn. This may occur because older adults are providing JOLs based for the entire set of information as a whole, rather than on individual items (Matvey et al., 2002), proving again that older adults are more likely to be using general levels of representation.

Up to this point, we have seen a number of ways that older adults have greater trouble with memory than younger adults do. However, it is not true that memory inevitably gets worse. In the next section we highlight some aspects of memory that stay the same or might even improve. Before moving on to that, it is important to understand that attitude is very important. If a person *thinks* memory get worse with age, then the person's performance will be worse. This may occur at a subconscious level. In a study by Levy (1996), older adults were given a series of memory tests. They were then subliminally exposed to a number of age-positive words, such as "wisdom," "sage," or "guidance," or age-negative words, such as "senile," "dementia," and "decrepit." After this, a second series of memory tests were given. Even though the older adults were not aware that they had already seen the words, their performance was greatly affected by what they had seen. The data from this study are shown in Table 15.2. Specifically, older adults generally did worse following age-negative words but better following age-positive words. There was no influence when younger adults were tested. Thus, the implicit age-related stereotypes that can be activated in these sorts of studies can have a noticeable impact on how well memory actually works.

When goals are set for people to improve memory performance, both younger and older adults respond well to those goals. However, the improvement is sometimes greater for the older adults (West, Thorn, & Bagwell, 2003). This suggests that older adults may be more prone to discounting their memory abilities and perhaps may be making their situation worse by having self-handicapping thoughts.

Some Things Stay the Same

While aging is generally associated with the idea of a decline in memory. There are some aspects of memory that do not suffer any noticeable decline. Instead, these memory abilities remain constant and may even improve with increasing age. These memory abilities would roughly map onto general ideas of wisdom and sageness.

Semantic Memory. Although there are clear declines in weaker forms of memory, such as working memory or episodic memory, there is relatively little decline in semantic

TABLE 15.2   Effects of Age-Positive and Age-Negative Words on Memory. Difference in pre- and postexposure conditions.

	OLDER ADULTS		YOUNGER ADULTS	
	Negative	*Positive*	*Negative*	*Positive*
Immediate recall	−1.77	0.98	−0.36	−0.10
Learned recall	−0.46	0.49	0.43	0.07
Delayed recall	−1.11	0.20	0.33	−0.07
Photo recall	0.14	1.50	0.77	0.24
Auditory recall	−0.64	−0.02	−0.47	−0.60

Source: Levy, 1996

memory. As people age, they are exposed to a broader range of information, and this knowledge continues to accumulate in semantic memory. As a result, older adults often outperform younger adults on general measures of semantic knowledge. For example, if younger and older adults are given vocabulary tests, the older adults invariably outperform the younger adults. This does not seem to be related to educational factors, such as the older adults getting a "better" education, because this can be observed even in cases where some of the older adults have less education than the younger adults.

Another aspect of semantic memory that remains stable is priming effects. This includes both automatic semantic priming (Howard, McAndrews, & Lasaga, 1981), as well as more consciously controlled priming (Burke, White, & Diaz, 1987), such as with the Neely priming task (described in Chapter 9). This means that the ability of older adults to draw on their general world knowledge is just as intact as a younger person's. Moreover, the fact that the older person has a broader range of real-world knowledge can put him at an advantage in terms of this type of memory information.

Episodic Memory.   There is no doubt that episodic memory processing declines as a person ages, but this decline appears to have its limits. Some aspects of episodic memory remain at a high level of ability and may even improve. In general, the distinction between what is and is not retained in older adults is a distinction between quantitative and qualitative aspects of episodic memory (Small, Dixon, Hultsch, & Hertzog, 1999). Specifically, there is a near uniform quantitative decline in episodic memory. This means that older adults generally remember less overall. However, many qualitative aspects of episodic memory are preserved. This means that the way that information is remembered stays the same. For example, older adults show as much organization of information during episodic remembering as do younger adults and may even shown an increase, with their episodic recalls being more structured than those of the younger adults. This may reflect an increased reliance on the structural organization of semantic memory, which remains intact with old age.

Higher-Level Memory.   One area of memory that appears to be less affected by age-related changes in memory is processing at higher levels of thought, such as the mental model level. For example, younger and older adults appear to use mental models to the same degree when assessing whether information has been encountered before (Radvansky, Gerard, Zacks, & Hasher, 1990). That is, when both younger and older adults make errors in identifying information that was heard before, there is no age difference in the rate at which people mistakenly select information that is consistent with the previously described situation but that was not actually heard before. In some cases, it has been observed that while older adults show memory problems at lower levels, such as remembering verbatim or propositional information, their ability to remember information at higher levels, such as the mental model level, are unaffected (Radvansky, Zwaan, Curiel, & Copeland, 2001).

This preserved memory ability at higher levels of thought is seen in more everyday tasks, such as remembering news events (Frieske & Park, 1999). It has been observed that compared to younger adults older adults are better at remembering the content of news stories and remembering the sources of these stories (i.e., whether it was a television or radio broadcast).

Synopsis

Several changes occur in memory as a result of old age. Some of these are due to neurological changes, such as in the speed of neural firing and the functioning of the cortex, particularly the frontal lobes. A number of cognitive changes occur in memory processing, including reductions in working memory span and decreases in inhibitory and self-initiated processes. Some aspects of memory get worse with old age, including declines in some episodic memory processes, such as free recall and source monitoring, as well as changes in metamemory tasks such as prospective memory. Importantly, some aspects of memory are relatively unchanged, including much of semantic memory, the organization of episodic information, and the retention of information at higher levels of thought.

SUMMARY

In this chapter we looked at the consequences of development on memory. We saw that some memory systems and abilities are present at birth, whereas others, such as episodic and autobiographical memory, require some time for them to be at a level where they function adequately. As a person moves from infancy to childhood, memory continues to develop. During childhood, much of this development is related to increases in the speed of processing, as well as a greater self-knowledge of how memory works. This developing metamemory helps a person devise and implement various memory strategies, such as rehearsal, that can result in better memory later. Over the lifetime, there are continuous developmental changes. Near the other end of life, it is not unusual to see changes in memory as a result of the natural aging process. There are a number of declines in memory as a result of aging. These include declines in the speed of processing, a reduction in working memory capacity, and a decline in controlled memory processes, such as the suppression or irrelevant information and the self-initiation of various memory processes. Despite these changes, there are some parts of memory that are less affected by aging. These include things such as memory at higher levels of processing and some preservation in semantic memories.

STUDY QUESTIONS

1. What are some of the various ways of testing infants' memories, and how do they work?

2. What memory systems are well developed in infancy, and which are still immature?

3. What are some of the major changes in memory that are observed during childhood?

4. What important role does metamemory play in changes in memory during childhood?

5. What are some major neurological changes that occur with old age that can affect memory?

6. What are the dominant theories of age-related changes in memory? In what ways do they overlap? In what ways are they different?

7. What are the major changes in memory that occur as a result of the normal aging process?

8. What aspects of memory remain relatively unchanged, or even improve, with old age?

KEY TERMS

conjugate reinforcement, development, elicited imitation, inhibition theory, looking method, nonnutritive sucking, self-initiated processing deficit, speed theories, working memory deficit

CHAPTER SIXTEEN

AMNESIA

As we have seen, one of the most important issues in memory is not how much people remember but how much they forget. In this chapter we consider forgetting on a grand scale, to the extent that it is pathological, called amnesia. **Amnesia** is the loss of memories or memory abilities beyond what is expected in the normal course of forgetting, although there is otherwise normal intelligence and attention span (O'Connor, Verfaellie, & Cermak, 1995). There are various types of amnesia. While they vary in their scope and content, they are similar in that they all cripple memory processing in systematic ways, damaging some memories but leaving others more or less intact. Most of the amnesias that occur are a result of some organic damage to the brain. However, there is some suggestion that amnesia can result when there has been some psychological trauma. In such cases, the loss of memory functioning may be due to exclusively mental processes and not a problem with the underlying neurophysiology per se. Such amnesias are called psychogenic amnesia. In this chapter we first cover issues of organic amnesias with regard to retrograde and anterograde amnesia, followed by a consideration of the various types of psychogenic amnesia.

LONG-TERM MEMORY AMNESIA

The first types of amnesias we consider are the result of an organic disturbance that affects long-term memory. These amnesias can be divided into two types: retrograde and anterograde. Retrograde amnesia is a loss of long-term memories prior to a traumatic incident. This is amnesia backward in time. In contrast, anterograde amnesia is a loss of the ability to store new long-term memories. This is amnesia forward in time. Although we consider these two separately, it is actually rare to find a pure case of either one or the other. Whenever there is a trauma dramatic enough to produce amnesia, typically both are present to some degree. Some traumas result in much more retrograde amnesia than anterograde, whereas others have the opposite effect. The conditions that are described here are situations in which one type of amnesia is dominating a person's condition. A clear case of a mixing of the two is considered at the end of the anterograde section.

Retrograde Amnesia

Retrograde amnesia occurs when people lose the ability to access long-term memories that were previously available (see Kapur, 1999, for a review). Typically, with retrograde amnesia a person is losing her personal past. This is the sort of amnesia that people in soap operas tend to get. Usually, in those scenarios, people get hit on the head, and then they can't remember who they are, where they are, whether they're married, and so forth. In real life, the situation is much more complex, and retrograde amnesia has specific defining characteristics.

There are a number of things that cause retrograde amnesia. With each of these there is a trauma to the brain that disrupts normal processing. In general, retrograde amnesia disrupts a process called **consolidation** in long-term memory (McGaugh, 1966; but see Riccio, Millin, & Gisquet-Verrier, 2003, for an alternative view). Consolidation is a relatively slow process that makes memories more permanent. The easiest long-term memories to disrupt in retrograde amnesia are those that are not completely consolidated but where much of the information is being held in the temporary state, such as with long-term potentiation (see Chapter 2). In severe cases, more stable memories might be disrupted. This may occur either when there has been a disruption to the parts of the brain where the information is held or to the neural mechanisms that are used to retrieve and reconstruct that knowledge.

The presence of retrograde amnesia is determined by asking people to remember things from the past. One simple but effective approach is to ask people to recount facts from their life, including dates of events, schools attended, places lived, previous jobs, and so forth. The degree to which these questions cannot be answered indicates whether the person has retrograde amnesia. One difficulty with this is that it may not be possible to verify the facts that the person is asked to remember. There are other less idiosyncratic tests available. These include things such as asking about news events from the past or using the famous faces test (Sanders & Warrington, 1971) or the single season television program test (Cohen & Squire, 1981). These are both types of information that were widely available for limited periods in the past. In these tests, people are given items from different periods of time (either a photograph or the name of a show) and are asked to identify them. Different items come from different periods of time and make it easier to narrow down how much memory has been compromised.

What sorts of events can bring about retrograde amnesia? Severe blows to the head are a common way (and consistent with accounts provided by the entertainment industry). This physical trauma can affect the brain in a number of ways depending on the nature of the blow, such as its location and intensity. These blows to the head can disrupt consolidation or damage larger groups of cells, making the recovery of older memories more difficult.

Another event that can bring about retrograde amnesia is a cardiovascular incident, such as a stroke. During a stroke there is a disruption of the supply of oxygen and nutrients to parts of the brain. If this disruption is relatively brief, many of the cells will recover, and memory loss will be temporary. However, with longer periods of time, it is more likely that permanent cell damage and death will occur. With cell death, the patterns of neural information become disrupted, and there is a permanent loss of memories. This is why some stroke victims may need to relearn to speak and walk.

Characteristics of Retrograde Amnesia.   A number of characteristics typify retrograde amnesia. One is the graded nature of the memory loss in which newer, more recent memories are more easily disrupted. In contrast, older memories are more firmly established and thus are more difficult to disrupt, so there is a temporally graded loss of memories. As one goes back further in time, there is less memory loss. Memory loss is greater as the age of the memory approaches the time of the incident. This graded pattern of memory loss and retention is known as **Ribot's Law,** and it reflects the consolidation of memories in the nervous system. Basically, the older a memory becomes, the less susceptible it is to disruption (Brown, 2002).

Much of what is lost in retrograde amnesia are autobiographical memories—that is, memories that refer to events or episodes of one's own life, as well as more personal semantic information, such as addresses and jobs, and public events, such as news stories. Nondeclarative memories are largely preserved, as is semantic knowledge, although a person with retrograde amnesia may not be aware that he acquired this knowledge and may deny having it.

Another interesting aspect of retrograde amnesia is that the memory loss may not occur immediately. Instead, there may be a delay of a minute or two between the time of the injury and the onset of the amnesia. In a study by Lynch and Yarnell (1973), University of Colorado football players were tested after a concussive injury, after some other injury, or after simply coming off the field during a substitution. It was found that when tested immediately (within 30 seconds) after coming off the field, all of the players remembered the play that had just occurred. However, three to five minutes later, or longer, players who suffered a concussion could no longer remember the play that led to their injury. This delayed amnesia onset suggests that retrograde amnesia may take time to establish itself.

In cases where there has not been permanent damage to the brain, the recovery of memories in retrograde amnesia follows a regular pattern. Because older memories are more stable and well established, they are the first to return. As time goes on, more memories are recovered, again with the older memories being recovered sooner than newer memories. It is not unusual for many memories from the amnesic period to be recovered at or close to their level prior to the incident. However, there is also a period of time just prior to the trauma that is never recovered. This occurs because these memories have been permanently destroyed by the trauma. The disruption of consolidation hits these memories while they are in a very fragile state.

I have personal experience with retrograde amnesia. When I was 21 (a brief period when my personality slightly approached being cool), I worked as a bartender. One night, while driving home after work, I had stopped at a red light and was waiting to turn left onto my street. There was a car behind me, and behind that car was a police cruiser. When the light turned green, I started to take the left turn, when suddenly the police cruiser broadsided my car, pushing the driver's side door into the middle of the car (it turned out they had just gotten a call and had sped off to answer it with no flashing lights or siren—remember the witness in the car behind me). I was taken by ambulance to the hospital half a block away. During the night I was very disoriented, and when I woke up in intensive care the next morning, I had absolutely no memory of the accident. And even though it was July, I thought it was April. Over the next few days, my memories gradually returned, but even today, I have no memory of the day of the accident, the accident itself (thank goodness), or my admission to the hospital.

Case Studies of Retrograde Amnesia. Not all cases of retrograde amnesia follow the same pattern. What we have seen up to now is a typical pattern, but retrograde amnesia can appear in other ways. For example, Stracciari et al. (1994) describe two young men who had closed head injuries resulting in a temporally limited retrograde amnesia. These men had trouble remembering what had happened to them during the past year. This amnesia seemed to be limited to autobiographical memories but not more semantic and public memories (such as current events). So not all information was lost for the amnesic period. However, even important personal information was lost for that time period. For example, one of them forgot that he had been seeing a particular woman for the six months before the accident. This memory loss was profound enough that her name was not familiar to him—and he had her name tattooed on his forearm!

Although memories often return during recovery, in more severe cases they do not. One case of severe retrograde amnesia without much improvement is the case of P. S., who suffers profound anterograde amnesia as well (McCarthy & Hodges, 1995). As a result of a stroke when he was 67, P. S. sustained damage to his thalamus. The result of this was retrograde amnesia for all of his adult life, except for the period of time when he was in the British Navy during World War II. Because of his added problem with anterograde amnesia, he believes himself to be in this period of time. He interprets and places any knowledge he has within the framework of those war years. For example, while his autobiographical memory is severely compromised, he does have good memory for famous faces of the decades following World War II, and he can place them in the correct temporal sequence. However, when asked to date this information, he will place it in the early to mid-1940s. He does, however, have reasonably good memory for that period. For example, when asked to describe his hometown, he can be very specific, but his description is of the town as it appeared in the 1940s. In this case, the thalamus is not likely to be the storehouse of memories that were lost. Instead it is a connection between different sources of information in memory that would place information in time and in P. S.'s life. However, when this connection was severed, P. S. became trapped in time. (For another description of profound retrograde amnesia, see Hunkin, 1997, which describes a person who appears to have lost all memories before the age of 19.)

Electroconvulsive Therapy/Shock. Retrograde amnesia can also occur when a powerful electrical current is passed through the brain. In some cases this is done as part of a therapeutic treatment. This is known as **Electroconvulsive Therapy,** or **ECT.** For ECT, electrodes are placed on the head, either with one on each side of the head (the bilateral technique) or, more recently, on just one side of the head, usually the right (the unilateral technique). The unilateral technique results in less memory loss. During ECT, the patient is strapped securely to a table, and series of electrical pulses are passed through his brain. Unless a person is administered anticonvulsant drugs, these shocks can make the whole body convulse violently and possibly be injured. Basically, the ECT treatment is inducing a grand mal seizure. This process is repeated 6 to 12 times over a 3- to 5-week period (Cahill & Frith, 1995), and it is most often used with depressed patients after there has been little to no response to any other treatments and the patient is in a precarious state, such as being suicidal. ECT continues to be used and is effective at getting patients to a state where more conventional methods can be used.

ECT has a number of effects other that an alleviation of depressive symptoms. One of these is amnesia. Initially, after ECT, there is a brief period anterograde amnesia during

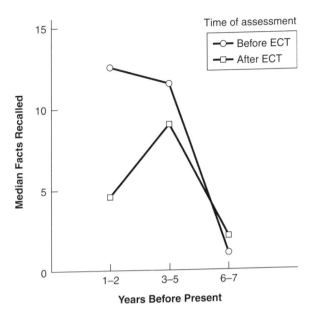

FIGURE 16.1   Graded Effects of Retrograde Amnesia

Source: Squire & Cohen, 1979

which the person has trouble learning new information. This gets worse with successive treatments (Cahill & Frith, 1995). There may also be long-term anterograde amnesic effects. More prominently, and important for this discussion, is the marked presence of retrograde amnesia (Cahill & Frith, 1995; Squire & Cohen, 1979). People undergoing this treatment lose memories from the recent past, including memories of the ECT session itself (which is probably a good thing). The amount of memory loss can vary, but it can be as long as one or two years prior to the ECT treatment (Squire, Slater, & Chace, 1975); see Figure 16.1. This graded loss of information is found for both personal autobiographical memories (a more episodic memory loss) and for community-shared public event memories (a more semantic memory loss).

When used to study memory and not as a treatment, this procedure is called **Electroconvulsive Shock,** or **ECS.** It is used on laboratory animals, such as rats. ECS provides a systematic assessment of retrograde amnesia for different types of information under different conditions of learning and retrieval. This is simply not possible with ECT treatments. When ECS is given to rats shortly after a fear experience, such as receiving a painful shock, retrograde amnesia occurs, and there is no subsequent fear of that situation (Duncan, 1949; Madsen & McGaugh, 1961). In another ECS study of memory by Chorover and Schiller (1965), rats were placed on a platform. If the rat stepped down from the platform, it received a shock, so it would no longer step down. Wires that delivered an ECS were attached to the rats' ears, and the amount of time between when the rat stepped off the platform and the delivery of the ECS was varied. As can be seen in Figure 16.2, the shorter the delay between the shock and the ECS, the less likely that rats learned to avoid stepping down,

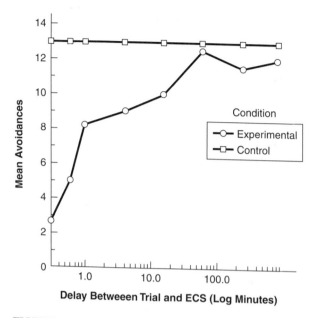

FIGURE 16.2   Retrograde Amnesia Following Electroconvulsive Shock
Source: Duncan, 1948

because the ECS had disrupted their memories. However, if there was a lengthy period between stepping down and the ECS, this information was stored in the rats' brains and thus was more permanent, stable, and resistant to the disruption caused by the ECS.

Transient Global Amnesia.   The type of retrograde amnesia that we have been talking about is the consequence of a clear traumatic injury to the brain. There is often no ambiguity about what brought about the amnesia, and the amnesia lasts for a substantial period of time. However, there is a rare form of amnesia that can occur where the cause is uncertain and the duration is relatively brief, but that still affects a broad range of memories. This is **transient global amnesia,** or **TGA.** During a TGA attack, a person reports having no memories of the recent past. This period of memory loss can be anywhere from a few hours to several decades, although in most cases the memory loss is for a few months. This range of memory loss in TGA is shown in Figure 16.3. This type of amnesia can be very dense. For example, one person was surprised to see that some fingers on his left hand were missing, although they were lost in a farm machinery accident four months before.

TGA episodes are relatively short-lived, lasting only a few hours (typically three to eight), although there may be some residual memory loss after the episode, typically for a few hours before the onset of the incident. A distribution of TGA durations is shown in Figure 16.4. This fleeting nature of TGA episodes makes them hard to study. So although the concept of transient global amnesia has been around since the 1950s, it has been difficult to systematically study until recently. Often, by the time a knowledgeable person is notified, much of the amnesia has begun to clear. Many of these incidents must go unreported.

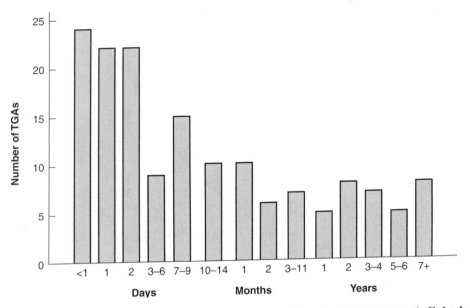

FIGURE 16.3   Degree of Retrograde Amnesia During a Transient Global Amnesia Episode

Source: Brown, 1998

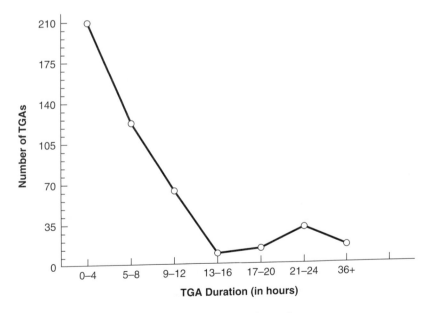

FIGURE 16.4   Duration of a Transient Global Amnesia

Source: Brown, 1998

Often during a TGA episode, people are confused and repeatedly ask the same questions. This is due to an anterograde amnesia component that prevents them from remembering that they had already asked the question or from remembering the answers. Although working memory span appears to be fine, more episodic knowledge is not retained or recovered after the episode has passed. Semantic and procedural knowledge seem to be unaffected.

Part of what makes TGA so mysterious is that there is no clear indicator of what causes it. The person seems fine one minute but is experiencing this dense memory loss the next. As illustrated in Figure 16.5, TGAs often occur in people between the ages of 50 and 70, and typically only occur once in a lifetime. It has been suggested that TGAs are brought about by an emotional or physical stress or exertion, such as having an argument, playing an exciting card game, having sex (the most popular way to get it), driving, taking a hot shower, or having a coughing spell. There has been some suggestion that TGAs are a result of ischemias in the brain. These are temporary disruptions of blood flow. The parts of the brain that are most often implicated are the temporal lobes, hippocampus, and thalamus. (For reviews of this phenomenon, see Brown, 1998, or Goldenberg, 1995.)

Synopsis

The loss of memories prior to an incident is known as retrospective amnesia. There is a graded loss of memories, with newer memories being more susceptible than older memo-

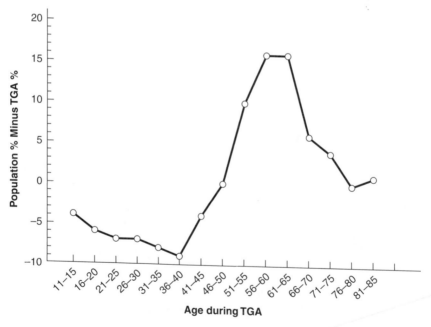

FIGURE 16.5   Age at Which a Transient Global Amnesia Episode Is Experienced
Source: Brown, 1998

ries, suggesting a disruption of consolidation. Often, many of the memories initially lost are recovered, although those near the traumatic event may be lost forever. In addition to random accidents, retrograde amnesia can be deliberately induced through electrical shocks. Finally, there is a form of amnesia known as transient global amnesia that is an odd loss of major periods of a person's life that can be triggered by mild to moderate stress during a person's early retirement years.

Anterograde Amnesia

Whereas retrograde amnesia is the loss of memories prior to an incident, **anterograde amnesia** is the inability to store new memories after an incident. This is a much more devastating condition. With anterograde amnesia, people lose the ability to fully benefit from their experiences, and they become, in some sense, frozen in time. For someone with severe anterograde amnesia, they need to be given the same information repeatedly because they have great difficulty retaining it. Here, we first look at anterograde amnesia in terms of what part of the brain is damaged. The first type is anterograde amnesia that arises as a result of damage to the medial temporal lobes and the hippocampus. The second type is damage to the diencephalon. After this, we consider issues of anterograde amnesia more generally.

Medial Temporal Lobe and Hippocampus. As discussed in Chapter 2, the temporal lobe is a part of the cerebral cortex. The medial part of the temporal lobe is the part toward the interior of the brain, near the middle. This part of the temporal lobe is adjacent to an important memory structure: the hippocampus, which is part of the limbic system. Damage to these areas of the brain as a result of surgical intervention, infection, stroke, or anoxia (lack of oxygen to the brain) can result in anterograde amnesia.

Perhaps the most famous amnesic is a man known as H. M. (Scoville & Milner, 1957). On August 23, 1953, at the age of 27, H. M. underwent brain surgery to alleve his severe epilepsy. H. M. was experiencing several petit mal seizures each day (up to 12 in a two-hour period) and weekly grand mal seizures, often resulting in injury. He was unable to work or otherwise lead a normal life. The surgeons removed much of his hippocampus and adjoining cortex on both sides of his brain. Recent MRI scans (Corkin et al., 1997) have shown that the brain damage included other structures, including portions of the amygdala and temporal cortex. The parts of the hippocampus that remain show evidence of atrophy. In terms of his epilepsy, the operation was a success. The rate and severity of his seizures greatly diminished, although they were still present. Also, his intelligence level stayed the same (if not improved), and his personality appeared to be unchanged. However, there was an unexpected side effect. H. M. had severe and dense anterograde amnesia. He was not able to learn new things. Because of the severity of this amnesia, the surgeons who performed the operation quickly wrote a paper on their findings so no one else would make the same mistake.

Although H. M. has difficulty storing new memories, he has above normal intelligence, and he does remember a great deal from before the operation (Scoville & Milner, 1957). However, he has difficulty in his daily life because he cannot remember much beyond the span of his short-term memory. He often comments that he feels as if he has just awakened from a dream. It is not unusual for him to do a jigsaw puzzle many times or to read the same magazine over and over and not have any memory of read it before. H. M. also has some retrograde amnesia for a period of time prior to the operation, but most of his preoperative memories remain intact. As an illustration of his preserved preoperative memories and the deficit he has with new ones, on one occasion he was going back to his house with some researchers (14 years after the operation). After getting off the highway he confidently directed them to his house. However, it was the house he used to live in and not the one to which his family moved after his amnesia. He only recognized how to get to his new home when he was within a block or two.

While H. M. has severe memory deficits, not all of his memory abilities are gone. For example, he has a reasonably well-preserved short-term memory (Wickelgren, 1968). Also, he is able to acquire new declarative memories if the information is salient enough and is repeatedly presented to him for a long period of time. For example, H. M. was eventually able to recall that there was a president named Kennedy and that he was assassinated. He was also able to remember his father's death after his father had been absent from the home for about one month (Milner, Corkin, & Teuber, 1968). He also shows some evidence of implicit memory processing, such as perceptual identification (Milner, Corkin, & Teuber, 1968), as well as procedural memory for various motor tasks, such as mirror tracing or pursuit rotor tasks (Corkin, 1968).

H. M. is not the only person to get such severe anterograde amnesia. Other ways of getting this condition include loss of oxygen to the brain, brain tumors, neurological disorders such as epilepsy, or viral attacks such as herpes simplex encephalitis.

Diencephalic Anterograde Amnesia.   The diencephalon is a collection of brain structures, including the thalamus, hypothalamus, and mammilary bodies. Like damage to the medial temporal lobes and the hippocampus, damage to this area can result in anterograde amnesia. The most common way of getting this condition is as a symptom of Korsakoff's syndrome. Korsakoff's syndrome occurs in people who are chronic and severe alcoholics. People with this syndrome have damage in many brain areas, including the dorsomedial thalamic neuclei, the mamillary bodies, and the frontal lobe. This extensive brain damage is a function of a deficiency in thiamine (vitamin B1) as a result of alcoholism rather than an effect of the alcohol itself. It is also possible for the diencephalon to be damaged in other ways to produce anterograde amnesia, such as through a stroke.

The diencephalon is closely associated with frontal lobe processing, which involves the coordination and control of thought. People with anterograde amnesia as a result of damage to these areas may confabulate. That is, they may make up information on the fly to account for some aspect of their life. They are not lying because there is no intention to deceive. However, this loss of mental control leads these people to report things that are clearly false as if they were true. There may also be changes in the person's personality and a decline in motivation.

Anterograde amnesia that results from damage to these structures may result in a decline in the ability to coordinate information in memory, making it difficult to recover memories in an effective manner. People with this sort of damage also have more extensive retrograde amnesia than those with medial temporal lobe damage. This may also be due to a lack of an ability to coordinate information in memory, which would make it difficult to retrieve old memories as well as lay down new ones.

Anterograde Amnesia More Generally.   The part of memory that is most affected in anterograde amnesia is declarative memory. People with this condition have difficulty acquiring new, conscious memories. This applies to both episodic or autobiographical information as well as new semantic knowledge. If you were to have a conversation with an anterograde amnesic, she might appear to be normal. However, if you were to get up, leave, and return ten minutes later, the amnesic would not recognize you and may claim that she never met you before. Even in cases where there is some preserved declarative memory abilities, other deficits may arise. For example, both types of anterograde amnesics do not show distinctiveness and novelty effects, such as the Von Restorff effect (Kishiyama, Yonelinas, & Lazzara, 2004). This occurs because, due to deficits in long-term memory encoding, these people do not have the pool of memories needed to keep track of context, since distinctiveness is defined by the context in which information is found (e.g., elephant is distinctive in a list of vehicles but not in a list of zoo animals).

While long-term memory is often affected, anterograde amnesics often have an intact short-term memory (Baddeley & Warrington, 1970) because amnesics forget things at a much faster rate (Warrington & Weiskrantz, 1968). They can consciously comprehend the experiences as they happen, but the experiences slip away quickly.

Although declarative memory is severely affected, nondeclarative memories may be relatively intact. For example, the procedural memories are mostly unaffected. Anterograde amnesics can learn new procedural tasks, although they may lack conscious awareness that they have a memory for the task. For example, amnesics might learn a motor task, such as mirror tracing, at a rate similar to normal people, even with their severe declarative memory deficits (Brooks & Baddeley, 1976). An example of the learning in an anterograde amnesic on a mirror tracing task is shown in Figure 16.6.

Suppose a person knew how to play the piano before becoming amnesic and then learned a new song while an amnesic. Later, if she were asked to play the song, the amnesic would deny knowing it. However, if she were coaxed into trying to play the song, she could do so. This is illustrated clearly in the case of Clive Wearing, a well-known British classical musician who suffered from herpes simplex encephalitis in 1985. Despite his very profound anterograde amnesia, his musical abilities remain largely intact, allowing him to play or conduct as he had done before, with degradations noticed only by expert musicians (Wilson & Wearing, 1995).

The preservation of nondeclarative memories not only applies to motor skills, but also to implicit, linguistic tasks (Schacter, 1987). For example, amnesics show as much semantic and episodic priming of words as normal people do (Graf & Schacter, 1985; Graf, Shimamura, & Squire, 1985). They are also able to perform similarly to normal people on word fragment completion (Warrington & Weiskrantz, 1970), word stem completion (Graf, Squire, & Mandler, 1984), and perceptual identification tasks. For example, amnesics are like normal people in that they spend less time viewing pictures that are repeated. However, if something in a picture has been altered (e.g., the relationship among elements are changed), normal people spend more time looking in the region where the change occurred, whereas amnesics do not (Ryan, Althoff, Whitlow, & Cohen, 2000). This is consistent with the idea that amnesia leaves an ability to implicitly recognize when things are old but not to detect changes in a current situation that require a comparison with information in long-term episodic memory. This reinforces the point that the problem of anterograde amnesia is

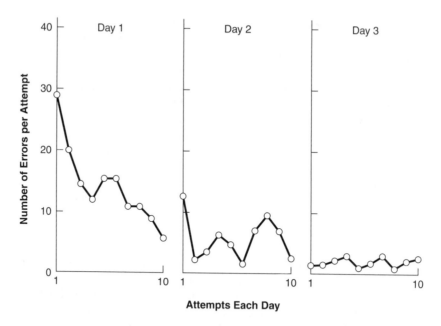

FIGURE 16.6   Performance of an Anterograde Amnesic on a Mirror Tracing Task.
Illustrating preserved implicit memory.

Source: Blakemore, 1977

not a problem in encoding or storage (consolidation) but in retrieval. When the information is tested for appropriately, it can be observed to be present in some form in long-term memory.

Again, although we have been talking about explicit and implicit memory, it is important to keep in mind that no memory test is process pure. There is always an influence of multiple memory components. For example, the combined influence of explicit and implicit memory on a direct memory task (where one is consciously trying to remember) in amnesics can be seen with recall and recognition. In Chapter 10, we saw how recall requires a great deal of mental effort to generate the information, whereas recognition requires only that a person, at a minimum, believes that the information is old. This feeling of familiarity does not require explicit conscious recollection, but it could involve unconscious, implicit influences. It has been reported that anterograde amnesics have greater difficulty with recall than with recognition. In some cases they may show no recognition deficit in conjuction with a clear recall deficit (Hirst et al., 1986; Hirst, Johnson, Phelps, & Volpe, 1988).

Other Case Studies of Anterograde Amnesia.   It is possible for people to have anterograde amnesia for some types of information but not others. One intriguing case is the amnesic A. B., who as a result of a hematoma had damage to his posterolateral (rear) frontal lobe and adjacent anterior (front) parietal lobe on the left side. What is intriguing about A. B. is his inability to retain word or sentence lists in short-term memory task. However,

A. B. can recall complex stories he reads or hears. Thus, A. B. has anterograde amnesia for words and simple unrelated sentences but has more normal memory for complex, interrelated sets of information such as meaningful stories (Romani & Martin, 1999). In terms of the levels of representation described in Chapter 8, A. B. has poor memory at the surface form and textbase levels but good memory at the situation model level. This also supports the idea that our ability to remember complex sets of information does not depend on our ability to remember the individual components that make it up.

Another amnesic with selective problems is the case of T. R. (Sirigu & Grafman, 1996). This man suffered cerebral anoxia after heart failure and then had amnesia consistent with damage to the hippocampus. Like many anterograde amnesics, T. R. has difficulty with new episodic memories. However, for him, it is only for certain types of information. He retains the ability to remember past events but only so far as it involves remembering what had happened and where it happened. However, he is amnesic for the identities of the people who were involved and for when it happened. This shows a selective loss of some episodic information (time and entities) but not for others (space and activities).

Irreversible brain damage is not the only way to experience anterograde amnesia. There are ways to temporarily induce this condition in normal people. It has been suggested that people taking benzodiazepines (e.g., Valium and Halcion) may have anterograde amnesia without retrograde amnesia, similar to what is seen in Korsakoff's syndrome patients (Curran, 1991; Mintzer & Griffiths, 2001).

Living with Anterograde Amnesia.   As you can imagine, anterograde amnesia has a profound effect on the ability to function normally. Is there anything that can be done to help people with this condition? An important thing to keep in mind is that it depends on how severe the person's amnesia is. The more severe the amnesia, the more severe the symptoms. Some people may have a relatively mild form of amnesia, which allows them some independence, whereas others are more profoundly affected and require constant supervision. This section describes some amnesics and some of the changes in their daily lives that have occurred as a result of their condition.

One of these is a special education teacher, Sheila Moakes (Kapur & Moakes, 1995). She became amnesic when a case of herpes simplex encephalitis at the age of 32 damaged parts of her temporal lobe and hippocampus, leaving her with some retrograde amnesia and profound anterograde amnesia. While she was nearly incapacitated after the onset of her condition, she eventually did recover some abilities. Although she can no longer work as a regular teacher, tracking students across the school year, she is able to tutor students on a lesson-by-lesson basis, and only with supervision. She has also regained the ability to do many household tasks but only by keeping to a strict schedule (otherwise she does not do some things and does others repeatedly), and she can do light grocery shopping if she has a list and does not have to go to a new store. Amazingly, she can still drive well, with her only problem being that she may become lost if she ventures too far from home. She does watch television but avoids shows that have a plot that must be remembered and followed. She also does not read much for the same reason. Some parts of her life have continued to deteriorate. She has become distant to her son and has lost many of her old friends and has not been able to make new ones. She has also lost the motivation to learn new tasks because she knows the enormous effort that is involved.

If a person's amnesia is milder, he may be aware of the problem and develop strategies to compensate for the loss. An example of this is the case of J. C. (Wilson, J. C., & Hughes, 1997). J. C., a former law student, became amnesic after an attack of herpes simplex encephalitis. Because of some spared memory ability and his high intelligence and motivation, he was able to overcome this disability to some degree. Although he had to quit law school, he was able to train to become a professional furniture refinisher. Still, it took him 20 trips to learn where to get off the bus for refinishing school. He also went on to start his own business. To keep his life in order, he developed a complex system using a watch with multiple alarms and a color-coded filofax for keeping notes about events in his life. Keep in mind, however, that he does have anterograde amnesia. If he goes to a new restaurant with friends, he needs to write down that he went and what he ate, or he won't remember. J. C. was functioning to the extent that he started a new relationship, but he must record facts about his activities with the woman in his filofax. He also needs to leave himself constant reminders, such as "clean contact lenses" or "check the oven." His life critically depends on sticky notes.

J. C. was able to show remarkable adaptation to go on to lead a relatively productive life. This is due in large part to the tremendous amount of support and monitoring he receives from his family and friends. However, not all anterograde amnesics are so fortunate. For example, Mr. S. became amnesic in his 70s as the result of a stroke (Squires, Hunkin, & Parkin, 1997). Although he used a notebook for reminders in the beginning, a lack of reinforcement from his wife and friends, as well as his own lack of motivation, made him soon stop. Thus, there was little to no improvement for Mr. S.

Mixture of Retrograde and Anterograde Amnesia

As noted earlier, it is rare to have only retrograde or anterograde amnesia. In this section we consider in detail a case of severe head trauma in which both retrograde and anterograde amnesia were present and how this changed over time (as reported in Barbizet, 1970).

An overview of the situation is given in Figure 16.7. Initial testing occurred five months after the trauma in which there was both retrograde and anterograde amnesia. For the retrograde amnesia, the person was unable to remember events from the two years prior to the accident and only had partial memories for the time before that. This is a classic retrograde amnesia temporal gradient. For the anterograde amnesia, the person was not able to remember much of what happened after coming out of the coma, and he was having trouble storing new memories.

As time progressed, things changed. With retrograde amnesia, the severity of the situation eases over time. By 8 months after the trauma, there was dense amnesia for only 1 year and partial amnesia for 4 years prior to that, although most other memories had returned to a normal or near normal state. Ten months after that, almost all of the retrograde amnesia had lifted, leaving only dense amnesia for the two weeks prior to the trauma. It is unlikely that those memories will ever be recovered. As for the anterograde amnesia, Figure 16.7 shows that there is some improvement in the ability to successfully acquire new memories as well. By 8 months after the trauma, some new information is being stored in long-term memory, and by 18 months memory performance has returned to a normal range. It is only the 3.5-month period after the person emerged from the coma that there are no

First examination: 5 months after trauma

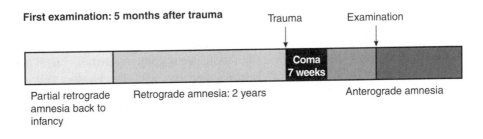

Second examination: 8 months after trauma

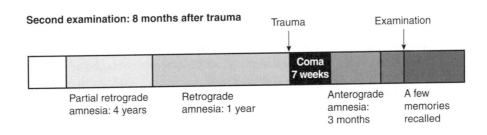

Third examination: 18 months after trauma

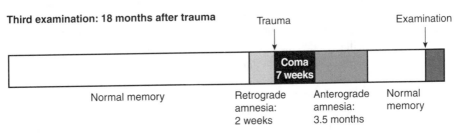

FIGURE 16.7   Illustration of Brain Damage Resulting in Both Retrograde and Anterograde Amnesias

Source: Barbizet, 1970

memories. Presumably, during this period the person was not able to store information effectively, so it will never be remembered.

Synopsis

The loss of the ability to encode new memories is anterograde amnesia. Sometimes this deficit is quite severe, as with H. M. Anterograde amnesia can occur as a result of damage to either the hippocampus and medial temporal lobes or to the diencephalon. This amnesia results in profound loss of declarative memory abilities, whereas nondeclarative memory systems are less affected, if at all. People with anterograde amnesia need to be monitored for their own safety. However, people with less severe forms of this condition can have some limited independence.

SHORT-TERM MEMORY AMNESIA

Most amnesias involve a loss in long-term memory, with a preserved short-term memory. However, there are cases where short-term memory, often verbal short-term memory (e.g., Belleville, Caza, & Peretz, 2003), is damaged, but long-term memory is unaffected. One example is the case of K. F. (Shallice & Warrington, 1970), who had deficits in short-term memory tasks, such as having a serial position curve recency effect of only one item (normal people have recency effects of five or six) and not being able to detect whether a probe letter was in a list if it was not the most recent letter heard. However, long-term memory was relatively intact. Another example is the case of P. V. (Vallar & Baddeley, 1984; Vallar & Papagno, 1995), who had difficulty remembering spoken word lists over the short term but had normal short-term memory for visually presented lists and good long-term retention. This deficit leads P. V. to have problems "understanding" short sequences of information that required verbal short-term memory, such as phone numbers or the prices of goods. She also had trouble doing mental calculations.

Many of these verbal short-term memory amnesias involved damage to the left parietal lobe (Vallar & Papagano, 1995)—in particular, the supramarginal gyrus, which is part of the inferior (bottom) portion of the parietal lobe, near the frontal lobe. In some cases, parts of the premotor areas of the frontal lobe are also implicated (e.g., Broca's area). These result in disruptions of short-term memory rehearsal. This can also have a spillover effect and influence more complex mental activity, such as sentence comprehension. For example, a person with verbal short-term memory amnesia would have difficulty understanding sentences like "Touch the small green square and the large black circle," or "The cat that the dog chased was white." Comprehension of these sentences requires that a person keep track of both the exact words and the order in which they were heard. A person is less able to guess the intended message if there is some forgetting of some of the words or their order. The ability to learn new foreign languages is, of course, also severely compromised.

Other short-term memory amnesias follow damage to the right parietal/occipital lobe. These result in visuo-spatial working memory problems (Vallar & Papagano, 1995), such as having difficulty counting the number of dots on a computer screen, identifying unfamiliar faces, doing mental rotation, or learning their way around an unfamiliar house.

The fact that such amnesias occur makes salient the fact that the modal model of memory is a convenient heuristic, an adequate description of memory. As you read in Chapter 1, from this view, information enters the short-term store before going to long-term memory. If the short-term system were damaged, long-term memory should be affected as well. The fact that some amnesics can have trouble with short-term but not long-term memory suggests that information can be stored in long-term memory without always requiring the involvement of short-term memory. Long-term memory has its own direct and privileged access to new information.

This loss of short-term memory ability highlights different qualities of information that have been described by working memory theories. As a reminder, one general classification that can be made is to divide up working memory into the phonological loop and the visuo-spatial sketchpad. Each of these may be selectively affected in short-term memory amnesia.

People with damage to the phonological loop portion have word or digit spans of one or two items. A loss of this part of working memory is associated with damage to the left hemisphere (where many language skills are localized), often to the parietal or temporal lobes. Damage to the left parietal lobe is associated with problems in the phonological short-term store, whereas damage to the left temporal lobe is more associated with damage to the rehearsal process. People who have this kind of short-term memory amnesia must rely on other sources of information. For example, patient, I. R. could not use phonological information to help her remember but could use semantic information from long-term memory (Belleville, Caza, & Peretz, 2003).

People with damage to the visuo-spatial sketchpad have difficulty with spatial tasks. A loss of this part of working memory is associated with damage to the right hemisphere (where more holistic processing generally occurs). Again, this sort of amnesia is associated with damage to the parietal and temporal lobes, as well as some involvement of the frontal lobes. Damage to more posterior regions of the brain are associated with more perceptual aspects of working memory, whereas more anterior portions are more associated with retention and control.

Synopsis

Whereas most amnesias strike long-term memory, it is also possible to have short-term memory damaged, with long-term memory relatively intact. Rather than damaging short-term memory as a whole, different components of working memory appear to be compromised. This form of amnesia also deemphasizes the idea that long-term memory learning requires a fully functioning short-term memory.

PSYCHOGENIC AMNESIA

The amnesias we have seen so far are the result of physical damage to the brain, and in most cases, this is clearly the underlying cause of memory loss. However, there are other types of amnesia that are thought to arise based on psychological content, not the functioning of the nervous system. That is, a person may be so psychologically disturbed by something that it causes them to forget on a massive scale. These are known as **psychogenic amnesias** because they are brought about by psychological rather than neurological mechanisms. In most of these cases, the memory loss is associated with some traumatic event or circumstances in the person's life, and the knowledge lost is usually episodic or autobiographical in nature. Semantic and procedural memories remain intact. The memory loss can be viewed as one way of coping with the trauma. If the oppressive knowledge is not consciously remembered, then it will no longer be stressful and anxiety provoking.

Repression

One of the best-known forms of psychogenic amnesia is **repression.** This concept is largely associated with Freud and his followers, although it has been adapted by other people. This finding states that there are times in people's lives when they have experiences that are traumatic or threatening to the point of potentially damaging the ability to function adequately in the world. These threats can be any number of traumas, including sexual abuse, severe violence, or even inappropriate sexual desires or feelings. To protect people from these damaging memories, there is a part of the mind that actively represses them to keep them from entering consciousness. As such, repression is a defense mechanism.

This type of repression is different from the suppression or inhibition we have seen elsewhere in the book. In short, inhibition is a general mechanism to control the flow of thought. Information that is inhibited is related to what is being thought about but is irrelevant to their current goals. This memory loss is relatively mild and short-lived. In contrast, repression is a defense mechanism that keeps damaging thoughts from ever entering awareness. It may be information that is vitally important to a person but is still prevented from entering conscious awareness because of its vicious nature. This loss of memories is severe and pervasive, capable of lasting an entire lifetime.

The experimental support for the Freudian concept of repression is scarce. By its very nature, repression would be difficult to study. First, one must recover repressed memories, but the problem is determining how accurate such memories are. As we saw in Chapter 12, it is easy for false memories to be generated, and there is no clear way, apart from gathering independent evidence, to distinguish real recovered memories from false ones generated while searching for repressed memories (Loftus, 1993). Thus, to study repressed memories, one needs to know what actually happened. However, in many cases when a claim of repression is made, such as childhood sexual abuse, the independent evidence is often meager and unreliable.

One of the more emotional debates in memory research has been whether or not recovered repressed memories are real. Some people have argued that there is no such thing as repression. All recovered repressed memories are either false memories or not really repressed in the first place. There are two lines of argument for this view. One is that many of the methods used to recover repressed memories are similar to those that would be used to generate false memories. Thus, many recovered memories are actually false memories. Another point is that the typical outcome for highly traumatic experiences is that people remember them very vividly and have difficulty forgetting them, even when they want to do so. This is the opposite of repression.

Dissociative Amnesia

Another psychogenic amnesia is **dissociative amnesia,** which occurs when a person is unable to remember segments of information about her life (Kihlstrom & Schacter, 1995). Typically, in this condition, the forgotten knowledge is either traumatic itself or is associated with a traumatic event. For example, suppose you were the driver of a car in an accident that resulted in someone's death. If this pathologically troubled you, you might acquire dissociative amnesia in which you do not remember any of the events of that day. This amnesia is almost exclusively a retrograde amnesia, with a person being unable to remember events from his past. What makes this condition distinct from repression is that a person is aware of the memory loss and is troubled by it, whereas this may not be the case with repression.

There are three ways that dissociative amnesia can manifest itself (Nemiah, 1979). The first is as a **systematized amnesia,** where people are amnesic for information related to a traumatic event, regardless of when or where it occurred. Second, there is a **localized**

amnesia, where a person has trouble remembering events within a block of time, such as a period of hours or weeks. Finally, there is **generalized amnesia,** in which nearly all of a person's life is forgotten. These different ways that dissociative amnesia manifests itself illustrates the psychological influence of the origins of this amnesia. This sort of selectivity or breadth of coverage is almost never seen with organic amnesia. There is more flexibility in what can be forgotten when there is a psychological mechanism. It is also possible that these different types of dissociative amnesia are the result of different conditions.

Dissociative Fugue

A more profound psychogenic amnesia occurs with a **dissociative fugue,** in which memory is disrupted to the point that a person forgets fundamental aspects of his identity, such as who he is, where he lives, what he does for a living, and so forth (Kihlstrom & Schacter, 1995). Like dissociative amnesia, a dissociative fugue is almost exclusively a retrograde amnesia.

There are different types of fugue states, depending on the nature and extent of the loss (Fisher, 1945; Fisher & Joseph, 1949). First, there may be a change in both identity and location (where the person lives)—what we can call **fugue and flight.** Second, there may be a loss of memories, but the core identity is intact. We can call **memory fugue.** Finally, there may be a reversion to an earlier state of life, with an inability to remember events after that period. We can call this **regression fugue.** Again, the nature of the memory loss illustrates the psychological nature of this type of amnesia, which is not seen with organic damage, and underlines the flexibility in the systematic forgetting of information.

Although conscious awareness of previous memories is rendered inaccessible in the fugue state, if this is like other amnesias, one would expect implicit memory to be unaffected. This has been difficult to test, especially because the fugue state is so rare. However, there is some anecdotal evidence that is consistent with the idea. A dramatic illustration of preserved implicit memory of a fugal amnesic is a case of a woman who had been found wandering around but could provide no information about herself. She was asked on several occasions to dial a random number on a telephone. This number turned out to be her mother's (Lyon, 1985).

What is more fascinating is that when a person comes out of the fugue state, even if it had been going on for years, not only do memories from the original identity return, but memories from the fugue identity become forgotten. This return to the original identity can be slow or fast. Thus, even when there has been a recovery of the original identity, there is still an amnesic state associated with this condition.

Dissociative Identity Disorder

Perhaps the most intriguing psychogenic amnesia comes in the form of **dissociative identity disorder** (formerly called multiple personality disorder), in which a person acts as if she has many separate personalities or identities, each with its own autobiographical history. In some cases these alternative identities are even aware of the others. Often one identity has no conscious memories of what another identity learned while he or she was dominant. One of the interesting things about dissociative identity disorder is that there may be assymetrical amnesia across various identities (Kihlstrom & Schacter, 1995). That is, one identity may be able to remember information that was learned when a second identity was dominant but not vice versa. This bears some resemblance to dissociative fugue, where the shift from one identity to another results in some amnesic forgetting of information learned while involved with a previous identity.

Although some amnesia occurs when a person switches from one identity to another, this does not apply to all memories. For example, like organic amnesia, explicit memories may be compromised, but implicit memories may escape unscathed. For example, a person can learn procedural knowledge learned with one identity dominant and then be able to use that knowledge when another personality is dominant with no evidence of forgetting, even when the second identity is amnesic of the first (Kihlstrom & Schacter, 1995). Similarly, implicit memory is also spared in the case of priming. Priming is observed across identities where amnesia is claimed, showing the continued, stable operation of implicit memory (Huntjens et al., 2002).

Synopsis

In addition to organic amnesias, it may also be possible for people to be amnesic due to a psychological trauma. These are called psychogenic amnesias, and they include repression, dissociative amnesia, dissociative fugue, and dissociative identity disorder.

SUMMARY

In this chapter we looked at a number of ways memory can be altered to lead to a state of pathological forgetting. Often this amnesia results from some sort of organic disturbance to the brain. In some cases, as with retrograde amnesia, a person is unable to remember a large number of events from his recent past. This can be the result of many events, such as a blow to the head or from electroconvulsive therapy treatments. Although the consequences of retrograde amnesia are generally long lasting, there is a condition known as transient global amnesia, where a person may become amnesic for a period of only a day. In other cases, as with anterograde amnesia, a person is unable to acquire new memories. Sometimes this occurs as a result of damage to the hippocampus or the medial temporal lobe. In other cases it is a result of damage to diencephalic structures of the brain, such as the thalamus. In either case, a person with anterograde amnesia is effectively trapped in the present, with little to no abilities to adapt and change as a result of new information they are given. However, there may be a preservation of some unconscious memories, such as procedural memory. If a person were to acquire anterograde amnesia, life is changed dramatically, and with only a great deal of effort and support will the person be able to approach living a normal life.

Other types of amnesia have no clear organic source but seem to be due to more psychological stressors. For example, the Freudian concept of repression, if it exists, would be a broad-based defense mechanism that actively prevents threatening memories from entering conscious awareness. Well-documented cases of dissociative amnesia can occur if a person has certain memories that are highly traumatic. When pushed to an extreme, a person may become amnesic for his or her entire identity, as in a fugue state, and possibly wander off to form a new life as a new person. In one of the more intriguing psychopathologies that can arise, a person with dissociative identity disorder will behave as though they have different personalities with different identities. What is interesting is that some of these personalities may be amnesic for information that was learned when a different personality was dominant, at least for declarative memories.

STUDY QUESTIONS

1. How does retrograde amnesia occur? What are some of its defining characteristics?

2. What do electroconvulsive shocks do to memory? How extensive can the damage be?

3. What is transient global amnesia? How extensive is the loss? How long does it last? Who does this happen to?

4. What is anterograde amnesia? Damage to which brain structures produce this condition?

5. What types of memories are damaged in anterograde amnesia? What types of memories are preserved? What is the general prognosis for people with this condition?

6. What sorts of memory losses occur with short-term memory amnesias?

7. What is psychogenic amnesia? What is repression? What is dissociative amnesia? What is a psychogenic fugue? What memory losses can occur in dissociative identity disorder?

KEY TERMS

amnesia, anterograde amnesia, consolidation, dissociative amnesia, dissociative fugue, dissociative identity disorder, Electroconvulsive Shock (ECS), Electroconvulsive Therapy (ECT), fugue and flight, generalized amnesia, memory fugue, organic amnesia, psychogenic amnesia, regression fugue, repression, retrograde amnesia, Ribot's Law, systematized amnesia, transient global amnesia (TGA)

CHAPTER SEVENTEEN

OTHER MEMORY DISORDERS

The disruption of memory that is seen with the various types of amnesia discussed in the previous chapter can be quite devastating. There are other ways that memories can be damaged or hindered. These additional disorders are the focus of this chapter. Each of these is associated with some disruption of neurological activity. The memory deficits that are seen in these conditions are only part of a larger set of problems that are associated with each of them. Because many of these disorders fall outside the realm of what have traditionally been considered studies of amnesia, they have been given their own chapter. However, it should be noted that many of these memory disorders do involve some kind of amnesia in that there is a profound loss of memory content or abilities beyond what is observed in normal forgetting.

This chapter first covers memory disorders that arise in various types of dementia that a person might be unfortunate enough to develop. These include conditions such as Alzheimer's, Parkinson's, and Huntington's diseases, as well as multiple sclerosis. Following this, there is an overview of how a serious psychotic condition, like schizophrenia, can have a profound and negative impact on memory. Other, milder psychological conditions, such as anxiety and depression, can also disrupt the normal functioning of memory. Finally, a number of specific memory losses that occur with more localized and limited forms of brain damage are examined.

DEMENTIA

Dementia is a condition where a person develops serious impairments in thinking along a number of dimensions, only one of which is memory, but without any impairment of consciousness. The memory problems that occur in dementias include both a decline in the ability to learn new information as well as a loss of previous memories. Because of the widespread degradation of the brain, this memory loss can even extend to fairly well-ingrained memories that are otherwise preserved, as with amnesics. Finally, people often think of dementias as illnesses of only the elderly. Although it is true that many older adults will acquire some form of dementia (15 percent over the age of 65 and 25 to 47 percent over the age of 85), many younger people contract these diseases as well (Brandt & Rich, 1995). In this section we consider a number of the more prominent dementias in detail. These include Alzheimer's disease, Parkinson's disease, Huntington's disease, and the dementia associated with Multiple Sclerosis.

Alzheimer's Disease

Alzheimer's disease is a condition that was originally described by Alois Alzheimer in 1907. It is now one of the most rapidly expanding health concerns in our country, and as our population ages, more people will succumb to its effects. It should be noted that Alzheimer's disease is a condition that occurs only in certain people as a result of the presence of certain neurological conditions. It is not a natural consequence of growing old. While far too many older adults will contract Alzheimer's, most will not. Also, unfortunately, this is a condition in which the person is often very aware of his progressive memory loss.

Characteristics.   Alzheimer's disease is a cortical dementia, which means that it primarily affects the cerebral cortex. This condition is marked by a severe degradation in brain structure and function. In essence, with Alzheimer's disease, a person's mind and memory deteriorate. Three primary changes occur in the brain as a result of this condition (Hodges, 2000). The first is a loss in the number of neurons and neural connections in the brain. This loss is primarily focused in the frontal and temporal lobes of the brain, which are critical for effective memory processing, with areas used primarily for sensory and motor processing being better preserved. The second change is the presence of **neurofibrillary tangles.** These tangles occur with individual neurons themselves and impede their ability to effectively transmit a signal. They continue to grow over time, eventually pushing other neural structures, such as the nucleus, mitochondria, and ribosomes to one side, thereby disrupting their function and filling up the interior of the axons and dendrites. Finally, the third change is the presence of **amyloid plaques.** These are growths of old neural tissue with a central core of amyloid proteins that occupy the regions around neurons. These plaques are surrounded by various microglia. These plaques are about 70 microns in diameter, much larger than the surrounding neurons, which are often only 10 to 30 microns in diameter. Their presence makes it difficult for the neurons to function because they degenerate the neurons' axons.

In addition to these structural changes, Alzheimer's disease is also accompanied by a change in the cholinergic system (Bartus, Dean, Beer, & Lippa, 1982), particularly the manufacturing of the neurotransmitter acetylcholine (ACh), which is critical to learning and memory. Because of the nature of the condition, it is difficult to verify positively that a person has Alzheimer's disease, and not some other neurodegenerative condition, while he or she is alive. Alzheimer's disease is typically only verified during an autopsy.

Causes of Alzheimer's Disease.   Given the number of people who are susceptible to contracting Alzheimer's and the high costs associated with living with this condition, it is critical that the causes—and a cure—for this disease be discovered soon. Right now, no one knows for sure what causes Alzheimer's. However, a number of preconditions that indicate the likelihood of contracting the disease are known (Small, 1998). There appears to be a strong genetic component to the disease. If one of your relatives has Alzheimer's, there is a 25 to 50 percent probability that you will develop it as well. (As you can see, the wide range of percentages illustrates how much more work needs to be done on this issue to understand the true correspondences.) If not, then the probability is only 10 percent. In identical twins, if one of the twins contracts this condition, there is a 40 to 50 percent chance that the other will as well, and a 10 to 50 percent chance for fraternal twins. There is also a higher rate of occurrence of the disease in people with Down's syndrome, also suggesting a genetic component.

Alzheimer's is also more likely to occur as a result of external, environmental experiences as well. For example, people who have suffered head traumas or long periods of depression are more likely to succumb. There do seem to be some protective factors as well. For example, people who have been exposed to estrogen or antioxidants are less likely to get the disease. Similarly, people who experience inflammations in the body, such as arthritis, are less likely to contract Alzheimer's disease later. There may also be some DNA combinations that are more resistant to the development of this condition. Thus, there many factors that impact whether a person will one day have to live with Alzheimer's disease.

Stages of Alzheimer's Disease.   Alzheimer's disease progresses through a series of well-defined stages (Brandt & Rich, 1995); see Table 17.1. The initial stage is a level of mild forgetfulness, such as forgetting where objects had been placed and familiar names. Often it is difficult to distinguish people who have acquired Alzheimer's disease and those who are merely suffering the natural effects of old age. However, there are measurable differences in the episodic, but not short-term, memories of people who will eventually contract the condition up to six years before the condition becoming clinically apparent (Bäckman, Small, & Fratiglioni, 2001).

As the condition progresses, more profound memory loss emerges. In the next stage, the frequency of tip-of-the-tongue situations increases, indicating problems in semantic memory. There is also a decline in spatial memory. At first, a person might be lost only in unfamiliar locations but will then start getting lost in familiar surroundings, such as the grocery store, and may eventually become lost in her own home.

During the next stage of the disease, problems with memory increase along with general cognitive deficits in reasoning and judgment. People in this stage require assistance and cannot function outside the home. They often require help even in the most common daily tasks, such as feeding and bathing. As the disease progresses, memory deficits are so severe

TABLE 17.1   Stages of Alzheimer's Disease

STAGE	CHARACTERISTICS
Initial Stage	Mild forgetfulness
Early Stage	Increased word-finding problems, decline in spatial memory
Intermediate Stage	General cognitive deficits in reasoning and judgment; help needed in common daily tasks, such as feeding and bathing
Late Stage	Person may not recognize family members or even his or her own reflection; loss of communicative skills; infantile reflexes may reemerge
End Stage	Death

that the person may not recognize close family members like a spouse or children, or even his own reflection in a mirror. Eventually, the person's condition deteriorates to a point where she is not communicative, and infantile reflexes may reemerge, leaving little sign of a lifetime's worth of memories. All this is because memories have largely been destroyed. This late stage of the disease may end in the person's death.

Memory Changes.   People with Alzheimer's disease suffer from problems in working memory. These tend not to be problems with maintaining information in the phonological loop and visuo-spatial sketchpad but with controlling the flow of thought through the central executive. That is, these people seem to have normal working memory spans for both verbal and spatial information. However, they do not show normal recency effects for larger sets of information. Furthermore, these people have trouble controlling the flow of thought and regulating the contents of their memories. For example, they have much more trouble than normal people in managing their memories under dual-task conditions where a person needs to keep track of two things at once. As such, a person with this condition can become more easily confused and overwhelmed when there is a need to take note of and process multiple pieces of information at once.

Alzheimer's also has a profound effect on episodic memories, although this loss is not uniform. Instead, there is a temporal gradient to the loss, with newer memories being more likely to be compromised and older memories being more likely to remain intact. This temporal gradient of memory loss can be extensive, reaching back several decades into the person's life. As the disease progresses, and autobiographical memories are affected, losses in earlier and earlier autobiographical memories can result in changes and losses in a person's identity (Addis & Tippett, 2004).

This temporal gradient of memory loss suggests that part of the problem in this condition is the encoding of information into memory and the subsequent retention of information over time. The evidence to date suggests that people with Alzheimer's disease primarily have difficulty with the encoding process. This is supported by neurological work using fMRI scanning showing that the prefrontal lobes of Alzheimer's patients are not functioning as well as normal people's (Corkin, 1998). The rate with which they forget episodic information, once it has been encoded, is the same as that of people without the disease (White & Ruske, 2002). Thus, much of the problem in episodic memory in this condition can be viewed as a form of anterograde amnesia. This results in shallower learning curves and more rapid forgetting rates. Retrieval, while difficult, is less of a problem, at least in the earlier stages of the disease. This deficit is more profound with recall than with recognition.

Although semantic memory is initially more resistant to the effects of Alzheimer's, it does eventually get affected. People with this condition often lose the ability to identify the names of objects in their environment. When this occurs, the person may substitute similar words for the appropriate one—for example, using the word "tiger" or "animal" for "lion." Thus, there is a degree of noise and error that is introduced into semantic memory processing. This influence of Alzheimer's on semantic memory can also be seen in the rate at which different semantic memory abilities are lost. For example, semantic knowledge about how something is used to interact with other objects—that is, its functional relations—is lost sooner than semantic knowledge about its parts and properties, with knowledge about categorical relations being the most resistant (Johnson & Hermann, 1995), although they can become compromised as well later on. Also, with memory for older information, patients with Alzheimer's are more likely to have trouble remembering public information (such as the names of people who were famous some time ago) as compared to autobiographical information (Greene & Hodges, 1996). Here is a case where more stable, and somewhat semanticlike, information is more vulnerable to the disease than the more episodiclike information. What may be causing this is that the public information, in these cases, is more likely to be tied to events of that time and are not like semantic memories in the more standard sense. In this case, the autobiographical information is more resistant to loss because of the greater degree of rehearsal it has had over time.

Although there are many memory systems that are affected by Alzheimer's, as we have seen with more general forms of amnesia, some memory systems are left relatively intact. For example, implicit memory processes are less affected by this condition than are explicit memory processes. This also spills over into related metamemory processes. For example, using the remember-know distinction, Alzheimer's patients show marked declines in memory for information that is marked as "remember" but not for information that is marked as "know" (Barba, 1997). There are some implicit memory processes that do seem to be disrupted. For example, Alzheimer's patients often show impaired performance on semantic priming tasks.

Parkinson's Disease

The diseases we look at now—Parkinson's, Huntington's, and multiple sclerosis—are called subcortical diseases. This is in contrast to Alzheimer's disease, which is a cortical dementia. It should also be noted that not all of the people who contract these diseases become clearly demented. That is, these diseases primarily involve damage to brain structures other than the lobes of the cortex. These subcortical dementias are also often associated with movement difficulties, as well as problems with memory and thinking.

Parkinson's disease is a condition in which there is some damage to or loss of neurons in the basal ganglia and the substantia nigra. This is also accompanied by a disruption in the processing of the neurotransmitter dopamine in the brain. This damage produces problems in coordinating movements, such as tremors, "pill rolling" (rubbing fingers together as if rolling a pill), problems in facial expression, and difficulty in walking. This condition usually begins around the age of 50. In addition to the movement problems, there are general cognitive and emotional deficits, including problems with memory (Brandt & Rich, 1995; Prizzolo et al., 1982).

People with Parkinson's disease have some working memory problems. First, there appear to be problems with their spatial working memories. So with regard to the visuo-spatial sketchpad, people with Parkinson's disease have difficulty updating spatial information. For example, when they travel through a new space in which there are twists and turns, they may become more disoriented and unsure of the direction of their starting location (Montomery et al., 1993). In addition, people with this condition experience problems in the ability to identify the locations of previously seen pictures on a simple display grid (Pillon et al., 1997). They are not keeping track of spatial contextual information the way that a normal person would do almost automatically. Thus, overall, people with Parkinson's disease have trouble remembering the locations of objects they've recently seen in the world and so also have trouble encoding this information into long-term memory.

In addition to the visuo-spatial information processing, it has also been observed that people with Parkinson's disease have trouble with more general, central executive aspects of working memory (Brown & Marsden, 1988). As such, they have some difficulty regulating and controlling their stream of thought and how they are using their memories. For example, these people have difficulty changing strategies when appropriate and will continue doing things the way they've always done them before, such as sorting cards by suit when they should be sorting by value (Canavan et al., 1989).

Like Alzheimer's, with Parkinson's disease there is a loss of episodic memories that follows a temporal gradient, with older memories being more preserved than newer memories. However, with Parkinson's, the extent of the temporal gradient is often not as great. In general, episodic memory loss with the condition is not as noticeable, and forgetting is more normal. Again, not all types of information in memory are handled similarly, and this difference can be seen in how memory for event content is differentially forgotten relative to memory for the date of an event. So while the forgetting of event content is less compromised in Parkinson's than in Alzheimer's, the opposite is true for event date memories.

People with Parkinson's also have a greater difficulty locating events in time (Sagar, Cohen et al., 1988; Sagar, Sullivan, et al., 1988). For example, they have trouble putting pieces of information in the correct sequence, such as a telephone number. Similarly, they have trouble dating events that occurred in their lives. There is also some suggestion that part of the problem with memory for this condition is trouble in coordinating or planning retrieval strategies and not so much the encoding or storage of information. This may be due to a difficulty in properly retrieving script information from semantic memory (Godbout & Doyon, 2000). Specifically, when recalling the components of a common script, such as going to the doctor, people with Parkinson's disease are more likely to leave out some of the more minor components, retrieve script components in the incorrect order, and have more irrelevant intrusions. Thus, there is a general decline in the ability to properly sequence information in memory.

Huntington's Disease

Huntington's disease is a condition characterized by uncontrolled muscle spasms, resulting in jerky movements. This is caused by damage to the basal ganglia and the caudate nucleus. This disease often strikes around the age of 40, and the victim often dies by the age of 60. There is no known cure for this condition. In addition to the movement problems, and some general cognitive and emotional deficits, there are problems in memory (Brandt & Rich, 1995).

People with this condition have problems with the central executive component of working memory, resulting in a reduced memory span and difficulties with dual-task situations (Hodges, 2000). However, unlike Alzheimer's disease, the rate of forgetting in episodic memory may be preserved along with recognition memory performance. Also, importantly, there is no temporal gradient to episodic memory loss. The loss is more uniform across time. This suggests that the problem in this condition is with memory retrieval rather than the encoding and storage of memories.

With Huntington's disease, in episodic memory there may be problems with free recall, although recognition performance is often near normal. This is consistent with the idea that people with this condition have trouble planning how to retrieve information from memory. In general, the memory deficits are often similar to those observed with Parkinson's disease patients. However, these people are more likely to have trouble with memory for nonverbal information, such as faces, spatial layouts, or visual images. Also, unusually, these people also have trouble with procedural memory, even though this memory system is often preserved in people with neurologically related memory loss.

Multiple Sclerosis

Multiple sclerosis is a condition in which there is a demyelinization of various neurons in the nervous system. Although this is generally associated with problems in muscle control, it can have effects on memory as well. One of the more striking impacts this condition has is on short-term memory. There seem to be problems in both creating and retrieving memory traces (Pelosi et al., 1997). There is also a decline in the speed with which short-term memory is scanned, but not so much in the capacity of this memory system (Janculjak, Mubrin, Brinar, & Spilich, 2002). Again, there is also a greater disturbance of explicit memory over implicit memory (Janculjak et al., 2002).

Synopsis

Memory can be devastatingly altered if someone contracts a disease that produces dementia. Alzheimer's, the most common, results in memory being systematically destroyed as drastic changes are made to the structure of the brain. These memory changes are subtle at first but eventually spread to even well-learned, nondeclarative memory systems. Other conditions, such as Parkinson's, Huntington's, and multiple sclerosis, are subcortical diseases that can each have a memory loss component to them but are not as devastating to memory as Alzheimer's. How each condition affects memory depends on the brain structures that are damaged.

MEMORY PROBLEMS ASSOCIATED WITH OTHER CONDITIONS

In this section we consider the problems people can experience as a consequence of other conditions. These are not conditions where memory loss is necessarily the focus, nor are they formally considered dementias. They are confabulation, or the inadvertent generation of false information, schizophrenia, depression, and anxiety.

Confabulation

Some brain-damaged patients report memories that are clearly not based on reality but that make some sort of false memory generated by the patient. This is called **confabulation.** Although this is more of a symptom than a memory syndrome, it is discussed here because of the interesting role memory plays in producing this condition. The false reports that are provided during confabulation are inconsistent with the patient's past and current situations. As with many false memories, these confabulated reports are not lies because there is no intent to deceive. Instead, the patient is reporting what she believes to be the truth. Even when the confabulations are very bizarre, the person is often unaware of any memory problems. Confabulations often occur when a person suffers damage to the frontal lobes. Thus, there is some damage to the central executive processes in working memory. In this case, a person is not able to effectively monitor memory retrieval and evaluate the results of retrieval. As a result, incorrect information is reported as if it corresponded to a true memory.

Confabulatory reports are often confined to episodic memory, with a strong meta-memory sense of remembering or recollecting. Semantic memory is largely unaffected (Barba, 1993). That is, people are unconsciously inventing information about events in their lives. However, their general understanding of how the world is structured and operates is relatively intact.

Schizophrenia

Schizophrenia is a serious mental disorder in which a person becomes detached from reality because of a disruption in the patterns of thinking and perception. There are four basic types of schizophrenia: paranoid, hebephrenic, catatonic, and simple. Thus, schizophrenia is not a single, unitary condition. Instead, this is a term used to describe a wide class of related conditions. The cause of schizophrenia is not completely understood, although it may be related to an imbalance of neurotransmitters, such as dopamine.

Schizophrenics may have amnesia for portions of their episodic memory. Often there is a temporal gradient to the retrograde component of the amnesia, with more severe memory impairment occurring closer to the present and lessening as one progresses backward in time. It is unclear to what degree this memory deficit reflects actual problems with memory per se or is instead only reflective of the general psychological disturbance these people are suffering. More generally, if people have disrupted and fragmented thought processes, it naturally follows that they will have trouble structuring and organizing information. As a result of this low degree of structure, memory will be poorer. With regard to semantic memory, the ability to retain information remains stable, although schizophrenics appear to be less organized in their use of this semantic information.

While schizophrenics may have damage for explicit memory, their implicit memory seems to be better preserved. For example, when given a recognition test and asked to make remember-know distinctions, memory performance is deficient for "remember" responses but not for "know" responses (Huron, et al., 1995). Also, short-term memory appears to remain fairly intact for schizophrenics in the presence of more long-term memory problems (McKenna, Clare, & Baddeley, 1995). When looking at working memory in particular, the phonological loop and visuo-spatial sketchpad appear to be less affected, but there are noticeable problems with the central executive component of working memory. This is not surprising given that one role of the central executive is to help control the flow of thought, and schizophrenics' thinking patterns are very disturbed.

Depression

Memory problems can occur not only with severe pathologies, such as brain damage and schizophrenia, but as a result of other psychological conditions as well. One condition that can also introduce memory problems is **depression.** Depression is an emotional state that, if it persists for long periods of time, can result in problems with memory (Watts, 1995). People who are depressed find it more difficult to successfully encode new information, particularly positive information. Part of this may be due to a decline in the motivation level necessary to perform well. This decreased motivation not only affects the amount of information produced on a free recall test, but it can also be observed as worse memory performance on forced recall and recognition tests. Part of this deficit in long-term memory may reflect a decreased likelihood that depressed people will actively organize information in long-term memory.

It is also interesting to note that depressed people may have selective memory problems. For example, normal people tend to show a preference for remembering positive experiences over negative experiences, something known as the **Pollyanna Principle.** However, depressed people show a greater tendency to remember negative experiences. This seems to be due to a decline in memory for positive information rather than an increase in memory for negative information. For example, in a study by Deldin, Keller, Gergen, and Miller (2001) people were first given a series of faces to look at. These faces expressed positive, neutral, or negative emotions. When taking a later memory test for those faces, during which ERPs were recorded, normal people showed a substantial P300 when they saw positive faces they had seen before, indicating that they recognized the faces. However, depressed people did not show a P300, indicating an absence of recognition processing of this positive information in the brain.

This tendency to remember more negative information is further harmful. Because what is remembered is negative and depressing, the person is always depressed, making her recovery from this condition more difficult. In addition to the mood-congruent effects that are observed in long-term memory, compared to people in positive moods, people who are in negative moods appear to be limited in the amount of information that is activated in semantic memory (Bolte, Goschke, & Kuhl, 2003). So because the range of concepts that becomes available during thinking, people in negative moods may be less able to think creatively because not as much information is available from semantic memory.

Although some aspects of long-term memory are affected with depression, short-term memory tends to remain undisturbed. These people have normal memory spans, and they show normal recency effects, although the primacy effects might be compromised because of problems with long-term memory. This latter finding reflects the fact that depressed people are less likely to exert the effort needed to rehearse information and thus transfer it to long-term memory. Also, in addition to more preserved short-term memory processing, depressed people also do not appear to be suffering from problems in implicit memory.

In very extreme and rare cases, a person's depression can become so extensive that he suffers from the **Cotard delusion.** The Cotard delusion is a mistaken belief that one is dead or even that the world does not exist. This is a condition first described by a French psychiatrist, Jules Cotard, in 1882. A person may come to this condition if there is profound depression with very little emotional response, accompanied by a decline in the ability to access episodic and semantic memories that would help identify the current surroundings and make them seem real (Leafhead & Koplman, 1997). In essence, there is almost a complete lack of feeling of familiarity that would normally accompany memory retrieval.

Anxiety and Stress

Anxiety and **stress** are other mental conditions that can influence memory. Unlike depression, where there is less mental effort expended at making memory work, with anxiety the opposite is true. People exert a great deal of effort to resolve memory problems. These memory problems are more likely to occur with state anxiety (when an otherwise normal person is in an anxious state) than with trait anxiety (for people for whom anxiety is a part of their basic personality) (Watts, 1995).

Unlike depression, there are noticeable problems with short-term memory for those with anxiety. Because the person is actively pursuing one or more lines of thought because of his anxiety, there is less working memory capacity available for maintaining other information. As a result, short-term memory performance suffers, but if a long-term memory task is easy, very little disturbance is observed in long-term memory. If the memory tasks are more difficult, however, such as involving a number of memory failures, an anxious person's memory will show a noticeable deficit. Factors that can assist memory performance, such as providing some semantic structure to the information, can actually lead anxious people to perform better than nonanxious people.

Synopsis

Memory loss can also be a symptom or side effect of other pathological conditions. Confabulation is a symptom of memory problems, in which a person has a great deal of difficulty monitoring the contents and configurations of information that are retrieved from memory. Memories that would normally be rejected are accepted as genuine memories in those with this condition. People with severe mental disturbances, such as schizophrenia, have their conditions worsened by memory problems, such as metacognitive awareness of where memories come from. The conditions of depression and anxiety also have strong memory components. People with severe depression often have difficulty remembering positive information. In contrast, people with severe anxiety have trouble because they are remembering too much, with this extra information crowding out desired working memory processes.

LOSS OF MEMORY OF SPECIFIC KNOWLEDGE OR SKILLS

One distinction that has been made in this book is between autobiographical memories and semantic memories. This difference between these two types of information is also observed in certain types of amnesia. For example, it is possible for a person to have trouble with semantic memory but not autobiographical memory. Yasuda, Watanabe, and Ono (1997) describe a patient, M. N., who sustained (from a tumor) damage to her right hemisphere in the areas where the frontal and temporal lobes meet. She was able to give accurate accounts of her own autobiographical memories, such as where she had gone to school, the places she had worked, and the various illnesses she had throughout her life. However, in marked contrast, she had great difficulty identifying and remembering public events, remembering only 20 percent of events that most people could recall at a near 100 percent level. She had similar problems with historical figures and famous monuments. Other problems can arise within autobiographical memory itself, with people being able to remember information at the event specific but not higher levels, or the reverse (Conway, 1996). This problem with semantic memory leads us to a condition called semantic amnesia.

Semantic Amnesia

Another memory disorder that has not been studied in much detail is **semantic amnesia** (Hodges, Patternson, Oxbuy, & Funnell, 1992; Snowden, Goulding, & Neary, 1989). In this condition a person has a deficit in the ability to retrieve semantic knowledge, often as a result of damage to the temporal lobes, particularly in the anterolateral portions and more likely with damage to the left hemisphere than the right (Patterson & Hodges, 1995). This is a rare condition in the absence of any other neurological syndrome, such as Alzheimer's disease, because many of the main sources of neurological damage tend to affect other areas as well and because this part of the brain is particularly well supported. For example, this portion of the temporal lobe is maintained by two major arteries. This makes it less likely to be the source of damage when a stroke occurs, so semantic amnesia is less common, although it does occur.

People with semantic amnesia are unable to retrieve the meanings of various, even common, words, despite otherwise normal language abilities. For example, a person with semantic amnesia would not be able to remember what a cat or a robin was or whether a mouse has a beak or a long, skinny tail (Funnell, 1995). This loss of an ability to retrieve word meanings in semantic amnesia is called **anomia.** This anomia can sometimes be very specific. For example, one patient, G. R., had difficulty with famous names but not with the names of friends or the names of historical or literary figures (Lucchelli, Muggia, & Spinnler, 1997). G. R.'s memory for knowledge about the person was intact, such as knowing her line of work and any distinguishing achievements or physical features. The only trouble was with remembering the names of these celebrities.

With semantic amnesia and anomia, other parts of memory, including nondeclarative and episodic memories, appear to remain relatively intact (although see following). What distinguishes this condition from aphasia is that people with this condition also have difficulty with semantic judgments that do not require the use of language, suggesting that semantic memory in general has been damaged (Bozeat et al., 2000).

People with semantic amnesia have difficulty not only identifying the names of objects and their semantic associates, but also how these objects are used. People may attempt to use objects in the incorrect manner, such as trying to use a match as a pencil. However, it should be noted that people with this condition may be able to use objects appropriately and even use unfamiliar objects correctly. However, these are typically cases where the use of the objects is fairly clear and constrained by the situation (Hodges et al., 2000)—for example, using a pair of scissors with a piece of paper. There are only a limited number of ways that the scissors lend themselves to being used in that situation, and many people with semantic amnesia would perform normally.

Semantic amnesias can be restricted to very particular types of information. This is clearly illustrated in a person known as A. B. R., who suffers from semantic amnesia as a result of a period of anoxia during open heart surgery. A. B. R. has problems identifying pictures (but not names) of famous people (e.g., Queen Elizabeth and Napoleon) and landmarks (e.g., the White House and the Parthenon). The rest of his semantic and other types of memories appear to be relatively intact (Kartsounis & Shallice, 1996). Another distinction of information in semantic memory that may be affected is the difference between abstract and concrete ideas. In normal people, concrete ideas (such as sock, pencil, dog, etc.) are easier to remember than abstract ideas (truth, love, redemption). There is also a report of the case of a patient, D. M., could identify abstract words but not concrete words. This is the opposite of the normal pattern. In this case, D. M.'s semantic amnesia has affected memory for concrete ideas but left abstract knowledge more intact (Breedin, Saffran, & Coslett, 1994). A similar isolation in semantic amnesia can occur for knowledge of natural kinds versus artifacts (Patterson & Hodges, 1995).

As you can see, there are a wide variety of ways memory can be affected in semantic amnesia, with no clear patterns of memory loss. Some types of memories are damaged, whereas others are preserved. In an effort to bring some coherence to the understanding of semantic amnesia and to illustrate the complexity of the deficits discovered, Cree and McRae (2003) listed the trends seen in the various deficits found in semantic amnesias.

Trend 1. Animals
Trend 2. Nonliving things, excluding foods and musical instruments
Trend 3. Fruits and vegetables
Trend 4. Fruits and vegetables with either animals or nonliving things
Trend 5. Foods with living things
Trend 6. Musical instruments with living things
Trend 7. Living things problems more frequent than nonliving things (p. 167)

From these trends, Cree and McRae were able to extract four dimensions around which semantic memory was organized and the deficits observed. Essentially, these dimensions capture salient characteristics of knowledge, each of which is handled by a different part of the brain. Each type of deficit is a result of damage to a particular part of the brain. Although they appear different on the surface, they all involve the same semantic memory system operating on the same basic principles.

Dimension 1. Visual motion/complexity versus frequency/function
Dimension 2. Distinctive sounds versus distinctive features or names
Dimension 3. Touch/taste/color versus parts/textures
Dimension 4. Smell/correlated features/encyclopedic features versus parts/textures (p. 190)

Each of these dimensions separates out different types of knowledge. For example, Dimension 1 helps distinguish between living and nonliving things. Dimension 2 helps distinguish musical instruments (and guns) from other things. Dimension 3 distinguishes fruits, vegetables, and food from other things. Finally, Dimension 4 distinguishes things like fish, buildings, and foods from musical instruments.

This breakdown helps us understand the complexity of semantic information storage in normal people. Our semantic memories appear to be organized and structured along such dimensions, and future theories of semantic memory will need to take these sorts of findings into account. Moreover, it also helps us understand the problems that people with semantic amnesia faced. Once we better understand their deficits, we can then more confidently link them with underlying neurological or psychological problems and be better prepared to treat them.

Before leaving the topic of semantic amnesia, let's think about what is going on in episodic memory a little more. As a reminder, despite problems in semantic memory, even complex forms of episodic memory, such as laying down new autobiographical memories, appear to be preserved (Simons, Graham, & Hodges, 2002). These preserved autobiographical memories can be used to guide the semantic dementia patient to derive semantic-like knowledge. Using memories of previous autobiographical experiences of what happened during particular events can help people derive some sort of semantic understanding, even though semantic memory itself may be severely compromised (Graham, Ralph, & Hodges, 1997). For example, a person could remember the names of other people she played golf with frequently by using these autobiographical memories, but she would not be able to remember the names of people she had played with in the distant past or the names of famous golfers. However, although there is some preservation of episodic memory, this preservation is incomplete. In an odd reversal of Ribot's Law, what is typically seen in retrograde amnesia, there is a temporal gradient of memory loss. However, rather than poorer memory for recent autobiographical events and better memory for older ones, in semantic amnesia the reverse is true, particularly for semantic aspects of those events, such as people's names (Piolino et al., 2003).

Aphasia, Amusia, and Agnosia

Some forms of semantic amnesia are so exclusive to certain types of knowledge that they can be identified as separate conditions. In some cases, people may lose the ability to remember how to use language, called **aphasia.** Because language is usually located in the left hemisphere of the brain, this is typically a result of damage to that area. There are two general kinds of aphasia that can occur. One type, known as **Broca's aphasia,** occurs when there is damage to the anterior portion of the temporal lobe and the adjoining portions of the frontal lobe. This area is near the motor cortex portion of the frontal lobe. In this condition, a person has difficulty speaking, but language comprehension is relatively well preserved.

The other type of aphasia is called **Wernicke's aphasia.** This aphasia occurs when there is damage to the posterior temporal lobe and the adjoining portions of the parietal lobe. In this condition, a person has difficulty comprehending language, but language production is better preserved. This decline in language comprehension can get to the point where people cannot even monitor their own language. As a result, when they speak, they produce a word salad that is grammatically correct but semantically anomalous. Unlike people with Broca's aphasia, people with Wernike's aphasia are less aware of their deficit. A condition that is very related to aphasia is called **amusia.** People with this deficit may have trouble either comprehending or producing music.

Another specific loss of a certain type of information in memory is **prospagnosia,** or a failure to recognize faces. Essentially, a person with this condition retains memories of who different people are, but he is unable to recognize a person's face, even when he knows the person well. The person may not even be able to recognize his or her own face in a mirror. People with this condition must rely on other cues to identify someone, such as the person's voice. This tells us that different types of knowledge about people are stored or processed using different parts of the brain. Memory retrieval is not a discrete process of remembering or not. Instead, people may be in situations in which they are able to partially remember some information but not all of it.

Phantom Limbs

One final interesting memory condition where people have strong memories of something that no longer exists is **phantom limbs.** When people lose a body part, such as a finger, arm, or leg, due to some trauma, they may feel as though the body part is still present. They report various sensations from the body part, such as pain, cramps, or itching (which, of course, they cannot scratch). This is an interesting memory condition because the person's mind has a memory for the missing body part and how it should feel. These are memories and processes that are part of nondeclarative memory that persist even in the absence of external support.

    The reason for phantom limbs is because over a person's life a portion of his or her brain is devoted to managing the sensory experiences and motor control over that body part, so the neural nets have become highly ingrained. When the body part is lost, those portions of the cortex remain dedicated to it. Because of the stimulation this part of the brain receives from activity in other parts of the nervous system, the well-ordered sets of neurons will continue to fire. This gives these people the sensation than an amputated body part is still there.

Synopsis

It is possible for people to have selective deficits that target memory for certain types of information but that leave other types of information relatively intact. In semantic amnesia, people have difficulty retrieving semantic information about the world, which makes it difficult for them to understand what is going on around them. However, their episodic and autobiographical memories are comparatively well preserved. Memory loss can also target specific abilities, such as loss of language skill memories with aphasia, loss of music skill memories with amusia, and loss of object name knowledge with anomia. Thus, different parts of the brain play specialized roles in remembering various different types of knowledge. Finally, memory can sometimes be erroneous when it causes a person to continue to remember something that no longer exists, as in the case of phantom limbs.

SUMMARY

In this chapter we discussed a number of disorders a person may suffer from in addition to more standard forms of amnesia. The most common of these memory disorders are the various dementias. Some of these, such as Alzheimer's disease, are primarily a result of damage to cortical structures that are important for memory. Others, such as Huntington's and Parkinson's diseases, are primarily a result of damage to subcortical structures. The fact that memory can be profoundly disrupted by damage to this wide variety of neurological structures shows that memory is a complex system made up of many different interlocking components. There was some discussion of how memory can be compromised when people suffer from other sorts of disturbances, such as schizophrenia, or general frontal lobe damage (resulting in confabulation). We also discussed how memory can be disrupted by more normal changes in psychological functioning, such as depression and anxiety. Finally, we discussed some problems that can occur with other forms of memory, such as semantic and nondeclarative memory. Semantic memory deficits often leave a person with a decreased ability to store or retrieve certain types of information, such as words or music. Nondeclarative memory can also have trouble, such as when a person continues to have sensations of limbs that are no longer present. These phantom limbs are memory echoes of physical experiences that had occurred repeatedly in the past and that are projecting themselves into the present.

STUDY QUESTIONS

1. What are the characteristics of Alzheimer's disease? What parts of the brain are affected? How is memory affected?

2. What are some of the subcortical dementias? What parts of the brain are affected? How is memory affected?

3. How does confabulation occur, and how does this inform us about the normal operation of memory?

4. What sorts of memory deficits occur in pathologies involving serious mental disturbances, such as schizophrenia?

5. What sorts of memory problems occur in affective disturbances? With depression? With anxiety?

6. What sort of memory disturbances occur with semantic amnesia? How does this relate to anomia? What types of memory systems are preserved in this condition?

7. What is interesting about episodic memory loss in semantic amnesia?

8. What are aphasia, amusia, and agnosia? What sorts of memories are lost in each of these conditions?

9. How can phantom limbs indicate a problem with memory?

KEY TERMS

Alzheimers' disease, amusia, amyloid plaques, anomia, anxiety, aphasia, Broca's aphasia, confabulation, Cotard delusion, depression, Huntington's disease, neurofibrillary tangles, Parkinson's disease, phantom limbs, Polyanna Principle, prospagnosia, semantic amnesia, stress, Wernike's aphasia

MEMORY METHODS

This appendix provides students who are taking a lab course in memory methods that can be used to calculate various aspects of memory. This is intended to be in addition to any statistical course you may have taken. The qualities of these methods are discussed in Chapter 3, as well as other places throughout the book.

The appendix is divided into three sections. The first describes a signal detection analysis method using easy-to-calculate measures of discrimination and bias. The second is a measure of clustering that can be applied to recall data. The third is a way to use the process dissociation method to provide estimates of implicit and explicit memory processes.

SIGNAL DETECTION ANALYSIS

As described in Chapter 3, by using signal detection analysis, a memory researcher can better correct for guessing and tease apart the influences of discrimination and bias in a person's responses. Signal detection analyses are typically applied to yes-no recognition data—that is, when people are presented with individual items of some sort and are asked to indicate whether each item is old or new. The following is a description of nonparametric measures of discrimination and bias that are relatively easy to calculate and interpret.

The measure of discrimination is A', which is a lot like d' but easier to calculate (following Snodgrass & Corwin, 1988; see also Pollack, 1970). Here is the equation for calculating A' when the number of hits is greater than or equal to the number of false alarms:

$$A' = .5 + [(H - FA)(1 + H - FA)] / [(4H(1 - FA)]$$

However, when the number of hits is less than the number of false alarms, the following formula should be used:

$$A' = .5 - [(F - H)(1 + FA - H)] / [(4FA(1 - H)]$$

B" is a measure of bias, much like β, but, again, easier to calculate and based on the same principles as A'. Here is how to calculate B" when the number of hits is greater than or equal to the number of false alarms:

$$B'' = [H(1 - H) FA(1 FA)] / [H(1 H) + FA(1 FA)]$$

However, when the number of hits is less than the number of false alarms, this formula should be used:

$$B'' = [FA(1 - FA) - H(1 - H)] / [FA(1 - FA) + H(1 - H)]$$

For these formulas, an A' value of .5 corresponds to chance discrimination (i.e., no discrimination). That is, when A' values are around .5, it is unlikely that a person is reliably recognizing old information and rejecting new information. An A' value of 1 corresponds to perfect discrimination. That is, the person is perfectly detecting old information in memory and rejecting new information. A' values of less than .5 indicate below chance identification. This may mean that the person is using memory in a consistent and reliable way but not in the way you are intending or hypothesizing. If A' is negative, then you've calculated it wrong.

With regard to the bias measure, negative B" values correspond to conservative responses. That is, people are being very careful about what they are willing to identify as recognized. In contrast, positive B" values correspond to liberal responses. That is, people are very willing to say that any given item has been encountered before and is remembered. B" values of zero correspond to no bias. Finally, B" values greater than 1 or less than −1 indicate that you've done something wrong in your calculations.

CLUSTERING

Another thing a person doing a memory study may want to know is how information is structured or organized in memory. One way to do this is verifying if the way a person structures information in memory corresponds to a predetermined structure the researcher hypothesizes people will use. For example, if a person knows that experts tend to organize information in a certain way, you can assess the degree to which a given person's own organization of this information in memory matches that of the expert. This would tell you something about the level of this person's expertise.

This measure of organization is called an ARC score, for Adjusted Ratio of Clustering. ARC scores are applied to data from recall tests. Essentially, what is going to happen is that people will be asked to recall a set of information that was learned earlier. Then, using a preconceived idea about how the information could be organized in memory, the researcher will assess the degree to which the organization approaches that ideal, taking chance into account. The basic formula for calculating an ARC score is as follows:

$$ARC = (R - E(R)) / (maxR - E(R))$$

In this formula, R stands for the number of observed categorical repetitions—that is, how many times during a person's recall were two items from the same predetermined category recalled together—for example, recalling two animal names one after the other. E(R) is the number of categorical repetitions that would be expected by chance given the categories being tested for and how much the person actually recalled. In some sense, this is the amount of error that might be expected in the data. This is the formula for calculating E(R):

$$E(R) = \frac{\Sigma n_i^2}{N} - 1$$

Here, n refers to the number of items recalled from a given category i, and N is the number of items recalled by the person.

Finally, maxR refers to the maximum number of repetitions possible if clustering perfectly conformed to expectations, again given the categories being tested and the amount of information actually recalled. The formula for calculating maxR is as follows:

$$maxR = N - k$$

Here, the value for N, again, is the number of items recalled by the person, and k is the number of categories present in a person's recall. This calculation will result in a number that is something like a ratio, although not quite. Perfect clustering will result in an ARC score of 1, whereas chance clustering will result in a score of 0. Variations in the degree of clustering will result in values between these two. It should also be noted that it is possible to get negative ARC scores. This indicates clustering below chance. If this value is a relatively large negative number, it might suggest that people have organized the information in memory in some way other than the categories defined by the experimenter.

A related measure is the ARC' score (Pelligrino, 1971) which looks at sequential order across multiple recall attempts, rather than categorical groupings. Here is a simplified version for pairs of repetitions (rather than triples or larger units) and assuming unidirectional recall. The basic structure of the formula is similar to the ARC score. The formula for ARC' is as follows:

$$ARC' = O(ITR) - E(ITR) / max(ITR) - E(ITR)$$

Here *ITR* refers to intertrial repetitions. *O(ITR)* are the number of observed repetitions, which is derived by counting up the number of times a particular item follows another. For example, if people were to recall the months of the year, this would count as 1 if July followed June on trial t and $t+1$. The formula for *E(ITR)*, the number of times a repetition would occur across trials by chance, is as follows:

$$E(ITR) = (N - 1)!(M - 3 + R) / N!$$

Here *M* is the number of items recall on trial t, *N* is the number of items recalled on trial $t+1$, and *R* is number of items pairs that are recalled on trial t, but one or both of these items are not recalled on trial $t+1$. The explanation point is a mathematical symbol of a factorial function. Finally, the formula for *max(ITR)*, the maximum number of intertrial repetitions, is as follows:

$$max(ITR) = M - 3$$

PROCESS DISSOCIATION

The process dissociation procedure is a simple way of trying to separate out the influence of conscious and unconscious memory processes. Although this method is not completely precise and reliable in all cases, for the purposes of course work, it should be just fine. Essentially, the way the method works is by comparing people's performance in two conditions. In one condition, both conscious and unconscious processes are hypothetically working in the same way. This is called the *inclusion condition*. In the second, these processes would be working in opposition to one another. This is called the *exclusion condition*. By looking at the difference in memory performance in these two conditions, one can derive estimates of how each process is being affected by the manipulation of interest.

In the inclusion condition, people are asked to do some task that theoretically would involve implicit and explicit memory working together—for example, asking a person to report words, such as animal names, that had been seen earlier on a list of animal names. A person can do this task using either conscious or unconscious influences. The basic idea is that in the inclusion condition people can do the task using both explicit and implicit memory performance to produce words that were on the previous list. This is expressed in the following formula:

$$I = R + F - RF$$

In this formula, I stands for the inclusion condition, R stands for recollection—the explicit, conscious process—and F stands for familiarity—the implicit, unconscious process. So the rate of remembering old items on the inclusion condition reflects the rate of explicitly recollecting items, plus the rate of remembering items based solely on implicit familiarity, minus the portion where these two overlap (e.g., if you recall something consciously, the additional unconscious familiarity doesn't give you any additional benefit).

In contrast, in the exclusion condition, people are asked to do something that puts implicit and explicit memory processes in opposition. For example, people might see a list of animal names at the initial part of the study. Then a person would be asked to report a list of animals as long as she did not use any from the list heard earlier. Thus, words from the previous list that are reported are almost certainly due to unconscious memory processes because if the person consciously remembered them, she should not report it. This is expressed in this formula:

$$E = F (1 - R)$$

In this formula, E stands for the exclusion condition. So the rate of remembering old items is the rate at which the implicit memory processes retrieve this information, minus those that are rejected because they are also consciously remembered.

Thus, by separating out performance in the exclusion condition from performance on the inclusion condition, one is left with the contribution of explicit memory. This can be expressed by this formula:

$$R = I - E$$

What is due to implicit memory can also be estimated using this conceptualization. The estimate for familiarity can be expressed as follows:

$$F = E / (1 - I + E)$$

acetylcholine   A neurotransmitter important for establishing new memories. For example, low levels of acetylcholine are implicated in Alzheimer's disease

action potential   The electrical component of neural communication. The action potential occurs when a neuron "fires" by shifting the electrical charge of the neuron from –70 mv to +40 mv

additive factors logic   A method of using response times, developed by Sternberg, to study human thought processes. This process is done by comparing various conditions of different levels of complexity

ad hoc categories   Categories that are not stored previously in long-term memory but are generated on the fly in the service of some goal

"aha" effect   This refers to better memory for problem solutions that are generated as compared to those that are simply provided

amnesia   An inability to remember beyond what is observed with normal forgetting

amygdala   A portion of the limbic system that is critical for processing emotional aspects of memory

anorthoscopic perception   An iconic memory phenomenon in which people are able to identify an object rapidly passed behind a narrow slit

anterograde amnesia   Amnesia forward in time. An inability to acquire new memories

articulatory loop   The portion of the phonological loop in working memory that actively rehearses verbal/auditory information

associative interference   Interference that occurs during memory retrieval as a result of increased numbers of associations with a concept (see also fan effect)

autobiographical memory   Memory for one's life narrative

backward telescoping   The finding that very recent memories will be reported as being older than they actually are

Baddeley and Hitch model   A popular model of working memory involving a central executive and two slave systems: the phonological loop and the visuo-spatial sketchpad

basal ganglia   A collection of subcortical structures that are involved in memory. These structures include the caudate nucleus, the putamen, the globus pallidus, and the subthalamic nucleus and are located above and around the thalamus. Important for memories involving habits and motor skills

behaviorism   A school of psychological thought, dominant in the mid-twentieth century, that placed a heavy emphasis on studying observable behavior and actively avoided making assumptions about or studying thought

bias   A tendency to be more liberal or conservative in reporting information from memory

category   A semantic memory representation in which several separate entities are treated as if they are functionally equivalent in some way

Category Adjustment Theory   A fuzzy trace theory of memory that assumes that people use coarse-grained, categorical representations and fine-grained, detailed representations to make decisions about what is remembered from the past

cerebellum   A subcortical structure located at the back of the brain and involved in memory. This structure is involved in memory for fine motor skills

chunking   The process of organizing multiple units of information into a single mental representation in memory

classical conditioning   A form of nondeclarative memory that involves creating associations between environmental stimuli and ensuing responses

cognitive revolution   The period in time during the 1950s and 1960s when there was a shift from behaviorism to an accepted study of mental processes (cognitive psychology)

collaborative facilitation   Increased performance on a recognition test that occurs when people work in groups

collaborative inhibition   Decreased performance on a recall test that occurs when people work in groups

computer-assisted tomography   Also known as a CT or CAT scan. A neuroimaging technique that involves taking multiple x-ray "slices" of the brain

concreteness effect   The finding that information that refers to concrete ideas (e.g., tree) is better remembered than information that refers to abstract ideas (e.g., truth)

connectionist models   See parallel distributed processing models

consolidation   The process of solidifying memory traces in the neural structure over very long periods of time

cryptomnesia   Unconscious plagiarism brought about by lack of memory for source information

cued recall   A recall method in which a person is given part of the information as a cue for the recall of the rest

decay   Forgetting caused by the passage of time alone

declarative memory   A portion of memory that is open to conscious inspection and verbalization

dendrites   The part of an individual neuron that is primarily specialized for receiving signals from other neurons

diencephalon   A portion of the brain including the thalamus and hypothalamus that primarily serves as a routing station. It is involved in memory for conscious, factual knowledge

directed forgetting   The intentional forgetting of information. This usually occurs when people are instructed to forget or disregard some set of information

discrimination   A component of signal detection theory of memory that refers to the ability to distinguish old from new information

distributed practice   When the rehearsing of information in memory is spread out over several occasions rather than lumped into a single session (see massed practice). This leads to better memory

distributed storage models   Models of memory that assume that information in memory traces are distributed across a large set of relatively simple individual units

dopamine   This is a neurotransmitter that is important for memory. For example, people with Parkinson's disease have lower than normal dopamine levels

Dual Code Theory   A theory of memory that assumes that people are able to store information in either perceptual codes and/or verbal codes

dual process theories   Models of memory that assume there are two retrieval processes: an automatic activation one and a deliberative search one

Easterbrook hypothesis   The theory that at heightened levels of emotion, attention becomes increasingly focused on a small subset of details, leaving memory for peripheral details poorer

echoic memory   The sensory register dedicated to the brief retention of auditory information

eidetic imagery   A term used to describe a type of photographic memory

elaborative rehearsal   Rehearsing information in memory by building on and elaborating the information that is provided with other information that is already known. Thus, inferences make for more complex and elaborate memory trace

embodied cognition   The theoretical idea that cognitive processes, including memory, are strongly influenced and guided by the fact that we inhabit bodies that interact with the world in certain ways. That is, our bodily interactions with the world are incorporated into how we think about things

emergent property   A property of a system that does not exist in any of its parts but that emerges out of the combination of the parts into a new system

enactment effect   The finding that memory is better for information that was actually performed

encoding specificity   The finding that memory retrieval can sometimes be better when the retrieval context matches the encoding context

engram   Another name for a memory trace

episodic memory   Memory for the individual events a person experiences

executive controller   A portion of working memory that manage attentional resources and the processing of the two slave systems

explicit memory   Memory that involves conscious awareness—that is, a person is aware that she is using her memory to perform some task

false fame effect   Inappropriately labeling a nonfamous person as famous because his name elicits a feeling of familiarity

false memories   Memories for events that never actually occurred

fan effect   An increase in response times or error rates, with an increase in the number of associations with a concept

feeling of knowing   A metacognitive judgment a person can make about the likelihood of later recognizing something that cannot be currently recalled

field memories   The experience of remembering an event from one's own perspective

flashbulb memories   Highly detailed memories for the events of learning highly surprising and significant news

forced recall   A type of recall test in which a person is forced to recall a certain amount of information

forced choice recognition A type of recognition test in which a person must select one item from among a set of alternatives, such as a multiple-choice test

forgetting curve A change in memory performance over time as information is being lost over the retention period. Most forgetting curves are negatively accelerated functions, with the most forgetting occurring early on and less forgetting occurring later (per unit of time)

forward telescoping The finding that older memories will be reported as being more recent than they actually are

free recall A recall measure in which people are provided with very little information but are expected to generate and report as much as possible

frequency effect The influence of prior frequency of information on memory retrieval

frontal lobes The lobes of the cortex located at the front of the head. These lobes are involved in memory by controlling the flow and coordination of various memory processes, including both long-term memory and working memory

functional magnetic resonance imaging The neuroimaging technique of tracking oxygen level concentrations to measure cerebral blood flow under various conditions

fuzzy trace theories These are theories of memory that assume that memory performance is a reflection of multiple types of mental representations working in combination

generation effect The finding that information that was generated by a person is remembered better than information that was only seen or heard

Gestalt psychology An early school of psychological thought, originating in Germany, that emphasized molar levels of analysis. Known for the concepts that the whole is different from the sum of its parts and representational isomorphism

global matching models Models of memory that assume that memory retrieval occurs through a massively parallel process in which all memory traces are compared with information in a memory probe but for which only some are activated

HERA model The Hemispheric Encoding/Retrieval Asymmetry model. It suggests that the left frontal lobes are primarily involved in semantic retrieval and episodic encoding, whereas the right frontal lobes are primarily involved in episodic retrieval

hindsight bias The tendency to misremember the past in a way consistent with a person's current state of mind

hippocampus The limbic system structure that is often implicated in memory encoding

hypermnesia The phenomenon of greater memory retrieval after subsequent retrieval attempts

iconic memory The sensory register dedicated to the brief retention of visual information

imagination inflation The greater likelihood of remembering something as having been experienced before when a person tries to imagine the event

implicit memory This refers to memory that is unconscious and out of awareness. That is, a person is not aware that they are using his or her memory to perform some task

incidental learning Situations in which a person memorizes information without explicitly trying to

indirect memory tasks Tasks that assess memory performance that minimize a person being consciously aware that his memory is being used and/or tested

infantile amnesia Difficulty remembering life events from the period of infancy

inhibition A mental mechanism that actively suppresses related but irrelevant memory traces

instrumental conditioning A form of learning that involves either reinforcing or extinguishing associations between a response produced by an organism and the ensuing consequences of that response

intentional learning Situations in which a person explicitly memorizes information

interference A primary source of forgetting in memory in which different memory traces compete with one another for retrieval, making it difficult to access the desired information

intrusions Information that is reported on a recall test that was not experienced previously

judgments of learning Metamemory ratings of how well a person feels that he has learned something

knew-it-all-along effect The tendency for people to misremember and think that they knew more in the past than they actually did

laterality The primary localization of a function in either the left or right hemisphere of the brain. Often laterality does not imply that one function is completely in one hemisphere but that one hemisphere is dominant for that function and does it much better than the other

learning Any change in the potential of a person to change her behavior as a consequence of some experience

learning curve   A change in memory performance over time as information is being acquired. Most learning curves are negatively accelerated functions, with the most learning occurring early on and less learning occurring later (per unit of time)

levels of processing   The idea that more elaboratively (or deeply) processed information is remembered better than more superficially (or shallowly) processed information

lexical decision task   A commonly used indirect memory task that requires people to indicate whether a given string of letters is a word or not. Both response time and error rates are considered dependent variables

long-term memory   This part of the modal model of memory is where information is held for longer periods of time (generally longer than 30 seconds) and that has a functionally unlimited capacity

long-term potentiation   Relatively long-lasting durability of neural connections that may serve as one of the initial encoding aspects to move information into long-term memory

long-term working memory   A set of retrieval cues assembled in working memory to make accessing information in long-term memory more efficient. This develops in parallel with a cognitive skill

Magnetic Resonance Imaging   A neuroimaging technique that relies on the natural oscillations of atoms that make up various components of the brain and nervous system

massed practice   When the rehearsing of information in memory is lumped into a single session rather than spread out over several occasions (see **distributed practice**). This leads to poorer memory

mediated priming   Priming of concepts that are mediated by a related concept—for example, the priming of "stripes" by "lion" through the concept of "tiger"

memorists   People with an exceptional memory ability of some sort

memory   The retention of information over a period of time involving encoding, storage, and retrieval

mere exposure effect   The finding that people prefer things that they have been exposed to before relative to things they have not been exposed to, even if they are unaware of this exposure

metamemory   Conscious knowledge of one's own memory contents, processes, and effectiveness

mnemonic   Any device (broadly speaking) used to help a person remember

modal model of memory   This is the standard model of memory developed by Atkinson and Shiffrin (1968). This model is composed of the sensory registers, a short-term store, control processes, and a long-term store

mood-congruent memory   The finding that people remember information better when they are in the same mood at retrieval as they were in during encoding

naming task   An indirect memory task that requires a person to name words that are visually presented. Response time is the typical dependent measure

negative transfer   The decreased ability to learn new information because of prior known information that is related to it

network theories   Theories of memory that assume that associative relations among concepts are stored directly in long-term memory

neural networks   See parallel distributed processing models

neuron   An individual cell that serves as the basic building block of the nervous system and, hence, memory

neurotransmitters   Chemicals in the nervous system that are released from the terminal buttons of one neuron into a synapse. These neurotransmitters then affect the firing pattern of the postsynaptic neurons

nondeclarative memory   A portion of memory that is not open to conscious inspection and verbalization

nonsense syllable   A type of stimulus used to study memory performance in the absence of prior knowledge. These often come in the form of consonant-vowel-consonant (CVC) trigrams

observer memories   The experience of remembering an event in which one sees oneself from a third-person perspective

occipital lobes   These are the lobes of the neocortex located at the back of the brain. These lobes are primarily responsible for visual processing

old-new recognition   A form of recognition test in which a person is to indicate whether each item is either old (remembered) or new (not remembered)

overlearning   Continuing to study information even after perfect memory retrieval has been achieved. This often results in a greater resistance to forgetting

paired associate   A pair of items presented during learning in a memory experiment. One word would serve as the context or cue for the retrieval of the other word during a memory test

parallel processing When memory encoding or retrieval involves engaging multiple processes at the same time, possibly toward a common end

parallel distributed processing models Theories of memory that assume that information is represented in a massively interconnected network in which information is encoded by the strength of the associations among the units

parietal lobes The lobes of the cerebral cortex located in front of the occipital lobes and behind the frontal lobes. Often involved in working memory processes, such as those involving the visuo-spatial sketchpad

part-set cuing The finding that it is harder to retrieve any given item from a set after a person has been given a subset of that set as a retrieval cue

permastore Memory traces that are in a long-term state in which very little is susceptible to forgetting

phantom limbs Memory traces that produce sensations of body parts that have been amputated

phonological loop One of the slave systems of working memory that is primarily responsible for processing auditory and verbal information

phonological store The portion of the phonological loop part of the working memory system that maintains auditory and verbal information over short periods of time

picture superiority effect The finding that memory is generally better for pictures than for words

Pollyanna Principle The idea that positive information tends to be remembered better than negative information

positron Emission Tomography Also known as PET. This is a neuroimaging technique that involves tracking blood flow under various conditions. This tracking is done by measuring concentrations of a radioactive isotope that has been injected into the bloodstream

primacy effect Better memory for information presented at the beginning of a series

priming A process of making some memories more available by previously retrieving memories that are similar to them in some way

proactive interference Interference forward in time. When previously known information makes it more difficult to retrieve information learned later that is related to it

prospagnosia An inability to use memory for faces

prospective memory Memory to engage in actions in the future at a predetermined time or event

psychogenic amnesia Amnesia that is a result of psychological causes with no known underlying neurological abnormalities

recall A type of memory test that requires a person to generate information

recency effect Better memory for information presented at the end of a series

recognition A type of memory test that requires a person to assess whether information that is presented has been encountered before

reminiscence The remembering of previously forgotten information

recognition failure Information that is recalled but not recognized

reminiscence bump A bump in a memory curve reflecting an increase in memory reports from the period between ages 15 and 25

repetition blindness Failing to consciously identify an entity (such as a word) in the environment when it follows soon after a person sees an initial entity of that type

retrieval-induced inhibition Any finding in which the act of retrieval of some information makes it harder to remember other, related pieces of information

retrieval plan A system of retrieval cues subjectively devised by a person to aid in the recall of large sets of information

retroactive interference Interference backward in time. When newly learned information makes it more difficult to retrieve older, learned information that is related to it

retrograde amnesia Amnesia backward in time. An inability to retrieve memories of things that happened prior to an injury

retrospective memory The opposite of prospective memory. Memory for the past

revelation effect The increasing in reporting something as remembered (either accurately or not) when it is slowly revealed over time rather than revealed all at once

rote rehearsal The practice of trying to memorize information simply by repeating it over and over, and ignoring the meaning of the information

savings A reduction in the amount of effort needed to learn a set of information on a subsequent attempt after some forgetting has already occurred

scale effect The finding that when people are asked to locate memories in time, they may be accurate at one scale (e.g., day of the week) but inaccurate at another (e.g., number of weeks in the past)

semantic amnesia   Severe loss of memory for general knowledge about the world

semantic memory   Memory for general world, encyclopedic knowledge that is generally shared with one's community

sensory registers   A part of the modal model of memory where sensory information is held in modality specific stores. Sensory registers generally have a very large capacity but a very short duration

serial position curve   Memory performance changes as a function of when items appeared in the series. Often there is a primacy effect and a recency effect

serial processing   When memory encoding or retrieval involves engaging multiple processes in sequence

short-term memory   A part of the modal model of memory is where information is held for a period of generally no longer than 30 seconds unless rehearsed. Control processes can operate on information in this memory store. Finally, short-term memory has a very limited capacity of 7 ± 2 chunks of information

signal detection theory   A data analytical approach that allows researchers to separate out the influences of discrimination and bias on performance

sleeper effect   The finding that people are more willing to accept previously rejected opinions over time when a low credible source is forgotten

source monitoring   Remembering where information in memory came from

state-dependent memory   The finding that it is easier to remember information when people are in a similar physiological state during retrieval as they were during the original encoding of the information

subtractive factors logic   A method of using response times, developed by Donders, to study human thought processes. This is done by comparing various conditions in which the process of interest is present in one condition but absent in the other

suffix effect   A decreased recency effect in a short-term memory serial position curve as a result of presenting an additional, nominally unrelated item at the end

temporal lobes   One of the lobes of the neocortex located below and behind the frontal lobes. Probably the portion of the cortex most strongly associated with memory storage

terminal buttons   Part of a neuron at the end tips of an axon where the neurotransmitters are stored before being released into the synapse

thalamus   A midbrain structure that is involved in memory by coordinating different types of information from different parts of the brain

threshold model   A model of memory that assumes that retrieval occurs when the activation of a memory trace exceeds some preset level

tip-of-the-tongue state   The feeling of imminent remembering in a case where a person has forgotten something, such as a word or name

transfer appropriate processing   The finding that it is easier to remember information when the mental processes used at retrieval are more similar to the ones used at encoding

Transient Global Amnesia   A brief period of amnesia typically lasting 24 hours or less

triarchic theory of memory   A theory of memory by Endel Tulving that assumes that memory is divided into three primary components: (1) procedural memory, (2) semantic memory, and (3) episodic memory

Tulving-Wiseman Function   A formal, mathematical function that describes recognition failure

verbal learning   A research tradition in memory that existed in the context of a behaviorist psychology and stemmed from Ebbinghaus's work with nonsense syllables. People working in this tradition often used tasks such as the learning of paired-associate lists of words

verbal overshadowing   Poorer memory for information that is later described as compared to information that is not described

verbal reports   A method of studying memory by asking people to report the contents of their current state of consciousness—that is, what they are currently thinking about

visuo-spatial sketchpad   The slave system of working memory primarily responsible for processing visual and spatial information

Von Restorff effect   The finding that information is remembered better if it is relatively distinct compared to other information a person was exposed to at the time

weapon focus effect   The finding that attention, and hence memory, for an event is altered toward a weapon when one is present in an event, leading to poorer memory for nonweapon components of the event

working memory   The portion of memory dedicated to processing information in the short term, including the active manipulation of that information. The Baddeley and Hitch model is a common framework for understanding working memory

Yerkes-Dodson law   The theory that memory performance overall declines at high levels of arousal. This theory is not well supported

BIBLIOGRAPHY

Abbot, V., Black, J. B., & Smith, E. E. (1985). The representation of scripts in memory. *Journal of Memory and Language, 24,* 179–199.

Addis, D. R., & Tippett, L. J. (2004). Memory of myself: Autobiographical memory and identity in Alzheimer's disease. *Memory, 12,* 56–74.

Ahn, W., Kim, N. S., Lassaline, M. E., & Dennis, M. J. (2000). Causal status as a determinant of feature centrality. *Cognitive Psychology, 41,* 361–416.

Alba, J. W., & Hasher, L. (1983). Is memory schematic? *Psychological Bulletin, 93,* 203–231.

Albert, M. S., & Kaplan, E. (1980). Organic implications of neuropsychological deficits in the elderly. In L. W. Poon, J. L. Fozard, L. S. Cermak, D. Arenberg, & L. W. Thompson (Eds.), *New Directions in Memory and Aging,* pp. 403–432. Hillsdale, NJ: Erlbaum.

Algom, D. (1992). Memory psychophysics: An examination of its perceptual and cognitive prospects. In D. Algom (Ed.), *Psychophysical Approaches to Cognition,* pp. 441–513. New York: North Holland.

Algom, D., & Lubel, S. (1994). Psychophysics in the field: Perception and memory for labor pain. *Perception & Psychophysics, 55,* 133–141.

Algom, D., Wolf, Y., & Bergman, B. (1985). Integration of stimulus dimensions in perception and memory: Composition rules and psychophysical relations. *Journal of Experimental Psychology: General, 114,* 451–471.

Alley, T. R., & Cunningham, M. R. (1991). Averaged faces are attractive, but very attractive faces are not average. *Psychological Science, 2,* 123–125.

Anderson, J. R. (1974). Retrieval of propositional information from long-term memory. *Cognitive Psychology, 6,* 451–474.

Anderson, J. R. (1976). *Language, Memory, and Thought.* Hillsdale, NJ: Erlbaum.

Anderson, J. R. (1983). *The Architecture of Cognition.* Cambridge, MA: Harvard University Press.

Anderson, J. R. (2000). *Learning and Memory: An Integrated Approach.* New York: Wiley.

Anderson, M. C. (2003). Rethinking interference theory: Executive control and the mechanisms of forgetting. *Journal of Memory and Language, 49,* 415–455.

Anderson, M. C., & Bell, T. (2001). Forgetting our facts: The role of inhibitory processes in the loss of prepositional knowledge. *Journal of Experimental Psychology: General, 130,* 544–570.

Anderson, M. C., Bjork, E. L., & Bjork, R. A. (2000). Retrieval-induced forgetting: Evidence for a recall-specific mechanism. *Psychonomic Bulletin & Review, 7,* 522–530.

Anderson, M. C., Green, C., & McCulloch, K. C. (2000). Similarity and inhibition in long-term memory: Evidence for a two-factor theory. *Journal of Experimental Psychology: Learning, Memory, and Cognition, 26,* 1141–1159.

Anderson, M. C., & McCulloch, K. C. (1999). Integration as a general boundary condition on retrieval-induced forgetting. *Journal of Experimental Psychology: Learning, Memory, and Cognition, 25,* 608–629.

Anderson, M. C., & Neely, J. H. (1996). Interference and inhibition in memory retrieval. In E. L. Bjork & R. A. Bjork (Eds.), *Memory: Handbook of Perception and Cognition,* pp. 237–313. San Diego, CA: Academic Press.

Anderson, M. C., & Spellman, B. A. (1995). On the status of inhibitory mechanisms in cognition: Memory retrieval as a model case. *Psychological Review, 102,* 68–100.

Anderson, R. B., Garavan, H., Rivardo, M. G., & Chadwick, R. (1997). Inhibitory consequences of memory selection. *Acta Psychologica, 96,* 155–166.

Anderson, R. C., and Pichert, J. W. (1978). Recall of previously unrecallable information following a shift in perspective. Journal of Verbal Learning and Verbal Behavior, 17, 1–12.

Anderson, S. J., & Conway, M. A. (1993). Investigating the structure of autobiographical memories. *Journal of Experimental Psychology: Learning, Memory and Cognition, 19,* 1178–1196.

Anderson, S. J., & Conway, M. A. (1997). Representations of autobiographical memories. In M. A. Conway (Ed.), *Cognitive Models of Memory.* Cambridge, MA: MIT Press.

Andrade, J. (1995). Learning during anaesthesia: A review. *British Journal of Psychology, 86,* 479–506.

Andrés, P., Van der Linden, M., & Parmentier, F. B. R. (2004). Directed forgetting in working memory: Age-related differences. *Memory, 12,* 248–256.

Anisfeld, M., & Lambert, W. E. (1966). When are pleasant words learned faster than unpleasant words. *Journal of Verbal Learning and Verbal Behavior, 5,* 132–141.

Arbuckle, T. Y., & Cuddy, L. L. (1969). Discrimination of item strength at time of presentation. *Journal of Experimental Psychology, 81,* 126–131.

Arkes, H. R., Wortman, R. C., Saville, P. D., & Harkness, A. R. (1981). Hindsight bias among physicians weighing the likelihood of diagnosis. *Journal of Applied Psychology, 66,* 584–588.

Armstrong, S. L., Gleitman, L. R., & Gleitman, H. (1983). What some concepts might not be. *Cognition, 13,* 263–308.

Assefi, S. L., & Garry, M. (2003). Absolute memory distortions: Alcohol placebos influence the misinformation effect. *Psychological Science, 14,* 77–80.

Atkinson, R. C., & Juola, J. F. (1973). Factors influencing speed and accuracy of word recognition. *Attention and Performance, 6,* 583–612.

Atkinson, R. C., & Juola, J. F. (1974). Search and decision processes in recognition memory. In D. H. Krantz, R. C. Atkinson, R. D. Luce, & P. Suppes (Eds.), *Contemporary Developments in Mathematical Psychology,* pp. 243–293. San Francisco, CA: Freeman.

Atkinson, R. C., & Shiffrin, R. M. (1968). Human memory: A proposed system and its control processes. *The Psychology of Learning and Motivation, 2,* 89–195.

Auble, P. M., Franks, J. J., Soraci, S. A. J. (1979). Effort toward comprehension: Elaboration or "aha!"? *Memory & Cognition, 7,* 426–434.

Averbach, E. (1963). The span of apprehension as a function of exposure duration. *Journal of Verbal Learning and Verbal Behavior, 2,* 60–64.

Ayers, T. J., Jonides, J., Reitman, J. S., Egan, J. C., & Howard, D. A. (1979). Differing suffix effects for the same physical suffix. *Journal of Experimental Psychology: Human Learning and Memory, 5,* 315–321.

Bäckman, L., Small, B. J., & Fratiglioni, L. (2001). Stability of preclinical episodic memory deficit in Alzheimer's disease. *Brain, 124,* 96–102.

Baddeley, A. D. (1966). Short-term memory for word sequences as a function of acoustic, semantic, and formal similarity. *Quarterly Journal of Experimental Psychology, 18,* 302–309.

Baddeley, A. D. (1986). *Working Memory.* Oxford: Oxford University Press.

Baddeley, A. D., & Andrade, J. (2000). Working memory and the vividness of imagery. *Journal of Experimental Psychology: General, 129,* 126–145.

Baddeley, A. D., & Hitch, G. (1974). Working memory. *Psychology of Learning and Motivation, 8,* 47–89.

Baddeley, A. D., Thomson, N., & Buchanan, M. (1975). Word length and the structure of short-term memory. *Journal of Verbal Learning and Verbal Behavior, 14,* 575–589.

Baddeley, A. D., & Warrington, E. K. (1970). Amnesia and the distinction between long- and short-term memory. *Journal of Verbal Learning and Verbal Behavior, 9,* 176–189.

Baddeley, A. D., & Wilson, B. (1985). Phonological coding and short-term memory in patients without speech. *Journal of Memory and Language, 24,* 490–502.

Bahrick, H. P. (1983). The cognitive map of a city: 50 years of learning and memory. *The Psychology of Learning and Motivation, 17,* 125–163.

Bahrick, H. P. (1984). Semantic memory content in permastore: Fifty years of memory for Spanish vocabulary learned in school. *Journal of Experimental Psychology: General, 113,* 1–29.

Bahrick, H. P. (2000). Long-term maintenance of knowledge. In E. Tulving & F. I. M. Craik (Eds.), *The Oxford Handbook of Memory,* pp. 347–362. New York: Oxford University Press.

Bahrick, H. P., Bahrick, P. O., & Wittlinger, R. P. (1975). Fifty years of memory for names and faces: A cross-sectional approach. *Journal of Experimental Psychology: General, 104,* 54–75.

Bahrick, H. P., & Hall, L. K. (1991). Lifetime maintenance of high school mathematics content. *Journal of Experimental Psychology: General, 120,* 20–33.

Ballard, P. B. (1913). Oblivescence and reminiscence. *British Journal of Psychology Monograph Supplements, 1,* 1–82.

Banks, W. P. (1970). Signal detection theory and human memory. *Psychological Bulletin, 74,* 81–99.

Banks, W. P. (1977). Encoding and processing of symbolic information in comparative judgments. *The Psychology of Learning and Motivation, 11,* 101–159.

Banks, W. P., Clark, H. H., & Lucy, P. (1975). The locus of the semantic congruity effect in comparative judgments. *Journal of Experimental Psychology: Human Perception and Performance, 104,* 35–47.

Barba, G. D. (1993). Confabulation: Knowledge and recollective experience. *Cognitive Neuropsychology, 10,* 1–20.

Barba, G. D. (1997). Recognition memory and recollective experience in Alzheimer's disease. *Memory, 5,* 657–672.

Barbizet, J. (1970). *Human Memory and Its Pathology.* San Francisco: Freeman.

Barsalou, L. W. (1983). Ad hoc categories. *Memory & Cognition, 11,* 211–227.

Barsalou, L. W. (1988). The contents and organization of autobiographical memories. In U. Neisser & E. Winograd (Eds.) *Remembering Reconsidered: Ecological and Traditional Approaches to the Study of Memory.* New York: Cambridge University Press.

Barsalou, L. W., & Sewell, D. R. (1985). Contrasting the representation of scripts and categories. *Journal of Memory and Language, 24,* 646–665.

Bartlett, F. C. (1932). *Remembering: A study in experimental and social psychology.* Cambridge University Press.

Bartlett, J. C., & Snelus, P. (1980). Lifespan memory for popular songs. *American Journal of Psychology, 93,* 551–560.

Barton, S. B., & Sanford, A. J. (1993). A case study of anomaly detection: Shallow semantic processing and cohesion establishment. *Memory & Cognition, 21,* 477–487.

Bartus, R. T., Dean, R. L., Beer, B., & Lippa, A. S. (1982). The cholinergic hypothesis of geriatric memory dysfunction. *Science, 217,* 408–417.

Basden, B. H., Basden, D. R., Bryner, S., & Thomas, R. L. (1997). A comparison of group and individual remembering: Does collaboration disrupt retrieval strategies? *Journal of Experimental Psychology: Learning, Memory, and Cognition, 23,* 1176–1189.

Basden, B. H., Basden, D. R., & Morales, E. (2003). The role of retrieval practice in directed forgetting. *Journal of Experimental Psychology: Learning, Memory, and Cognition, 29,* 389–397.

Basden, B. H., Basden, D. R., & Stephens, J. P. (2002). Part-set cuing of order information in recall tests. *Journal of Memory and Language, 47,* 517–529.

Basden, D. R., Basden, B. H., & Galloway, B. C. (1977). Inhibition with part-list cuing: Some tests of the item strength hypothesis. *Journal of Experimental Psychology: Human Learning and Memory, 3,* 100–108.

Batchelder, W. H., & Riefer, D. M. (1980). Separation of storage and retrieval factors in free recall of clusterable pairs. *Psychological Review, 87,* 375–397.

Batchelder, W. H., & Riefer, D. M. (1999). Theoretical and empirical review of multinomial process tree modeling. *Psychonomic Bulletin & Review, 6,* 57–86.

Bauer, P. J. (1996). What do infants recall of their lives? *American Psychologist, 51,* 29–41.

Bauer, P. J. (2002). Long-term recall memory: Behavioral and neuro-developmental changes in the first two years of life. *Current Directions in Psychological Science, 11,* 137–141.

Bauer, P. J., Wiebe, S. A., Carver, L. J., Waters, J. M., & Nelson, C. A. (2003). Developments in long-term memory late in the first year of life: Behavioral and electrophysiological indices. *Psychological Science, 14,* 629–635.

Bäuml, K. (2002). Semantic generation can cause episodic forgetting. *Psychological Science, 13,* 356–360.

Bäuml, K., & Hartinger, A. (2002). On the role of item similarity in retrieval-induced forgetting. *Memory, 10,* 215–224.

Bäuml, K., & Kuhbandner, C. (2003). Retrieval-induced forgetting and part-list cuing in associatively structured lists. *Memory & Cognition, 31,* 1188–1197.

Bayen, U. J., Nakamura, G. V., Dupuis, S. E., & Yang, C. (2000). The use of schematic knowledge about sources in source monitoring. *Memory & Cognition, 28,* 480–500.

Bayes, U. J., Nakamura, G. V., Dupuis, S. E., & Yang, C. (2000). The use of schematic knowledge about sources in source monitoring. *Memory & Cognition, 28,* 480–500.

Begg, I. M., Robertson, R. K., Gruppuso, V., Anas, A., & Needham, D. R. (1996). The illusory-knowledge effect. *Journal of Memory and Language, 35,* 410–433.

Beilock, S. L., Bertenthal, B. I., McCoy, A. M., & Carr, T. H. (2004). Haste does not always make waste: Expertise, direction of attention, and speed versus accuracy in performing sensorimotor skills. *Psychonomic Bulletin & Review, 11,* 373–379.

Beilock, S. L., & Carr, T. H. (2001). On the fragility of skilled performance: What governs choking under pressure? *Journal of Experimental Psychology: General, 130,* 701–725.

Belleville, S., Caza, N., & Peretz, I. (2003). A neuropsychology argument for a processing view of memory. *Journal of Memory and Language, 48,* 686–703.

Bellezza, F. S. (1992). Recall of congruent information in the self-reference task. *Bulletin of the Psychonomic Society, 30,* 275–278.

Belli, R. F., Lindsay, D. S., Gales, M. S., & McCarthy, T. T. (1994). Memory impairment and source misattribution in postevent misinformation experiments with short retention intervals. *Memory & Cognition, 22,* 40–54.

Bentin, S. (1989). Electrophysiological studies of visual word perception, lexical organization, and semantic processing: A tutorial review. *Language and Speech, 32,* 205–220.

Bentin, S., McCarthy, G., & Wood, C. C. (1985). Event-related potentials, lexical decision and semantic memory. *Electroencephalography and Clinical Neurophysiology, 60,* 343–355.

Berkerian, D. A., & Bowers, J. M. (1983). Eyewitness testimony: Were we misled? *Journal of Experimental Psychology: Learning, Memory, and Cognition, 9,* 139–145.

Bernstein, D. M., Godfrey, R. D., Davidson, A., & Loftus, E. F. (2004). Conditions affecting the revelation effect for autobiographical memory. *Memory & Cognition, 32,* 455–462.

Bernstein, D. M., Whittlesea, B. W. A., & Loftus, E. F. (2002). Increasing confidence in remote autobiographical memory and general knowledge: Extensions of the revelation effect. *Memory & Cognition, 30,* 432–438.

Berntsen, D., & Rubin, D. C. (2002). Emotionally charged autobiographical memories across the life span: The recall of happy, sad, traumatic, and involuntary memories. *Psychology and Aging, 17,* 636–652.

Berntsen, D. & Rubin, D. C. (2004). Cultural life scripts structure recall from autobiographical memory. *Memory & Cognition, 32,* 427–442.

Biederman, I., Cooper, E. E., Fox, P. W., & Mahadevan, R. S. (1992). Unexceptional spatial memory in an exceptional memorist. *Journal of Experimental Psychology: Learning, Memory, and Cognition, 18,* 654–657.

Bieman-Copland, M. C., & Charness, N. (1994). Memory knowledge and memory monitoring in adulthood. *Psychology and Aging, 9,* 287–302.

Bishop, D. V. M., & Robson, J. (1989). Unimpaired short-term memory and rhyme judgment in congenitally speechless individuals: Implications for the notion of "articulatory coding." *Quarterly Journal of Experimental Psychology, 41A,* 123–140.

Bjork, E. L., & Bjork, R. A. (2003). Intentional forgetting can increase, not decrease, residual influences of to-be-forgotten information. *Journal of Experimental Psychology: Learning, Memory, and Cognition, 29,* 524–531.

Bjork, R. A. (1970). Positive forgetting: The noninterference of items intentionally forgotten. *Journal of Verbal Learning and Verbal Behavior, 9,* 255–268.

Bjork, R. A. (1989). Retrieval inhibition as an adaptive mechanism in human memory. In H. L. Roediger & F. I. M. Craik (Eds.), *Varieties of Memory and Consciousness,* pp. 309–330. Hillsdale, NJ: Erlbaum.

Bjorklund, D. F., & Zeman, B. R. (1982). Children's organization and metamemory awareness in their recall of familiar information. *Child Development, 53,* 799–810.

Björkman, M., Lundberg, I., & Tärnblom, S. (1960). On the relationship between percept and memory: A psychophysical approach *The Scandinavian Journal of Psychology, 1,* 136–144.

Blakemore, C. (1977). *Mechanics of the Mind.* Cambridge, England: Cambridge University Press.

Blakemore, C., & Cooper, G. F. (1970). Development of the brain depends on the visual environment. *Nature, 228,* 477–478.

Blanchet, S., Desganges, B., Denise, P., Lechevalier, B., Eustache, F., & Faure, S. (2001). New questions on the hemispheric encoding/retrieval asymmetry (HERA) model assessed by divided visual-field tachistoscopy in normal subjects. *Neuropsychologia, 39,* 502–509.

Blaney, P. H. (1986). Affect and Memory: A Review. *Psychological Bulletin, 99,* 229–246.

Blank, H., Fischer, V., & Erdfelder, E. (2003). Hindsight bias in political elections. *Memory, 11,* 491–504.

Blaxton, T. A., (1989). Investigating dissociations among memory measures: Support for a transfer-appropriate processing framework. *Journal of Experimental Psychology: Learning, Memory, and Cognition, 15,* 657–668.

Blaxton, T. A., & Neely, J. H. (1983). Inhibition from semantically related primes: Evidence of a category-specific inhibition. *Memory & Cognition, 11,* 500–510.

Bliss, J. C., Crane, H. D., Mansfield, P. K., & Townsend, J. T. (1966). Information available in brief tactile presentations. *Perception & Psychophysics, 1,* 273–283.

Bliss, T. V. P., & Collingridge, G. L. (1993). A synaptic model of memory: Long-term potentiation in the hippocampus. *Nature, 232,* 31–39.

Bliss, T. V. P., & Lomo, T. (1973). Long-lasting potentiation of synaptic transmission in the dentate area of the anaesthetized rabbit following stimulations of the preforant path. *Journal of Physiology, 232,* 331–356.

Bolte, A., Goschke, T., & Kuhl, J. (2003). Emotion and intuition: Effects of positive and negative mood on implicit judgments of semantic coherence. *Psychological Science, 14,* 416–421.

Bornstein, R. F. (1989). Exposure and affect: A review and meta-analysis of research, 1968–1987. *Psychological Bulletin, 106,* 265–289.

Bornstein, B. H., & Neely, C. B. (2001). The revelation effect in frequency judgment. *Memory & Cognition, 29,* 209–213.

Bousfield, A. K., & Bousfield, W. A. (1966). Measurement of clustering and of sequential constancies in repeated free recall. *Psychological Reports, 19,* 935–942.

Bousfield, W. A., (1953). The occurrence of clustering in the recall of randomly arranged associates. *Journal of General Psychology, 49,* 229–240.

Bower, G. H. (1981). Mood and memory. *American Psychologist, 36,* 129–148.

Bower, G. H., Black, J. B., & Turner, T. J. (1979). Scripts in memory for text. *Cognitive Psychology, 11,* 117–220.

Bower, G. H., Clark, M. C., Lesgold, A. M., & Winzenz, D. (1969). Hierarchical retrieval schemes in recall of categorized word lists. *Journal of Verbal Learning and Verbal Behavior, 8,* 323–343.

Bower, G. H., Karlin, M. B., & Dueck, A. (1975). Comprehension and memory for pictures. *Memory & Cognition, 3,* 216–220.

Bower, G. H., & Rinck, M. (2001). Selecting one among many referents in spatial situation models. *Journal of Experimental Psychology: Learning, Memory, and Cognition, 27,* 81–98.

Bozeat, S., Lamdon Ralph, M. A., Patterson, K., Garrard, P., & Hodges, J. R. (2000). Non-verbal semantic impairment in semantic dementia. *Neuropsychologia, 38,* 1207–1215.

Bradburn, N. M., Rips, L. J., & Shevell, S. K. (1987). Answering autobiographical questions: The impact of memory and inference on surveys. *Science, 236,* 157–161.

Bradley, M. M., Greenwald, M. K., Petry, M. C., & Lang, P. J. (1992). Remembering pictures: Pleasure and arousal in memory. *Journal of Experimental Psychology: Learning, Memory, and Cognition, 18,* 379–390.

Brainerd, C. J., Payne, D. G., Wright, R., & Reyna, V. F. (2003). Phantom recall. *Journal of Memory and Language, 48,* 445–467.

Brainerd, C. J., Reyna, V. F., & Mojardin, A. H. (1999). Conjoint recognition. *Psychological Review, 106,* 160–179.

Brainerd, C. J., Wright, R., Reyna, V. F., & Mojardin, A. H. (2001). Conjoint recognition and phantom recognition. *Journal of Experimental Psychology: Learning, Memory, and Cognition, 27,* 307–327.

Brandt, J., & Rich, J. B. (1995). Memory disorders in the dementias. In A. D. Baddeley, B. A. Wilson, & F. N. Watts (Eds.), *Handbook of Memory Disorders,* pp. 243–270. New York: Wiley.

Bransford, J. D., Barclay, J. R., & Franks, J. J. (1972). Sentence memory: A constructive versus interpretive approach. *Cognitive Psychology, 3,* 193–209.

Bransford, J. D., & Franks, J. J. (1971). The abstraction of linguistic ideas. *Cognitive Psychology, 2,* 331–350.

Bransford, J. D., & Johnson, M. K. (1972). Contextual prerequisites for understanding: Some investigations of comprehension and recall. *Journal of Verbal Learning and Verbal Behavior, 11,* 717–726.

Bransford, J. D., & Stein, B. S. (1984). *The Ideal Problem Solver.* New York: Freeman.

Braver, T. S., Barch, D. M., Keys, B. A., Carter, C. S., Cohen, J D., Kaye, J. A., Janowsky, J. S., Taylor, S. F., Yesavage, J. A., Mumenthaler, M. S., Jagust, W. J., & Reed, B. R. (2001). Context processing in older adults: Evidence for a theory relating cognitive control to neurobiology in healthy aging. *Journal of Experimental Psychology: General, 130,* 746–763.

Brédart, S., Lampinen, J. M., & Defeldre, A. C. (2003). Phenomenal characteristics of cryptomnesia. *Memory, 11,* 1–11.

Breedin, S. D., Saffran, E. M., & Coslett, H. B. (1994). Reversal of the concreteness effect in a patient with semantic dementia. *Cognitive Neuropsychology, 11,* 617–660.

Brewer, W. F., & Treyens, J. C. (1981). Role of schemata in memory for places. *Cognitive Psychology, 13,* 207–230.

Brigham, J. C., & Cairns, D. L. (1988). The effect of mugshot inspections on eyewitness identification accuracy. *Journal of Applied Social Psychology, 18,* 1394–1410.

Brooks, D. N., & Baddeley, A. D. (1976). What can amnesic patients learn? *Neuropsychologia, 14,* 111–122.

Brown, A. S. (1991). A review of the tip-of-the-tongue experience. *Psychological Bulletin, 109,* 204–223.

Brown, A. S. (1998). Transient global amnesia. *Psychonomic Bulletin & Review, 5,* 401–427.

Brown, A. S. (2002). Consolidation theory and retrograde amnesia in humans. *Psychonomic Bulletin & Review, 9,* 403–425.

Brown, A. S., & Halliday, H. E. (1991). Cryptomnesia and source memory difficulties. *American Journal of Psychology, 104,* 475–490.

Brown, E., Deffenbacher, K., & Sturgill, W. (1977). Memory for faces and the circumstances of encounter. *Journal of Applied Psychology, 62,* 311–318.

Brown, G. D. A. (1997). Formal models of memory for serial order: A review. In M. A. Conway (Ed.), *Cognitive Models of Memory,* pp. 47–78. Cambridge, MA: MIT Press.

Brown, J. (1958). Some tests of the decay theory of immediate memory. *Quarterly Journal of Experimental Psychology, 10,* 12–21.

Brown, N. R. (1990). Organization of public events in long-term memory. *Journal of Experimental Psychology: General, 119,* 297–314.

Brown, N. R., Rips, L. J., & Shevell, S. K. (1985). The subjective dates of natural events in very-long-term memory. *Cognitive Psychology, 17,* 139–177.

Brown, N. S., & Schopflocher, D. (1998a). Event clusters: An organization of personal events in autobiographical memory. *Psychological Science, 9,* 470–475.

Brown, N. S., & Schopflocher, D. (1998b). Event cueing, event clusters, and the temporal distribution of autobiographical memories. *Applied Cognitive Psychology, 12,* 305–319.

Brown, R., & Kulik, J. (1977). Flashbulb memories. *Cognition, 5,* 73–99.

Brown, R., & McNeill, D. (1966). The "tip of the tongue" phenomenon *Journal of Verbal Learning and Verbal Behavior, 5,* 325–337.

Brown, R. G., & Marsden, C. D. (1988). Internal versus external cues and the control of attention in Parkinson's disease. *Brain, 111,* 323–345.

Bruner, J. (1991). The narrative construction of reality. *Critical Inquiry, 18,* 1–21.

Bruner, J. S., Goodnow, J. J., & Austin, G. A. (1956). *A study of thinking.* Oxford, England: Wiley.

Buckner, R. L. (1996). Beyond HERA: Contributions of specific prefrontal brain areas to long-term memory retrieval. *Psychonomic Bulletin & Review, 3,* 149–158.

Burgess, A. P., & Ali, L. (2002). Functional connectivity of gamma EEG activity is modulated at low frequency during conscious recollection. *International Journal of Psychophysiology, 46,* 91–100.

Burgess, N., & Hitch, G. J. (1992). Toward a network model of the articulatory loop. *Journal of Memory and Language, 31,* 429–460.

Burgess, P. W., & Shallice, T. (1997). The relationship between prospective and retrospective memory: Neurological evidence. In M. A. Conway (Ed.), *Cognitive Models of Memory,* pp. 247–272. Cambridge, MA: MIT Press.

Burke, D. M., White, H., & Diaz, D. L. (1987). Semantic priming in young and older adults: Evidence for age constancy in automatic and attentional processes. *Journal of Experimental Psychology: Human Perception and Performance, 13,* 79–88.

Burns, D. J. (1989). Proactive interference: An individual-item versus relational processing account. *Journal of Memory and Language, 28,* 345–359.

Burns, D. J. (1992). The consequences of generation. *Journal of Memory and Language, 31,* 615–633.

Burt, C. D. B. (1992). Retrieval characteristics of autobiographical memories: Event and date information. *Applied Cognitive Psychology, 6,* 389–404.

Burt, C. D. B., Kemp, S., & Conway, M. A. (2003). Themes, events, and episodes in autobiographical memory. *Memory & Cognition, 31,* 317–325.

Burt, C. D. B., Mitchell, D. A., Raggatt, P. T. F., Jones, C. A., & Cowan, T. M. (1995). A snapshot of autobiographical memory retrieval characteristics. *Applied Cognitive Psychology, 9,* 61–74.

Burt, C. D. B., Watt, S. C., Mitchell, D. A., & Conway, M. A. (1998). Retrieving the sequence of autobiographical event components. *Applied Cognitive Psychology, 12,* 321–338.

Butler, J., & Rovee-Collier, C. (1989). Contextual gating of memory retrieval. *Developmental Psychobiology, 22,* 533–552.

Cahill, C., & Frith, C. (1995). Memory following electroconvulsive therapy. In A. D. Baddeley, B. A. Wilson, & F. N. Watts (Eds.), *Handbook of Memory Disorders,* pp. 319–335. New York: Wiley.

Cameron, T. E., & Hockley, W. E. (2000). The revelation effect for item and associative recognition: Familiarity versus recollection. *Memory & Cognition, 28,* 176–183.

Campbell, R., & Dodd, B. (1982). Some suffix effects on lipread lists. *Canadian Journal of Psychology, 36,* 508–514.

Canas, J. J., & Nelson, D. L. (1986). Recognition and environmental context: The effect of testing by phone. *Bulletin of the Psychonomic Society, 24,* 407–409.

Canavan, A. G. M., Passingham, R. E., Marsden, C. D., Quinn, N., Wyke, M., & Polkey, C. E. (1989). The performance on learning tasks of patients in the early stages of Parkinson's disease. *Neuropsychologia, 27,* 141–156.

Candel, I., Merckelbach, H., & Zandbergen, M. (2003). Boundary distortions for neutral and emotional pictures. *Psychonomic Bulletin & Review, 10,* 691–695.

Cann, A., & Ross, D. A. (1989). Olfactory stimuli as context cues in human memory. *American Journal of Psychology, 102,* 91–102.

Cantor, J., & Engle, R. W. (1993). Working-memory capacity as long-term memory activation: An individual differences approach. *Journal of Experimental Psychology: Learning, Memory, and Cognition, 19,* 1101–1114.

Cantor, J., Engle, R. W., & Hamilton, G. (1991). Short-term memory, working memory, and verbal abilities: How do they relate? *Intelligence, 15,* 229–246.

Carmichael, L., Hogan, H. P., & Walter, A. A. (1932). An experimental study of the effect of language on the reproductions of visually perceived forms. *Journal of Experimental Psychology, 15,* 73–86.

Carrier, L. M., & Pashler, H. (1995). Attentional limits in memory retrieval. Journal of Experimental Psychology: Learning, Memory, and Cognition, 21, 1339–1348.

Carter, H. D. (1936). Emotional correlates of errors in learning. *Journal of Educational Psychology, 27,* 55–67.

Carter, H. D., Jones, H. E., & Shock, N. W. (1934). An experimental study of affective factors in learning. *Journal of Educational Psychology, 25,* 203–215.

Case, R. (1972). Validation of a neo-Piagetian mental capacity construct. *Journal of Experimental Child Psychology, 14,* 287–302.

Cech, C. G., Shoben, E. J., & Love, M. (1990). Multiple congruity effects in judgments of magnitude. *Journal of Experimental Psychology: Learning, Memory, and Cognition, 16,* 1142–1152.

Ceci, S. J., & Bruck, M. (1993). Suggestibility of the child witness: A historical review and synthesis. *Psychological Bulletin, 113,* 403–439.

Cerella, J. (1994). Generalized slowing in Brinley plots. *Journal of Gerontology: Psychological Sciences, 49,* P65-P71.

Cermak, L. S., & O'Connor, M. (1983). The anterograde and retrograde retrieval ability of a patient with amnesia due to encephalitis. *Neuropsychologia, 21,* 213–234.

Charles, S. T., Mather, M., & Carstensen, L. L. (2003). Aging and emotional memory: The forgettable nature of negative images for older adults. *Journal of Experimental Psychology: General, 132,* 310–324.

Chase, W. G., & Simon, H. A. (1973). Perception in chess. *Cognitive Psychology, 4,* 55–81.

Chen, Y., & Blanchard-Fields, F. (2000). Unwanted thought: Age differences in the correction of social judgments. *Psychology and Aging, 15,* 475–482.

Chew, E. I., & Richardson, J. T. E. (1980). The relationship between perceptual and memorial psychophysics. *Memory & Cognition, 16,* 25–26.

Chi, M. T. H., & Koeske, R. D. (1983). Network representation of a child's dinosaur knowledge. *Developmental Psychology, 19,* 29–39.

Chiappe, P., Hasher, L., & Siegel, L. S. (2000). Working memory, inhibitory control, and reading disability. *Memory & Cognition, 28,* 8–17.

Chin-Parker, S., & Ross, B. H. (2002). The effect of category learning on sensitivity to within-category correlations. *Memory & Cognition, 30,* 353–362.

Chorover, S. L., & Schiller, P. H. (1965). Short-term retrograde amnesia in rats. *Journal of Comparative and Physiological Psychology, 59,* 73–78.

Christiaansen, R. E., & Ochalek, K. (1983). Editing misleading information from memory: Evidence for the co-existence of original and postevent information. *Memory & Cognition, 11,* 467–475.

Christianson, S. (1989). Flashbulb memories: Special, but not so special. *Memory & Cognition, 17,* 435–443.

Christianson, S. (1992). Emotional stress and eyewitness memory: A critical review. *Psychological Bulletin, 112,* 284–309.

Chu, S., & Downes, J. J. (2002). Proust nose best: Odors are better cues of autobiographical memory. *Memory & Cognition, 30,* 511–518.

Chugani, H. T., Phelps, M. E., & Mazziotta, J. C. (1986). Positron emission tomography study of human brain functional development. *Annals of Neurology, 22,* 487–497.

Chwilla, D. J., Kolk, H. J., & Mulder, G. (2000). Mediated priming in the lexical decision task: Evidence from event-related potentials and reaction time. *Journal of Memory and Language, 42,* 314–341.

Ciranni, M. A., & Shimamura, A. P. (1999). Retrieval-induced forgetting in episodic memory. *Journal of Experimental Psychology: Learning, Memory, and Cognition, 25,* 1403–1414.

Clare, J., & Lewandowsky, S. (2004). Verbalizing facial memory: Criterion effects in verbal overshadowing. *Journal of Experimental Psychology: Learning, Memory, and Cognition, 30,* 739–755.

Clark, S. E., & Gronlund, S. D. (1996). Global matching models of recognition memory: How the models match the data. *Psychonomic Bulletin & Review, 3,* 37–60.

Clark, S. E., Hori, A., Putnam, A., & Martin, T. P. (2000). Group collaborations in recognition memory. *Journal of Experimental Psychology: Learning, Memory and Cognition, 26,* 1578–1588.

Clayton, K., & Chattin, D. (1989). Spatial and semantic priming effects in tests of spatial knowledge. *Journal of Experimental Psychology: Learning, Memory, & Cognition, 15,* 495–506.

Clayton, K., & Habibi, A. (1991). Contributions of temporal contiguity to the spatial priming effect. *Journal of Experimental Psychology: Learning, Memory, & Cognition, 17,* 263–271.

Cockburn, J. (1995). Task interruption in prospective memory: A frontal lobe function? *Cortex, 31* 87–97.

Cohen, N. J., & Squire, L. R. (1981). Retrograde amnesia and remote memory impairment, *Neuropsychologia, 19,* 337–356.

Colcombe, S. J., & Wyer, R. S. (2002). The role of prototypes in the mental representation of temporally related events. *Cognitive Psychology, 44,* 67–103.

Coles, M. G. H., Gratton, G., & Fabiani, M. (1990). Event-related brain potentials. In J. T. Cacioppo & L. G. Tassinary (Eds.), *Principles of Psychophysiology: Physical, Social, and Inferential Elements,* pp. 413–455. Cambridge, England: Cambridge University Press.

Colle, H. A., & Welsh, A. (1976). Acoustic masking in primary memory. *Journal of Verbal Learning and Verbal Behavior, 15,* 17–32.

Collins, A. M., & Loftus, E. F. (1975). A spreading activation theory of semantic processing. *Psychological Review, 82,* 407–428.

Collins, A. M., & Quillian, M. R. (1969). Retrieval time from semantic memory. *Journal of Verbal Learning and Verbal Behavior, 8,* 240–247.

Collins, A. M., & Quillian, M. R. (1972). How to make a language user. In E. Tulving & W. Donaldson (Eds.), *Organization and Memory,* pp. 309–351. New York: Academic Press.

Conrad, R. (1960). Very brief delay of immediate recall. *Quarterly Journal of Experimental Psychology, 12,* 45–47.

Conrad, R. (1965). Order error in immediate recall of sequences. *Journal of Verbal Learning and Verbal Behavior, 4,* 161–169.

Conrad, R. & Hull, A. (1964). Information, acoustic confusion, and memory span. *British Journal of Experimental Psychology, 55,* 75–84.

Conway, A. R. A., & Engle, R. W. (1994). Working memory and retrieval: A resource-dependent inhibition model. *Journal of Experimental Psychology: General, 123,* 354–373.

Conway, M. A. (1996). Autobiographical memory. In E. L. Bjork & R. A. Bjork (Eds.), *Memory.* San Diego: Academic Press.

Conway, M. A. (1996). Failures in autobiographical memory. In D. J. Herrmann, C. McEvoy, C. Hertzog, P. Hertel, & M. K. Johnson (Eds.), *Basic and Applied Memory Research: Theory in Context,* pp. 295–315. Mahwah, NJ: Erlbaum.

Conway, M. A., Anderson, S. J., Larsen, S. F., Donnelly C. M., McDaniel, M. A., McClelland, A. G. R., Rawles, R. E., & Logie, R. H. (1994). The formation of flashbulb memories. *Memory & Cognition, 22,* 326–343.

Conway, M. A., & Berkerian, D. A. (1987). Organization of autobiographical memory. *Memory & Cognition, 15,* 119–132.

Conway, M. A., Cohen, G., & Stanhope, N. (1991). On the very long-term retention of knowledge acquired through formal education: Twelve years of cognitive psychology. *Journal of Experimental Psychology: General, 120,* 395–409.

Conway, M. A., Harries, K., Noyes, J., Racma'ny, M., & Frankish, C. R. (2000). The disruption and dissolution of directed forgetting: Inhibitory control of memory. *Journal of Memory and Language, 43,* 409–430.

Conway, M. A. & Pleydell-Pearce, C. W. (2000). The construction of autobiographical memories in the self-memory system. *Psychological Review, 107,* 261–288.

Cooke, N. J., & Breedin, S. D. (1994). Constructing naive theories of motion on the fly. *Memory & Cognition, 22,* 474–493.

Copeland, D. E., & Radvansky, G. A. (2001). Phonological similarity in working memory. *Memory & Cognition, 29,* 774–776.

Corkin, S. (1968). Acquisition of motor skill after bilateral medial temporal-lobe excision. *Neuropsychologia, 6,* 255–265.

Corkin, S. (1998). Functional MRI for studying episodic memory in aging and Alzheimer's disease. *Geriatrics, 53,* S13-S15.

Corkin, S., Amaral, D. G., González, R. G., Johnson, K. A., & Hyman, B. T. (1997). H. M.'s medial temporal lobe lesions: Findings from magnetic resonance imaging. *Journal of Neuroscience, 17,* 3964–3979.

Costermans, J., Lories, G., & Ansay, C. (1992). Confidence level and feeling of knowing in question answering: The weight of inferential processes. *Journal of Experimental Psychology: Learning, Memory, & Cognition, 18,* 142–150.

Cowan, N. (2000). The magical number 4 in short-term memory: A reconsideration of mental storage capacity. *Behavioral and Brain Sciences, 24,* 87–185.

Cowan, N., Baddeley, A. D., Elliott, E. M., & Norris, J. (2003). List composition and the word length effect in immediate recall: A comparison of localist and globalist assumptions. *Psychonomic Bulletin & Review, 10,* 74–79.

Cowan, N., Suomi, K., & Morae, P. A. (1982). Echoic storage in infant perception. *Child Development, 53,* 984–990.

Crabb, B. T., & Dark, V. J. (2003). Perceptual implicit memory relies on intentional load-sensitive processing at encoding. *Memory & Cognition, 31,* 997–1008.

Craik, F. I. M., & Byrd, M. (1982). Aging and cognitive deficits: The role of attentional resources. In F. I. M. Craik & S. Trehub (Eds.), *Aging and Cognitive Processes,* pp. 191–211. New York: Plenum Press.

Craik, F. I. M., & Lockhart, R. S. (1972). Levels of processing: A framework for memory research. *Journal of Verbal Learning and Verbal Behavior, 12,* 671–684.

Cree, G. S., & McRae, K. (2003). Analyzing the factors underlying the structure and computation of the meaning of chipmunk, cherry, chisel, cheese, and cello (and many other such concrete nouns). *Journal of Experimental Psychology: General, 132,* 163–201.

Crowder, R. G. (1972). Visual and auditory memory. In J. F. Kavanagh & I. G. Mattingly (Eds.), *Language by Ear and by Eye.* Cambridge, MA: MIT Press.

Crowder, R. G., & Morton, J. (1969). Precategorical acoustic storage (PAS). *Perception & Psychophysics, 5,* 365–373.

Curiel, J. M., & Radvansky, G. A. (1998). Mental organization in maps. *Journal of Experimental Psychology: Learning, Memory, & Cognition, 24,* 202–214.

Curran, T., & Friedman, W. J. (2003). Differentiating location- and distance-based processes in memory for time: An ERP study. *Psychonomic Bulletin & Review, 10,* 711–717.

Curran, H. V. (1991). Benzodiazapines, memory, and mood: A review. *Psychopharmacology, 105,* 1–8.

Cutting, J. E. (2003). Gustave Caillebotte, French Impressionism, and mere exposure. *Psychonomic Bulletin & Review, 10,* 319–343.

Dagenbach, D., Horst, S., and Carr, T. H. (1990). Adding new information to semantic memory: How much learning is enough to produce automatic priming? *Journal of Experimental Psychology: Learning, Memory, and Cognition, 16,* 581–591.

Daneman, M., & Carpenter, P. A. (1980). Individual differences in working memory and reading. *Journal of Verbal Learning and Verbal Behavior, 19,* 430–466.

Daneman, M., and Merikle, P. M. (1996). Working memory and language comprehension: A meta-analysis. *Psychonomic Bulletin and Review, 3,* 422–433.

Darwin, C. J., Turvey, M. T., & Crowder, R. G. (1972). An auditory analogue of the Sperling partial report procedure: Evidence for brief auditory storage. *Cognitive Psychology, 3,* 255–267.

Davis, G., Shepherd, J., & Ellis, H. (1979). Effects of interpolated mugshot exposure on accuracy of eyewitness identification. *Journal of Applied Psychology, 64,* 232–237.

Deese, J. (1959). On the prediction of occurrence of particular verbal intrusions in immediate recall. *Journal of Experimental Psychology, 58,* 17–22.

De Groot, A. M. B. (1983). The range of automatic spreading activation in word priming. *Journal of Verbal Learning and Verbal behavior, 22,* 417–436.

Dehon, H., & Brédart, S. (2004). False memories: Young and older adults think of semantic associates at the same rate, but young adults are more successful at source monitoring. *Psychology and Aging, 19,* 191–197.

Deldin, P. J., Keller, J., Gergen, J. A., & Miller, G. A. (2001). Cognitive bias and emotion in neuropsychological models of depression. *Cognition and Emotion, 15,* 787–802.

DeLoache, J. S., Cassidy, D. J., & Brown, A. L. (1985). Precursors of mnemonic strategies in very young children's memory. *Child Development 56,* 125–137.

Dempster, F. N. (1992). The rise and fall of the inhibitory mechanism: Toward a unified theory of cognitive development and aging. *Developmental Review, 12,* 454–75.

Detmer, D. E., Fryback, D. G., & Gassner, K. (1978). Heuristics and biases in medical decision making. *Journal of Medical Education, 53,* 682–683.

Deutsch, D. (2002). The puzzle of absolute pitch. *Current Directions in Psychological Science, 11,* 200–204.

Dietrich, D., & Olson, M. (1993). A demonstration of hindsight bias using the Thomas confirmation vote. *Psychological Reports, 72,* 377–378.

Dinges, D. F., Whitehouse, W. G., Orne, E. C., Powell, J. W., Orne, M. T., & Erdelyi, M. H. (1992). Evaluating hypnotic memory enhancement (hypermnesia and reminiscence) using multitrial forced recall. *Journal of Experimental Psychology: Learning, Memory, and Cognition, 18,* 1139–1147.

Diwadkar, V. A., & McNamara, T. P. (1997). Viewpoint dependence in scene recognition. *Psychological Science, 8,* 302–307.

Dodd, D. H., & Bradshaw, J. M. (1980). Leading questions and memory: Pragmatic constraints. *Journal of Verbal Learning and Verbal Behavior, 19,* 695–704.

Dodson, C. S., Johnson, M. K., & Schooler, J. W. (1997). The verbal overshadowing effect: Why descriptions impair face recognition. *Memory & Cognition, 25,* 129–139.

Dodson, C. S., & Riesberg, D. (1991). Indirect testing of eyewitness memory: The (non)effect of misinformation. *Bulletin of the Psychonomic Society, 29,* 333–336.

Dodson, C. S., & Shimamura, A. P. (2000). Differential effects of cue dependency on item and source memory. *Journal of Experimental Psychology: Learning, Memory, and Cognition, 26,* 1023–1044.

Donders, F. C. (1868). Over de snelheid van psychische processen. Onderzoekingen gedaan in het Physiologisch Laboratorium der Utrechtsche Hoogeschool, 1868–1869, Tweede reeks, II, 92–120.

Dopkins, S., & Ngo, C. T. (2002). Inhibition of verbal memory retrieval as a consequence of prior retrieval. *Journal of Memory and Language, 46,* 606–621.

Duchek, J. M., & Neely, J. H. (1989). A dissociative word-frequency X levels-of-processing interaction in episodic recognition and lexical decision tasks. *Memory & Cognition, 17,* 148–162.

Dulany, D. E., Carlson, R. A., & Dewey, G. L. (1984). A case of syntactical learning and judgment: How conscious and how abstract? *Journal of Experimental Psychology: General, 113,* 541–555.

Duncan, C. P. (1949). The retroactive effect of electroshock on learning. *Journal of Comparative Physiological Psychology, 42,* 32–44.

Dunlosky, J. & Hertzog, C. (2000). Updating knowledge about encoding strategies: A componential analysis of learning about strategy effectiveness from task experience. *Psychology and Aging, 15,* 462–474.

Dunlosky, J., & Nelson, T. O. (1994). Does the sensitivity of judgments of learning (JOLs) to the effects of various activities depend on when the JOLs occur? *Journal of Memory and Language, 33,* 545–565.

Dysart, J. E., Lindsay, R. C. L., Hammond, R., & Dupuis, P. (2001). Mug shot exposure prior to lineup identification: Interference, transference, and commitment effects. *Journal of Applied Psychology, 86,* 1280–1284.

Dywan, J., Segalowitz, S. J., & Webster, L. (1998). Source monitoring: ERP evidence for greater reactivity to nontarget information in older adults. *Brain and Cognition, 36,* 390–430.

Eagle, M., & Leiter, E. (1964). Recall and recognition in intentional and incidental learning. *Journal of Experimental Psychology, 68,* 58–63.

Eakin, D. K., Schreiber, T. A., & Sergent-Marshall, S. (2003). Misinformation effects in eyewitness memory: The presence and absence of memory impairment as a function of warning and misinformation accessibility. *Journal of Experimental Psychology: Learning, Memory, and Cognition, 29,* 813–825.

Easterbrook, J. A. (1959). The effect of emotion on cue utilization and the organization of behavior. *Psychological Review, 66,* 183–201.

Ebbinghaus, H. (1885/1964). *Memory: A Contribution to Experimental Psychology.* Translated by H. A. Ruger & C. E. Bussenius. New York: Dover.

Eich, E. (1995). Mood as a mediator of place dependent memory. *Journal of Experimental Psychology: General, 124,* 293–308.

Eich, J. E., Weingartner, H., Stillman, R. C., & Gillin, J. C. (1975). State-dependent accessibility of retrieval cues in the retention of a categorized list. *Journal of Verbal Learning and Verbal Behavior, 14,* 408–417.

Eich, J. M. (1982). A composite holographic associative recall model. *Psychological Review, 89,* 627–661.

Eich, J. M. (1985). Levels of processing, encoding specificity, elaboration and CHARM. *Psychological Review, 92,* 1–38.

Eichenbaum, H. (2002). *The Cognitive Neuroscience of Memory: An Introduction.* New York: Oxford.

Eimas, P. D., & Quinn, P. C. (1994). Studies on the formation of perceptually based basic-level categories in young infants. *Child Development, 65,* 903–917.

Einstein, G. O., & Hunt, R. R. (1980). Levels of processing and organization: Additive effects of individual-item and relational processing. *Journal of Experimental Psychology: Human Learning and Memory, 6,* 588–598.

Einstein, G. O., & McDaniel, M. A. (1990). Normal aging and prospective memory. *Journal of Experimental Psychology: Learning, Memory, and Cognition, 16,* 717–726.

Einstein, G. O., McDaniel, M. A., Owen, P. D., & Cote, N. C. (1990). Encoding and recall of texts: The importance of material appropriate processing. *Journal of Memory and Language, 29,* 566–581.

Einstein, G. O., McDaniel, M. A., Richardson, S. L., Guynn, M. L., & Cunfer, A. R. (1995). Aging and prospective memory: Examining influences of self-initiated retrieval processes. *Journal of Experimental Psychology: Learning, Memory, and Cognition, 21,* 996–1007.

Einstein, G. O., McDaniel, M. A., Smith, R., & Shaw, P. (1998). Habitual prospective memory and aging: Remembering instructions and forgetting actions. *Psychological Science, 9,* 284–288.

Eldridge, M. A., Barnard, P. J., & Bekerian, D. A. (1994). Autobiographical memory and daily schemas at work. *Memory, 2,* 51–74.

Elliot, R., & Dolan, R. J. (1998). Neural response during preference and memory judgments for subliminally presented stimuli: A functional neuroimaging study. *The Journal of Neuroscience, 18,* 4697–4704.

Ellis, A. W., Young, A. W., & Critchley, E. M. R. (1989). Loss of memory for people following temporal lobe damage. *Brain, 112,* 1469–1483.

Engelkamp, J., & Zimmer, H. D. (1997). Sensory factors in subject-performed tasks. *Acta Psychologica, 96,* 43–60.

Engle, R. W., Fidler, D. S., & Reynolds, L. H. (1981). Does echoic memory develop? *Journal of Experimental Child Psychology, 32,* 459–473.

Epstein, R., DeYoe, E. A., Press, D. Z., Rosen, A. C., & Kanwisher, N. (2001). Neuropsychological evidence of a topographical learning mechanism in parahippocampal cortex. *Cognitive Neuropsychology, 18,* 481–508.

Epstein, R., & Kanwisher, N. (1998). A cortical representation of the local visual environment. *Nature, 392,* 598–601.

Erdelyi, M. H., & Becker, J. (1974). Hypermnesia for pictures: Incremental memory for pictures but not words in multiple recall trials. *Cognitive Psychology, 6,* 159–171.

Erickson, T. D., & Mattson, M. E. (1981). From words to meaning: A semantic illusion. *Journal of Verbal Learning and Verbal Behavior, 20,* 540–551.

Ericsson, K. A., Chase, W. G., & Faloon, S. (1980). Acquisition of a memory skill. *Science, 208,* 1181–1182.

Ericsson, K. A., & Kintsch, W. (1995). Long-term working memory. *Psychological Review, 102,* 211–245.

Ericsson, K. A., & Simon, H. A. (1980). Verbal reports as data. *Psychological Review, 87,* 215–251.

Estes, W. K. (1972). An associative basis for coding and organization in memory. In A. W. Melton & E. Martin (Eds.), *Coding Processes in Human Memory*, pp. 161–190. New York: Wiley.

Estes, W. K. (1985). Levels of association theory. *Journal of Experimental Psychology: Learning, Memory, and Cognition, 11,* 450–454.

Evans, G. W., & Pezdek, K. (1980). Cognitive mapping: Knowledge of real-world distance and location information. *Journal of Experimental Psychology: Human Learning and Memory, 6,* 13–24.

Fein, S., McCloskey, A. L., & Tomlinson, T. M. (1997). Can the jury disregard the information? The use of suspicion to reduce the prejudicial effects of pretrial publicity and inadmissible testimony. *Personality and Social Psychology Bulletin, 23,* 1215–1226.

Ferguson, R. P., & Hegarty, M. (1994). Properties of cognitive maps constructed from texts. *Memory & Cognition, 22,* 455–473.

Ferguson, R. P., & Martin, P. (1983). Long-term temporal estimation in humans. *Perception & Psychophysics, 33,* 585–592.

Finlay, F., Hitch, G. J., & Meudell, P. R. (2000). Mutual inhibition in collaborative recall: Evidence for a retrieval-based account. *Journal of Experimental Psychology: Learning, Memory, and Cognition, 26,* 1556–1567.

Finkenhauer, C., Luminet, O., Gisle, L., El-ahmadi, A., van der Linden, M., & Philipott, P. (1998). Flashbulb memories and the underlying mechanisms of their formation: Toward an emotional-integrative model. *Memory & Cognition, 26,* 516–531.

Fischhoff, B. (1975). Hindsight does not equal foresight: The effect of outcome knowledge on judgment under uncertainty. *Journal of Experimental Psychology: Human Perception and Performance, 1,* 288–299.

Fischhoff, B. (1977). Perceived informativeness of facts. *Journal of Experimental Psychology: Human Perception and Performance, 3,* 349–358.

Fisher, C. (1945). Amnesic states in war neuroses: The psychogenesis of fugues. *Psychoanalytic Quarterly, 14,* 437–468.

Fisher, C., & Joseph, E. D. (1945). Fugue with awareness of loss of personal identity. *Psychoanalytic Quarterly, 18,* 480–493.

Fisher, R. P., Geiselman, R. E., & Amador, M. (1989). Field test of the cognitive interview: Enhancing the recollection of actual victims and witnesses of crime. *Journal of Applied Psychology, 74,* 722–727.

Flavell, J. H., Beach, D. H., & Chinsky, J. M. (1966). Spontaneous verbal rehearsal in a memory task as a function of age. *Child Development, 37,* 283–299.

Flexser, A. J., & Tulving, E. (1975). Retrieval independence in recognition and recall. *Psychological Review, 85,* 153–171.

Freud, S. (1899/1938). Childhood and concealing memories. In A. A. Brill (Ed.), *The Basic Writings of Sigmund Freud.* New York: The Modern Library.

Freyd, J. J. (1987). Dynamic mental representations. *Psychological Review, 94,* 427–438.

Freyd, J. J., & Finke, R. A. (1984). Representational momentum. *Journal of Experimental Psychology: Learning, Memory, and Cognition, 10,* 126–132.

Freyd, J. J., & Finke, R. A. (1985). A velocity effect for representational momentum. *Bulletin of the Psychonomic Society, 23,* 443–446.

Freyd, J. J., Pantzer, T. M., & Cheng, J. L. (1988). Representing statics as forces in equilibrium. *Journal of Experimental Psychology: General, 117,* 395–407.

Friedman, A., & Brown, N. R. (2000a). Reasoning about geography. *Journal of Experimental Psychology: General, 129,* 193–219.

Friedman, A., & Brown, N. R. (2000b). Updating geographical knowledge: Principles of coherence and inertia. *Journal of Experimental Psychology: Learning, Memory, and Cognition, 26,* 900–914.

Friedman, A., Brown, N. R., & McGaffey, A. P. (2002). A basis for bias in geographical judgments. *Psychonomic Bulletin & Review, 9,* 151–159.

Friedman, A., Kerkman, D. D., & Brown, N. R. (2002). Spatial location judgments: A cross-national comparison of estimation bias in subjective North American geography. *Psychonomic Bulletin & Review, 9,* 615–623.

Friedman, N. P., & Miyake, A. (2000). Differential roles for visuospatial and verbal working memory in situation model construction. *Journal of Experimental Psychology: General, 129,* 61–83.

Friedman, S. (1972). Newborn visual attention to repeated exposure of redundant vs. "novel" targets. *Perception & Psychophysics, 12,* 291–294.

Friedman, W. J. (1993). Memory for the time of past events. *Psychological Bulletin, 113,* 44–66.

Frieske, D. A., & Park, D. C. (1999). Memory for news in young and old adults. *Psychology and Aging, 14,* 90–98.

Frigo, L. C., Reas, D. L., & LeCompte, D. C. (1999). Revelation without presentation: Counterfeit study list yields robust revelation effect. *Memory & Cognition, 27,* 339–343.

Frost, P. (2000). The quality of false memory over time: Is memory for misinformation "remembered" or "known"? *Psychonomic Bulletin & Review, 7,* 531–536.

Furnham, A. (1986). The robustness of the recency effect: Studies using legal evidence. *The Journal of General Psychology, 113,* 351–357.

Gagne, C. L., & Shoben, E. J. (2002). Priming relations in ambiguous noun-noun combinations. *Memory & Cognition, 30,* 637–646.

Galambos, J. A., & Rips, L. J. (1982). Memory for routines. *Journal of Verbal Learning and Verbal Behavior, 21,* 260–281.

Gallo, D. A., & Roediger, H. L. (2003). The effects of associations and aging on illusory recollection. *Memory & Cognition, 31,* 1036–1044.

Gardiner, J. M. (1988). Functional aspects of recollective experience. *Memory & Cognition, 16,* 309–313

Gardiner, J. M., & Java, R. I. (1993). Recognizing and remembering. In A. F. Collins, S. E. Gathercole, M. A. Conway, & P. E. Morris (Eds.), *Theories of Memory,* pp. 163–188. Hillsdale, NJ: Erlbaum.

Gardiner, J. M., & Parkin, A. J. (1990). Attention and recollective experience in recognition memory. *Memory & Cognition, 18,* 579–583.

Gardiner, J. M., & Richardson-Klavehn, A. (2000). Remembering and knowing. In E. Tulving & F. I. M. Craik (Eds.), *The Oxford Handbook of Memory,* pp. 229–244. New York: Oxford University Press.

Garnham, A. (1981). Mental models as representations of text. *Memory & Cognition, 9,* 560–565.

Garry, M., & Polaschek, D. L. L. (2000). Imagination and memory. *Current Directions in Psychological Science, 9,* 6–10.

Garsoffky, B., Schwan, S., & Hesse, F. W. (2002). Viewpoint dependency in the recognition of dynamic scenes. *Journal of Experimental Psychology: Learning, Memory, and Cognition, 28,* 1035–1050.

Gathercole, S. E. (1997). Models of verbal short-term memory. In M. A. Conway (Ed.), *Cognitive Models of Memory,* pp. 13–45. Cambridge, MA: MIT Press.

Geiselman, R. E., Fisher, R. P., Firstenberg, L. Hutton, L. A., Sullivan, S., Avetissian, I., & Prosk, A. (1984). Enhancing eyewitness memory: An empirical evaluation of the cognitive interview. *Journal of Police Science and Administration, 12,* 74–80.

Geiselman, R. E., Fisher, R. P., MacKinnon, D. P., & Holland, H. L. (1985). Eyewitness memory enhancement in the police interview: Cognitive retrieval mnemonics versus hypnosis. *Journal of Applied Psychology, 70,* 401–412.

Gelman, S. A. (1988). The development of induction within natural kind and artifact categories. *Cognitive Psychology, 20,* 65–95.

Gelman, S. A., & O'Reilly, A. W. (1988). Children's inductive inferences within superordinate categories: The role of language and category structure. *Child Development, 59,* 876–887.

Ghetti, S. (2003). Memory for nonoccurrences: The role of metacognition. *Journal of Memory and Language, 48,* 722–739.

Gilbertson, L. J., Dietrich, D., Olson, M., & Guenther, R. K. (1994). A study of hindsight bias: The Rodney King case in retrospect. *Psychological Reports, 74,* 383–386.

Gillund, G., & Shiffrin, R. M. (1984). A retrieval model for both recognition and recall. *Psychological Review, 91,* 1–67.

Gilovich, T. (1981). Seeing the past in the present: The effect of associations to familiar events on judgments and decisions. *Journal of Personality and Social Psychology, 40,* 797–808.

Glanzer, M., & Cunitz, A. R. (1966). Two storage mechanisms in free recall. *Journal of Verbal Learning and Verbal Behavior, 5,* 351–360.

Glaze, J. A. (1928). The association value of nonsense syllables. *Journal of Genetic Psychology, 35,* 255–269.

Glenberg, A. M. (1976). Monotonic and nonmonotonic lag effects in paired-associate and recognition memory paradigms. *Journal of Verbal Learning and Verbal Behavior, 15,* 1–16.

Glenberg, A. M. (1979). Component-levels theory of the effects of spacing of repetitions on recall and recognition. *Memory & Cognition, 7,* 95–112.

Glenberg, A. M. (1997). What is memory for? *Behavioral and Brain Sciences, 20,* 1–55.

Glenberg, A. M., Bradley, M. M., Stevenson, J. A., Kraus, T. A., Tkachuk, M. J., Gretz, A. L., Fish, J. H., and Turpin, B. M. (1980). A Two-process account of long-term serial position effects.

Journal of Experimental Psychology: Human Learning and Memory, 6, 355–369.

Glenberg, A. M., & Lehmann, T. S. (1980). Spacing repetitions over 1 week. *Memory & Cognition, 8,* 528–538.

Glenberg, A. M., Meyer, M., & Lindem, K. (1987). *Journal of Memory and Language, 26,* 69–83.

Glenberg, A. M., Smith, S. M., & Green, C. (1977). Type I rehearsal: Maintenance and More. *Journal of Verbal Learning and Verbal Behavior, 16,* 339–352.

Glisky, E. L., Rubin, S. R., & Davidson, P. S. R. (2001). Source memory in older adults: An encoding or retrieval problem? *Journal of Experimental Psychology: Learning, Memory, and Cognition, 27,* 1131–1146.

Glucksberg, S., & McCloskey, M. (1981). Decisions about ignorance: knowing that you don't know. *Journal of Experimental Psychology: Human Learning and Memory, 7,* 311–325.

Godbout, L., & Doyon, J. (2000). Defective representation of knowledge in Parkinson's disease: Evidence from a script-production task. *Brain and Cognition, 44,* 490–510.

Godden, D. B., & Baddeley, A. D. (1975). Context-dependent memory in two natural environments: On land and underwater. *British Journal of Psychology, 66,* 325–331.

Goldenberg, G. (1995). Aphasic patients' knowledge about the visual appearance of objects. *Aphasiology, 9,* 50–56.

Golding, J. M., Fowler, S. B., Long, D. L., & Latta, H. (1990). Instructions to disregard potentially useful information: The effects of pragmatics on evaluative judgments and recall. *Journal of Memory and Language, 29,* 212–227.

Golding, J. M., & Hauselt, J. (1994). When instructions to forget become instructions to remember. *Personality and Social Psychology Bulletin, 20,* 178–183.

Goldinger, S. D., Kleider, H. M., Azuma, T., & Beike, D. R. (2003). "Blaming the victim" under memory load. *Psychological Science, 14,* 81–85.

Goldstein, A. G., & Chance, J. E. (1970). Visual recognition memory for complex configurations. *Perception & Psychophysics, 9,* 237–241.

Goldstone, R. L., Steyvers, M., & Rogosky, B. J. (2003). Conceptual interrelatedness and caricatures. *Memory & Cognition, 31,* 169–180.

Gómez-Ariza, C. J., & Bajo, M. T. (2003). Interference and integration: The fan effect in children and adults. *Memory, 11,* 505–523.

Goodwin, D. W., Powell, B., Bremer, D., Hoine, H., & Stern, J. (1969). Alcohol and recall: State-dependent effects in man. *Science, 163,* 2358–2360.

Gorenstein, G. W., & Ellsworth, P. C. (1980). Effect of choosing an incorrect photograph on a later identification by an eyewitness. *Journal of Applied Psychology, 65,* 616–622.

Gottesman, C. V., & Intraub, H. (2002). Surface construal and the mental representation of scenes. *Journal of Experimental Psychology: Human Perception and Performance, 28,* 589–599.

Graesser, A. C., Gordon, S. E., & Sawyer, J. D. (1979). Recognition memory for typical and atypical actions in scripted activities: Tests of the script pointer + tag hypothesis. *Journal of Verbal Learning and Verbal Behavior, 18,* 319–332.

Graesser, A. C., & Nakamura, G. V. (1982). The impact of a schema on comprehension and memory. *The Psychology of Learning and Motivation, 16,* 59–109.

Graesser, A. C., Woll, S. B., Kowalski, D. J., & Smith, D. A. (1980). Memory for typical and atypical actions in scripted activities. *Journal of Experimental Psychology: Human Learning and Memory, 6,* 503–515.

Graf, P., Mandler, G., & Haden, P. E. (1982). Simulating amnesic symptoms in normal subjects. *Science, 218,* 1243–1244.

Graf, P., & Schacter, D. L. (1985). Implicit and explicit memory for new associations in normal and amnesic subjects. *Journal of Experimental Psychology: Learning, Memory, and Cognition, 11,* 501–518.

Graf, P., Shimamura, A. P., & Squire, L. R. (1985). Priming across modalities and priming across category levels: Extending the domain of preserved function in amnesia. *Journal of Experimental Psychology: Learning, Memory, and Cognition, 11,* 386–396.

Graf, P., Squire, L. R., & Mandler, G. (1984). The information that amnesic patients do not forget. *Journal of Experimental Psychology: Learning, Memory, and Cognition, 10,* 164–178.

Graham, K. S., Ralph, M. A. L., & Hodges, J. R. (1997). Determining the impact of autobiographical experience on "meaning": New insights from investigating sport-related vocabulary and knowledge in two cases with semantic dementia. *Cognitive Neuropsychology, 14,* 801–837.

Gray, C. R., & Gummerman, K. (1975). The enigmatic eidetic image: A critical examination of methods, data, and theories. *Psychological Bulletin, 82,* 383–407.

Greene, J. D. W., & Hodges, J. R. (1996). The fractionation of remote memory: Evidence from a longitudinal study of dementia of Alzheimer type. *Brain, 119,* 129–142.

Greene, R. L. (1989). Spacing effects in memory: Evidence for a two-process account. *Journal of Experimental Psychology: Learning, Memory, and Cognition, 15,* 371–377.

Gustafsson, B., & Wigstrom, H. (1988). Physiological mechanisms underlying long-term potentiation. *Trends in Neuroscience, 11,* 156–163.

Haber, R. N. (1979). Twenty years of haunting eidetic imagery: Where's the ghost? *Behavioral and Brain Sciences, 2,* 583–629.

Haber, R. N., & Nathanson, L. S. (1968). Post-retinal storage? Some further observations on Parks' camel as seem through the eye of a needle. *Perception & Psychophysics, 3,* 349–355.

Haberlandt, K., & Bingham, G. (1984). The effect of input direction on the processing of script statements. *Journal of Verbal Learning and Verbal Behavior, 23,* 162–177.

Habib, R., Nyberg, L., & Tulving, E. (2003). Hemispheric asymmetries of memory: The HERA model revisited. *Trends in Cognitive Science, 7,* 241–245.

Halberstadt, J. & Rhodes, G. (2000). The attractiveness of nonface averages: Implications for an evolutionary explanation for the attractiveness of average faces. *Psychological Science, 11,* 285–289.

Halberstadt, J., & Rhodes, G. (2003). It's not just average faces that are attractive: Computer-manipulated averageness makes birds, fish, and automobiles attractive. *Psychonomic Bulletin & Review, 10,* 149–156.

Hannigan, S. L., & Reinitz, M. P. (2001). A demonstration and comparison of two types of inference-based memory errors. *Journal of Experimental Psychology: Learning, Memory, and Cognition, 27,* 931–940.

Harnishfeger, K. K., & Pope, R. S. (1996). Intending to forget: The development of cognitive inhibition in directed forgetting. *Journal of Experimental Child Psychology, 62,* 292–315.

Hart, J. T. (1965). Memory and the feeling-of-knowing experience. *Journal of Educational Psychology, 56,* 208–216.

Hasher, L., Attig, M. S., & Alba, J. W. (1981). I knew it all along: Or did I? *Journal of Verbal Learning and Verbal Behavior, 20,* 86–96.

Hasher, L., & Griffin, M. (1978). Reconstructive and reproductive processes in memory. *Journal of Experimental Psychology: Human Learning and Memory, 4,* 318–330.

Hasher, L., & Zacks, R. T. (1979). Automatic and effortful processes in memory. *Journal of Experimental Psychology: General, 108,* 356–388.

Hasher, L., & Zacks, R. T. (1988). Working memory, comprehension, and aging: A review and a new view. *Psychology of Learning and Motivation, 22,* 193–225.

Hashtroudi, S., Ferguson, S. A., Rappold, V. A., & Chrosniak, L. D. (1988). Data-driven and conceptually driven processes in partial-word identification and recognition. *Journal of Experimental Psychology: Learning, Memory and Cognition, 14,* 749–757.

Hashtroudi, S., Johnson, M. K., & Chrosniak, L. D. (1990). Aging and qualitative characteristics of memories for perceived and imagined complex events. *Psychology and Aging, 5,* 119–126.

Hashtroudi, S., Johnson, M. K., Vnek, N., & Ferguson, S. A. (1994). Aging and the effects of affective and factual focus on source monitoring and recall. *Psychology and Aging, 9,* 160–170.

Hayes-Roth, B., & Hayes-Roth, F. (1977). The prominence of lexical information in memory representations of meaning. *Journal of Verbal Learning and Verbal Behavior, 16,* 119–136.

Healy, A. F., Havas D. A., & Parker, J. T. (2000). Comparing serial position effects in semantic and episodic memory using reconstruction of order tasks. *Journal of Memory and Language, 42,* 147–167.

Heaps, C. M., & Nash, M. (2001). Comparing recollective experience in true and false autobiographical memories. *Journal of Experimental Psychology: Learning, Memory, and Cognition, 27,* 920–930.

Hebb, D. O. (1949). The *Organization of Behavior.* New York: Wiley.

Hedden, T., & Park, D. (2001). Aging and interference in verbal working memory. *Psychology and Aging, 16,* 666–681.

Hege, A. C. G., & Dodson, C. S. (2004). Why distinctiveness information reduces false memories: Evidence for both impoverished relational-encoding and distinctiveness heuristics accounts. *Journal of Experimental Psychology: Learning, Memory, and Cognition, 30,* 787–795.

Heit, E., Brockdorff, N., & Lamberts, K. (2004). Strategic processes in false recognition memory. *Psychonomic Bulletin & Review, 11,* 380–386.

Henderson, J. M., & Anes, M. D. (1994). Roles of object-file review and type priming in visual identification within and across eye fixations. *Journal of Experimental Psychology: Human Perception and Performance, 20,* 826–839.

Henkel, L. A. (2004). Erroneous memories arising from repeated attempts to remember. *Journal of Memory and Language, 50,* 26–46.

Henkel, L. A., Franklin, N., & Johnson, M. K. (2000). Cross-modal source monitoring confusions between perceived and imagined events. *Journal of Experimental Psychology: Learning, Memory, and Cognition, 26,* 321–335.

Henry, J. D., MacLeod, M. S., Philips, L. H., & Crawford, J. R. (2004). A meta-analytic review of prospective memory and aging. *Psychology and Aging, 19,* 27–39.

Hess, T. M. & Bolstad, C. A. (1998). Category-based versus attribute-based processing in different-aged adults. *Aging, Neuropsychology, and Cognition, 5,* 27–42.

Hess, T. M., & Flannagan, D. A. (1992). Schema-based retrieval processes in young and older adults. *Journal of Gerontology: Psychological Sciences, 47,* P52–P58.

Hess, T. M., & Follett, K. J. (1994). Adult age differences in the use of schematic and episodic information in making social judgments. *Aging and Cognition, 1,* 54–66.

Hess, T. M., Follett, K. J., & McGee, K. A. (1998). Aging and impression formation: The impact of processing skills and goals. *Journal of Gerontology: Psychological Sciences, 53B,* P175–P187.

Hicks, J. L., & Cockman, D. W. (2003). The effect of general knowledge on source memory and decision processes. *Journal of Memory and Language, 48,* 489–501.

Hicks, J. L., & Marsh, R. L. (1998). A decrement-to-familiarity interpretation of the revelation effect from forced-choice tests of recognition memory. *Journal of Experimental Psychology: Learning, Memory, & Cognition, 24,* 1105–1120.

Hicks, J. L., & Marsh, R. L. (2001). *Journal of Experimental Psychology: Learning, Memory, & Cognition, 27,* 375–383.

Hicks, J. L., & Marsh, R. L. (2002). On predicting the future states of awareness for recognition of unrecallable items. *Memory & Cognition, 30,* 60–66.

Hicks, J. L., Marsh, R. L., & Ritschel, L. (2002). The role of recollection and partial information in source monitoring. *Journal of Experimental Psychology: Learning, Memory, & Cognition, 28,* 503–508.

Hicks, J. L., Marsh, R. L., & Russell (2000). The properties of retention intervals and their affect on retaining prospective memories. *Journal of Experimental Psychology: Learning, Memory, & Cognition, 26,* 1160–1169.

Hicks, J. L., & Starns, J. J. (2004). Retrieval-induced forgetting occurs in tests of item recognition. *Psychonomic Bulletin & Review, 11,* 125–130.

Hill, H., Strube, M., Roesch-Ely, D., & Weisbrod, M. (2002). Automatic vs. controlled processing in semantic memory: Differentiation by event-related potentials. *International Journal of Psychophysiology, 44,* 197–218.

Hill, J. W., & Bliss, J. C. (1968). Modeling a tactile sensory register. *Perception & Psychophysics, 4,* 91–101.

Hinsz, V. B. (1990). Cognitive and consensus processes in group recognition memory performance. *Journal of Personality and Social Psychology, 59,* 705–718.

Hintzman, D. L. (1986). "Schema abstraction" in a multiple-trace memory model. *Psychological Review, 93,* 411–428.

Hintzman, D. L. (1987). Recognition and recall in MINERVA 2: Analysis of the 'recognition-failure' paradigm. In P. Morris (Ed.) *Modelling congition,* p. 215–229. Oxford, England: Wiley.

Hintzman, D. L. (1988). Judgments of frequency and recognition memory in a multiple-trace memory model. *Psychological Review, 95,* 528–551.

Hintzman, D. L. (1990). Human learning and memory: Connections and Dissociations. *Annual Review of Psychology, 41,* 109–139.

Hintzman, D. L., (2003). Robert Hooke's mode of memory. *Psychonomic Bulletin & Review, 10,* 3–14.

Hintzman, D. L., Summers, J. J., and Block, R. A. (1975). Spacing judgments as an index of study-phase retrieval. *Journal of Experimental Psychology: Human Learning and Memory, 1,* 31–40.

Hirst, W., Johnson, M. K., Kim, J. K., Phelps, E. A., Risse, G., & Volpe, B. T. (1986). Recognition and recall in amnesics. *Journal of Experimental Psychology: Learning, Memory, and Cognition, 12,* 445–451.

Hirst, W., Johnson, M. K., Phelps, E. A., & Volpe, B. T. (1988). More on recognition and recall in amnesics.

Journal of Experimental Psychology: Learning, Memory, and Cognition, 14, 758–762.

Hitch, G. J., & Ferguson, J. (1991). Prospective memory for future intentions: Some comparisons with memory for past events. *European Journal of Cognitive Psychology, 3,* 285–295.

Hobson, J. A. (1988). *The dreaming brain.* New York, NY,: Basic Books, Inc.

Hochberg, J., & Brooks, V. (1962). Pictorial recognition as an unlearned ability: A study of one child's performance. *American Journal of Psychology, 75,* 624–628.

Hodges, J. R. (1995). Retrograde amnesia. In A. D. Baddeley, B. A. Wilson, & F. N. Watts (Eds.), *Handbook of Memory Disorders,* pp. 81–108. New York: Wiley.

Hodges, J. R., Bozeat, S., Lambdon Ralph, M. A., Patterson, K., & Spatt, J. (2000). The role of conceptual knowledge in object use: Evidence from semantic dementia. *Brain, 123,* 1913–1925.

Hodges, J. R., Patternson, K., Oxbuy, S., & Funnell, E. (1992). Semantic dementia: Progressive fluent aphasia with temporal lobe atrophy. *Brain, 115,* 1783–1806.

Hoffman, H. G., Granhag, P. A., See, S. T. K., & Loftus, E. F. (2001). Social influences on reality-monitoring decisions. *Memory & Cognition, 29,* 394–404.

Holcomb, P. J., Kounios, J., Anderson, J. E., & West, W. C. (1999). Dual-coding, context availability, and concreteness effects in sentence comprehension: An electrophysiological investigation. *Journal of Experimental Psychology: Learning, Memory, and Cognition, 25,* 721–742.

Hollingworth, A., & Henderson, J. M. (2003). Testing a conceptual locus for the inconsistent object change detection advantage in real-world scenes. *Memory & Cognition, 31,* 930–940.

Holloway, F. A. (1978). State dependent retrieval based on time of day. In B. Ho, D. Richards, D. Chute (Eds.), *Drug Discrimination and State Dependent Learning,* pp. 319–344. New York: Academic Press.

Holyoak, K. J., & Mah, W. A. (1982). Cognitive reference points in judgments of symbolic magnitude. *Cognitive Psychology, 14,* 328–352.

Hoosain, R., & Salili, F. (1988). Language differences, working memory, and mathematical ability. In M. M. Gruneberg, P. E. Morris, & R. N. Sykes (Eds.), *Practical Aspects of Memory: Current Research and Issues,* pp. 512–517. Chichester, England: Wiley.

Hornstein, S. L., Brown, A. S., & Mulligan, N. W. (2003). Long-term flashbulb memory for learning of Princess Diana's death. *Memory, 11,* 293–306.

Howard, D. V., McAndrews, M. P., & Lasaga, M. I. (1981). Semantic priming of lexical decisions in young and old adults. *Journal of Gerontology, 36,* 707–714.

Howe, M. L. (2003). Memories from the cradle. *Current Directions in Psychological Science, 12,* 62–65.

Hovland, C. I., & Weiss, W. (1951). The influence of source credibility on communication effectiveness. *Public Opinion Quarterly, 15,* 635–650.

Howe, M. L., & Courage, M. L. (1993). On resolving the enigma of infantile amnesia. *Psychological Bulletin, 113,* 305–326.

Hubel, D. H., & Wiesel, T. N. (1960). Receptive fields of optic nerve fibres in the spider monkey. *Journal of Physiology, 154,* 572–580.

Hubbard, T. L. (1990). Cognitive representation of linear motion: Possible direction and gravity effects in judged displacement. *Memory & Cognition, 18,* 299–309.

Hubbard, T. L. (1995a). Cognitive representation of motion: Evidence for friction and gravity analogues. *Journal of Experimental Psychology: Learning, Memory, and Cognition, 21,* 241–254.

Hubbard, T. L. (1995b). Environmental invariants in the representation of motion: Implied dynamics and representational momentum, gravity, friction, and centripetal force. *Psychonomic Bulletin & Review, 2,* 322–338.

Hubbard, T. L. (1996). Representational momentum, centripetal force, and curvilinear impetus. *Journal of Experimental Psychology: Learning, Memory, and Cognition, 22,* 1049–1060.

Hubbard, T. L. (1997). Target size and displacement along the axis of implied gravitational attraction: Effects of implied weight and evidence of representational gravity. *Journal of Experimental Psychology: Learning, Memory, and Cognition, 23,* 1484–1493.

Hubbard, T. L., & Bharucha, J. J. (1988). Judged displacement in apparent vertical and horizontal motion. *Perception & Psychophysics, 44,* 211–221.

Hulme, C. Maughan, S., & Brown, G. D. A. (1991). Memory for familiar and unfamiliar words: Evidence for a long-term memory contribution to short-term memory span. *Journal of Memory and Language, 30,* 685–701.

Hulme, C., Suprenant, A. M., Bireta, T. J., Stuart, G., & Neath, I. (2004). Abolishing the word-length effect. *Journal of Experimental Psychology: Learning, Memory, and Cognition, 30,* 98–106.

Hulme, C., Thomson, N., Muir, C., & Lawrence, A. (1984). Speech rate and the development of short-term memory span. *Journal of Experimental Child Psychology, 38,* 241–253.

Hunkin, N. M. (1997). Focal retrograde amnesia: Implications for the organization of memory. In A. J. Parkin (Ed.), *Case Studies in the Neuropsychology of Memory,* pp. 63–82. Hove, England: Psychology Press.

Hunt, R. R. (1995). The subtlety of distinctiveness: What von Restorff really did. *Psychonomic Bulletin & Review, 2,* 105–112.

Hunt, R. R., Ausley, J. A., & Schultz, E. E. (1986). Shared and item-specific information in memory for event descriptions. *Memory & Cognition, 14,* 49–54.

Hunt, R. R., & Einstein, G. O. (1981). Relational and item-specific information in memory. *Journal of Verbal Learning and Verbal Behavior, 20,* 497–514.

Hunt, R. R., & McDaniel, M. A. (1993). The enigma of organization and distinctiveness. *Journal of Memory and Language, 32,* 421–445.

Hunt, R. R., & Seta, C. E. (1984). Category size effects in recall: The roles of relational and individual item information. *Journal of Experimental Psychology: Learning, Memory, and Cognition, 10,* 454–464.

Huntjens, R. J. C., Postma, A., Hamaker, E. L., Woertman, L., van der Hart, O., & Peters, M. (2002). Perceptual and conceptual priming in patients with dissociative identity disorder. *Memory & Cognition, 30,* 1033–1043.

Huron, C., Danion, J. M., Giacomoni, F., Grange, D., Robert, P., & Rizzo, L. (1995). Impairment of recognition memory with, but not without, conscious recollection in schizophrenia. *American Journal of Psychiatry, 152,* 1737–1742.

Hutenlocher, J., and Hedges, L. V., and Bradburn, N. M. (1990). Reports of elapsed time: Bounding and rounding processes in estimation. *Journal of Experimental Psychology: Learning, Memory, and Cognition, 16,* 196–213.

Huttenlocher, J., Hedges, L. V., & Duncan, S. (1991). Categories and particulars: Prototype effects in estimating spatial locations. *Psychological Review, 98,* 352–376.

Huttenlocher, J., and Hedges, L. V., and Prohaska, V. (1992). Memory for day of the week: A 52 day cycle. *Journal of Experimental Psychology: General, 121,* 313–325.

Hyde, T. S., & Jenkins, J. J. (1973). Recall for words as a function of semantic, graphic, and syntactic orienting tasks. *Journal of Verbal Learning and Verbal Behavior, 12,* 471–480.

Intons-Peterson, M. J., & Roskos-Ewoldsen, B. B. (1989). Sensory-perceptual qualities of images. *Journal of Experimental Psychology: Learning, Memory, and Cognition, 15,* 188–199.

Intraub, H., Bender, R. S., & Mangels, J. A. (1992). Looking at pictures but remembering scenes. *Journal of Experimental Psychology: Learning, Memory, and Cognition, 18,* 180–191.

Intraub, H., & Berkowits, D. (1996). Beyond the edges of a picture. *American Journal of Psychology, 109,* 581–598.

Intraub, H., & Bodamer, J. L. (1993). Boundary extension: Fundamental aspect of pictorial representation or encoding artifact? *Journal of Experimental Psychology: Learning, Memory, and Cognition, 19,* 1387–1397.

Intraub, H., Gottesman, C. V., & Bills, A. J. (1998). Effects of perceiving and imagining scenes on memory for pictures. *Journal of Experimental Psychology: Learning, Memory, and Cognition, 24,* 186–201.

Intraub, H., Gottesman, C. V., Willey, E. V., & Zuk, I. J. (1996). Boundary extension for briefly glimpsed photographs: Do common perceptual processes result in unexpected memory distortions? *Journal of Memory and Language, 35,* 118–134.

Intraub, H., & Hoffman, J. E. (1992). Reading and visual memory: Remembering scenes that were never seen. *American Journal of Psychology, 105,* 101–114.

Intraub, H., & Richardson, M. (1989). Wide-angle memories of close-up scenes. *Journal of Experimental Psychology: Learning, Memory, and Cognition, 15,* 179–187.

Irwin, D. E. (1991). Information integration across saccadic eye movements. *Cognitive Psychology, 23,* 420–456.

Irwin, D. E. (1996). Integrating information across saccadic eye movements. *Current Directions in Psychological Science, 5,* 94–100.

Irwin, D. E., & Brockmole, J. R. (2000). Mental rotation is suppressed during saccadic eye movements. *Psychonomic Bulletin & Review, 7,* 654–661.

Irwin, D. E., Brown, J. S., & Sun, J. S. (1988). Visual masking and visual integration across saccadic eye movements. *Journal of Experimental Psychology: General, 117,* 276–287.

Irwin, D. E., Yantis, S., & Jonides, J. (1983). Evidence against visual integration across saccadic eye movements. *Perception & Psychophysics, 34,* 49–57.

Jacobs, L. F., & Schenk, F. (2003). Unpacking the cognitive map: The parallel map theory of hippocampal function. *Psychological Review, 110,* 285–315.

Jacoby, L. L. (1991). A process dissociation framework: Separating automatic from intentional uses of memory. *Journal of Memory and Language, 30,* 513–541.

Jacoby, L. L., & Dallas, M. (1981). On the relationship between autobiographical memory and perceptual learning. *Journal of Experimental Psychology: General, 110,* 306–340.

Jacoby, L. L., Kelley, C., Brown, J., & Jasechko, J. (1989). Becoming famous overnight: Limits on the ability to avoid unconscious influences of the past. *Journal of Personality and Social Psychology, 56,* 326–338.

Jacoby, L. L., Woloshyn, V., & Kelley, C. (1989). Becoming famous without being recognized: Unconscious influences of memory produced by dividing attention. *Journal of Experimental Psychology: General, 118,* 115–125.

Janculjak, D., Mubrin, Z., Brinar, V., & Spilich, G. (2002). Changes of attention and memory in a group of patients with multiple sclerosis. *Clinical Neurology and Neurosurgery, 104,* 221–227.

Janowski, J. S., Shimamura, A. P., & Squire, L. R. (1989). Memory and metamemory: Comparisons between patients with frontal lobe lesions and amnesic patients. *Psychobiology, 17,* 3–11.

Jenkins, J. G., & Dallenbach, K. M. (1924). Oblivescence during sleep and waking. *American Journal of Psychology, 35,* 605–622.

Johnson, M. K., De Leonardis, D. M., Hashtroudi, S., & Ferguson, S. A. (1995). Aging and single versus multiple cues in source monitoring. *Psychology and Aging, 10,* 507–517.

Johnson, M. K., Foley, M. A., & Leach, K. (1988). The consequences of memory of imagining in another person's voice. *Memory & Cognition, 16,* 337–342.

Johnson, M. K., Hashtroudi, S., & Lindsay, S. (1993). Source monitoring. *Psychological Bulletin, 114,* 3–28.

Johnson, M. K., & Hermann, A. M. (1995). Semantic relations and Alzheimer's disease: An early and disproportionate deficit in functional knowledge. *Journal of the International Neuropsychological Society, 1,* 568–574.

Johnson, M. K., Kounios, J., & Reeder, J. A. (1994). Time-course studies of reality monitoring and recognition. *Journal of Experimental Psychology: Learning, Memory, and Cognition, 20,* 1409–1419.

Johnson, M. K., & Raye, C. L. (1981). Reality monitoring. *Psychological Review, 88,* 67–85.

Johnson, S. J., & Anderson, M. C. (2004). The role of inhibitory control in forgetting semantic knowledge. *Psychological Science, 15,* 448–453.

Johnson-Laird, P. N. (1983). *Mental Models.* Cambridge, MA: Harvard University Press.

Johnson-Laird, P. N., Hermann, D. J., & Chaffin, R. (1984). Only connections: A critique of semantic networks. *Psychological Bulletin, 96,* 292–315.

Joslyn, S., Loftus, E., McNoughton, A., & Powers, J. (2001). Memory for memory. *Memory & Cognition, 29,* 789–797.

Just, M. A., Carpenter, P. A., Maguire, M., Diwadkar, V., & McManis, S. (2001). Mental rotation of objects retrieved from memory: A functional MRI study of spatial processing. *Journal of Experimental Psychology: General, 130,* 493–504.

Kahana, M. J., & Wingfield, A. (2000). A functional relation between learning and organization in free recall. *Psychonomic Bulletin & Review, 7,* 516–521

Kahneman, D., Treisman, A., and Gibbs, B. J. (1992). The reviewing of objects files: Object-specific integration of information. Cognitive *Psychology, 24,* 175–219.

Kail, R. (1991). Processing time declines exponentially during childhood and adolescence. *Developmental Psychology, 27,* 259–266.

Kail, R. (1997). Processing time, imagery, and spatial memory. *Journal of Experimental Child Psychology, 64,* 67–78.

Kaiser, M. K., Proffitt, D. R., & Anderson, K. (1985). Judgments of natural and anomalous trajectories in the presence and absence of motion. *Journal of Experimental Psychology: Learning, Memory, and Cognition, 11,* 795–803.

Kalakoski, V., & Saarilouma, P. (2001). Taxi drivers' exceptional memory of street names. *Memory & Cognition, 29,* 634–638.

Kalish, C. W. (2002). Essentialist to some degree: Beliefs about the structure of natural kinds categories. *Memory & Cognition, 30,* 340–352.

Kane, M. J., & Engle, R. W. (2000). Working-memory capacity: Proactive interference, and divided attention: Limits on long-term memory retrieval. *Journal of Experimental Psychology: Learning, Memory, and Cognition, 26,* 336–358.

Kane, M. J., & Engle, R. W. (2002). The role of pre-frontal cortex in working-memory capacity, executive attention, and general fluid intelligence: An individual-differences perspective. *Psychonomic Bulletin & Review, 9,* 637–671.

Kanwisher, N. (1987). Repetition blindness: Type recognition without token individuation. *Cognition, 27,* 117–143.

Kapur, N. (1999). Syndromes of retrograde amnesia: A conceptual and empirical synthesis. *Psychological Bulletin, 125,* 800–825.

Kapur, N., & Moakes, D. (1995). Living with amnesia. In R. Campbell & M. A. Conway (Eds.), *Broken Memories: Case Studies in Memory Impairment,* pp. 1–7. Malden, MA: Blackwell.

Karney, B. R., & Coombs, R. H. (2000). Memory bias in long-term close relationships: Consistency or improvement? *Personality and Social Psychology Bulletin, 26,* 959–970.

Kelemen, W. L., & Weaver, C. A. (1997). Enhanced memory at delays: Why do judgments of learning improve over time? *Journal of Experimental Psychology: Learning, Memory, and Cognition, 23,* 1394–1409.

Kemp, S. (1988). Memorial psychophysics for visual area: The effect of retention interval. *Memory & Cognition, 16,* 431–436.

Kennedy, Q., Mather, M., & Carstensen, L. L. (2004). The role of motivation in the age-related positivity effect in autobiographical memory. *Psychological Science, 15,* 208–214.

Kensinger, E. A., & Corkin, S. (2003a). Memory enhancement for emotional words: Are emotional words more vividly remembered than neutral words? *Memory & Cognition, 31,* 1169–1180.

Kensinger, E. A., & Corkin, S. (2003b). Effect of negative emotional content on working memory and long-term memory. *Emotion, 3,* 378–393.

Keppel, G., & Underwood, B. J. (1962). Proactive inhibition in short-term retention of single items. *Journal of Verbal Learning and Verbal Behavior, 1,* 153–161.

Kerst, S. M., & Howard, J. H. (1978). Memory psychophysics for visual area and length. *Memory & Cognition, 6,* 327–335.

Kerst, S. M., & Howard, J. H. (1983). Mental processes in magnitude estimation of length and loudness. *Bulletin of the Psychonomic Society, 21,* 141–144.

Kerstholt, J. H., & Jackson, J. L. (1998). Judicial decision making: Order of evidence presentation and availability of background information. *Applied Cognitive Psychology, 15,* 445–454.

Khaneman, D., Triesman, A., & Gibbs, B. J. (1992). The reviewing of object files: Object-specific integration of information. *Cognitive Psychology, 24,* 175–219.

Kihlstrom, J. F., & Schacter, D. L. (1995). Functional disorders of autobiographical memory. In A. D. Baddeley, B. A. Wilson, & F. N. Watts (Eds.), *Handbook of Memory Disorders,* pp. 337–364. New York: Wiley.

Kim, N. S., & Ahn, W. (2002). Clinical psychologists' theory-based representations of mental disorders predict their diagnostic reasoning and memory. *Journal of Experimental Psychology: General, 131,* 451–476.

Kimball, D. R., & Bjork, R. A. (2002). Influences of intentional and unintentional forgetting on false memories. *Journal of Experimental Psychology: General, 131,* 116–130.

Kimball, D. R., & Metcalfe, J. (2003). Delaying judgments of learning affects memory, not metamemory. *Memory & Cognition, 31,* 918–929.

Kintsch, W. (1968). Recognition and free recall of organized lists. *Journal of Experimental Psychology, 78,* 481–487.

Kintsch, W. (1970). Models for free recall and recognition. In D. A. Norman (Ed.), *Models of Human Memory,* pp. 331–373. New York: Academic Press.

Kintsch, W., & Bates, E. (1977). Recognition memory for statements from a classroom lecture. *Journal of Experimental Psychology: Human Learning and Memory, 3,* 150–159.

Kintsch, W., Mandel, T. S., & Kozminsky, E. (1977). Summarizing scrambled stories. *Memory & Cognition, 5,* 547–552.

Kintsch, W., Welsch, D., Schmalhofer, F., & Zimny, S. (1990). Sentence memory: A theoretical analysis. *Journal of Memory and Language, 29,* 133–159.

Kishiyama, M. M., & Yonelinas, A. P. (2003). Novelty effects on recollection and familiarity in recognition memory. *Memory & Cognition, 31,* 1045–1051.

Kishiyama, M. M., Yonelinas, A. P., & Lazzara, M. M. (2004). The Von Restorff effect in amnesia: The contribution of the hippocampal system to novelty-related memory enhancements. *Journal of Cognitive Neuroscience, 16,* 15–23.

Klein, K., & Boals, A. (2001). Expressive writing can increase working memory capacity. *Journal of Experimental Psychology: General, 130,* 520–533.

Klein, S. B., Cosmides, L., Tooby, J., & Chance, S. (2002). Decisions and the evolution of memory: Multiple systems, multiple functions. *Psychological Review, 109,* 306–329.

Kliegel, M., McDaniel, M. A., & Einstein, G. O. (2000). Plan formation, retention, and execution in prospective memory: A new approach and age-related effects. *Memory & Cognition, 28,* 1041–1049.

Klimesch, W. (1996). Memory processes, brain oscillations and EEG synchronization. *International Journal of Psychophysiology, 24,* 61–100.

Klimesch, W. (1999). EEG alpha and theta oscillations reflect cognitive and memory performance: A review and analysis. *Brain Research Reviews, 29,* 169–195.

Klimesch, W., Doppelmayr, M., Russegger, H., & Pachinger, T. (1996). Theta band power in the human scalp EEG and the encoding of new information. *Neuroreport, 7,* 1235–1240.

Klimesch, W., Schimke, H., Dopplemayr, M., Ripper, B., Schwaiger, J., & Pfurtscheller, G. (1996). Event-related deschronization (ERD) and the Dm effect: Does alpha desychronization during encoding predict later recall performance? *International Journal of Psychophysiology, 24,* 47–60.

Knight, B. G., Maines, M. L., & Robinson, G. S. (2002). The effects of sad mood on memory in older adults: A test of the mood congruence effect. *Psychology and Aging, 17,* 653–661.

Kolers, P. A. (1976). Reading a year later. *Journal of Experimental Psychology: Human Learning and Memory, 2,* 554–565.

Kolers, P. A., & Palef, S. R. (1976). Knowing not. *Memory & Cognition, 4,* 553–558.

Kolers, P. A., & Roediger, H. L. (1984). Procedures of mind. *Journal of Verbal Learning and Verbal Behavior, 23,* 425–449.

Koriat, A. (1993). How do we know that we know? The accessibility model of the feeling of knowing. *Psychological Review, 100,* 609–639.

Koriat, A. (1995). Dissociating knowing and the feeling of knowing: Further evidence for the accessibility model. *Journal of Experimental Psychology: General, 124,* 311–333.

Koriat, A. (1997). Monitoring one's own knowledge during study: A cue utilization approach to judgments of learning. *Journal of Experimental Psychology: General, 126,* 349–370.

Koriat, A. (2002). Comparing objective and subjective learning curves: Judgments of learning exhibit increased underconfidence with practice. *Journal of Experimental Psychology: General, 131,* 147–162.

Koriat, A., & Levy-Sadot, R. (2001). The combined contributions of the cue-familiarity and accessibility heuristics to feelings of knowing. *Journal of Experimental Psychology: Learning, Memory, and Cognition, 27,* 34–53.

Koriat, A., Levy-Sadot, R., Edry, E., & de Marcas, S. (2003). What do we know about what we cannot remember? Accessing the semantic attributes of words that cannot be recalled. *Journal of Experimental Psychology: Learning, Memory, and Cognition, 29,* 1095–1105.

Koriat, A., & Pearlman-Avnion, S. (2003). Memory organization of action events and its relationship to memory performance. *Journal of Experimental Psychology: General, 132,* 435–454.

Kosslyn, S. M. (1975). Information representation in visual images. *Cognitive Psychology, 7,* 341–370.

Kosslyn, S. M. (1980). *Image and Mind.* Cambridge, MA: Harvard University Press.

Kosslyn, S. M., Alpert, N. M., Thompson, W. L., Melijkovic, V., Weise, S. B., Chabris, C. F., Hamilton, S. E., Rauch, S. L., & Buonanno, F. S. (1993). Visual mental imagery activates topographically organized visual cortex: PET investigations. *Journal of Cognitive Neuroscience, 5,* 263–287.

Kosslyn, S. M., Ball, T. M., and Reiser, B. J. (1978). Visual images preserve metric spatial information: Evidence from studies of image scanning. *Journal of Experimental Psychology: Human Perception and Performance, 4,* 47–60.

Kosslyn, S. M., & Pomerantz, J. R. (1977). Imagery, propositions, and the form of internal representations. *Cognitive Psychology, 9,* 52–76.

Kounios, J., & Holcomb, P. J. (1994). Concreteness effects in semantic processing: ERP evidence supporting dual-coding theory. *Journal of Experimental Psychology: Learning, Memory, and Cognition, 20,* 804–823.

Kounios, J., & Holcombe, P. J. (1994). Concreteness effects in smenatic processing: ERP evidence supporting dual-code theory. *Journal of Experimental Psychology: Learning, Memory, and Cognition, 20,* 804–823.

Kounios, J., Montgomery, E. C., & Smith, R. W. (1994). Semantic memory and the granularity of semantic relations: Evidence from speed-accuracy decomposition. *Memory & Cognition, 22,* 729–741.

Koutstaal, W., Reddy, C., Jackson, E. M., Prince, S., Cendan, D. L., & Schacter, D. L. (2003). False recognition of abstract versus common objects in older and younger adults: Testing the semantic categorization account. *Journal of Experimental Psychology: Learning, Memory and Cognition, 29,* 499–510.

Koutstaal, W., & Schacter, D. L. (1997). Gist-based false recognition of pictures in older and younger adults. *Journal of Memory and Language, 37,* 555–583.

Kozhevnikov, M., & Hegarty, M. (2001). Impetus beliefs as default heuristics: Dissociation between explicit and implicit knowledge about motion. *Psychonomic Bulletin & Review, 8,* 439–453.

Kramer, T. H., Buckout, R., & Eugenio, P. (1990). Weapon focus, arousal, and eyewitness memory. *Law and Human Behavior, 14,* 167–184.

Krause, W., Gibbons, H., & Schack, B. (1998). Concept activation and coordination of activation procedures require two different networks. *Neuroreport, 9,* 1649–1653.

Kroll, N. E. A., & Klimesch, W. (1992). Semantic memory: Complexity or connectivity. *Memory & Cognition, 20,* 192–210.

Kunst-Wilson, W. R., & Zajonc, R. B. (1980). Affective discrimination of stimuli that cannot be recognized. *Science, 207,* 557–558.

Kutas, M., & Hillyard, S. A. (1980). Reading senseless sentences: Brain potentials reflect semantic incongruity. *Science, 207,* 203–205.

Lampinen, J. M., Copeland, S. M., & Neuscatz, J. S. (2001). Recollections of things schematic: Room schemas revisited. *Journal of Experimental Psychology: Learning, Memory, and Cognition, 27,* 1211–1222.

Lancaster, J. S., & Barsalou, L. W. (1997). Multiple organizations of events in memory. *Memory, 5,* 569–599.

Landau, J. D. (2001). Altering the balance of recollection and familiarity influences the revelation effect. *American Journal of Psychology, 114,* 425–437.

Landauer, T. K. (1969). Reinforcement as consolidation. *Psychological Review, 76,* 82–96.

Langlois, J. H., & Roggman, L. A. (1990). Attractive faces are only average. *Psychological Science, 1,* 115–121.

Langlois, J. H., Roggman, L. A., & Musselman, L. (1994). What is average and what is not average about attractive faces. *Psychological Science, 5,* 214–220.

Lashley, K. S. (1950). In search of the engram. *Symposia of the Society for Experimental Biology: Physiological Mechanisms of Animal Behavior,* Vol. 4. New York: Academic Press.

LaVoie, D. J., & Malmstrom, T. (1998). False recognition effects in younger and older adults' memory for text passages. *Journals of Gerontology: Psychological Sciences, 53B,* P255–P262.

Leary, M. R. (1981). The distorted nature of hindsight. *Journal of Social Psychology, 115,* 25–29.

Leary, M. R. (1982). Hindsight distortion and the 1980 Presidential election. *Personality and Social Psychology Bulletin, 8,* 257–263.

LeBoe, J. P., & Whittlesea, B. W. A. (2002). The inferential basis of familiarity and recall: Evidence for a common underlying process. *Journal of Memory and Language, 46,* 804–829.

LeCompte, D. C. (1995). Recollective experience in the revelation effect: Separating the contributions of recollection and familiarity. *Memory & Cognition, 23,* 324–334.

Levin, D. T., & Simons, D. J. (1997). Failure to detect changes to attended objects in motion pictures. *Psychonomic Bulletin & Review, 4,* 501–506.

Levine, B., Svaboda, E., Hay, J. F., Winocur, G, & Moscovitch, M. (2002). Aging and autobiographical memory: Dissociating episodic from semantic retrieval. *Psychology and Aging, 17,* 677–689.

Levine, L. J., Prohaska, V., Burgess, S. L., Rice, J. A., & Laulhere, T. M. (2001). Remembering past emotions: The role of current appraisals. *Cognition and Emotion, 15,* 393–417.

Levine, M., Jankovic, I. N., & Palij, M. (1982). Principles of spatial problem solving. *Journal of Experimental Psychology: General, 111,* 157–175.

Levy, B. (1996). Improving memory in old age through implicit self-stereotyping. *Journal of Personality and Social Psychology, 71,* 1092–107.

Levy, B. A., & Kirsner, K. (1989). Reprocessing text: Indirect measures of word and message level processes. *Journal of Experimental Psychology: Learning, Memory, and Cognition, 15,* 407–417.

Lewandowsky, S., & Murdock, B. B. (1989). Memory for serial order. *Psychological Review, 96,* 25–57.

Li, X., Schweickert, R., & Gandour, J. (2000). The phonological similarity effect in immediate recall: Positions of shared phonemes. *Memory & Cognition, 28,* 1116–1125.

Libby, L. K. (2003). Imagery perspective and source monitoring in imagination inflation. *Memory & Cognition, 31,* 1072–1081.

Light, L. L., & Capps, J. L. (1986). Comprehension of pronouns in young and older adults. *Developmental Psychology, 22,* 580–585.

Light, L. L., Hollander, S., & Kayra-Stuart, F. (1981). Why attractive people are harder to remember. *Personality and Social Psychology Bulletin, 7,* 269–276.

Lindberg, M. A. (1980). Is knowledge base development a necessary and sufficient condition for memory development? *Journal of Experimental Child Psychology, 30,* 401–410.

Lindsay, D. S., Allen, B. P., Chan, J. C. K., & Dahl, L. C. (2004). Eyewitness suggestibility and source similarity: Intrusions of details from one event into memory reports of another event. *Journal of Memory and Language, 50,* 96–111.

Lindsay, D. S., Hagen, L., Read, J. D., Wade, K. A., & Garry, M. (2004). True photographs and false memories. *Psychological Science, 15,* 149–154.

Lindsay, D. S., & Johnson, M. K. (1991). Recognition memory and source monitoring. *Bulletin of the Psychonomic Society, 29,* 203–205.

Lindsay, R. C. L., & Wells, G. L. (1980). What price justice? *Law and Human Behavior, 4,* 303–313.

Lindsay, R. C. L., & Wells, G. L. (1985). Improving eyewitness identifications from lineups: Simultaneous versus sequential lineup presentations. *Journal of Applied Psychology, 70,* 556–564.

Liu, L. L., & Park, D. C. (2004). Aging and medical adherence: The use of automatic processes to achieve effortful things. *Psychology and Aging, 19,* 318–325.

Liu, T., & Cooper, L. A. (2001). The influence of task requirements on priming in object decision and matching. *Memory & Cognition, 29,* 874–882.

Liu, T. & Cooper, L. A. (2003). Explicit and implicit memory for rotating objects. *Journal of Experimental Psychology: Learning, Memory and Cognition, 29,* 554–562.

Lloyd-Jones, T., & Vernon, D. (2003). Semantic interference from visual object recognition on visual imagery. *Journal of Experimental Psychology: Learning, Memory and Cognition, 29,* 563–580.

Lockhart, R. S., & Murdock, B. B. (1970). Memory and the theory of signal detection. *Psychological Bulletin, 74,* 100–109.

Loftus, E. F. (1971). Memory for intentions: The effect of presence of a cue and interpolated activity. *Psychonomic Science, 23,* 315–316.

Loftus, E. F. (1979). The malleability of human memory. *American Scientist, 67,* 312–320.

Loftus, E. F. (1980). Impact of expert psychological testimony on the unreliability of eyewitness identification. *Journal of Applied Psychology, 65,* 9–15.

Loftus, E. F. (1993). The reality of repressed memories. *American Psychologist, 48,* 518–537.

Loftus, E. F. (2004). Memories of things unseen. *Current Directions in Psychological Science, 13,* 145–147.

Loftus, E. F., & Loftus, G. R. (1980). On the permanence of stored information in the human brain. *American Psychologist, 35,* 409–420.

Loftus, E. F., Loftus, G. R., & Messo, J. (1987). Some facts about "weapon focus." *Law and Human Behavior, 11,* 55–62.

Loftus, E. F., Miller, D. G., & Burns, H. J. (1978). Semantic integration of verbal information into a visual memory. *Journal of Experimental Psychology: Human Learning and Memory, 4,* 19–31.

Loftus, E. F., & Palmer, J. C. (1974). Reconstruction of automobile destruction: An example of the interaction between language and memory. *Journal of Verbal Learning and Verbal Behavior, 13,* 585–589.

Loftus, E. F., & Zanni, G. (1975). Eyewitness testimony: The influence of the wording of a question. *Bulletin of the Psychonomic Society, 5,* 86–88.

London, K., & Nunez, N. (2000). The effect of jury deliberations on jurors' propensity to disregard inadmissible evidence. *Journal of Applied Psychology, 85,* 932–939.

Long, D. L., & Prat, C. S. (2002). Memory for *Star Trek:* The role of prior knowledge in recognition revisited. *Journal of Experimental Psychology: Learning, Memory, and Cognition, 28,* 1073–1082.

Lucchelli, F., Muggia, S., & Spinnler, H. (1997). Selective proper name anomia: A case involving only contemporary celebrities. *Cognitive Neuropsychology, 14,* 881–900.

Luo, C. R. (1993). Enhanced feeling of recognition: Effects of identifying and manipulating test items on recognition memory. *Journal of Experimental Psychology: Learning, Memory, and Cognition, 19,* 405–413.

Luria, A. R. (1968). *The Mind of a Mnemonist: A Little Book About a Vast Memory.* New York: Basic Books.

Luus, C. A. E., & Wells, G. L. (1994). The malleability of eyewitness confidence: co-witness and perseverance effects. *Journal of Applied Psychology, 79,* 714–723.

Lynch, S., & Yarnell, P. R. (1973). Retrograde amnesia: Delayed forgetting after concussion. *American Journal of Psychology, 86,* 643–645.

Lyon, L. S. (1985). Facilitating telephone number recall in a case of psychogenic amnesia. *Journal of Behavior Therapy and Experimental Psychiatry, 16,* 147–149.

Maass, A., & Köhnken, G. (1989). Simulating the "weapon effect." *Law and Human Behavior, 13,* 397–408.

Macken, W. J. (2002). Environmental context and recognition: The role of recollection and familiarity. *Journal of Experimental Psychology: Learning, Memory, and Cognition, 28,* 153–161.

MacLeod, C. M. (1989). Directed forgetting affects both direct and indirect tests of memory. *Journal of Experimental Psychology: Learning, Memory, and Cognition, 15,* 13–21.

MacLeod, C., Dodd, M. D., Sheard, E. D., Wilson, D. E., & Bibi, U. (2003). In opposition to inhibition. *The Psychology of Learning and Motivation, 43,* 163–214.

MacPherson, S. E., Phillips, L. H., & Sala, S. D. (2002). Age, executive functioning, and social decision making: A dorsolateral prefrontal theory of cognitive aging. *Psychology and Aging, 17,* 598–609.

Macrae, C. N., & Roseveare, T. A. (2002). I was always on my mind: The self and temporary forgetting. *Psychonomic Bulletin & Review, 9,* 611–614.

Madsen, M. C., & McGaugh, J. L. (1961). The effect of ECS on one-trial avoidance learning. *Journal of Comparative and Physiological Psychology, 54,* 522–523.

Mahmood, D., Manier, D., & Hirst, W. (2004). Memory for how one learned of multiple deaths from AIDS: Repeated exposure and distinctiveness. *Memory & Cognition, 32,* 125–134.

Mahrer, P., & Miles, C. (1999). Memorial and strategic determinants of tactile memory. *Journal of Experimental Psychology: Learning, Memory and Cognition, 25,* 630–643.

Mahut, H., Zola-Morgan, S., & Moss, M. (1982). Hippocampal resections impair associative learning and recognition memory in the monkey. *The Journal of Neuroscience, 2,* 1214–1229.

Malmberg, K. J., Steyvers, M., Stephens, J. D., & Shiffrin, R. M. (2002). Feature frequency effects in recognition memory. *Memory & Cognition, 30,* 607–613.

Malpass, R. S., & Devine, P. G. (1981). Eyewitness identification: Lineup instructions and the absence of the offender. *Journal of Applied Psychology, 66,* 482–489.

Mandler, G. (1967). Organization and memory. In K. W. Spence and J. T. Spence (Eds.), *The Psychology of Learning and Motivation.* New York: Academic Press.

Mandler, G. (1980). Recognizing: The judgment of previous occurrence. *Psychological Review, 87,* 252–271.

Mandler, J. M., Bauer, P. J., & McDonough, L. (1991). Separating the sheep from the goats: Differentiating global categories. *Cognitive Psychology, 23,* 263–298.

Mandler, J. M., Fivush, R., & Reznick, J. S. (1987). The development of contextual categories. *Cognitive Development, 2,* 339–354.

Mandler, J. M., & McDonough, L. (1996). Drinking and driving don't mix: Inductive generalization in infancy. *Cognition, 59,* 307–335.

Mandler, J. M., & Ritchey, G. H. (1977). Long-term memory for pictures. *Journal of Experimental Psychology: Human Learning and Memory, 3,* 386–396.

Mäntylä, T. (2003). Assessing absentmindedness: Prospective memory complaint and impairment in middle-aged adults. *Memory & Cognition, 31,* 15–25.

Maratos, E. J., Dolan, R. J., Morris, J. S., Henson R. M. A., & Rugg, M. D. (2001). Neural activity associated with episodic memory for emotional context. *Neuropsychologia, 39,* 910–920.

Mark, M. M., & Mellor, S. (1991). Effect of self-revelence of an event on hindsight bias: The foreseeability of a layoff. *Journal of Applied Psychology, 76,* 569–577.

Marsh, E. J., Dolan, P. O., Balota, D. A., & Roediger, H. L. (2004). Part-set cuing effects in younger and older adults. *Psychology and Aging, 19,* 134–144.

Marsh, E. J., Edelman, G., & Bower, G. H. (2001). Demonstrations of a generation effect in context memory. *Memory & Cognition, 29,* 798–805.

Marsh, E. J., Meade, M. L., & Roediger, H. L. (2003). Learning facts from fiction. *Journal of Memory and Language, 49,* 519–536.

Marsh, R. L., Hicks, J. L., Cook, G. I., Hansen, J. S., & Pallos, A. L. (2003). Interference to ongoing activities covaries with the characteristics of an event-based intention. *Journal of Experimental Psychology: Learning, Memory, and Cognition, 29,* 861–870.

Marsh, R. L., Hicks, J. L., Hancock, T. W., & Munsayac, K. (2002). Investigating the output monitoring component of event-based prospective memory performance. *Memory & Cognition, 30,* 302–311.

Martin-Loeches, M., Hinojosa, J. A., Fernandez-Frias, C., & Rubia, F. J. (2001). Functional differences in the semantic processing of concrete and abstract words. *Neuropsychologia, 39,* 1086–1096.

Mather, M., & Johnson, M. K. (2000). Choice-supportive source monitoring: Do our decisions seem better to us as we age? *Psychology and Aging, 15,* 596–606.

Mather, M., Johnson, M. K., & De Leonardis, D. M. (1999). Stereotype reliance in source monitoring: Age differences and neuropsychological test correlates. *Cognitive Neuropsychology, 16,* 437–458.

Mather, M., Shafir, E., & Johnson, M. K. (2000). Misremembrance of options past: Source monitoring and choice. *Psychological Science, 11,* 132–138.

Mather, M., Shafir, E., & Johnson, M. K. (2003). Remembering chosen and assigned options. *Memory & Cognition, 31,* 422–433.

Matvey, G., Dunlosky, J., Shaw, R. J., Parks, C., & Hertzog, C. (2002). Age-related equivalence and deficit in knowledge updating of cue effectiveness. *Psychology and Aging, 17,* 589–597.

Mayer, R. E. (1983). Can you repeat this? Qualitative effects of repetition and advanced organizers on learning from scientific prose. *Journal of Educational Psychology, 75,* 40–49.

Mayes, A. R., & Montaldi, D. (1999). The neuroimaging of long-term memory encoding processes. *Memory, 7,* 613–659.

Maylor, E. A. (2002). Serial position effects in semantic memory: Reconstructing the order of versus of hymns. *Psychonomic Bulletin & Review, 9,* 816–820.

Mazzoni, G. A. L., Loftus, E. F., & Kirsch, I. (2001). Changing beliefs about implausible autobiographical events: A little plausibility goes a long way. *Journal of Experimental Psychology: Applied, 7,* 51–59.

Mazzoni. G. A. L., & Memon, A. (2003). Imagination can create false autobiographical memories. *Psychological Science, 14,* 186–188.

McAdams, D. P. (2001). The psychology of life stories. *Journal of General Psychology, 5,* 100–122.

McCarthy, R. A., & Hodges, J. R. (1995). Trapped in time: Profound autobiographical memory loss following thalamic stroke. In R. Campbell & M. A. Conway (Eds.), *Broken Memories: Case Studies in Memory Impairment.* Cambridge, MA: Blackwell.

McCarthy, R. A., & Warrington, E. K. (1992). Actors but not scripts: The dissociation of people and events in retrograde amnesia. *Neuropsychologia, 30,* 633–644.

McClelland, J. L. (2000). Connectionist models of memory. In E. Tulving & F. I. M. Craik (Eds.), *The Oxford Handbook of Memory,* pp. 583–596. New York: Oxford University Press.

McCloskey, M., Caramazza, A., & Green, B. (1980). Curvilinear motion in the absence of external forces: Naive beliefs about the motion of objects. *Science, 210,* 1139–1141.

McCloskey, M., & Kohl, D. (1983). Naive physics: The curvilinear impetus principle and its role in interactions with moving objects. *Journal of Experimental Psychology: Learning, Memory, and Cognition, 9,* 146–156.

McCloskey, M., & Watkins, M. J. (1978). The seeing-more-than-is-there phenomenon: Implications for the locus of iconic storage. *Journal of Experimental Psychology: Human Perception and Performance, 4,* 553–564.

McCloskey, M. Wible, C. G., & Cohen, N. J. (1988). Is there a special flashbulb-memory mechanism? *Journal of Experimental Psychology: General, 117,* 171–181.

McCloskey, M. & Zaragoza, M. (1985). Misleading postevent information and memory for events: Arguments and evidence against memory impairment hypotheses. *Journal of Experimental Psychology: General, 114,* 1–16.

McConnell, J. V. (1962). Memory transfer through cannibalism in planarians. *Journal of Neuropsychiatry (Supplement),* 42–48.

McDaniel, M. A., & Einstein, G. O. (1986). Bizarre imagery as an effective memory aid: The importance of distinctiveness. *Journal of Experimental Psychology: Learning, Memory, and Cognition, 12,* 54–65.

McDaniel, M. A., Einstein, G. O., Dunay, P. K., & Cobb, R. E. (1986). Encoding difficulty and memory: Toward a unifying theory. *Journal of Memory and Language, 25,* 645–656.

McDaniel, M. A., Einstein, G. O., & Lollis, T. (1988). Qualitative and quantitative considerations in encoding difficulty effects. *Memory & Cognition, 16,* 8–14.

McDaniel, M. A., Guynn, M. J., Einstein, G. O., & Breneiser, J. (2004). Cue-focused and reflexive-associative processes in prospective memory retrieval. *Journal of Experimental Psychology: Learning, Memory, and Cognition, 30,* 605–614.

McDaniel, M. A., & Waddill, P. J. (1990). Generation effects for context words: Implications for item-specific and multifactor theories. *Journal of Memory and Language, 29,* 201–211.

McFarland, C., & Ross, M. (1987). The relation between current impressions and memories of self and dating partners. *Personality and Social Psychology Bulletin, 13,* 228–238.

McGaugh, J. L. (1966). Time-dependent processes in memory storage. *Science, 153,* 1351–1358.

McGeoch, J. A. (1932). Forgetting and the law of disuse. *Psychological Review, 39,* 352–370.

McGovern, J. B. (1964). Extinction of associations in four transfer paradigms. *Psychological Monographs, 78,* no. 16.

McGuire, M. J., & Maki, R. H. (2001). When knowing more means less: The effect of fan on metamemory judgments. *Journal of Experimental Psychology: Learning, Memory, and Cognition, 27,* 1172–1179.

McIsaac, H. K., & Eich, E. (2004). Vantage point in traumatic memory. *Psychological Science, 15,* 248–253.

McNamara, T. P. (1986). Mental representations of spatial relations. *Cognitive Psychology, 18,* 87–121.

McNamara, T. P., & Altarriba, J. (1988). Depth of spreading activation revisited: Semantic mediated priming occurs in lexical decisions. *Journal of Memory and Language, 27,* 545–559.

McNamara, T. P., Altarriba, J., Bendele, M., Johnson, S. C., & Clayton, K. N. (1989). Constraints on priming in spatial memory: Naturally learned and experimentally learned environments. *Memory & Cognition, 17,* 444–453.

McNamara, T. P., Halpin, J. A., & Hardy, J. K. (1992a). Spatial and temporal contributions to the structure of spatial memory. *Journal of Experimental Psychology: Learning, Memory, and Cognition, 18,* 555–564.

McNamara, T. P., Halpin, J. A., & Hardy, J. K. (1992b). The representation and integration in memory of spatial and nonspatial information. *Memory & Cognition, 20,* 519–532.

McNamara, T. P., Hardy, J. K., & Hirtle, S. C. (1989). Subjective hierarchies in spatial memory. *Journal of Experimental Psychology: Learning, Memory, and Cognition, 15,* 211–227.

McNamara, T. P., & LeSueur, L. L. (1989). Mental representations of spatial and nonspatial relations. *The Quarterly Journal of Experimental Psychology, 41A,* 215–233.

McNamara, T. P., Ratcliff, R. & McKoon, G. (1984). The mental representation of knowledge acquired from maps. *Journal of Experimental Psychology: Learning, Memory and Cognition, 10,* 723–732.

McNamara, T. P., Rump, B., & Werner, S. (2003). Egocentric and geocentric frames of reference in memory for large-scale space. *Psychonomic Bulletin & Review, 10,* 589–595.

Meade, M. L., & Roediger, H. L. (2002). Explorations in the social contagion of memory. *Memory & Cognition, 30,* 995–1009.

Medin, D. L. (1989). Concepts and conceptual structure. *American Psychologist, 44,* 1469–1481.

Medin, D. L., & Shaffer, M. M. (1978). Context theory of classification learning. *Psychological Review, 85,* 207–238.

Medin, D. L., & Shoben, E. J. (1988). Context and structure in conceptual combination. *Cognitive Psychology, 20,* 158–190.

Medin, D. L., & Smith, E. E. (1984). Concepts and concept formation. *Annual Review of Psychology, 35,* 113–138.

Medin, D. L., Wattenmaker, W. D., & Hampson, S. E. (1987). Family resemblance, conceptual cohesiveness, and category construction. *Cognitive Psychology, 19,* 242–279.

Meissner, C. A., Brigham, J. C., & Kelley, C. M. (2002). The influence of retrieval processes in verbal overshadowing. *Memory & Cognition, 29,* 176–186.

Melton, A. W., & Irwin, J. M., (1940). The influence of degree of interpolated learning on retroactive inhibition and the overt transfer of specific responses. *American Journal of Psychology, 53,* 173–203.

Memon, A., Hope, L., Bartlett, J., & Bull, R. (2002). Eyewitness recognition errors: The effects of mugshot viewing and choosing in young and old adults. *Memory & Cognition, 30,* 1219–1227.

Merrill, A. A., & Baird, J. C. (1987). Semantic and spatial factors in environmental memory. *Memory & Cognition, 15,* 101–108.

Metcalf, J. (2000). Metamemory: Theory and data. In E. Tulving & F. I. M. Craik (Eds.), *The Oxford Handbook of Memory,* pp. 197–211. New York: Oxford University Press.

Metcalfe, J. (2002). Is study time allocated selectively to a region of proximal learning? *Journal of Experimental Psychology: General, 131,* 349–363.

Metcalfe, J., & Kornell, N. (2003). The dynamics of learning and allocation of study time to a region of proximal learning. *Journal of Experimental Psychology: General, 132,* 530–542.

Meyer, D. E., Irwin, D. E., Osman, A. M., & Kounios, J. (1988). The dynamics of cognition and action: Mental processes inferred from speed-accuracy decomposition. *Psychological Review, 95,* 183–237.

Meyer, D. E. & Schvanevelt, R. W. (1971). Facilitation in recognizing pairs of words: Evidence of a dependence between retrieval operations. *Journal of Experimental Psychology, 90,* 227–234.

Miles, C., & Jenkins, R. (2000). Recency and suffix effects with immediate recall of olfactory stimuli. *Memory, 8,* 195–206.

Miller, A. R., Baratta, C., Wynveen, C., & Rosenfeld, J. P. (2001). P300 latency, but not amplitude or topography, distinguishes between true and false recognition. *Journal of Experimental Psychology: Learning, Memory, and Cognition, 27,* 354–361.

Miller, G. A. (1956). The magical number seven, plus or minus two: Some limits on our capacity for processing information. *Psychological Review, 63,* 81–97.

Milner, B., Corkin, S., & Teuber, H. L. (1968). Further analysis of the hipocampal amnesic syndrome: 14-year follow-up study of H. M. *Neuropsychologia, 6,* 215–234.

Minsky, M. L. (1986). *The Society of Mind.* New York: Simon & Schuster.

Mintzer, M. Z., & Griffiths, R. R. (2001). False recognition in triazolam-induced amnesia. *Journal of Memory and Language, 44,* 475–492.

Mishkin, M., & Appenzeller, T. (1987). The anatomy of memory. *Scientific American, 256,* 80–89.

Montomery, P., Siverstein, P., Wichmann, R., Fleischaker, K., & Andberg, M. (1993). Spatial updating in Parkinson's disease. *Brain and Cognition, 23,* 113–126.

Morris, C. D., Bransford, J. D., & Franks, J. J. (1977). Levels of processing versus transfer appropriate processing. *Journal of Verbal Learning and Verbal Behavior, 16,* 519–533.

Morrow, D. G., Greenspan, S. L., & Bower, G. H. (1987). Accessibility and situation models in narrative comprehension. *Journal of Memory and Language, 26,* 165–187.

Morton, J., Crowder, R. G., & Prussin, H. A. (1971). Experiments with the stimulus suffix effect. *Journal of Experimental Psychology: Monograph, 91,* 169–190.

Moyer, R. S., Bradley, D. R., Sorensen, M. H., Whiting, J. C., & Mansfield, D. P. (1977). Psychophysical functions for perceived and remembered size. *Science, 200,* 330–332.

Moyer, R. S., Sklarew, P., & Whiting, J. (1982). Memory psychophysics. In H. Geissler & P. Patzold (Eds.), *Psychophysical Judgment and the Process of Perception,* pp. 35–46. New York: North-Holland.

Muller, R. U., Kuble, J. L., & Ranck, J. B. (1987). Spatial firing patterns of hippocampal complex-spike cells in a fixed environment. *The Journal of Neuroscience, 7,* 1935–1950.

Mulligan, N. W. (2001). Generation and hypermnesia. *Journal of Experimental Psychology: Learning, Memory, and Cognition, 27,* 436–450.

Munger, M. P., Solberg, J. L., & Horrocks, K. K. (1999). The relationship between mental rotation and representational momentum. *Journal of Experimental Psychology: Learning, Memory, and Cognition, 25,* 1557–1568.

Murdock, B. B. (1962). The serial position effect of free recall. *Journal of Experimental Psychology, 64,* 482–488.

Murdock, B. B. (1974). *Human memory: Theory and data.* Potomac, MD: Erlbaum.

Murdock, B. B. (1982a). A theory for the storage and retrieval of item and associative information. *Psychological Review, 89,* 609–626.

Murdock, B. B. (1982b). A distributed memory model for serial-order information. *Psychological Review, 90,* 316–338.

Murdock, B. B. (1993). TODAM2: A model for the storage and retrieval of item, associative, and serial-order information. *Psychological Review, 100,* 183–203.

Murdock, B. B. (1995). Developing TODAM: Three models for serial-order information. *Memory & Cognition, 23,* 631–645.

Murray, D. J. (1967). The role of speech responses in short-term memory. *Canadian Journal of Psychology, 21,* 263–276.

Myers, J. L., O'Brien, E. J., Balota, D. A., & Toyofuku, M. L. (1984). Memory search without interference: The role of integration. *Cognitive Psychology, 16,* 217–242.

Myerson, J., Hale, S., Wagstaff, D., Poon, L. W., & Smith, G. A. (1990). The information-loss model: A mathematical theory of age-related cognitive slowing. *Psychological Review, 97,* 475–487.

Myerson, J., Wagstaff, D., & Hale, S. (1994). Brinley plots, explained variance, and the analysis of age differences in response latencies. *Journal of Gerontology: Psychological Sciences, 49,* P72-P80.

Nadel, L., & Zola-Morgan, S. (1984). Infantile amnesia: A neurobiological perspective. In M. Moscovitch (Ed.), *Infant Memory.* New York: Plenum Press.

Nakamura, G. V., Graesser, A. C., Zimmerman, J. A., & Riha, J. (1985). Script processing in a natural situation. *Memory & Cognition, 13,* 140–144.

Neath, I., Surprenant, A. M., & Crowder, R. G. (1993). The context-dependent stimulus suffix effect. *Journal of Experimental Psychology: Learning, Memory and Cognition, 19,* 698–703.

Neely, J. H. (1977). Semantic priming and retrieval from lexical memory: Roles of inhibitionless spreading activation and limited-capacity attention. *Journal of Experimental Psychology: General, 106,* 226–254.

Neisser, U. (1981). John Dean's memory: A case study. *Cognition, 9,* 1–22.

Neisser, U. (1982). Snapshots or benchmarks? In U. Neisser (Ed.), *Memory Observed: Remembering in Natural Contexts,* pp. 43–48. San Francisco: Freeman.

Nelson, K. (1993). The psychological and social origins of autobiographical memory. *Psychological Science, 4,* 7–14.

Nelson, K., & Fivush, R. (2004). The emergence of autobiographical memory: A social cultural developmental theory. *Psychological Review, 111,* 486–511.

Nelson, T. O. (1978). Detecting small amounts of information in memory: Savings for nonrecognized items. *Journal of Experimental Psychology: Human Learning and Memory, 4,* 453–468.

Nelson, T. O., & Dunlosky, J. (1991). When people's judgments of learning (JOLs) are extremely accurate at predicting subsequent recall: The "Delayed-JOL effect." *Psychological Science, 2,* 267–270.

Nelson, T. O., & Leonesio, R. J. (1988). Allocation of self-paced study time and the "labor-in vain effect." *Journal of Experimental Psychology: Learning, Memory, and Cognition, 14,* 676–686.

Nemiah, J. C. (1979). Dissociative amnesia: A clinical and theoretical reconsideration. In J. F. Kihlstrom and F. J. Evans (Eds.), *Functional Disorders of Memory.* Hillsdale, NJ: Erlbaum.

Newcombe, N. S., Drummy, A. B., Fox, N. A., Lie, E., & Ottinger-Alberts, W. (2000). Remembering early childhood: How much, how, and (why or why not). *Current Directions in Psychological Science, 9,* 55–58.

Newcombe, N., Huttenlocher, J., Sandberg, E., Lie, E., & Johnson, S. (1999). What do misestimations and asymmetries in spatial judgment indicate about spatial representation? *Journal of Experimental Psychology: Learning, Memory and Cognition, 25,* 986–996.

Newtson, D. (1976). Foundations of attribution: The perception of ongoing behavior. In J. H. Harvey, W. J. Ickes, & R. F. Kidd (Eds.), *New Directions in Attribution Research.* New York: Erlbaum.

Nickerson, R. S. (1984). Retrieval inhibition from part-set cuing: A persistent enigma in memory research. *Memory & Cognition, 12,* 531–552.

Nickerson, R. S., & Adams, M. J. (1979). Long-term memory for a common object. *Cognitive Psychology, 11,* 287–307.

Niedwieska, A. (2003). Misleading postevent information and flashbulb memories. *Memory, 11,* 549–558.

Niewiadomski, M. W., & Hockley, W. E. (2001). Interrupting recognition memory: Tests of familiarity-based accounts of the revelation effect. *Memory & Cognition, 29,* 1130–1138.

Nigro, G., & Neisser, U. (1983). Point of view in personal memories. *Cognitive Psychology, 15,* 467–482.

Nisbett, R. E., & Wilson, T. D. (1977). Telling more than we can know: Verbal reports on mental processes. *Psychological Review, 84,* 231–259.

Nissen, M. J., & Bullemer, P. (1987). Attentional requirements of learning: Evidence from performance measures. *Cognitive Psychology, 19,* 1–32.

Nittono, H., Suehiro, M., & Hori, T. (2002). Word imagability and N400 in an incidental memory paradigm. *International Journal of Pychophysiology, 44,* 219–229.

Nosofsky, R. M. (1988). Exemplar-based accounts of relations between classification, recognition, and typicality. *Journal of Experimental Psychology: Learning, Memory, and Cognition, 14,* 700–708.

Nyberg, L., Cabeza, R., & Tulving, E. (1996). PET studies of encoding and retrieval: The HERA model. *Psychonomic Bulletin & Review, 3,* 135–148.

Nyberg, L., Maitland, S. B., Rönnlund, M., Bäckman, L., Dixon, R. A., Wahlin, A., & Nilsson, L. (2003). Selective adult age differences in an age-invariant multifactor model of declarative memory. *Psychology and Aging, 18,* 149–160.

O'Connor, M., Verfaellie, M., & Cermak, L. S. (1995). Clinical differentiation of amnesic subtypes. In A. D. Baddeley, B. A. Wilson, & F. N. Watts (Eds.), *Handbook of Memory Disorders,* pp. 53–80. New York: Wiley.

O'Keefe, J., & Dostrovsky, J. (1971). The hippocampus as a spatial map. *Brain Research, 34,* 171–175.

Olafson, K. M., & Ferraro, F. R. (2001). Effects of emotional state on lexical decision performance. *Brain and Cognition, 45,* 15–20.

O'Reilly, R. C., & Rudy, J. W. (2001). Conjunctive representations in learning and memory: Principles of cortical and hippocampal function. *Psychological Review, 108,* 311–345.

Ornstein, P. A., Naus, M. J., & Liberty, C. (1975). Rehearsal and organization processes in children's memory. *Child Development 46,* 818–830.

Ortony, A., Turner, T. J., & Antos, S. J. (1983). A puzzle about affect and recognition memory. *Journal of Experimental Psychology: Learning, Memory, and Cognition, 9,* 725–729.

Otani, H., & Hodge, M. H. (1991). Does hypermnesia occur in recognition and cued recall? *American Journal of Psychology, 104,* 101–116.

Pansky, A., & Koriat, A. (2004). The basic-level convergence effect in memory distortions. *Psychological Science, 15,* 52–59.

Papanicolaou, A. C., Simos, P. G., Castillo, E. M., Breier, J. I., Katz, J. S., & Wright, A. A. (2002).

The hippocampus and memory of verbal and pictoral material. *Learning and Memory, 9,* 99–104.

Paris, S. C., & Lindaur, B. K. (1976). The role of inference in children's comprehension and memory for sentences. *Cognitive Psychology, 8,* 217–227.

Park, D. C., Nisbett, R., & Heeden, T. (1999). Aging, culture, and cognition. *Journals of Gerontology: Psychological Sciences, 54B,* P75–P84.

Parks, T. E. (1965). Post-retinal visual storage. *American Journal of Psychology, 78,* 145–147.

Parmentier, F. B. R., Tremblay, S., & Jones, D. M. (2004). Exploring the suffix effect in serial visuospatial short-term memory. *Psychonomic Bulletin & Review, 11,* 289–295.

Patternson, K. E., Meltzer, R. H., & Mandler, G. (1971). Inter-response times in categorized free recall. *Journal of Verbal Learning and Verbal Behavior, 10,* 417–426.

Pavio, A. (1969). Mental imagery in associative learning and memory. *Psychological Review, 76,* 241–263.

Payne, D. G. (1987). Hypermnesia and reminiscence in recall: A historical and empirical review. *Psychological Bulletin, 101,* 5–27.

Pearse, S. A., Isherwood, S., Hrouda, D., Richardson, P. H., Erskine, A., & Skinner, J. (1990). Memory and pain: Tests of mood congruity and state dependent learning in experimentally induced and clinical pain. *Pain, 43,* 187–193.

Pellegrino, J. W. (1971). A general measure of organization in free recall for variable unit size and internal sequential consistency. *Behavior Research Methods & Instruments, 3,* 241–246.

Pelosi, L., Geesken, J. M., Holly, M., Hayward, M., & Blumhardt, L. D. (1997). Working memory impairment in early multiple sclerosis: Evidence from an event-related potential study of patients with clinically isolated myelopathy. *Brain, 120,* 2039–2058.

Penfield, W. (1955). The permanent record of the stream of consciousness. *Acta Psychologica, 11,* 47–69.

Pennington, N., & Hastie, R. (1986). Evidence evaluation in complex decision making. *Journal of Personality and Social Psychology, 51,* 242–258.

Pennington, N., & Hastie, R. (1988). Explanation-based decision making: Effects of memory structure on judgment. *Journal of Experimental Psychology: Learning, Memory and Cognition, 14,* 521–533.

Pennington, N., & Hastie, R. (1992). Explaining the evidence: Tests of the story model for juror decision making. *Journal of Personality and Social Psychology, 62,* 189–206.

Perfect, T. J. (1994). What can Brinley plots tell us about cognitive aging? *Journal of Gerontology: Psychological Sciences, 49,* P60–P64.

Perfect, T. J., Moulin, C. J. A., Conway, M. A., & Perry, E. (2002). Assessing the inhibitory account of retrieval-induced forgetting with implicit-memory tests. *Journal of Experimental Psychology: Learning, Memory and Cognition, 28,* 1111–1119.

Pesta, B. J., Murphy, M. D., & Sanders, R. E. (2001). Are emotionally charged lures immune to false memory? *Journal of Experimental Psychology: Learning, Memory and Cognition, 27,* 328–338.

Peters, R., & McGee, R. (1982). Cigarette smoking and state-dependent memory. *Psychopharmacology, 76,* 232–235.

Peterson, L. R., & Johnson, S. F. (1971). Some effects of minimizing articulation of short-term retention. *Journal of Verbal Learning and Verbal Behavior, 10,* 346–354.

Peterson, L. R., & Peterson, M. J. (1959). Short-term retention of individual verbal items. *Journal of Experimental Psychology, 58,* 193–198.

Peynirc̆glu, Z. F., & Tekcan, A. I. (1993). Revelation effect: Effort or priming does not create the sense of familiarity. *Journal of Experimental Psychology: Learning, Memory and Cognition, 19,* 382–388.

Pezdek, K., Finger, K., & Hodge, D. (1997). Planting false childhood memories: The role of event plausibility. *Psychological Science, 8,* 437–441.

Pickel, K. L. (1998). Unusualness and threat as possible causes of "weapon focus." *Memory, 6,* 277–295.

Pickel, K. L. (2004). When a lie becomes the truth: The effects of self-generated misinformation on eyewitness memory. *Memory, 12,* 14–26.

Pike, R. (1984). A comparison of convolution and matrix distributed memory systems. *Psychological Review, 91,* 281–294.

Pillemer, D. B. (2001). Momentous events and the life story. *Journal of General Psychology, 5,* 123–134.

Pillon, B., Ertle, S., Deweer, B., Bonnet, A. Vidailhet, M., & Dubois, B. (1997). Memory for spatial location in "de novo" Parkinsonian patients. *Neuropschologia, 35,* 221–228.

Piolino, P., Belliard, S., Desgranges, B., Perron, M., & Eustache, F. (2003). Autobiographical memory and autonoetic consciousness in a case of semantic dementia. *Cognitive Neuropsychology, 20,* 619–639.

Pirolli, P. L., & Anderson, J. R. (1985). The role of practice in fact retrieval. *Journal of Experimental Psychology: Learning, Memory, and Cognition, 11,* 136–153.

Plumert, J. M. (1994). Flexibility in children's use of spatial and categorical organizational strategies in recall. *Developmental Psychology, 30,* 738–747.

Pollack, I. (1970). A nonparametric procedure for evaluation of true and false positives. *Behavioral Research Methods & Instruments, 2,* 155–156.

Pollio, H. R., Richards, S., & Lucas, R. (1969). Temporal properties of category recall. *Journal of Verbal Learning and Verbal Behavior, 8,* 529–536.

Porter, S., Birt, A. R., Yuille, J. C., & Lehman, D. R. (2000). Negotiating false memories: Interviewer and rememberer characteristics relate to memory distortion. *Psychological Science, 11,* 507–510.

Posner, M. I., & Keele, S. W. (1968). On the genesis of abstract ideas. *Journal of Experimental Psychology, 77,* 353–363.

Posner, M. I., & Keele, S. W. (1970). Retention of abstract ideas. *Journal of Experimental Psychology, 83,* 304–308.

Posner, M. I., & Raichle, M. E. (1994). *Images of Mind.* New York: Scientific American Library.

Postman, L., & Adams, P. A. (1956). Studies in incidental learning: IV. The interaction of orienting tasks and stimulus materials. *Journal of Experimental Psychology, 51,* 329–333.

Postman, L., Adams, P. A., & Philips, L. W. (1955). Studies in incidental learning: II. The effects of association value and of the method of testing. *Journal of Experimental Psychology, 49,* 1–10.

Postman, L., & Keppel, G. (1977). Conditions of cumulative proactive inhibition. *Journal of Experimental Psychology: General, 106,* 376–403.

Postman, L., & Stark, K. (1969). Role of response availability in transfer and interference. *Journal of Experimental Psychology, 79,* 168–177.

Potts, G. R. (1972). Information processing strategies used in the encoding of linear orderings. *Journal of Verbal Learning and Verbal Behavior, 11,* 727–740.

Powell, J. L. (1988). A test of the knew-it-all-along effect in the 1984 presidential statewide elections. *Journal of Applied Social Psychology, 18,* 760–773.

Presson, C. C., DeLange, N., & Hazelrigg, M. D. (1989). Orientation specificity in spatial memory: What makes a path different from a map of a path? *Journal of Experimental Psychology: Learning, Memory and Cognition, 15,* 887–897.

Pretkanis, A. R., Greenwald, A. G., Leippe, M. R., & Baumgarder, M. H. (1988). In search of reliable persuasion effects: III. The sleeper effect is dead: Long live the sleeper effect. *Journal of Personality and Social Psychology, 54,* 203–218.

Prizzolo, F. J., Hansch, E. C., Mortimer, J. A., Webster, D. D., & Kuskowski, M. A. (1982). Dementia in Parkinson's disease: A neuropsychological analysis. *Brain and Cognition, 1,* 71–83.

Pulvermüller, F., Lutzenberger, W., & Preissl, H. (1999). Nouns and verbs in the intact brain: Evidence from event-related potentials and high-frequency cortical responses. *Cerebral Cortex, 9,* 497–506.

Quinn, P. C., Eimas, P. D., & Rosenkrantz, S. L. (1993). Evidence for representations of perceptually similar natural categories by 3-month-old and 4-month-old infants. *Perception, 22,* 463–475.

Raaijmakers, J. G. W., & Shiffrin, R. M. (1980). SAM: A theory of probabilistic search of associative memory. *The Psychology of Learning and Motivation, 14,* 207–262.

Raaijmakers, J. G. W., & Shiffrin, R. M. (1981). Search of associative memory. *Psychological Review, 88,* 93–134.

Raaijmakers, J. G. W., & Shiffrin, R. M. (1992). Models for recall and recognition. *Annual Review of Psychology, 43,* 205–234.

Radvansky, G. A. (1999). Memory retrieval and suppression: The inhibition of situation models. *Journal of Experimental Psychology: General, 128,* 563–579.

Radvansky, G. A., Carlson-Radvansky, J., & Irwin, D. E. (1995). Uncertainty in estimating distances from memory. *Memory & Cognition, 23,* 596–606.

Radvansky, G. A., Fleming, K. J., & Simmons, J. A. (1995). Timbre reliance in nonmusicians' and musicians' memory for melodies. *Music Perception, 13,* 127–140.

Radvansky, G. A., Gerard, L. D., Zacks, R. T., & Hasher, L. (1990). Younger and odler adults' use of mental models as representations of text materials. *Psychology and Aging, 5,* 209–214.

Radvansky, G. A., and Potter, J. K. (2000). Source cuing: Memory for melodies. *Memory and Cognition, 28,* 693–699.

Radvansky, G. A., Spieler, D. H., & Zacks, R. T. (1993). Mental model organization. *Journal of Experimental Psychology: Learning, Memory, and Cognition, 19,* 95–114.

Radvansky, G. A., Wyer, R. S., Curiel, J. M., & Lutz, M. F. (1997). Situation models and abstract ownership relations. *Journal of Experimental Psychology: Learning, Memory, and Cognition, 23,* 1233–1246.

Radvansky, G. A., & Zacks, R. T. (1991). Mental models and the fan effect. *Journal of Experimental Psychology: Learning, Memory, and Cognition, 17,* 940–953.

Radvansky, G. A., Zwaan, R. A., Federico, T., & Franklin, N. (1998). Retrieval from temporally organized situation models. *Journal of Experimental Psychology: Learning, Memory, and Cognition, 24,* 1224–1237.

Radvansky, G. A., Zwaan, R. A., Curiel, J. M., & Copeland, D. E. (2001). Situation models and aging. *Psychology and Aging, 16,* 145–160.

Ranganath, C., & Pallar, K. A. (1999). Frontal brain activity during episodic and semantic retrieval: Insights from event-related potentials. *Journal of Cognitive Neuroscience, 11,* 598–609.

Rahhal, T. A., May, C. P., & Hasher, L. (2002). Truth and character: Sources that older adults can remember. *Psychological Science, 13,* 101–105

Rajaram, S. (1993). Remembering and knowing: Two means of access to the personal past. *Memory & Cognition, 21,* 89–102.

Rand, G., & Wapner, S. (1967). Postural states as a factor in memory. *Journal of Verbal Learning and Verbal Behavior, 6,* 268–271.

Raney, G. E. (2003). A context-dependent representation model for explaining text repetition effects. *Psychonomic Bulletin & Review, 10,* 15–28.

Read, J. D. (1994). Understanding bystander misidentifications: The role of familiarity and contextual knowledge. In D. F. Ross, J. D. Read, and M. P. Toglia (Eds.), *Adult Eyewitness Testimony: Current Trends and Developments,* pp. 56–79. Cambridge: Cambridge University Press.

Reber, A. S. (1967). Implicit learning of artificial grammars. *Journal of Verbal Learning and Verbal Behavior, 6,* 855–863.

Reber, A. S. (1969). Transfer of syntactic structure in synthetic languages. *Journal of Experimental Psychology, 81,* 115–119.

Reder, L. M. (1987). Strategy selection in question answering. *Cognitive Psychology, 19,* 90–138.

Reder, L. M., & Cleermans, A. (1990). The role of partial matches in comprehension: The Moses illusion revisited. *Psychology of Learning and Motivation, 25,* 233–258.

Reder, L. M., & Kusbit, G. W. (1991). Locus of the Moses Illusion: Imperfect encoding, retrieval or match? *Journal of Memory and Language, 30,* 385–406.

Reder, L. M. & Ritter, F. E. (1987). What determines initial feeling of knowing? Familiarity with question terms, not the answer. *Journal of Experimental Psychology: Learning, Memory, and Cognition, 18,* 435–451.

Reed, C. L., & Vinson, N. G. (1996). Conceptual effects on representational momentum. *Journal of Experimental Psychology: Human Perception and Performance, 22,* 839–850.

Rehder, B., & Hastie, R. (2001). Causal knowledge and categories: The effects of causal beliefs on categorization, induction, and similarity. *Journal of Experimental Psychology: General, 130,* 323–360.

Rehder, B., & Ross, B. H. (2001). Abstract coherent categories. *Journal of Experimental Psychology: Learning, Memory, and Cognition, 27,* 1261–1275.

Reitman, J. S., & Rueter, H. H. (1980). Organization revealed by recall orders and confirmed by pauses. *Cognitive Psychology, 12,* 554–581.

Reysen, M. B. (2003). The effects of social pressure on group recall. *Memory & Cognition, 31,* 1163–1168.

Rhodes, G., Jeffery, L., Watson, T. L., Clifford, C. W. G., & Nakayama, K. (2003). Fitting the mind to the world: Face adaptation and attractiveness after effects. *Psychological Science, 14,* 558–566.

Rhodes, G., & Tremewan, T. (1996). Averageness, exaggeration, and facial attractiveness. *Psychological Science, 7,* 105–110.

Richarson, R., Guanowsky, V., Ahlers, S. T., & Riccio, D. D. (1984). Role of body temperature in the onset of, and recovery from, hypothermia-induced anterograde amnesia. *Physiological Psychology, 12,* 125–132.

Riccio, D. C., Millin, P. M., & Gisquet-Verrier, P. (2003). Retrograde amnesia: Forgetting back. *Current Directions in Psychological Science, 12,* 41–44.

Riefer, D. M., & Batchelder, W. H. (1988). Multinomial modeling and the measurement of cognitive processes. *Psychological Review, 95,* 318–339.

Riefer, D. M., & Rouder, J. N. (1992). A multinomial modeling analysis of the mnemonic benefits of bizarre imagery. *Memory & Cognition, 20,* 601–611.

Rilling, M. (1996). The mystery of the vanished citations: James McConnell's forgotten 1960's quest for planarian learning, a biochemical engram, and celebrity. *American Psychologist, 51,* 589–598.

Rinck, M., Haehnel, A., & Becker, G. (2001). Using temporal information to construct, update, and retrieve situation models of narratives. *Journal of Experimental Psychology: Learning, Memory, and Cognition, 27,* 67–80.

Rinck, M., and Bower, G. H. (1995). Anaphora resolution and the focus of attention in situation models. *Journal of Memory and Language, 34,* 110–131.

Rinck, M., Haehnel, A., Bower, G. H., & Glowalla, U. (1997). The metrics of spatial situation models. *Journal of Experimental Psychology: Learning, Memory, and Cognition, 23,* 622–637.

Rips, L. J., Shoben, E. J., & Smith, E. E. (1973). Semantic distance and the verification of semantic relations. *Journal of Verbal Learning and Verbal Behavior, 12,* 1–20.

Robinson, M. D., & Johnson, J. T. (1998). How not to enhance the confidence-accuracy relation: The detrimental effects of attention to the identification process. *Law and Human Behavior, 22,* 409–428.

Roediger, H. L. (1980). Memory metaphors in cognitive psychology. *Memory & Cognition, 8,* 231–246.

Roediger, H. L., & Blaxton, T. A. (1987). Effects of varying modality, surface features, and retention interval on priming in word-fragment completion. *Memory & Cognition, 15,* 379–388.

Roediger, H. L., and Crowder, R. G. (1976). A serial position effect in recall of United States presidents. *Bulletin of Psychonomic Society, 8,* 275–278.

Roediger, H. L., & McDermott, K. B. (1995). Creating false memories: Remembering words not presented in lists. *Journal of Experimental Psychology: Learning, Memory, and Cognition, 21,* 803–814.

Roediger, H. L., Meade, M. L., & Bergman, E. T. (2001). Social contagion of memory. *Psychonomic Bulletin & Review, 8,* 365–371.

Roediger, H. L., Neely, J. H., & Blaxton, T. A. (1983). Inhibition from related primes in semantic memory retrieval: A reappraisal of Brown's (1979) paradigm. *Journal of Experimental Psychology: Learning, Memory, and Cognition, 9,* 478–485.

Roediger, H. L., Stellon, C. C., & Tulving, E. (1977). Inhibition from part-list cues and rate of recall. *Journal of Experimental Psychology: Human Learning and Memory, 3,* 174–188.

Roediger, H. L., Watson, J. M., McDermott, K. B., & Gallo, D. A. (2001). Factors that determine false recall: A multiple regression analysis. *Psychonomic Bulletin & Review, 8,* 385–407.

Roenker, D. L., Thompson, C. P, & Brown, S. C. (1971).Comparison of measures for the estimation of clustering in free recall. *Psychological Bulletin, 76,* 45–48.

Rohrer, D. (2003). The natural appearance of unnatural incline speed. *Memory & Cognition, 31,* 816–826.

Rohrer, D. & Pashler, H. E. (2003). Concurrent task effects on memory retrieval. *Psychonomic Bulletin & Review, 10,* 96–103.

Romani, C., & Martin, R. (1999). A deficit in the short-term retention of lexical-semantic information: Forgetting words but remembering a story. *Journal of Experimental Psychology: General, 128,* 56–77.

Rosch, E. (1975). Cognitive representations of semantic categories. *Journal of Experimental Psychology: General, 104,* 192–233.

Rosch, E., & Mervis, C. B. (1975). Family resemblances: Studies in the internal structure of categories. *Cognitive Psychology, 7,* 573–605.

Rosch, E., Mervis, C. B., Gray, W. D., Johnson, D. M., & Boyes-Braem, P. (1976). Basic objects in natural categories. *Cognitive Psychology, 8,* 382–439.

Ross, D. F., Ceci, S. J., Dunning, D., & Toglia, M. P. (1994). Unconscious transference and mistaken identity: When a witness misidentifies a familiar but innocent person. *Journal of Applied Psychology, 79,* 918–930.

Rossano, M. J., Warren, D. H, & Kenan, A. (1995). Orientation specificity: How general is it? *American Journal of Psychology, 108,* 359–380.

Rovee-Collier, C., Borza, M. A., Adler, S. A., & Boller, K. (1993). Infants' eyewitness testimony: Effects of postevent information on a prior memory representation. *Memory & Cognition, 21,* 267–279.

Rovee-Collier, C., & Fagan, J. W. (1981). The retrieval of memory in early infancy. *Advances in Infancy Research, 1,.*

Rubin, D. C. (1998). Knowledge and judgments about events that occurred prior to birth: The measurement of the persistence of information. *Psychonomic Bulletin & Review, 5,* 397–400.

Rubin, D. C., and Baddeley, A. D. (1989). Telescoping is not time compression: A model of the dating of autobiographical events. *Memory and Cognition, 17,* 653–661.

Rubin, D. C., & Berntsen, D. (2003). Life scripts help to maintain autobiographical memories of highly positive, but not highly negative, events. *Memory & Cognition, 31,* 1–14

Rubin, D. C., Rahhal, T. A., & Poon, L. W. (1998). Things learned in early adulthood are remembered best. *Memory & Cognition, 26,* 3–19.

Rubin, D. C., Schrauf, R. W., & Greenberg, D. L. (2003). Belief and recollection of autobiographical memories. *Memory & Cognition, 31,* 887–901.

Rundus, D. (1971). Analysis of rehearsal processes in free recall. *Journal of Experimental Psychology, 89,* 63–77.

Russo, R., Parkin, A. J., Taylor, S. R., & Wilks, J. (1998). Revising current two-process accounts of spacing effects in memory. *Journal of Experimental Psychology: Learning, Memory, and Cognition, 24,* 161–172.

Ryan, J. D., Althoff, R. R., Whitlow, S., & Cohen, N. J. (2000). Amnesia is a deficit in relational memory. *Psychological Science, 11,* 454–460.

Rypma, B., Prabhakaran, V., Desmond, J. E., & Gabriei, D. E. (2001). Age differences in prefrontal cortical activity in working memory. *Psychology and Aging, 16,* 371–384.

Sachs, J. S. (1967). Recognition memory for syntactic and semantic aspects of connected discourse. *Perception & Psychophysics, 2,* 437–442.

Sachs, J. S. (1974). Memory in reading and listening to discourse. *Memory & Cognition, 2,* 95–100.

Sadalla, E. K., Burroughs, J., & Staplin, L. J. (1980). Reference points in spatial cognition. *Journal of Experimental Psychology: Human Learning and Memory, 5,* 516–528.

Safer, M. A., Bonanno, G. A., & Field, N. P. (2001). "It was never that bad": Biased recall of grief and long-term adjustment to the death of a spouse. *Memory, 9,* 195–204.

Sagar, H. J., Cohen, N. J., Sullivan, E. V., Corkin, S., & Growden, J. H. (1988). Remote memory function in Alzheimer's disease and Parkinson's disease. *Brain, 111,* 185–206.

Sagar, H. J., Sullivan, E. V., Gabrieli, J. D. E., Corkin, S., & Growdon, J. H. (1988). Temporal ordering and short-term memory deficits in Parkinson's disease. 525–539.

Salame, P., & Baddeley, A. (1989). Effects of background music on phonological short-term memory. *Quarterly Journal of Experimental Psychology, 41A,* 107–122.

Salzman, I. J. (1953). The orienting task in incidental and intentional learning. *American Journal of Psychology, 64,* 593–598.

Salzman, I. J. (1956). Comparisons of incidental and intentional learning with different orienting tasks. *American Journal of Psychology, 69,* 274–277.

Samuel, A. G. (1978). Organizational vs. retrieval factors in the development of digit span. *Journal of Experimental Child Psychology, 26,* 308–319.

Sanders, H. I., & Warrington, E. K. (1971). Memory for remote events in amnesic patients. *Brain, 94,* 661–668.

Sanna, L. J., & Schwartz, N. (2004). Integrating temporal biases: The interplay of focal thoughts and accessibility experiences. *Psychological Science, 15,* 474–481.

Sanna, L. J., Schwartz, N., & Small, E. M. (2002). Accessibility experiences and the hindsight bias: I knew it all along versus it could never have happened. *Memory & Cognition, 30,* 1288–1296.

Schacter, D. L. (1987). Implicit memory: History and current status. *Journal of Experimental Psychology: Learning, Memory, and Cognition, 13,* 501–518.

Schacter, D. L., & Badgaiyan, R. D. (2001). Neuroimaging of priming: New perspectives on implicit and explicit memory. *Current Directions in Psychological Science, 10,* 1–4.

Schacter, D. L., Cooper, L. A., & Delaney, S. M. (1990). Implicit memory for unfamiliar objects depends on access to structural descriptions. *Journal of Experimental Psychology: General, 119,* 5–24.

Schacter, D. L., Eich, J. E., & Tulving, E. (1978). Richard Semon's theory of memory. *Journal of Verbal Learning and Verbal Behavior, 17,* 721–743.

Scheck, P., Meeter, M., & Nelson, T. O. (2004). Anchoring effects in the absolute accuracy of immediate versus delayed judgments of learning. *Journal of Memory and Language, 51,* 71–79.

Schmidt, S. R. (2004). Autobiographical memories for the September 11th attacks: Reconstructive errors and emotional impairment of memory. *Memory & Cognition, 32,* 443–454.

Schmolck, H., Buffalo, E. A., & Squire, L. R. (2000). Memory distortions over time: Recollections of the O. J. Simpson trial verdict after 15 and 32 months. *Psychological Science, 11,* 39–45.

Schnorr, J. A., & Atkinson, R. C. (1969). Repetition versus imagery instructions in the short- and long-term retention of paired-associates. *Psychonomic Science, 15,* 183–184.

Schooler, J. W., & Engstler-Schooler, T. Y. (1990). Verbal overshadowing of visual memories: Some things are better left unsaid. *Cognitive Psychology, 22,* 36–71.

Schrauf, R. W., & Rubin, D. C. (1998). Bilinguial autobiographical memory in older adult immigrants: A test of cognitive explanations of the reminiscence bump and the linguistic encoding of memories. *Journal of Memory and Language, 39,* 437–457.

Schreiber, T. A. (1998). Effects of target set size on feelings of knowing and cued recall: Implications for the cue effectiveness and partial-retrieval hypotheses. *Memory & Cognition, 26,* 553–571.

Schreiber, T. A. & Nelson, D. L. (1998). The relation between feelings of knowing and the number of neighboring concepts linked to the test cue. *Memory & Cognition, 26,* 869–883.

Schwartz, B. L. (1994). Sources of information in metamemory: Judgments of learning and feelings of knowing. *Psychonomic Bulletin & Review, 1,* 357–375.

Schwartz, B. L. (2001). The relation of tip-of-the-tongue states to retrieval time. *Memory & Cognition, 29,* 117–126.

Schwender, D., Kaiser, A., Klasing, S., Peter, K., and Poeppel, E. (1993). Explicit and implicit memory and mid-latency auditory evoked potentials during cardiac surgery. In B. Bonke (Ed.), *Memory and awareness in anesthesia.* (pp. 85–98). Upper Saddle River, NJ: Prentice-Hall.

Scoville, W. B., & Milner, B. (1957). Loss of recent memory after bilateral hippocampal lesions. *Journal of Neurology, Neurosurgery, and Psychiatry, 20,* 11–21.

Seamon, J. G., Luo, C. R., Kopecky, J. J., Price, C. A., Rothschild, L., Fung, N. S., & Schwartz, M. A. (2002). Are false memories more difficult to forget than accurate memories? The effect of retention interval on recall and recognition. *Memory & Cognition, 30,* 1054–1064.

Searleman, A., & Herrmann, D. (1994). *Memory From a Broader Perspective.* New York: McGraw-Hill.

Segal, S. J., & Fusella, V. (1970). Influence of imaged pictures and sounds on detection of visual and auditory signals. *Journal of Experimental Psychology, 83,* 458–464.

Segal, S. J., & Fusella, V. (1971). Effect of images in six sense modalities on detection of visual signal from noise. *Psychonomic Science, 24,* 55–56.

Sehulster, J. R. (1989). Content and temporal structure of autobiographical knowledge: Remembering twenty-five seasons at the Metropolitan Opera. *Memory & Cognition, 17,* 590–606.

Seiler, K. H., & Engelkamp, J. (2003). The role of item-specific information for the serial position curve in free recall. Journal of Experimental Psychology: *Learning, Memory, and Cognition, 29,* 954–964.

Senkfor, A. J., & Van Petten, C. (1998). Who said what? An event-related potential investigation of source and item memory. *Journal of Experimental Psychology: Learning, Memory, and Cognition, 24,* 1005–1025.

Shafto, M., & MacKay, D. G. (2000). The Moses, mega-Moses, and Armstrong illusions: Integrating language comprehension and semantic memory. *Psychological Science, 11,* 372–378.

Shah, P., & Miyake, A. (1996). The separability of working memory resources for spatial thinking and language processing: An individual differences approach. *Journal of Experimental Psychology: General, 125,* 4–27.

Shallice, T., Fletcher, P., & Dolan, R. (1998). The functional imaging of recall. In M. A. Conway, S. E. Gathercole, and C. Cornoldi (Eds.), *Theories of Memory: Volume II,* pp. 247–258. Hove, England: Psychology Press.

Shallice, T., & Warrington, E. K. (1970). Independent functioning of verbal memory stores: A neuropsychological study. *Quarterly Journal of Experimental Psychology, 22,* 261–273.

Shapiro, M. L., Tanila, H., & Eichenbaum, H. (1997). Cues that hippocampal place cells encode: Dynamic and hierarchical representation of local and distal stimuli. *Hippocampus, 7,* 624–642.

Shaw, J. S. (1996). Increases in eyewitness confidence resulting from postevent questioning. *Journal of Experimental Psychology: Applied, 2,* 126–146.

Shaw, J. S. & Kerr, T, K. (2003). Extra effort during memory retrieval may be associated with increases in eyewitness confidence. *Law and Human Behavior, 27,* 315–329.

Shaw, J. S., & McClure, K. A. (1996). Repeated postevent questioning can lead to elevated levels of eyewitness confidence. *Law and Human Behavior, 20,* 629–653.

Shelton, A. L., & McNamara, T. P. (1997). Multiple views of spatial memory. *Psychonomic Bulletin & Review, 4,* 102–106.

Shelton, A. L., & McNamara, T. P. (2004). Orientation and perspective dominance in route and survey learning. *Journal of Experimental Psychology: Learning, Memory, and Cognition, 30,* 158–170.

Shepard, R. N. (1967). Recognition memory for words, sentences, and pictures. *Journal of Verbal Learning and verbal Behavior, 6,* 156–163.

Shepard, R. N. (1984). Ecological constraints on internal representation: Resonant kinematics of perceiving, imagining, thinking, and dreaming. *Psychological Review, 9,* 417–447.

Shepard, R. N., & Chipman, S. (1970). Second-order isomorphs of internal representations: Shapes of states. *Cognitive Psychology, 1,* 1–17.

Shepard, R. N., & Metzler, J. (1971). Mental rotation of three-dimensional objects. *Science, 171,* 701–703.

Sherman. R. C., & Lim, K. M. (1991). Determinants of spatial priming in environmental memory. *Memory & Cognition, 19,* 283–292.

Sherry, D. F., & Schacter, D. L. (1987). The evolution of multiple memory systems. *Psychological Review, 94,* 439–454.

Shiffrin, R. M. & Steyvers, M. (1997). A model for recognition memory: REM—retrieving effectively from memory. *Psychonomic Bulletin & Review, 4,* 145–166.

Shoben, E. J., Cech, C. G., Schwanenflugel, P. J., & Sailor, K. M. (1989). Serial position effects in comparative judgments. *Journal of Experimental Psychology: Human Perception and Performance, 15,* 273–286.

Sholl, J. M. (1987). Cognitive maps as orienting schemata. *Journal of Experimental Psychology: Learning, Memory, and Cognition, 13,* 615–628.

Simcock, G., & Hayne, H. (2002). Breaking the barrier? Children fail to translate their preverbal memories into language. *Psychological Science, 13,* 225–231.

Simons, D. J., & Levin, D. T. (1998). Failure to detect changes to people during real-world interaction. *Psychological Bulletin & Review, 5,* 644–649.

Simons, J. S., Graham, K. S., & Hodges, J. R. (2002). Perceptual and semantic contributions to episodic memory: Evidence from semantic dementia and Alzheimer's disease. *Journal of Memory and Language, 47,* 197–213.

Sirigu, A., & Grafman, J. (1996). Selective impairments within episodic memories. *Cortex, 32,* 83–95.

Slamecka, N. J. (1968). An examination of trace storage in free recall. *Journal of Experimental Psychology, 4,* 504–513.

Slamecka, N. J., & Graf, P. (1978). The generation effect: Delineation of a phenomenon. *Journal of Experimental Psychology: Human Learning and Memory, 4,* 592–604.

Sloman, S. A., Bower, G. H., & Rohrer, D. (1991). Congruency effects in part-list cuing inhibition. *Journal of Experimental Psychology: Learning, Memory, and Cognition, 17,* 974–982.

Small, B. J., Dixon, R. A., Hultsch, D. F., & Hertzog, C. (1999). Longitudinal changes in quantitative and qualitative indicators of word and story recall in young-old and old-old adults. *Journal of Gerontology: Psychological Sciences 54B,* P107–P115.

Small, G. W. (1998). The pathogenesis of Alzheimer's disease. *Journal of Clinical Psychiatry, 59,* 7–14.

Smith, E. E. (2000). Neural bases of human working memory. *Current Directions in Psychological Science, 9,* 45–49.

Smith. E. E., Adams, N., & Schorr, D. (1978). Fact retrieval and the paradox of interference. *Cognitive Psychology, 10,* 438–464.

Smith, M. C. (1983). Hypnotic memory enhancement of witnesses: Does it work? *Psychological Bulletin, 94,* 387–407.

Smith, R. E., & Hunt, R. R. (2000). The influence of distinctive processing on retrieval-induced forgetting. *Memory & Cognition, 28,* 503–508.

Smith, S. M., (1979). Remembering in and out of context. *Journal of Experimental Psychology: Human Learning and Memory, 5,* 460–471.

Smith, S. M. (1984). A comparison of two techniques for reducing context-dependent forgetting. *Memory & Cognition, 12,* 477–482.

Smith, S. M. (1985). Background music and context-dependent memory. *American Journal of Psychology, 98,* 591–603.

Smith, S. M., (1988). Environmental context–dependent memory. In G. M. Davies & D. M. Thomas (Eds.), *Memory in Context: Context in memory,* pp. 13–34. New York: Wiley.

Smith, S. M., Glenberg, A., & Bjork, R. A. (1978). Environmental context and human memory. *Memory & Cognition, 6,* 342–353.

Smith, S. M., & Vela, E. (2001). Environmental context-dependent memory: A review and meta-analysis. *Psychonomic Bulletin & Review, 8,* 203–220.

Snodgrass, J. G., & Corwin, J. (1988). Pragmatics of measuring recognition memory: Applications to dementia and amnesia. *Journal of Experimental Psychology: General, 117,* 34–50.

Snodgrass, J. G., Volvovitz, R., & Walfish, E. R. (1972). Recognition memory for words, pictures, and words + pictures. *Psychonomic Science, 27,* 345–347.

Snowden, J., Goulding, J., & Neary, D. (1989). Semantic dementia: A form of circumscribed cerebral atrophy. *Behavioral Neurology, 2,* 167–182.

Solomon, K. O., & Barsalou, L. W. (2001). Representing properties locally. *Cognitive Psychology, 43,* 129–169.

Solomon, K. O., & Barsalou, L. W. (2004). Perceptual simulation in property verification. *Memory & Cognition, 32,* 244–259.

Son, L. K. (2004). Spacing one's study: Evidence for a metacognitive control strategy. *Journal of Experimental Psychology: Learning, Memory, and Cognition, 30,* 601–604.

Souchey, C., Isingrini, M., & Espagnet, L. (2000). Aging, episodic memory feeling-of-knowing, and frontal functioning. *Neuropsychology, 14,* 299–309.

Spear, N. E., & Riccio, D. C. (1994). *Memory: Phenomena and Principles.* New York: Allyn and Bacon.

Sperling, G. (1960). The information available in brief visual presentations. *Psychological Monographs: General and Applied, 74 (11),* 1–29.

Sporer, S. L., Penrod, S., Read, D., & Cutler, B. (1995). Choosing, confidence, and accuracy: A meta-analysis of the confidence-accuracy relation in eyewitness identification studies. *Psychological Bulletin, 118,* 315–327.

Sprecher, S. (1999). "I love you more today than yesterday": Romantic partners' perceptions of change in love and related affect over time. *Journal of Personality and Social Psychology, 76,* 46–53.

Squire, L. R. (1986). Mechanisms of memory. *Science, 232,* 1612–1619.

Squire, L. R. (1987). *Memory and Brain.* New York: Oxford University Press.

Squire, L. R., & Cohen, N. (1979). Memory and amnesia: Resistance to disuption develops for years after learning. *Behavioral and Neural Biology, 25,* 115–125.

Squire, L. R., Slater, P. C., & Chace, P. M. (1975). Retrograde amnesia: Temporal gradient in very long term memory following electroconvulsive therapy. *Science, 187,* 77–79.

Squires, E. J., Hunkin, N. M., & Parkin, A. J. (1997). Take note: Using errorless learning to promote memory notebook training. In A. J. Parkin (Ed.), *Case Studies in the Neuropsychology of Memory,* pp. 191–203. Hove, England: Psychology Press.

Srivinas, K., & Roediger, H. L. (1990). Classifying implicit memory tests: Category association and anagram solution. *Journal of Memory and Language, 29,* 389–412.

Stagner, R. (1933). Factors influencing the memory value of words in a series. *Journal of Experimental Psychology, 16,* 129–137.

Standing, L. (1973). Learning 10,000 pictures. *Quarterly Journal of Experimental Psychology, 25,* 207–222.

Stebbins, G. T., Carrillo, M. C., Dorfman, J., Dirksen, C., Desmond, J. E., Turner, D. A., Bennett, D. A., Wilson, R. S., Glover, G., & Gabrieli, J. D. E. (2002). Aging effects on memory encoding in the frontal lobes. *Psychology and Aging, 17,* 44–55.

Steblay, N. M. (1992). A meta-analytic review of the weapon focus effect. *Law and Human Behavior, 16,* 413–424.

Steblay, N. M. (1997). Social influence in eyewitness recall: A meta-analytic review of lineup instruction effects. *Law and Human Behavior, 21,* 283–297.

Steffens, M. C., Buchner, A., Martensen, H., & Erdfelder, E. (2000). Further evidence on the similarity of memory processes in the process dissociation procedure and in source monitoring. *Memory & Cognition, 28,* 1152–1164.

Steffens, M. C., Buchner, A., & Wender, K. F. (2003). Quite ordinary retrieval cues may determine free recall of actions. *Journal of Memory and Language, 48,* 399–415.

Sternberg, S. (1966). High-speed scanning in human memory. *Science, 153,* 652–654.

Sternberg, S. (1969). The discovery of processing stages: Extensions of Donders' method. *Acta Pscyhologica, 30,* 276–315.

Sternberg, S. (1975). Memory scanning: New findings and current controversies. *Quarterly Journal of Experimental Psychology, 27,* 1–32.

Stevens, A. & Coupe, P. (1978). Distortions in judged spatial relations. *Cognitive Psychology, 10,* 422–437.

Stevens, S. S., & Galantner, E. H. (1957). Ratio scales and category scales for a dozen perceptual continua. *Journal of Experimental Psychology, 54,* 377–411.

Stracciari, A., Ghidoni, E., Guarino, M., Poletti, M., & Pazzaglia, P. (1994). Post-traumatic retrograde amnesia with selective impairment of autobiographical memory. *Cortex, 30,* 459–468.

Stuss, D. T., Craik, F. I. M., Sayer, L., Franchi, D., & Alexander, M. P. (1996). Comparison of older people with frontal lesions: Evidence from word list learning. *Neuropsychologia, 37,* 1005–1027.

Summers, W. V., Horton, D. L., & Diehl, V. A. (1985). Contextual knowledge during encoding influences sentence recognition. *Journal of Experimental Psychology: Learning, Memory, and Cognition, 11,* 771–779.

Sun, H. J., Chan, G. S. W., & Campos, J. L. (2004). Active navigation and orientation-free spatial representations. *Memory & Cognition, 32,* 51–71.

Swaab, T. Y., Baynes, K., & Knight, R. T. (2002). Separable effects of priming and imageability on word processing: An ERP study. *Cognitive Brain Research, 15,* 99–103.

Swanson, J. M., & Kinsbourne, M. (1976). Stimulant-related state-dependent learning in hyperactive children. *Science, 192,* 1354–1356.

Taft, M. (1979). Recognition of affixed words and the word frequency effect. *Memory & Cognition, 7,* 263–272.

Talarico, J. M., & Rubin, D. C. (2003). Confidence, not consistency, characterizes flashbulb memories. *Psychological Science, 14,* 455–461.

Taylor, H. A., & Tversky, B. (1992). Spatial mental models derived from survey and route descriptions. *Journal of Memory and Language, 31,* 261–292.

Tekcan, A. İ., Ece, B., Gülgöz, S., & Er, N. (2003). Autobiographical and event memory for 9/11: Changes across one year. *Applied Cognitive Psychology, 17,* 1057–1066.

Terry, W. S. (2000). *Learning and Memory: Basic Principles, Processes, and Procedures.* Boston: Allyn & Bacon.

Thomas, A. K., Bulevich, J. B., & Loftus, E. F. (2003). Exploring the role of repetition and sensory elaboration in the imagination inflation effect. *Memory & Cognition, 31,* 630–640.

Thomas, A. K., & Loftus, E. F. (2002). Creating bizarre false memories through imagination. *Memory & Cognition, 30,* 423–431.

Thompson, C. P., Cowan, T. M. & Frieman, J. (1993). *Memory Search by a Memorist.* Hillsdale, NJ: Erlbaum.

Thompson, C. P., Cowan, T. M., Frieman, J., Mahadevan, R. S., & Vogl, R. J. (1991). Rajan: A study of a memorist. *Journal of Memory and Language, 30,* 702–724.

Thompson, C. P., Skowronski, J. J., & Lee, D. J. (1988). Telescoping in dating naturally occurring events. *Memory & Cognition, 16,* 461–468.

Thompson, C. P., Skowronski, J. J., Larsen, S. F., & Betz, A. L. (1996). *Autobiographical Memory: Remembering What and Remembering When.* Mahwah, New Jersey: Erlbaum.

Thompson, D. M., & Tulving, E. (1970). Associative encoding and retrieval: Weak and strong cues. *Journal of Experimental Psychology, 86,* 255–262.

Thompson, W. C., Fong, G. T., & Rosenhan, D. L. (1981). Inadmissible evidence and juror verdicts. *Journal of Personality and Social Psychology, 40,* 453–463.

Thompson-Schill, S. L., Kurtz, K. J., & Gabrieli, J. D. E. (1998). Effects of semantic and associative relatedness on automatic priming. *Journal of Memory and Language, 38,* 440–458.

Thorndyke, P. W. (1981). Distance estimation from cognitive maps. *Cognitive Psychology, 13,* 526–550.

Toglia, M. P., & Kimble, G. A. (1976). Recall and use of serial position information. *Journal of Experimental Psychology: Human Learning and Memory, 2,* 431–445.

Tolman, E. C. (1948). Cognitive maps in rats and men. *Psychological Review, 55,* 189–208.

Toppino, T. C., & Bloom, L. C. (2002). The spacing effect, free recall, and two-process theory: A closer look. *Memory & Cognition, 28,* 437–444.

Toth, J. P., Reingold, E. M., & Jacoby, L. L. (1994). Toward a redefinition of implicit memory: Process dissociations following elaborative processing and self-generation. *Journal of Experimental Psychology: Learning, Memory, and Cognition, 20,* 290–303.

Townsend, J. T. (1990). Serial vs. parallel processing: Sometimes they look like Tweedledum and Tweedledee but they can (and should) be distinguished. *Psychological Science, 1,* 46–54.

Trabasso, T., & Bower, G. (1964). Presolution reversal and dimensional shifts in concept identification. *Journal of Experimental Psychology, 67,* 398–399.

Trabasso, T., & van den Broek, P. W. (1985). Causal thinking and the representation of narrative events. *Journal of Memory and Language, 24,* 612–630.

Trafimow, D., & Wyer, R. S. (1993). Cognitive representations of mundane social events. *Journal of Personality and Social Psychology, 64,* 365–376.

Tulving, E. (1962). Subjective organization in free recall of "unrelated" words. *Psychological Review, 69,* 344–354.

Tulving, E. (1972). Episodic and semantic memory. In E. Tulving & W. Donaldson (Eds.), *Organization of Memory,* pp. 381–403. New York: Academic Press.

Tulving, E. (1985a). How many memory systems are there? *American Psychologist, 40,* 385–398.

Tulving, E. (1985b). Memory and consciousness. *Canadian Psychology, 26,* 1–12.

Tulving. E., & Hastie, R. (1972). Inhibition effects of intralist repetition in free recall. *Journal of Experimental Psychology, 92,* 297–304.

Tulving, E., & Madigan, S. A. (1970). Memory and verbal learning. *Annual Review of Psychology, 21,* 437–484.

Tulving. E., & Pearlstone, Z. (1966). Availability versus accessibility of information in memory for words. *Journal of Verbal Learning and Verbal Behavior, 5,* 381–391.

Tulving, E., & Psotka, J. (1971). Retroactive inhibition in free recall: Inaccessibility of information available in the memory store. *Journal of Experimental Psychology, 87,* 1–8.

Tulving, E., & Schacter, D. L. (1990). Priming in human memory systems. *Science, 247,* 301–306.

Tulving, E., Schacter, D. L., McLachlan, D. R., & Moscovitch, M. (1988). Priming of semantic autobiographical knowledge: A case study of retrograde amnesia. *Brain and Cognition, 8,* 3–20.

Tulving, E., Schacter, D. L., & Stark, H. A. (1982). Priming effects in word-fragment completion are independent of recognition memory. *Journal of Experimental Psychology: Learning, Memory and Cognition, 8,* 336–342.

Tulving, E., & Watkins, O. C. (1977). Recognition failure of words with a single meaning. *Memory & Cognition, 5,* 513–522.

Tulving, E., & Wiseman, S. (1975). Relation between recognition and recognition failure of recallable words. *Bulletin of the Psychonomic Society, 6,* 79–82.

Turkheimer, E. (1998). Heretibility and biological explanation. *Psychological Review, 105,* 782–791.

Turner, M. L., & Engle, R. W. (1989). Is working memory capacity task dependent? *Journal of Memory and Language, 28,* 127–154.

Tversky, B. (1981). Distortions in memory for maps. *Cognitive Psychology, 13,* 417–433.

Tversky, B., & Hemenway, K. (1984). Objects, parts, and categories. *Journal of Experimental Psychology: General, 113,* 169–193.

Tzeng, O. J. L. (1976). A precedence effect in the processing of verbal information. *American Journal of Psychology, 89,* 577–599.

Underwood, B. J. (1957). Interference and forgetting. *Psychological Review, 64,* 49–60.

Underwood, J., & Pezdek, K. (1998). Memory suggestibility as an example of the sleeper effect. *Psychonomic Bulletin & Review, 5,* 449–453.

Ungerleider, L. G., & Haxby, J. V. (1994). "What" versus "where" in the human brain. *Current Opinion in Neurobiology, 4,* 157–165.

Vaidya, C. J., Zhao, M., Desmond, J. E., & Gabrieli, J. D. E. (2002). Evidence for cortical encoding specificity in episodic memory: Memory-induced re-activation of picture processing areas. *Neuropsychologia, 40,* 2136–2143.

Valiquette, C. M., McNamara, T. P., & Smith, K. (2003). Locomotion, incidental learning, and the selection of spatial reference systems. *Memory & Cognition, 31,* 479–489.

Vallar, G., & Baddeley, A. D. (1985). Fractionation of working memory: Neuropsychological evidence for a phonological short-term store. *Journal of Verbal Learning and Verbal Behavior, 23,* 151–161.

Vallar, G., & Papagano, C. (1995). Neuropsychological impairments of short-term memory. In A. D. Baddeley, B. A. Wilson, & F. N. Watts (Eds.), *Handbook of Memory Disorders,* pp. 135–165. New York: Wiley.

van Dijk, T. A., & Kintsch, W. (1983). *Strategies in Discourse Comprehension.* New York: Academic Press.

Veling, H., & van Knippenberg, A. (2004). Remembering can cause inhibition: Retrieval induced inhibition as cue independent process. *Journal of Experimental Psychology: Learning, Memory, and Cognition, 30,* 315–318.

Verfaillie, K., & Y'dewalle, G. (1991). Representational momentum and event course anticipation in the perception of implied periodic motions. *Journal of Experimental Psychology: Learning, Memory, and Cognition, 17,* 302–313.

Verkoeijen, P. P. J. L., Rikers, R. M. J. P., & Schmidt, H. G. (2004). Detrimental influence of contextual change on spacing effects. *Journal of Experimental Psychology: Learning, Memory, and Cognition, 30,* 796–800.

Viney, W., & King, D. B. (1998). *A History of Psychology: Ideas and Context.* Boston, Allyn and Bacon.

Vollrath, D. A., Sheppard, B. H., Hinsz, V. B., & Davis, J. H. (1989). Memory performance by decision-making groups and individuals. *Organizational Behavior and Human Decision Processes, 43,* 289–300.

Von Essen, J. D., & Nulsson, L. (2003). Memory effects of motor activation in subject-performed tasks and sign language. *Psychonomic Bulletin & Review, 10,* 445–449.

Wagenaar, W. A. (1986). My memory: A study of autobiographical memory over six years. *Cognitive Psychology, 18,* 225–252.

Wagner, S. M., Nusbaum, H., & Goldin-Meadow, S. (2004). Probing the mental representation of gesture: Is handwaving spatial? *Journal of Memory and Language, 50,* 395–407.

Walker, W. R., Skowronski, J. J., & Thompson, C. P. (2003). Life is pleasant—and memory helps keep it that way! *Review of General Psychology, 7,* 203–210.

Walker, W. R., Vogl, R. J., & Thompson, C. P. (1997). Autobiographical memory: Unpleasantness fades faster than pleasantness over time. *Applied Cognitive Psychology, 11,* 399–413.

Waller, D., Loomis, J. M., & Haun, D. B. M. (2004). Body-based senses enhance knowledge of directions in large-scale environments. *Psychonomic Bulletin & Review, 11,* 157–163.

Waller, D., Montello, D. R., Richardson, A. E., & Hegarty, M. (2002). Orientation specificity and spatial layout updating of memories for layouts. *Journal of Experimental Psychology: Learning, Memory and Cognition, 28,* 1051–1063.

Wang, Q. (2004). Infantile amnesia reconsidered: A cross-cultural analysis. *Memory, 11,* 65–80.

Warrington, E. K., & Weiskrantz, L. (1968). A study of learning and retention in amnesic patients. *Neuropsychologia, 6,* 283–291.

Warrington, E. K., & Weiskrantz, L. (1970). Amnestic syndrome: Consolidation or retrieval? *Nature, 228,* 628–630.

Waters, G. S., & Caplan, D. (1996). The measurement of verbal working memory capacity and its relation to reading comprehension. *Quarterly Journal of Experimental Psychology, 49A,* 51–79.

Watkins, M. J., & Peynircioulu, Z. F. (1990). The revelation effect: When disguising test items induces recognition. *Journal of Experimental Psychology: Learning, Memory and Cognition, 16,* 1012–1020.

Waugh, N. C., & Norman, D. A. (1965). Primary memory. *Psychological Review, 72,* 89–104.

Wegner, D. M. (1989). *White Bears and Other Unwanted Thoughts: Suppression, Obsession, and the Psychology of Mental Control.* New York: Viking.

Weiss, W. (1953). A "sleeper" effect in opinion change. *Journal of Abnormal and Social Psychology, 48,* 173–180.

Weldon, M. S., & Bellinger, K. D. (1997). Collective memory: Collaborative and individual processes in remembering. *Journal of Experimental Psychology: Learning, Memory, and Cognition, 23,* 1160–1175.

Weldon, M. S., Blair, C., & Huebsch, P. D. (2000). Group remembering: Does social loafing underlie collaborative inhibition? *Journal of Experimental Psychology: Learning, Memory and Cognition, 26,* 1568–1577.

Wells, G. L. (1984). The psychology of lineup identification. *Journal of Applied Social Psychology, 14,* 89–103.

Wells, G. L., & Bradfield, A. L. (1998). "Good, you identified the suspect": Feedback to eyewitnesses distorts their reports of the witnessing experience. *Journal of Applied Psychology, 83,* 360–376.

Wells, G. L., & Bradfield, A. L. (1999). Distortion in eyewitnesses' recollections: Can the postidentification-feedback effect be moderated? *Psychological Science, 10,* 138–144.

Wells, G. L., Malpass, R. S., Lindsay, R. C. L., Fisher, R. P., Turtle, J. W., & Fulero, S. M. (2000). From the lab to the police station: A successful application of eyewitness research. *American Psychologist, 55,* 581–598.

West, R. L. (1988). Prospective memory and aging. In M. M. Gruneberg, P. E. Morris, & R. N. Sykes (Eds.), *Practical aspects of memory,* pp. 119–125. Chichester, England: Wiley.

West, R. L., Thorn, R. M., & Bagwell, D. K. (2003). Memory performance and beliefs as a function of goal setting and aging. *Psychology and Aging, 18,* 111–125.

Westerman, D. L. (2000). Recollection-based recognition eliminates the revelation effect in memory. *Memory & Cognition, 28,* 167–175.

Westerman, D. L., & Greene, R. L. (1996). On the generality of the revelation effect. *Journal of Experimental Psychology Learning, Memory, and Cognition, 22,* 1147–1153.

Westerman, D. L., & Greene, R. L. (1998). The revelatin that the revelation effect is not due to revelation. *Journal of Experimental Psychology Learning, Memory, and Cognition, 24,* 377–386.

Westerman, D. L., & Larsen, J. D. (1997). Verbal-overshadowing effect: Evidence for a general shift in processing. *American Journal of Psychology, 110,* 417–428.

Westmacott, R., & Moscovitch, M. (2003). The contribution of autobiographical significance to semantic memory. *Memory & Cognition, 31,* 761–774.

Wheeler, M. A., & Roediger, H. L. (1992). Disparate effects of repeated testing: Reconciling Ballard's (1913) and Barlett's (1932) results. *Psychological Science, 3,* 240–245.

White, K. G., & Ruske, A. C. (2002). Memory deficits in Alzheimer's disease: The encoding hypothesis and cholinergic function. *Psychonomic Bulletin & Review, 9,* 426–437.

White, K. K., & Abrams, L. (2002). Does priming specific syllables during tip-of-the-tongue states facilitate word retrieval in older adults? *Psychology and Aging, 17,* 226–235.

Whitten, W. B., & Leonard, J. M. (1981). Directed search through autobiographical memory. *Memory & Cognition, 9,* 566–579.

Wickelgren, W. A. (1968). Sparing of short-term memory in an amnesic patient: Implications for strength theory of short-term memory. *Neuropsychologia, 6,* 235–244.

Wickens, D. D. (1972). Characteristics of word encoding. In A. W. Melton & E. Martin (Eds.), *Coding Processes in Human Memory,* pp. 191–215. New York: Wiley.

Widner, R. L., Otani, H., & Smith, A. D. (2000). Hypermnesia: Age-related differences between young and older adults. *Memory & Cognition, 28,* 556–564.

Wiest, W. M., & Bell, B. (1985). Stevens's exponent for psychophysical scaling of perceived, remembered and inferred distance. *Psychological Bulletin, 98,* 457–470.

Wiggs, C. L., Weisberg, J., & Martin, A. (1999). Neural correlates of semantic and episodic memory retrieval. *Neuropsychologia, 37,* 103–118.

Wilding, E. L. (2000). IN what way does the parietal ERP old/new effect index recollection? *International Journal of Psychophysiology, 35,* 81–87.

Wilkinson, L., Scholey, A., & Wesnes, K. (2002). Chewing gum selectively improves aspects of memory in healthy volunteers. *Appetite, 38,* 235–236.

Wills, T. W., Soraci, S. A., Chechile, R. A., & Taylor, H. A. (2000). "Aha" effects in the generation of pictures. *Memory & Cognition, 28,* 939–948.

Wilson, B. A., J. C., & Hughes, E. (1997). Coping with amnesia: The natural history of a compensatory memory system. In A. J. Parkin (Ed.), *Case Studies in the Neuropsychology of Memory,* pp. 179–190. East Sussex, England: Psychology Press.

Wilson, B. A., & Wearing, D. (1995). Prisoner of consciousness: A state of just awakening following herpes simplex encephalitis. In R. Campbell & M. A. Conway (Eds.), *Broken Memories: Case Studies in Memory Impairment.* Cambridge, MA: Blackwell.

Wilson, M. (2002). Six views of embodied cognition. *Psychonomic Bulletin & Review, 9,* 625–636.

Winer, G. A., Cottrell, J E., Gregg, V., Fournier, J. S., & Bica, L. A. (2002). Fundamentally misunderstanding visual perception. *American Psychologist, 57,* 417–424.

Winkielman, P., & Schwartz, N. (2001). How pleasant was your childhood? Beliefs about memory shape inferences from experienced difficulty of recall. *Psychological Science, 12,* 176–179.

Wood, G. (1978). The knew-it-all-along effect. *Journal of Experimental Psychology: Human Perception and Performance, 4,* 345–353.

Wyer, R. S., & Unverzagt, W. H. (1985). Effects of instructions to disregard information on its subsequent recall and use in making judgments. *Journal of Personality and Social Psychology, 48,* 533–549.

Yasuda, K., Watanabe, O., & Ono, Y. (1997). Dissociation between semantic and autobiographical memory: A case report. *Cortex, 33,* 623–638.

Yerkes, R. M., & Dodson, J. D. (1908). The relation of strength of stimulus to rapidity of habit-formation. *Journal of Comparative Neurology and Psychology, 18,* 459–482.

Yonelinas, A. P. (2002). The nature of recollection and familiarity: A review of 30 years of research. *Journal of Memory and Language, 46,* 441–517.

Zacks, R. T., Hasher, L., Sanft, H., and Rose, K. C. (1983). Encoding effort and recall: A cautionary note. *Journal of Experimental Psychology: Learning, Memory, and Cognition, 9,* 747–756.

Zacks, R. T., Radvansky, G. A., & Hasher, L. (1996). Studies of directed forgetting in older adults. *Journal of Experimental Psychology: Learning, Memory, and Cognition, 22,* 143–156.

Zajonc, R. B. (1968). Attitudinal effects of mere exposure. *Journal of Personality and Social Psychology Monograph Supplement, 9,* 1–27.

Zajonc, R. B. (2001). Mere exposure: A gateway to the subliminal. *Current Directions in Psychological Science, 10,* 224–228.

Zaragoza, M. S., & Koshmider, J. W. (1989). Misled subjects may know more than their performance implies. *Journal of Experimental Psychology: Learning, Memory, and Cognition, 15,* 246–255.

Zaragoza, M. S., & Lane, S. M. (1994). Source misattributions and the suggestibility of eyewitness memory. *Journal of Experimental Psychology: Learning, Memory, and Cognition, 20,* 934–945.

Zaragoza, M. S., Payment, K. E., Ackil, J. K., Drivdahl, S. B., & Beck, M. (2001). Interviewing witnesses: Forced confabulation and confirmatory feedback increase false memories. *Psychological Science, 12,* 473–477.

Zechmeister, E. B., & Shaughnessy, J. J. (1980). When you think that you know and when you think that you know but you don't. *Bulletin of the Psychonomic Society, 15,* 41–44.

Zimmer, H. D., & Engelkamp, J. (2003). Signing enhances memory like performing actions. *Psychonomic Bulletin & Review, 10,* 450–454.

Zimmerman, J., and Underwood, B. J. (1968). Ordinal position knowledge within and across lists as a function of instructions in free-recall learning. *Journal of General Psychology, 79,* 301–307.

Zwaan, R. A., & Radvansky, G. A. (1998). Situation models in comprehension and memory. *Psychological Bulletin, 123,* 162–185.